God Grant It

DAILY DEVOTIONS FROM C.F.W. WALTHER

From the sermons of the sainted Professor Dr. C. F. W. Walther

Translated by Gerhard P. Grabenhofer

Compiled by August Crull

CONCORDIA PUBLISHING HOUSE · SAINT LOUIS

3558 S. Jefferson Avenue, St. Louis, MO 63118-3968
1-800-325-3040 • www.cph.org

Written by C. F. W. Walther
Translated by Gerhard P. Grabenhofer
Compiled by August Crull
Cover Art: Art Resource, NY. The Wetterhorn, Switzerland by Albert Bierstadt.

This publication may be available in braille, in large print, or on cassette tape for the visually impaired. Please allow 8 to 12 weeks for delivery. Write to the Library for the Blind, 7550 Watson Rd., St. Louis, MO 63119-4409; call 1-866-215-6852; or e-mail to blind.mission@blindmission.org.

Manufactured in the United States of America

Library of Congress Cataloging-in-Publication Data

Walther, C. F. W. (Carl Ferdinand Wilhelm, 1811-1887.
[Sermons. English. Selections]
God grant it: daily devotions from C. F. W Walther / C. F. W Walther; translated by Gerhard P. Grabenhofer; compiled by August Crull.
p. cm.

ISBN 0-7586-0834-9

1. Devotional calendars. 2. Lutheran Chruch–Sermons. 3. Sermons, German –Translations into English. I. Crull, August, 1845-1923. II. Title.

BV4811.C365 2006

242'.2--dc22

2006014383

---

1 2 3 4 5 6 7 8 9 10 15 14 13 12 11 10 09 08 07 06

PUBLISHER'S PREFACE

DR. C.F.W. WALTHER WAS FAMOUS for preaching sermons that were powerfully and passionately delivered, with intensity and conviction. His sermons were filled with doctrinal content. These sermons stayed with hearers long after they left the church. So popular was Walther as a preacher that his sermons were gathered and collected in various editions and widely circulated. Readers will be impressed by the directness of Dr. Walther. Sermons were not times to amuse or entertain for Dr. Walther. They were not opportunities to pander to hearers, or to talk down to them, or to wander far afield from a clear outline and theme. These are thoroughly Lutheran sermons and as such readers will notice Dr. Walther not shying away from the faithful proclamation of the whole counsel of God, in line with the Lutheran Confessions. His rejection of the errors and erring teachers and movements of his day come through clearly. His comments about Roman Catholicism or Reformed theology or Methodism may sound harsh to the 21st century ear, but this is Pastor Walther discharging his duty to warn and guard his flock from false teaching. We do well to listen to what he has to say. May God bless all who, through this book, have the opportunity to spend time daily with the "American Luther," Dr. C.F.W. Walther, and through these devotions based on his sermons grow in the truth of God's Holy Word and in the grace and mercy of our Lord Jesus Christ.

FOREWORD

AS THE TITLE PAGE STATES, the devotions in this book contain portions from the collected sermons ("Sermon Book on the Gospels," "Sermon Book on the Epistles," "Brosamen," and "Casual Sermons and Speeches") of Professor Dr. C. F. W. Walther who was highly esteemed by the American Lutheran Church. The devotions are arranged according to the Church Year so the note struck by Sunday's readings in church may continue to sound throughout the entire week in the homes of Christians. The sainted Dr. Walther was a mighty man of God. In the spirit and power of Luther, he was influential and looked after American Lutheran Christendom. The hope is certainly justified that the witness of this faithful servant, who has now entered the joy of his Lord, will be blessed also in this form. May God grant it! Amen.

A. C.

Translator's Preface

THE VOICE OF C. F. W. WALTHER is one that needs to be heard today, not because he is a founding father of our Synod, but because he preached nothing but the truths of Scripture. Although written more than 150 years ago, these sermons still apply to us today. We will do well as a Synod to listen to the voice of our founding father, seminary professor and president, and our first synodical president proclaiming the timeless truths of Scripture as we navigate through the twenty-first century, seeking to be a faithful and confessional Lutheran Synod.

Walther, the champion of the congregation and the laypeople, wrote and preached these sermons for laypeople. By reading these devotions daily, the layperson will certainly grow tremendously in the faith. These devotions were translated with the twenty-first century reader in mind. The original lengthy sentences were broken down into the shorter sentences of today. Some rhetorical devices and redundancies were removed or consolidated to have free-flowing modern English. This was done while maintaining accurate content and meaning.

At times, the original hymn stanza at the end of the devotion could not be located in English. In those cases, another hymn stanza was chosen that reflected the content of the original or the content of the devotion. These are marked with a cross (†).

These devotions follow the Church's historic one-year lectionary, which today is used by only a minority of our congregations. About the only time a great difference occurs between the order of the historic and modern Church Years is in the Epiphany season. The modern Church Year goes directly from Epiphany into Lent. The historic Church Year has a three-week pre-Lenten season that begins three Sundays before Ash Wednesday with the week of Septuagesima. This translation also contains an index of Bible verses used as the text of the devotions and another with verses quoted in the devotions to help the reader study Scripture.

The translator thanks the people of Immanuel Lutheran Church, Copperas Cove, Texas, and of Faith Lutheran Church, Corning, New York, who read some early translations of these devotions in their newsletters or heard them before meetings. Thanks also to Mr. Daniel Fraser for his consistent encouragement to have these devotions published, and to Mrs. Shirley Olinger for her work on the preparation of the manuscript. A very special thanks goes to Mr. Richard Price who spent untold hours typing the manuscript and offered countless, invaluable suggestions to make this translation possible in its current form.

Gerhard Grabenhofer
Corning, New York
15 January 2004

GOD GRANT IT

C.F.W. WALTHER

Sunday

Read Matthew 21:1–5

EVER SINCE THE FIRST CENTURY, Christ has been continually coming, and He has made His presence known in many thousands of hearts. But even in these last years of the Church, few have received Him. Many have turned their backs to Him or, following a period of belief, they have become unfaithful to Him. Can we be sure, then, that Christ will come again in the new Church Year that begins today? Could He, perhaps, have grown tired of coming since He has already been so often rejected? No! Christ does not grow weary of coming. Today's Gospel reading testifies to that. That visible entry into Jerusalem is a symbol of His continual invisible coming to the New Testament Jerusalem of His dear Church in accordance with this promise: "If anyone loves Me, he will keep My word; and My Father will love him, and We will come to him and make Our home with him" (John 14:23), and "Behold, I am with you always, to the end of the age" (Matthew 28:20).

However, is it comforting for us to know that Christ will come again in this new Church Year? Isn't He the holy Son of God, and aren't we all sinners who fail to offer the praise we should properly show to God? Shouldn't we expect that, when Christ comes, He will come in wrath to punish us according to our deeds?

It may seem that way, but let us look at today's text to determine what kind of Jesus will come again this year. It is true that our Gospel presents Jesus as high and exalted. It tells us that He is all-knowing. From afar, He even knows the thoughts and words of the inhabitants of Bethphage. It tells us that He is almighty. From a distance, He can guide, according to His will, the heart of one who owns two beasts of burden. Our text also tells us that He did not come as a Judge, but as a humble King of grace and mercy.

In the Church Year that begins today, we have the comfort that Jesus will again come to us. He is all-knowing. He knows all of the sins we have committed (even those we have forgotten), as well as those we will commit in the future. He knows the condition of our heart better than we do ourselves, and He is all too well aware of the magnitude of our corruption by sin. Nevertheless, He does not come to punish our sins, but to forgive them, to wipe them away, and to throw them into the depths of the sea. He knows the trouble we are in, the sorrows that depress us, the tears that we secretly shed, and the enemies that oppress us. Our plight is great, but our King of grace wants to provide us with everything we need, both bodily and spiritually. He wants to hear our prayers and sighs, to dry our tears, to deflect our dangers, to protect us from our enemies, and, finally, to redeem us from all despair by His blessed death.

But Christ is not only willing to help us, He is also able to do so because He is the almighty Son of God. Therefore, He can support us in a manner that no one else can equal, and He can offer counsel that no one else can supply. Everything is in His hands. He can also direct the hearts of people and make everything work together for our temporal and eternal salvation.

When the call "Jesus comes again!" is heard today, we must lift up our heads and greet Him as did those we read about in today's Gospel: "Hosanna to the Son of David! Blessed is He who comes in the name of the Lord! Hosanna in the highest!" (Matthew 21:9).

Redeemer, come! I open wide
My heart to Thee; here, Lord, abide!

Let me Thine inner presence feel,
Thy grace and love in me reveal;
Thy Holy Spirit guide us on
Until our glorious goal is won.
Eternal praise and fame
We offer to Thy name. Amen.

(TLH 73:5)

Dec. 3

Monday

Read Matthew 21:4–5

TODAY'S READING INFORMS US that Jesus came to the "daughter of Zion." Zion was a mountain. At its summit was the temple of Jerusalem, and the city itself was located on one side of the mountain. Therefore, in one sense, the inhabitants of Jerusalem were the daughter of Zion because the mountain held them just as a mother holds her children in her womb. In a figurative or spiritual sense, however, the Old and New Testament Church is the daughter of Zion. It is these believers who hold the promise that Jesus will come to them continually in the Church Year that is just beginning.

Are there not many who fear that Jesus will not come to them because they are not certain they belong to the daughter of Zion as true believers and true members of Christ's Church? By no means! When Jesus entered Jerusalem, He visited His spiritual, believing Zion, but He also came to all who had entered the city, even the most miserable and lost sinners. And so it is today. Jesus comes, first, to His Church, His true believers, but He also visits all who cling to His Church, even if they are still miserable and lost sinners. Christ's Church is wherever His Word is proclaimed and His precious Sacraments are administered. Where these means of grace are absent, His Church is also absent. In such a place, there is no Christ, no salvation, and no blessedness. Anyone who does not want to keep God's Word and Sacraments hopes in vain for Christ's coming. Only the daughter of Zion, who has His Word and Sacraments, will hear these words: "Rejoice greatly, O daughter of Zion! Shout, O daughter of Jerusalem! Behold, your King is coming to you, . . . humble" (Zechariah 9:9).

For this reason, it is well with all who are determined to listen diligently to the precious Word of God in the new Church Year. If they do not yet belong to the daughter of Zion, if they cannot yet be numbered among the citizens of the true spiritual Jerusalem, they are still like those Israelites who witnessed Jesus' entrance into the visible Jerusalem so many years ago. The joyful message applies to all who let themselves be found among those who hear Christ's Word. Jesus also comes to them in this new Church Year. There are those who, in the year just past, did not completely forget, forsake, and lose the Lord Jesus, but they were often unfaithful to Him. They did not keep much of the vow they had made to Him; they were overcome by many sins, and, in many respects, they went more backward than forward. Yet they should not despair. A new Church Year begins, and Jesus, the King, comes again with new grace.

Whoever in the old Church Year was outwitted by his flesh, the world, or Satan, losing the Savior who had dwelt in his heart, should yet be encouraged. He may have spent the last year without peace and rest, without light and comfort, and without power and hope, oppressed by the feeling of displeasure from his God. But a new year has dawned, and Jesus is returning, bringing with Him a fresh supply of grace.

Have you not yet experienced the blessedness of having Jesus as your King of Grace? Have you, until now, wandered about in fleshly security, without care for the salvation of your immortal soul? Have you sought, above all else, money and goods, quiet days and a comfortable life, caring not at all for Jesus from your heart? Perhaps you have even been His bitter enemy. If you have recognized that you cannot be saved on this path, and if you are now anxiously asking "What must I do to be saved?" God wants to extend to you, too, the new grace of the new Church Year. You may be bound with a thousand bands of sin, but if, with a heart full of repentance, you grasp in faith the hand of grace He is extending to you, He will speak to you as before: "Loose him and lead him to Me." And you will indeed be free.

Come, Thou precious ransom, come,
Only Hope for sinful mortals!
Come, O Savior of the world!
Open are to Thee all portals.
Come, Thy beauty let us see;
Anxiously we wait for Thee.

Enter now my waiting heart,
Glorious King and Lord most holy.
Dwell in me and ne'er depart,
Tho' I am but poor and lowly.
Ah, what riches will be mine
When Thou art my Guest Divine. Amen.

(TLH 55:1, 2)

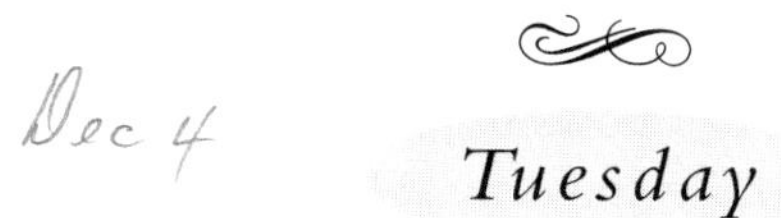

Tuesday

Read Matthew 21:6–9

AS THE WORD SPREAD in Jerusalem that Jesus was about to enter the city, multitudes, awakened by God, hurried to meet Him, crying, "Hosanna (which means, Oh, help!) to the Son of David!" Their cry of "Hosanna" was a fervent prayer for Christ at the beginning of His Messianic rule. Their prayer was that God would permit His kingly Messiah to succeed in overcoming all His enemies, that His kingdom would grow, and that He would rule in joy and blessing. The crowds then added: "Blessed is He who comes in the name of the Lord! Hosanna in the highest!" This zeal was revealed not only in their words but also in their actions. To glorify Christ, some removed their outer garments and placed them on the path, while others cut branches from trees and spread them on the road.

Here is a picture of people who are zealous for the joyful progress of the kingdom of Christ on earth. It begins with a burning heart that furthers Christ's kingdom with words and works. Many mean well when they belong to a Christian congregation, faithfully attending church, sending their children to a Christian school, and giving regular offerings for the support of the church. No one would deny that such people are committed to the advancement of Christ's kingdom. But it all depends not on their works, but on the condition of their heart. Therefore, only the one who is faithful and diligent in all his earthly dealings and whose heart lives in and for Christ's kingdom, regarding everything else as of secondary importance, has the proper zeal.

When that kind of zeal resides in the heart, it cannot

remain there, but must spill out in words and deeds. When the heart is full, the mouth overflows in prayers for the affairs of the kingdom of God. This is the daily "Hosanna" that is cried to the heavenly King. Such a person is also active in spreading the Kingdom, offering his abilities, his spiritual gifts, his time, and his influence to further the cause of Christ. These are the "clothes" and "palm branches" he daily lays at Jesus' feet.

Oh, may our whole life be such a constant "Hosanna" and a spreading of palm branches on the path before Christ. If we remain in this mind until we die, it is well with us! On that terrible Judgment Day, when the books are opened, we will discover, to our amazement, that He entered into our account everything good—even our humblest works—that we did in faith for His kingdom. Then, when Christ finally enters with His own through the gates of the heavenly Jerusalem, we will find ourselves among this holy multitude, and our petitioning "Hosanna" will be transformed into an eternally rejoicing "Hallelujah!"

Thy Zion strews before Thee
Green boughs and fairest palms,
And I, too, will adore Thee
With joyous songs and psalms.
My heart shall bloom forever
For thee with praises new
And from Thy name shall never
Withhold the honor due. Amen.

(TLH 58:2)

Wednesday

Read Lamentations 3:22–23

JEREMIAH OFFERED COMFORT to Old Testament believers when they groaned in heavy captivity following the fall of Jerusalem. The city and its temple lay in ruins. But the prophet reminded the people that the mercy of the Lord is new every morning, and there can be no greater, richer, more precious comfort for the sinner. Let us consider what these words mean.

"His mercies . . . are new every morning." On earth, as long as a new morning follows the evening, those mercies never cease. Although God has shown mercy to the whole sinful human race for centuries, and although He follows each individual with mercy for many years, that mercy does not end. As human beings, we have a small amount of mercy and we all too soon reach the limit of our patience in dealing with our fellow sinners. If we have already demonstrated mercy toward someone several times, we deem that to be enough. If the one to whom we have shown mercy is ungrateful, if he uses that mercy against us, the fountains of our mercy toward him easily and quickly dry up forever. The fountains of divine mercy, however, flow continually and even the basest ingratitude and the most wanton misuse cannot stop them. This is a bottomless sea of love and it can never be exhausted.

There is more. When Scripture says, "His mercies . . . are new every morning," it indicates that these mercies not only continue without ceasing, but they also do not diminish. They are always the same, always as great and fervent as they were in the beginning. Our mercy may burn brightly for a time, but as soon as it is tested, it becomes weaker until it finally drips like the last drops from an emptied vessel. But God's mercy flows over us in full streams from the first day of our life, and on every following evening we must again sing, "Praise to the Lord, who doth prosper thy work and defend thee, Who from the heavens the streams of His mercy doth send thee" (*TLH* 39:4). Just as the visible sun rises every morning in splendor over the whole world, upon which it has already shone for millennia, so does the invisible sun of God's mercy rise every day with the same brightness so it shines upon us continually.

God never thinks about the amount of mercy He has already shown or the length of time in which He has shown it to an individual. It is not as if each person has a certain amount of mercy allotted to him and God subtracts a bit of that mercy each day until the account is emptied. Each day, God treats us as if He were extending His mercy to us for the first time. He seeks us, and He shows Himself to us as a God who earnestly desires our salvation. Millions of proofs of God's grace may already lie behind us, and until now they may have proven futile. But each morning, without fail, God lifts us up, like a newborn baby to a mother's bosom, and grants us His grace anew.

This word of Scripture is especially comforting at the start of a new Church Year, when we may reflect sadly on the often futile use we have made of God's mercy during the previous years. That mercy remains with us, however. It is new every morning and every year.

Ev'ry morning mercies new
Fall as fresh as morning dew;
Ev'ry morning let us pay
Tribute with the early day;
For Thy mercies, Lord, are sure,
Thy compassion doth endure. Amen.

† *(TLH 537:1)*

Thursday

Read Romans 13:11

THE SLEEP OUT OF WHICH Saint Paul seeks to awaken us here is the spiritual sleep of sin. It is a sleep from which man must awaken daily until he dies so, in the end, he does not sink into eternal death. The unconverted person lies in this sleep, as in death, so he does not see, hear, and understand anything spiritual. However, even true, awakened Christians cannot escape a certain amount of spiritual drowsiness. If they do not want to fall back into the old spiritual sleep of death, they must continually rouse themselves.

This word of the apostle also applies to us. "Besides this you know the time, that the hour has come for you to wake from sleep. For salvation is nearer to us now than when we first believed." By "salvation," Paul clearly does not mean God's grace and forgiveness of sins because the Roman Christians already had these. Rather, he is referring to the return of Christ on the Last Day to take His children home to heaven and to blessedness. The apostle is not suggesting there ever would have been a time in which man had no reason to awaken from his spiritual sleep. He says instead that as long as Christ had not come in the flesh, it was not possible for Him to return in judgment, ending the time of grace for all mankind (namely, the time of the old covenant). Naturally, at that time, a person could have reasoned that his awakening from sleep could be delayed awhile longer. But, beloved Christians, our salvation is closer than when we first believed. Christ has come, and He can return at any moment! Now is the time to arise from sleep so the Day of the Lord may not fall upon us as upon the foolish virgins who awakened too late, only to find the door to the heavenly marriage eternally shut.

If the approaching return of Christ was considered a reason to awaken hastily from sleep in the days of the apostles, how much more is it a reason for us! Many centuries have passed since Paul wrote the words of today's text, and everything has come to pass that, according to the prophecies of Christ and His apostles, herald the Last Day. The Judge is already at the door. God stands, bearing His torch of wrath before the world, but still His boundless patience struggles with His justice, a justice that wants to set the world, which is becoming a great Sodom, on fire in order to destroy it. The whole world, which is already lying in death throes amid a thousand fulfilled signs of the Last Day, calls to Christians and to all who want to be Christians, "[T]he hour has come for you to wake from sleep." It would be insanity and folly of the heart not to want to awaken now from the sleep of sin, for already the flames of divine wrath are approaching the straw house of the world, and heaven calls, as with a voice of thunder: "The hour is here! Awaken from sleep!"

Help me as the morn is breaking,
In the spirit to arise,
So from careless sloth awaking,
That, when o'er the aged skies
Shall the Judgment Day appear,
I may see it without fear. Amen.

(TLH 549:4)

Friday

Read Romans 13:12

IT IS NO WONDER THAT MOST people lie in spiritual darkness because they remain in their sins and seek their heaven in the earth and its glory. Unfortunately, this applies not only to poor, blind heathens, but also to most baptized, so-called Christians. They do not understand how frightful sin is. Each sin, no matter how small, earns hell and eternal damnation. They also do not know how blessed are those who cling to God alone, possess His grace, and stand in communion with Him. Few of those who are surrounded by the dark night are ashamed, even if they wear the most wretched clothes, the clothes of repeated sinfulness.

It is different with the faithful Christian. Of him it is said, "The night is far gone; the day is at hand." In the heart of such a Christian, the natural darkness is fading and the day of the knowledge of salvation has dawned. Christ Himself has risen in his heart as the bright morning star. The faithful Christian knows what sin is. When he was converted to Christ, he recognized that sin is a horrible offense to God. He experienced the torment of conscience on account of his sin and he understood that sin separated him from God, stirring up His wrath. No man can atone for his own sins, and for that reason God's Son had to die on the cross. The faithful Christian has also learned that the whole world, with all its glory, cannot make anyone happy, cannot provide peace and rest, and cannot offer comfort in a time of trouble. God alone, with His grace and His communion, is the highest good of man.

Isn't this an urgent reason for a faithful Christian to awaken from the sleep of sin and to walk in a new life? Certainly!

Just as a man cannot remain in his bedclothes when the night is over, the Christian, in whose heart the day has dawned, cannot continue to wear the night clothes of sin. He must, instead, don the garb of good works and live a God-pleasing life.

Therefore, let all of us who want to be faithful Christians remember three things in this new Church Year: (1) the hour is here to awaken from sleep, (2) our salvation is drawing closer, and (3) the night has passed and the day has dawned. By the grace of Jesus, we will reach our beautiful destination.

Comfort my desponding heart;
Thou my Strength and Refuge art.
I am weak, and cunningly
Satan lays his snares for me. Amen.

† *(TLH 91:7)*

Saturday

Read Romans 13:12–14

If a person has been awakened from his sleep by God's Word, he has come to know his miserable, damnable condition. If he no longer wishes to become lost, he must rise, take something off and put something on, just like the individual who, rising from bodily sleep, removes his night clothes and puts on his day clothes.

According to our text, what he must put off is everything that belongs to the "works of darkness." This includes all the things that a person seeks in the darkness but wishes no one else, above all the holy God, to discover. These may be the evil thoughts and desires of the heart, or sinful and hypocritical words and deeds. They are, in short, anything that fights against God's Word and Spirit. The person who does not daily seek to rid himself of these works of darkness comforts himself in vain that God's Word has awakened him and that he no longer resides in carnal security without care for his salvation. All his religious "awakening" has made him nothing more than a two-faced child of hell, about whom the Lord says, "And that servant who knew his master's will but did not get ready or act according to his will, will receive a severe beating" (Luke 12:47).

It is not enough for one who has been awakened to put off the works of darkness. He must also put on the armor of light. This gives him a clear conscience before God and man. He no longer has anything to hide or to be ashamed of, and this makes him rejoice before God. This new garb is not called "works" but "armor" because it not only clothes him but also arms him for the battle for the crown. The armor of light consists, first of all, of the belt of truth, that is, sincerity in the whole walk before God and man. It also includes the breastplate of righteousness toward everyone, the shoes that are ready to bring the Gospel of peace to friend and foe, the shield of faith to extinguish all of Satan's fiery darts, the helmet of salvation (that is, a living trust full of the hope of eternal life), and the sword of the Spirit (that is, the Word of God). This armor provides the means to battle victoriously against the flesh, the world, and the devil.

To put all of this even more clearly, Saint Paul writes in today's text: "Let us walk properly as in the daytime, not in orgies and drunkenness, not in sexual immorality and sensuality, not in quarreling and jealousy. But put on the Lord Jesus Christ, and make no provision for the flesh, to gratify its desires." The putting off of the works of darkness must be revealed in a life and walk that are unblemished by the world.

Whoever says that he has put off the works of darkness but continues to walk with the world—a world that lives in revelry and drunkenness, giving rise to fleshly desires, strife, envy, anger, dissension, and sometimes even murder—is a liar. A Christian must look after his body, not so he can live in luxury, but so he can remain fit to serve God and his neighbor.

But there is still more! Only the one who has been truly awakened from spiritual sleep is able to keep himself unblemished. Instead of conforming to the world, he has put on Christ as his garment so the world sees in him not the old man, but a new man who presents the image of his loving, humble, chaste, pure, and heavenly-minded Savior.

Before the dawning day
Let sin's dark deeds be gone,
The old man all be put away,
The new man all put on. Amen.

† *(TLH 68:5)*

Sunday

Read Luke 21:25–27

CERTAIN SIGNS WILL PRECEDE the Last Day and announce its nearness to all mankind. Many people believe they can remain calm about the Last Day because these signs must still come before this great and terrible day. They intend to wait for their arrival before they become concerned. But they are in error, for all these signs have already occurred. Haven't the sun and moon often become darkened? Haven't remarkable appearances in the stars often been observed? Haven't people languished in fear and doubt about the events that are to take place? Haven't the seas become turbulent and swallowed up men? Haven't the powers of the heavens often been shaken? Astronomers report that stars that were observable for centuries have suddenly disappeared.

Didn't all these signs, which according to the Word of God will precede the Last Day, take place long ago? People and kingdoms have rebelled against one another. Pestilence and earthquakes have struck our world repeatedly. Unrighteousness among baptized Christians has increased, and the love of many has grown cold. Many false prophets have risen and led many astray. And, for a long time, the Gospel has been preached in the whole world. This has not always resulted in conversion, but as Christ Himself says, it has served as "a testimony to all nations" (Matthew 24:14). Wasn't the great falling away—which, according to divine prophecy, precedes the Day of the Lord—fulfilled long ago when Christendom came under the dominion of the papacy? In the long papal line, hasn't the Antichrist openly sat in the temple of God, that is, the Christian Church? And wasn't that falling away brought down at the time of the Reformation for all who preserve God's Word? Finally, haven't there also been mockers inside Christ's Church, as was predicted by the apostle Peter?

There can be no doubt: All of the signs that precede the coming of the Last Day appeared long ago. The unbelieving world does not regard these events as omens. It thinks these are simply natural phenomena that have always taken place and are easy to explain. Indeed, some of these occurrences, such as solar and lunar eclipses, can be calculated and predicted precisely by astronomers. It is therefore foolish, unbelieving people maintain, to ascribe a special meaning to these events.

Scientists may be able to explain the natural reasons for the formation of a rainbow, but believers know that God created the rainbow to be a sign that He would never again destroy the earth with a flood. In the same way, He created eclipses and other heavenly appearances, as well as the horrible roarings of the sea, as certain signs of the approaching Last Day, no matter how much science may dismiss them as natural occurrences.

Every bodily sickness in a man reminds him of his mortality and exhorts him to set his house in order. In the same way, the signs in the heavens and on earth that mankind has witnessed through the centuries have been a repeated warning that the last hour is soon to strike. God has sounded these warnings with the unmistakable clarity of a trumpet call, yet people profess to be secure and unconcerned, as if to say, "My Lord won't come for a long time." From such false security may the Lord, by His grace, preserve us!

E'en now, when tempests round us fall
And wintry clouds o'ercast the sky,
Thy words with pleasure we recall
And deem that our redemption's nigh.

† *(TLH 64:2)*

O Christ, who diedst and yet dost live,
To me impart Thy merit;
My pardon seal, my sins forgive,
And cleanse me by Thy Spirit.
Beneath Thy cross I view the day
When heav'n and earth shall pass away,
And thus prepare to meet Thee. Amen.

† *(TLH 604:4)*

Monday

Read Luke 21:34

WITH THESE WORDS, Christ warns Christians not to let themselves succumb, in these last days, to the world's penchant for a secure, carefree, and luxurious life. That life is marked, in part, by drunkenness and revelry and by cares, covetousness, and striving for temporal things. When we compare the condition of our world with that described in Holy Scripture, can we doubt for a moment that we live in the last times? The evidence is everywhere, both in Scripture and in life.

> The doctrinal evidence is just as Christ proclaimed. The Gospel of the kingdom of heaven has been preached among all peoples. The great falling away has been revealed both in the rise of the papacy and in open unbelief. Many charismatic sects and a mixture of religions have given rise to an entire army of baptized scoffers and blasphemers. These seek to overturn religion under the guise of progress and enlightenment and to reject all of the holy doctrines and foundations of Christianity as superstition. They make jokes about the Bible and the Creator, and they mock the belief in the Last Day.

The world now seems to operate according to the motto, "Let us eat and drink, for tomorrow we die." All sinners proceed on the assumption that there is no God whom men must fear and no judgment in which man must give an account. People make no secret of their sins; they even boast about them. As at the time of the flood and the destruction of Sodom and Gomorrah, sinners regard themselves as secure and carefree. They seek money, bigger houses, and other worldly pleasures. They dismiss as laughable those who witness to the truth of God's anger and punishment. New movements continue to arise for the purpose of overturning Christian discipline and order and for stirring up children against their parents, citizens against their government, students against their teachers, and the poor against the rich. Perhaps we should be grateful that the world has not yet demonstrated the impudence to impugn the estate of marriage and to declare that prostitution, adultery, and all other sins are to be legally permissible.

Whoever cannot see from all this that the world has descended into a pit of vileness must have already drunk deeply from the cup of shame. Are we permitted to be secure in any of this? Surely not! Heaven and earth are calling us with a voice of thunder, warning that the Judge is at the door and Satan has launched the final rebellion of mankind against its Creator. Therefore, let us not sleep but instead be armed for war, so when Jesus Christ comes to judge the living and the dead, we will be ready to receive Him with joy.

Soon will the Lord, my Life, appear;
Soon shall I end my trials here,
Leave sin and sorrow, death and pain.
To live is Christ, to die is gain.

Soon will the saints in glory meet,
Soon walk through every golden street,
And sing on every blissful plain:
To live is Christ, to die is gain. Amen.

† *(TLH 608:4, 5)*

Tuesday

Read Luke 21:35–36

IF GOD WERE TO ANNOUNCE mankind's Last Day even one hour before the fact, many would continue to think they had time for conversion. They would comfort themselves with the notion that, just before the end of the time of grace, they could still turn to God and plead for His acceptance because He is a merciful God.

But God has cut off this false comfort from man. Scripture tells us that the Last Day will come suddenly and unforeseen. Just as many die without the warning signs of declining health, increasing sickness, and the debility of old age, there will be nothing to announce the arrival of the Last Day that was not made known long ago. It will come like a thief in the night, like a lightning bolt from heaven, and, as today's text informs us, "upon all who dwell on the face of the whole earth." Even the godly will receive no additional advance notice of it.

The hunter lays and conceals his snares for the game he wants to catch and he anxiously avoids any noise that could betray how close he is to his quarry. As the animal wanders without care through the grass, the hunter suddenly bursts out of the thicket and throws the snare over his unsuspecting prey. The trembling animal is quickly and firmly bound until it is unable to move. The hunter then carries it away to receive the stab of death with a sharp, shiny blade. So, in this same way, God prepares His Last Day in secret for a falsely secure world. No human soul, earthly creature, or heavenly angel knows the precise moment when that great and terrible event will occur.

Until the arrival of the Last Day, the world will continue to sleep in sin, living as it has always lived: eating and drinking, buying and selling, building and planting, laughing and joking, mocking and blaspheming. To the faithful, the world says: "Don't talk to me about this Last Day, about hell and punishment. These are all farces created by priests merely to frighten us." But behold! While the world proceeds in its carefree, mocking manner, the heavens will suddenly open, and Jesus Christ will appear. He will be dressed in the raiment of the great Judge of all mankind, and He will be surrounded by thousands upon thousands of angels with flaming swords. The archangel will sound the trumpet, and like a thousand storms, its blaring tones will thunder through the quaking creation. The dead will rise and all the world will tremble in fear. The enemies of Christ will already feel in their hearts the expected damnation and their howling will fill the earth. Only the company of the godly will raise their voices in shouts of "Hallelujah!" as they rejoice at the appearance of their Savior.

There will now be no time for the unconverted to change their mind. The time of grace will have ended with the appearance of the Judge. In this moment, God's wrath will press like mountains upon the souls of all who have not prepared themselves for the Day of Wrath with true repentance. All of them will shout in mourning, curse the day of their birth, and find themselves with nowhere to flee and hide. In their misery, they will cry "to the mountains and rocks, 'Fall on us and hide us from the face of Him who is seated on the throne, and from the wrath of the Lamb, for the great day of their wrath has come, and who can stand?'" (Revelation 6:16–17). The form of the world will come crashing down, and hell will rush in, open its fiery jaws, and swallow up all of its children for eternity.

This terrible scene can happen today, even this very hour,

and it should prompt us to rise immediately and to flee into the wounds of Jesus Christ. Let us remain there and "stay awake at all times, praying that you may have strength to escape all these things that are going to take place, and to stand before the Son of Man" (Luke 21:36).

O'er the distant mountains breaking
Comes the redd'ning dawn of day.
Rise, my soul, from sleep awaking;
Rise and sing and watch and pray.
'Tis thy Savior, 'Tis thy Savior,
On His bright returning way. Amen.

† *(TLH 606:1)*

Dec. 12

Wednesday

Read Genesis 3:15

MOSES TELLS US THAT GOD created man in His image. A child loves his father and has an innocent, heartfelt confidence in him. Man also once walked before the face of his Creator as before his dear father. But he then fell, having been led into sin by Satan, who approached him in the form of a snake. With this act of rebellion, man came into the kingdom of Satan, in which hostility toward God and His own reigns. In forsaking God, man descended into great misery, blindness, shame, and disgrace. Because of this, he had no desire to return to God. From that hour, he was able to die a bodily death and his soul died a spiritual death—just as God had promised.

Nevertheless, God turned His face, full of mercy, toward man. He appeared in visible form in Eden, and full of fear, Adam and Eve drew near to their returning Creator. Reminding them of their fall, He turned to the snake, in whose form Satan was still present, and said to it, "I will put enmity between you and the woman, and between your offspring and her offspring; He shall bruise your head, and you shall bruise His heel."

That promise is now fulfilled in Jesus Christ. He is the promised Seed of the woman, for He had no human father, but only a human mother, namely, the most favored Virgin Mary, who conceived Him by the overshadowing of the Holy Ghost. Almost immediately after His birth, the hellish snake slithered after Him, prompting Herod to seek His death. As soon as Christ appeared to teach the people, the evil enemy incited spiritual and worldly powers—the Pharisees and scribes, Herod and Pilate, and the entire Jewish people—to kill Him. Satan finally succeeded. He inflicted his sting in Christ's heel, and it was horrible. Christ suffered blows from fists and ridicule, He was spat upon, a crown of thorns was forced upon His head, He was scourged, and He was finally nailed, hand and foot, to the cross, where He poured out His blood. Yet only His heel was pierced. Christ's human nature could suffer death, but because He was truly God as well as truly man, death could not hold Him. After three days, all of His wounds were healed.

By all of this, Christ fulfilled the promised crushing of the serpent's head. With His incarnation, Jesus entered the field of battle against Satan's power. With His preaching and His miracles, He attacked Satan earnestly. With His suffering and death, He overcame Satan. By letting Himself be slaughtered and sacrificed, Christ received the punishment for mankind's sin, satisfying fully the righteousness of God. All of Satan's accusations against fallen man thus came to an end. Christ destroyed Satan's kingdom and severed the bands of death and damnation. Moreover, by His descent into hell, His resurrection, and His ascension, Christ finally celebrated a public triumph over the greatest enemy of the human race and bound him in darkness eternally.

Scripture's first promise of the Savior of the world was fulfilled in Jesus Christ alone. He alone is the Seed of the woman or, as Isaiah calls Him, the Son of the Virgin. He alone had to feel the sting in the heel. But He alone, with His life, His suffering, His death, and His glorious resurrection, crushed the serpent's head forever.

Comfort my desponding heart;
Thou my Strength and Refuge art.
I am weak, and cunningly
Satan lays his snares for me.

Bruise for me the Serpent's head
That, set free from doubt and dread,
I may cleave to Thee in faith,
Safely kept through life and death. Amen.

(TLH 91:7, 8)

Thursday

Read Ephesians 5:14

THE SPIRITUAL CONDITION OF ALL people, before they experience the wonder of grace and are changed by God's Word and Spirit, is like the physical condition of someone who is asleep. He knows nothing about the visible sun that has risen in the sky and casts its rays upon him. He knows nothing of the evil or the good that surround him. Empty dreams hover around him but none of them are real.

Every man, by nature, lies in a deep spiritual sleep. He knows nothing of the sun of the Gospel that seeks to enlighten him. He regards the heavenly light as darkness and the divine wisdom as foolishness. He may rage against it, as if it were a terrible hindrance to true human happiness.

Some people hear the Gospel with their bodily ears but the ears of their spirit remain firmly shut to it. They are like those dangerously sick individuals who sleep with open eyes. They are illumined with the heavenly rays of God's Word, but their mind and heart remain unenlightened. They may come to historical knowledge of the Christian faith, but that faith is found only in their head. They do not learn to recognize the danger that confronts their soul, the danger of being eternally lost. They never understand their great natural corruption and that their natural mind is hostile toward God. They are unable to distinguish the evil from the good, the important from the vain, the happy from the unhappy. Finally, they do not sense how great is the grace that caused Jesus Christ to enter the world to save sinners. For them, Jesus remains a stranger, and the world remains their highest good. They do not come to hate sin or to understand that everything the world offers and everything man strives after avails nothing. They never understand, as Solomon did, that "all is vanity" (Ecclesiastes 1:2).

Such people spend their entire life as in a dream. They intend to wake up, but still they sleep. They intend to live, but they are dead. When God blesses them temporally, attempting, with His goodness, to lead them to repentance, they take this good only as a sign of their condition of grace and they feel a false sense of security. When God sends them distress and misery, hoping to rip them loose from the world and move them toward Himself, they want only to quarrel with God, regarding Him as an enemy who has dealt with them more harshly than they deserve.

How unfortunate is the condition of those who have not awakened from this natural spiritual sleep. It is the certain forerunner of eternal death and damnation. Everywhere in God's Word, we hear warnings against this. As today's text tells us, "Awake, O sleeper, and arise from the dead, and Christ will shine on you." May God grant that these warnings will enter our hearts as well as our ears, that they will frighten us out of the sleep of sin, and that they will awaken us to a new life in Christ!

Rise, my soul, to watch and pray,
From thy sleep awaken;
Be not by the evil day
Unawares o'ertaken.
For the Foe,
Well we know,
Oft his harvest reapeth
While the Christian sleepeth. Amen.

† *(TLH 446:1)*

Dec. 14

Friday

Read Romans 15:4

WITHOUT THE OLD TESTAMENT, we would know nothing about the beginning and end of the world and ourselves. It reveals to us how God called the world into existence out of nothing, how He preserves and governs it, how man was created good and in the image of God, how man was tempted by the devil and fell into sin and death, and how, from the very beginning, a Redeemer was promised. What foundation does the New Testament have without Old Testament revelations? The New Testament is nothing but an announcement that the promises of the Old Testament have been fulfilled. Without the Old Testament, we would not be sure that Jesus is the Savior of the world, whose coming was promised beforehand. There we learn that He would be descended from Abraham, Isaac, Jacob, Judah, and David. We learn when and where He would appear, the works He would do, and the teachings of the prophets about Him. We learn that He would be the Seed of the woman, the Son of the Virgin, and the Lord of righteousness.

Without the Old Testament, the New Testament would be a building without a foundation, a tree without roots, a doctrine without evidence. Thus, when the New Testament teaches us about Christ's person, His work, and His doctrine, we can readily prove this from the books of Moses, the Psalms, and the prophets, which say, "It is written" or "Have you not read?" The holy apostles and evangelists offer proofs of Christ's divinity from the Old Testament when they report that "this was to fulfill" and "as the Holy Ghost has spoken." The Bereans are highly praised in Scripture because they received the preaching of Paul and Silas "with all eagerness," but they were also "examining the Scriptures daily to see if these things were so" (Acts 17:11).

Who can doubt that the Old Testament remains of the greatest relevance for New Testament Christians? "But," someone may interject, "aren't there accounts in the Old Testament history of completely horrible sins, reports of wars and slaughters, and extremely detailed descriptions of ceremonies, equipment, clothing, buildings, and sayings that are often hard to understand? How can any of this have been written for us Christians for doctrine?"

The terrible sins described in the Old Testament are not reported just as history but as an earnest warning that God is greatly angered by sin and punishes it unto the children's children. But it also reports that God forgives these sins when people truly repent of them and bring forth the honest fruits of faith. The history of these sins is given to us for our instruction and correction so we can recognize how great the corruption of fallen man is and how we must pray and fight against it. As Saint Paul tells us, following a report of serious sins and the resulting divine judgments from the Old Testament, "They were written down for our instruction, on whom the end of the ages has come" (1 Corinthians 10:11).

The accounts of devastating wars and bloody killings are also loud witnesses of mankind's wickedness and God's divine wrath and judgment. The detailed descriptions of ceremonies, clothing, and buildings are types of the spiritual things of the New Testament, and they offer us comfort in that our Christian freedom delivers us from these heavy burdens of the Law. The darkness of Old Testament speech should move us to reflect that what was hidden to the faithful at the time those books were written has now been revealed in the writings of the New Testament.

There can thus be no doubt. Everything contained in the Old Testament Scriptures remains essential reading for Christians everywhere.

Preserve Thy Word, O Savior,
To us this latter day
And let Thy kingdom flourish,
Enlarge Thy Church, we pray.
Oh, keep our faith from failing,
Keep hope's bright star aglow.
Let naught from Thy Word turn us
While wand'ring here below. Amen.

† *(TLH 264:1)*

Dec. 15

Saturday

Read Romans 15:4

THE NEW TESTAMENT SCRIPTURES contain the history of the life, suffering, and death of our Savior, but the descriptions of the lives of the apostles and other believers are only fragmentary. The Old Testament, by contrast, offers complete accounts of the lives of many faithful servants and children of God. What do we learn about them? They did not seek God, but God sought them. They were not always true to God, but God was always true to them. God always comforted them in times of trouble, and He delivered them out of every distressing circumstance. When they cried out to Him, He heard them. When they stumbled, He lifted them up. When they traveled along the path of error, God sought them and put their feet upon the right path. When they fell into serious sin, God punished them and let them feel His wrath, but He did not eternally reject them. Remembering the covenant of grace He had established with them, He attended to them, led them to repentance, and accepted them again in grace.

Here we can remember Adam and Eve, the first people; Noah, the second father of the human race; Abraham, Isaac, and Jacob, the holy patriarchs; Job, the man of endurance; Moses, the mediator of the old covenant; Aaron, the first high priest; David, the kingly prophet who greatly sinned and received a great pardon; Daniel, the faithful confessor in the exile; and all the holy prophets. God led all of them on miraculous paths until they died, blessed in the faith to which they had come. Here, we have vivid examples of the Lord's promise, as given to us by the Holy Ghost: "My sheep hear My voice, and I know them, and they follow Me. I give them eternal life, and they will never perish, and no one will snatch them out of My hand" (John 10:27–28). We also have here clear examples of the words of Saint Paul: "No temptation has overtaken you that is not common to man. God is faithful, and He will not let you be tempted beyond your ability, but with the temptation He will also provide the way of escape, that you may be able to endure it" (1 Corinthians 10:13). Finally, we have these words from the same apostle: "And I am sure of this, that He who began a good work in you will bring it to completion at the day of Jesus Christ" (Philippians 1:6).

How can we then read the Old Testament without being strengthened in the hope of eternal life? How can we read the Old Testament and still doubt our salvation? Why should God, through His Holy Spirit, have given us all these examples of great sinners who were led to salvation on the wonderful path of grace if He did not desire that we, too, seize the hope Christ offers, a hope that comforts us in this life and allows us to die in full confidence?

Let us, then, recognize what an unspeakably great treasure we have in the Old Testament Scriptures. Let us not rob ourselves of it, either by our own blind reason or by those who vilely mock religion. Let us diligently read and sincerely pray for enlightenment from the Holy Ghost. With his own mind and strength, no person can understand either the Old or New Testament for his salvation. Let us also compare the Old and New Testaments, just as Christ opened the Scriptures of Moses and the prophets to the Emmaus disciples so they understood them and their hearts burned with heavenly joy. Above all, let us seek Christ in both Testaments, for, as Saint Peter tells us, this is the One to whom all of the prophets bore witness, and all who believe in Him shall receive the forgiveness of their sins. Thus, we too will be able to say from our hearts regarding the Old Testament:

Thy Word doth deeply move the heart,
Thy Word doth perfect health impart,
Thy Word my soul with joy doth bless,
Thy Word brings peace and happiness.

(TLH 5:2)

Preserve Thy Word and preaching,
The truth that makes us whole,
The mirror of Thy glory,
The power that saves the soul.
Oh, may this living water,
This dew of heavenly grace,
Sustain us while here living
Until we see Thy face! Amen.

(TLH 264:5)

Dec. 16

Sunday

Read Matthew 11:2–5

IF JESUS HAD NOT PERFORMED miracles, He could not have been the promised Savior whose coming was foretold by the prophets. He allowed His miraculous power to be seen from time to time, and His miracles identified Him as the messenger of God.

The first to recognize Jesus as a worker of miracles were the astonished crowds of people who gathered around Him. From the time He began His teaching ministry, He was given to healing a great multitude of suffering people in the course of a single day. The miracles of Christ are distinguished by their special glory. The people who witnessed them confessed, "Never since the world began has it been heard that anyone opened the eyes of a man born blind" (John 9:32). Jesus provoked even greater wonder when He said, "Destroy this temple, and in three days I will raise it up" (John 2:19). He was referring, of course, to the temple of His body. He also explained that, with His own power, He would rise again. And Jesus fulfilled that prediction when, three days following His crucifixion, He brought Himself to life again.

Part of the superiority of Christ's miracles resides in their extraordinary variety. He performed miracles on all sorts of creatures, including evil spirits that He cast out of possessed people, and in doing this, He revealed their most secret thoughts. Christ healed individuals who suffered from fever, dropsy, paralysis, and bleeding. He made the deaf hear, the dumb speak, the blind see, the lame walk, the lepers clean, and even the dead alive. Some of these people were healed when Jesus was present with them, but on other occasions, He healed them from a great distance. He helped them without having to speak to them or even to see them. He also displayed His power over other creatures. At His command, the fish in the sea gathered and a fish provided Him with a coin for the payment of taxes. At His blessing, bread and fish multiplied thousands of times to feed the masses. At His word, the fig tree that produced no fruit withered immediately and water was turned into wine. At His beckoning, the surface of the sea served Him as a solid floor to walk on. And at His threat, the storm and the turbulent waves subsided, prompting the relieved disciples to cry out, "What sort of man is this, that even winds and sea obey Him?" (Matthew 8:27).

What distinguished Christ as a miracle worker, what set Him apart from the prophets and apostles, was that He performed His miracles in His own name and by His own power, revealing Himself to be the Son of God. When the leper pleaded, "Lord, if You will, You can make me clean," Jesus replied, "I will; be clean" (Matthew 8:2–3), and the miracle occurred. To the daughter of Jairus, who was already dead, He called, "Child, arise" (Luke 8:54); to the son of the widow at Nain, who was already in the coffin, He said, "Young man, I say to you, arise" (Luke 7:14); and to Lazarus, who was already decomposing in the grave, He cried, "Lazarus, come out" (John 11:43). And behold! At these mighty words of Jesus, death and decay fled!

Moses could not have spoken in this way. When he performed miracles, he said, for example, "Thus says the Lord. . . . I will strike the water that is in the Nile" (Exodus 7:17). Moses spoke in the name of the Lord and his power derived from the Lord as well. The apostles also spoke differently from Christ. Indeed, they received their miracle-working power from Christ, along with the command that they use it in His name. Therefore, Peter called to the lame man in the temple, "In the name of Jesus Christ of Nazareth, rise up and walk!" (Acts 3:6).

Unlike the prophets, whose miracles were often destructive and frightening, the miracles of Jesus were always beneficial and delightful. While Moses turned water into blood, Jesus turned it into wine. While Elisha struck an unfaithful servant with leprosy, Christ healed those who were afflicted. Elijah called down fire from heaven upon the enemies of God, but when the apostles requested something similar from Jesus, He replied: "You do not know what manner of spirit you are of; for the Son of Man came not to destroy people's lives but to save them" (Luke 9:55–56). When Peter cut off Malchus's ear in the Garden of Gethsemane, Christ immediately healed him, although Malchus was among those who had come to arrest Him.

These are the glorious, miraculous works of Christ, by which He undeniably proves that we must believe Him when He declares that He is the Son of God and the Savior of the world.

Immanuel, we sing Thy praise,
Thou Prince of life and Fount of grace,
Thou Flower of heaven and Star of morn,
Thou Lord of lords, Thou Virgin-born.
Hallelujah!

With all Thy saints to Thee we sing,
Praise, honor, thanks to Thee we bring,
That Thou, O long-expected Guest,
Hast come at last to make us blest!
Hallelujah! Amen.

(ELHB 161:1, 2)

Monday

Read Matthew 11:6

THERE CANNOT BE THE SLIGHTEST doubt that Christ truly performed the miraculous works that the writers of the Gospels relate, for these evangelists are the most unobjectionable witnesses. In their writings, they reveal their own errors with the greatest openness and impartiality. Would they have done this if they were not lovers of the truth? Whom could we believe if we were unable to trust such witnesses? Why would they not have wanted to tell the truth? Did the apostles acquire some earthly benefit by their preaching on the works of Christ? Were they not forced, on the contrary, to take upon themselves poverty, disgrace, persecution, and even the most gruesome death? Will a person tell an untruth in order to plunge himself into unhappiness? Nothing could be more absurd than such a notion.

Moreover, Christ's miracles were not performed in secret. They did not occur only before the eyes of His friends, like the alleged miracles of the deceiver. Instead, they took place before many thousands of witnesses, including some of Jesus' most bitter enemies. For this reason, following His resurrection, when the apostles referred to His miracles in their preaching, no one dared to contradict them. If what the apostles related about Jesus had not happened, there surely would have been some in the crowd ready to respond, "You lie!"

Even the unbelieving Jews could not deny Christ's miracles, and these are attested in the Talmud itself. Instead, in order to reject Jesus, the rabbis devised laughable fables, such as the one that ascribes His power for miracles to His invocation of the secret name "Jehovah." During the first centuries of the Christian era, pagans wrote entire books against Christianity. We still have these books, either in their entirety or in fragments. But remarkably, none of them seeks to refute Christianity by denying the truth of the accounts of miracles found in the Scriptures. On the contrary, they admit that the miracles took place, although in heathen blindness they attribute them to magical powers. Even Muhammad, in his Koran, recognized the miracles of Christ, so no Muslim can deny them.

How, then, can anyone continue to reject Christ? And what more could Jesus Himself have done to prove He is the Son of God and the Savior of the world? He said, "If I had not done among them the works that no one else did, they would not be guilty of sin, but now they have seen and hated both Me and My Father" (John 15:24). Even in our day, we are surrounded by thousands of witnesses who remain convinced of the certainty of Christ's miracles.

If Jesus had only spoken God's Word and failed to perform God's works, a person could excuse himself by saying that in spiritual matters he is like a blind man and unable to examine and appraise the excellence of His doctrine. But anyone, even a child, can and must recognize the divinity of His works. There is no one other than Christ who could with but a word make a blind man see, restore to the lame the ability to walk, and even bring the dead back to life. Even the simplest among us can understand this. The true God has given testimony, and we can believe Him. Indeed, we must believe Him or fear His eternal displeasure and the loss of our eternal salvation.

The Scriptures tell us that the one who sees Jesus also sees the Father, for the Father is in Jesus and Jesus is in the Father. Our Lord also calls Himself the Door, the Good Shepherd, the Bread of life, the Light of the world, and the Resurrection and the Life. He also informs us that whoever believes in Him will live even though he dies. How, then, will those who have not believed excuse themselves on the Last Day? Jesus' glorious miracles will come forward against them, accusing them and condemning them, and they will have no rejoinder.

Therefore, let us with the open eyes of faith examine Christ's great signs and wonders and say, with Peter: "Lord, to whom shall we go? You have the words of eternal life, and we have believed, and have come to know, that You are the Holy One of God" (John 6:68–69).

My Jesus is my Splendor
My Sun, my Light, alone;
Were He not my Defender
Before God's awe-full throne,
I never should find favor
And mercy in His sight,
But be destroyed forever
As darkness by the light. Amen.

† *(TLH 528:4)*

Dec. 18

Tuesday

Read Isaiah 62:11

THE OPENING WORDS OF TODAY'S text inform us that this promise of salvation is intended for the time of the New Testament. What is prophesied here first took place when the apostles were alive, and it continues now until the Last Day. Jesus initially came to the world of the first century, and He will come again to judge all mankind. However, He also comes daily to enter the hearts of the faithful. It is this coming that is spoken of here by the prophet Isaiah.

"Behold, your salvation comes!" What a mighty and joyful invitation for each of us! Anyone who hears God's Word is visited and called by the Savior. Therefore, even the poor individual should rejoice. No one should consider himself too small, too lowly, too despised. Man looks on the outward appearance of a person, considering those of humble station to be insignificant. Such an attitude soon causes the poor and miserable to lose their human joy, and they can never hope to entertain a wealthy and distinguished person as their houseguest. But Jesus is not like that. It is the house of the heart the Savior wants to visit, and the heart of a poor man is as dear to Him as that of a king. Simple or wise, poor or rich, miserable or happy, lowly or grand—it is all the same to Jesus. In fact, the more lowly a person is in his own eyes, the more Jesus will desire to reside with him. Therefore, the poor man, too, should rejoice: "Behold, your salvation comes!"

For those of you who have, until now, loved sin more than Christ and His Word, do not think that Jesus will pass you by. Do not add to your sins with despair and doubt. The words "Behold, your salvation comes!" are also intended for you. Your sins in no way hinder Jesus from coming to you, for He is the Savior and the Friend of sinners. In fact, He earnestly seeks after sinners as for the lost lamb in the fold of one hundred. If you recognize yourself as lost, He wants to find you, too. Oh, believe it and rejoice!

There are also those who say: "Jesus was once in my heart, but I have lost Him again. I have cast Him out by my sins. I have sunk back into the cares and desires of the world, and there I must stay. Jesus has already often returned to me, but I told Him to go away, and now, I fear, He is eternally gone from me." Poor man, know this: Jesus does not tire of returning to the house of your heart. You have only to say: "Come, Jesus, again to me. Behold, my heart stands open to You." How quickly will your groanings be heard! It is also to you that Isaiah speaks the words, "Behold, your salvation comes!"

Welcome, O my Savior, now!
Hail! My Portion, Lord, art Thou.
Here, too, in my heart, I pray,
Oh, prepare Thyself a way!

King of Glory, enter in;
Cleanse it from the filth of sin,
As Thou hast so often done;
It belongs to Thee alone. Amen.

(TLH 91:4, 5)

Wednesday

Read Revelation 3:20

NO ONE COULD HINDER the arrival of Jesus in the flesh, and no one will be able to oppose His appearance for judgment. However, His advent into the heart is resistible and we can hinder Him from coming into our hearts. It is true that Christ, like the Father, is omnipresent, filling everything in heaven and on earth. In Him, we live and move and have our being. Again, no one can hinder this. But Christ's entrance into the individual human heart is not part of the kingdom of power and nature but of the kingdom of grace. Here, no force is used and free hearts are required. In such an advent, the heart of man becomes worthy by the presence of Christ's grace, and His Spirit and power come to the faithful.

"What," we may ask, "did Christ do and what does He still do so He may come into our hearts?" We must answer this question according to God's Word. Everything that Christ has already done and still does for us is based on His desire to enter our hearts and to live there forever. He became a man, lived and suffered, died and was buried, rose from the dead and ascended into heaven, and sits at the right hand of God and intercedes for us all so He can come to us in grace, live in us, and make us holy and eternally blessed. When our text tells us, "Behold, I stand at the door and knock," we are reminded of the means by which Christ prepares His entrance into our hearts. These means are the Word of God and the holy Sacraments.

When we read or hear the divine Law, it enters into our souls and lets us feel God's wrath. At such times, Christ knocks with the hammer of the Law, the staff of grief, upon the firmly latched iron doors of our unyielding hearts. His goal is not to destroy us, but to be admitted. When the largest and firmest bolts of our hearts have burst open and the Gospel is then preached to us, we are enticed to faith by its sweetness. Then, Christ knocks on the doors of our hearts with the staff of gentleness. When this happens, we should respond with the passionate cry: "Oh, come in, You blessed of the Lord. Why do You want to stand outside?" It is the same with the holy Sacraments. With our Baptism we put on Christ, He enters us, and He purifies the walls of our heart with the blood of the atonement. In Holy Communion, He lets us eat and drink His true body and blood, and He marries Himself with our soul so He is in us and we are in Him, flesh of His flesh and bone of His bone.

With the Law and the Gospel, Christ often combines some outward afflictions, sicknesses, and accidents, along with some gracious deliverances and blessings. These, too, are the means by which He knocks on our hearts. Oh, that we would always have them open to Him!

Lord, open Thou my heart to hear
And through Thy Word to me draw near;
Let me Thy Word e'er pure retain,
Let me Thy child and heir remain. Amen.

(*TLH* 5:1)

Dec. 20

Thursday

Read Mark 1:3

God's Advent call, "Prepare the way of the Lord," admonishes us poor sinners and makes us desire to celebrate the joyful season of Christmas. Not the one who is full, but only the one who is tormented by hunger and thirst can rejoice from his heart when food and drink are offered to him. Not the one who is well, but only the one who painfully feels his sickness can rejoice from his heart when he is assured that he will soon be well. Not the one who is free, but only the one who knows he is a prisoner can rejoice from his heart when his freedom is announced. Not the one who is rich, but only the one who is oppressed and frightened by his debts can rejoice from his heart when he hears that those debts have been paid. In the same way, only the one who vividly recognizes that he is a poor, lost sinner can rejoice from his heart when he hears that the Savior of sinners is here.

If a person wants to recognize himself as a poor sinner and to prepare the way of the Lord, how must he begin? No one can do this for himself. First, he must take the holy Ten Commandments in his hand, quietly look in this bright mirror, and examine his whole life and being according to them. He stops at each commandment and says to himself: "God has here commanded this. Did I also do it? God has forbidden this. Did I also omit it?" Above all, however, he must go into his heart and say to himself: "According to God's commandment, this is how my heart should be. I must love, fear, and trust God above everything else, and I must love my neighbor, even my enemy, as myself. Is my heart so composed?" The person for whom this examination is a serious matter does not try to deceive himself by it. He does not wantonly and stubbornly struggle against the Holy Ghost. Instead, he cries out, with David, "My iniquities . . . are more than the hairs of my head" (Psalm 40:12).

There is more to preparing the way of the Lord than this, however. Many recognize that their sins are innumerable and yet they are not poor sinners. A person must also rightly consider what God has threatened against all transgressors of His Commandments. This is what He says: "I the LORD your God am a jealous God, visiting the iniquity of the fathers on the children to the third and fourth generations . . ." (Exodus 20:5). God also speaks through Moses: "'Cursed by anyone who does not confirm the words of this law by doing them.' And all the people shall say, 'Amen!'" (Deuteronomy 27:26). Whoever takes these terrible words, not as a joke, but earnestly to heart, will then from his heart be frightened over his sins and say with David, "For my iniquities have gone over my head; like a heavy burden, they are too heavy for me" (Psalm 38:4).

Oh, blessed Advent time, when a person has such experiences! By preparing a way for the Lord, he has become a poor sinner and the gates of his heart stand open for the Lord to enter in grace. He embraces the Gospel, which is rich in comfort for sinners, and then, with inner longing, he welcomes the joyful Christmas celebration.

Come from on high to me;
I cannot rise to Thee.
Cheer my wearied spirit,
O pure and holy Child;
Thro' Thy grace and merit,
Blest Jesus, Lord most mild,
Draw me unto Thee!
Draw me unto Thee! Amen.

(TLH 92:2)

Friday

Read 1 Corinthians 4:1

WITH THESE WORDS, Saint Paul clearly states the qualities that all upright preachers should possess and display in order for their congregations to follow them according to God's Word.

The first requirement is that they be "servants of Christ." The true preacher is the only one whom Christ Himself has placed in his office. The preacher is called by Christ into the holy office of the ministry through the congregation. Christ has granted to His faithful congregation the keys of the kingdom of heaven and with them the power to choose, ordain, and install its servants. Only the servant of Christ, sent and called by Christ Himself, can show the call of the congregation whose shepherd he is supposed to be. The enthusiast, by contrast, can only boast that the "Spirit" leads him.

In our text, the apostle does not call true preachers Christ's lords, rulers, masters, or persons in authority. Instead, they are "servants of Christ." In the original Greek, Paul uses a word that literally means "oarsmen." Christ is and will remain the Lord of the ship of His Church. He will steer the rudder, and the preachers will man the oars. Christ says to His disciples: "[Y]ou have one teacher, and you are all brothers" (Matthew 23:8). He also says: "You know that the rulers of the Gentiles lord it over them, and their great ones exercise authority over them. It shall not be so among you. But whoever would be great among you must be your servant, and whoever would be first among you must be your slave" (Matthew 20:25–27).

Therefore, the apostle Peter warns the preachers of his time, "[N]ot domineering over those in your charge, but being examples to the flock" (1 Peter 5:3). Paul also says: "What then is Apollos? What is Paul? Servants through whom you believed" (1 Corinthians 3:5); "Not that we lord it over your faith, but we work with you for your joy" (2 Corinthians 1:24); and "For what we proclaim is not ourselves, but Jesus Christ as Lord, with ourselves as your servants for Jesus' sake" (2 Corinthians 4:5).

In our reading today, Paul tells us that true preachers are more than servants of Christ. They are also "stewards of the mysteries of God." Such preachers do not come with their own mysteries but only with those of the great God Himself as revealed in the Scriptures. They do not preach the word of man but the Word of God. The Scriptures of the apostles and prophets, from which everything pure flows, must be the source of what they teach.

Preachers are not just proclaimers of the mysteries of God, however, but also "stewards" of them. This is a matter of great importance. A steward is neither an unlimited lord nor merely a distributor of goods. He does much more than administer goods that are not his. He has precise instructions directing him to give to each member of the household only what he needs. Thus, a true preacher is not one who merely preaches God's Word, the Law and the Gospel, purely, clearly, and fully. In addition, he is a true steward of that Word, "rightly handling the word of truth" (2 Timothy 2:15), and he also strives for his congregation "to give them their portion of food at the proper time" (Luke 12:42).

O blessed ministry Of reconciliation,
That shows the way to God And brings to us salvation!
By Thine evangel pure, Lord, Thou preserv'st Thy fold,
Dost call, enlighten, keep, Dost comfort and uphold.
Amen.

† *(TLH 485:3)*

Saturday

Read 1 Corinthians 4:2

GOD HAS DISTRIBUTED GIFTS among His preachers. "To one," says Paul, "is given through the Spirit the utterance of wisdom, and to another the utterance of knowledge according to the same Spirit, to another faith [that is, heroic faith], . . . to another prophecy [that is, a special aptitude in the interpretation of the Scriptures], to another the ability to distinguish between spirits, to another different kinds of tongues, to another the interpretation of tongues" (1 Corinthians 12:8–10). No individual preacher has all these gifts, but only his appointed portion. The holy apostles themselves did not possess the same amount of gifts. To Paul, above all the others, was granted the gift of a deep and rich knowledge. John received the gift of looking into the future, and Apollos had the gift of eloquence.

It is the same today. One gift is granted to a certain preacher and a different gift is given to another preacher. And just as a person does not demand certain things from a steward, only that which is required by his master, so shall a congregation not seek this or that gift in its preacher, but only the gift God has awarded. The congregation that seeks more than this commits both an injustice and a cruelty, and, in addition, it is guilty of having a preacher who holds his office not with joy but with sighing. In that case, the congregation will be shortchanged because it will not have the full benefit and full blessing God intended it to have in its preacher.

Our text warns that a congregation should seek in a preacher nothing more than that he be found faithful. At the same time, however, it is commanded to seek nothing less. Faithfulness in doctrine and in life is of vital importance to a preacher, and it should be no less important to the congregation. Woe, therefore, to the congregation whose preacher wants to be faithful to biblical doctrine, but which insists, instead, that he preach, either openly or secretly, something other than God's pure Word. Woe to the congregation whose preacher wants to be faithful in refuting all errors dangerous to the soul, but which demands that he remain silent for the sake of temporal peace. Woe to the congregation whose preacher wants to be faithful in punishing all ungodly conduct, but requires him, as did the Jews of Isaiah's time, to "speak to us smooth things, prophesy illusions" (Isaiah 30:10). Woe to the congregation whose preacher wants to be faithful in administering to the church the discipline that Christ prescribed, but wants to know only about the releasing key and not about the binding key. Woe to the congregation whose preacher wants to remain faithful by making no distinctions among his parishioners, but which demands that he have regard for them. Finally, woe to the congregation whose preacher wants to remain faithful in a Christian, God-pleasing life, but which seeks from him perfect angelic holiness, having no forgiveness for any weakness in him, or merely wants him to be good company and to serve the world and the flesh.

In a certain sense, then, God's grace has placed in the hands of congregations the key to whether a preacher's office is blessed or unblessed. Our preachers, as God's stewards, must give a terrible guarantee that they want to remain faithful. They must pledge to us, the whole Church, and to their God nothing less than their souls' salvation. Therefore, let us not demand from them what God has forbidden them or forbid them what God has commanded them. God has admonished them to preach His Word without diminishing and without adding. Let us, then, demand of our preachers God's Word, His whole counsel for our salvation, for God has directed them as follows: "Cry aloud; do not hold back; lift up your voice like a trumpet; declare to my people their transgression, to the house of Jacob their sins" (Isaiah 58:1). Let us also receive with gentleness our preachers' words even when they chastise us, for God has spoken to them: "For I am not ashamed of the gospel, for it is the power of God for salvation to everyone who believes" (Romans 1:16). Let us, as poor sinners, always open our hearts and ears to this message of joy and receive it in faith.

In these last days of sore distress
Grant us, dear Lord, true steadfastness
That pure we keep, till life is spent,
Thy holy Word and Sacrament. Amen.

† *(TLH 292:2)*

Sunday

Read John 1:19–28

JOHN SPENT HIS YOUTH in the Judean desert. In admirable self-denial, he clothed himself with a coarse garment of camel's hair and managed to exist only on locusts and wild honey. With his extraordinary appearance, he quickly captured people's attention. When he entered manhood, he began to preach repentance, emphasizing that the long-expected Messiah's kingdom was near. He also baptized those who believed his preaching. Everywhere among the people, the thought arose that John was the promised Messiah himself; Elijah, who they thought would return to life in the days of the Messiah; or the great Prophet, who, according to a common delusion of that day, would be found next to the Messiah. Each day, John's authority among the people grew. So popular did he become that the authorities sent a delegation of priests and Levites to him, posing the question, "Who are you?" If John had answered, "I am Christ, the promised Messiah," the people would undoubtedly have paid him homage immediately and enthusiastically. No official would have been in a position to stop the uproar if John had placed himself at the head of the people. But today's text informs us that John "confessed, and did not deny, but confessed 'I am not the Christ.'"

The delegation then asked him if he was Elijah or the Prophet. To both of these questions, he responded in the negative. However, by Christ's own utterance (Matthew 11:14), wasn't John the Elijah who should go before the Messiah? Wasn't he likewise, according to Christ's own testimony, a prophet—indeed, greater than all other prophets? In a certain sense, he was. Yet John denied both of these identifications.

From John's restraint, we see how careful a person must be in confessing his faith. The Jews wondered if John was the returning Old Testament prophet Elijah. However, John was called Elijah only because he was a man in the spirit and power of Elijah. Therefore, he answered his questioners according to the meaning they had in mind when they asked him. He was neither the Elijah nor the Prophet they were awaiting, and he answered them decisively and without hesitation, wanting to avoid even the slightest ambiguity in his confession.

But the delegation pressed him further, asking, "Who are you? We need to give an answer to those who sent us. What do you say about yourself?" John then characterized himself as "the voice of one crying out in the wilderness, 'Make straight the way of the Lord,' as the prophet Isaiah said." Note how carefully John framed his response. He identified himself as the herald, the forerunner, and the one who arrived on the scene first to prepare people's hearts for the Messiah by preaching repentance.

Now the tone of the delegation changed from friendly to potentially threatening: "Then why are you baptizing, if you are neither the Christ, nor Elijah, nor the Prophet?" With joy, John seized the opportunity to give a clear and true testimony of Jesus of Nazareth, that He is the Christ or the Messiah, and that John himself is merely a subject in His kingdom. He answered: "I baptize with water, but among you stands one you do not know, even He who comes after me, the strap of whose sandal I am not worthy to untie."

So that, might and firmness gaining,
Hope in danger, joy in grief,
Now and evermore remaining
In the one and true belief,
Resting in my Savior's merit,
Strengthened with the Spirit's strength
With Thy saints I may inherit
All my Father's joy at length. Amen.

† *(TLH 333:3)*

Dec. 24

Monday

Read Romans 10:10

IF WE WANT TO BE CHRISTIANS, we are called to be heralds of Christ and to declare His name with word and deed, even with our whole life. The Second Commandment obliges each of us not to use the name of Christ in vain, which occurs each time we deny Him. Whenever we pray the second petition, we ask God to help us in hallowing Christ's name, that is, confessing that name before the entire world. When we were baptized, we were enlisted in Christ's army as His soldiers for battle. Therefore, whenever we deny Him, we transgress a holy commandment of God, we deride our own daily "Our Father," we break our baptismal covenant, and we forsake the multitude of faithful confessors standing under the cross of Christ. We become instead faithless deserters entering the camp of His enemies, the world and Satan. Therefore, though our reason or our heart may advise us to deny some truth for some good appearance, we must always regard God's commandment and our holy oath as a higher requirement, as dear to us as God's grace and our salvation.

Even if we had not already bound ourselves to Christ and received God's commandment, we should still be moved by the love and thanks we owe to Christ not to deny Him under any circumstance. Don't we consider it to be the most shameful display when someone denies a faithful friend behind his back? How much more shameful, then, must we regard the denial of our best Friend in heaven and on earth, who for our sake forsook His own life (even heaven and its glory), who redeemed us from death and hell by a life of humiliation and the shedding of His blood, and who loved us from eternity? When it concerned our salvation, "Christ Jesus, who in His testimony before Pontius Pilate made the good confession" (1 Timothy 6:13), although He knew He would be whipped, ridiculed, spat upon, crowned with thorns, and finally killed on the cross for it. What small thanks our confession, bound together with a little disgrace, is for a love of this magnitude!

Do we not also have an obligation to our brothers and sisters to never deny Christ before them? Christ tells us that "the truth will set you free" (John 8:32), and that should motivate us to confess the full truth to our neighbor. Is it not a horrible deception of our heart when we think we can show love to our neighbor by denying the one truth that can free and save him?

Christ has given us the glorious promise, "[E]veryone who

acknowledges Me before men, I will also acknowledge before My Father who is in heaven" (Matthew 10:32). But He has also warned us that "whoever is ashamed of Me and My words, of him will the Son of Man be ashamed when He comes in His glory and the glory of the Father and of the holy angels" (Luke 9:26). What, then, would we gain by denying Christ, even if it should bring us the favor of all people and the goods of the whole world? In the end, at our death, we would lose all this, and we would also discover we had forfeited our soul and salvation in exchange for eternal punishment. What would it harm us, therefore, if we, like John the Baptizer, were to shed our blood because we, too, did not want to deny Christ with a single word? We would then inherit eternal life for our lost temporal life, eternal honor for our temporal shame, and eternal joy and blessedness for our temporal pain.

May our hearts, through faith, have Jesus above all. May we confess Him in our heart, with our mouth, and indeed, with everything that we are and have. If we confess Him in such faith, we will also obtain the end of that faith, eternal salvation, and Christ will acknowledge us in heaven. For thus Saint Paul testifies to us through the Holy Ghost: "For with the heart one believes and is justified, and with the mouth one confesses and is saved."

My hope is built on nothing less
Than Jesus' blood and righteousness;
I dare not trust the sweetest frame,
But wholly lean on Jesus' name.
On Christ, the solid Rock, I stand;
All other ground is sinking sand. Amen.

† *(TLH 370:1)*

Tuesday

Read Psalm 116:10a

DAVID TESTIFIES HERE THAT when he has faith in his heart, he must speak it with his mouth. The prophet Jeremiah says something similar in relating how he had the misfortune to prophesy to the apostate people of Israel and how he received nothing for it but the most bitter scorn and derision. He resolved to remain completely silent from then on. However, he adds, "there is in my heart as it were a burning fire shut up in my bones, and I am weary with holding it in, and I cannot" (Jeremiah 20:9).

Both of these examples show us that true faith is a fire God Himself lights in a person's heart, and wherever it truly burns, it forcibly makes a path for itself. It is like an enclosed fire that bursts forth in a confession of the mouth. History has provided plenty of supporting evidence of this. Whenever faith has flamed up in Christendom, it has been accompanied by a special zeal that results in the boldest and most open confession. That zeal was already evident in the age of the holy apostles, who seized every opportunity to declare what resided in their hearts. Saint Paul, although he was in chains, continued to confess Christ crucified before the governors Felix and Festus and before King Agrippa and his wife, Bernice. Fearlessly, the apostles Peter and John stood before the Sanhedrin, calling: "[L]et it be known to all of you and to all the people of Israel that by the name of Jesus Christ of Nazareth, whom you crucified, . . . by Him this man is standing before you well. This Jesus is the stone that was rejected by you, the builders, which has become the cornerstone" (Acts 4:10–11). When they were ordered to say nothing further on the subject of this name, they answered, "We cannot but speak of what we have seen and heard" (Acts 4:20).

Such zeal in confession was a common occurrence in the first three centuries of Christianity. No stake, no sword still colored with the blood of confessors, no lions' jaws, and no terrible torture could deter the faithful from identifying themselves as Christians, even before the cruelest rulers. Women and children joined the chorus of those who joyously and fearlessly proclaimed their faith despite threats from the authorities.

At the time of the Reformation, the Gospel was again poured out, touching many thousands of hearts with a spirit of faith that was immediately sounded from many thousands of lips. While the Roman pope angrily threatened evangelical Christians with excommunication, and while the Holy Roman emperor attempted to treat believers as outlaws, the confession "I am a Lutheran Christian" continued to be heard. Despite the bodily danger to the faithful, their hearts were full, and thus they could not be silent with their mouths. They believed, and therefore they spoke.

In our day, we must wonder where the beautiful golden ages of true confessors have gone. Isn't Christ now slandered instead of confessed by many of those who call themselves Christians? Don't many so-called Christian preachers deny that Christ is the true God and Reconciler of all sinners? From time to time, there are great and glorious awakenings to faith, but where is the bold confession of the entire truth as it was expressed by the first Christians and our forefathers? Don't we long for a Christian who both recognizes and acknowledges that type of faith? Those who want to pray, "God, let me find the truth against which all else is error," are frequently dismissed as arrogant. Oh, Christ is truly denied more often than we might care to think!

Would to God that I might even
As the martyred saints of old,
With the helping hand of Heaven,
Steadfast stand in battle bold!
O my God, I pray Thee,
In the combat stay me.
Grant that I may ever be
Loyal, staunch, and true to Thee. Amen.

† *(TLH 470:4)*

Wednesday

Read Philippians 4:5

SAINT PAUL STATES THE CASE simply and succinctly. He offers no addition, as did the Psalmist: "The Lord is near to all who call on Him, to all who call on Him in truth" (Psalm 145:18). By omitting all explanatory clauses, Paul can mean only that Christ's promised return on the Last Day is near. Christ informed His disciples that He would leave the world, but He assured them that He would return so they would be with Him forever. At His ascension, angels called to the holy apostles, "This Jesus, who was taken up from you into heaven, will come in the same way as you saw Him go into heaven" (Acts 1:11). From that time, the apostles proclaimed that now is the last time, the evening of the world, and Christians have nothing more to wait for than Christ's second coming, His return in divine majesty and glory. That return, they insisted, is near. As Saint James explained: "The coming of the Lord is at hand.

. . . Behold, the Judge is standing at the door" (5:8–9). "The end of all things is at hand," wrote Saint Peter (1 Peter 4:7). Saint John added, "Children, it is the last hour" (1 John 2:18).

Many centuries have come and gone since then, and those who do not earnestly keep the word of the holy apostles believe these prophecies of the nearness of Christ's return were mistaken. But there was no error. Although Paul wrote, "The Lord is at hand," he also informed Timothy, his helper, "the time of my departure has come" (2 Timothy 4:6). This demonstrates that Paul had no expectation of being alive when Christ returned. Paul wrote further about the Christians of his time "on whom the end of the ages has come" (1 Corinthians 10:11). When many in the congregation at Thessalonica were convinced "that the day of Christ is already at hand," Paul cautioned in his second epistle to them, "Let no one deceive you in any way. For that day will not come, unless the rebellion comes first, and the man of lawlessness is revealed, the son of destruction" (2 Thessalonians 2:3), that is, the Antichrist.

How, then, could the apostles still say, "The Lord is near"? Peter explains, "But do not overlook this one fact, beloved, that with the Lord one day is as a thousand years, and a thousand years as one day" (2 Peter 3:8). Two thousand years have passed since those words were written, but in the Lord's manner of calculating that is no more than two days.

If someone asks why the apostles spoke in this way, we can note that they had to speak thus because no person can know the day of Christ's return, the Last Day, beforehand. Instead, all people, at all times, every hour of their life, must keep themselves ready for this final day of the world. Therefore, woe to him who says in his heart, "My Lord is not coming for a long time!" Christ calls him a "wicked servant," whom He will condemn and who will receive his reward with the hypocrites. On the contrary, blessed is he who is always ready to receive the Lord with joy! Christ will receive him with joy, set him at His right hand, and crown him with the crown of eternal glory.

Prepare my heart, Lord Jesus,
Turn not from me aside,
And grant that I receive Thee
This blessed Advent-tide.
From stall and manger low
Come Thou to dwell within me;
Loud praises will I sing Thee
And forth Thy glory show. Amen.

† *(TLH 75:4)*

Thursday

Read Philippians 4:4–5

ALL BELIEVING CHRISTIANS should always rejoice in the Lord because He is near. Isn't it wondrous? However, isn't the nearness of Christ's return for judgment more a reason to tremble than to rejoice? Indeed, for the unbelieving world there are no more frightening words in the whole Christian faith than those of the Second Article: "From thence He will come to judge the living and the dead." For woe to the world when the Last Day, which it mocks, finally comes upon it unexpectedly like a snare! Woe to the world when it sees, like a bolt of lightning from heaven, the appearance of Christ. The One who had been despised and rejected will now be seen sitting in the clouds in glory, attended by all of His holy angels. Then all peoples upon the earth will cry out and say to the mountains and cliffs: "Fall on us and hide us from the face of Him who is seated on the throne, and from the wrath of the Lamb, for the great day of their wrath has come, and who can stand?" (Revelation 6:16–17).

How, in the light of all this, could Saint Paul say in our text that we should "rejoice in the Lord always"? These words are not written to the unbelieving world but to believing Christians. We thus recognize just how blessed the faithful are. What is most terrible to the unbelieving world—the coming of the Lord for the final judgment—is the greatest comfort and richest joy to the believing Christian.

The sound of the last trumpet, which will cause all of the unbelieving children of this world to tremble, will fall upon the ears of believing Christians as a joyful fanfare of victory. If unbelievers are terrified when they see Christ coming in the clouds of heaven and clothed with divine majesty, they were his enemies on earth and He will now come upon them as their enemy. But believing Christians, who loved and confessed their Lord before the world, will rejoice in His majesty as a bride rejoices at the sight of her bridegroom. For the unbelievers, the sight of Christ seated upon His judgment throne and opening their debt books will produce additional terror, for then all of their countless sins will rise against them and accuse them. Believing Christians, on the other hand, will rejoice in Christ's sentence because they know that all of their sins have been forgiven and their debts have been paid with the blood of the atonement. Standing before Christ's throne, the unbelieving children of the world will confront the One whose eyes penetrate like fire into their heart of sin. But believing Christians will learn that the last roots of sin have been wiped out of their heart. As their bodies are raised from the dead, they will be awakened in the image of God, or, if they are still living when the Last Day dawns, they will be transfigured in a moment.

Finally, the unbelievers of this world will look on with horror as the world they loved so much passes away and as the abyss of hell opens to devour them for eternity. The believing Christians, however, will see the world and its woes consumed by fire and the gates of heaven opening to admit them. Then they will hear Christ's welcome voice saying, "Come, you who are blessed by My Father, inherit the kingdom prepared for you from the foundation of the world!" (Matthew 25:34).

For this reason, then, the holy apostle writes in our text: "Rejoice in the Lord always; again I will say, Rejoice. . . . The Lord is at hand." Nothing can more urgently invite believing Christians to rejoice in their Lord than His nearness.

To Thee alone we cling,
For Thee all else forsaking;
On Thee alone we build
Tho' heav'n and earth be quaking.
To thee alone we live,
In Thee alone we die;
O Jesus, dearest Lord,
With Thee we reign on high. Amen.

(TLH 93:4)

Friday

Read Philippians 4:5

THE GENTLENESS TO WHICH Saint Paul exhorts us here does not consist in a person, contrary to truth and righteousness, making light from darkness and sweet from sour. Instead, this gentleness, which is worked by the Holy Ghost and is a quality of true Christians, flows from faith. As a result, they do not judge their neighbor harshly, but leniently and considerately. In word and deed, they act in a gracious and friendly manner toward that neighbor, and especially do they offer comforting words to those who recognize that they are fallen. Finally, in relating to their neighbor, they do not claim their rights, preferring instead to forgo some of those rights to preserve the bond of love and peace.

Even if all true Christians have made a beginning in this gentleness, it is still mostly very imperfect. Many believe they can demonstrate their progress in Christianity by judging their neighbor strictly, laying his words and deeds on the scale, overlooking no weaknesses, accepting no excuses, putting the worst construction on something questionable, and judging everything strictly according to the letter of the Law.

A Christian has plenty of reasons to let his gentleness be known to all people. First, there is the commandment to love, as Christ says, "So whatever you wish that others would do to you, do also to them, for this is the Law and the Prophets" (Matthew 7:12). What person does not want someone else to show him gentleness in thoughts, words, and deeds? The additional command of the Lord, "Be merciful, even as your Father also is merciful" (Luke 6:36), should move the Christian to gentleness toward everyone. Finally, Christians should also be prompted by their own frailty and stumbling, recalling that they themselves live only by mercy. As Saint Peter reminds us, "count the patience of our Lord as salvation" (2 Peter 3:15).

Nevertheless, one of the strongest reasons for a Christian to show gentleness is the one Paul places before us in today's text: "The Lord is at hand." How do all Christians want the Lord to judge on the day of His return? Surely it is gently rather than severely according to the Law. Even believing Christians confess that if the Lord did not judge them with mercy, He would have to condemn them. As David sighed, "Enter not into judgment with Your servant, for no one living is righteous before You" (Psalm 143:2), and "If You, O Lord, should mark iniquities, O Lord, who could stand?" (Psalm 130:3). But who can expect to receive lenient judgment from the Lord when he himself deals severely with his neighbor? Doesn't Christ admonish us always to pray, "forgive us our debts, as we also have forgiven our debtors" (Matthew 6:12)? Didn't He regard as an "unfaithful servant" the one who, after his lord released him from a debt of 10,000 talents, choked and threw into prison his fellow servant who owed him 100 denarii?

Oh, may the words of the apostle, "The Lord is at hand," penetrate deeply into our hearts. Let us think of them whenever we are tempted by our corrupt heart to judge our neighbor harshly, and let us right away pray that God would grant us a gentle heart. Would it not be a sacrilege to boast of the letter of the Law and deal severely with those around us, hoping all the while that God would impose a more lenient set of standards in judging us? Surely we should expect instead that the Lord will adhere to the principle He espoused long ago: "And with the measure you use it will be measured to you" (Matthew 7:2).

"The Lord is at hand," not to judge us but to absolve us. That, above all, should prompt us to let our gentleness become known to all people. Let us think of that most blessed goal day and night. In this way, our heart will become kinder and gentler toward our neighbor, both friend and enemy, and Christ will recognize us as His own, leading us with joy into the kingdom of His eternal love.

And let me with all men,
As far as in me lieth,
In peace and friendship live.
And if Thy gift supplieth
Great wealth and honor fair,
Then this refuse me not,
That naught be mingled there
Of goods unjustly got. Amen.

† *(TLH 395:5)*

Saturday

Read Philippians 4:5–7

BELIEVING CHRISTIANS SEEM TO have good reason to worry about living in the last time, as the call "The Lord is near" sounds continually in their ears. For, according to the teaching of Christ and His apostles, the last time, in which the Christian Church has lived since the apostolic age, is an exceedingly difficult time, a time of the greatest temptations. Some are tempted to unbelief, to false faith, or to falling away from Christ because of carnal security, worldly-mindedness, or the fear of persecution and despair. As Christ says of the last time, "For false christs and false prophets will arise and perform great signs and wonders, so as to lead astray, if possible, even the elect" (Matthew 24:24). Saint Paul adds, "But understand this, that in the last days there will come times of difficulty" (2 Timothy 3:1).

But the call "The Lord is near" should not prompt a feeling of anxiety in believing Christians. On the contrary, Paul admonishes us: "[D]o not be anxious about anything, but in everything by prayer and supplication with thanksgiving let your requests be made known to God." Believing Christians should regard themselves as people in a fortress that is surrounded and assailed by countless mighty and well-armed enemies. Nevertheless, they can be certain the Lord is close by with His angelic army, and when His hour arrives, He will bring relief to the besieged Christians, conquering all their enemies and celebrating with them the victory feast of eternal life. Instead of worrying, then, Christians should cast all their cares upon the Lord, bring all their requests before Him, call to Him day and night for gifts of every good, and implore Him to turn away all evil, all the while thanking and praising God for the benefits of grace they have experienced.

Let us not be so foolish as to surrender ourselves to anxiety. Let us, instead, recognize that, next to the Word of God, we have, in prayer, an almighty and unconquerable weapon. And if we use this weapon daily, even hourly, victory for us is certain. The Church has always won with the weapons of Scripture, prayer, and tears. Let us recall the words of the poet who was strong in faith and rich in experience:

> By anxious sighs and grieving
> And self-tormenting care
> God is not moved to giving;
> All must be gained by prayer. Amen. (TLH 520:2)

Above all, whenever hardship seems to flow like a flood over our souls, let us, in faith, remember these words of our

Lord: "And will not God give justice to His elect, who cry to Him day and night? Will He delay long over them? I tell you, He will give justice to them speedily" (Luke 18:7–8).

To ensure that the Christian is moved to all of this by the call "The Lord is at hand," Saint Paul, in our text, adds to his admonition this very comforting wish: "And the peace of God, which surpasses all understanding, will guard your hearts and your minds in Christ Jesus." If we will rejoice in the certainty of the nearness of the Lord, let our gentleness be made known to all people and prayerfully cast all our worries upon the Lord, "the peace of God, which surpasses all understanding," will enter our hearts. Then we will have peace in the midst of war, a peace that will guard our heart and mind, our will and understanding, like a wall as high as the heavens. So protected, we will be secure against both the flesh and the world. Neither will be able to rob us of our treasure, and we will remain well protected in our fortress of faith.

I am trusting Thee, Lord Jesus,
Trusting only Thee;
Trusting Thee for full salvation,
Great and free.

I am trusting Thee, Lord Jesus;
Never let me fall.
I am trusting Thee forever
And for all. Amen.

† *(TLH 428:1, 6)*

December 25

Read Luke 2:1–14

CHRIST HAD HARDLY BEEN BORN in a manger in Bethlehem when outside, in the fields, the angel of the Lord, shining from His glory, appeared and called to the shepherds: "Fear not, for behold, I bring you good news of a great joy that will be for all the people. For unto you is born this day in the city of David a Savior, who is Christ the Lord." As the heavens opened, the whole multitude of the heavenly host came down and sang before the astonished shepherds: "Glory to God in the highest, and on earth peace among those with whom He is pleased!" Here, in Bethlehem and its environs, was everything that properly belongs in heaven. The Lord of the heavens Himself was lying as a child in the manger. The glory of the Lord shone around the shepherds and illuminated the night with heavenly light. The heavenly host gathered before men who were speechless with joy. Heaven's music sounded. It was as if heaven had descended to earth and taken up and enclosed the earth within itself.

But what happened here did not apply solely to the residents of Bethlehem, but to all whose nature the Son of God assumed, everyone who is called human and a sinner. For, as the angel of the Lord proclaimed, "I bring you good news of a great joy that will be for all the people."

An unspeakably great, unexplorable divine mystery is at the bottom of all this. God's holiness and righteousness must shut the doors of heaven to us sinners, and He knows that neither we ourselves nor any creature in heaven or on earth can open them for us. He had therefore determined from eternity that what we could not do, He would do Himself, and He would do it in such a way that His divine, wonderful, incomprehensible, and infinite love would be made known to all creatures, to His eternal praise and glory. God had decreed that His dear, only-begotten Son Himself would be sent into the world, that He would become man, that all of our sins would be laid on Him, and that those sins would be completely and eternally blotted out by His deep humiliation and death on a cross.

What happened in Bethlehem was the fulfillment of that eternal decree of the heavenly Father. As soon as His Son became man, the unbearable burden of all humanity's sin was laid upon Him. And so, as Christ, God's sacrificial Lamb for the sins of the whole world, lay in a hard crib in the dark stable, the eyes of God looked into the future to see His Son already dying on the cross. Therefore, this atonement for sins, by which God's offended holiness and righteousness were satisfied and men were reconciled to Him, was already as good as accomplished. For this reason, God immediately opened the gates of heaven as a sign of this glorious event. The heavenly host announced the wonder of His eternal love (which He wants each person to receive) to the humblest of people, the poor shepherds, and when the heavenly choir had concluded its festival hymn of reconciliation with the world, He filled them with joy.

Let us, then, rejoice and be happy today. Let our mouths be full of laughter and our tongues full of praise. For the holy message of Christmas is that heaven's gates stand open for us.

From heav'n above to earth I come
To bear good news to ev'ry home;
Glad tidings of great joy I bring,
Whereof I now will say and sing:

Ah, dearest Jesus, holy Child,
Make Thee a bed, soft, undefiled,
Within my heart, that it may be
A quiet chamber kept for Thee. Amen.

✝ *(TLH 85:1, 13)*

December 26

Read Luke 2:11

WHO WAS HE, THIS CHILD lying in the bosom of a poor maidservant? He had the form of a mere human child. No visible, radiating glory glittered around His kind face. But what did the angel of the Lord declare to the astonished shepherds? He said that this child "is Christ the Lord," Jehovah, God over everything, highly praised in eternity.

O wonderful message! With this birth, God and man were united; God became a man, and a man became God! The eternal united itself with a mortal creature. The Almighty joined Himself with powerless dust. The eternal Love joined in marriage with the one who hates Him. The Most Holy united with the sinner. The Creator of all things joined Himself with a creature and became just like him. The Lord of lords, at whose feet all angels and archangels, as His servants, lay prostrate with covered faces, was linked with the servant of sin and Satan. He who carries the universe in His hands and sowed the myriad stars like grain in the field of the firmament became one with weak and helpless humanity and allowed Himself to be lifted up and carried in the hands of sinners. He who shared the heavenly Father's divine majesty, who was begotten in His eternal "today," true Son of the living God, became the child of a man, a brother of sinners, a descendant of the fallen father of the children of death, and a member of the miserable family of mankind. That family had lost its human nobility and become an abomination before the angels and all creatures. Christ, the eternal Light, came into the world to be a companion of those who sit in darkness and in the shadow of death. He whom the heavens cannot contain and for whom the earth serves as His footstool came down to share with the inhabitants of dust their huts of earth and clay. He who alone is the One who writes in the Book of Life, at Christmas let His name be written in the list of men as the humblest and poorest among them.

O great, godly mystery: God is revealed in the flesh! What mind of man or the highest angel can look into the depth of this divine counsel and find the reason? The holy angels surely desired to make inquiry, but finding no reason, they could only call out in worship, "Glory to God in the highest!" (Luke 2:14). What can compare with this supreme miracle: The Word of God became flesh? What is the miracle of the world created out of nothing, the miracle of the building of the heavenly vaults upon invisible pillars with countless stars running through their appointed paths, the miracle of the preservation of the universe and all that lives and moves in it? What are these wonders against the miracle that the great God divested Himself of His divine glory, descended from His heavenly throne to earth, and assumed the form of a creature that had fallen away from Him?

Where is the language that has words to express the importance of such a birth? At first, the angels praised this birth in an earthly language. Then they hurried back into heaven to begin there, before the throne of God, an eternal song of praise in the language of heaven. As for us, we can do nothing except throw ourselves into the dust and worship with cries of "Hallelujah!" to the holy Lord who, to the amazement of all creatures everywhere, consented to become man.

O Jesus Christ,
Thy manger is
My paradise at which my soul reclineth.
For there, O Lord,
Doth lie the Word
Made flesh for us; herein Thy grace forth shineth.
Amen.

(TLH 81:1)

December 27

Read Titus 2:11

IN TODAY'S TEXT, we see Saint Paul, as it were, standing in a high pulpit before the manger at Bethlehem, from which he preaches the Christmas sermon to the whole world. And how does he begin it? Does he say, "The strict righteousness of God has appeared" or even "The eternal love of God has appeared"? No. Instead, he says, "For the grace of God has appeared, bringing salvation for all people."

If the apostle had said, "The strict righteousness of God has appeared," it would not have come as joy to us, but rather as a frightening sermon indeed. For are we not all sinners, and is not God's righteousness the quality according to which He hates all sins and must punish all sinners? If Paul had said only,

"The eternal love of God has appeared," it would have sounded exceedingly lovely, but what would it have helped us? Do not proper parents, who love their children fervently, nevertheless discipline them earnestly when they are disobedient? Would we have to fear that, if only the love of God had appeared, it would have come as a rod to discipline us for our disobedience toward Him? However, it is well with us! Paul's Christmas sermon begins, "For the grace of God has appeared, bringing salvation for all people." Grace is both the theme and the entire content of the Christmas message, and it is precisely the sermon we need to hear.

But mustn't grace often be silent when the righteousness of God stands against it? For example, what good does a gracious judge do an evil man who cannot pay his debt? If the judge wishes to rule justly, he cannot absolve the man from his debt until he has paid it or has arranged for someone else to pay it. But Paul announces the arrival, not merely of grace, but of "the grace of God . . . bringing salvation." What does he mean by this? Christ has appeared to pay man's debt of sin, and for that reason, man is indeed blessed. The Lord of all lords has become the servant of all servants. God had to humble Himself so deeply to pay our debt. He began to pay it while lying in deepest misery in the manger, and He did not stop paying it until, forsaken by God, He was about to breathe His last upon the cross. Then and only then, after having paid the very last cent of our debt, could He cry out triumphantly, "It is finished!" (John 19:30). The God who became man had then effected the pardon of sinful men and their reconciliation with God, who opened the gates of heaven to them once again.

"The grace of God . . . bringing salvation" did not appear to all pious men or to all penitent men or even to all believing men. It appeared to "all men," without exception. There is thus no one in the whole world—from Adam, the first created, to the last person born—who is shut out from God's grace.

Oh, let us go in spirit to Bethlehem and fall on our knees in worship before the manger. For here the most beautiful drama in heaven and on earth presents itself to us. Here lies the grace of God, the One who brings us salvation and blessedness. Hallelujah!

Thou comest in the darksome night
To make us children of the light,
To make us in the realms divine,
Like Thine own angels, round Thee shine.
Hallelujah! Amen.

† *(TLH 80:4)*

December 28

Read 1 Timothy 1:15

WHEN LUTHER TRANSLATED THIS PASSAGE, he began with the words "It is certainly true." This means it is completely reliable. Saint Paul tells us here that the Son of God came into the world and became a man in order to save sinners. It seems implausible, but a few moments' reflection on this great miracle should convince us how highly believable it is.

God's nature is made up of two glorious qualities. On the one hand, He is absolutely holy, just, and true. On the other hand, He is full of unending love, grace, and mercy. What was God to do when man transgressed His holy Law? Should He, perhaps, have forgiven man his sin and received him into heaven without anything further? No, never! For if God had done this, He would have had to ignore the part of His nature that is holy and just. God wrote His Law into the heart of man at his creation, and He threatened man with the punishment of temporal and eternal death if he should transgress that Law. If God had pardoned fallen man without anything further, He would have declared before all creatures that He is not faithful. He would be just like a poor earthly father who commands and threatens his children, but who follows through on neither his orders nor his punishments.

But God is also full of unending love, grace, and mercy. He is an eternally overflowing sea of love with which He embraces all of His creation. By virtue of this love, He could want nothing less than to rescue the human race from its sin. How could God do this without compromising His holiness, righteousness, and faithfulness? He determined to become a man and to suffer Himself the consequences of man's sinfulness. Already, as a newborn child, we see Him in deepest humility, covered in miserable swaddling clothes, lying in a stall. This is the Lamb of God, who bears the world's sins, and in Him, holiness and love, righteousness and grace, and faithfulness and mercy are reconciled.

But Paul, in today's text, goes further. What he says is not only "trustworthy," or exceedingly believable. It is also "deserving of full acceptance." If the great Christmas miracle were only true, if we could not or would not be able to receive it, it would only have called forth a passing amazement. It would, then, have brought us no salvation and have worked in us no joy. But God be praised! This miracle is worthy of acceptance precisely because it happened for the salvation of all people, all sinners. Paul writes "of whom I am the foremost" to show that he applied the Christmas miracle to himself. His words recall those of the prophet Isaiah, who rejoiced, "For unto us a child is born, to us a son is given" (Isaiah 9:6). The Christmas angel calls to the shepherds and to all people everywhere, "For unto you is born this day in the city of David a Savior" (Luke 2:11). In faith, each of us should be able to say, "Christ Jesus came into the world to save me, the sinner."

Guilt no longer can distress me;
Son of God, Thou my load
Bearest to release me.
Stain in me Thou findest never;
I am clean,
All my sin
Is removed forever. Amen.

(TLH 77:13)

December 29

Read Galatians 4:4–5

HERE WE SEE THAT CHRIST did not come into the world to reveal to men that they were already children of God, as the rationalists of our day teach. Indeed, He taught just the opposite. He came to gain for men the right of divine adoption and to redeem them from the guardianship of the Law.

However, according to God's Word, there was a time when all people were children of God, when all men shared in the divine nature, carried the image of their heavenly Father in them, had the mind of God, and were filled with the Holy Spirit. That was the time when people were still in Paradise in the state of innocence. But when man fell into sin, he lost God's image, the divine nature and mind, the Spirit of God, and innocence and righteousness. Now man is no longer born a child of God but a child of sin and darkness. As Paul writes, man is a child of wrath, death, hell, and damnation. Out of His unfathomable mercy, however, God decided from eternity to make us, the fallen and degenerate, His children. For this to happen, however, sin had to be destroyed. How could we again share in the divine grace and the divine nature? God destroyed sin by sending His only-begotten Son into the world to assume our burden of sin and to pay the penalty for it. Now all who believe in Him share in His divine nature. They are renewed in His image and they receive the Holy Spirit.

The number of the children of men in the world is great, but the number of the children of God is small. Only the one who has experienced a double birth can become a child of God. This involves both a bodily birth, from his parents, and a spiritual birth. As Christ says, "Unless one is born of water and the Spirit, he cannot enter the kingdom of God" (John 3:5). A child of God is one whom God not only created, like other men, but also bore and begot. Therefore, James writes: "Of His own will He brought us forth by the word of truth, that we should be a kind of firstfruits of His creatures" (1:18). The child of God carries in himself more than the natural light of his own understanding. He also bears the higher, divine, heavenly light that comes from above and enters his soul. Therefore, Paul says of the children of God, "at one time you were darkness, but now you are light in the Lord" (Ephesians 5:8).

Furthermore, the child of God carries in himself a double life, one that is both natural and supernatural. According to his natural life, he lives on earth; according to his supernatural life, he lives in heaven. According to his natural life, he is related to his father and mother; according to his supernatural life, he is related to Jesus Christ. As Paul says, "It is no longer I who live, but Christ who lives in me" (Galatians 2:20). The child of God also enjoys double nourishment. His bodily nourishment is food and drink, and his spiritual nourishment is the Word of God and the holy Sacraments. Peter tells us: "Like newborn infants, long for the pure spiritual milk, that by it you may grow up to salvation" (1 Peter 2:2). Another advantage of the child of God is that he has a double spirit, both the one created in him and the Holy Spirit. Paul writes, "Or do you not know that your body is the temple of the Holy Spirit within you, whom you have from God? You are not your own" (1 Corinthians 6:19). Finally, the child of God cannot wantonly and knowingly sin. John says, "No one born of God makes a practice of sinning, for God's seed abides in him, and he cannot keep on sinning because he has been born of God" (1 John 3:9).

Thus, whoever is a child of God is not so because he loves God like a child and God loves him like a father. That would make him only like a child of God. Children of God are truly what their name says, for all of the reasons outlined above.

Lord, at Thy word, Amen, I say;
Increase my feeble faith, I pray.
Thou lead'st me with a father's care;
Oh, let me be Thy child and heir! Amen.

(ELHB 517:4)

December 30

Read Luke 2:33–35

"BEHOLD, THIS CHILD is appointed for the fall and rising of many in Israel, and for a sign that is opposed." This is what the aged Simeon proclaimed about Christ's reception among men. He says "many in Israel" not to suggest that such a disposition would appear only among those in Israel. If this is how He will be received even among His chosen people, how much more so elsewhere. And so it is. Christ was an offense to most people when He lay as a poor, naked baby in the manger, and even now He remains "a sign that is opposed," after all the world has seen His glory. Many people appear to be of the noblest mind but as soon as Christ is preached to them, they fulfill Simeon's prophecy by dismissing Him. The more purely and loudly He is proclaimed, all the more is He a stumbling block and a rock of offense to most people. Opposition arises from all sides. Pride and human understanding prompt hearts to arise against this unbelievable teaching. The wise ones of the world unite to refute and reject the Gospel, which is foolishness to them. Kings of the earth take counsel to banish from their kingdoms this religion, which appears dangerous to them. Men who think themselves holy, righteous, and godly pronounce the doctrine of Christ to be pernicious.

However, we cannot say that Christ would find such opposition only among the crass unbelievers and mockers. Let us look inside our own hearts. There we will find additional proof of the truth of Simeon's utterance: Christ is "a sign that is opposed." Why did God give mankind such a Savior and prescribe a way to salvation that is so offensive to our minds and hearts? Why did He not allow a Gospel to be preached that would immediately move the wise ones of the world to say "Yes" and "Amen"? Why did God allow His dear Son to appear in a form and to present a doctrine that seem to annoy the natural soul of every man? The answer is that if God is to help us, He had to send us a Savior who would not delight our natural hearts. For our natural hearts are full of natural pride and virtue, imagined wisdom and righteousness, and fleshly desires, all of which shut us away from God and His holy communion. A true Savior must be such that, when we receive Him, all of what is false in us is destroyed.

The sweetest Friend of man Thou art.
Yet many hate Thee in their heart;
By Herod's heart Thou art abhorred,
Yet Thou art our Salvation, Lord.
Hallelujah!

But I, Thy humblest servant, may
Confess my love and freely say,
I love Thee truly, but I would
That I might love Thee as I should.
Hallelujah!

I have the will, the power is weak,
Yet, Lord, my humble offering take
And graciously the love receive
Which my poor heart to Thee can give.
Hallelujah! Amen.

(ELHB 161:10–12)

December 31

Read Daniel 9:7

Today, the last day of the year, is an important day in our life. We stand, as it were, on the border between two great regions through which the way of our life, the way to salvation, leads us. Today we leave the one through which we have already traveled and to which no return is possible. The past is past. We will soon enter, full of expectation, the other as a land that is completely unknown to us.

Could we have allowed this day to pass without taking a look back before stepping forward into the new year? It is not possible. But what do we see when we look back? First, we consider what God has done. We see nothing but evidence of His goodness, His love, His mercy, His long-suffering, and His patience, and we are bound to thank and glorify Him for all of it. How many times during the year were we and our families in need of nourishment, clothing, and shelter? And behold! The Lord never let us lack what was necessary. Yes, He has blessed most of us with excess. We must say, with Saint Paul, "Yet He did not leave Himself without witness, for He did good by giving you rains from heaven and fruitful seasons, satisfying your hearts with food and gladness" (Acts 14:17). Furthermore, how many dangers were we exposed to during the year? How many kinds of misfortune could have befallen our bodies and souls? But behold! As on the wings of an eagle, He carried us above all dangers. He stood by our side when we awoke, and He was on guard when we slept. His eye was always upon us. He has proved Himself to be the guardian of Israel, and we must cry out, with David: "Sing praises to the Lord, O you His saints, and give thanks to His holy name. For His anger is but for a moment, and His favor is for a lifetime. Weeping may tarry for the night, but joy comes with the morning" (Psalm 30:4–5).

We may begin to think that the Word of grace did not resound to many millions in the past year, but how richly God let it be proclaimed to us, both by mouth and in writing! How kindly He always offered us His grace anew, showing us the way to heaven and inviting us into His holy kingdom! Mustn't we cry out: "Lord, how shall we repay You for all Your mercy and faithfulness You have shown us? Oh, if only each pulse were thanks and each breath a hymn!"

Yet what do we see when we look back at what we have done? Is there one commandment that we have not transgressed? Is there one day in which we have not sinned? Is there one gift for which we have been perfectly thankful and which we have used in complete accord with the will of the heavenly Giver? Is there one rescue from trouble for which we offered the proper praise to God? Is there one vow we have kept perfectly? Is there one sermon, one exhortation to repentance, one call to faith, one encouragement to holiness with which we have fully complied? At each of these questions, must we not cast our eyes down in shame before the most holy God, beat our breast and say with the tax collector, "God, be merciful to me, a sinner!" (Luke 18:13)? With David, must we not sigh, "If You, O LORD, should mark iniquities, O Lord, who could stand?" (Psalm 130:3), and "Enter not into judgment with Your servant, for no one living is righteous before You" (Psalm 143:2)? Must we not agree with Daniel, who says, "To You, O Lord, belongs righteousness, but to us open shame" (9:7)?

Hearty thanks and deepest humiliation are the two things required of us today as we review the past year. No one of us is excluded. May all of us, then, end this year as reconciled children of the heavenly Father. Only the ones who do this will make a joyful and blessed close to the year.

The old year now hath passed away;
We thank Thee, O our God, today,
That Thou hast kept us through the year
When danger and distress were near.

Oh, help us to forsake all sin,
A new and holier course begin!
Mark not what once was done amiss;
A happier, better year be this. Amen.

(TLH 125:1, 4)

January 1

Read Luke 2:21

THOSE WHO ARE STILL CHILDREN of the world are those in whom the desire for eternal life and their soul's salvation and blessedness has not been awakened. They concern themselves only with this life. Such people think that a good beginning for the new year is when they and theirs are alive and healthy, when they plan to acquire more goods than they now possess, and when new pleasures and new days of joy may come to them. These children of the world, therefore, begin the God-given new year of grace mostly with worldly vanities: dancing, game-playing, laughing, and joking. People who know no better joys are certainly to be pitied, for they are still walking in darkness. The light of divine grace has not yet risen upon them. They still do not know what a completely different joy and blessedness God desires for them. They still do not know that their riches are really nothing but a burden of cares for their soul, their joy nothing but an empty shadow, and their hope nothing but a vain dream. They still do not know how happy and blessed they could be if only they wanted to recognize what serves for their peace.

The most necessary thing for a truly happy and blessed beginning to a new year is that we do not carry forward the sins of the old year. Isn't the rich person very poor if he still lacks the most important good—the grace of God? How can such a person be truly happy if he cannot rejoice in the forgiveness of sins? And how can he truly be at peace today if he must still fear that God is angry with him, that he has not been reconciled with his heavenly Father? Indeed, only the person who carries this comfort in his heart can enter the new year truly happy and blessed. He knows that all of his past sins are forgiven and buried in the depths of the sea. He can draw near to God as a child draws near to his dear father. On our own, we can merit nothing before God. Even if we could cry bloody streams of tears, perform the greatest work of repentance, and submerge ourselves in the deepest sorrow and contrition, we could not wash from our soul even one of the past year's sins and we could not satisfy the offended righteousness of God.

There is only One who can wipe out our debt of sin. It is He who made atonement for us all with His blood. This is Jesus Christ, the most holy God-man, who today, as an eight-day-old boy, was circumcised according to the divine command. This holy child allowed this act, which is disgraceful in the eyes of human reason, to happen to Him. He was obedient to the divine Law and He fulfilled its humblest demand as if He were a sinner like us. But this was not necessary for Jesus, the most holy Son of the living God. He was not a servant and a subject, but the Lord of all human and divine laws. For our sake, however, He submitted Himself freely to what was commanded only of us men, and by it He wiped out the sins we commit by violating the divine Law. The drops of blood Christ shed at His circumcision were the first of the payments He made for the immeasurable debt of the world's sins.

Oh, let us in faith and with joy embrace the holy Christ Child, who today so willingly submitted Himself to the most humble divine Law for us. Now no law that we have transgressed can damn us. Now God Himself, whom we have offended, can no longer be angry with us. Now, like the old year itself, all of our old sins have eternally disappeared.

O Lord Christ, our Savior dear,
Be Thou ever near us.
Grant us now a glad New Year;
Amen, Jesus, hear us! Amen.

(TLH 97:4)

January 2

Read Luke 1:47

OF ALL THE FESTIVALS celebrated by the Christian Church during the year, the one that most captivates the world at large is New Year's. The world stays awake as the last midnight hour of the old year passes, and after the last bell has sounded it greets the new year with rejoicing and well-wishers exchange greetings and express their hopes for the months to come. Oh, if only the world knew its true condition, it would not rejoice, but weep. It would not put on festive clothing, but would instead cover itself with mourning clothes. There would be no shouts of joy in the air, but rather sighs for mercy from the throne of grace. The person who lacks a Savior is immeasurably unhappy. As he reflects on the old year, he cannot look back with joy, like a hiker toward the mountains behind, for the joys of his past have vanished, but the stain of sins committed during that time has not departed with them. Those sins have been entered into God's book of debts, and he has no Savior to strike them out with atoning blood. His sins have left the world, but they have gone up into heaven and there they stand before the throne of God and accuse him. They hover over his head like storm clouds of divine wrath and there is no one to scatter them.

The person without a Savior is even less comforted by looking forward into the new year. That year lies dark and gloomy before him, like a thick curtain no human eye can penetrate and no human hand can lift. No one knows what will befall him in the new year, and how and where and if he will end it. Upon whom can the person without a Savior rely? He cannot say, "I rely upon God," for he does not know God. What guarantee can he have that, in the new year, God has not written in His book for him sickness rather than health, poverty rather than enrichment, disgrace rather than honor, suffering rather than joy, and death rather than life? What assurance is there that God's patience toward him will not end in this new year? Perhaps He will say: "Behold, I have come now each year and looked for fruit on this fig tree, fruit of repentance and faith, but I do not find it. Come, death, cut it down. Why does it use up the ground?"

Oh, how many began last year with the most joyful hopes, and where are they now? Do not seek them in their palaces, for they have moved out and others have taken their place. Their bodies already decay outside in their graves and their souls stand before God's judgment. Their hopes at the start of the year rested upon the most unholy deception, for only the person who celebrates a happy Christmas can also celebrate a happy new year. Only the person who knows that he has a Savior can set out comforted on the pilgrim's journey of his life. Such a person may always be a poor sinner, but he does not deceive himself when he looks into the future with great joys, hopes, and confidence. In him, God will do more than he can ask for and understand. He has the Savior as helmsman and His cross as sail. He can, then, rejoicingly weigh anchor and boldly pilot on the open sea of life. His ship does not run aground, it is not wrecked, and it does not go under. Instead, it will certainly arrive in safe harbor, in this year or another one.

Jesus is the name we treasure,
Name beyond what words can tell;
Name of gladness, name of pleasure,
Ear and heart delighting well;
Name of sweetness, passing measure,
Saving us from sin and hell. Amen.

† *(TLH 116:2)*

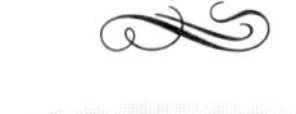

January 3

Read Psalm 103:22

PEOPLE WHO DO NOT HAVE FAITH in their heart marvel when they are asked to praise God for a year that is already past. They are, after all, happy and relieved to have overcome that year, with its toils and deluded hopes. They are even more astonished, however, when it is suggested they should praise God in advance for the coming year. They respond: "Why should I praise God when I cannot know what will meet me during the new year? Who can know if I will be sick or healthy during that time, richer or poor, and alive or dead? Will I experience more good or more evil, more joy or more suffering?"

The faithful Christian can no more look into the future than the child of the world, but the Christian can look into the Word of God, that telescope into the heart of his heavenly Father, and there he can read his future. Scripture calls upon him to praise God, regardless of the circumstances. He does not know if he will be poorer or richer during the new year, but he does know he will not lack any necessary thing, for God says in His Word: "Therefore do not be anxious, saying, 'What shall we eat?' or 'What shall we drink?' or 'What shall we wear?' For the Gentiles seek after all these things, and your heavenly Father knows that you need them all. But seek first the kingdom of God and His righteousness, and all these things will be added to you" (Matthew 6:31–33).

Moreover, the Christian cannot know if he will experience more suffering than joy in the new year, but he does know he has a God who is his Father. Without His will, nothing can happen to him; God weighed out from eternity his sufferings and joys. God is the leader who holds him by his right hand and will guide him according to His counsel. God is the watchman of His faithful Israel, who neither slumbers nor sleeps, keeping His eyes upon them when they have closed theirs.

But the greatest comfort for the faithful Christian is that his God is, at the same time, his merciful Savior who wants to save him. Whatever may happen to him in the new year, God has a plan of peace for him. God will never intend evil for him. Everything—health or sickness, glory or disgrace, suffering or joy—will lead him to salvation and serve him for the best. Whatever burden God lays on him, He will also help him carry it.

No Christian knows what temptations and tests of faith await him in the new year. But he does know that, however weak his faith, God will not quench a smoking flax nor break a bruised reed. Although man's heart is fickle, God's covenant of grace is eternally constant: "For the mountains may depart and the hills be removed, but My steadfast love shall not depart from you, and My covenant of peace shall not be removed" (Isaiah 54:10). While the Christian may despair of his steadfastness, he knows God wants to bring to completion on the Last Day the good work that He began in him. The Savior says: "My sheep hear My voice, and I know them, and they follow Me. I give them eternal life, and they will never perish, and no one will snatch them out of My hand" (John 10:27–28).

Finally, the Christian cannot know whether he will die in the new year, but he does know this: "For none of us lives to himself, and none of us dies to himself. If we live, we live to the Lord, and if we die, we die to the Lord. So then, whether we live or whether we die, we are the Lord's" (Romans 14:7–8). If he lives, then, he will live in faith and see the goodness of the Lord in the land of the living. And if he dies, he will die reconciled to God and his death will be the end of all distress and the beginning of eternal glory.

Therefore, faithful Christian, do not stand before the future as if it were a closed world about which you can know nothing, whether you will find good or evil in it. Know that whatever the path on which God will lead you—up the mountain or down the valley, through flowers or over thorns, on rocky terrain or on level ground, through darkness or through light, for a long time or a short time—that path leads through the kingdom of grace and its end is salvation.

Great God, we sing that mighty hand
By which supported still we stand.
The op'ning year Thy mercy shows;
Let mercy crown it till it close.

In scenes exalted or depressed
Be Thou our Joy and Thou our Rest.
Thy goodness all our hopes shall raise,
Adored through all our changing days. Amen.

† *(TLH 119:1, 4)*

January 4

Read Matthew 2:12–13

TODAY'S TEXT TEACHES US that Christ fled to save His life for the salvation of the world. Like Him, we cannot be oblivious to distress in danger, and we too must seize the opportunity to flee as long as this does not offend the divine glory or shortchange our neighbor and if God Himself provides that opportunity for safety. In the first centuries of the Christian era, some believers gave themselves up to their persecutors when it was not demanded of them. By doing this, they hoped to obtain a martyr's crown. But this was a false zeal. In such cases, the suffering is both self-willed and self-imposed, and it has no promise of grace. God cannot reward this suffering; instead, it must be forgiven. Moreover, when a person has the means for his preservation but refuses to use them, relying instead on God's protection and care, he has a false trust and only tempts God by it. The

Son of God, who could have miraculously helped Himself out of any difficulty, did not despise the means bestowed by man. How much less can we afford to despise them?

When the holy child was persecuted by His enemies and fled from them, those who were entrusted by God had to flee with Him. This teaches us that whoever receives Jesus in faith is in no way guaranteed peace and good days by Him. Instead, he will come upon great distress as readily as His mother, Mary, did. When the world discovers that a person is a faithful Christian, it will hate him, persecute him, and tempt him, doing everything possible to kill the Child in him and snatch Him out of his heart. The Christian can then only go the way of the persecuted Savior and His holy mother before him. He will go the way of the cross. With Jesus, he will flee from the world, severing intimate friendship with the unbelieving world and its sins and vanities. He will prefer to lose anything rather than Christ.

Our text also tells us that no sooner was Christ revealed to man by the angels and Wise Men than He had to conceal Himself again quickly. It is still that way today. One day, Christ gives Himself to be recognized in our heart, but the next day He hides Himself again from us and it seems as if He has forsaken us. What, then, should we do? Where should we seek Him? Our text tells us, relying on the prophecy of Hosea. When we no longer feel Christ in our hearts, we must still seek Him in the Word. Whoever firmly holds to Hosea's teaching will soon be rescued from his affliction.

Herod's attempts to kill Christ were clever but unsuccessful, and this enemy of our Lord perished miserably. This same end continues to befall Christ's enemies. However clever their plotting to eradicate Christ and His holy Word from the earth, their wisdom will come to shame and they themselves will come to a terrible end. People can drive Christ away, for He does not force Himself on anyone. However, they will never push Him out of the world.

So, then, let us take courage at this time of an almost universal falling away. Christ still lives and His Church will remain even if the whole world should conspire against Him. Therefore, let us faithfully follow Him, though He may lead us through wilderness and desert, knowing we will finally arrive with Him in the true fatherland.

Thine honor rescue, Christ our Lord!
Hear Zion's sighs, and help afford;
Destroy the wiles of mighty foes,
Who now Thy Word and truth oppose.

That Thou art with us, loud proclaim,
Who put'st our enemies to shame,
Dost all their haughtiness suppress.
And help Thine own in their distress. Amen.

(ELHB 275:1, 4)

January 5

Read Matthew 2:16–23

THE MURDERS OF THE CHILDREN of Bethlehem provide us with an important teaching. If we want to remain with Christ, we cannot expect anything in this world other than the dear cross: persecution, distress, and death. As soon as the world learns that our heart and mind live in Bethlehem, we must be prepared to find a Herod pursuing us, and we must therefore seal our confession with patient suffering—even, perhaps, with our blood. We should also learn from our text, however, that if we want to reject Christ out of aversion to the cross of the Bethlehem children, that will not free us from suffering. We have a choice to make. We can suffer with Christ now, like those children, and then enter with Him into glory. Or we can rejoice without Christ, like the fathers and mothers of Bethlehem, and then go without Christ into the land of eternal tears.

There is more. When Herod caused the blood bath in Bethlehem, he did not consider himself to be a persecutor of the pious. Instead, he declared the Wise Men from the East to be deceivers and the residents of Bethlehem to be treacherous receivers of stolen goods. We should learn from this to recognize the methods of Christ's enemies. If you are a Christian, the world will be hostile to you and persecute you because of Christ and the truth. It will nevertheless insist, however, that it has every right to pursue you, that you are only suffering for the sake of your sins.

Yet there is a very rich comfort to be derived from the murder of the children of Bethlehem. We can, indeed, be comforted when God allows our dear children to suffer much, for this shows us that God wants to glorify Himself by their sufferings. They, too, become martyrs of Christ, bearing the cross for their Savior. By their suffering, they, too, will enter into glory. When you look upon the sickbed of your dear little one and your weak heart wants to break because of his suffering, do not murmur against your God! He, the all-loving heavenly Father, loves your children as much as you do, and precisely for that reason, He often lets them suffer greatly and bitterly here on earth. They now sow with many tears, but they will one day harvest with much joy. They may now experience great misery, but one day they will be very glorious. You cry over them now, but you will rejoice with them in eternity. Therefore you should say: "Lord, as You will. Your will be done!"

When we suffer much and are troubled by the thought that God is angry with us, we should remember this comfort from the suffering of the Bethlehem children. God often lays great suffering upon the unbelieving world in wrath for the punishment of its sins, but He also allows His dear children to suffer out of love that He may be glorified in them. The bloody end of the Bethlehem children was not a punishment but a glorious deliverance and the greatest grace God could show them. Therefore, we who believe in Christ cannot doubt God's fatherly love, even when He lays upon us much suffering in this life. God punishes and disciplines those whom He loves, knowing that one day He will make them glorious. He may let them struggle here, but He will one day bring them to a celebration of eternal victory. Those who mourn now will find eternal comfort.

Thro' deserts of the cross Thou leadest;
I follow, leaning on Thy hand.
From out the cloud Thy child Thou feedest
And givest water from the sand.
I trust Thy ways, howe'er distressing;
I know my path will end in blessing;
Enough that Thou wilt be my Stay.
For whom to honor Thou intendest
Oft into sorrow's vale Thou sendest;
The night must e'er precede the day. Amen.

(TLH 362:3)

January 6

Read Matthew 2:1–12

THE WAY IN WHICH the first Gentiles were led to Christ was wonderful. In a country lying far to the east of Judea, probably Persia, a star appeared to several Wise Men, and God revealed to them that this star signified the birth of the long-expected King of grace from the Jewish people. At once, the Wise Men began their journey to the capital city of Jerusalem, and when they arrived, they asked: "Where is He who has been born king of the Jews? For we saw His star when it rose and have come to worship Him." King Herod immediately assembled all of his chief priests and scribes and asked them where, according to the Scriptures, the Messiah was to be born. He learned, from the Book of Micah, that the Messiah must be born in Bethlehem. The king then directed the Wise Men to this little city. They followed the words of the prophet, and behold! They found Him whom they were seeking, knelt down before Him, worshiped Him, opened their treasures to Him, and returned to their own country with the eternal treasure of this saving knowledge.

Even more wonderful than the circumstances of this account is the fact that God chose to lead the Wise Men to Bethlehem, not exclusively by the star, but also via a detour. The Jewish king, with his chief priests and scribes, first had to show them from God's Word that Bethlehem was the place where Christ could be found. We cannot imagine that the all-wise God would have done this without a most important reason. God wanted to show all future generations that He did not lead the Gentiles to His dear Son by miracles, by stars, by angels, or by some other extraordinary heavenly appearance.

Instead, He directed them by means of men, His already existing church. We see from this that the mission to the Gentiles is a duty of the Church.

Unfortunately, in our day, far too many people, including those who are undeniably Christians, think that the mission to the Gentiles, while laudable, is something they can do or not do. With so much distress in the world, they believe that the burden of missions should not be imposed on the Church as a potential hindrance to other important work. Such Christians are in error. The Christian Church is a debtor to the whole world that remains outside Christ. They are responsible for the lighting of the heavenly star of the Word for the poor Gentiles and leading them to Bethlehem. The Church is the fruitful mother out of whose womb more children should be born for God.

O Jesus, King of Glory,
Both David's Lord and Son!
Thy realm endures forever,
In heav'n is fixed Thy throne.
Help that in earth's dominions,
Thro'out from pole to pole,
Thy reign may spread salvation
To each benighted soul. Amen.

(TLH 130:1)

January 7

Read Matthew 28:19–20

WITH THESE WORDS, Christ sends His apostles out to all nations and makes all mankind their field of work. But the ones who heard these words were by no means alone. Rather, they were the roots of the tree planted by Christ that finally overshadowed the whole world, and representatives of the entire Church. Christ gave this commission to all the ages of His Church, for it was to the Church that He entrusted His Word as the right key to the kingdom of heaven. To His command, He added this promise: "And behold, I am with you always, to the end of the age." The holy apostles have been dead for many centuries, and although they filled the entire earth with the sound of the Gospel, millions of people continue to sit in darkness and in the shadow of death. Therefore, the command, "Go therefore and make disciples of all nations," still sounds loudly in the ear of Christ's Church, and it will continue to sound until the Gentiles have concluded their entry into His kingdom, that is, until the Last Day. The Church for which the command was intended consists, not solely of the clergy, but of all believing Christians.

Even if Christ had never spoken these words, the Church would still be obligated to spread the Gospel throughout the world. Doesn't each Christian have an eternal debt of love toward God? How, then, can he say that he loves God if he is able to look on peacefully as the enemy of God, Satan, holds in his snares millions of people who were created for fellowship with God? Can a Christian say that he loves God and allow Christ to have suffered for these millions and gained salvation for them in vain? How can a Christian profess to love

God while remaining silent as these millions serve Satan and sin, blaspheming God's holy name?

As certainly as the Christian's obligation to love God remains with him for all eternity, so too does the obligation to participate in mission work to the Gentiles remain with him for his earthly lifetime. In this way, the kingdom of Satan will be destroyed, the booty he stole from God will be taken away, and God's kingdom of light, grace, righteousness, and salvation will be increased. A Christian must love his brother as well as God, as Saint Paul instructs us: "Owe no one anything, except to love each another" (Romans 13:8). Aren't the poor, miserable Gentiles also our brothers and sisters according to the flesh? Can Christians say they love them when so many are without God, without comfort in suffering, without hope in death? Can we allow them to be lost, body and soul, for eternity? Never!

For this reason, the mission to the Gentiles remains the Christian's obligation. It is an obligation that has been imposed on him both by Christ's command and by the requirement to love God and man. It is a requirement that lasts for eternity.

O Christ, our true and only Light,
Enlighten those who sit in night;
Let those afar now hear Thy voice
And in Thy fold with us rejoice. Amen.

(TLH 512:1)

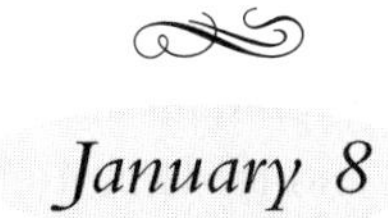

January 8

Read Malachi 1:11

THERE WERE TIMES when Christians devoutly wished, but in vain, to contribute something to the conversion of the heathen world. These were times when almost all heathen countries, controlled by Satan, were closed to Christians. Christians could then do nothing except pray that God would have mercy on their lost brothers according to the flesh and that He would open the entrance that was closed to them. These times are past. Today, Christians have access to almost every country. The expansion of world trade in earthly goods has opened to Christians the gates of all kingdoms of the world and all islands of the sea. Ships are traveling faster than ever, bringing countries closer together, and language barriers have fallen.

The world, of course, does not suppose that all of these changes are following a higher goal, namely, advancing the kingdom of God. Nevertheless, as it has become easier to send heralds of the Gospel to all regions of the earth, so it has become essential for Christians to carry on, with great zeal, the daily work of converting the Gentiles. God obviously desires to have the fullness of the Gentiles, the elect of heathendom, enter into His kingdom of grace. As John says, He wants to "gather into one the children of God who are scattered abroad" (11:52). Christians should therefore faithfully and carefully use the glorious time of grace that has dawned to gather into Christ's fold the many sheep that have gone astray in the desert of this world. Not all of us, of course, can or should go out as missionaries to all the places where darkness covers the peoples and the earth. Some of us fulfill the duties of our spiritual priesthood to the heathen around us wherever an opportunity presents itself. But for a person to leave his present calling and to dedicate himself exclusively to the service of holy mission, special gifts are required, as well as clear signs that it is the Lord's will.

Those who possess the necessary gifts and who are free and willing to perform this service of love should receive every encouragement to become missionaries. We can and should help to fund this effort. What we have is not ours. It is all part of God's cashbox and we are only the stewards of it. The baby Jesus, who lies so poor in His crib, earnestly desires that we, along with the Wise Men of the East, open our treasures and lay them down before Him as traveling money for His representatives to distant heathen lands.

Oh, let us not wait until the hour of our death to pay off our debt, for it could then be too late! Let us not be harder than Herod, who showed the Gentile Wise Men the way to Bethlehem and the Christ Child. Let us ensure that the bright star of the Word of God that now illuminates us is illuminated for our poor heathen brothers as well. Let us consider that even one soul is worth more than the entire world. For the world will pass away, but a converted soul lives eternally to behold God. Therefore, if we can assist even one soul to be won for Christ, how richly we will all be rewarded for the offered sacrifice.

God does not tire of doing good to us, and we must not tire of doing good to our brothers. God allows the Gospel to be preached to the poor, and because we too belong to the poor of the world, let us present a mite from our poverty to advance His kingdom. It is the same to God whether He helps with little or much. For this reason, let us add our portion to the earthly gift of missions as well as our fervent prayers to heaven that God will bless our offering abundantly.

May God bestow on us His grace,
With blessings rich provide us,
And may the brightness of His face
To life eternal guide us
That we His saving health may know,
His gracious will and pleasure,
And also to the heathen show
Christ's riches without measure
And unto God convert them. Amen.

(TLH 500:1)

January 9

Read 1 Timothy 2:4

IF A PERSON ONLY superficially considers the reign of God in the distribution of His means of grace among the peoples, it is easy to think that God wants only certain people to have a share in His grace. The Old and New Testaments, however, declare just the opposite. First, they tell us that God's grace is universal and extends to all people. "[T]here is no injustice with the LORD our God, or partiality or taking bribes," we read in 2 Chronicles 19:7, and these words are repeated by Peter in Acts 10:34. The prophet Ezekiel makes this even clearer: "'As I live,' declares the Lord GOD, 'I have no pleasure in the death of the wicked, but that the wicked turn from his way and live'" (33:11). In today's text, Paul says "[God desires] all people to be saved and to come to the knowledge of the truth," and Peter adds, "[God is not willing] that any should perish, but that all should reach repentance" (2 Peter 3:9). From these passages, it is obvious that God does not want any sinner to die, but that each one should come to the knowledge of the truth that saves.

From the beginning of the world, God revealed that the Redeemer promised in Paradise is for all peoples, including the Gentiles. The Lord said to Abraham, Isaac, and Jacob, from whom the Jewish people descended, that by one of their descendants, not only their people and race, but all peoples and races of the earth would be blessed. Thus, Jacob, on his deathbed, calls the expected Redeemer the man of rest whom the peoples would obey (Genesis 49:10). In addition, the entire line of holy prophets, from Moses to Malachi, entreats all Gentiles to wait for and rejoice in the Messiah, the Comfort of all Gentiles. As soon as the forerunner of the Messiah was born, God opened the mouth of Zechariah so he loudly could proclaim that the Dayspring from on high has visited the Jewish people "to give light to those who sit in darkness and in the shadow of death" (Luke 1:79).

On three occasions, God proclaimed His decree of grace to all people without exception, calling them into His kingdom of grace. The first time was in Paradise, through Adam as the root and head of the entire human race. The second proclamation was through Noah, the second ancestor of humanity, and the third was made by the apostles, who were commissioned to go into all the world, teaching the heathen and preaching the Gospel to every creature. This commission was faithfully carried out, allowing Paul to affirm, "Their voice has gone out to all the earth, and their words to the ends of the world" (Romans 10:18). In another place, this same apostle testifies that the Gospel "has been proclaimed in all creation under heaven" (Colossians 1:23).

Despite these arrangements by God to give His saving

Word to all the Gentiles, there are still countless millions who have been robbed of that Word by the guilt of their forefathers, and they have sunk back into the night of uncertainty and superstition. We cannot blame God that so many who have never heard about their Savior have already perished and continue to perish. But all of the heathens who languish in despair and hopelessness without God's Word are accusers of those Christians who, in indifference and lovelessness, care not at all about the salvation of their poor brothers. The conversion of the heathen remains a duty of everyone who calls himself a Christian. The neglected heathen is lost on account of his sins, but God still demands his blood from the hands of Christians.

May our zeal to help the heathen
Be increased from day to day
As we plead in true compassion
And for their conversion pray.
For the many faithful heralds,
For the Gospel they proclaim,
Let us all be cheerful givers
To the glory of Thy name. Amen.

† *(TLH 498:5)*

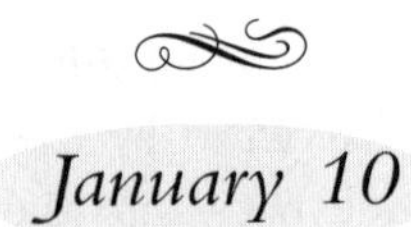

January 10

Read Isaiah 60:2

IF WE LOOK AT MIDDLE and eastern Asia, inner Africa, Australia, and the countless islands of the Pacific Ocean, we see that the largest and most beautiful surfaces of the earth are still enveloped in the night of heathendom. Even our beautiful fatherland still has thousands of heathen inhabitants. Christian eastern Europe, which has been highly blessed for more than a millennium, and western Asia and northern Africa, where the Gospel was once abundantly heard, are now filled with millions of worshipers of that false god that Muhammad preached. Of the approximately one billion people who inhabit the earth at this time, about two-thirds are still without the light of the Gospel.

Like us, they all have one God in heaven, who wants to be their Father, and one Savior. They, too, are reconciled with God, and all their sins have been paid for. They are all destined to eternal life and eternal communion with God. Paradise in heaven and on earth has again been opened to them. But they know none of this because no one proclaimed it to them. They do not know where they originated and where they are going. In vain, they ask, "What is truth?" Like us, they have a feeling heart that longs for perfect happiness, rest, and the peace that this world and all its glory cannot bestow. But they know nothing of the One who calls the weary and heavy-laden to Himself, refreshes them, and gives them rest and peace for their souls. They are sinners, as we are; the imaginings and desires of their hearts are evil from childhood. But they have no power to resist sin.

Millions of them are also poor in earthly goods, but they

know nothing of a Father in heaven upon whom they can cast all their worries because He cares for them. They are weighed down by the inexpressible sufferings of this age. They groan from their sickbeds and cry in the valley of misery. For them, the earth is a waiting room for hell. They do not have the comfort that those who sow here with tears shall harvest with joy in heaven. They are persecuted, rejected, and given up to the rage of their enemies, but they cannot say, "If God is for us, who can be against us?" (Romans 8:31). Millions die miserably in anxiety, fear, and pain because they know nothing of Him who took the power from death and brought life and immortality to light. As they live without God, they also die without hope. They have a holy and just Judge into whose hands they will fall after this life, but they do not have, as we do, an Intercessor who speaks for them. It is said that those who sin apart from the Law will also perish apart from the Law. Their existence on the other side of the grave is eternal death.

Let us look upon the terrible darkness that still surrounds millions of our brothers. It is more horrible than if the earthly sun were not to shine upon them. Their silent distress and their temporal and eternal misery call loudly into our ears, "O Christians, do not place your light under a bushel, but set it on a high place so that it may burn brightly, shedding light into our poor, desolate, hopeless, and eternally lost heathen world!"

And let Thy Word have speedy course,
Thro' ev'ry land be glorified,
Till all the heathen know its force
And fill Thy churches far and wide.
Oh, spread the conquest of Thy Word
And let Thy kingdom come, dear Lord! Amen.

† *(TLH 494:4)*

January 11

Read Isaiah 60:3–6

OUR TEXT IS A VIVID prophetic picture, and in all of Holy Scripture, there is almost nothing that is similar. Isaiah lived 800 years before the birth of Christ, but before his prophetic eyes the dark room of the coming centuries was opened. He clearly beheld the birth of the Savior, as well as His resurrection and ascension. This prompted him to call to the small flock of believers, "Lift up your eyes all around, and see: they all gather together, they come to You." Already he could see the apostles of the Lord going out into all the world and gathering millions of heathens to the Church of Jesus Christ.

All of this was most gloriously fulfilled. At Pentecost, thousands from every region of the globe were won for Christ by Peter's sermon. Some of the converted, Isaiah says in verse 5 of today's reading, are "the abundance of the sea." If, in the Old Testament, the word "sea" was mentioned without any further details, the Mediterranean was meant. This sea not only borders Palestine but also washes against the coasts of three continents: Asia, Africa, and Europe. The Gospel achieved its first and greatest victory from among the multitude living along this sea. There, Paul worked, filling all of Asia Minor, Greece, and Italy with the Gospel. It also appears that he journeyed to Spain. Mark, meanwhile, was founding the African congregations, especially in Egypt, with his preaching.

Isaiah adds, "A multitude of camels shall cover you, the young camels of Midian and Ephah." Even those who live in the homelands of the camels will receive the Gospel. These are the regions of the East and Near East, namely from Persia and Arabia to the East Indies and Ethiopia. The Wise Men testify to the rise of the Gospel in the Eastern regions. The treasurer of the Ethiopian Queen Candace, whom Philip brought to faith and baptized, provides evidence that the Gospel spread to the lands south of Egypt. Church history also tells us that the apostle Thomas, in particular, preached Christ crucified to the Medes and Persians and that Bartholomew sealed his witness of Christ with his blood in the East Indies. It is also known that Matthew was the herald of the Gospel in southern Ethiopia and the inhabitants of outermost northern Russia recognize Andrew as their apostle, who also confirmed his evangelical preaching with his martyr's death.

Therefore, that which Isaiah prophetically described many centuries before—"Lift up your eyes all around, [O church of the living God] and see; they all [from the four corners of the earth] gather together, they come to You [and fall down before the incarnate Son of God]"—was fulfilled before all eyes by the time the apostles died. Where, now, are the borders of the kingdom of God? Where is there an earthly ruler with a kingdom as extensive as that of the One who died in disgrace upon the cross? Is there a single country in the world without subjects who, in Holy Baptism, pledged themselves to the blood flag of their eternal Redeemer? Yes, the voice of the Gospel has gone out with power into all lands and it has sounded to the ends of the earth. It has penetrated the impenetrable jungles of Africa, reached the icy heights of the furthest north, resounded through the Pacific islands, and made its way through the gates of America that Satan had long held shut with powerful bolts. Jesus Christ is the only King, and He rules among His enemies just as the Scriptures prophesied. There is no language in which the name of Jesus will not be called. All distinctions of national origin and race have fallen. Everywhere, people confess that

Jesus is Lord, to the glory of God the Father. Countless emperors, kings, princes, and lords have laid down their scepters, crowns, and royal garments before the staff of the Good Shepherd, humbly worshiping at the foot of the cross.

Come, Holy Ghost, God and Lord!
Be all Thy graces now outpoured
On each believer's mind and heart;
Thy fervent love to them impart.
Lord, by the brightness of Thy light
Thou in the faith dost men unite
Of ev'ry land and ev'ry tongue;
This to Thy praise, O Lord, our God, be sung.
Hallelujah! Hallelujah! Amen.

(TLH 224:1)

January 12

Read Isaiah 60:6

TODAY'S TEXT TELLS US that there are two ways that those who have come to faith may demonstrate their joy in the work of missions. They can offer the necessary means, and they can pray.

God has wonderfully arranged things so earthly means are necessary for the support and advancement of the spiritual kingdom of the Church, the kingdom of heaven on earth. God could have preserved humanity and the Church without means, but He chose to sustain life through the means of food and drink and to support His Church with certain earthly means that people must present. A Christian congregation must, at great cost, furnish itself with preachers and teachers, establish seminaries, and build churches and schools. If the Church wants to carry on missions, it must find the often considerable funding to educate and support missionaries. God has so ordered all of this in His great wisdom and love. This is not because God needs man or his gold and silver. As He Himself has said, "The silver is Mine, and the gold is Mine" (Haggai 2:8). Instead, God wants those who have come to faith to share in the glorious work of saving the world of sinners. He is not attempting to impose a heavy burden on the faithful, but to bestow upon them the highest and greatest honor that can be shown to a poor, sinful person.

When they are called upon to offer "gold and frankincense," as our text puts it, for the holy work of missions, all true Christians regard this as an honor that cannot be shared by any unbeliever. Not all of them are able to go out themselves as missionaries to call Christ's lost sheep, but they delight in presenting their offerings so others are able to do the glorious work in their place.

God wants to repay this honorable sacrifice with a great and gracious reward in eternity. All heathens who were converted by the work of missions will one day appear before God's judgment throne and give witness of all those who parted with some of their earthly goods for the sake of their conversion and salvation. There, the Word of the Lord will be most gloriously fulfilled: "Make friends for yourselves by means of unrighteous wealth, so that when it fails they may receive you into the eternal dwellings" (Luke 16:9). There, even the smallest mite presented in faith will become a pure, shining jewel in the crown of eternal life that the generous friends of missions will wear.

As important and necessary as earthly means are for the work of holy missions, they are not the main manner in which believers demonstrate their joy in this great undertaking. The principal activity of the faithful is, and remains, prayer. Even an unbeliever who has no heart for missions can throw money into a missions box, but he cannot pray for the work of conversion. Only the true believer can do this. Whenever he prays the Lord's Prayer, with its first and second petitions, "Hallowed be Thy name" and "Thy kingdom come," he also prays that God's Word and saving kingdom of grace would come to the poor heathens. Whenever he presents a gift for missions, he prays, "Lord, bless them!" He carries missionaries in his praying heart, and he is occasionally moved by the Holy Ghost to get on his knees in the quiet of his chamber and ask God to add His blessing to their work.

How is it with our gifts and intercessions for missions? If it hasn't occurred to us to pray for the conversion of others, then we ourselves are much in need of a missionary. If we have prayed only occasionally, we must scold ourselves for our idleness. Let us, then, arouse ourselves today to a new, active zeal for the work of missions.

Lord Jesus, help, Thy Church uphold,
For we are sluggish, thoughtless, cold.
Oh, prosper well Thy Word of grace
And spread its truth in ev'ry place! Amen.

(TLH 292:3)

Su

TODAY'S READING IS the onl
concerning the holy famil
Savior. This one account, h
vivid picture of the entire childhood of
entered His public teaching office.

The first thing we learn from this account is the way Mary and Joseph discharged their office as the human parents of Christ. After the holy child was circumcised according to the Law of the Lord, they brought Him up with the greatest diligence. From the age of 12, He was required to accompany them when they traveled to Jerusalem, according to the Law, in order to serve the Lord publicly where the only temple of the people of God was located, and to celebrate the Passover with the whole congregation of Israel.

What a rich lesson this is for us parents, to whom God has entrusted children as pledges of His love. Mary and Joseph must have carefully raised the holy child in whom the Lord had clothed His glory. They could not imagine that this child would develop by Himself, without their help, and that, without them, God would protect Him. How much more should we recognize our calling to be God's instruments for the raising of our helpless little ones! If the parents of the most holy God-man recognized it as their duty to lead Him into the house of the Lord, how much more should we recognize our duty to lead our children, who are sinners in need of grace, to the Lord early on! To be sure, we do not have the power to convert our children, to cleanse their sinful hearts, and to keep them in God's grace. Nevertheless, we can be guilty of neglect and the loss of their

ve should be God's handymen in effecting their
ildren are not given to us as toys and pleasantries
ervants. Instead, they are entrusted to us by God, so
en they know nothing about Him we would lead them
eir heavenly Father. God will thus demand from us one day
e souls and the blood of our children, saying, "Where are they, My children, which I have given to you?"

It is our first duty as Christian parents that, immediately after the birth of our children, we bring them to the Holy Baptism of Jesus. For He says, "Let the children come to Me; do not hinder them, for to such belongs the kingdom of God" (Mark 10:14). However, this in no way completes the payment of our parental debt to them. No, if our children have been baptized, they then carry Jesus Himself in their hearts, and then, like Mary and Joseph, we each have a little Child Jesus in our house and in our arms. At this point, our heartfelt care for the protection of that child is doubled. The salvation of that precious child is then the object of our daily cares and prayers.

Each day, along with providing mother's milk, we should teach our children the love of Jesus and the fear of God. As soon as they are able to grasp the significance of their Baptism, we should teach them to say with joy: "I am baptized! My Jesus is mine! My sins are forgiven me!" This instruction should not wait until our children go to school. Even before that time, we must become their teacher and leader to God.

Let Thy holy Word instruct them;
Fill their minds with heavenly light;
Let Thy powerful grace constrain them
To approve whate'er is right;
Let them feel Thy yoke is easy,
Let them prove Thy burden light. Amen.

✝ *(TLH 627:4)*

Monday

Read Luke 2:49–52

THE EXAMPLE OF JESUS teaches our dear children two things above all else: (1) How they should serve God in childhood, and (2) How they should be subject to their parents.

The Son of God could have entered the world as an adult, but He did not want to do this. Instead, He wanted to be a child, and by His holy childhood, He wanted to redeem us from the sins of our childhood and to provide all boys and girls with a model of godly childhood they should follow. Because the holy Child Jesus was God's Son, He was not obligated to appear in the temple at Jerusalem according to the Law and to celebrate the Passover. Nevertheless, He accompanied His parents with joy, undertaking the long, difficult, and tiring trip on which Mary and Joseph, being poor, could certainly not have supplied Him with the necessary refreshments. In this holy child, all the treasures of wisdom and knowledge lay hidden, and the teachers must have wondered about the great understanding He displayed both in the asking and the answering of questions. Full of God's wisdom, He nevertheless went, as soon as He arrived in Jerusalem, into the temple and sat amid the teachers.

Since Jesus was God's Son, it is not surprising that He was already godly as a child. However, many wonder if the same can truly be expected of our children. Of course it can. Many children have already followed the example of Jesus and become like Him. Saint Paul says of Timothy that as a child he knew the Holy Scriptures. We read of the God-fearing Samuel, "Now the young man Samuel continued to grow both in stature and in favor with the LORD and also with man" (1 Samuel 2:26). And this is said concerning the eight-year-old Josiah: "And he did what was right in the eyes of the LORD, ... and he did not turn aside to the right or to the left" (2 Kings 22:2).

Already in childhood, a person can be godly. The godly child does not share the great cares, expectations, and work-related concerns that face the godly adult. In addition, the child is not hated and persecuted on account of his godliness. Everyone loves a godly child. Godly children, therefore, are happy children. Godless children, on the other hand, are very unhappy because they are an abomination to God and even men do not want anything to do with them. In their own strength, of course, children are as unable as men to make themselves godly. Only Jesus was holy, innocent, and separated from sin from His birth. The rest of us entered the world with an evil heart. But in Holy Baptism, God sends His Holy Ghost into the hearts of young and old alike, purifying them through faith. They now believe in their dear Savior, having been persuaded that He redeemed them and washed all their sins from them. He also gives them the power to walk according to His holy example. Therefore, godly children also follow Him, gladly and faithfully entering the house of the Lord like the holy Child Jesus. Evil children may attempt to lead them away from the place where they can receive instruction in God's Word, but godly children do not follow them, saying instead, with the Child Jesus, "Did you not know that I must be in My Father's house?"

It is also reported of the Child Jesus that, when His parents found Him in the temple and wanted to return home, "He went down with them and came to Nazareth and was submissive to them." Oh, that these words would stand written with indelible ink in every child's heart. Christ's humility is worthy of worship in that He, to whom all creatures are subject and before whom all angels and men must bow, was subject to His parents. Let all children resolve to imitate this glorious example and to follow the guidance of their parents.

Gracious Child, we pray Thee, hear us,
From Thy lowly manger cheer us,
Gently lead us and be near us
Till we join th' angelic choir. Amen.

† *(TLH 90:8)*

Tuesday

Read Matthew 19:16–22

IN TODAY'S TEXT, we meet a young man who, according to the usual way of thinking, did not need anything else to be happy. He was rich. He had all the necessary means to take part in the pleasures of the world. He had a distinguished position. Luke reports that he was a ruler, a member of the council (Luke 18:18). He was also a young man of thoroughly blameless character and conduct. And so, without blushing, he could dare to say he had observed the Commandments, particularly the fourth through eighth, from his youth on.

Shouldn't such a young man be happy? This young man was not. Above all, he did not know how he stood with God, whether he would be saved when he died. This uncertainty gave him no peace. He feared that, perhaps soon, he would have to leave all his glory, that he would then be lost, and that, in the meantime, the world could not satisfy him with its goods, joys, and glories. The condition of his soul had made him anxious and he wanted to hear Christ preach. Therefore, when Christ came nearby one day, he made his way to Him, fell down before Him, and said, "Teacher, what good deed must I do to have eternal life?" He certainly considered Christ to be a prophet, but only a mere man. Christ reprimanded him for calling Him "good," noting that no one is good except the only God. Moreover, Christ knew that this young man had still not learned how to regard himself properly—thinking himself to be good rather than a sinner in need of redemption. Thus, He told the young man that he must observe the Commandments. When the young man responded that he had kept the Commandments from his youth perfectly, Christ put him to the test—a test in which he would learn to examine himself in the correct manner. To his question, "What do I still lack?" Christ replied, "If you would be perfect, go, sell what you possess and give to the poor, and you will have treasure in heaven; and come, follow Me." What happened? Here is a living proof that young men who do not dedicate their youth to the service of their Savior remain unhappy regardless of their other advantages. The rich young man could not bring himself to sacrifice everything to Christ, and he went away full of sorrow.

If a young man dedicates his youth to the service of the Savior, he will be truly happy. Joy enters his heart and divine grace makes him sure. He looks happily to a future that is full of hope. God's blessing rests upon all his works, and the love of Christians is a rich replacement for the friendship of the world that he has forsaken. As the sun rising in the sky gilds the mountain's summit and illuminates the valley, so also does the rising of the heavenly Sun of grace make the morning of life beautiful, illuminating first the heights and valleys of youth.

On those that rule our country,
Oh! shower Thy blessings down,
And in Thy loving-kindness
Adorn, as with a crown,
With piety our youth,
With godliness our nation,
That all, to gain salvation,
May know Thy heavenly truth. Amen.

(ELHB 252:10)

Wednesday

Read 1 Peter 2:9

THERE IS A GREAT DIFFERENCE in the status of the children of God in the Old and New Testaments. In the Old Testament, as Saint Paul writes, those children stood under guardianship. They were not allowed to deal with God directly in all things. The mediators between them and God were the priests. In the name of the people, the priests arranged the public worship services, brought God all kinds of sacrifices, and entered into the holy place of the temple in the grace of the God, who was present there. The priests explained the Law of God, decided between clean and unclean, bestowed the blessing of the Lord, and represented the people with their prayers to God. Therefore, whenever an Israelite wanted to be reconciled with God or cleansed from sin, desired to bring Him a sacrifice, or sought to turn to Him in petition, he was directed to the priests. This did not happen because Old Testament believers did not yet stand before God in grace, but rather as a testimony that the promised and expected Messiah would first have to reconcile man with God and provide free access to Him. Therefore, after the New Testament was established by the death of Christ, the curtain that had hidden the holy of holies from the covenant people of the Old Testament was ripped in two as a sign that the Levitical priesthood, with its privileges, was now finished. A new, holy, priestly covenant people was hereby created, making everyone a priest of the Most High God.

And so it is. According to the testimony of the holy apostles, all believing Christians are priests and the whole Christian Church is the temple, the house of God in which they serve under their only High Priest, Jesus Christ, who by His own blood once entered into the holy of holies, that is, heaven, and established an eternal redemption. Saint Peter emphatically declares this new status for believers in today's reading. Here we see that as soon as a person becomes a Christian by Holy Baptism and receives the Holy Ghost, he is anointed a spiritual priest. As long as a person preserves his baptismal grace—or, having lost it by unbelief, he obtains it again by true repentance—he is and remains adorned with the holy privileges of a priest of God.

A Christian needs no mediator in order to deal with God. Day and night, he has free access to his heavenly Father and His throne of grace, and he receives grace upon grace from Christ's fullness. To be sure, God provided in the New Testament that particular persons should handle His means of grace in public offices: preaching His Word, administering His holy Sacraments, and shepherding Christ's flock. However, preachers do not form a particular class like the priests of the Old Testament, who alone were entrusted with certain spiritual gifts and rights. Therefore, throughout the New Testament, the Church's servants are never called priests, but instead they are known as elders, teachers, servants, and stewards. They have an outflowing of the rights and gifts of the spiritual priesthood of the Christians they serve. They are not lords or exclusive possessors of certain treasures that the so-called Christian laity does not have. They are, rather, stewards in public offices of the rights and gifts that all Christians possess. Therefore, through their faith, Christians are free lords over everything, and by love, they are the servants of all others. In judgment over spiritual things, they are subject to no man, but alone to the Word of God. God has established them to be watchmen and judges over their teachers.

Thou art, O Holy Spirit,
The true anointing Oil,
Through which are consecrated
Soul, body, ease, and toil
To Christ, whose guardian wings,
Where'er their lot appointed,
Protect His own anointed,
His prophets, priests, and kings. Amen.

(ELHB 252:4)

Thursday

Read Romans 12:1

TO BE A PRIEST of the Most High God is the highest honor and blessedness in which a created being can participate. Whoever is a priest of God always has the office, the call, and the privilege to stand before God, to cultivate an intimate relationship with Him, and to serve Him as a mighty one of His great kingdom. However, the duties of the priest of God are just as great. The main duty of a priest is to sacrifice. Bringing sacrifices is inseparable from the office of a priest, just as preaching is inseparable from the office of a preacher and teaching from the office of a teacher. What is the sacrifice a Christian, as a spiritual priest, is obligated to bring to God? Saint Paul shows us in the words of today's reading. Here we see that Christians do not have to offer God the kinds of things the priests of the Old Testament offered: bulls, rams, lambs, turtledoves, the first of the fruits of the field, oil, incense, and the like. All of these were types of the Levitical priesthood, which was itself a type. The spiritual priests of the New Testament sacrifice to God their bodies, together with everything they are and have.

But how can a Christian sacrifice himself? He does this when, by the power of the Holy Spirit, he daily and even hourly kills everything evil that is in and of him, and lays at God's feet everything he has that is good. When he notices in himself the desires of the eyes, that is, anything earthly, covetousness, and avarice, he immediately seeks to be rid of them. When he senses in himself the desires of the flesh—lust, craving for pleasure, and love for a comfortable life—he strives to root them out. When he finds arrogance in himself, that is, desire for his own glory, pride, haughtiness, and self-satisfaction, he takes great pains to rip this weed out of his heart. In short, when he is daily intent upon becoming free of all his sins, sinful longings, emotions, and thoughts, then, and only then, does he live before God as a spiritual priest who sacrifices to Him.

Yet it is not enough for a Christian to strive to kill the evil in himself. He must also lay the good that he has at God's feet.

He tries to make everything he is and has serve to the glory of God. He lives as if his body and soul were not his own, but God's. He sees all his goods as belonging to God, and he lives so those goods can be employed for God's glorification. He is ready to give up everything that is dear and pleasant to him—his honor and his good name, his joy and rest, his friends and relatives, his wisdom and skills, even his life—so he can contribute something to God's praise. When he wishes, like Saint Augustine, to be a beaming light that pines for service to God, then he has sacrificed himself to God.

In this life, a Christian is never completely sacrificed to God. He has to struggle with his flesh and blood until he dies. However, even this is a sign that he is a Christian, a spiritual priest. With prayer and God's Word, he wages a daily battle to become an ever more complete sacrifice to his God. Although such a Christian is not perfect, his sacrifice is holy and, for the sake of Christ, pleasing to God.

From morn till eve my theme shall be
Thy mercy's wondrous measure;
To sacrifice myself to Thee,
My foremost aim and pleasure.
My stream of life shall flow for Thee,
Its steadfast current ceaselessly
In praise to Thee outpouring;
And all that Thou hast done for me,
I'll treasure in my memory,
Thy gracious love adoring. Amen.

(ELHB 191:6)

Friday

Read Romans 12:2

MANY WHO CALL THEMSELVES Christians readily agree that it is not proper for a preacher to be worldly. They say he should not go to places of public pleasure, such as taverns and theaters, where all kinds of people come together, all kinds of sins are incited, and modesty is scorned. It isn't appropriate, they maintain, for a preacher to play and dance, to dress ostentatiously, and to promote wastefulness in his household. In short, they insist, a "spiritual person" must separate himself from the worldly. However, they caution, such narrow borders and such great earnestness cannot be demanded of one who is in a secular estate. One who wants to regard himself as a preacher will become a laughingstock, appearing holy while being a hypocrite. Such notions are all too common in our day, and they are entirely false.

It is, of course, a sin for a preacher to be worldly, since he should be an example to his flock. But what is a sin for the preacher is also a sin for every Christian. It is against God's Word to divide the Christian between the worldly and the spiritual. A worldly Christian is a non-Christian, a man without a soul. Every Christian should be spiritual, that is, anointed with the Holy Ghost. He should be one who is both chosen and called by God out of sin and the world. As a preacher, every Christian should, with his words and his works, proclaim the praises of Him who called him from the darkness into His wonderful light. In short, every Christian should be a holy priest, dedicated to God, and a servant and disciple of Christ. Whoever does not want this is no Christian.

In our text, Paul's declaration, "Do not be conformed to this world," is addressed not just to preachers, but to all Christians. Any Christian who wants to be a spiritual priest must separate himself from the world. He cannot walk through life in a wild, disorderly manner or participate in its vain desires. He cannot go to places where the world gathers to serve its god: dancing halls or to houses of drink, games, and theater. He cannot take his rest and pleasure where mockers sit or join their secret societies. He cannot indulge in the world's pursuit of splendor and delights or behave as a child of the world: free, impudent, proud, and foolish. In his entire outward behavior, he must demonstrate that he is in the world but is not of the world.

But Paul doesn't stop there. In addition to the command, "Do not be conformed to this world," he adds, "But be transformed by the renewal of your mind, that by testing you may discern what is the will of God, what is good and acceptable and perfect." If a person wants to be a Christian, a spiritual priest, it is not enough for him merely to separate himself outwardly from the world. A person can still be a false Christian or an unbeliever even in the most secluded settings, removed from all worldly associations. The Christian who truly separates himself from the world must have another mind. What pleases the world must displease him. What the world seeks, he must flee. What the world considers precious, he must disdain. What the world enjoys must be disgusting to him. If the world seeks riches, he must be satisfied with his poverty. If the world pursues good days, he must regard his suffering in Christ as more dear. If the world delights in glory, then scorn for the sake of Christ must please him most of all. If long life is the world's chief aim, he must long for a blessed departure. In this way, God's will, which the world hates, must always appear perfect and acceptable to the Christian.

Renew me, O eternal Light,
And let my heart and soul be bright,
Illumined with the light of grace
That issues from Thy holy face.

Grant that I only Thee may love,
And seek those things which are above,
Till I behold Thee face to face,
O Light eternal, through Thy grace. Amen.

(ELHB 350:1, 4)

Saturday

Read Romans 12:3–6

SAINT PAUL SAYS SO MUCH with these words. The gifts that are given to Christians are indeed diverse. One can miraculously heal sickness, while another can speak foreign languages. One has the gift to prophesy and interpret the Scriptures, while another is able to govern the church and the like. One has greater gifts, while another's gifts are more humble. However, the more gifted ones are not permitted to exalt themselves over the less gifted ones, and the less gifted are not allowed to envy the more gifted. The only right measure by which gifts can be judged is faith, and according to faith, we are all one in Christ and members of one another. When a person has great gifts, he isn't more righteous before God. Even when a person's gifts are so humble as to make him seem to be the most insignificant member of Christ's body, the more important members still serve him. Isn't the eye, that most precious member of the body, the servant of the foot? Doesn't the head serve the hand? Doesn't the heart nourish every member of the body? We see from this that humility and love are our principal duties toward our brothers.

One who has greater knowledge or stronger faith or an office of higher honor is not permitted to extol himself over his brother, for before God, they are alike. Both have the same faith, the same Christ, the same righteousness, the same salvation, and the same heaven. As soon as one extols himself, he excludes himself from Christians and becomes the last instead of the first. But those who are less gifted are not permitted to be envious because they, too, are members of Christ's body. A brother's glorious gifts are at their service, as the light of the eye serves the foot. Another's gifts are also your gifts. If you let envy prevail in your heart instead of brotherly love, you have ceased to be a member of Christ's body and a spiritual priest.

All of us who are spiritual priests through faith should not boast of this privilege as if we were arrogant enthusiasts. Instead, let us consider what a high and holy duty this privilege lays on us. Let us offer ourselves to God with everything that we are and have. Let us separate ourselves from the world with our whole lives. Finally, let us, in humility, regard our brothers as better than ourselves. Thus we will proceed in true priestly adornment. When our last day arrives, the curtain before the Most Holy Place of heaven will be torn in two before our eyes, and we will go in with joy to stand eternally before God as priests and kings, bringing Him eternal sacrifices of praise. May Jesus Christ help us all! Amen.

To Thee my heart I offer,
O Christ-child sweet and dear,
Upon Thy love relying;
Oh, be Thou ever near!

Take Thou my heart and give me Thine
And let it be forever mine,
O Jesus, holy, undefiled,
My Savior meek and mild.

Let me be Thine forever,
O Christ-child sweet and dear;
Uphold me with Thy mercy,
And be Thou ever near.
From Thee I gladly all receive,
And what is mine to Thee I give,
My heart, my soul, and all I own.
Let these be Thine alone. Amen.

† *(TLH 89:1, 5)*

Sunday

Read John 2:1–11

We first rightly recognize the glory of marriage in the light of the divine Word.

Jesus Christ, the Son of the living God, has come to seek and to save what was lost. He lived the first thirty years of His life on earth in relative obscurity, with only one known interruption, in His twelfth year. Finally, he left His concealment, publicly entered His office as Messiah, and began to gather a circle of disciples. At that time, there was a wedding in Cana of Galilee, probably among the relatives of Mary, the mother of the Lord. Jesus appeared in Galilee with His disciples, and they were invited to attend the wedding. A person who thinks that Christ came to establish a heavenly kingdom on earth supposes that He would have declined the invitation. Not only did Christ accept the invitation and dignify this wedding with His presence and that of His apostles, but He also performed His first miracle, revealing His glory. And what was this miracle? Did He heal a sick person? Did He raise a person back to life? No. He revealed His glory and His power as Creator in that, when the wine was gone, He turned water into excellent wine.

This miracle revealed the glory of marriage in four ways. First, we see that marriage is a holy institution that God Himself ordained. Second, it is an institution that God preserves by His almighty power. Third, God Himself provides for the needs of this institution. Finally, in it, God wants to reveal Himself to man.

God's Word tells us that He instituted marriage as soon as He had created heaven and earth and the first two people, so that, by a man and a woman in an indissoluble holy union, the human race could be reproduced until the end of days. According to God's holy decree, marriage is a divine institution. The Most High Lawgiver Himself says, "You shall not commit adultery" (Romans 13:9) and "What therefore God has joined together, let not man separate" (Matthew 19:6). Oh, what a holy, sacred institution marriage is, according to God's Word! God also acts to preserve marriage throughout the world. Can anyone be so blind as to consider the durability of marriage to be the result of mere blind chance? No, it is evident that God must care mightily for the preservation of this institution.

Furthermore, God cares for the needs of marriage. What Christ did at the wedding at Cana is a reflection of what God does in all marriages. When there was no wine (which was not a necessity, but only a means of refreshment and amusement), behold! The Lord could not long permit the wedding party to be embarrassed, so He used this opportunity to provide quickly and in a miraculous way, so as to reveal His glory. Our Lord always acts in this way. Millions of couples enter into the state of matrimony with empty hands, but do they not find daily what they need? Isn't this faithful care by God for the necessities of the household clear evidence of the way in which God honors marriage as His institution?

God does still more. As Christ once went to the wedding at Cana and there revealed His glory by a miracle, so today He uses marriage as a way to reveal Himself to all who do not wantonly shut their eyes and hearts to Him. In no way is marriage a hindrance to serving God and living a godly life. Instead, marriage, with its sorrows and joys, is a way in which countless couples, relying on Christ, have had their faith strengthened and preserved. For them, marriage has become a source of both temporal and eternal blessings.

This, then, is the fourfold glory with which God has honored the state of holy matrimony. He instituted it, preserves it, provides for those who enter into it, and makes it a school of faith and love.

O blessed home where man and wife
Together lead a godly life,
By deeds their faith confessing!
There many a happy day is spent,
There Jesus gladly will consent
To tarry with His blessing. Amen.

† *(TLH 624:1)*

Monday

Read Proverbs 18:22

TODAY'S TEXT COMES from Solomon, and it is a truly remarkable expression. He does not talk about taking a wife, but about finding her. That a spouse is found is an integral part of the true marriage. From eternity, God intended for each person one who would walk through life with him. The happiness of marriage depends upon finding the person whom God has selected for us. It is clear, therefore, that whoever does not inquire of God about his choice, depending on his own wisdom or following impure motives, takes a spouse but does not find her. He may make his choice on the basis of fleeting beauty, uncertain riches, quickly dwindling honor, or the hope of good days or a voluptuous life.

What is the correct manner in which to conduct that search? The faithful God has already prepared the choice for us. We must therefore begin by turning to Him in heartfelt prayer and calling upon Him for direction and guidance. We must implore Him to open our eyes, to govern our hearts, and to graciously superintend the particulars. God has already shown us in His Word how a right spouse must be supplied. The second step in our search is to determine whether the person to be chosen truly loves the Lord, is on the path of salvation, and possesses the qualities necessary for a happy and blessed marriage that is pleasing to the Lord. But even this is not enough. In such important matters, we too easily deceive ourselves, for our heart is roguish and always gravitates toward the erring way. It is therefore necessary that we seek good counsel from experienced, conscientious, and reliable Christians—in particular, pious parents. If we do all of this, we can rest assured that we have found the one whom God intended for us from eternity.

Whoever follows this prescribed course for marriage finds in his spouse a good and precious treasure. Solomon also tells us: "An excellent wife who can find? She is far more precious than jewels" (Proverbs 31:10). With a virtuous wife, a faithful husband receives a helper who lightens for him the burdens of life. That wife receives in her husband a lord who governs her with the reins of love, a protector who makes himself a shield for her against all attacks, a friend who lovingly cares for her, and a bishop who heartily takes care of her soul. Each of them finds in the other a heart that is faithful in love and in sorrow, in sickness and in health, in honor and in shame, in distress and in death.

In today's text, Solomon declares that the one who finds a wife "obtains favor from the Lord." Sinful weaknesses, which even pious spouses find in marriage, will be covered by God with His cloak of grace. And that grace is never idle. God always accompanies His grace with doing good, pouring out a thousand blessings in earthly and heavenly goods.

Well He knows what best to grant me;
All the longing hopes that haunt me,
Joy and sorrow, have their day.
I shall doubt His wisdom never—
As God wills, so be it ever—
I to Him commit my way. Amen.

† *(TLH 425:5)*

Tuesday

Read Ephesians 5:24–25

THERE IS A UNION that the eternal Love instituted among men in Paradise, whose fragrance lingers by His creating power. It is the covenant of holy matrimony. Without marriage, the life of man in this selfish world would be like an endless icy winter. Marriage ties a warm band of love around millions and produces precious family circles of natural love.

Only believers experience all of this in the fullest sense. Their marriages are an image of the marriage of Christ and His Church, His bride. By himself, what man can be to his wife what Christ is to His Church? Can a man redeem his wife, as Christ did His Church? Can he give satisfaction for her sins, reconcile her with God, keep her in the faith until the end, and finally bring her into the glory of heaven? No, he can do none of these. But God be praised! None of this is required of him. What makes the marriage of believers an image of the marriage of Christ and His Church is a husband's self-sacrificing love for his wife. Saint Paul writes, "Husbands, love your wives, as Christ loved the church and gave Himself up for her."

How does Christ love His Church? He loves her, first of all, from the heart, fervently, giving her drink with His own heart's blood. The Christian husband should love his wife no less fervently. Second, Christ loves His Church although she is full of stains. He does not separate from her; instead, He covers her sins with His own righteousness. The Christian husband should love his wife just as patiently, despite her weaknesses and faults. He should bear them and not desire to be rid of her on account of them. Third, Christ loves His Church with deeds so she does not lack anything. He eternally cares for her. He is her intercessor with the Father; He protects her in danger, He comforts her in sorrow, and He fills her with peace and joy. The Christian husband should love his wife just as actively, caring for her body and soul, praying for and with her, providing for her, protecting and comforting her, and seeking to give her daily joy as his second self. Finally, Christ loves His Church continuously. He loved her from eternity and chose her to be His bride. Therefore, even when she has proved unfaithful to Him at times, He remains devoted in love to her until death. In this way also should a Christian husband constantly love his wife. No storm of unhappiness should extinguish the flames of his love, and even long years of invalidism should only make that love more fervent.

The marriage of believers is also an image of the marriage of Christ and His Church from the side of the wife. The apostle writes, "Now as the church submits to Christ, so also wives should submit in everything to their husbands." The true Church reveals and proves herself faithful by this alone: she is subject to Christ, who rules her with His Word as the scepter of His eternal love. Every word of Christ is a command for her that she carries out with joy, even if it costs her blood and life. So, too, is the Christian wife. Her husband's scepter of love is holy to her. She does not seek to rule over anything, but instead, she desires to serve him whom God has placed as her head. She does not require hard commands; rather, she can learn how to care for her husband by observing with her eyes. She considers herself blessed to be able to do this.

Oh, blessed is the marriage in which the husband loves his wife as Christ loves His Church! And blessed is the marriage in which the wife is subject to her husband as the Church is to Christ! Such a marriage is the earthly reflection of the marriage of the Bridegroom in heaven and His bride on earth.

Lo, stained with blood,
The Lamb of God,
The Bridegroom, lies before thee,
Pouring out His life that He
May to life restore thee. Amen.

† *(TLH 167:4)*

Wednesday

Read 1 Timothy 4:8

IF WE ASK THE WORLD, "When can we expect that the marriage of a young couple will be happy and blessed?" the world will answer as follows: "First of all, if the couple have happy hearts; second, if they are rich; third, if they are bound by an ever-present love for each other; and fourth, if they have helpful friends at their side in time of need. Then there is no doubt that their marriage is well advised and not to be regretted." However, in the true sense of the word, these things can be found only in the godliness about which Saint Paul writes in today's text.

It is true that in order to have a happy marriage a happy heart is required above all else. But it is godliness that provides a truly happy heart. According to the Holy Scriptures, this means that a person believes in Christ and faithfully and fervently serves Him. Whoever believes in Christ certainly knows that his sins are forgiven, that God has written his name in the Book of Life, and that God is his gracious Father who looks upon him with favor as His dear child of grace. When pious spouses know this about themselves, how can they not have a happy heart? Unlike worldly spouses, they do not seek joy outside of their home in the places where the wild desires of the world hold sway. In the simple quiet of their home, they have the benefit of hidden joys about which the poor world knows nothing. Their hearts are filled with the peace of God, which is sweeter than all the world, and therefore their hearts remain bright even when their eyes are wet with tears.

It is also true, in a certain sense, that riches are required in order for a marriage to be blessed. Even in the short space of a single year, a family's needs are great. However, married people are truly rich and well cared for when they are godly, for then they have a rich Father in heaven whose treasuries are inexhaustible and whose hands are always tenderly open. Even if their house were otherwise completely empty, they could move in, for godliness is the richest dowry of the bride and the richest capital of the bridegroom. It brings about God's blessing, and wherever this blessing is, there is abundance.

Mutual love is another prerequisite for a truly happy marriage. Burning newlywed love can be found in the hearts of those who do not fear God, but how quickly it changes into indifference, and even hate. How soon the children of this world forget and break the vow that was spoken to their spouse. Godliness is a much more certain pillar of married love and faithfulness. When bride and bridegroom love each other in the Lord, when at their wedding they swear faithfulness both to each other and to the Lord, they begin a dear communion. If, in time, something comes between them and threatens to separate their hearts, they will then, because of their fear of the Lord, immediately implore Him once again to fan their love. Therefore, that love can never grow completely cold. If it appears to be about to die, God works in such a way that the resulting flames are even brighter than before.

Finally, in order for a marriage to be happy, there must be friends in time of need. Every marriage encounters many kinds of woe, but blessed are those whose marriage is grounded in godliness. They have a true Friend in their time of need. It is not the poor, mortal, fickle, and unreliable friendship of man. Instead, this Friend is always great in counsel and mighty in deed. He does not die or change, and He never forsakes those who call upon Him. They can appear before Him at any hour with their petitions, and they will be heard. He will give them comfort from all fears, rescue them from all dangers, and help them through all distresses. He who is their best Friend is also their God and Father in heaven.

Oh, how blessed is the marriage that is godly! It is then a picture of the marriage of Christ and His Church, and an earthly prelude of the communion of saints in heaven. It is also the most dear and beautiful flower, which continues to bloom in this vale of tears.

O Holy Spirit, grant us grace
That we our Lord and Savior
In faith and fervent love embrace
And truly serve Him ever,
So that when death is drawing nigh,
We to His open wounds may fly
And find in them salvation. Amen.

† *(TLH 293:1)*

Thursday

Read Romans 12:6–8

IN ORDER TO UNDERSTAND the words of today's text correctly, we must know that, in apostolic times, when God distributed so many different and glorious gifts, there were, especially in the larger congregations where the preacher could not supply every need, various church offices that were founded on these gifts. There was a special office for prophecy, that is, for those who had the gift of interpreting the Scriptures. There were also special offices for charity, teaching, administering the money of the church, leadership, and showing mercy, particularly in the care of the sick and imprisoned. For each of these offices, Saint Paul here provides an exhortation.

To those who prophesy, he says they should prophesy in proportion to faith. This means they should interpret the Scriptures so their interpretation harmonizes well with the whole of Christian doctrine. To those who offer charity and those who teach, he instructs them to administer their offices faithfully. To those in charge of money, he says they should give freely and with integrity, not regarding the person or acting with partiality. The ones who lead, he adds, should be alert watchmen whose decisions are taken to please God rather than men. Finally, those who attend the sick should show mercy, not because they are forced to, but because they want to.

Here we see that Christians should justify their faith before the world, above all, by conscientiousness and faithfulness in their offices and callings. Unfortunately, many who show themselves as zealous Christians in pious exercises are slow, careless, and unfaithful in their callings. They think the essence of Christianity consists of diligent praying and reading and churchgoing, of refraining from the vanity of the world, of pious speech, and of the holy appearance of many works. When the world sees that those who boast of faith are indeed diligent in such seemingly holy exercises but are unfaithful in their work, as well as terrible spouses, parents, and workers, the world concludes that the faith of Christians is an idle speculation, making people useless for this life. In addition, it views Christians as either poor beggars or hypocritical deceivers.

Therefore, whoever wants to be a Christian must justify his faith before the world by the manner in which he conducts himself in his vocation. The faith of a husband and father leads him to care for the temporal needs and the eternal salvation of his family, to love his wife as Christ loved the Church and to raise his children in the fear and admonition of the Lord. The faith of a wife and mother prompts her to be subject to her husband in all humility, standing at his side as a true helper, caring for her children with tenderness, and teaching them the first letters of saving knowledge. The faith of the businessman results in good work for his customers; if he works for himself, he does not enrich himself from the sweat of the poor, but rather regards his poor workers as better than himself. The faith of the servant or day laborer is revealed in work that is performed, not for the sake of mere wages or for display before the eyes of men, but to serve men as Jesus Christ Himself. The faith of those who work in churches, schools, and communities causes them to act out of love for their Savior rather than for financial or other worldly gain.

In all our pursuits, let us demonstrate that faith makes us the best we can be. In this way, we justify our faith before the world.

And grant me, Lord, to do,
With ready heart and willing,
Whate'er Thou shalt command,
My calling here fulfilling;

To do it when I ought,
With all my strength; and bless
The work I thus have wrought,
For Thou must give success. Amen.

(ELHB 346:2)

Friday

Read Romans 12:9–11

ACCORDING TO THE WORD of God, Christians must reject and condemn the wisdom and works of the world when they seek to come before God. Therefore, the world regards Christians as loveless enemies of man, as people with a blind faith that blots out the natural love from the heart. Christians must consider how to refute this judgment by the revelation of the love that resides in them. They confess that God loved the whole world so much that He gave His only-begotten Son that all who believe in Him would not be lost but have eternal life. How can the world regard this faith as true when Christians who confess this faith show no love toward the world and its greatest sinners? Christians confess that all have one Father in heaven through a new birth in the Holy Spirit, but the world is disinclined to believe this when Christians show themselves to be unbrotherly, cold, and disrespectful toward one another. Whoever does this dishonors his confession, commits an inexcusable offense, and becomes a hindrance to the kingdom of God.

Therefore, let us who confess the Christian faith before the world listen to Saint Paul's exhortation in today's reading: "Let love be genuine. Abhor what is evil; hold fast to what is good." Let us prove to the world that we carry love for it in our heart—not a pretended love, but a true, natural love, a love that reveals itself, not merely with the tongue, but principally in action directed by the heart. Such a love includes our enemies as well as those who love us. Let us prove to the world that when we chastise it, we do so, not in hatred, but in sympathy and pity. We abhor what is evil and cling to what is good. Let us prove to the world that it can count on us, in its every need, to be ready with an untiring willingness to help. Let us prove to the world that we can embrace in love, just as we are embraced by the bond of one faith. We not only love one another as brothers and sisters, but we also honor one another as children of the Most High and as a temple of the Holy Spirit. Let us prove to the world that this is no hypocrisy, that we are burning in love. "Do not be slothful in zeal, be fervent in spirit."

Oh, if we all would justify our faith before the world, what enormous success we would see! How many who still belong to the world would observe us with astonishment and remark: "Behold, what love these despised Christian people have! Their faith must really come from God! Let us seek out their congregation and learn their heavenly secrets of faith." It happened just this way in the days of the apostles. Whole crowds converted to Christianity. By their love to the world, these Christians preached as loudly and urgently as their bishops with their words. Therefore, let your light shine before people that they may see your good works and praise your Father in heaven.

Thou sacred Love, grace on us bestow,
Set our hearts with heav'nly fire aglow
That with hearts united we love each other,
Of one mind, in peace with ev'ry brother.
Lord, have mercy! Amen.

(TLH 231:3)

Saturday

Read Romans 12:12–16

CHRISTIANS CONFESS THE FAITH, arguing that no one, without God's will, can harm a hair on the head of any person. All troubles, they maintain, come from God, but they are only a father's rod that strikes in love, and the suffering of this time is not worth the glory that shall be revealed in them. However, when some Christians are in distress, they show themselves despondent, hopeless, and impatient, murmuring against their fate. They forsake their brothers in a time of distress and repay their persecutors evil for evil. Sometimes, they seek revenge for themselves or want to resist persecution with force. In all of this, do they not bring dishonor to the faith that they confess with their mouths? Don't they openly give weapons into the hand of the world so it can dispute their faith and declare it to be a deception?

Therefore, all who confess the Christian faith before the world consider: The time of distress is precisely the right time to let our faith shine before all the world. We should reveal the power that overcomes the world. We will then justify our faith by a godly resigning of ourselves to the evil times. We do this, Saint Paul says in today's text, "[rejoicing] in hope," proving to the world that *it* is in distress, without hope; meanwhile, our faith never disappoints and leads us to doubt, for we know that suffering leads to glory, and death to life.

The apostle characterizes us next as "patient in tribulation." We must prove to the world that our faith gives us power to endure everything patiently as a burden that the eternal Love has placed on us.

Next, Paul advises us to remain "constant in prayer." We

must prove to the world that our faith does not waver when it storms and it does not doubt that our prayers are heard, even when help is delayed. As the distress continues, we continue steadfast in prayer.

Paul goes on to say, "Contribute to the needs of the saints and seek to show hospitality." We must prove to the world that our faith does not bind us only on good days. Instead, the bond becomes even firmer in distress, disgrace, and persecution. In addition, we are not ashamed of those who are disgraced, but instead regard those who suffer for Christ all the more highly. Our goods belong to our poor brothers, and our homes are places of refuge for those who are persecuted.

The apostle adds, "Bless those who persecute you; bless and do not curse them." We must prove to the world that our faith does more than prevent us from taking revenge on our enemies. Indeed, we must show our love to them, repaying their evil with good, their cursing with blessing, and their blasphemy with intercession to God, just as Christ interceded for those who crucified Him and Stephen interceded for those who stoned him.

In our text, Paul makes one additional demand on Christians: "Rejoice with those who rejoice, weep with those who weep. Live in harmony with one another. Do not be haughty, but associate with the lowly." Here, He teaches us that Christians should also justify their faith by mutual concord in humility. Nothing makes a stronger negative impression on the world than the viewing of discord and pride ruling among those who confess the Christian faith. And it is in no way wrong.

We Christians confess with the apostle: "For in one Spirit we were all baptized into one body [in the Holy Supper] . . . and all were made to drink of one Spirit" (1 Corinthians 12:13). Before God, we have earned nothing but wrath, and everything we have received was not from ourselves, but from grace. What a demand to concord and deepest humility this is! What are we doing, then, when we maintain quarreling, divisions, envy, a lack of forgiveness, and the like among ourselves? What are we doing when we are haughty with our gifts and our knowledge, seeking honor for ourselves and despising our despised brothers? We are then disavowing with deed what we confess with our mouth and declaring that our faith is a lie. Instead of attracting the world to our faith, we cast suspicion on it. Our life is then a public warning that others should not believe as we do.

Wherever we go, then, let us be mindful of the calling that we have, not only to confess the Christian faith before the world, but also to justify it by mutual concord in humility.

May we Thy precepts, Lord, fulfill
And do on earth our Father's will
As angels do above;
Still walk in Christ, the living Way,
With all Thy children and obey
The law of Christian love. Amen.

† *(TLH 412:1)*

Sunday

Read Matthew 8:5–10

FROM THE CENTURION at Capernaum, we learn the basis of faith. He says to Christ, "But only say the word, and my servant will be healed." He is certain that Christ will help his servant. He does not require Christ's personal presence or a sign or anything visible or tangible. He desires only one thing: a word from Christ's mouth that promises him the help for which he wishes. The centurion is completely earnest, since he even seeks to prove before Christ Himself that His word would be sufficient. He says: "For I too am a man under authority, with soldiers under me. And I say to one, 'Go,' and he goes, and to another, 'Come,' and he comes, and to my servant, 'Do this,' and he does it." If the word of a mere man who submits to the authority of other men has so much power, how could he doubt the ability of the word of the true and almighty Son of God Himself to accomplish what it commands or promises? His faith astonishes Christ. On what is that faith based? It is based on the Word alone. This, and nothing else, is the proper foundation of faith.

Some believing Christians ground their faith on God's Word, but not on that Word alone. One also relies on feeling, another on sanctification, and still another on the witness of other men. What is the result of this? Their faith is like a reed that the wind blows to and fro. If they feel rest, peace, courage, and strength, then they also truly believe that their sins are forgiven and that they are children of God. However, as soon as this feeling leaves them and a cold, dark winter night of tribulation arises in their heart, they begin to doubt. They now fear that the faith and comfort that they had earlier were a mere delusion.

Others can show all kinds of good works, as well as great diligence in prayer and in the study of God's Word. They think they have taken steps forward in a pious life, and they do not notice that sinful desires stir in them. Then they are happy, believing firmly that they stand by God in grace. However, at another time, when their sanctification does not progress correctly, they feel the laziness of their flesh in the exercise of holiness and they acknowledge that their heart is still a source of evil thoughts and desires. Now, they think, they have lost their previous state of grace.

Finally, there are still others who are considered and called good Christians, even by their pastors. This gives them a great peace although it is without proof from God's Word. Then, as soon as their supporters lose faith in them and no longer regard them as true Christians, all their peace and certainty vanish.

Such Christians are in a truly lamentable condition. At one time, they are brave, but then they are forced to struggle with doubt. At that time, they hover between heaven and hell. What prompted this unhappy state? They did not ground their faith on God's Word alone.

If we want to have our faith as it should be, firm and constant, we must lose sight of everything except God's Word. Whoever grounds his faith on that Word alone has a support that no storm can destroy and no flood can wash away.

I know my faith is founded
On Jesus Christ, my God and Lord;
And this my faith confessing,
Unmoved I stand upon His Word.
Man's reason cannot fathom
The truth of God profound;
Who trusts her subtle wisdom
Relies on shifting ground.
God's Word is all-sufficient,
It makes divinely sure,
And trusting in its wisdom,
My faith shall rest secure. Amen.

† *(TLH 381:1)*

Monday

Read Matthew 8:11–12

The example of the Gentile centurion at Capernaum offers a striking proof that honest disciples of Christ—including the humblest, purest, and most faithful souls who far surpass and shame the members of the orthodox Church—are often found among the heterodox. Does this suggest that we should regard truth and error as of equivalent value or that it does not matter which church one attends? Since there are children of God among the heterodox, should we stop contending for purity of doctrine and against false teaching? Should Christians call all parties brothers and should we merge all churches? Heaven forbid! Many in the midst of heterodoxy come to true faith in Christ in their heart and are therefore saved. However, it does not follow that one can attain true faith and salvation through error, and many do indeed err out of simplicity and ignorance. But if they can recognize the truth, faithfully accept and appropriate it, and remain in it by God's grace, the errors that still hold them captive do not work toward their death. Whoever has been saved in simplicity but then does not seek the truth, willfully remaining in error and in a false religion, or even forsaking the true religion to side with the heterodox, moves from grace to malice and is rejected by God as an unfaithful servant. The correct interpretation of Christ's true disciples among the heterodox is found in today's text. Here, without doubt, Christ wants to sound a warning against security to all who belong to the communion of the orthodox.

In carnal security, the Jews relied upon the fact that they were the children of Abraham, to whom God had given great promises. They were God's chosen people, and they possessed the revealed Word of God, pure and clear, as well as the temple and the true worship. When the prophets of God threatened them with punishment, they replied: "Here is the Lord's temple! He surely would not destroy this holy place!" When Christ chastised the Jewish people, particularly the high priests, scribes, and Pharisees, proclaiming their temporal and eternal destruction, they ignored Him. They were, after all, the orthodox Church, and they therefore thought they were not in danger. But our Lord insisted that, while God would call guests to His heavenly table from every region under heaven, these outward participants in the "true church," these "children of the kingdom" would be cast into the outermost darkness.

We, who possess the pure Gospel and the genuine Sacraments, certainly have a great advantage over those who, perhaps from their youth, were victimized by false preaching. But let us not think that our membership in the orthodox Church and our adherence to the pure doctrine will be sufficient for us. To whom much is given, from him will much be demanded. The purer our doctrine, the more firmly we must cling to it and the more carefully we must guard against the invasion of false doctrine. The richer the comfort we receive from the Gospel, the more faithful we must be in the faith. The more numerous the spiritual blessings we receive from God, the more fervent must be our love and the works in which we demonstrate our gratitude. If we walk as children of the kingdom and not as children of this world, we are blessed, for then we will not be cast out. Instead, we will be taken into the kingdom of eternal glory.

Increase my faith, dear Savior,
For Satan seeks by night and day
To rob me of this treasure
And take my hope of bliss away.

But, Lord, with Thee beside me,
I shall be undismayed;
And led by Thy good Spirit,
I shall be unafraid.
Abide with me, O Savior,
A firmer faith bestow;
Then I shall bid defiance
To ev'ry evil foe. Amen.

(TLH 381:2)

Tuesday

Read Hebrews 11:6

FOR MANY IN OUR DAY, the most offensive thing about the Christian religion is that faith is its most important and necessary requirement. Why, they wonder, does God place such a premium on faith that He saves the one who believes something and damns another who does not believe this? Is the one who believes better than the one who does not believe? Because God is holy, shouldn't it matter more to Him that one is pious, lives honestly, and does good works?

Those who do not believe themselves to be wicked people fail to understand what Christianity teaches about faith and unbelief. No one can deny that all people are sinners. Thus, no one can be saved except by grace. To enjoy the salvation that was earned for him by grace and that is offered to him by the Gospel, a person must believe that God sent His only-begotten Son into the world and that He earned salvation for all people by His bitter suffering and death. Whoever does not accept this remains, according to his own will, excluded, and he will ultimately be lost. This is the teaching of Holy Scripture: salvation is solely by grace, not by work or merit. If a person is lost, it is because he refused the salvation God freely offered; he did not want to be saved by grace. Therefore, Saint Paul says, "That is why [righteousness] depends on faith, in order that the promise may rest on grace" (Romans 4:16).

Faith is important and precious before God for another reason as well: it is man's way back to God. Man was created in such a manner that he subjected himself in humility to his Lord and Creator, clinging to God as his highest good in childlike trust and giving Him all honor. But when man fell into sin, a great, sad change occurred in his heart. From that moment, he wanted to be independent of God, to be like God, to be his own god. Instead of trusting God, he relied upon himself. He now feared God, fled from Him, and robbed Him of the honor that was due Him, appropriating it instead to himself.

However, as soon as a person starts to believe, he recognizes himself as a poor, vain creature, and he subjects himself once again to God as his Creator and Lord. He lets go of all trust in himself, and places that trust in God alone. He desires salvation from God and accords Him the honor He is due. Before the world, faith appears to be so humble, but before God, it is the most precious thing one can offer. Through faith, man begins to fulfill the first and highest commandment: to make God his God and to trust in Him above all things. Therefore, today's reading instructs us, "Without faith it is impossible to please Him."

In faith, Lord, let me serve Thee;
Tho' persecution, grief, and pain

Should seek to overwhelm me,
Let me a steadfast trust retain;
And then at my departure
Take Thou me home to Thee
And let me there inherit
All Thou has promised me.
In life and death, Lord, keep me
Until Thy heav'n I gain,
Where I by Thy great mercy
The end of faith attain. Amen.

(TLH 381:3)

Wednesday

Read Ezekiel 13:3,10

IN 1817, A NEW CHURCH arose in Germany. It assumed the beautiful name "Evangelical Church." This Church was built on the principle that if people are united in the main doctrines of Christianity, the remaining points of faith are not worth quarreling about, and each one can believe whatever he wants. It was said: "The Protestant Church has been split long enough, since the time of the Reformation, into the Lutheran and Reformed parties. People have lovelessly fought long enough over a few important points. It is time for this dispute to end, and each Christian should extend the hand of broth erly love to another for the sake of unity. The song of the angels over the Savior's crib, 'Peace on earth,' must become a reality."

It is true that God's Word urgently exhorts Christians to peacefulness and unity. Does it follow from this that for the sake of peace and friendship we should not fight against those who deny the clearly revealed truths in that Word concerning our salvation, perverting and falsifying the Holy Scriptures in many places? Should we unite with them as dear brothers in the faith? Heaven forbid!

As sinful and godless as it is to quarrel over mere words or indifferent questions, it is just as reprehensible to ignore differences concerning precious, certain, divine truths instead of fighting for them. In the Book of Revelation, the Lord speaks about such indifferent people: "So, because you are lukewarm, and neither hot nor cold, I will spit you out of my mouth" (3:16). Such lukewarm people are more repulsive to Christ than the open enemies of the truth. Didn't the prophets and apostles of the Lord struggle constantly against falsifiers of God's Word? Didn't most of Christ's talks contain warnings against the leaven, or false doctrine, of the Pharisees, Sadducees, and scribes, as well as threats of punishment for this?

Saint Paul wrote to the Galatians about false brothers who had attacked the doctrine of Christian liberty, "to them we did not yield in submission even for a moment, so that the truth of the gospel might be preserved for you" (2:5). The same apostle wrote to Titus about a faithful bishop, stating that he should hold "firm to the trustworthy word as taught, so that he may be able to give instruction in sound doctrine and also to rebuke those who contradict it" (1:9). He added: "If anyone teaches a different doctrine and does not agree with the sound words of our Lord Jesus Christ and the teaching that accords with godliness, he is puffed up with conceit and understands nothing. . . . Flee these things" (1 Timothy 6:3–4,11). Paul thus insists that no false doctrine should be regarded as minor, that no deviation from God's Word, no matter how seemingly insignificant, is insignificant: "A little leaven leavens the whole lump" (1 Corinthians 5:6). He also pronounces this sentence on the falsifiers of doctrine: "But even if we or an angel from heaven should preach to you a gospel contrary to the one we preached to you, let him be accursed" (Galatians 1:8).

As much as God's Word exhorts us to seek true peace, doesn't it just as earnestly warn against a false peace? In today's text, the prophet Ezekiel rebukes the peacemakers who do not have truth.

According to God's Word, the church that wants to make peace by leaving some of the truth behind and declaring false doctrine to be acceptable is a house of whitewashed walls that are neither mortared nor built upon solid ground. As a result, any wind can blow it down, and any rain can wash it away. Such a church is more dangerous than the most awful sect, for at least the sect recognizes that only pure doctrine should be preached in a church. A so-called united church stands on rotten ground. No one in it can find and possess the pure truth because no one is willing to fight for it. May God protect every pious Christian from such false peace with man and against God.

O God, how sin's dread works abound!
Throughout the earth no rest is found,
And falsehood's spirit wide has spread,
And error boldly rears its head.

The haughty spirits, Lord, restrain
Who o'er Thy Church with might would reign
And always set forth something new,
Devised to change Thy doctrine true. Amen.

(TLH 292:5, 6)

Thursday

Read Romans 12:16b

BEING PEACEABLE is an absolutely necessary sign of a true Christian who is on the right path to salvation and who stands in the faith. A person who delights in strife and discord, who does not earnestly long to live in peace and friendship with all people, and who declines the opportunity to establish harmonious relationships when it is offered to him, cannot be a true Christian. Such a person's faith is hypocrisy. The moment he is converted and experiences the grace of rebirth and renewal in his heart, he will be filled with the holy desire to act toward his neighbors, and especially toward his brothers and sisters in Christ, as God acted toward him.

At times, of course, even true Christians cannot prevent the disturbance of the peace between themselves and others. Nevertheless, they do everything in their power to preserve the peace or to obtain it once again. What is required of the Christian who would live in peace with all people? Saint Paul tells us in today's reading: "Never be conceited."

The greatest and most powerful disturber of peace and harmony among people is pride in one's wisdom. As Solomon, who was known for his wisdom, writes, "By insolence comes nothing but strife" (Proverbs 13:10). If someone imagines that he is especially wise because many things have turned out well for him, he is always dogmatic and obstinate. Such a person likes to hear himself talk, and when he speaks, he wants all others, whom he despises as little lights, to be silent. Everything, he imagines, should go just as he wishes. Take, for example, the false friends who visited and quarreled with Job. Job had to tell them, "No doubt you are the people, and wisdom will die with you" (12:2). The conceited person believes that everyone should concur with his opinions. Everyone should yield to him, but he will yield to no one. If a decision is made to pursue a course of action with which he disagrees, he will have nothing to do with it, or he will participate only with inner resentment. He imagines that even the entire congregation should give in to his conceit. If it does not, he quits, or his heart is no longer with it and its endeavors. Even if he becomes convinced that he has erred, he will not admit it, but instead he will insist on his opinion. Wherever such arrogance is found, peace and harmony are impossible. Self-will and obstinacy are usually stumbling blocks on which the completion of all blessed common works is shattered. Either the matter deteriorates into an open quarrel or disunion, or the harmony is only skin-deep, while inner discord divides the hearts.

Therefore, Saint Paul calls to Christians, "Do not be conceited." As pride is the real father of all discord, so humility is the true mother of peace. Whoever in sincere humility does not consider himself wise will not deviate in the slightest from God's Word. A person who does not trust in his own wisdom believes instead that God is the only wise person and that His Word is divine wisdom. If the business at hand must be decided by men, he will always be ready to hear the opinions of others. He will let himself be easily convinced that he himself is in error, that another can see the matter more clearly, and that he must give up his false notion. Yes, a truly humble person will gladly admit the possibility that he has erred, even when he cannot make a definitive determination he has done so. In any event, he is glad to sacrifice his opinions for the sake of peace and harmony.

Today's text should always resound in the hearts of Christians. Then most quarrels would be put aside, and peace and harmony would dwell in their place.

O gentle Dew, from heaven now fall
With power upon the hearts of all,
Thy tender love instilling,
That heart to heart more closely bound,
In kindly deeds be fruitful found,
The law of love fulfilling.
Dwell thus in us;
Envy banish; Strife will vanish
Where thou livest.
Peace and love and joy Thou givest. Amen.

† *(TLH 235:7)*

Friday

Read Romans 12:16–21

UNFORTUNATELY, THERE ARE far too many people who think that if they did not instigate discord, and especially if the offender does not take the first step toward reconciliation, then it is not their fault if they cannot live in peace with the offender. If they are obvious non-Christians, they rejoice when it does not go well for their offender. They watch for a suitable opportunity when they can repay him the injustice he did them. If they are not Christians who carefully guard themselves, they often allow a bitter root to grow up in their heart against their offender, from which bitter fruits are produced. This is especially true if they have been insulted by a Christian. It is usually the case that careless Christians can no longer, from their hearts, pray for their offender and all his temporal and spiritual needs. They are no longer able to rejoice with him, to speak to him in a friendly manner, and to do good to him. Such Christians are of the opinion that only their offender bears responsibility for the discord.

But what does Saint Paul say in today's reading? "Live in harmony with one another." Therefore, "repay no one evil for evil." We see from this that even if a person has not provided the first occasion for discord, if he lets the offense that he has suffered at the hands of his neighbor serve as an excuse for not loving him as before and for not being friendly to him in deeds and words, that person has not done "so far as it depends on you" to live in peace with all men.

In the concluding words of our text, the apostle makes two points. First, he says, "Beloved, never avenge yourselves, but leave it to the wrath of God; for it is written, 'Vengeance is Mine, I will repay,' says the Lord." If the Christian wants to be peace-loving in God's eyes, he dare not repay his offender with the least evil, even if the offense was ever so great and grievous. Either the offense is not worth the strife, or else it earns God's wrath and punishment. In the event that the offense deserves the latter, the Christian must give way to God's wrath. He must not take the least bit of revenge himself, seizing God's office and thus hindering Him by taking vengeance on the evil by himself. A Christian must value peace and harmony so highly that he will suffer considerable harm if he can thereby purchase peace and harmony.

Yet even this is not enough. Saint Paul demands still more. He says: "To the contrary, 'if your enemy is hungry, feed him; if he is thirsty, give him something to drink; for by so doing you will heap burning coals on his head.' Do not be overcome by evil, but overcome evil with good." If a Christian wants to be peace-loving in God's eyes, he must repay evil with good. The darker and more sullen the offender is against him, the more friendly the Christian must show himself toward his offender. He must not become tired of heaping coals of fire on his antagonist's head, overwhelming him with love and benefits to the extent that he is finally conquered by that love, moved to give up his wrath, and prompted to love the person he offended.

Oh, if only all Christians would do all they can to live in peace with their neighbors, then peace would bloom in all hearts, in homes and in families, in cities and in congregations, throughout the world.

And give us Thy peace: peace in Church and school;
Peace to the powers who o'er our country rule;
Peace to the conscience, peace within the heart,
Do Thou impart. Amen.

(ELHB 279:3)

Saturday

Read Romans 12:17

IN THIS VERSE, Saint Paul says that a person should take great pains to act in such a manner that it is seen by all men as good, honorable, and laudable. Too many people who want to be good Christians believe that if their behavior is not wrong, it doesn't matter what people think and say about it. If they can justify their actions before the judgment seat of their own conscience, they can be indifferent to others' views of those same actions. Such people believe that a Christian must not ask if people regard him as faithful or unfaithful, as zealous or idle, as proud or humble, as sincere or hypocritical, as a Christian or a non-Christian, and as pious or godless. They imagine that Paul was of like mind when he wrote, "If I were still trying to please man, I would not be a servant of Christ" (Galatians 1:10).

This interpretation is in error. It is both harmful and sinful. What the apostle says with this remark is that he would not depart from the Word of God to please men. He adds that he has judged himself, in all his words and actions, according to other people's perceptions: "For though I am free from all, I have made myself a servant to all, that I might win more of them. . . . To the weak I became weak, that I might win the weak. I have become all things to all people, that by all means I might save some" (1 Corinthians 9:19,22). The inconsiderateness of many Christians destroys peace and unity. How could it be otherwise when they are unconcerned that others have taken offense and are annoyed with them?

If a Christian truly wants to live in peace with all people, at least as much as it lies in him, it is absolutely necessary that, as the apostle writes, he "give thought to do what is honorable in the sight of all." He must act, not only rightly, but also with diligence. He must behave in a manner that everyone regards as proper. He must not only avoid everything evil but also everything that appears evil. He must guard his Christian freedom in his conscience and in his outward life for the sake of the weak, and wherever it is necessary, he must limit and forgo its use. To act in a God-pleasing manner, he must, with Paul, in fervent love of his neighbor, conduct himself so he pleases his neighbor for his betterment. In short, in both words and deeds, he must seek his neighbor's good, not his own.

How wonderful life would be if all of us did everything in our power to establish peace with our neighbors. The love of peace is not just a beautiful adornment, but also an important sign of a justified Christian. Whoever has not sought peace has not attained it. Whoever abandons the love of peace when his flesh is attacked must recognize that he is still a child of God's wrath. May he hurry to rescue his unsaved soul, to repent and convert, and to become a child of peace. Whoever is idle or slow in pursuing peace must become zealous in it. May every zealous Christian let his light shine brighter and brighter before people so they can see his good works and praise the Father in heaven.

Give us this day our daily bread
And let us all be clothed and fed.
From war and strife be our Defense,
From famine and from pestilence,
That we may live in godly peace,
Free from all care and avarice. Amen.

(TLH 458:5)

Sunday

Read Matthew 8:23–24

IT HAD BEEN an especially difficult day for Jesus. When evening finally came, He called His disciples to make a boat ready for a trip to the other side of the Sea of Galilee. This was no great merchant ship, but one of the small, simple fishing boats owned by Peter, who was living in Capernaum. No vessel had ever held a more precious cargo, for it carried both the

Savior of the world and His twelve apostles, who one day would carry the message of salvation through all the earth. If any vessel should have had a safe and blessed trip, one would naturally think it would be this one. But our text says, "there arose a great storm on the sea, so that the boat was being swamped by the waves." When the boat left the land, the evening sky was clear and bright and the air and sea were calm. But a fierce storm quickly arose, and the waves lifted the boat to a towering height and then pulled it down into the depths. Saint Mark writes that a "furious squall" came up and "nearly swamped" the boat (Mark 4:37 NIV). Heaven, air, and sea all appeared to have been thrown into an uproar. Covered by the waves, the boat seemed sure to sink. Wisdom, power, and all other human resources would avail nothing against such a storm. The fishermen aboard the boat, who knew the sea, despaired of the likelihood of rescue. And where was Jesus the Lord in the midst of this turmoil? Our text says, "He was asleep." He appeared neither to know nor to be concerned about the danger His disciples were facing.

This is a portrait of the great danger that confronts the Christian Church at all times. Just like this boat, the Church travels on the sea of the world. Its pilot is Christ, its oarsmen are the preachers of the Gospel, its gangplank is faith and Baptism, its anchor is hope, its mast is the cross, its sail is the Word swelled by the Holy Ghost, its flag is our confession, its crew is faithful Christians, and the harbor to which it is traveling is heaven. As soon as this ship of the Church weighed anchor, at the time of the apostles, and set out on its voyage, a tempest arose from below and a windstorm from above. Hell, the world, and even the heavens seemed to be united in a conspiracy to disrupt and destroy the Church. A tempest of bloody persecution beset it, to be soon followed by a whirlwind of false doctrines. From that time on, the ship of the

Church has always been in danger of being smashed to pieces and sinking in the deep.

This is especially true today. To be sure, in many places, Christians no longer groan under the bloody rod of persecution; and especially in America, God has provided the blessing of a religious freedom that is largely unknown elsewhere. Nevertheless, the ship of the Church is in greater danger. Sects continue to preach their false faith everywhere. The enemies of Christ and His Church are numerous and very powerful. If God does not prevent it, they could take our freedom from us at any moment.

The ship of the Church continues to be tossed about by fierce storms. The spirit of the age quickly raises it to a towering height then casts it down into the depths of the sea. Many baptized Christians have been lost and more are following them daily. And once again, it appears as if Christ is asleep while the sail of the Word is torn, the mast of the cross is broken, and the ship of the church is flooded by sin and unbelief.

Preserve in wave and tempest
Thy storm-tossed little flock;
Assailed by wind and weather,
May it endure each shock.
Take Thou the helm, O Pilot,
And set the course aright;
Thus we shall reach the harbor
In Thine eternal light. Amen.

(TLH 264:6)

Monday

Read Matthew 8:25–26

THE STORY OF THE BOAT on the Sea of Galilee presents a picture, not just of the dangers facing the Church, but also of its members. Today's text tells us two things about those who were on board the vessel: they were true believers but their faith was still exceedingly weak. They had forsaken the world and its enticements to follow Jesus. Now, in the face of great danger and with all human help gone, they did not doubt. They turned to Christ, awakened Him, and pleaded with Him to help them. If they had not truly believed in Jesus as the almighty Son of God, they would not have turned to Him at a time when only an experienced seaman might have been able to effect a rescue.

Had they been strong in faith, they would have recalled the many miracles of Jesus they had already witnessed. In the midst of the storm, they would have been so certain their prayers for help would be heard that they could have sung a hymn of praise and thanks, without entertaining a momentary thought that the boat could sink. They would also have remembered, as the psalmist reflected, that no matter where we go, the Lord is with us. But their prayer of faith, "Save us, Lord," is full of fear and anxiety, for they immediately add, "We are perishing!" Mark's Gospel reports that several of them cried out, "Teacher, do You not care that we are perishing?" (4:38). Their faith was so weak that it bordered on unbelief. It was nothing more than a smoldering wick and a bruised reed. Christ replies, chastising them, "Why are you so afraid? O you of little faith?"

Here is a picture of those on board the ship of the

Church. They include, first of all—may God be praised!—people who have forsaken the world and its enticements and glories, clinging to Christ, confessing Him as the Son of God, and in the midst of distresses, calling on Him in true faith, "Lord, help us!" But the age of the strong believers, the heroes of faith who were prevalent in the first three centuries of the Christian era and during the Reformation, is past. The believers of our age are, with few exceptions, weak and of little faith. The storms that beset them are much milder than the one the apostles encountered on the Sea of Galilee, yet afflictions and temptations cause Christians to waver and stumble. If a bloody persecution should arise and believers do not respond with a stronger faith than they are now displaying, it is likely that most of them would deny the Lord and fall away.

Does this not leave us with a sad outlook? Do we not have to fear that the Church will finally perish? For surely, in these last times, it will face greater distresses, afflictions, and temptations. We must expect difficulties, but they do not portend the death of the Church. Christ does not condemn the weak in faith, quench a smoldering wick, or break a bruised reed.

O God, forsake me not!
Take not Thy Spirit from me
And suffer not the might
Of sin to overcome me.
Increase my feeble faith,
Which Thou Thyself hast wrought.
Be Thou my Strength and Pow'r—
O God, forsake me not! Amen.

† *(TLH 402:2)*

Tuesday

Read Matthew 8:26–27

IT IS TRUE that Christ slept as the disciples in the boat were in the greatest danger. It certainly seemed as if He was utterly unaware of their plight, but appearances can be deceiving. Christ slept, but only according to His human nature. He also remained the protector of Israel, who neither slumbers nor sleeps. According to His divinity, He was awake and aware of everything that was happening. And He saw to it that the boat would not be wrecked, despite the storm and the waves. His sleeping before the eyes of the disciples was a test to strengthen their faith through affliction and to awaken them to prayer. When He was bodily awakened by the disciples' cries for help, He let the stormy sea rage on while He first attended to the storm in the hearts of His followers, who were trembling and weak in faith.

"Then," our text tells us, "He rose and rebuked the winds and the sea. And there was a great calm." This was a totally incomprehensible miracle, which demonstrated that Christ is also the Lord of nature. It sometimes happens that a heavy gale at sea dies down, but the waves continue to tower for some time before they gradually diminish. However, as Mark reports, as soon as Christ rebuked the sea and wind, "Peace! Be still!" (Mark 4:39) both immediately complied. The howling storm was replaced by silence, and the surface of the sea became smooth and clear, reflecting the glittering stars. Full of amazement, all of those in the boat cried out, "What sort of man is this, that even winds and sea obey Him?"

Here we have an inexpressibly comforting picture of today's Church. The world, with its learning and power, is like a sea stirred up by a strong storm. It attacks the ship of the Church, whose destruction appears to be inevitable, and it seems as if Christ is asleep at the helm. The members of the Church, who are still of little faith, already cry out in despair: "Save us, Lord; we are perishing!" Many, full of doubts, may abandon the ship of the Church and plunge back into the sea of the world. Yet there is no cause for alarm. Christ remains aboard our ship, and according to His divine omniscience, omnipotence, and care, He does not sleep. When His hour comes, He will rise up, rebuke us for our little faith, and say to the wind-driven sea of the world, "Peace! Be still!" Then the world will be stilled, and the ship of the Church will enter into the harbor of heaven. For Christ has promised, "On this rock [He means Himself] I will build My church, and the gates of hell shall not prevail against it" (Matthew 16:18), and "Behold, I am with you always, to the end of the age" (Matthew 28:20).

So let us not lose heart, even in these last, troubled times. Let us not forsake the ship of the Church, thinking it will soon sink. We would eternally regret our decision, for outside this ship, there is no salvation, just as there was no rescue for those who were not aboard Noah's ark. As that ark smoothly navigated through the flood and finally came to rest, safe and sound on Mount Ararat, so too will the ship of the Church pass through the world's stormy sea and finally rest on the eternal mountains of divine grace. Then we who have remained true in the faith will have our turn to cry out, full of amazement, "What sort of man is this, that even winds and sea obey Him?" And we will have all of eternity to rejoice in the answer to that question.

Preserve, O Lord, Thy Zion,
Bought dearly with Thy blood;
Protect what Thou hast chosen
Against the foes' dread brood.

Be Thou her great Defender
When dangers gather round;
E'en tho' the earth be crumbling,
Safe will Thy Church be found. Amen.

(*TLH 264:3*)

Wednesday

Read Psalm 46:5

IF WE READ THE HISTORY of the Christian Church, we will find that, in the eyes of man, it was always in great danger of going under, but it invariably rose up once more. When Christ left the world after completing His work of redemption, His Church was very small. It consisted of no more than a few hundred souls and most of them were poor, simple people. Even the twelve apostles, who had already lost one of their number (Judas, the betrayer), were not educated men, but these timid souls would soon begin, by their preaching of the crucified Christ, to spread the Church throughout the world.

At the time, this would have seemed impossible. But at Pentecost, the Holy Ghost equipped the apostles with the gifts they would need to preach the Gospel to everyone. And behold! No more than thirty years later, the apostle Paul, who had once been a persecutor of the Church, could write that the Good News had now been "proclaimed in all creation under heaven" (Colossians 1:23). Thus, at the time of the apostles' death, there were already Christian churches in every land on earth.

The Christian Church was established amid bloody persecutions that commenced as soon as it was founded. There is no imaginable form of torture that the heathen Caesars and their officials did not employ in an effort to force the Church to fall away from Christ and thus be destroyed. Those who confessed Christ as Lord and Savior were decapitated, drowned, strangled, and burned. Persecutors turned to ever more agonizing means of killing believers. They were thrown as food to wild animals. They were slowly roasted over fires. They were suffocated. They were crucified upside down and left to be devoured by ravenous animals. With glowing pincers, piece after piece of Christians' flesh was torn from their bones. Boiling oil and pitch were poured down their throats. Naked bodies were tied to corpses and tossed into dark and stinking holes to starve and rot. In this way, many hundreds of thousands of Christians became martyrs in the first centuries of the church age.

When the persecution of Diocletian ended in the year 310, edicts were issued to mark the victory of the Caesars over the Christians. They bore such titles as "After the Destruction of the Name of the Christians Who Wanted to Overthrow the Empire" and "After the Completed Destruction Everywhere of the Christian Superstition." But were these proud titles accurate? No! As Tertullian, one teacher of the Church, had already written: "The more they cut us down, the more we become. The blood of the martyrs is seed." It should also be noted that all of the persecutors met with a terrible end.

When Constantine himself became a Christian in 323, Christians were granted, with short interruptions, peace from outward persecutions. However, far more dangerous enemies arose in their midst. These were the false teachers, who sought to kill the Church not bodily but spiritually. But God responded by awakening the hearts of men to uncover the false teachers and defend the truth.

With the rise of the papacy, the Church encountered even greater dangers. It appeared to have been transformed into a worldly kingdom in which Christ was thrust from His throne and the saving Gospel was abolished. The Church finally seemed to have perished. The bloody persecutions that had hounded the Church in its first years were now repeated, but this time they were directed from inside its ranks. But behold! Just when all hope for help appeared to have vanished, God awakened Dr. Martin Luther to lead a complete and glorious reformation of the Church.

Christ, Thou the Champion of the band who own
Thy cross, O make Thy succor quickly known!
The schemes of those who long our blood have sought
Bring Thou to naught. Amen.

(ELHB 279:1)

Thursday

Read Matthew 24:12

NEVER HAVE PEOPLE spoken as much about love as they do in our own time. "Love" has now become a catchword that is employed both by those who want to be Christians and by those who want nothing whatsoever to do with the faith.

But what do many Christians mean when they employ the term "love"? Above all, they understand it to mean this: As a person expresses himself in matters of faith, he should show himself tolerant, that is, long-suffering, lenient, and easygoing.

He should not take purity of doctrine as seriously and rebuke deviation from God's Word as sharply as in the earlier years of the Church. He should also regard as dear brothers those who accept some main articles of faith but do not wish to subject themselves to the Word of God in all things.

How does all of this square with Scripture? Not well at all. Indeed, God's Word says just the opposite: "[Love] does not rejoice at wrongdoing, but rejoices with the truth" (1 Corinthians 13:6). Those who preach tolerance and overlook deviations in doctrine are like a man who demonstrates love and generosity toward the poor, but who is later revealed to have taken his gifts, not from his own goods, but by way of theft from others. They appropriate God's Word, His truth, and His glory for their own purposes, and by their use—and misuse—of them, they appear to possess more love than others. But most of them are full of resentment, malice, and enmity against those who take them to task because they despise the truth.

Those who do not want to be Christians regard love as the mere exercise of outward works of charity. In addition, they say that individuals who are seeking only their own advancement succeed in fulfilling the demands of love if the benefit that they receive also trickles down to those in need. Thus they attend the theater, concerts, dinner parties, and other pleasures. Some of them establish secret societies and contribute to the support of their fellow members, but only with the expectation that in time they will receive as much or more than they have given. This, they believe, is a beautiful covenant of brotherly love. With contempt, they look down on the believing Christian and think to themselves, "You boast of faith, but we, on the contrary, love."

How can such works be works of love? Poor, deceived men! Love has so completely vanished from their hearts that those who lack can anticipate help only if those who have are able to reap an added benefit for themselves from an act of "charity." Those who encounter misfortune can look for relief only to those with whom they have entered into a contract for mutual support. And woe to those who get unwelcomely close with requests for help. They are met with an unforgiving hatred. Still, people boast of our age as an age of love! The life of the children of this world is marked by fraud, envy, and malice.

There is no doubt that the time about which our Lord once prophesied has arrived: "And because lawlessness will be increased, the love of many will grow cold." This is not an age of love, but an age of lovelessness.

And let me do to others
As Thou hast done to me:
Love all men as my brothers,
And serve them willingly,
With ready heart, nor seek my own,
But as Thou, Lord, hast helped us,
From purest love alone. Amen.

(ELHB 197:7)

Friday

Read Romans 13:8

TODAY, MANY PEOPLE believe that love is an entirely free matter of an individual's heart. A person, they say, does not owe love to all men. Instead, he can choose to love or to hate another, and he can choose to do good or evil to that individual. The only limitation on the exercising of this freedom is that he cannot trample on another's legal rights or damage his property.

How does the Word of God judge all of this? Today's reading supplies the answer. Saint Paul does not say that our love for our brother depends upon our heart's inclination. He does not admonish us to love only a beautiful thing that stirs us by its praiseworthiness and loveliness. Instead, he demands that we extend our love as a debt. He says this because God has commanded us to love in His Law.

We are not at liberty to choose whom we will love. And if we love all people from our heart and demonstrate this with our deeds, we are doing nothing remarkable. Love is our debt. Every other person is our creditor, and we are his debtor. Even if we do not otherwise owe anyone, we owe him love. In vain we boast that we have given each person what is his, even when we have not loved each one. In vain we boast of our generosity and high-mindedness when we show love to our enemies. We are then doing only what we are obligated to do.

It is true that there is no court in the world that collects the debts of love, and there is none that punishes the person who does not pay these debts. But God's judgment is different. In His heaven, before all, the debt book of love is examined, and even if all our other debts are found to have been canceled, terrible judgment still meets us if we have not paid the debt of love.

According to God's Word, love is the debt of an exceptionally wonderful condition. In the verses that precede today's reading, Paul has maintained that we should not be in debt to anyone. Then he suddenly turns and instructs us to be in debt in regard to love. And this debt is both constant and unceasing. Every other debt becomes smaller by repayment until finally it is retired. Not so the debt of love we have toward our neighbor. It is our holy duty to strive after it, and while we may rid ourselves of every other debt, we can never discharge the debt of love. It is always the same, always as great today as it was yesterday. And while every other debt can obligate us only until death, we take the debt of love with us to the grave, into eternity, and into heaven. There, faith changes into beholding, and hope is transformed into having. Love, however, remains as long as there is a kingdom of God, that is, eternally.

Salvation free
By faith in Thee,
That is Thy Gospel's preaching,
The heart and core
Of Biblelore
In all its sacred teaching.
In Christ we must
Put all our trust,
Not in deeds or labor;
With conscience pure
And heart secure
Love Thee, Lord, and our neighbor. Amen.

† *(TLH 266:2)*

Saturday

Read Romans 13:9–10

In this passage, Saint Paul gives us two reasons why love for our fellow man is our only debt. First, without love, it would be impossible to fulfill any of God's commands. Love is really the intent of all of God's Commandments. Second, when love is perfect, no command of God is unfulfilled. The true fulfillment of the Law lies in love.

All of God's Commandments are contained in this: "You shall love God above all things, and your neighbor as yourself." God gave us the Ten Commandments, but not because man had exactly ten kinds of duties. Instead, these Commandments give us ten examples of the commandment to love, and they are met only when they are addressed with an attitude of love. Doing what the Commandments mandate, and failing to do what they forbid, will not be sufficient. You may honor your parents according to the Fourth Commandment. You may refrain from killing with your fist according to the Fifth Commandment. You may not commit adultery with an outward act according to the Sixth Commandment. You may not take another's property by force or cunning according to the Seventh Commandment. You may not bear false witness with your mouth against your neighbor according to the Eighth Commandment. And you may not knowingly covet—even once—your neighbor's good fortune according to the Ninth and Tenth Commandments. But even if you do all of this, you will not have fulfilled even one letter of the whole Law unless the true, pure, and fervent love of God and your neighbor dwells in your heart. Everything must flow from this spring of love inside you.

Whoever does not have this love, although he may live ever so honorably, harmlessly, and blamelessly, is still a trespasser before God, an idolater, a profaner of His name, a desecrater of His Sabbath, a despiser of his parents and other authorities, a murderer, an adulterer, a thief, a false witness, and a coveter. His heart is the dwelling place of ungodly impulses and desires. For love is the sum of all our debts, and if we do not love our neighbor as ourselves, we have failed to make even a single payment.

We cannot think, however, that having love in our hearts allows us to transgress the Commandments with works. The Law is not fulfilled merely by means of love. Instead, the apostle writes, "Love does no wrong to a neighbor; therefore love is the fulfilling of the law." Wherever love is, it does not allow any commandment to remain unfulfilled, and it does the works of all the Commandments. How could it be otherwise? Whoever loves God above all things could not transgress any of the commandments of the first table without denying his love of God. And whoever loves his neighbor as himself cannot transgress any of the commandments of the second table without denying that love. No, "love does no wrong to a neighbor," only good. All evil stems from the absence of love for God and neighbor. True love does not first inquire, "Should I be obligated to God and my neighbor?" No, it regards everything it has as belonging to God, and so it wants nothing except to break out, to overflow, and to be totally consumed in service both to God and to neighbor. The blessedness of love is not in taking but in giving, not in being loved but in loving, and not in being served but in serving.

Let us ever walk with Jesus,
Follow His example pure,
Flee the world, which would deceive us
And to sin our souls allure.
Ever in His footsteps treading,
Body here, yet soul above,
Full of faith and hope and love,
Let us do the Father's bidding.
Faithful Lord, abide with me;
Savior, lead, I follow Thee. Amen.

† *(TLH 409:1)*

Sunday

Read Matthew 13:24–26

AS LONG AS GOD'S CHURCH is on earth, there are people who will look more closely at its life than at its doctrine. Some have always asserted that if a church really wants to be the Church of God, it must be completely pure. Sin and godlessness, they say, should not be found in the true Church. All of its members must be believers, born again, and pious, and the most blessed peace must prevail among them. Many people remain in heterodox fellowships because they find many sins in the orthodox Church. Even some of those within the Church itself are vexed for the same reason, and they may separate from it and join a sect that has a holy appearance.

It is for such people as these that Jesus related the parable in our text about weeds among the wheat. It should serve to publicly shame those who are offended at the evil in the Church. Christ's Church on earth cannot be purified from all evil. Jesus therefore compares the Church to "a man who sowed good seed in his field, but . . . his enemy came and sowed weeds among the wheat" (Matthew 13:24–25). Matthew tells us that when Jesus' disciples asked Him for the meaning of the parable, He answered: "The one who sows the good seed is the Son of Man. The field is the world, and the good seed is the children of the kingdom. The weeds are the sons of the evil one, and the enemy who sowed them is the evil one" (13:37–39).

Christ sows only good seed in His true Church. This means that the doctrine that is preached in the true Church leads no one to sin or error. Instead, it makes people into true, pious believers. But what happens? Satan sows his weeds among the wheat, that is, he does everything possible to bring children of wickedness into Christ's Church. In part, he deludes people, making them impenitent and hardening them so, despite the pure doctrine they hear, they do not convert to God. He also works so those who have already converted will fall away. He tempts and provokes them so they take no notice of the exhortations and chastisements they receive, and so they still serve the world and sin in the midst of the orthodox Church. By their unchristian life, both in words and in deeds, they cause all kinds of offenses that bring disgrace and shame to the Church and its pure doctrine.

If a church has pure doctrine, it does not become a false church on account of the sins that occur in it. In fact, if a church is really a Christian Church, it is inevitable that many sins will occur in it. The purer the doctrine in a church, the more hostile Satan is toward it and the more he strives to shame it. Wherever souls are truly rescued from sin and brought to peace with God by the pure preaching of Christ, Satan angrily attacks and seeks to make the Church appear to be a haven for every type of sin. Wherever there is true unity of faith, Satan creates an illusion of discord and strife. It is quiet and peaceful wherever the devil rules. But wherever his power is taken from him by Word and Sacraments, he rages with all his might as the prince of darkness. In short, wherever Christ sows His good seed, we can be certain Satan will scatter his weeds there also.

Therefore, those who take offense at the entire Church because of the evil ones, rejecting it and separating themselves from it, should be ashamed of themselves. Their vexation is really directed at God Himself. They are despising and rejecting Him even when He is not ashamed of His stained Church and still acknowledges it when His pure Word and genuine Sacraments are found there.

Grant me, Lord, Thy Holy Spirit
That in all I follow Him
Lest the light of faith grow dim.
Let me ever trust Thy merit,
Let Thy blessing me attend,
From all evil me defend. Amen.

† *(TLH 408:3)*

Monday

Read Matthew 13:27–30

Does Jesus wish to say here that those to whom the governing of the Church is entrusted should do nothing to hinder the weeds? Far from it! As our Lord said in yesterday's reading, "While his men were sleeping, his enemy came and sowed weeds among the wheat" (Matthew 13:25). Therefore, the upright members of the Church, and especially their called and appointed watchmen, should not sleep. Instead, they should be vigilant and see to it that Satan does not bring his weeds—evil Christians, hypocrites, and false brethren—into the Church. A Christian should not accept or tolerate those who want to hold fast to error, live in sin, walk as something other than true Christians, refuse to subject themselves to God's Word, decline to bid farewell to the world and sin, and reject a life of godliness. Whenever a member of a congregation gives offense by any sin, he should be punished. If the offense was secret, the punishment should be private as well; if the offense was public, the punishment should also take place publicly. If a congregation fails to do this, it makes itself a participant in the sin of its member and fosters the growth of weeds in its midst.

If members of a Christian congregation openly commit sins and, with impenitence and stubbornness, want to persist in them, the Church has the duty to cut them off as rotten and dead members from its body. It must announce to them God's wrath and eternal condemnation, regard and declare them to be heathens, and avoid fellowship with them. In short, it must excommunicate them. And woe to him whom the Church must exclude from its fellowship, for he retains his sin and is excluded from the communion of saints until he repents and is reconciled with the Church. Scripture says of every Christian congregation, "If you forgive the sins of anyone, they are forgiven; if you withhold forgiveness from anyone, it is withheld" (John 20:23), and "Whatever you bind on earth shall be bound in heaven, and whatever you loose on earth shall be loosed in heaven" (Matthew 16:19).

What, then, does Christ mean when He says, "Let both grow together until the harvest"? He means that, until the end of the world arrives, His Church will never be a visible, glorious kingdom, completely purified from sins and weaknesses. But He also says here that He will preserve His Church until the Last Day. The Church should not punish anyone, even the most godless heretic, with death. In addition, it should not deny fellowship with any sinner forever; instead, if he repents, it should again comfort him with the forgiveness of sins and receive him anew as a lost child who has been found again. For these reasons, the sword has never been used against the weeds that are both inside and outside the Church, except in the church that is directed by the papacy. Under the pretense of gathering together the weeds, that church tore out the wheat, and while professing to fight against heretics, it fought against the confessors of the truth.

The true Church of Christ acts in a completely different manner. It sees to it, through both doctrine and discipline, that the weeds do not get the upper hand in its field and choke the wheat. But it also does not gather the weeds together with bodily force or premature judgment. Instead, following Christ's admonition, it allows them to grow together until the harvest, confident that Christ will preserve His Church and one day present it as a holy congregation, although it is now defaced and disfigured by sinners.

There are those who, not having converted from the heart, still adhere to a true congregation and outwardly present themselves as Christians. By their sins, they bring disgrace upon Christ and His Word, which they confess, and upon the congregation, to which they belong. Even so, they will be tolerated and endured here among the Christians. But one day, the day of the great harvest, they will be separated from the wheat, discarded as weeds by the holy angels, and thrown into the fiery ovens of hell.

Lord, write my name, I pray Thee,
Now in the Book of Life
And with all true believers
Take me where joys are rife.
There let me bloom and flourish,
Thy perfect freedom prove,
And tell, as I adore Thee,
How faithful was Thy love. Amen.

(TLH 407:5)

Tuesday

Read John 8:31

IN AMERICA, EVERYONE has the freedom to worship as he chooses. Here, the power of government is not used to force upon a congregation a preacher it does not want. Here, no church is preferred by the state over any other and there is no obstacle to the existence and expansion of any church. Every citizen and every fellowship can live here completely unhampered in their belief.

A person should use this glorious freedom to adhere to the Holy Scriptures and to believe, teach, and base his worship on them alone. But many people employ that freedom to depart from God's Word shamelessly, to establish new sects, and to divide and tear apart Christ's Church. No one wants to subject his reason and his heart to the Word of God in humility. Instead, everyone wants to follow his own mind and to obtain followers for his peculiar teaching. As a result, we have many teachers with widely varied beliefs competing for attention. When a person immigrates to America, he is greeted by shouts of "Come to us! Here is Christ! Here you will find the right way to heaven! Here is the true Church!"

In America, therefore, it is absolutely necessary for a Christian to know how he can recognize the true Church. It is not just that we are surrounded by so many sects here. In addition, they are always seeking to outdo one another. One offers an attractive outward appearance, a second supports institutions that are beneficial to the community (such as temperance groups and Sunday schools), a third performs many great works for the advancement of the kingdom of God (such as missions and Bible societies), and a fourth attempts to demonstrate its piety by offering almost incessant worship exercises.

Woe to him who lacks the proper touchstone to distinguish among all the opposing voices in his midst. If he is deceived by the glittering appearance of a sect, he will soon become its victim, and if he previously stood in the true faith, he will replace it with false doctrine, an impure zeal, and spiritual pride.

Only one thing can rescue a Christian in America and preserve him from error. He must direct all his attention to the place where the Word of God is rightly preached and the holy Sacraments are administered purely, according to Christ's institution. Whoever does not do this will be lost. He will surely be tempted, for Scripture tells us that the false churches often appear to possess a more godly zeal than the true Church. We read that the Israelites were more zealous when they set up idolatrous and false worship than when proper worship was conducted among them by the faithful servants of God. When, for example, Aaron made the golden calf for the people, they were ready to joyfully sacrifice their golden treasures for this idol worship. However, when Moses insisted upon the worship of the only true God, these same people were annoyed with him and slow to agree. And so it has been in all ages.

Every one of us has a natural inclination to false devotion and is incapable of works of true worship. Grace alone can correct this deficiency. Therefore, if a person seeks the true Church, he must look for a place where God's Word alone is preached, where the Church is built on the foundation of the prophets and the apostles, where Jesus Christ is the cornerstone, and where nothing is added to or taken away from the divine Word. Such a person cannot be deceived by the good appearance of the heterodox churches, and he cannot take offense at the weaknesses of the true Church.

Preserve Thy little flock in peace,
Nor let Thy boundless mercy cease;
To all the world let it appear
That Thy true Church indeed is here. Amen.

(TLH 265:5)

Wednesday

Read John 6:37b

IT IS AN EXCEEDINGLY PRECIOUS and comforting truth, firmly grounded in God's Word, that God always receives a person when he repents, even if it is in the hour of his death. It is firmly grounded in God's Word, first, because the promises of grace contained in it are universal and unconditional. The Lord says: "Come to Me, all who labor and are heavy laden, and I will give you rest. . . . I am gentle and lowly in heart, and you will find rest for your souls" (Matthew 11:28–29), and "All that the Father gives Me will come to Me, and whoever comes to Me I will never cast out" (John 6:37). Christ thus invites all those who are weary and heavy-laden to Himself, without appointing any time. He wants to refresh and give rest to all, casting none away. Therefore, whoever turns to Him, even in the hour of his death, is received.

Moreover, in Holy Scripture, a person's entire lifetime is presented as a time of grace. "Today," it says in the Epistle to the Hebrews (and so the call is continually going out), "if you hear His voice, do not harden your hearts. . . . But exhort one another every day, as long as it is called 'today'" (3:7–8,13).

We also read, in the Book of Lamentations: "The steadfast love of the LORD never ceases; His mercies never come to an end; they are new every morning; great is Your faithfulness" (3:22–23). Finally, Solomon writes in Ecclesiastes, "But he who is joined with all the living has hope" (9:4). We see here that as long as it is still today for a person, the portals of salvation remain open to him, and in each new morning in which the sun rises above him, so also the sun of divine goodness shines anew upon him. A person can still cry out to a dying man, "Seek the LORD while He may be found; call upon Him while He is near" (Isaiah 55:6). He is saying, "It is still the time of grace. Heaven still stands open to you. You still have hope for salvation."

Holy Scripture offers us express assurances of all this. Especially important is the parable of the workers in the vineyard. We read there that many will be hired in the eleventh hour and enjoy the goodness of the master. This means that a person can still find grace even in the last hours of his life. There really have been sinners who first sought grace at the portals of eternity and received it. Take, for example, the malefactor whose crime brought him to the cross. Here, for the first time, his eyes were opened to his perilous condition. He confessed that he was worthy only of damnation and turned for grace to the Savior, who was crucified next to him. And behold! The Savior replied, "Truly, I say to you, today you will be with Me in Paradise" (Luke 23:43). God declares: "I have no pleasure in the death of anyone . . . ; so turn, and live" (Ezekiel 18:32). He extends His arms of mercy toward us, even when we are already surrounded by death.

Oh, how important this truth is! How many would have had to despair in their last distress and perish if the Word of God did not contain this comfort! How many first come to this knowledge when the world closes behind them and eternity, with all of its terrors, opens before them!

Yet this truth is not given for the comfort of those who are healthy so they may delay their repentance until the last hour. Whoever uses it in this manner is like a criminal who throws himself from a boat into the ocean because he has heard that many have escaped to shore from a shipwreck upon a piece of wood. Will such a one succeed? Certainly not. Of him, it is said:

Then woe to those who scorned the Lord
And sought but carnal pleasures,
Who here despised His precious Word
And loved their earthly treasures!
With shame and trembling they will stand
And at the Judge's stern command
To Satan be delivered. † *(TLH 611:4)*

I, a sinner, come to Thee
With a penitent confession;
Savior, mercy show to me
Grant for all my sins remission.
Let these words my soul relieve: THL
Jesus sinners doth receive. Amen.

† *(TLH 324:5)*

Thursday

Read Psalm 90:12

ONE DAY, WE WILL DIE. Nothing is more certain than this. But there is nothing more uncertain than the time, place, and manner of our death. Certainly, a hundred years from now, not one of us will still be alive. If the world still exists at that time, other people will be living in our homes, our bodies will have turned to ashes, and our souls will have been removed to the place where God's judgment has assigned them. Not one of us can be certain that he will not be dead tomorrow and that, next Sunday, it will be said of him, "It has pleased the Lord of life and death to call out of the temporal into eternity." Many have left their homes vigorous and healthy, only to be returned as corpses. Many have gone to bed at the end of the day hale and hearty, never to awaken again. No matter how long we live, our hour of death will eventually arrive, and our time of grace will have run its course.

Why has God made death such a certainty but the circumstances of death so uncertain? It can only have been to underscore the importance of seizing the opportunity to repent without delay. No one may hesitate for a day, or even an hour, thinking, "My Lord will not come for a long time." Our Lord may return at any time, and thus we must be ready to meet Him at any time. But what do many people, even those who regard themselves as Christians, do instead? Either they do not believe in the necessity of true repentance and conversion or they delay them from one day to the next, thinking they will be able to discern at some future time that their end is near, and then they will tear from their heart the fetters of sin, offer their repentance, and receive God's grace.

But death has a way of racing upon them suddenly, without warning, while they are still in their unconverted state. Even in their final sickness, they have a tendency to believe they will recover and can therefore delay their repentance even longer. For this reason, it says in the hymn:

> Who knows when death may overtake me!
> Time passes on, my end draws near.
> How swiftly can my breath forsake me!
> How soon can life's last hour appear! . . .
>
> The world that smiled when morn was breaking
> May change for me ere close of day
> For while on earth my home I'm making
> Death's threat is never far away. † *(TLH 598:1, 2)*

Oh, foolishness of all foolishness! To live as a non-Christian and yet wanting to die as a Christian! To go the wrong way while wanting to reach the right goal! Desiring to obtain the victor's crown without engaging in the battle! May God preserve us all from this terrible self-deception.

> *My end to ponder teach me ever*
> *And, ere the hour of death appears,*
> *To cast my soul on Christ, my Savior,*
> *Nor spare repenting sighs and tears.*
> *My God, for Jesus' sake I pray*
> *Thy peace may bless my dying day. Amen.*
>
> *(TLH 598:3)*

Friday

Read Luke 2:25–29

THE FIRST THING Saint Luke tells us about the aged Simeon is that "this man was righteous and devout." By "righteous," he means Simeon acted rightly toward his neighbor, and "devout" tells us he was zealous in the service of God. However, when Luke adds that Simeon was "waiting for the consolation of Israel, and the Holy Spirit was upon him," he indicates that Simeon's piety and fear of God were not merely good habits, accepted family customs, or the result of a good natural disposition. Instead, they were fruits of his living faith in the Messiah, who had been promised by the prophets, and a working of the Holy Ghost in him.

We see Simeon's attitude toward his neighbors in that, as soon as he recognized the promised Messiah in the baby Jesus, he praised God for sending the One whom the Father had "prepared in the presence of all peoples, a light for revelation to the Gentiles, and for glory to [His] people Israel" (Luke 2:31–32). Simeon was not one of those self-seeking and fleshly and narrow-minded Jews who desired from the Messiah only riches, honor, power, and good days that would be for the Jews alone. No, his loving heart embraced "all peoples," even the "Gentiles" sitting in darkness and the shadow of death—in other words, the entire world of sinners. The fact that the Redeemer had also come for them made him so happy that he would have gladly died then and there. His dearest wish for this world had been fulfilled.

Luke clearly describes not only Simeon's piety toward his neighbor but also the nature of his worship of God. He writes, "He came in the Spirit into the temple." Thus, Simeon did not approach the temple out of habit or self-righteousness, performing an outward work of worship so as to earn something from God, but "by the Spirit." He entered the house of God with a burning heart that was full of spiritual life and a holy hunger for God's Word. When the evangelist says Simeon *"was* just and devout," we see that he did not delay his repentance and conversion until old age, but that he had turned to God early on and remained devoted to Him throughout his long life.

But the most remarkable thing we learn about Simeon is that he had received a revelation from God "that he would not see death before he had seen the Lord's Christ." Did this knowledge give him a sense of security and a desire to enjoy life without any worry? Far from it. The more certain Simeon was of his life, the more he used it with greater zeal as a godly preparation for a blessed end.

If Luke wanted to present to us Simeon's joy at the prospect of death, why did he so carefully convey the fact that he was "just and devout" during his life? He doubtless wished to tell us that if we also want to die in a joyful and blessed manner, we must, like Simeon, prepare ourselves for our death by a truly godly and God-fearing life.

Let us, O Lord, be faithful
Like Simeon to the end,
So that his prayer exultant
May from our hearts ascend:
"O Lord, now let Thy servant
Depart in peace, I pray,
Since I have seen my Savior
And here beheld His day." Amen.

(TLH 138:4)

Saturday

Read Luke 2:29–32

IT WAS IMPORTANT for the aged Simeon that in the hour of his death his conscience not accuse him of having lived a life without God. His just and devout life, however, was in no way the foundation of his comfort in death. Luke praises him highly, but Simeon does not praise his own works. He does not say: "Lord, now You are letting Your servant depart in peace because I have lived justly and godly. I have earned eternal life with my works. Now I expect my reward from Your righteousness." Instead, the pious, dying old man says, "For my eyes have seen your salvation that You have prepared in the presence of all peoples, a light for revelation to the Gentiles, and for glory to Your people Israel." He places himself among the greatest sinners of heathendom. The grace which alone can save them is also his only comfort. He believed in and waited throughout his long life for the Savior of sinners as the Consolation of Israel, carrying Him continually in his heart. He was his only comfort—even then in death. Now, having lifted Him up in his arms and looked into His kind eyes, Simeon was ready to die. Soon thereafter, we can be sure, he fell asleep, gently and blessed.

If we, too, want someday to die blessed, it is essential that we exercise ourselves daily and even hourly, taking the Savior up in the arms of our faith and placing all our comfort in Him alone. As eager as a person should be to walk in a just and godly manner, he must even more eagerly grasp Christ as his comfort in his heart. The deeper this comfort penetrates into his heart, the more his heart will be cleansed and sanctified from sin and the love of the vain things of this world. For, as

David says, "[When You comfort me] I will run in the way of Your commandments" (Psalm 119:32), and as Paul adds, "For sin will have no dominion over you, since you are not under law but under grace" (Romans 6:14).

What, then, should a person do when death finally approaches? Should he, perhaps, look around anxiously for witnesses of his good works? Or should he quickly do good works and try to buy heaven by rich bequests to the poor, the church, or other charitable organizations? No, no! When a person still has time, he can certainly arrange his temporal house appropriately and, if he can, remember the poor and the church. But he must know this: The time for good works is already past. Although a just and godly life may lie behind him, he cannot rely on this. No, he must throw everything he has, including his sins and his good works, overboard into the sea of divine mercy and in faith take hold of Jesus as the only and certain lifesaver. It is well with the one who does this! The waves of death will close over him, but by grabbing hold of Jesus with his heart, he will reach the blessed shore of eternal life. For it is written, "Everyone who calls on the name of the LORD shall be saved" (Joel 2:32).

May God send all of us grace so we may live like Simeon, but above all, so we may die as he did. Then, when our end comes, with Jesus in the arms of our faith, we, too, can sing, "Lord, now you are letting Your servant depart in peace, according to Your word; for my eyes have seen your salvation that You have prepared in the presence of all peoples, a light for revelation to the Gentiles, and for glory to Your people Israel."

My Savior, I behold Thee
With faith's enlightened eye;
Of Thee no foe can rob me,
His threats I can defy.

Within Thy heart abiding,
As Thou, O Lord, in me,
Death can no longer frighten
Nor part my soul from Thee. Amen.

(TLH 138:5)

Sunday

Read Matthew 22:14

All of the things God does in time are executions of decrees that He had already made in eternity, for God does nothing in time that He had not already decided to do in eternity. Therefore, the eternal destiny of man was first decided, not in time, but in eternity—before his creation and even before the foundation of the world. God knows the exact numbers of people who will be saved and lost. Already from eternity, He had elected a part of mankind for salvation. Those who will be saved are few in comparison with those who will be lost. These truths are so clearly taught in the Holy Scriptures that no one who believes in the Bible can deny them. In today's text, our Lord speaks with clear words, "For many are called, but few are chosen." The Book of Acts says: "When the Gentiles heard this, they began rejoicing and glorifying the word of the Lord, and as many as were appointed to eternal life believed" (13:48).

Our human reason has a hard time comprehending all this. If God really wanted all people to be saved, we may think, then they would certainly all be saved. Since this does not happen, we then conclude, it must be the fault of God's will. But what does God's Word say? It says, on every page, that God has not consigned any man to damnation. Rather, from eternity, He loved and desired that all would be saved. In 1 Timothy, Saint Paul writes that God "desires all people to be saved and to come to the knowledge of the truth. For there is one God, and there is one Mediator between God and men, the man Christ Jesus, who gave Himself as a ransom for all, which is the testimony given at the proper time" (2:4–6). Saint Peter says, "[The Lord] is patient toward you, not wishing that any should perish, but that all should reach repentance" (2 Peter 3:9). And Saint John adds, "For God so loved the world, that He gave His only Son, that whoever believes in Him should not perish but have eternal life" (John 3:16).

We cannot be in the slightest doubt about God's intention for, already in the Old Testament, He had sworn and sealed before the whole world an inviolable, precious oath that no person is excluded from His eternal love. The prophet Ezekiel says: "And you, son of man, say to the house of Israel, Thus have you said: 'Surely our transgressions and our sins are upon us, and we rot away because of them. How then can we live?' Say to them, As I live, declares the Lord GOD, I have no pleasure in the death of the wicked, but that the wicked turn from his way and live" (33:10–11).

Again, our reason rebels. If all people, by nature, are equally corrupt, and if God must begin and bring to completion all good in them, it must then be God's fault if a person is not converted or does not persevere until his end. Indeed, we conclude, if someone fails to stay the course, God must not have wanted it. But what does God's Word say? The Lord Himself speaks to the inhabitants of Jerusalem: "O Jerusalem, Jerusalem, the city that kills the prophets and stones those who are sent to it! How often would I have gathered your children together as a hen gathers her brood under her wings, and you would not!" (Matthew 23:37). The inhabitants of Jerusalem did not convert, but not because Christ did not desire them to do so.

It is true that all people by nature are equally sinful and God must first take the opposition from them. Nevertheless, no one is lost because of this, for when God comes with His Word, He also comes with His Holy Ghost who desires to remove the natural opposition. But God cannot help the one who obstinately opposes the working of the Holy Ghost. He cannot help because He does not force anyone to convert. A forced conversion is no conversion.

Our reason rises to the challenge one more time. If Scripture says that God hardened the hearts of many people, God Himself must also work so that people do not convert and are not saved. But what does God's Word say? It testifies to us that, in righteous judgment, God does punish certain people with terrible impenitence—but only those upon whom He first used all grace in vain. These people first hardened themselves against His grace and were therefore irretrievably lost. In 1 Samuel, we read, "Why should you harden your hearts as the Egyptians and Pharaoh hardened their hearts?" (6:6). We are faithfully warned against this: "Today, if you hear His voice, do not harden your hearts" (Hebrews 3:7–8).

Our ruin God hath not intended,
For our salvation He hath yearned;
For this His Son to earth descended
And then to heav'n again returned;
For this so patient evermore
He knocketh at our heart's closed door.

O depth of love, to me revealing
The sea where my sins disappear!

In Christ my wounds find perfect healing,
There is no condemnation here;
For Jesus' blood through earth and skies
Forever "Mercy! Mercy!" cries. Amen.

✝ *(TLH 385:3, 4)*

Monday

Read Matthew 20:1–16

THERE ARE MANY PEOPLE who will admit that those who are lost do not perish by God's determination but by their own sin. Unfortunately, these same people still think that, from eternity, God chose the elect for salvation because He saw beforehand how repentant, believing, holy, and steadfast they would be. Such people attribute good to unholy man, while the other group attributes evil to the holy God. Both of these viewpoints are in error.

Today's reading serves as a corrective to this first error. Peter had asked Jesus: "See, we have left everything and followed You. What then will we have?" (Matthew 19:27). Our Lord responded by assuring Peter that all would be well rewarded, and He offered the parable of the workers in the vineyard. He said that those who came to work in the last hour received the same payment as those who had endured the burden and heat of the whole day. Those who had worked longer complained about this and they lost the grace of the landowner, who announced: "So the last will be first, and the first last."

What did Christ want, above all, to show Peter with this parable, which serves as a warning for his soul? A man can indeed, by his own fault, become last rather than first and he can be lost. It is nothing except goodness, grace, and mercy when a person becomes first from the last, a saint from a sinner, and a chosen one from a called one. A person can lose grace but he can never merit it. Therefore, the payment for the work in God's vineyard is not earned. Instead, it is a payment of grace, a gift of God's free goodness.

If we recognize that God could not elect many to salvation because He foresaw that they would not believe and be converted, we must not think, on the contrary, that God elected others because He foresaw that they would be better than others, believe, and be converted. God did elect only those in whom He saw this, but that was not the cause of their election.

God was moved to save a number of people because of His love in Christ and the people's misery and need. God did not choose the elect because He knew they would remain in faith; instead, their election is the reason they persevere in believing. God did not choose them because He knew they would be saved; rather, they will be saved because they were elected. In eternity, God saw only sin, distress, and death in all people. Therefore, He did not base His election on something good He foresaw in certain people. It is as a result of His election that they will be holy Christians and saved people. God's free election of grace is the basis of the salvation of the elect. As it says in the 11th article, the last confession, of the Formula of Concord:

> God's eternal election, however, not only foresees and foreknows the salvation of the elect, but by God's gracious will and pleasure in Christ Jesus it is also a cause which creates, effects, helps, and furthers

salvation and whatever pertains to it. Our salvation is based on it in such a way that "the gates of hell" are not able to do anything against it (Matthew 16:18) [8]. It is therefore false and wrong when men teach that the cause of our election is not only the mercy of God and the most holy merit of Christ, but that there is also within us a cause of God's election on account of which God has elected us unto eternal life [88].

From eternity, O God,
In Thy Son Thou didst elect me;
Therefore, Father, on life's road
Graciously to heav'n direct me;
Send to me Thy Holy Spirit
That His gifts I may inherit.

Oh, create a heart in me
That in Thee, my God, believeth
And o'er the iniquity
Of my sins most truly grieveth.
When dark hours of woe betide me,
In the wounds of Jesus hide me. Amen.

(TLH 411:1, 4)

Tuesday

Read Matthew 20:15

THERE CAN HARDLY be any doubt about which goodness of God is referred to in today's text. It is not the goodness of God in the kingdom of nature, but rather His goodness in the kingdom of grace. God proves His great goodness by offering, out of pure grace, His dear Son, the forgiveness of sins, righteousness, life, and salvation to all whom He called into His kingdom as into His vineyard. He does not ask for merit because all people are equally unworthy and deserving only of wrath. However, because they are redeemed and reconciled by Christ, God offers the same grace to all.

Many follow the call into the kingdom of Christ while they are still children. Others heed the call in their youth, following a miserable childhood without God. Some first hear God's Word in middle age, after they have served the world in their youth. And still others are elderly when they first think about salvation. Many have lived honorable lives, while others have fallen into great and serious sin. During their lives, many have carried a heavy load of suffering, while others are spared this. What is God doing? He is so good that He makes no distinction, but offers the same grace to all, saying: "Come, for everything is ready! Whoever comes to Me, I will not cast him away. Whoever calls on the name of the Lord shall be saved." And does this not happen by God's gracious command? Do not all true preachers of the Gospel call all sinners without distinction to the Lord's table of grace—young and old, great and small, children and elderly, honorable and godless? No one is shut out.

But where do many people now stand? In our text, the

Lord says, "Or is your eye evil because I am good?" We have an example of this evil eye in the Jewish people, particularly in the Pharisees. They lived under the yoke of the Law and, therefore, they thought they would get a Messiah who would honor them by making all people subject to them. However, when Christ declared that He came to have mercy on all, accepting both the honorable and sinners, they were offended and said, "Why should we, who so scrupulously concerned ourselves with the Law, be made like these sinners?" Instead of accepting Christ, they slandered, persecuted, and crucified Him.

It is still the same today. When someone preaches that a person must be virtuous to earn his way into heaven, people praise this as a sermon of righteousness. However, when these same people hear the message "Come unto Me all you who are weary and heavy-laden, and I will give you rest," offering grace to all sinners without distinction, they are offended by it and consider it to be a false doctrine. They reply: "How should this or that great sinner be able to come into heaven just as well as I, who from childhood have been intent on virtue and uprightness? Away with such a religion!" These people look upon God's goodness with evil. What a horrible sin! God's Word tells us that the angels in heaven rejoice over a sinner who repents and finds grace. Therefore, whoever does not wish the Gospel of grace to be received by a sinner becomes a devil, and his wish is that all of humanity would perish. He becomes a devil even against himself, for whoever looks with evil because a sinner has been offered grace rejects the Gospel, shuts himself off from grace, and becomes irretrievably lost.

Oh, let us not look with evil at God's goodness, but let us rejoice and comfort ourselves in it. Let us thank the Lord and praise Him because He calls all sinners—including us—to Himself.

Oh, how great is Thy compassion,
Faithful Father, God of grace,
That upon our wretchedness,
That upon man's sinful station
Thou took'st pity, so that we
Might be saved eternally! Amen.

(ELHB 317:1)

Wednesday

Read 1 Corinthians 1:4–5

ACCORDING TO TODAY'S READING, pure doctrine and knowledge are never the fruits of human will, ability, and effort, but a free gift from above.

Human desire is of no use in the quest for truth. Desire for the truth arises after a person has already begun to recognize the truth. To be sure, the question "What is truth?" fills the hearts of thousands, but where the Holy Ghost Himself has not prompted the question by giving a person a taste of its sweet light, the search for truth is nothing more than an arrogant, idolatrous thirst for knowledge that only hinders the effort to find the truth.

Human ability is equally useless where truth is concerned. Human proficiency in thinking is sufficient to attain the world's knowledge, but not the wisdom that comes from God. His truth is not the work of human speculation. The divine truth of salvation is above all understanding, both of men and of angels. It is also against the thinking of the natural man. The more wisdom of this world a person acquires, the more he advances in the knowledge of art and science, but this makes it all the harder for him to see and recognize the divine truth that has clothed itself in the preaching of the Gospel he regards as foolishness.

Finally, no human diligence in seeking, studying, and discovering leads to success in attaining divine wisdom. The natural man cannot find pure doctrine and knowledge simply by looking for it. The Lord tells His apostles, "To you has been given the secret of the kingdom of God" (Mark 4:11), and this also applies to all who have attained divine knowledge. It is not enough to have the Holy Scriptures and to search them day and night. Many thousands of people have eagerly searched God's Word and continue to do so. However, because they are still shrouded in their natural thinking, they remain blind to knowledge of the truth. Although they read the Bible carefully, it remains a closed book to them.

According to our text, pure doctrine and knowledge are a gift from above. They are also a free gift, one that derives from divine grace. God showed no regard for merit in bestowing His Word upon the entire world, and He offers every person the power to recognize the need for His salvation. It is often the case that God grants wisdom to an individual or an entire church fellowship at precisely the moment when unfaithfulness and apostasy have increased to the highest possible level. God thus acts according to His absolute freedom to do what He wants with His own.

Pure doctrine and knowledge are granted to us this very hour. We have not earned them. We have not merited them by any work. And we are not more worthy than those who do not have them. Instead, we have inherited them from our fathers as God's free gifts. He has given them to us purely out of grace. The only thing God now demands from us is that we thank Him for them. Let us therefore be quick to offer praise to God. Let us never forget how great is God's goodness. And let us faithfully use these gifts in the service of others.

Wisdom's highest, noblest treasure,
Jesus, lies concealed in Thee;
Grant that this may still the measure
Of my will and actions be,
Humility there and simplicity reigning,
In paths of true wisdom my steps ever training.
Oh, if I of Christ have this knowledge divine,
The fullness of heavenly wisdom is mine. Amen.

† *(TLH 366:5)*

Thursday

Read Jeremiah 15:16

GOD'S GRACE in granting Christians the opportunity to possess and read His Word is so great that it cannot be fully comprehended and worthily praised. First of all, Holy Scripture presents us with a bright, burning light. There is nothing for us to know regarding the necessity of the salvation of our souls that is not thoroughly explained in God's Word. It offers clear answers to all important questions about God and man, about the past and the future, and about time and eternity. While the heathen world, which does not have Scripture, is forever asking, "What is truth?" it must stand forever in doubt and fumble in the dark. But Christians, who have the Word, also have the perfect solution for all of their doubts.

The Word of God also offers Christians a treasury of information regarding the forgiveness of sins. It not only proclaims that the sins of all people have been washed away by Christ's blood and that there is a way for people to attain that forgiveness. It is also the hand of God that presents this precious good to man. The entire teaching of the Gospel is a God-given absolution to all people that everyone receives for himself as soon as he believes it.

Holy Scripture is an inexhaustible source of comfort for Christians. There is no type of loss—property and goods, honor and good name, health, freedom and family, even life itself—however great and difficult, for which the Bible does not supply a comfort that will bring total reassurance. Those who do not have God's Word will be thrown into despair by such setbacks, but those who are grounded in Scripture will be able to praise and glorify God in every circumstance.

With the Word of God, all Christians have a sword with which they can defend themselves against every enemy and win every battle. No matter how much power and cunning the world and hell employ in attacking them, those who have and use God's Word cannot be conquered and destroyed. Even if they appear to have been vanquished, fallen Christians can shout from the dust, like the church of the Old Testament: "Rejoice not over me, O my enemy; when I fall, I shall rise; when I sit in darkness, the LORD will be a light to me. I will bear the indignation of the LORD because I have sinned against Him, until He pleads my cause and executes judgment for me. He will bring me out to the light; I shall look upon His vindication" (Micah 7:8–9).

Finally, Holy Scripture presents Christians with the key to heaven. When death comes to them, when they must leave the world and enter into eternity, their conscience may whisper to them: "You cannot be saved. Your sins, your unworthiness, and your whole reprehensible life before God will shut the gates of heaven to you." But they have no cause for despair. They have only to seize the Word of God, which says, "The saying is trustworthy and deserving of full acceptance, that Christ Jesus came into the world to save sinners" (1 Timothy 1:15), and "But where sin increased, grace abounded all the more" (Romans 5:20). As soon as they hold to this Word, even if it is only with sighing and struggling faith, the heavens are opened to them and the holy angels come and carry their souls into the mansions of perfection and eternal peace.

O great grace, which God has given to all whom He permitted to be born in Christendom! If only all people could recognize how great a blessing we have received in God's holy Word! Then they would all confess with David that the Word is dearer to them than many thousands of pieces of gold and silver. And with Jeremiah they would regard it as their heart's joy and comfort.

A trusty weapon is Thy Word,
Thy Church's buckler, shield, and sword.
Oh, let us in its power confide
That we may seek no other guide!

Oh, grant that in Thy holy Word
We here may live and die, dear Lord;
And when our journey endeth here,
Receive us into glory there. Amen.

✝ *(TLH 292:8, 9)*

Friday

Read 1 Corinthians 10:1–4

THE PEOPLE OF ISRAEL, the people of the Old Testament, were the recipients of a totally inexpressible grace from God. It was not enough that God spoke with them, gave them His Word, declared them to be His people, and promised them His grace and help. He also added outward, visible signs of that grace. He promised to lead the people to Canaan and He sealed that promise by the pillars of cloud and fire and by the wonderful parting of the sea. He pledged to provide for the people and He confirmed that pledge by a rain of bread from heaven and by a stream of water from a dry rock.

Why does Saint Paul say in our text that the Israelite fathers at that time were baptized with the cloud and the sea and were nourished with the same spiritual food and drink? He wants to show that the signs of the cloud and the sea were types of the New Testament Baptism and the manna and the water from the rock were types of the New Testament Holy Communion.

What great grace those who share in the holy Sacraments enjoy! As God gave His Word to His people and added visible signs to confirm it, so He grants to the people of Christ the grace of the Gospel and added the visible signs of the holy Sacraments as a seal. Just as the pillars of fire and cloud were once a certain sign of God's presence in grace to all for whom they lightened the night and gave shade in the day, so Holy Baptism is now a sign to all who receive it that God remains with them in grace. At one time, those who went through the Red Sea untouched as Pharaoh and his army drowned had a sign that God recognized them as children of

His covenant of grace and would bring them into the earthly Canaan He promised. Today, Holy Baptism is a sign for all who receive it that their sins are swallowed up by the sea of Christ's blood, that God has accepted them as children of His covenant of grace, and that He will bring them into the heavenly Canaan promised in the Gospel. The Israelites, with their eating of the manna from heaven and their drinking of the water from the rock, enjoyed the presence of Christ spiritually, and their faith in the promised Redeemer was thus strengthened. In like manner, Christ gives Himself spiritually to all those who participate in faith in His New Testament Supper.

In the New Testament, where the types have ceased, grace is still greater. The signs of the Old Testament were connected with the promise but the New Testament signs are accompanied by heavenly goods. The Holy Spirit is richly poured out at the Baptism of one who believes he is born again and renewed to eternal life. Whoever receives the blessed bread and the blessed cup in the holy Supper is also fed with Christ's true body and true blood.

We are rightly amazed at the past displays of God's goodness, such as His appearance in the cloud and His parting of the sea. But wherever Holy Baptism is administered, we see something much greater. God is more than present in this water. In addition, all of the sins of the baptized one are drowned in the water, and when he receives this bath in faith, he emerges from the water as a pardoned, holy, and pure man. God's gifts of bread from heaven and water from the rock were also amazing manifestations of His care for His people. But the holy Supper offers a more astonishing demonstration of God's love, for there the communicants eat of the true heavenly bread and drink the true water of eternal life from the rock of salvation and blessedness.

In these last days of sore distress
Grant us, dear Lord, true steadfastness,
That pure we keep, till life is spent,
Thy holy Word and Sacrament. Amen.

(ELHB 110:2)

Saturday

Read 1 Corinthians 10:5

GOD LED THE ISRAELITES out of Egypt with a strong hand, in great wonders and signs. God went before these people in a pillar of cloud, leading them Himself. He miraculously opened a way for them through the sea, and He used that same sea to destroy Pharaoh and his entire army. God also sustained the people with miraculous food and drink. With these and many other miracles, some wonderful and some terrible, God told the people of His presence. God appeared to be covering these people with His grace, and thus they would have appeared certain to reach the Promised Land.

But what happened? Of the 600,000 men who left Egypt, all of whom witnessed numerous signs of God's presence during their forty years of wandering, only two, Joshua and Caleb, were permitted to enter the Promised Land. The others perished miserably in the desert. Even Moses himself was allowed to see Canaan only from afar; he had to die on Mount Nebo outside the borders of the Promised Land.

Just as the signs of grace the Israelites had once received from God were types of the holy Sacraments of Christendom, so is God's wrath upon those highly favored people a type of His wrath upon those who are not believers but who share in the Sacraments of the New Testament.

If you recognize that at your Baptism you were moistened by God's cloud of grace, it is well with you! But consider: If you have cast God out of your heart by your sins, you comfort yourself in vain that He came to you at your Baptism in grace. If you have taken to heart that at your Baptism your sins were drowned like Pharaoh and his army, it is well with you! But consider: If, after your Baptism, you let your sins dominate you, allowing yourself to sin knowingly and wantonly, you comfort yourself in vain that your sins were thrown into the deep of the sea at your Baptism. If you acknowledge that your Baptism marked a new birth and a renewal of the Holy Ghost, who was richly poured out over you, it is well with you! But consider: If you do not now walk as a new man in a new life, with a new heart, in the power of the Holy Ghost—if you do not fight against sin and pursue holiness—you comfort yourself in vain that you became a child of God and an heir of eternal life at your Baptism. You have broken your baptismal covenant, lost your baptismal grace, and removed your baptismal dress. You are thus a lost son who must return to his father in true repentance and conversion, else you will never see the heavenly Canaan.

Moreover, it is well with you if you do not belong to those despisers of the holy Supper, who regard it as an empty ceremony and therefore make use of it infrequently, if at all. You then are diligent in being fed with the heavenly food of Christ's true body and in receiving the heavenly drink of His true blood. But consider: If you are sacramentally connected with the Son of God but renounce Him by your friendship with the world and your unchristian life, you comfort yourself in vain with this most holy means of grace. Because you use it unworthily, it does not help you and you are also using it for your judgment. You will be guilty of the body and blood of the Lord. What is given to you for life will become death for you. What is given to you as a blessing will become a curse to you. What is given to you for salvation will become damnation to you. If you do not get rid of your sins, it would be better for you if you had never used these means of grace.

Oh, let us carefully consider the terrible examples of the Israelite fathers!

The guest that comes with true intent
To turn to God and to repent,
To live for Christ, to die to sin,
Will thus a holy life begin.

They who His Word do not believe
This food unworthily receive,
Salvation here will never find—
May we this warning keep in mind! Amen.

† *(TLH 163:7, 8)*

Sunday

Read Luke 8:5, 11–12

OUR TEXT TEACHES that all people are like a field. A field by itself produces only weeds if it is not sown with good seed. In like manner, nothing but the weed of sin grows in the field of an individual's heart if the seed of the divine Word is not sown there. Most people will not be saved because they do not want to read or hear God's Word; instead, they reject it as foolishness.

At least those who diligently read and hear God's Word may be saved. But what happens? When many learn how important the hearing of God's Word is for salvation, they do indeed listen earnestly to it. They do not fail to attend any worship service. They also read Holy Scripture in their homes. But they then think that they have done everything necessary to attain salvation. They regard the hearing of the Word as a good work by which a person proves he is a Christian and earns his own salvation.

How awfully such poor people deceive themselves! By imagining that the hearing of Scripture earns a person salvation, that hearing actually becomes a hindrance to them for their salvation. What was given to them for life becomes death to them. Why? Christ tells us in our text. And, according to Matthew's account, Christ explained that the ones who hear the Word of the kingdom do not understand (13:19).

Here we see that the Word of God is like the seed in the parable. If the seed is to be useful, it is not enough that it is only scattered. The main thing is that it must fall into good land and sprout there. If the seeds of grain fall on a well-trampled path so they cannot mix with the soil, the birds of the air will quickly come and eat them. It is the same with the Word. A person must do more than hear Scripture with his ears. It must take root in his heart in order to work true faith in him by its divine power. If the Word merely lies on the surface of the heart, so to speak, and does not penetrate deeper, Satan comes and rips the Word out of the heart. As a result, the person does not believe and is not saved.

God has given us His Word that it may produce a great, divine change in our hearts. The Word should enlighten us, revealing our great misery of sin so forcefully that we become sorrowful over it. Then, reading further by the light of the Holy Ghost, we learn to know Jesus Christ as our Redeemer and believe in Him from our hearts. If the heavenly fire of the Word does not engulf the heart, setting it ablaze for Christ, then the Word has been preached to a person in vain. Instead of saving that individual, it only accuses him before God, pointing out that he allowed this means of grace to be fruitless in him.

Therefore, whoever wants to be saved must listen to God's Word with great attention, and the divine thoughts it reveals must fill his whole heart, creating a living faith in Christ and a new life. Whoever does not want this must also give up the hope of being saved. For, as Christ says, "Truly, I say to you, unless one is born again he cannot see the kingdom of God" (John 3:3).

Precious Jesus, I beseech Thee,
May Thy words take root in me;
May this gift from heav'n enrich me
So that I bear fruit for Thee!
Take them never from my heart
Till I see Thee as Thou art,
When in heav'nly bliss and glory
I shall greet Thee and adore Thee. Amen.

† *(TLH 296:4)*

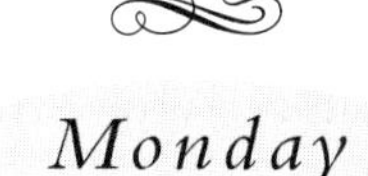

Monday

Read Luke 8:6,13

AS IT IS WITH THE SEED, so it is with the Word. The picture in this portion of the parable is of rocks upon which only a thin covering of good ground lies. The sower scatters good seeds on such ground, and when the seeds do indeed spring up, he concludes that this is fertile ground and awaits a bountiful harvest. But what happens? When the sun shines brightly and rainfall is sparse, the green plants begin to dry up as quickly as they shot up. Their roots had not descended far enough to secure for them an adequate supply of moisture.

This is also a picture of many who hear God's Word. By the working of the Holy Ghost, they come to understand that they are poor sinners who must be saved, and they respond by forsaking the world. They are filled with joy over Christ and His grace. They begin to believe in Him, and they demonstrate a great eagerness: praying daily on their knees, seeking out zealous Christians to discuss their concerns about being saved, and even confessing their faith before the world. But that eagerness lasts only for a while and they are ultimately lost. Perhaps they are attacked by their old sins and succumb to them. Perhaps they associate with nonbelievers and find themselves beginning to doubt, a process that ultimately leads them to open unbelief. Perhaps they are enticed by the children of the world to participate in some sinful activity and find themselves attracted to it. Perhaps they are ridiculed for their faith and gradually come to be ashamed of their Savior. Perhaps they are tempted by laziness, causing them to stop praying and reading God's Word diligently. Or perhaps they follow the example of other so-called Christians who lead unchristian lives and, like them, become Christians only in name. Who can count all the ways in which people lose the faith?

Why does this happen? The reason is that, as these individuals begin to become Christians, they do not permit God's Word to become deeply rooted in their heart, and so they do not take their sinful corruption seriously. As a result, they never come to understand how false their heart is, how powerless they are without Christ, and how easily they could once again fall away. They are never properly terrified about sin, God's wrath, and hell. They never learn how great a sinner they are. They do not calculate the cost of becoming a Christian. They promise God they will become different people, but they do not know that without God's grace they lack the power to accomplish this goal. They never relinquish reliance on their own power and thus quickly fall with the first attack, surrendering themselves to the world and forsaking, either outwardly or inwardly, the fellowship of Christ and Christians. And they never repent of this either because they regard their former confession and experience as a deception or because they comfort themselves that their former repentance is sufficient to save them. Thus, they are finally lost.

Let us never forget that we are saved, not merely by coming to faith, but by persevering in it. We do not reach our heavenly goal because we were once zealous to avoid the sins of the world, but because we remain on that path all our days. We are not heirs of eternal life because we were once united with Christ, but because we maintain fellowship with our Savior until our death.

Let me be Thine forever,
Thou faithful God and Lord;
Let me forsake Thee never
Nor wander from Thy Word.
Lord, do not let me waver,
But give me steadfastness,
And for such grace forever
Thy holy name I'll bless. Amen.

(TLH 334:1)

Tuesday

Read Luke 8:7,14

SEED CAN BE LOST in a variety of ways. As we saw in our first reading of this week, it can be lost when it falls upon the trampled path, where it does not mix with the ground and is eaten by the birds. Yesterday's text showed us that seed can also spring up quickly, but if it does not send down a deep root, it withers and dries up with the first heat of the sun. Today, we learn that seed can be lost even if it produces a deep root. In this case, it falls between thorns that choke the green growth. Our Lord is using these illustrations to demonstrate how the hearing of the pure Word can be in vain for some people. There are those who do not listen attentively. Some do not understand it correctly, and therefore they never come to faith. Others receive the Word with joy, but this is not accompanied by a deep foundation of repentance and therefore they fall away in the time of temptation. But it can also happen that those who have laid a deep foundation and produced a well-rooted faith still lose the crown.

How is this possible? Anyone who farms the land can supply the answer. A tiller of the soil knows that even when roots are deep, he has no hope of a bountiful crop unless he also roots out the weeds, thorns, and thistles that shoot up next to the growing plants. It is the same with the Christian. Even if his heart is a field well cultivated by the Word, it retains something of its old, evil thoughts and desires, and the weed of sin can thus continue to grow. Even the best and most experienced Christian must be diligent, or it will not be long before the weed of sin overgrows the crop of the Word and chokes it. There are two weeds in particular that threaten the Christian.

One is the cares of this world, and the other is riches.

A firmly grounded Christian will not easily fall away because of fear of ridicule, persecution, the allurements and flatteries of the world, or disillusionment caused by the evil lives of many who want to be Christians. Nevertheless, many strong heroes of faith have fallen because of such cares as poverty, shame, and sickness, or because of such riches as wealth, good days, and honor. Worry, discontentment with one's lot in life, and sadness over earthly losses can readily choke the Word and faith. Love for the earthly and trust in the temporal gradually establish themselves firmly even in the best Christians when they feel forsaken and so drive away the Holy Ghost. The desire to become rich can lure the true Christian "into temptation, into a snare, into many senseless and harmful desires that plunge people into ruin and destruction" (1 Timothy 6:9).

There is considerable value, therefore, in remaining vigilant, examining ourselves with the Word of God, and praying in order to root out the weeds. When we discover that we cannot root out everything, we are ashamed of ourselves and are reminded that we are poor, miserable, hungry, and thirsty sinners. This realization causes us to drink daily from the fountain of God's grace.

Oh, let us not be secure! Let us not only hear God's Word, but also seek to understand it and to let it penetrate deeply into our hearts. Let us also lay a deep foundation in true, earnest, and daily repentance so our faith does not wither and dry up in the heat of temptation. By rooting out the weeds that always threaten to spring up in our hearts, we can bring forth fruit in patience.

Though earthly trials should oppress me
And cares from day to day increase;
Though earth's vain things should sore distress me

And rob me of my Savior's peace;
Though I be brought down to the dust,
Still His mercy I will trust. Amen.

† *(TLH 385:7)*

Wednesday

Read Psalm 26:8

THERE HAVE BEEN TIMES when Christians could not gather together openly and freely to worship God and to hear His Word. In Holy Scripture, we read that during the apostolic period believers could assemble only in private homes. But even there they were at risk on account of their enemies and they usually conducted their congregational worship behind locked doors. During the first three centuries of the Christian era, believers had to seek out deserted places unknown to others—including forests, caves, and even empty burial vaults—whenever they wanted to hear the Word of life and to unburden their hearts before the Lord in their distress. The more benevolent heathen emperors occasionally allowed them to build beautiful and spacious churches, but those same emperors were likely to later demolish these structures. On some occasions, the churches of Christians were set afire while they were gathered inside and they were burned to death. At the beginning of the fourth century, the church historian Nicephorus informs us, the entire Christian congregation at Nicomedia in Asia Minor was suddenly attacked on the orders of the emperor Maximian. They had been instructed to sacrifice to the gods, but instead were celebrating the joyous Christmas festival. Their attackers quickly surrounded and burned the church, killing more than a thousand worshipers.

These were indeed hard, sad times. It is still a sad situation when a Christian is unable to gather with his brothers in his church without the threat of persecution. Yet it is incomparably sadder—and more dangerous—when Christians possess a beautiful church where they are free to gather peaceably and unhindered and they either abandon or falsify God's Word. A church in which man's delusion and wit are proclaimed instead of Holy Scripture is nothing but an open gate to hell, a butchering table of Satan, and a house of plagues to the soul. Whoever enters such a church of unbelievers and enemies of Christ would have done better to come into a den of robbers and murderers, for there only his mortal body would have been killed. In a church of unbelievers, it is his immortal soul that is slain. There are also churches in which the Word of God is indeed read aloud, but is either taught only in part or interpreted falsely. Here souls are led on dangerous detours and Satan sows handfuls of poisonous weeds next to the good seed of the Scriptures, tempting the hearts of the hearers. Christ Himself said of such churches, "'My house shall be called a house of prayer,' but you make it a den of robbers" (Matthew 21:13). A person would be better advised to read the Word of God alone at home, even in tears of loneliness, than to attend such a church.

What a blessing it is, then, when Christians can freely assemble in a church where God's Word is purely and clearly proclaimed and where the holy Sacraments are administered according to Christ's institution. Such a church, no matter how small and poor it may appear, is of more value than all of the splendid palaces of the world. In such a church, poor sinners can speak to God in fellowship with other Christians and hear the voice of God through a human mouth. Here they learn the correct path to heaven, and grace and salvation are opened wide to them. Whoever enters such a church has reason to cry out, with Jacob: "How awesome is this place! This is none other than the house of God, and this is the gate of heaven!" (Genesis 28:17).

Open now Thy gates of beauty,
Zion, let me enter there,
Where my soul in joyful duty
Waits for Him who answers prayer.
Oh, how blessed is this place,
Filled with solace, light, and grace! Amen.

† *(TLH 1:1)*

Thursday

Read Psalm 5:5

SELF-PRAISE AND BOASTFULNESS are certainly detestable vices, which God has forbidden in His Word. Jeremiah says: "Thus says the LORD: 'Let not the wise man boast in his wisdom, let not the mighty man boast in his might, let not the rich man boast in his riches, but let him who boasts boast in this, that he understands and knows Me, that I am the LORD who practices steadfast love, justice, and righteousness in the earth. For in these things I delight, declares the LORD'" (9:23–24). Even the natural man, who has no aversion to sinning, finds it extraordinarily repulsive to listen to someone who talks only about himself, his good qualities, his great deeds and riches, his skills and wisdom, and even his godliness. Such boasting makes everyone suspicious. People are inclined to think that those who praise themselves do so only because no one else is willing to do so. In any event, those who endlessly trumpet their good qualities lack the crown of all good qualities: humility.

Whoever is humble does not make much fuss about himself. He goes about quietly, giving each one his glory but seeking no glory for himself. Normally, when such an individual encounters shame, he finds his fellow men far readier to sympathize with him than with one who is always attempting to make something great out of himself. Who had sympathy for proud Nebuchadnezzar, who was deeply humbled shortly after declaring, "Is not this great Babylon, which I have built by my mighty power as a royal residence and for the glory of my majesty?" (Daniel 4:30). Who would not rejoice at the sight of the loud-mouth Goliath slain in the sand with a stone from the sling of a little shepherd who was regarded by his foe as too insignificant to fight because he lacked a sword, a spear, and a shield? Whose heart would not warm a thousand times faster to the publican, although he was a deeply fallen man, than to the Pharisee? For the former said, "God, be merciful to me, a sinner," while the latter, full of presumption regarding his holiness, prayed, "God, I thank You that I am not like other men, extortioners, unjust, adulterers, or even like this tax collector" (Luke 18:13, 11).

True Christians cannot tolerate boastfulness. Indeed, they became Christians by the working of the divine Spirit, who made them recognize that they are sinners and utterly without merit before God. Nevertheless, by God's grace and through faith in Christ, they are redeemed. Saint Paul says: "Then what becomes of our boasting? It is excluded. By what kind of law? By a law of works? No, but by the law of faith"

(Romans 3:27). Faithful Christians, then, gladly confess themselves to be poor and sinful creatures upon whom God has shown great mercy. Even Christ Himself speaks this way: "Yet I do not seek My own glory; . . . If I glorify Myself, My glory is nothing" (John 8:50, 54).

What, then, should a poor man say about himself, even if he is the best of Christians? Instead of boasting of his wisdom, he recognizes his blindness. Instead of pointing to his virtues—his good works, his tender heart, and his righteousness—he admits his sinfulness. Instead of extolling his power, skills, and wealth, he focuses on his nothingness! He remembers the words of the apostle Paul, who said: "What do you have that you did not receive? If then you received it, why do you boast as if you did not receive it?" (1 Corinthians 4:7). Whoever is pleased with himself and seeks to glory in this is certainly no true Christian.

When all my deeds I am reviewing,
The deeds that I admire the most,
I find in all my thought and doing
That there is naught whereof to boast.
Yet this sweet comfort shall abide—
In mercy I can still confide. Amen.

† *(TLH 385:8)*

Friday

Read 2 Corinthians 12:6

TODAY'S TEXT MAKES it clear that there may come a time when boasting about oneself is not sinful. It did not matter to Paul that his standing had been lowered in the eyes of the Corinthians and that he had been covered with disgrace and shame. He could easily bear that, for as a servant of God he was already used to it. He may have thought that the world had already spit in the face of the Son of God and that His slave could hardly expect to receive better treatment. Indeed, he regarded his shame as his glory. However, it touched his heart that his dear Corinthians were being tempted to reject him so they would also reject his doctrine and true faith in Jesus Christ. Paul recognized that if, in false humility, he now remained silent in the face of the blasphemies of the false apostles, many Corinthian Christians would doubt both him and Christ's Gospel. He had always spoken humbly about himself, but now he was in a position that required him to assume another voice. It was not a question of his vindication, but of the eternal salvation of many immortal souls and the glory of God, whose Word he proclaimed. He was compelled to show the Corinthians that he could boast of things the false apostles could not. In opposing their empty bragging, he was boasting in the truth.

We see from this that there are certain instances in which it is permissible and even God-pleasing to boast of self. These instances involve the glory of the divine name and the salvation of a neighbor's soul. In such circumstances, self-boasting is not only allowed, but also commanded as a holy obligation.

Many Christians are inclined to believe it doesn't matter

what people think about them, whether they are regarded as sincere believers or hypocrites, as servants of the belly or servants of Christ, or as guilty or innocent. They are also of the opinion that a Christian may not inquire after anything because only God knows the purity of the heart. They therefore remain silent before all defamations by their enemies and refuse to justify and defend themselves. The last thing they would think of doing is boasting in the presence of their enemies. Instead, they prefer to let their opponents continue their slanders until they become exhausted or to commend everything to God.

Such behavior may have a good appearance, but the true Christian, like Paul, cannot be indifferent to the judgments of others. In regard to his person, the Christian does well to be unconcerned about whether the world honors or despises him. As Paul writes, "If I were still trying to please man, I would not be a servant of Christ" (Galatians 1:10). But it is an entirely different matter if evil rumors about a Christian threaten the glory of the divine name and the salvation of a neighbor's soul. If, for example, an eager Christian is labeled as a hypocrite or a secret criminal, nonbelievers will be hardened against the faith all the more and weak believers will begin to have doubts. Then, if the insulted person does nothing to clear his name, he will become guilty of all the slanderings of the name and Word of God and all the offenses of the weak that arise from his inactivity. This is one reason why Christians must earnestly seek a good reputation among those who are both inside and outside the church.

There are cases in which a Christian cannot defend himself or in which he has only God as a witness to his innocence. In other instances, the world can readily recognize the untruth of a circulating rumor. Then it is time to remain silent. But if it stands in the power of a Christian to unmask the slanderer, then he should do it, and, for the sake of God and his neighbor, recover his good name.

Help me speak what's right and good
And keep silence on occasion;
Help me pray, Lord, as I should,
Help me bear my tribulation;
Help me die and let my spirit
Everlasting life inherit. Amen.

† *(TLH 411:7)*

Saturday

Read 2 Corinthians 11:12–12:9

NO OBLIGATION SEEMS EASIER to meet than to boast of oneself to the glory of God and for the salvation of a neighbor. But it only seems so. This duty is among the hardest of those that come to a Christian, and only a few are capable of fulfilling it. Paul provides the example of how this should be done.

Let us begin with his disposition: the deepest humility. He explains in our text that he would become a fool if he wanted to boast of his own glory because he had nothing to boast about in himself and everything is by grace. Yet we cannot think this humility stemmed from unfaithfulness, lukewarmness, or laziness on Paul's part. No, he was adorned with the most glorious virtues and works. What things could he boast about before the false teachers? He enumerates a long list of dangers and persecutions he courageously endured, pains he suffered on behalf of Christ and His Gospel, and works he assumed for the sake of the souls that had been entrusted to him. Finally, he disclosed to the Corinthians that God had dignified him fourteen years earlier with a rapture into the third heaven (that is, the heaven of the saints that exists above the heavens of the clouds and stars, or the paradise of God) while he was still alive. This experience was followed by one in which the angel of Satan was allowed to beat Paul with fists so he would not be overbearing because of the great revelation he had been privileged to witness.

Here is the model for those who, with Paul, want to justify themselves to their opponents and, in a certain sense, boast of themselves. It is not necessary, of course, that they attain as high a degree of holiness and suffer as much for Christ's sake as Paul had. But it is true that only a heartily humble, eager, and self-denying Christian is capable, with joy, of rebuking the lies that are spread about him.

Only the person who considers himself unworthy of praise can, without sin, praise himself before his enemies. Only the person who gives God alone all glory and seeks no glory of his own can, without sin, boast of himself when God's glory demands it. Only the person who does not live for himself, but who always seeks the best for others, can, without sin and out of pure love for the souls of those who might otherwise become offended and tempted, refer to his honest walk and his good works. Finally, only the person of pure and upright heart and mind, who lives honorably and blamelessly both before the world and before God, can approach his enemies and, without sin, save his good name.

In certain circumstances, the Christian has both the freedom and the obligation to appeal to his walk and his works, and thus to be justified before men. This includes an urgent demand for self-examination to determine whether one is qualified to do this. Anyone who fails this test is still not a true Christian.

Oh, let me never speak
What bounds of truth exceedeth;
Grant that no idle word
From my mouth proceedeth;
And then, when in my place
I must and ought to speak,
My words grant pow'r and grace
Lest I offend the weak. Amen.

(TLH 395:3)

Sunday

Read Luke 18:31

TODAY, MANY SELF-LEARNED PEOPLE believe it is time to revise our thinking about the life of Jesus. Until now, they maintain, people have been looking for divine secrets in that life. But since Christ was a true man, they insist that the only right way of thinking about His life is in purely human terms. This also includes His suffering and death. That Christ had to suffer so much and so terribly, they say, is an accidental and easily explainable thing. Jesus publicly expressed a doctrine that was both opposed and offensive to that of the wicked authorities of church and state, and this called forth from them the most bitter vindictiveness. The natural outcome was that Christ became a victim of the cunning, power and cruelty of His opponents.

All of this is nothing more than an empty fabrication of the most blind and wanton unbelief that is entirely pulled out of the air. As today's text informs us, the prophets of the Old Testament had foretold Christ's suffering and death long before. Indeed, it was determined by God Himself from eternity and revealed in time by His servants, the prophets. God spoke "through" or "by" them. The death of Jesus was not by chance. He did not suffer because His enemies wanted to outwit and overpower Him, but because God—and even Christ Himself—wanted it.

When Christ made His first public appearance, preaching in Nazareth, His hearers rose in great anger, casting Him from the city and forcibly leading Him to the steepest slope in the vicinity in order to throw Him down and kill Him. But because God's prescribed hour for His death had not yet arrived, He was able to escape, "passing through their midst" (Luke 4:30). Later, when Jesus affirmed in the temple, "Before Abraham was I AM," thus maintaining that He is the eternal God, many in the great assembly raised stones to kill Him. But once again, the appointed hour of His suffering and death had yet to come. Scripture tells us that "Jesus hid Himself and went out of the temple" (John 8:59), passing through the midst of them, meaning that He made Himself invisible as He left.

When the opponents of Jesus finally arrived to take Him prisoner, He felled the entire armed band by uttering three little words: "I am He!" He showed by this how easy it would have been for Him to flee, if that had been His desire. If it had not been the Father's will—and therefore Jesus' will also—that He should suffer and die, no bands would have been able to bind Him, no army of any size would have been able to take Him prisoner, and no power on earth would have been able to fasten Him to the cross. With a simple word or the force of His own will, He could have smashed and destroyed all of His enemies. Instead, Herod and Pilate did what God had decreed beforehand. As Peter said in his Pentecost sermon: "Men of Israel, hear these words: Jesus of Nazareth, a man attested to you by God with mighty works and wonders and signs that God did through Him in your midst, as you yourselves know—this Jesus, delivered up according to the definite plan and foreknowledge of God, you crucified and killed by the hands of lawless men" (Acts 2:22–23).

There is no doubt: the suffering and death of Christ were not accidentally forced upon Him by the decree of man. Rather, they were decided, appointed, and administered by God Himself.

A Lamb goes uncomplaining forth,
The guilt of all men bearing;
And laden with the sins of earth,
None else the burden sharing!
Goes patient on, grows weak and faint,
To slaughter led without complaint,
That spotless life to offer;
Bears shame, and stripes, and wounds and death,
Anguish and mockery, and saith,
"Willing all this I suffer." Amen.

† *(TLH 142:1)*

Monday

Read Luke 18:31

THAT CHRIST HAD TO SUFFER and die is clear from the fact that it was announced beforehand by God through the prophets. Moreover, as today's reading shows, Christ's death was absolutely necessary for the redemption of the world. Why does Jesus refer to Himself here as "the Son of Man"? He clearly wants to refer the disciples to the Seed of the woman, who had been promised to the fallen man in Eden. He would crush the head of the serpent that would otherwise kill Him with a poisonous sting in His heel. In addition, Christ wanted the disciples to recall the words of the prophet who announced that a child would be born for fallen mankind, a Son who would be "wounded for our transgressions" and "crushed for our iniquities" (Isaiah 53:5). The life of this Son would be given as a sacrifice for sin. Jesus referred to Himself in this way to underscore the necessity of His death for the redemption of the world, as had been foretold by the prophets.

So we can avoid error in reflecting on all of this, let us look at the various accounts of the suffering and resurrection of the Lord. When Christ began His spiritual suffering in Gethsemane, He said, "My Father, if it be possible, let this cup pass from Me" (Matthew 26:39). But the cup of inexpressible suffering did not pass from Him; He had to empty it. God's answer to Christ's prayer was, in effect, "No, My dear Son, in whom I am well pleased, it is not possible if the world is to be redeemed." When, soon thereafter, Peter wielded his sword to save Christ from the bodily suffering that stood before Him, Jesus said to him: "Do you think that I cannot appeal to My Father, and He will at once send Me more than twelve legions of angels? But how then should the Scriptures be fulfilled, that it must be so?" (Matthew 26:53–54). And later, when Christ had risen from the dead, He spoke thus to the disciples on the road to Emmaus, who could still not resign themselves to His suffering: "O foolish ones, and slow of heart to believe all that the prophets have spoken! Was it not necessary that the Christ should suffer these things and enter into His glory?" (Luke 24:25–26).

Even Christ's enemies had to be conformed to the divine will. They by no means wanted to kill Jesus during the Passover, when so many people had gathered in Jerusalem, "lest there be an uproar from the people" (Mark 14:2). But God's hour, the hour of the redemption of the world, had come and hell had already been unleashed against Christ.

It is such an important truth that Christ's suffering and death were absolutely necessary for our salvation. We see from this that God is by no means only a dear, lenient Father, as most people suppose. Instead, He is a holy and just being. He hates sin, and His wrath burns against it. Had Christ, the Son of God, been unwilling to take all of man's sins upon Himself and to atone for them with His inexpressible suffering and agonizing death, God neither could nor would have been able to save any man.

We also see here how foolish it is for people to think they can hope for God's grace while they continue to cling to open or secret sin. Such people make a devil out of God. For it is the devil, not the holy God, who takes no notice of sin. Therefore, whoever has been clearly and convincingly shown that some behavior of his is a sin, who nevertheless refuses to let go of that sin, and who comforts himself with the thought that God's great grace applies to him is actually sinning against grace, trampling upon the Son of God who bled for his sins, considering the blood of the testament impure, and insulting the Spirit of grace. What awaits him is the judgment and the fire that will consume the enemies of God.

Grant that I Thy passion view
With repentant grieving
Nor Thee crucify anew
By unholy living.
How could I refuse to shun

Ev'ry sinful pleasure
Since for me God's only Son
Suffered without measure? Amen.

(TLH 140:4)

Tuesday

Read Luke 18:32–33

MANY THINK THAT IF FAITH in Christ's atoning suffering and death is the only means by which every person could be saved, Christ would have needed to enter the world immediately after the fall of man. How could faith in something that would happen 4,000 years after the fall be the only redemption for all men, regardless of when they lived? But this objection would be valid only if, during those 4,000 years, people had known nothing about Christ's redeeming suffering and death. But that is not so. Already in Eden, help from a suffering and dying Man was promised to the first people, and all of the prophets referred to this Messiah who would redeem the world. They described His atoning suffering most precisely, just as Jesus does in today's reading. Indeed, the prophetic writings offer so much detailed information on this subject as to make it appear that the prophets had already accompanied Christ from Gethsemane to Golgotha.

Why did God make such an exact announcement of this event through the prophets? First, He wanted to ensure that, through expectant faith in this saving, substitutionary, and atoning suffering of One who would come, all those who lived before Christ could have the certain comfort of the forgiveness of their sins, divine grace, and eternal salvation. All those who were lost before Christ's coming were damned only because they did not want to hear and know anything about these richly comforting prophecies. Instead, they rejected them with ridicule and regarded them as empty fables.

Even after Christ's appearance, the prophecies of His suffering and death did not lose their meaning and power. On the contrary, they are especially significant and powerful because all of these prophecies have been fulfilled before the eyes of all the world, and the One who was crucified in weakness really rose from the dead in glory. Therefore, the prophecies call to all people, "Christ *has* died for our sins according to the Scripture. God was reconciling the world to Himself in Christ. Let us be reconciled with God!" During the time of the Old Testament, these prophecies invited all people to quench their thirst in the wide stream of grace and salvation that had issued from God. From the time of the New Testament, however, the prophecies and the apostolic preaching flow everywhere as a double stream wherever there are sinners in need of salvation by grace. The crucified One stands in the middle of world history as the banner to whom the prophets pointed forward and to whom the apostles and evangelical preachers point back as the Lamb of God, who bears the sins of the world. And, as John writes in the Book of Revelation, He was crucified "before the foundation of the world" (Revelation 13:8).

May all of this move us daily during the Lenten season before us to search the writings of the prophets in holy silence, both to find references to the suffering and dying Christ and to see, as in a mirror, the abomination of our sins and God's anger over them. There, too, we will find the complete atonement of our sins and the riches of divine love and grace. We are completely blind to this by nature, but let us, in simple faith, call on Christ to open our eyes. In this way, we will experience the power of the holy Word: "Recover your sight; your faith has made you well" (Luke 18:42).

Ev'ry wound that pains or grieves me,
By Thy stripes, Lord, is made whole;
When I'm faint, Thy cross revives me,
Granting new life to my soul.
Yea, Thy comfort renders sweet
Ev'ry bitter cup I meet;
For Thy all atoning passion
Has procured my soul's salvation. Amen.

† *(TLH 144:4)*

Ash Wednesday

Read Galatians 5:6

THE HOLY SCRIPTURES undeniably describe faith as the only thing necessary for salvation. They also teach that good works cannot justify a person before God or contribute in the least toward the attainment of salvation. The Old Testament says that Abram "believed the LORD, and He counted it to him as righteousness" (Genesis 15:6). Habakkuk testifies that "the righteous shall live by his faith" (2:4), and Jeremiah cries, "LORD, aren't You looking for loyalty?" (5:3 AAT).

This doctrine stands in even stronger light in the books of the New Testament. They remind us that faith, not works, is the way to salvation and blessedness. Whenever a person sought help from Christ, we read that Christ looked only for faith. "All things are possible for one who believes" (Mark 9:23), Jesus told the father who needed help for his son and had failed to find it in the disciples. To another father who had lost all hope for help with the report that his daughter was already dead, Jesus said, "Do not fear; only believe, and she will be well" (Luke 8:50). When another suffering father directed his petition to Him, after seeking help from the disciples in vain, Jesus replied, "Let it be done for you as you have believed" (Matthew 8:13). This was His usual answer to those who sought His help. Therefore, the apostles' Epistles speak in this manner: "And to the one who does not work but trusts Him who justifies the ungodly, his faith is counted as righteousness" (Romans 4:5); "For we hold that one is justified by faith apart from works of the law" (Romans 3:28); and "For by grace you have been saved through faith. And this is not your own doing; it is the gift of God, not a result of works, so that no one may boast" (Ephesians 2:8–9). There is still more. In John's Gospel, we are told that the Jews once asked Jesus, "What must we do, to be doing the works of God?" Jesus replied by pointing to faith: "This is the work of God, that you believe in Him whom He has sent" (6:28–29).

Many are ashamed to seek salvation through faith in Christ, the Savior of the sinner, and instead they build their hope for eternity on their upright life. They carelessly regard themselves as good, without having examined their heart, their thoughts, their words, and their works. Even if a man lives uprightly, he will daily perceive how his conscience accuses him and declares him guilty. If a person examines himself according to the Law of God revealed in the Holy Scriptures, he will see countless flaws and weaknesses. If he fails to find them, he must be completely blind, wantonly closing the eyes of his soul to the mirror God holds before us.

Although our sin caused us to forfeit our claim to a blessed eternity, God once again opened to us the possibility of salvation through the offer of faith. If He had not revealed this to us, all who had come to a knowledge of their sinfulness would have had to live in despair and doubt.

May no one think that this doctrine is too holy for those who are weighed down by the knowledge of their sin. However, it is dangerous to those who are happy in the midst of their sin. Although love and good works save no one, both are still necessary as evidences that a person is truly standing in the saving faith. Faith and love are related and inseparably connected like a father and his child. Whoever says he is justified through faith before God must prove himself by his love before man. Otherwise he is a liar, for faith works through love.

Faith clings to Jesus' cross alone
And rests in Him unceasing;
And by its fruits true faith is known,
With love and hope increasing.
Yet faith alone doth justify,
Works serve thy neighbor and supply
The proof that faith is living. Amen.

† *(TLH 377:9)*

Thursday

Read 1 Corinthians 13:1–3

OUR TEXT IS NOT a peaceful instruction about love. Instead, it is glowing psalm of praise in which Saint Paul, ascending on the wings of true Christian inspiration, praises love in its heavenly beauty and incomparable glory. He says, "If I speak in the tongues of men and of angels, but have not love, I am a noisy gong or a clanging cymbal." What he imagines here is a person who speaks all the languages of man, and even the language of angels, so all the world might be astonished and listen to him and be moved and converted to Christ. But if the heart of such a person were empty of love, if he spoke so gloriously about God's Word to sinners out of a love of selfishness and vanity rather than a desire for the rescue of souls, if he spoke so he would be praised by others, then he would be no more than an instrument that delights others with its lovely ringings but neither perceives nor experiences them himself. He awakens others to life, but he himself is dead. He brings others to the grace of God, but he himself remains under God's wrath. He leads others to heaven, but he himself goes to hell.

The holy apostle continues, "And if I have the prophetic powers, and understand all mysteries and all knowledge, and if I have all faith, so as to remove mountains, but have not love, I am nothing." If a person could interpret all of Scripture and decipher its secret sense, if he had such knowledge that he could judge everything about Christian life and doctrine correctly, if his faith were such that he could surpass all miraculous deeds, even to the extent of removing mountains, if his heart remained devoid of love, then he would view his gifts not as a means of serving others but as a way to seek his own praise and glory. Thus, on account of his works, he would be highly regarded by men but of no value before God.

Finally, Paul adds, "If I give away all I have, and if I deliver up my body to be burned, but have not love, I gain nothing." That is, even if a person accomplishes great deeds that are considered to be works of love, distributing everything he has among the poor so as to become poor himself, and letting himself be burned as a Christian by the enemies of the Gospel, an absence of love in his heart would make his generous alms, voluntary poverty, and martyr's death a means of gaining a reputation for holiness and a posthumous fame in the world. For all the good he had performed for others with his works, he would have his reward in that alone.

We see here just how important love is. A person may speak like an angel, in lovely tones and powerfully, so his speaking is like golden apples in silver skins. He may know all of Scripture by heart. He may even be adorned with apostolic knowledge and the ability to perform amazing miracles. He may be rich in works. Everyone may praise him as a noble benefactor of mankind and boast of him as a zealous promoter of the kingdom of Christ. He may even end his life in martyrdom. But if all of this does not flow out of love, everything he has accomplished is a dirty stream from a polluted spring. Without love, he is no Christian, despite all his gifts and visible works of love. Love is the true crown of all gifts, the true weight in the scale of all deeds. Where it is lacking, all works and the entire life of a person, are sinful, lost, and rejected before God.

Let each of us examine himself to see if love dwells in his heart and if all of his visible Christian works flow from this source.

O gentle Dew, from heaven now fall
With power upon the hearts of all,
Thy tender love instilling,
That heart to heart more closely bound,
In kindly deeds be fruitful found,
The law of love fulfilling.
Dwell thus In us;
Envy banish;
Strife will vanish
Where thou livest.
Peace and love and joy Thou givest. Amen.

(TLH 235:7)

Friday

Read 1 Corinthians 13:4–7

IN OUR TEXT, Saint Paul names fifteen virtues that result from true love. Let us briefly consider each of them.

He says, first, "Love is patient." This means that a person who has love in his heart can wait a long time, peacefully and without becoming angry, when another does all kinds of evil to him. He can wait however long it takes for the other to realize his wrong.

The second virtue is "Love is kind." Whoever has love in his heart will not appear surly and morose, but will reveal that he is filled with good will toward everyone. He will find his joy in making others happy and in serving them.

Third, "Love does not envy." A person with love in his heart is not jealous of the good another has. He does not envy him if he has more earthly goods or spiritual gifts, more blessings, and more honor and respect. He rejoices in what his neighbor has as if it were his own.

Fourth, "Love does not boast." Someone who is filled with true love will not want to use his wit at someone else's expense, carelessly making that individual a laughingstock.

Fifth, "Love is not arrogant." The person who is ruled by love does not look down on others with contempt. Instead, he regards the gifts of others as higher than his own, and he places himself among the lowly.

Sixth, "Love does not behave rudely." Where love dwells in the heart, a person is not coarse and rough in appearance and word, not impolite, but modest and unassuming in his outward behavior.

Seventh, "Love does not insist on its own way." Where love is, one does not seek to gain at the expense of his neighbor. His laudable works are not driven by selfishness, by the hope of thanks or reward, but only by the hope that the glory of God is furthered or that the neighbor is served. He rejoices more in drying the tears of a stranger than in drying his own, and in being able to heal a stranger's wounds instead of his own.

Eighth, "Love is not irritable." When a Christian is full of love, he cannot be prodded to anger. Rather, he guards his sweet peace in God quietly and meekly.

Ninth, "Love is not resentful." The one who has love does not wait for an opportunity to take revenge on his enemy. He wishes no one evil and does not pray to God that anything bad will happen to another. Instead, his only wish is that that individual will convert and that it will go well for him both here on earth temporally and in heaven eternally.

The next two characteristics of love are that it "does not

rejoice at wrongdoing, but rejoices with the truth." A person who has true love is gentle toward the sinner and the erring, but he is just as earnestly opposed to sin and error. True love is holy love. A love that does not hate unrighteousness and does not rejoice in the truth is only an illusion of love.

Finally, Paul says love "bears all things, believes all things, hopes all things, endures all things." The one whose heart is kindled by love "bears" the weaknesses of his neighbor as if they were his own. He covers them, excuses them, and turns everything for the best. He "believes" that the good he sees in his neighbor is just that. He does not nurse suspicion and distrust in his heart. He "hopes" for the conversion of a neighbor even when he sees obvious sin and evil in that individual. And, where hope no longer seems possible, the one motivated by love "endures" everything humbly, not letting himself be moved to hatred and a thirst for revenge, but waiting patiently and quietly for the Lord's return.

How glorious is this love! It is a heavenly diadem that Christ wears, and it presents a whole row of virtues that gleam like jewels.

Faith and hope and charity
Graciously, O Father, give me;
Be my Guardian constantly
That the devil may not grieve me;
Grant me humbleness and gladness,
Peace and patience in my sadness. Amen.

† *(TLH 411:6)*

Saturday

Read 1 Corinthians 13:8–13

In these words, Saint Paul places love above the gifts of languages, prophecy, and knowledge. But he also gives love a position superior to that of faith and hope. All five of these gifts will cease, while love remains.

In eternity, the angels and the elect will speak only one language. Therefore, the gift of speaking various languages will no longer be of value.

In eternity, Holy Scripture will be an unsealed and open book for all of the saints. God will give them a perfect understanding of His Word. Thus there will be no need of prophecy.

In eternity, the saints will finally see God face-to-face. Here, on earth, all great knowledge is piecemeal. What a man should know is put before him in Scripture, but only like a picture in a mirror. Even the greatest knowledge here is, on a heavenly scale, like the intelligence and thoughts of a child. As childish imaginings give way to the wisdom of man, and as the image gives way to the reality, so in eternity knowledge will give way to beholding God face-to-face.

As long as there are Christians in the world, faith and hope will be found. But in eternity, even they will cease, and only love will remain. Therefore, the greatest of these enumerated gifts is love. Faith is great because it makes the sinner righteous before God. It rescues him from hell and opens heaven to him. However, it ceases in eternity, where all promises, which are grounded in faith, are fulfilled. Thus, faith, like the other gifts, changes into beholding. The greatness of hope is that it fills the suffering with heavenly comfort and offers them a glimpse of eternity and the crown that awaits them.

But in eternity, there is no more future. Everything there is in the present, and the saints reside there in an eternal, blessed today. For this reason, even hope will cease.

While all of these other gifts will disappear in eternity, love will remain. It lasts beyond the grave and accompanies the Christian into that new world. As the small creek gradually grows into a stream and continues to expand until it finally flows into the ocean, so the creek of love, which originates with God, swells in the Christian life into a mighty river until it enters the sea of eternity.

Without love, our faith is merely appearance, and our Christianity is only an illusion. Therefore, if the flame of love is still lacking in your heart, repent, for you are still lacking faith. Where there is no faith, there is no grace, and where there is no grace, there is no salvation. But whoever can say to Christ, "Yes, Lord, You know all things, and You know that I love You and my brother," faithfully cultivates this heavenly plant in his heart by the use of the Word and the holy Sacraments and by uninterrupted daily sighs for the Spirit of love. Above all, however, he continuously draws near to the eternal love of his God and Christ, there warming his heart that otherwise would easily grow cold. By remaining in love, he remains in God and God remains in him. For now, indeed, in time, "faith, hope, and love abide, these three; but the greatest of these is love," for it remains eternally.

O Love, who once shalt bid me rise
From out this dying life of ours;
O Love, who once above yon skies
Shalt set me in the fadeless bowers—
O Love, I give myself to Thee,
Thine ever, only Thine, to be. Amen.

† *(TLH 397:6)*

Sunday

Read Matthew 4:1–11

AN EXCEEDINGLY WONDERFUL BATTLE is explained to us in our Gospel today. Shortly before, when Christ was baptized, the heavens opened up above Him as if they wanted to descend upon the earth. Immediately after His baptism, hell opened up under Christ and rushed upon Him with all its power. How wonderful! The Son of God in almighty power had once cast Satan out of heaven, but here on earth, He let Himself be attacked by him, let Himself be led around, sneered at, and ridiculed. He did not conquer Satan, as He very well could have, by one word of His omnipotence, but by the written Word of God. He who is the eternal Light battled with the spirit of darkness, the eternal Truth with the spirit of lies, the Most Holy with the spirit of impurity, the King of heaven with the powerless prisoner of hell. The Son of God allowed Himself to be placed on the pinnacle of the temple and permitted the tempter to demand that He worship him. What a wonderful battle!

When it says, at the beginning of today's text, "Then Jesus was led up by the Spirit into the wilderness to be tempted by the devil," we see that Christ's battle was not by chance. It was something arranged by God, the heavenly Father Himself. It happened according to God's eternal gracious decree, and Christ voluntarily undertook it to its completion. If Christ had not wanted it, Satan would not have appeared before Him, tempted Him, and attacked Him. But Christ here did not fight for Himself. Instead, He fought as surety, as a third party, as a substitute for the entire human race.

By sin, all people sold themselves to Satan, becoming

servants and subjects of his kingdom. Therefore, when Christ wanted to redeem men and save them, He came, as the true owner of all people's souls, to conquer Satan, to destroy his kingdom, to remove his plunder from him, to free us from his dark power, and to lead us through the kingdom of grace into the kingdom of eternal glory. Christ did this mainly by His bloody death of atonement on the cross for all the sins of the world. By this, the head of the snake was totally crushed and all people were completely redeemed. The battle with Satan described in our text was the beginning. It was the first engagement that had to be fought by the Prince of our salvation to trample Satan under His feet and to deal the first deadly wounds to him. It was the first defeat the hellish army had to experience to show them that the Stronger One had now come.

If Christ had been overcome in the wilderness, woe to us! But it is well with us! Christ gloriously won, not for Himself, but for us. The cord is broken in two and we are free. Everything we lost by the fall in Paradise, Christ regained by the battle in the wilderness. Man ate from the forbidden tree. For that, Christ fasted forty days and forty nights. Man wanted to be like God. For that, the Son of God endured Satan calling to Him in distrust and mockery: "If You are the Son of God." The snake said, "Did God actually say . . . ?" (Genesis 3:1). This led man to distort the divine Word. Here Satan tempted Christ, but He remained firm and spoke without wavering: "It is written! It is written!" The snake led man to pride and presumption when it deceived him: "For God knows that when you eat of it your eyes will be opened, and you will be like God, knowing good and evil" (Genesis 3:5). Here Satan also tempted Christ to pride and said, "All these things I will give You, if You will fall down and worship me." But Christ triumphed. Satan had to retreat. And "angels came and were ministering to Him."

With might of ours can naught be done,
Soon were our loss effected;
But for us fights the valiant One,
Whom God Himself elected.
Ask ye, Who is this?
Jesus Christ it is,
Of Sabaoth Lord,
And there's none other God;
He holds the field forever. Amen.

† *(TLH 262:2)*

Monday

Read Hebrews 12:1–2

WHOEVER HAS CONQUERED with Christ will also fight with Him. If Satan dared the Head, His members will not be secure. Christ is Commander in chief and all believing Christians are called to spiritual warfare. The God of the spiritual Israel is called the Lord of Sabaoth, that is, the Lord of hosts. Each little text is a horn calling the Christian to battle. At Baptism, we all vowed to renounce the devil and all his works and to fight against him. As Christ was led immediately after His Baptism into the wilderness to be tempted, so all who are baptized into Jesus Christ should expect to receive the same treatment.

Therefore, two things are necessary. A person must recognize Satan's cunning and he must know how to overcome him. We learn both things from the example of the temptations of our Lord in the wilderness. First, the devil pointed out to Christ the wretched condition in which He found Himself so he could lead Him to doubt that He is God's Son: "If You are the Son of God, command these stones to become loaves of bread" (Matthew 4:3). He wanted to say, "How can You imagine that You are God's Son if You must live in hunger and misery?" When this temptation was not successful, Satan placed Christ on the pinnacle of the temple and said: "If You are the Son of God, throw Yourself down, for it is written, 'He will command His angels concerning you,' and 'On their hands they will bear you up, lest you strike your foot against a stone'" (Matthew 4:6). Here Satan tried to tempt Christ by falsifying God's Word, for he indeed quoted Scripture, but he left important words out of it. Psalm 91 clearly states that angels shall "guard you in all your ways" (v. 11). Satan suggests that Christ should look away from these words and, tempting God, lower Himself to his desire. But when this temptation also did not succeed, Satan became even more impudent and took Christ "to a very high mountain and showed Him all the kingdoms of the world and their glory. And he said to Him, 'All these I will give You, if You will fall down and worship me'" (Matthew 4:8–9).

Satan finally wanted to dazzle and win Christ by riches, glory, and lust of this world. These are the three main temptations each believer in Christ faces. Satan may try to make the Christian despondent because of poverty, want, distress, misery, shame, ridicule, and all other kinds of misfortune. By falsifying God's Word, he may also try to move the Christian to all sorts of dangerous errors, heresies, and doubts about that Word. Finally, he may try, by deceptions of good days, riches, glory, and pleasures of the world, to ensnare the Christian's poor heart once again with his hellish nets.

How should the Christian defend himself from this onslaught? As Christ, the Commander in chief, leads the way,

His Christian soldiers will follow Him. But how did Christ fight and win? Satan tempted Him to unbelief, but He answered, "It is written." Satan tempted Him to false doctrine, and He answered again, "It is written." Satan tempted Him to pride, and He answered a third time, "It is written." With a few words from the Old Testament Scriptures, He destroyed all the entrenchments and bulwarks of the hellish spirit. How else could Christ have more clearly and undeniably shown to the whole world that the Bible is the imperishable Word of Him who created the heavens and the earth, and that this Word firmly stands when everything else perishes!

As Christians, we must also let the Word be our weapon in all temptations. We must learn from our Savior to answer all attacks of the devil only with "It is written." The Word of God is the sword of the Spirit. If we seize it in faith, we can fight, and all fiery darts of the villain will be extinguished and smashed on the shield of our faith.

Rise! To arms! With prayer employ you,
O Christians, lest the foe destroy you,
For Satan has designed your fall.
Wield God's Word, a weapon glorious!
Against each foe you'll be victorious;
Our God will set you o'er them all.
Is Satan strong and fell?
Here is Immanuel.
Sing hosanna! The strong ones yield,
With Christ our Shield,
And we as conqu'rors hold the field. Amen.

(TLH 444:1)

Tuesday

Read 1 Peter 5:8

ONE CHRISTIAN DOCTRINE that is frequently and vehemently denied states that there is a devil who fiercely and ceaselessly attacks man. Even among those who claim to believe all of Scripture, there are many who do not think that there is a devil or that he is at work among people. For those who reject God's Word, there is not much dispute here. The doctrine of Satan concerns the invisible spirit world, which cannot be unlocked for us by our reason but by the Word of the divine revelation. Of course, the doctrine of the mysterious power of darkness is foolishness to whoever simply rejects the entire divine revelation.

But as certainly as there is a God who revealed Himself in the Bible, it is just as certain that there is a Satan. In the Scriptures, the name "Satan" is not just mentioned here and there so a person could perhaps think it means only evil thoughts and desires. The whole history of his beginning, his being, his qualities, his works, his influence on the whole human race, his kingdom, his place of residence, and his destiny now and in the future is fully described for us in the Bible. The presence of Satan is so much a part of Scripture that the entire foundation of Christian doctrine collapses as soon as a person wants to deny the existence of the evil spirit.

The Bible tells us that God created both man and an untold number of higher spirits, namely angels, that He gave them great glory, and that, gathered around His throne, they should serve Him and execute His commands. However, one of the most glorious of these angels fell from God, and with him fell a great number of heavenly spirits. That fallen angel, therefore, was not allowed to keep his heavenly principality. After he had forsaken his dwelling, he was cast out of heaven to hell with chains of darkness. This evil enemy of God then decided to set up another kingdom in place of the one he lost and in it to annihilate God's works everywhere.

At that time, God created the first people in His image, holy and glorious in body and soul. Satan tried to make them fall away from God by driving them into sin. Man allowed himself to be led into temptation, forsook obedience to God, fell into sin, and thus became a subject in the kingdom of darkness instead of a child of God. From then on, sinful parents begot sinful children. Everything that is man's is now by nature not in the kingdom of God but in the kingdom of the enemy of God. With sin, God's kingdom vanished from earth. Scripture says that the prince and god of this world is Satan, and he now tries, unceasingly, to spread more sin, error, blindness, darkness, misery, and misfortune on earth. It also says that he rules in the air and, as today's text informs us, "prowls about like a roaring lion, seeking someone to devour."

Satan deludes the senses of the children of unbelief so they do not see the clearness of Christ in the bright light of the Gospel. We therefore do not have to struggle against flesh and blood, but with princes and powers, namely the lords who rule in the darkness of the world, the evil spirits under heaven.

But God's Word reveals to us more than our misery, how we all, through sin, have come into the kingdom of Satan. It also tells us how Jesus Christ, Son of God and Son of man, overcame Satan, redeemed us out of his kingdom, saved us from the authority of darkness, and by His blood established a new kingdom of God. In this kingdom of grace, all who believe in Him find freedom and salvation.

Do Thou Thyself for us, Thy children, fight,
Withstand the devil, quell his rage and might;
Whate'er assails Thy members left below,
Do Thou o'erthrow. Amen.

(ELHB 279:2)

Wednesday

Read Isaiah 63:3,5

IN SAYING THIS, the Messiah demonstrates that He alone can crush the head of the serpent, He alone can perform the work of redemption, and He alone can regain the salvation of imprisoned and lost mankind. No one else in heaven and on earth could have been an assistant or partner in this work.

This prophecy is literally fulfilled in the atoning and redeeming suffering of our Savior. When the Lord began this great suffering, He was immediately forsaken by all creatures. When, in Gethsemane, He writhed like a crushed worm in the dust, sweat bloody sweat, and struggled with death, all of His disciples—even Peter, who wanted to go with Him into death—were full of sleep and none would watch with Him for even one hour. One of His own disciples, Judas, was the instrument by which He was betrayed into the hands of sinners. Another, Peter, denied Him in order to avoid participating in the beginning of the suffering. All of the remaining disciples fled.

Another prophecy, this one in the Book of Zechariah, was fulfilled at the same time: "'Awake, O sword, against my shepherd, against the man who stands next to me,' declares the LORD of hosts. 'Strike the shepherd, and the sheep will be scattered'" (13:7). We do find John, along with Mary and other pious women, on Golgotha, not to suffer and die with Christ, but only to lament and weep for Him. Forsaken by God and man, Jesus had to cry out: "I have trodden the winepress alone, and from the peoples no one was with Me. . . . I looked, but there was no one to help." Finally, He called out, "My God, My God, why have You forsaken Me?" (Matthew 27:46).

It could not have been otherwise. God is just, and He must therefore punish sin. He can crown with eternal life only the One who has done His entire will and is perfectly just. Therefore, the One who wanted to redeem us fallen men from the misery of our sin, bringing salvation to the lost, had to be a perfectly holy and pure person in order to suffer innocently and die in our place. However, He also had to be God in order to fulfill God's Law for us without Himself being bound to it. Only in this way could He overcome sin, death, and hell and acquire for us perfect righteousness, innocence, and blessedness. No angel, let alone sinful, guilt-laden man, could accomplish this work. Jesus Christ, God and man in one person, alone could do it.

As God could not have had any assistant in creating the world, which He made out of nothing, so also the Son of God could not have been helped by any kind of creature at the second creation, the redemption of the world. He trod the winepress of God's wrath alone, and only He could have done this. Woe, therefore, to the person who wants to be saved but does not seek his salvation in Christ alone, who wants to merit something for himself before God. Therefore, it says in the hymn:

Christ says: "Come, ye heavy-laden,
I your weary hearts will gladden;

They that are yet strong and well,
Despise the best physician's skill.

"Couldst thou earn thine own salvation,
Useless were My death and Passion;
This feast is not spread for thee,
If thine own helper thou wilt be." *(ELHB 441:5, 6)*

Naught have I, O Christ, to offer
Naught but Thee, my highest Good.
Naught have I, O Lord, to proffer
But Thy crimson-colored blood.
Thy death on the cross hath Death wholly defeated
And thereby my righteousness fully completed;
Salvation's white raiments I there did obtain,
And in them in glory with Thee I shall reign.
Amen.

(TLH 366:6)

Thursday

Read Philippians 2:13

SOME SUPPOSE THAT MAN is good by nature and that a person becomes corrupt and evil as the result of a bad upbringing and a poor environment. Others believe that when a person is born, he is like a blank tablet upon which neither good nor evil is written, but he has free will to choose the good and reject the evil, even in spiritual things, things that concern his soul and salvation. According to this view, if a person wants the good, he has the power by nature to do it. Still others imagine that a person cannot complete the work of his conversion but he can begin it, and if he does this, the Holy Ghost helps him along. There is also a school of thought that man must at least prepare himself for grace and if he does so, grace extends him a helping hand. Finally, some believe that man cannot begin his conversion, but when God awakens the power of his will, which by nature lies dormant, the person himself can complete the work God began. However, all of these opinions about the free will of a person unconverted in spiritual matters are coarse, pernicious errors. They only make a person feel proud and secure, supporting him in his self-righteousness, and robbing the grace of God of its honor.

It is true that even after the fall, a person has by nature free will in temporal things and in the works of civil and worldly respectability. An unconverted person can freely determine to build or not to build a house, to cultivate a field or not to cultivate it, to learn a trade or not to do so, to read and hear God's Word or to avoid it, to curse or not to curse, to commit adultery or to remain faithful to his spouse, and to steal or not to steal. However, a person can be so deeply entangled in the snares of the devil that, unable to offer resistance, he is led, like an animal bound for sacrifice, from sin to sin. In spiritual things, in works pleasing to God, in the true fulfillment of the Law, in the knowledge and acceptance of the Gospel, in faith in Christ, in the fear and love of God, in trusting Him above all things—in short, in that which concerns his salvation, true repentance, and conversion of the heart—a person has no free will. He is completely helpless and powerless. In an unconverted person, there is not even a glimmer of true goodness.

Let us hear what Holy Scripture teaches about this. It says, in the first book of Moses: "The intention of man's heart is evil from his youth" (Genesis 8:21). In Psalm 53, it says, "God looks down from heaven on the children of man to see if there are any who understand, who seek after God. They have all fallen away; together they have become corrupt; there is none who does good, not even one (vv. 2–3). We read further, in John 15, "Apart from Me you can do nothing" (v. 5); in John 6, "No one can come to Me unless the Father who sent Me draws him" (v. 44); and in John 3, "That which is born of the flesh is flesh, and that which is born of the Spirit is spirit" (v. 6). Thus Saint Paul also writes, "The natural person does not accept the things of the Spirit of God, for they are folly to him, and he is not able to understand them because they are spiritually discerned (1 Corinthians 2:14); "No one can say 'Jesus is Lord' except in the Holy Spirit" (1 Corinthians 12:3); and "Not that we are sufficient in ourselves to claim anything as coming from us, but our sufficiency is from God" (2 Corinthians 3:5). Therefore, it finally says in our text, "For it is God who works in you, both to will and to work for His good pleasure."

All desires and thoughts of mine,
From my youth, are only evil;
Save me by Thy power divine
From myself and from the devil;
Give me strength in ample measure,
Both to will and do Thy pleasure. Amen.

(ELHB 343:4)

Friday

Read Ephesians 2:5

GOD'S WORD INFORMS US that, prior to conversion, every person is spiritually dead. Just as someone who is bodily dead cannot see, hear, feel, or do anything, so a natural, unconverted person cannot recognize or understand anything spiritual, anything concerning the salvation of his soul. If Scripture is not correctly taught and accepted by such a person, he will regard it as foolishness if the Holy Ghost does not enlighten him. If he is exhorted to true repentance and good works, he can do nothing but resist if the Holy Spirit does not work in him. Therefore, in spiritual things, man is *worse* than a stick or stone that can neither desire something nor do it. Man can also oppose the grace that works in him. The fallen Adam would not have returned to God if God had not come before him in grace, sought him out, and led him back. In the same way, God must come before all people by His grace; otherwise, not even one person in the whole world would convert to God.

We were unable to do anything about the fact that we were born into this world, and as fallen people, we can do nothing in our new creation, in the changing of our heart of stone, in our being born again. As little as a person who is bodily dead can contribute to his becoming alive bodily, so little can an unconverted, spiritually dead person contribute to his becoming alive spiritually. A person cannot convert himself or contribute to it in the least. He is awakened alone by God's power and grace, enlightened, brought to faith, and converted. The apostle Paul calls to the Philippians, "Work out your own salvation with fear and trembling" (2:12). He adds,

"For it is God who works in you, both to will and to work for His good pleasure" (2:13).

Because God alone can convert us, fear and trembling should be in us so we do not hinder the working of God's Word in us. Because we do not have the slightest power to work our conversion or even to cooperate in it, we must, for the sake of our salvation, not resist wantonly and obstinately whenever God wants to convert us. This also warns us not to delay our conversion even one hour, but to answer God right away when He greets us, to open up for God right away when He knocks on our hearts, to arise from the sleep of sin right away when He awakens us.

If we could convert ourselves, when would we want to do so? Perhaps we would say: "Not today, but tomorrow. Not this year, but next year. Not now in my youth and as long as I am healthy, but when I become old and sick." Because we can do nothing for our conversion and God alone must do everything, we should think, as soon as God begins to work in us, *Now, now is the time!* For it can happen that if God wants to convert us today but we prefer to wait until next year, God might not be willing to accommodate us, but would instead suddenly and unexpectedly tear us out of this life in our unconverted state to His severe judgment. Then we would have waited too long and we, past saving, would perish. Therefore, Scripture says: "Do not be deceived: God is not mocked" (Galatians 6:7). No one can excuse himself with his powerlessness. When we cannot come to God, He wants to draw us to Himself. When we cannot take God into our heart, He will open the heart for us. When we cannot see what serves our peace, He will enlighten us. When we cannot be rightly frightened of hell, He will work this fright in us.

But whoever then remains in his sins and unrepentance makes himself obdurate. He then will cry out when he goes to hell.

Though alive, I'm dead in sin,
To all good things lost by nature;
Holy Ghost, change me within,
Make of me a new-born creature;
For the flesh deserves damnation
And can never gain salvation. Amen.

(ELHB 343:2)

Saturday

Read 2 Corinthians 6:1

MOST UNCONVERTED PEOPLE think they can work their conversion themselves without the Holy Ghost. Many who have been converted believe they do not need to cooperate with the Holy Ghost. Both of these opinions are erroneous and dangerous.

Just as God must initiate our conversion and salvation, so, too, must He work their continuation and completion. Just as God alone makes us born again, so His power alone preserves us to salvation. Therefore, following conversion, no person can contribute anything out of his own powers for his perseverance and remaining in grace. But he can, and must, cooperate. Conversion is the freeing of the will, which beforehand was bound in sin and separated from God. The converted person is obligated no longer to serve sin but to serve God, for the Lord Himself has said, "So if the Son sets you free, you will be free indeed" (John 8:36). Through conversion, a person receives a divine light, a new and divine life and desires, and new and divine powers in his heart. This is a treasure of which the converted Christian now makes use, and from it he should bring God abundant tribute.

Even the converted can cooperate only as long as God governs and guides. If God removes His hand and takes His Holy Ghost from a converted person, that individual immediately falls back into his old spiritual death. Yet God does not forsake anyone who has not forsaken Him first. The Spirit of God continually drives the converted children of God forward to pursue sanctification, without which no one will see the Lord. A Christian who will not continually fight against sin, earnestly strive after the virtues that please God, faithfully watch over his heart and life, and always pray for new power and grace soon ceases to be a Christian. In him, the Word of the Lord is fulfilled: "For to everyone who has will more be given, and he will have an abundance. But from the one who has not, even what he has will be taken away" (Matthew 25:29). The oil in his lamp of grace, the living power of the Spirit, is exhausted; the flame is then extinguished, and when the Bridegroom comes, he cannot go to meet Him.

Most people are lost when they want to better themselves, even before they experience the working of the Holy Ghost, and therefore they never truly improve. But many are also lost when, after they have been converted by the grace of God, they do not cooperate with the Holy Ghost. They think that, having fought through the difficult battle of repentance, they immediately enter the harbor of peace. Believing that grace does everything, they are deceived into the sleep of security, although that thought of grace should fill them with a desire to be godly. They do not watch, fight, or pray. They do not work out their salvation with fear and trembling. And behold, they are lost.

Let us, then, hear the word of the holy apostle in our text: "Working together with Him, we appeal to you not to receive the grace of God in vain." What can be more frightening than to have received grace after wrath only to misappropriate that grace so as to reap wrath once again! What can be more frightening than, after being full of hope for salvation and heaven, being thrown suddenly into hell and damnation! Oh, may God protect us against this in grace, for Jesus' sake. Amen.

Grant that Thy Spirit's help
To me be always given
Lest I should fall again
And lose the way to heaven;
That He may give me strength
In mine infirmity
And e'er renew my heart
To serve Thee willingly. Amen.

† *(TLH 417:5)*

Sunday

Read Matthew 15:21–28

THE CANAANITE WOMAN demonstrates how God sometimes contends with His dear Christians. He may treat them as if they were people about whom He does not care, even as if He were their enemy instead of their friend. The first way in which God contends with His Christians is common earthly affliction. This is not always bodily torture by Satan. It may take the form of one's own sickness or the sickness and death of loved ones, poverty, the loss of a good name by poisonous tongues, the unfaithfulness and falsehood of trusted friends, and all other kinds of sorrow and unhappiness.

But, as we see with the Canaanite woman, there is another, more difficult struggle: God often does not answer the prayer of the Christian in distress but is silent to it. The distress goes on, and it will often become greater the more fervently the Christian prays.

God does not give in for a while. At first, Christ was silent to the cry for help from the Canaanite woman, and when He finally did speak, He spoke only angry words. When the disciples interceded, He explained that He had not been sent for the Gentiles, even comparing the woman to a dog that doesn't even deserve the children's breadcrumbs. Christians often experience this in the form of heavier inward temptations added to the outward cross. God takes all feelings of comfort out of their hearts. Their hearts condemn them as sinners about whom God doesn't want to know anything; they are not elected but rejected; they do not belong to the children of the kingdom but to the dogs, about which it is written that they are outside.

In the example of the Canaanite woman, however, we also see how Christians victoriously overcome God Himself when He contends against them. Their manner of battle is quite simple. They need three things: (1) patience and humility, (2) fervent and incessant prayer, and, as their main weapon, (3) a faith that holds fast to God's Word against the experiences and feelings of the heart.

If God contends with Christians by various sorts of misfortune, they do not say in their hearts, like the children of the world and false Christians: "What have I done to deserve this? Why must it go so badly for me while others, who are worse than I, sit in happiness?" Even less do they seek to help themselves in unjust ways. Instead, they first carry their cross in patience, and they think that they merit much worse than they have received—in fact, hell. Then they pray incessantly. Above all, however, they take refuge in God's Word and keep themselves in it. It is written: "Those whom I love, I reprove and discipline" (Revelation 3:19), and "We know that for those who love God all things work together for good" (Romans 8:28).

If God assails Christians with heavy, inner attacks, He lets them feel no comfort, but only darkness, sin, wrath, death, and hell. For them, it is as if they had already been rejected by God from eternity. Even then, they do not cease to pray. And if, after their prayer, it seems to be only worse instead of better, they persist in prayer. Above all, they seize the sword of the Spirit, which is the Word of God, and the shield of faith. They agree with God and say, "I have certainly deserved Your complete rejection of me," but they still cling to God's universal promises, such as "Whoever comes to Me I will never cast out" (John 6:37), "I have no pleasure in the death of the wicked" (Ezekiel 33:11), and "But where sin increased, grace abounded all the more" (Romans 5:20).

And behold, with one, the attack lasts a shorter time, and with another, a longer time. The attack is not removed from them, but the light of grace and joy once again rises more brightly. For ever so gladly, God lets Himself be overcome. He does not struggle against Christians to overcome them, but rather to be overcome by them.

I have Thy Word,
Christ Jesus, Lord;
Thou never wilt forsake me.
This will I plead
In time of need.
Oh, help with speed
When troubles overtake me! Amen.

† *(TLH 353:6)*

Monday

Read 1 Timothy 6:12

JOB SAYS: "Has not man a hard service on earth, and are not his days like the days of a hired hand?" (7:1). Christ calls to His disciples, "Strive to enter through the narrow door" (Luke 13:24). Finally, Paul adds, "An athlete is not crowned unless he competes according to the rules" (2 Timothy 2:5). Here we see that without fighting, striving, and competing—victoriously competing—there is no true Christian.

Many think that once a person has been converted, he is finished with the difficult work of repentance and he can then rest. He is like one who, after a stormy voyage at sea, has finally arrived in safe harbor; the danger of perishing is happily past, and the soul of such an individual is safely brought in and need no longer fear shipwreck. However, this is an extremely dangerous deception. It is precisely at the point of conversion that the true fight begins in him. When Christ says, "Strive to enter through the narrow gate," He is referring not just to the initial act of repentance but rather to the entire progress of the Christian life until death. All of this, taken together, is the narrow gate and the narrow path that lead to life.

When a person is converted, he is not pure spirit. He always retains a good portion of flesh. He is, indeed, no longer of the world but he is still in the world. And while he no longer stands under the authority of darkness, he continues to live where the prince of darkness, Satan, rules and "prowls around like a roaring lion, seeking someone to devour" (1 Peter 5:8). A converted Christian is therefore continually opposed by these three enemies: the flesh, the world, and the devil. If he does not continue to fight against them, he suddenly comes once again under their dominion, and then his faith and his salvation are forfeited. Wherever there is no struggle in a Christian, there is constant defeat.

Following conversion, the germ remains in the human heart, not only for this or that sin, but for all sins. Whoever does not believe this because he has not experienced it has, in fact, already sunk back again into spiritual death. And whoever is daily stirred up to all kinds of sins in thoughts, words, and works, and instead of fighting against these enticements, he rather considers them as trifles, is no less without the living, saving faith.

Even the Christian occasionally wrongs his neighbor in rashness, offends him, or judges him behind his back. In addition, a Christian can let himself be misled into speculating about becoming rich, taking advantage of his neighbor, and departing from the strict truth. Anger, resentment, envy, and joy in a neighbor's misfortune sometimes stir in the Christian. For we sin, Scripture says, in many ways. However, when a true Christian sins in such a way, it is as if he had a splinter in his flesh that continually hurts him. He cannot rest until he has removed this splinter from his conscience by true repentance. Every act of stumbling awakens him to inner battle, and if his fellow Christians show him his fault, he soon breaks down, admits his sin, and then is more humble and more watchful.

However, if someone falls into sin and is not disturbed by it, if he does not want to battle against it or be punished on account of it, if he is not chastened when he is reminded of his conduct, and if he does not want to see justice done, he is certainly no Christian. His supposed faith is dead. That which is not active in love and does not cleanse the heart of dead works is no faith. So, then, let us not deceive ourselves with a Christianity that does not involve constant battle, "For who bears not the battle's strain The crown of life shall not obtain" (*TLH* 421:5).

Destroy in me the lust of sin,
From all impureness make me clean.
Oh, grant me pow'r and strength, my God,
To strive against flesh and blood! Amen.

† *(TLH 398:2)*

Tuesday

Read Titus 3:5

ARE GOOD WORKS necessary for salvation? This question caused great commotion in our church soon after Luther's death. All faithful Christians, both then and now, have answered the question in the negative, while only a few suspect theologians have demurred on the basis of other points of doctrine. It seems extremely bold, even dangerous, for a person to declare that good works are not required for salvation. But we have only to open the Holy Scriptures, which are the infallible judge in all questions and disputes of faith and doctrine, and what do we find there? They tell us that all of man's works are completely excluded in his justification before God and in his salvation. Instead, both justification and salvation are attributed to the grace of God alone, Christ alone, and faith alone.

In the Epistle to the Romans, it says, "For we hold that one is justified by faith apart from works of the law" (3:28), and "To the one who does not work but trusts Him who justifies the ungodly, his faith is counted as righteousness, just as David also speaks of the blessing of the one to whom God counts righteousness apart from works" (4:5–6). We find the same thing in the Epistle to the Ephesians: "For by grace you have been saved through faith. And this is not your own doing; it is the gift of God, not a result of works, so that no one may boast" (2:8–9). We cannot think that man, by his works, earns either the beginning of his justification and salvation or his preservation in them. Peter expressly says, "Who by God's power are being guarded through faith for a salvation" (1 Peter 1:5). Also, Paul calls the salvation of the soul the goal of faith, not the goal of works.

These passages show us that it is against God's Word to say that works are necessary for salvation. Such a position overturns the clearly revealed doctrine of salvation by grace. As the apostle Paul then writes, "That is why [righteousness] depends on faith, in order that the promise may rest on grace and be guaranteed to all his offspring" (Romans 4:16), and "But if it is by grace, it is no longer on the basis of works; otherwise grace would no longer be grace" (Romans 11:6).

And it is well for us that this is so! For if God's Word informed us that, in addition to Christ, grace, and faith, works are required for salvation, we could never be happily certain of our state of grace and our salvation. Then we could never know for sure which works are pleasing to God and how many of them would be sufficient for us to earn our way into heaven. Then the Gospel would be no more comforting than the Law; Christ would not be the unmovable rock of our hope, and this would cast us forever into the hell of doubt.

But we know that all of our own works are excluded in our justification before God. Our works do not earn us heaven and eternal life. Instead, these are gifts of the free grace and mercy of God, which Christ alone has acquired for us. He offers them to us in Word and Sacrament, which are presented, sealed, and effected by us through faith alone. Thus, although we are and remain poor sinners, through faith we can become and remain certain of our state of grace and our future salvation. If, besides faith, only one work from our side were necessary for salvation, we would be robbed of all comfort. While we sit at the richly set table of the divine promises, that one work would hang over our heads like a double-edged sword, suspended by a hair, threatening and frightening us. However, it says in God's Word: "Come, everyone who thirsts, come to the waters; and he who has no money, come, buy and eat! Come, buy wine and milk without money and without price" (Isaiah 55:1). That is comfort indeed for such miserable and powerless people as we are. That is a Gospel for sinners, and we have need of it.

I know my faith is founded
On Jesus Christ, my God and Lord;
And this my faith confessing,
Unmoved I stand upon His Word.
Man's reason cannot fathom
The truth of God profound;
Who trusts her subtle wisdom
Relies on shifting ground.
God's Word is all-sufficient,
It makes divinely sure,
And trusting in its wisdom,
My faith shall rest secure. Amen.

† *(TLH 381:1)*

Wednesday

Read Philippians 3:12, 15

CERTAIN RELIGIOUS FELLOWSHIPS maintain that a Christian can and should be perfect already in this life. This doctrine is among those mighty errors that Paul says will arise in the last days, after people have refused the love of truth. Nevertheless, this error is a powerful temptation to the soul. Everyone thinks that a doctrine that demands perfect sanctification must be both good and holy. Moreover, in many places, Scripture itself speaks about Christian perfection. Now if an inexperienced Christian sees nothing more than the words "perfect" and "mature," which he also finds in the Bible, he can readily believe that Scripture teaches that a person can attain a perfect sanctification and a perfect love. However, upon closer examination, he would discover that Christian perfection means nothing more than the perfect righteousness of Christ, which God imputes out of grace to each believer. Thus, Saint Paul writes to the Corinthians, after explaining that he preached only the despised, crucified Christ to the world, "Yet among the mature we do impart wisdom" (1 Corinthians 2:6). He is referring here to those believers who, in faith, have received the crucified One and find their highest wisdom in Him. In the Epistle to the Colossians, the same apostle writes, "For in Him the whole fullness of deity dwells bodily, and you have been filled in Him" (2:9–10). Here, Paul explains in what way Christians are perfect: not in themselves, but rather in Christ or in faith in Him. God, out of grace, considers them perfect in Christ.

There are also places in Scripture where certain Christians are called "perfect" in contrast with others. Thus, the author of the Epistle to the Hebrews writes: "For though by this time you ought to be teachers, you need someone to teach you again the basic principles of the oracles of God. You need milk, not solid food, for everyone who lives on milk is unskilled in the word of righteousness, since he is a child. But solid food is for the mature, for those who have their powers of discernment trained by constant practice to distinguish good from evil" (5:12–14). When Holy Scripture speaks of mature Christians, then, it is referring to those individuals who have advanced to a certain level of adulthood in Christian knowledge, experience, faith, love, and hope. However, we find no word in the Bible about Christians who have become perfect in sanctification or in love. John speaks about those who are complete in love, but a careful inspection of these passages shows that he is talking not about the love of man for God but about the love of God for man. The people to whom he refers are those who rely solely and completely upon the love of God in Christ.

Scripture testifies, in countless places, that all people without exception are sinners and remain so until their death. Solomon says, "Surely there is not a righteous man on earth who does good and never sins" (Ecclesiastes 7:20). In the Book of Job, it says: "What is man, that he should be innocent, or the one born of a woman that he should be righteous? God doesn't trust His holy ones, and the heavens aren't pure in His sight" (Job 15:14, 15 AAT). David writes: "Who can discern his errors? Declare me innocent from hidden faults" (Psalm 19:12). John informs us, "If we say we have no sin, we deceive ourselves, and the truth is not in us" (1 John 1:8). James writes: "For we all stumble in many ways, and if anyone does not stumble in what he says, he is a perfect man" (3:2). Finally, Paul says: "I know that nothing good dwells in me, that is, in my flesh. For I have the desire to do what is right, but not the ability to carry it out" (Romans

7:18), and "I am not aware of anything against myself, but I am not thereby acquitted" (1 Corinthians 4:4).

Where, then, do perfect love and sanctification remain? They are nothing but the vain imagining of a self-deceived enthusiast. According to Saint Paul's clear doctrine, those who are among the mature through Christ confess that they still have not attained perfection.

Grant that Thy Spirit's help
To me be always given
Lest I should fall again
And lose the way to heaven;
That He may give me strength
In mine infirmity
And e'er renew my heart
To serve Thee willingly. Amen.

† *TLH 417:5)*

Thursday

Read 1 Thessalonians 4:1–2

It is a heavy task the apostle Paul places before all Christians in this passage. A Christian should never think that since he has faith and stands by God in grace that there is no danger for him and he can look forward peacefully and without care to a blessed eternity. No, the apostle says, a Christian should never think he is finished. Indeed, he should never be satisfied with himself, but rather should say with Paul, "Not that I have already obtained this or am already perfect, but I press on to make it my own, because Christ Jesus has made me His own" (Philippians 3:12). The Christian should be a person of progress. He should never stand still, but always seek to go forward. He should always be found actively doing the will of God, always in battle for the treasure, always in the race for the crown of glory. With each day, he should come closer to the goal, that is, seeking to become holier and more like Christ. In the narrow sense, sanctification is nothing but the restoration of the image in which God created us, that is, in His image. There are three parts to sanctification: (1) an always greater illumination of the mind, (2) an always greater purification and renewing of the heart, and (3) an always greater zeal for a life of good works.

Therefore, a Christian should not think it is enough if he knows only as much of the right doctrine as is necessary for salvation. No, Paul says, a Christian must always seek to become more complete in his knowledge. He must desire the Law of the Lord and meditate on it day and night. Without ceasing, he must seek, investigate and study God's Word to become better able to distinguish pure doctrine from false and to discern how the revealed doctrine fits together. He will then be able to answer more completely the question, "What do you believe?" He will cite Scripture more clearly and refute more powerfully those who contradict it. Christians should earnestly seek to "attain . . . the unity of the faith and of the knowledge of the Son of God, to mature manhood, to the measure of the stature of the fullness of Christ, so that we may no longer be children, tossed to and fro by the waves and carried about by every wind of doctrine, by human cunning, by craftiness in deceitful schemes" (Ephesians 4:13–14).

In addition, a Christian should not think his goal is merely to remain in the good state in which he is now placed by

God's grace, being careful not to fall into gross sin. No, says the apostle, a Christian should always become more perfect in purifying and renewing his heart. Where impurity, malice, corruption, or something else ungodly still shows itself in his heart, he should, with all earnestness, seek to sweep it out of every corner of his heart. He should also seek to become stronger in faith, more devoted to God's will, more heavenly minded, more humble before God and man, more burning and unselfish in love, more pure in his desires, and more watchful over his thoughts.

Finally, a Christian should not think that his goal in life is merely to give no one offense. No, Paul says, if he wants to be a Christian, he must always become more perfect in his zeal for a life of good works, for the service of God, for prayer, and for the hearing and reading of God's Word. He must always be more frank in the confession of his faith, more faithful in his office and calling, more friendly and zealous and peaceful toward everyone, more forgiving toward his enemies, more consoling toward his friends, more conscientious in his trade, more generous and charitable toward his poorer brothers, and more willing to devote himself to the things of the Church and the kingdom of God. In short, he must become an example for all and let his "light shine before others, so that they may see [his] good works and give glory to [his] Father who is in heaven" (Matthew 5:16).

Help us to serve Thee evermore
With hearts both pure and lowly;
And may Thy Word, that light divine,
Shine on in splendor holy
That we repentance show,
In faith ever grow;
The pow'r of sin destroy

And all that doth annoy.
Oh, make us faithful Christians! Amen.

† *(TLH 477:3)*

Friday

Read 1 Thessalonians 4:3–6

WHEN CHRISTIANS CONTINUALLY READ and hear about the free grace of God in Christ, about justification and salvation through faith alone, and about the willingness of the heavenly Father to forgive even the greatest sinners for the sake of Christ's merits, it is easy for them to think that God does not take sin very seriously. This thought may become even more deeply ingrained in them if they do not study God's Word, do not heed the impulses and chastenings of the Holy Ghost, and do not diligently watch and pray. To them, God is a good, lenient, dear Father, who does not ask much when they, His faithful children, still serve this or that sin as long as they remain earnestly intent upon sanctifying themselves in body and spirit.

Against such thoughts, the apostle Paul writes in our text, "For this is the will of God, your sanctification" (v. 3). God should hardly think differently about sin, following the reconciliation with sinners He accomplished through Christ, than He did before. He can hardly have become an old, weak father who regards his children's evil as good, who does not see their misbehavior and punish them for it. His divine Law can hardly have lost universal obligation. God always remains unchangeable. He is the same holy God He always was, and His will is the perfect holiness of all created beings, including man. Every sin is an offense to His holiness and an insolent rebellion of the creature against His unchangeable declared will. He remains the strong, zealous God who visits the sins of the fathers upon the children to the third and fourth generations. His anger continues to burn against every wanton sin. Because of believers' sins of weakness, the Son of God must continually stand as Intercessor until the Last Day in order to prevent God from pouring out His wrath upon sinners and so consuming them.

Woe, therefore, to those who, after they have come to faith in Christ, think they have now received a license freeing them from the earnest pursuit of sanctification. Woe to those who believe that because of their faith the heavenly Father will readily overlook in them the same sins He punishes in the unbelievers. Woe to them if they then secretly engage in whoremongering or adultery or shameful unnatural self-defilement of their bodies, or if their hearts give way to impure lusts and desires, thereby making their bodies, which should be a temple of the Holy Ghost, a cloak of the spirit of unchastity. Woe to them if they seek an ill-gotten gain in their trade, deceive their neighbor, or become covetous, stingy, or enamored of riches. Woe to them if they become drunk, lie to extricate themselves from difficulty, fill their tongues with slander, or become seized with anger to the point of plotting revenge against one who has offended them.

Such people still want to be Christians, but they do not stand with God in grace. God is not their friend, but their declared enemy. The apostle Paul clearly says in our text that all who, with their imagined faith, serve some sort of sin are just like the heathen "who do not know God." They have God, not as a good, lenient Father, but as the dreadful "avenger of all these things." For God is and remains a just, holy God who hates sin and strongly and zealously avenges it. His will is and remains our sanctification in body and soul, and in all our thoughts, desires, words, and works.

Come, Light serene and still,
Our inmost bosoms fill,
Dwell in each breast.
We know no dawn but Thine;
Send forth Thy beams divine
On our dark souls to shine
And make us blest.

Exalt our low desires,
Extinguish passion's fires,
Heal every wound.
Our stubborn spirits bend,
Our icy coldness end,
Our devious steps attend
While heavenward bound. Amen.

† *(TLH 227:3, 4)*

Saturday

Read 1 Thessalonians 4:7

THE APOSTLE PAUL SAYS here that pardoned Christians are not released from the duty of holiness but that all people are obligated to this duty. In fact, the call of grace, which they have received, has no purpose other than their holiness.

Additionally, as people created for fellowship with God, they are obligated to holiness. And so, believing Christians are doubly obligated.

With great earnestness, the apostle opposes certain false notions that many in Christendom have. These individuals wonder why Christ came into the world, why God allows the comforting Gospel of the forgiveness of sins to be preached, and why faith was decreed as the means of salvation if the believing Christian still has to fight against each sin and must continue to pursue greater holiness. If this is so necessary, what is the difference between Christ and Moses, between the Law and the Gospel, between one pardoned and one unpardoned? But how such people err!

If we were to be saved, it was indeed necessary for Christ to come into the world and to gain for us grace and a righteousness that avails before God. Above all, it is necessary for each person who would be saved, through faith in Christ, to take hold of that grace and that righteousness. However, all of this is hardly the final goal of the incarnation of Christ and of our call into His kingdom of grace. It is only the means, the way to the true goal. God did not send His Son into the world, pardoning man and reconciling him to Himself, solely to remove from man the worry that God is his enemy and after death he has to expect His punishments. The final and true goal of all of God's works of grace for and in man is nothing other than his holiness.

Man was originally created in the image of God, in righteousness and holiness. This image, which he lost by sin, must be restored and man must again become holy. For only if a person is holy can he also be saved. Therefore, a person is redeemed so he becomes holy once again. So he becomes holy, the Gospel is preached to him, faith is given to him and counted for righteousness, he is baptized, and his sins are forgiven. So he is comforted, he is fed with Christ's body and given to drink Christ's blood in Holy Communion. So he can attain salvation, heaven is opened to him.

Does it not follow that holiness is absolutely necessary for the believing Christian who has already been saved in hope? It is true that no one can earn salvation by holiness. Instead, a person must take hold of salvation through faith before he can pursue holiness. And while it is impossible to obtain salvation by holiness, it is entirely possible for a person to lose his salvation again by the neglect of his holiness. What does the person do who will not pursue holiness? God extends to him the means of grace (that is, the Word and the Sacraments) and gives him His grace through faith so he becomes holy again. Thus, if he resists God, and grieves and drives out of his heart the Holy Ghost (who alone can preserve him in faith), he suffers a shipwreck of his faith and he finally perishes.

Therefore, whoever wants to be saved first seeks grace in true repentance. If he has grace, he takes seriously the admonishment to become holy, for this is the will of God and to this Christians are called. We will certainly never bring this to perfection here below, but woe to him who pleads his weakness and imperfection to excuse his service to sin and his lukewarmness! Such a person will receive his reward with the hypocrites. But blessed are those who can say from their heart with Paul, "Not that I have already obtained this or am already perfect, but I press on to make it my own, because Christ Jesus has made me His own" (Philippians 3:12). Already, here on earth, a brightness is reflected in the faces of such people of the Lord, and they are transfigured from one brightness to another until they finally awake in heaven, perfect in His image.

But since my strength will nevermore suffice me
To crucify desires that still entice me,

To all good deeds, oh, let Thy Spirit win me
And reign within me! Amen.

† *(TLH 143:11)*

Sunday

Read Luke 11:14–26

THIS PASSAGE TELLS US that Christ cast the devil out of a man who was dumb, and the parallel account in the Gospel of Matthew adds that this man was also blind (Matthew 12:22). By doing this, Christ instantly gave the man sight, hearing, and speech. When the people were astonished at this great miracle, some, probably Pharisees, broke out in terrible blasphemy, "He casts out demons by Beelzebul, the ruler of the demons." Christ showed them that this assertion was not only wicked but also totally foolish. If Satan struggled this way against himself, his kingdom would not endure, and he would have destroyed it himself long ago. Christ also reminded them that even their own children used the name of Jesus when they wanted to cast a devil out of a person; thus, they only condemned themselves with their assertion. Convinced in their mind and beaten by their own conscience, they nevertheless persisted in their horrible blasphemy.

In these Pharisees, we see people who, while living amid Christians and the sound of the Gospel, still belong to the kingdom of the devil. All of them continue in open unbelief or in open sin against their own conscience. While some of them do not know the Bible and Christianity, others know them both and still reject them with mockery and scorn. What motivates this behavior is obviously greater than human spite; it shows that they are subjects and prisoners of the devil. On the other hand, there are some who blaspheme the doctrine of God's Word, not with their mouths (perhaps they even confess it), but as they live in open sin. They hear or read God's Word, wherein they are often urgently admonished. But everything is in vain. They always hope for grace, but they remain in their sins. This corruption is greater than normal. It is an obviously satanic delusion and it shows that these servants of sin operate under the hidden orders of the Prince of Darkness and are obedient subjects of his kingdom.

In our text, we also meet those who do not blaspheme but are certainly not of Christ. Rather, they "[sought] from Him a sign from heaven." They suggested that they were ready to make up their mind for Christ, but one thing was lacking. Jesus says about them, "Whoever is not with Me is against Me, and whoever does not gather with Me scatters." Here we see those who remain neutral in the war between Christ and the world, who want to perish neither with Christ nor with the world, who want to break radically neither from their old Adam nor from God. In short, they are straddling the fence, and thus do not belong in Christ's kingdom but in the kingdom of the devil. Such half-Christians are among the most accursed subjects of the devil. They think that, going down the middle of the road, they are on firm footing as members of Christ's kingdom. But their faith is imaginary, and they are, in the end, traveling the road to hell. Faithful pastors have even comforted such individuals on their deathbed.

Let us recognize how great the devil's kingdom is in the midst of Christendom. It is populated not only by open unbelievers and obvious servants of sin, but also by all hypocrites. Their godliness is not true earnestness, they still do not have a newborn heart by the Holy Ghost, and they do not want to be fools for Christ. If they do not want to be on Christ's side in everything, they are not on His side at all. For, as Christ clearly says, "Whoever is not with Me is against Me, and whoever does not gather with Me scatters."

Be Thou our Helper and our strong Defender;
Speak to our foes and cause them to surrender.
Yea, long before their plans have been completed,
They are defeated. Amen.

(TLH 269:3)

Monday

Read Luke 11:27–28

IF A PERSON IS TO BE RESCUED from the kingdom of the devil, three things are necessary. First, he must understand that he stands under the authority of darkness. Second, from his heart, he must be terrified by this and filled with an inner longing to be removed from this terrible and shameful power. Finally, Satan must give up the right to accuse him before God and the power to rule over him.

A person is no more able to rescue himself in this way than someone can awaken himself from death. The first hindrance is that, by his own mind, an individual is unable to recognize his true condition. Everyone, by nature, is completely blind in all spiritual things; no one can sense the natural enmity of his heart against God. Moreover, Satan deludes him into thinking that either there is no kingdom of the devil or that he is no part of it. The most deluded people are not those who manifest coarse unbelief and open sins, but those who are neutral, who do not openly reject Christ but fail to give Him their hearts completely.

A second hindrance is that because a person's heart, by nature, loves sin and the things of this world, he does not entirely wish to be rescued out of his disgraceful slavery, even loving the chains that bind him. A third hindrance is that a person does not forgive himself his sins, and he therefore cannot protect himself against the devil's accusation, cannot sever the cord by which Satan binds him in sin, and cannot change his heart. Thus, he cannot free himself from the dominion of Satan.

Where is deliverance to be found? By no creature, but only by Jesus Christ, the Son of God and the Redeemer of the world. Christ Himself says, "So if the Son sets you free, you will be free indeed" (John 8:36). Satan is strong, fully armed, and guards his palace with great power and considerable cunning. Nevertheless, Christ is, as He says, the stronger one, and when "He attacks him and overcomes him, He takes away his armor in which he trusted and divides his spoil" (Luke 11:22).

However, Christ compels no one by an irresistible grace, and He doesn't retrieve anyone from Satan's kingdom by outward power. Rather, He says, "Blessed rather are those who hear the word of God and keep it!" (Luke 11:28). This shows that the means He uses to rescue souls out of Satan's kingdom is the Word of God, for alone by this is the finger of God, the Holy Ghost, inseparably bound. A person must, then, hear and keep the Word of God. If a person does this, the Holy Ghost omnipotently pulls him with divine power out of the devil's cords. The Holy Ghost first convinces the person that until then he has stood under the authority of darkness. He then works in him a holy horror over it and a deep longing to be rescued from it. He allures him to faith in Jesus Christ, brings him to the forgiveness of his sins, and finally fills him with power to hate all of the devil's works, even the subtlest of sins. This allows him to break off obedience to the devil completely and eternally, to fight victoriously against him, and to walk with a new heart in a new life.

The Word of God is preached to many thousands who remain under the authority of darkness because they wantonly resist the Holy Ghost. However, there are always some who let themselves be rescued by the Word, like the woman in our text. When she heard all that Christ said, she was moved by the Holy Ghost and, full of divine courage in the midst of the furious, bloodthirsty enemies of Christ, she cried out, "Blessed is the womb that bore You, and the breasts which nursed You!" These words show how weak she still was in understanding. Therefore, Christ corrected her with the words, "Blessed are those who hear the Word of God and keep it!"

It is Thy work alone
That now I am converted,
Thy power o'er Satan's work
In me Thou hast asserted;
Thy mercy, that doth reach
Unto the clouds, O Lord,
Did break my stony heart
By Thine almighty Word. Amen.

(ELHB 344:3)

Tuesday

Read Psalm 90:11

THE MAIN REASON WHY nonbelievers reject the Old Testament is that God is often described therein as an angry God. These people say that any religion that attributes anger and wrath to God cannot possibly be the true religion, for God loves all people and certainly overlooks, as human weaknesses, the sins of His children. To suggest that God is not angry against sin is a terrible error. That so many hypocrites or nonbelievers who still consider themselves Christians hold this belief proves that they have fallen even farther than the heathen world had already sunk. For all heathens believed there is a God who is angry against sin, and they thus wanted to appease Him with certain sacrifices. Saint Paul says, "For the wrath of God is revealed from heaven against all ungodliness and unrighteousness of men, who by their unrighteousness suppress the truth [that is, their own natural better knowledge]" (Romans 1:18).

Nature writes in every human heart that God is angry against sin. As a result, all people feel uneasiness about an obviously evil deed, even when no one else knows it. Their own "conscience also bears witness, and their conflicting thoughts accuse or even excuse them" (Romans 2:15), testifies to them that their sin has angered an invisible Judge who is strong and zealous and who will either temporally or eternally punish them for it.

Why does death reign as the king of terrors in the world? It mercilessly takes the child from the cradle and from the mother's breast. It tears one spouse from the other and the father from his children. Death, from the beginning of time until this hour, ceaselessly stalks among humanity like an angel of vengeance, sparing neither the palace nor the hut, overlooking no one. This is another irrefutable proof that all people, by nature, are sinners and therefore children of death by God's righteous anger. Moses proclaims: "For we are brought to an end by Your anger; by Your wrath we are dismayed. . . . Who considers the power of Your anger, and Your wrath according to the fear of You?" (Psalm 90:7,11).

Another irrefutable proof is that the whole world is a vale of tears, full of trouble, misfortune, anxiety, and groans. No amount of intelligence and human effort has been able to change that. This shows us, once again, that the world has fallen away from its Creator, that it is a world of sin, that on account of its sins, it must already groan under God's holy wrath and punishment.

Do not even our histories reveal a God who is angry over sin and sits in judgment? What does the drowning of an entire human world, sunk in all sins and abominations, proclaim? What does the destruction of the bestial cities of Sodom and Gomorrah, still covered by the sulfur and salt floods of the Dead Sea, tell us? What does the terrible destruction of the murderous city of Jerusalem, prophesied by Christ forty years earlier, suggest? What does the destruction of all of the mighty states of antiquity, which always occurred after they had filled their measure of sin, indicate? O blind world! Everywhere—even into the deepest hell—God revealed His burning wrath against sin, but the world wants to know only of a God who only loves! A God who does not get angry also does not love, for only He who hates evil can love good. The all-loving God created by the unbelieving world is an empty image of an idol whose original is sinful man himself.

O Lord, my God, to Thee I pray:
Oh, cast me not in wrath away!

Let Thy good Spirit ne'er depart,
But let Him draw to Thee my heart
That truly penitent I be:
O God, be merciful to me! Amen.

† *(TLH 318:2)*

Wednesday

Read 1 John 2:15

MAN IS CREATED in such a way that he must love something. A person cannot go through the world indifferent. Inside of him, he carries the inextinguishable inclination, not only to know all sorts of things, but also to enjoy himself in something. The human heart cannot be empty of all love. If a person does not love God, he loves the world. If he does not love the Creator, he loves the creation. If he does not love the invisible, he loves the visible. If he does not love the heavenly, he loves the earthly. If he does not love the holy and pure, he loves the unholy and impure.

When man first came forth from the hand of God, the right, true, and holy love lived in his heart. He loved God above everything else, as the source of all goodness, joy, and blessedness. And he loved his fellow man, created like him, as a companion of his nature, as his second self. And in this holy love, man was happiest and most highly blessed. But when man fell into sin, a great, lamentable change took place. The love of God as the highest good and the love of his neighbor as himself ceased. Man retained his created heart with its longing, but he now filled his heart with another love: the love of the creature, of the perishable things of the world, even of sin itself.

As a person's bodily hunger always seeks to be satisfied, so too does love, the hunger of the soul. The prodigal son, who defiantly renounced the house of his wealthy father and the communion of his brother and ended up hungry in a foreign land, greedily devoured the food of the most disgusting animals. In the same way, a man who no longer loves God more than anything else, and who no longer loves his neighbor as himself, greedily devours even the food of the unclean spirits, sin. A heart that is empty of the love of God and of neighbor does not become completely empty. Just as a vessel that was once filled with the most expensive wine is now filled with only air when its sweet contents are gone, so too the heart of man, when it becomes empty of holy love, fills itself with the love of vanity and of emptiness.

All people born into the world are filled with this unholy love. Each person, by nature, has a heart that must love, a desire for happiness, and a longing for peace and quiet that he must satisfy. However, as long as God does not alter the heart of a person, that person does not seek his happiness in the love of God and his neighbor. Instead, one seeks it in riches, another in lust, and a third in glory.

Nevertheless, there is a small group of people in the world, known only by God, who have a heart that has been changed by God. The Epistle to the Hebrews describes them in this way: "These all died in faith, not having received the things promised, but having seen them and greeted them from afar, and having acknowledged that they were strangers and exiles on the earth" (11:13). Saint Paul sketches the following picture of them: "Those who have wives live as though they had none, and those who mourn as though they were not mourning, and those who rejoice as though they were not rejoicing, and those who buy as though they had no goods, and those who deal with the world as though they had no dealings with it. For the present form of this world is passing away" (1 Corinthians 7:29–31). Who, then, are they? They are the born-again children of God, the true Christians. They are in the world but not of the world. Their bodies are on earth, but their hearts are in heaven.

As long as Christians still live in this world, they are in great danger of losing the heavenly, holy sense of love God has planted in them. Therefore, they must always examine themselves to see if they still stand in such love, and they must always rouse themselves to it anew.

Thy light to every thought impart
And shed Thy love in every heart;
The weakness of our mortal state
With deathless might invigorate. Amen.

† *(TLH 233:4)*

Thursday

Read Ephesians 5:1–2

SAINT PAUL SAYS, "Therefore be imitators of God." But how does God love? Saint John expresses it simply: "God is love" (1 John 4:16). God does not just have and practice love; He is love itself. His whole being is love. He is a fire of love that is red-hot and blazing, both in heaven and on earth. He is a sea of love that is constantly flowing over everything. He has shown Himself, in particular, as an inexpressibly loving God of people. He loved us even before we existed. He loved us from eternity, and had already decided in eternity to pour all His sweet love over us. He created us, and when we fell into sin and became His enemies, He did not take away His love. Instead, He gave up His only-begotten Son to suffering, blood, and death on our behalf. He, the Son of eternal love, willingly gave Himself for us as an offering on the altar of the cross, gave Himself to God as a wholly acceptable sacrifice. By that sacrifice, God's righteousness, which had been offended by our sins, was appeased and we became acceptable in Him despite our sins.

This is the model of love Christians judge themselves by, the example of love they imitate, the heavenly original they strive to duplicate. Therefore, the apostle does not admonish us to have love or to practice love, but to "walk in love." By this, he means that the life of the Christian should be a constant love for God and for man. This holy love should fill and move his whole heart. It should be revealed in his speech, it should shine from his face, and it should be the motivation for all his works. God Himself, and the love of God, must dwell in the Christian.

This is a great demand that the holy apostle places upon Christians. But the underlying motive is just as urgent. Paul tells us to follow God "as beloved children." He recognizes that he cannot freely make this call to all people. For how could the poor man who still lies in the death of sin and vanity, who does not recognize God as the highest good, who wanders about like a blind man seeking his rest and peace in the things of this world, be a follower of God in love? If he hears the call to holy, divine love, he dismisses it as foolishness. Even if he wanted to soar to eternal love, his heart would pull him back to the ground. But Christians, through faith, experience the love by which God, from eternity, has loved as a father loves his children. By experiencing this love, they are begotten by God, participate in the divine nature, and become true children of the eternal, perfect love. They are obligated, as children of God, to love as their Father loves, and they receive from Him the holy, sweet power to love. Therefore, up! Arise! Walk now as dear children in love.

The children of God here below have still not been perfectly delivered out of the bonds of their natural corruption. The old, loveless heart often continues to stir in them bad thoughts, to cling to its love of the creature, and even to break out into loveless words and deeds. But all of this cannot rule the one who is a true child of God. When he succumbs to it, he at once falls on his face in the dust and asks, sighing and crying, for grace and forgiveness. God has no stillborn children. If someone is a true child of God, he is not only obligated to walk in holy love, he also has the desire and power and grace to do it.

Holy Spirit, all divine,
Dwell within this heart of mine;
Cast down every idol throne,
Reign supreme, and reign alone.
See, to Thee I yield my heart,
Shed Thy life through every part;
A pure temple I would be,
Wholly dedicate to Thee. Amen.

† *(TLH 234:5, 6)*

Friday

Read Ephesians 5:3–5

MOST PEOPLE SEEM TO THINK that the sins of uncleanness (fornication) and covetousness are not of much consequence. They may be improper, but they are not sinful, godless, and criminal. In these last troubled days, even most Christians seem to share this view. Sexual sins are in vogue everywhere, and they have ceased to be considered disgraceful. Instead, they are regarded as a very excusable weakness, and unchaste jokes are even looked upon as gallantry. As far as covetousness is concerned, if it doesn't reveal itself in dirty poverty, the world looks upon it not as a weakness but as a strength, as an enviable skill to make money. The miser who became rich by the sweat of the poor, or by all sorts of deceitful speculations and business dealings, is esteemed by the world. Everyone flatters him, hoping to get something from him.

Again, such blindness is hardly found only among those who do not know God's Word and do not want to become Christians. This weed, sown in the field of the church by the enemy, grows so luxuriantly there that even the faithful may almost lose heart. Even among those who regard themselves as Christians, there are many who live in various kinds of sexual sins and unchastity or in covetousness and unrighteousness, yet they still believe they have entered the kingdom of God. They think that if they show themselves as Christians in other respects, God will overlook the fact that they are not completely able to suppress that one passion. If they are living in covetousness, they do not recognize this but instead consider their behavior as "thrift" or "wise business." They recall that a

Christian is to be faithful in earthly things and industrious in his vocation to deflect any uneasiness that arises when they hear the preaching of God's Word.

But man is not his own judge. God is, and as we read in today's text, He has already judged in His Word: "For you may be sure of this, that everyone who is sexually immoral or impure, or who is covetous (that is, an idolater), has no inheritance in the kingdom of Christ and God." Fornication and all uncleanness, as well as covetousness, are not sins that are still to be found in a Christian, sins that he washes away with daily repentance, and for which he daily obtains forgiveness. These, rather, are sins by which a person has no share or inheritance, either here in Christ's kingdom of grace or there in God's kingdom of glory. The judgment has fallen and the condemnation comes: Whoever lives in these sins is an abomination before God. He stands under His wrath. He will not behold God, but will instead be cast out into the outermost darkness, where he will weep and gnash his teeth. Damnation will be the eternal lot of such a person, and his eternal dwelling will be hell. For Christ says, "Blessed are the merciful, for they shall receive mercy. Blessed are the pure in heart, for they shall see God" (Matthew 5:7–8).

Sinners may still comfort themselves with the thought that God will not be as severe and angry as He is portrayed in the preaching of the clergy. But God will one day prove that His threats were no joke but a terrible earnestness. When it is too late, then will faith come to the unchaste and to misers. Then they will cry over themselves and curse sin, which was once so sweet to them, as a hell. Let us all be frightened from the heart by all sins, but especially by the sins of fornication and covetousness. For the person whose conscience testifies that, until now, he has lived in one of these sins and continues in it, there is still time to escape the future wrath.

Destroy in me the lust of sin,
From all impureness make me clean.
Oh, grant me pow'r and strength, my God,
To strive against my flesh and blood! Amen.

(TLH 398:2)

Saturday

Read Ephesians 5:6–9

MANY WHO READ or hear these words wonder why grace exists if a person has to be very careful about sin. Didn't Christ fight for us? Why would Christ have fought for us if we must continue to fight so anxiously? Didn't Christ earn salvation for us? What would happen to His work if we also had to work out our salvation with fear and trembling? Hasn't Christ appeased God's wrath? What would become of His atonement if we still had to live in constant fear of His wrath? Who would and could then be saved?

Saint Paul tells us here that these are all empty words. They are void, absurd, and ungodly speech, speech that people, completely in vain, seek to excuse themselves. The sins Christians want to allow themselves are precisely those that cause the wrath of God to fall upon the children of unbelief. If these Christians now become partakers with them, God's wrath will also come upon them despite their imagined faith, and as they have loved with the world, they will be damned with the world.

Perhaps in no church more than ours is the blessed doctrine of reconciliation with God through Christ, God's endless love of sinners, and free grace so richly proclaimed. But there are many Christians who comfort themselves with God's grace, believing that it alone will ensure their salvation. They then proceed to live like the children of the world and unbelief, and to participate in their vanity. Each of them lives in secret service to some sin. Such unfortunate people think that because they pray, go to church, and partake of the Lord's Supper, they are faithful Christians who, for Christ's sake, still stand in grace before God. However, God's Word states that whoever lives in such prevailing sin is shut out from the kingdom of God and Christ. God's wrath, not His grace, rests upon him. In vain does such a person believe that his faith will still help him into heaven.

O foolishness! His faith is nothing but an empty thought, for no one can call Jesus Lord in true faith but by the Holy Ghost. However, the Holy Ghost does not live in any soul subjected to sin. If the wrath of God comes upon the children of unbelief because of their sins, how much more will it come upon those who boast of faith but disgrace God by those same sins! "For if they do these things when the wood is green, what will happen when it is dry?" (Luke 23:31). This truth about the wrath of God is not only an earnest warning for those who are or want to be believers. It is also an urgent admonition and encouragement, for Paul continues in our text, "For at one time you were darkness, but now you are light in the Lord. Walk as children of light (for the fruit of the light is found in all that is good and right and true)."

In these verses, the apostle clearly says that if a person wants to escape the wrath of God that comes upon the earth, it is his duty not to be a partaker of the sins of the world, but instead to walk and shine in this world as a child of the light in true holiness, in all kinds of goodness toward God, in righteousness toward his neighbor, and in truth and sincerity.

No one becomes just and holy before God by his sanctification. But whoever does not earnestly continue to seek a more perfect sanctification certainly falls back again under the complete power of some sin. Whoever does not fight anymore will be overcome; so, too, will the Christian. Like a light that does not burn anymore is the former child of the light who has become a child of darkness. The driving out of his good conscience has caused him to suffer a shipwreck in his faith.

O God, forsake me not!
Take not Thy Spirit from me
And suffer not the might
Of sin to overcome me.
Increase my feeble faith,
Which Thou Thyself hast wrought.
Be Thou my Strength and Pow'r—
O God, forsake me not! Amen.

(TLH 402:2)

Sunday

Read John 6:1–15

BEFORE CHRIST MIRACULOUSLY FED the people, "He began to teach them many things" (Mark 6:34) and He spoke about "the kingdom of God" (Luke 9:11).

Christ's sermon about His glorious kingdom seems to have made a deep impression on the people. They probably thought that the only reason He did not want to establish that kingdom immediately was because He feared He would have no subjects. They therefore wanted to use force to seize Christ, to declare themselves as His subjects, and to make Him their king. That this was foolish needs no proof, for Christ did not allow Himself to be seized by them, but quickly departed to a mountain. It is clear that the whole intention was a work and counsel of the flesh and thoroughly contrary to the sense of Christ.

All Christians certainly recognize this. However, most of them still commit the same foolishness displayed by the hearers of Christ in today's text. There, the foolishness began when they wanted to seize Christ and make Him their king. They were without repentance and without conversion, but they thought that by mere outward confession and clinging to Christ they became and were His subjects. How differently do most so-called Christians think and act now? They are baptized. They understand that Christ must really be the Savior of the world and confess this openly when they go to church and receive Holy Communion. By this, they think, they have made Christ their king and have become His subjects. But they, too, are deluded. Christ no more lets Himself be seized and made a king by people today than He did at the time of the incident described in our text.

The manner of entering into the kingdom of Christ is entirely different from that of entering into a kingdom of this world. A person enters into an earthly kingdom by coming to the place where the kingdom is situated. He is then recognized as a citizen of that kingdom when he swears the oath of citizenship, pays homage to the king, obeys the laws of the land, pays his tax, and perhaps, when necessary, joins the military and fights for the defense of the kingdom. The king and his officials do not inquire about the state of the heart of the person who does all of this.

It is completely different in the case of Christ's kingdom. This is an invisible, spiritual, heavenly kingdom, a kingdom of hearts and souls. It is everywhere. Therefore, a person can be everywhere in this kingdom and yet remain outside it. Wherever a person may find himself, he can enter into the kingdom of Christ. But wherever that person may go, he never passes through into this kingdom or comes closer to it. One does not enter into this kingdom by any outward means, but only by receiving a new heart. Everything external either does not belong in this kingdom or is only a means that should work the change of the heart by which a person is incorporated into this kingdom.

Moreover, a person does not come into this kingdom by any work. He may work earnestly for this kingdom, offer many gifts for it, fight for it, suffer and endure much for it, and even let himself be burned for it. But if he does not have that new, changed heart, he would be a tool, a worker, and a mercenary rather than a member, a subject, and a citizen of this kingdom. Wherever there are hearts in which the rule of sin has been replaced by the rule of Christ, in which He has truly placed His throne, and in which He directs and governs by His Spirit, there—and only there—is Christ's kingdom.

Therefore, the one who has not experienced this changed heart—or the one who has lost it—is no citizen of the kingdom of Christ. And whoever wants to be exactly like those who, in a foolish way, wanted to seize Christ and make Him their king are engaged in a vain effort.

When Jesus comes—O blessed story!—
He works a change in heart and life;
God's kingdom comes with pow'r and glory

To young and old, to man and wife;
Thro' Sacrament and living Word,
Faith, love, and hope are now conferred. Amen.

† *(TLH 65:4)*

Monday

Read John 6:26

ALTHOUGH CHRIST HAD ALREADY performed great miracles and signs—making the blind see, the lame walk, the deaf hear, the dumb speak, the lepers clean, and even the dead alive—the people had not yet, at those times, wanted to make Him king. But as soon as He had, a second time, fed thousands with a few loaves of bread and a few small fish, they were ready and eager to do it. Why? Without doubt, it was because they had concluded from this repeated miracle that Christ is a king in whose kingdom a person finds, without work, a table always set, freedom from all want and trial—in short, luxury and good days. Having witnessed this miracle, they quickly wanted to crown Christ king and to pay Him homage.

A true picture of most so-called Christians is sketched here. For how many baptized Christians are not truly earnest in things pertaining to salvation? God's Word says, "But seek first the kingdom of God and His righteousness, and all these things will be added to you" (Matthew 6:33), and "But if we have food and clothing, with these we will be content. But those who desire to be rich fall into temptation, into a snare, into many senseless and harmful desires that plunge people into ruin and destruction. For the love of money is a root of all kinds of evils. It is through this craving that some have wandered away from the faith and pierced themselves with many pangs" (1 Timothy 6:8–10). But if we look in this mirror of the Word of God at those who bear the name of Christian, what do we find? Do most of them really seek first the kingdom of God and His righteousness? Do they let themselves be content with food and clothing? Not at all! They want to be rich!

Christianity must serve many for that reason. What they save by not taking part in costly worldly pleasures, they do not give to God (that is, they do not give or lend it to the poor and suffering) or to the kingdom of God. Instead, in all quietness, they use it to enlarge their homes and to stockpile their wealth so they can always look more peacefully into the future and say to their gold nuggets, "My comfort!" They use it secretly for shameful usury, and they use it against the needy brother until he is poor. Others are satisfied only when they have enough bread and fish. A certain, carefree, and comfortable life is the heaven they seek. God's Word says, "Let not sin therefore reign in your mortal bodies, to make you obey their passions" (Romans 6:12), "Those who belong to Christ Jesus have crucified the flesh with its passions and desires" (Galatians 5:24), and "An athlete is not crowned unless he competes according to the rules" (2 Timothy 2:5).

What do most so-called Christians do? Are they grieved over their sins? Do they seek to recognize them more vividly and deeply? Do they fight against them? Despite their flesh, are they busy and diligent in watching, praying, and hearing and reading God's Word so as to sweep all sins from their hearts and lives and so to grow in sanctification? Not at all! Most think it is enthusiasm to torment themselves over sin; they regard it as pietism, Methodism, and a false legalism. Many also believe that because they have already repented and experienced the pain of sin, they are now, God be praised, rid of that.

What are all such people really seeking in the kingdom of Christ? Nothing except luxury and good days. They are like the Jews who wanted to make Christ king when He miraculously fed them. To them, Christ said, "Truly, truly, I say to you, you are seeking Me, not because you saw signs, but because you ate your fill of the loaves." How can we believe that such Christians are citizens of the kingdom of Christ? We cannot. Their whole Christianity is only appearance by which they only deceive themselves. They suppose that they still have the faith and must therefore be citizens of Christ's kingdom. However, they err, for it is written: "No one can serve two masters, for either he will hate the one and love the other, or he will be devoted to the one and despise the other. You cannot serve God and money" (Matthew 6:24). Also, it says, "So therefore, any one of you who does not renounce all that he has cannot be My disciple" (Luke 14:33).

The world seeks after wealth
And all that Mammon offers,
Yet never is content
Tho' gold should fill its coffers.
I have a higher good,
Content with it I'll be:
My Jesus is my Wealth—
What is the world to me! Amen.

✝ *(TLH 430:4)*

Tuesday

Read Galatians 4:26

What is the real church, the true mother of all Christians? According to Saint Paul, she is, first of all, "the Jerusalem above." Therefore, she is not of this world. She is not an earthly, bodily, visible kingdom, but an invisible, spiritual, heavenly one. She is not an institution perceptible to the senses, not a number of people who are bound by certain laws and customs. Instead, she is a kingdom of hearts that are bound by one understanding and one Spirit. What holds her together is unseen by the eyes of people. She is not a host of people who can be recognized by natural descent or by the country in which they reside. She is bound to no nation or city of the world. She is a congregation that is dispersed over the face of the entire earth, and she has members of every age and station among all people everywhere.

Furthermore, the apostle says, the Church is "free." There are no children of Hagar, no Ishmaels, none who by their human birth belong to her as servants of the Law. She is made up entirely of Sarah's children, of Isaac's, of pure children of the promise, namely those who are born again by the promise of grace as free children of God.

The true Church is thus the whole number of those who have sought and found their salvation, not on Sinai, but on Golgotha. They have chosen Christ rather than Moses to be their Mediator and Leader. They have desired to be saved, not by the works demanded by the Law, but by grace preached in the Gospel and offered to all people. They have clearly recognized themselves as poor, lost sinners. Hungry for grace, they have fled from the judgment seat of the just God to the seat of grace opened by Christ to all sinners. Although in themselves they are sinners, through faith they are God's saints and beloved in Christ. They need no longer slavishly fear before God. Instead, they can rely upon God as dear children rely upon their dear father. They can say with Paul: "What then shall we say to these things? If God is for us, who can be against us? He who did not spare His own Son but gave Him up for us all, how will he not also with Him graciously give us all things? Who shall bring any charge against God's elect? It is God who justifies. Who is to condemn? Christ Jesus is the one who died—more than that, who was raised—who is at the right hand of God, who indeed is interceding for us" (Romans 8:31–34). Yes, they can defy all enemies, before which the whole world trembles, ridiculing them, challenging them, and saying: "'O death, where is your victory? O death, where is your sting?' The sting of death is sin, and the power of sin is the Law. But thanks be to God, who gives us the victory through our Lord Jesus Christ" (1 Corinthians 15:55–57).

This is the true Church, which has received all of these glorious promises, authority, and power. The Lord speaks of its members when He says that not even the gates of hell can prevail against them. To them the Lord has given the keys to the kingdom of heaven. He has promised to be with them to the end of the world. He speaks of them when He says, "If he refuses to listen to them, tell it to the church. And if he refuses to listen even to the church, let him be to you as a Gentile and a tax collector" (Matthew 18:17). In the Song of Songs, Christ calls the church "virgins without number. My dove, my perfect one" (6:8–9). She is the true Noah's ark, in which all of the elect are saved. In short, she is, as the apostle says in our text, the mother of all believers.

Shine in our hearts, O most precious Light,
That we Jesus Christ may know aright,
Clinging to our Savior, whose blood hath bought us,
Who again to our homeland hath bro't us.
Lord, have mercy! Amen.

(TLH 231:2)

Wednesday

Read Galatians 4:29

ALTHOUGH ONE CANNOT SEE her or pick out her members, there are certain signs that identify the true Church. Saint Paul tells us that all members of the Church are children of the promise, that is, the Gospel. They were once servants of the Law but are now reborn as free children of God. God also says: "For as the rain and the snow come down from heaven and do not return there but water the earth, making it bring forth and sprout, giving seed to the sower and bread to the eater, so shall My word be that goes out from My mouth; it shall not return to Me empty, but it shall accomplish that which I purpose, and shall succeed in the thing for which I sent it" (Isaiah 55:10–11). We see from this that the Word of God, especially the Gospel, is the only seed from which the children of the promise, the Church, are born. Furthermore, whenever God sends His Word anywhere, it is never an unfruitful seed. Some are born through this Word, that is, they are brought to faith and are members of the Church.

One of the certain signs of the true Church is the preaching of the pure and clear Word of God with its seals, the holy Sacraments. And where this heavenly seed is sown, we can be certain that, according to the infallible promise of God, it will rise up in at least some hearts. As a result, there will be both weed and grain, sons of both Hagar and Sarah, both servants of the Law and children of the promise, true believers, right disciples, and members of Christ. Here is the true, invisible Church and here Christ Himself is present, along with the keys of the kingdom: grace, forgiveness of sins, righteousness, freedom, and an open heaven. Therefore, the seventh article of the unaltered Augsburg Confession very rightly says, "It is also taught that at all times a holy Christian church must be and remain, which is the assembly of all believers, in which the Gospel is purely preached and the holy Sacraments given according to the Gospel."

Thus, if a congregation finds itself with both of these, a pure Gospel and unadulterated Sacraments, the true Church certainly does not become visible, but she is still manifest. She is not tangible in any way, but she is recognizable. To be sure, not all members of the visible congregation are also members of the invisible true Church, but members of the invisible Church are certainly among them. Because of them, the entire congregation carries the name of Church, just as a field that also bears weeds is called a field on account of the grain. In the congregation, these children of God alone possess the power and authority given to the Church by Christ, and in His name alone they are practiced in the congregation.

The apostle gives us a sign by which the true Church is recognized when he writes, "But just as at that time he who was born according to the flesh persecuted Him who was born according to the Spirit, so also it is now." We see from this that the true Church will always bear the cross. As Ishmael, born of the maid Hagar, once persecuted Isaac, born of the free woman Sarah, so it is for all time. The false church persecutes and the true Church is persecuted. The false church walks along in glory and authority, and the true Church proceeds in disgrace and contempt. The true Church is thus also a suffering and fighting church. She is the rose of heaven among the thorns. She must go the same course on which her Lord, Jesus Christ, went before. The true Church is not recognized by outward glory, earthly well-being, and freedom from distress and affliction. Instead, she is recognized in the hate, persecution, and contempt of the world. Blessed, therefore, is the one to whom God has also given this mark.

Preserve Thy Word, O Savior,
To us this latter day
And let Thy kingdom flourish,
Enlarge Thy Church, we pray.
Oh, keep our faith from failing,
Keep hope's bright star aglow.
Let naught from Thy Word turn us
While wand'ring here below. Amen.

(TLH 264:1)

Thursday

Read Galatians 4:30

PEOPLE HAVE OFTEN THOUGHT the Church is nearing its end. The world sees so many religions that pretend to be based on divine revelation. These religions, however, have always won adherents only for a time. In the end, they have disappeared and made room for new religions. That is why the world believes this will also be the way with the Christian Church: "This one, too, had her heyday, but she too will finally collapse like a disintegrating building in the storm of time, and the temple of a more perfect religion will raise itself out of her ruins." Especially now, the enemies of the Church speak in such a way against her, as if the church were already lying as a rubbish heap at their feet.

The wretched fools! They do not want to believe Scripture, which clearly proclaims that the Lord will remain with His Church until the end of the world. History should have taught them that the church of Christ has something in her that no age can destroy, a germ of life that, even if one could bury the Church, would break through the stone of her grave and develop into a new fruit-bearing tree. Therefore, the world may even now delude itself in the sweet dream of having thrown down the building of the Church—but it is just a dream. All works of men, even if they tower ever so proudly into the clouds, must pass away with the age that produced them or fall by the hands that built them.

Christ's Church, however, is not a work of man. She rests upon an eternal foundation: Jesus Christ, God the Son. Whoever rebels against this foundation smashes himself to pieces. The foundation and the building resting upon it remain unmoved. Mankind is more likely to pull the stars down from the heavens, force the rivers of the earth to run backward to their source, hinder the sun from rising in the morning than cast Christ from the throne of His heavenly kingdom, dam up the course of His Word, and extinguish the light of the divine revelation. Heaven and earth will pass away, but Jesus' Word and Church will not pass away. The world will not bring an end to the Church, but the Church will bring an end to the world. When God permits the last member of His

Church to be born on the earth, then the last hour of the world will have struck. When God completes His Church, then He will show that this world was only a pilgrims' house for the members of His Church. Then God will demolish this pilgrims' house and lead His Church into a new earth with a new heaven where righteousness dwells.

Thus the apostle asks: "But what does the Scripture say? 'Cast out the slave woman and her son, for the son of the slave woman shall not inheirt with the son of the free woman.'" By this he points to the eternal goal of the Church. In the end, after the mocker Ishmael had caused much grief to Isaac, the legitimate son of the house, he and his slave mother were expelled from the house into the desert, with a bottle of water and a piece of bread, and the son of the free woman alone was the heir of the father. So will it be with the false churches and the true Church. And so it is: now Hagar's church of the servants of the Law and sin struts around gloriously. It boasts of itself, with its freedom and wisdom. It rules, and the true Church is subjected to it. It rejoices while the true Church laments and sighs. It moves in high glory, but the true Church lies in disgrace, shame, and contempt.

But patience! The Church on earth will suffer and fight insurmountably until the end. But she has a higher goal: to triumph eternally. The day is coming when it will finally be said about the whole church of Hagar: "Cast out the bondwoman and her son, for the son of the bondwoman shall not be heir with the son of the free woman." This will take place on the Last Day. Then all who have rejected Christ will be cast into the furthest darkness, without even Hagar's crumbs of bread and water bottle! In contrast, the Church of the promise will hear the Word of her King: "Come, you who are blessed by My Father, inherit the kingdom prepared for you from the foundation of the world" (Matthew 25:34).

Jesus, all Thy children cherish
And keep them that they never perish
Whom Thou hast purchased with Thy blood.
Let new life to us be given
That we may look to Thee in heaven
Whenever fearful is our mood.
Thy Spirit on us pour
That we may love Thee more—
Hearts o'erflowing;
And then will we
Be true to Thee
In death and life eternally. Amen.

† *(TLH 444:4)*

Friday

Read Revelation 21:1

A GLORIOUS DWELLING in another world is prepared for the church that sojourns and struggles in this world. She will enter that new world when she completes her pilgrimage in this land of trial. God did not wait until the last book of His revelation to uncover this truth. Adam and Eve, who were banished from Paradise because of their sin, received at the same time the promise of a Redeemer who would reopen the gates of paradise and allow them to enter a more beautiful, supernatural Eden. Scripture also says this about Abraham, the father of believers: "By faith he went to live in the land of promise, as in a foreign land. . . . For he was looking forward to the city that has foundations, whose designer and builder is God" (Hebrews 11:9–10). David calls this the land of the living; Solomon declares it to be the heaven of all heavens; and Isaiah describes it as the new heaven and the new earth.

Christ speaks about it even more clearly. He speaks about His Father's house and its many rooms He has prepared for His own. He speaks about eternal tabernacles into which they are received. He speaks about a paradise that the dying thief will enter with Him. He speaks about heavenly barns in which He gathers His grain, namely, the children of His kingdom. And He speaks and about a wedding hall into which He wants to lead the wise virgins. Saint Paul says, "For we know that if the tent, which is our earthly home, is destroyed, we have a building from God, a house not made with hands, eternal in the heavens" (2 Corinthians 5:1). Saint Peter says, "But according to His promise we are waiting for new heavens and a new earth in which righteousness dwells" (2 Peter 3:13). And in our text, Saint John says: "Then I saw a new heaven and a new earth, for the first heaven and the first earth had passed away, and the sea was no more."

This glorious view is revealed to all believers in Christ—His Church. As soon as Judgment Day ends, with the books of recompense closed and judgment made on all people, then the world with its air, the heavens with their stars, the earth with its mountains, and the sea with its waters will pass away and be no more. O blessed and double-blessed people who, here on earth, remained true in faith and were found to have been written in the Book of Life! While the things of this life will have passed away, these people will have lost nothing, for an indescribably more glorious dwelling has been prepared for them from the beginning of the world. Saint John says, "Then I saw a new heaven and a new earth."

Our present, visible world offers only a glimpse of that invisible world in which Christ's Church will one day rest from her struggles and celebrate her eternal triumph. Therefore, whatever in this earthly world is beautiful, sweet, and admirable will be found there by the saints, but the imperfections that now surround us will have been stripped away. As the firmament here surrounds us by day with its lovely blue sky and by night with its shining stars, so in heaven the saints will be surrounded by a heavenly light with unimaginable splendor. As our present earth spreads before us like a table set by God Himself, so in heaven the saints will walk in heavenly meadows full of inexhaustible springs of blessedness, full of trees of life that grow pure fruits of heavenly refreshment. What kind of sunshine that will be when God Himself will be the sun! What kind of stars will twinkle when millions of saints are illumined in starlight! What kind of morning dew will fall from the new heaven! What kind of flowers will bloom on the new earth! What a view will greet the glorified eyes of the saints when they gaze on the whole new creation with its eternal glories!

So I must hasten forward—
Thank God, the end will come!
This land of passing shadows
Is not my destined home.
The everlasting city,
Jerusalem above,
This evermore abideth,
The home of light and love.

There I shall dwell forever,
No more a parting guest,
With all Thy blood-bought children

In everlasting rest,
The pilgrim toils forgotten,
The pilgrim conflicts o'er,
All earthly griefs behind me,
Eternal joys before. Amen.

(TLH 586:5, 7)

Saturday

Read Revelation 21:3–4

IF GOD DID NOT DWELL with the saints in the New Jerusalem, they would not be blessed even in that beautiful heavenly city. This city, with its heavenly splendor and fountains of joy, would still be a lonely, bleak house of sorrow. But God will dwell with His saints like a dear father in the midst of his children, and this will make their condition perfectly blessed. There they will forever behold the triune God face-to-face, and He will never look at them with anger but only with eternal love. His face will never be covered by a cloud, as it so often is while we dwell here on earth. There, like a constant, shining sun of favor, grace, and kindness, He will shine over His saints. All servile fear will eternally vanish, and as children of the heavenly Father, all will call Him their sweet Abba.

Who can describe the glory of the condition of those who one day will be members of this holy, blessed family of God? The world has no colors for this painting for no eye has seen it and human language has no words to describe it for no ear has heard it. The human mind cannot even imagine what

God has prepared for those who love Him. Saint Paul, who was once taken up into this heavenly paradise, testifies that "he heard things that cannot be told, which man may not utter" (2 Corinthians 12:4). Even Saint John, as long as he lived in the dust, could not really describe to anyone what God had allowed him to see. He therefore related only what has passed away, adding God "will wipe away every tear from their eyes, and death shall be no more, neither shall there be mourning nor crying nor pain anymore, for the former things have passed away" (Revelation 21:4).

How blessed is the state of those who have finally gone home out of the vale of tears into the eternal house of the Father! Through death, they have entered into life, for there is no longer any death or sickness and their crying has ceased forever. There, no one is humbled by age; instead, there exists an eternal youth. No one groans on a sickbed. No one stands mourning at the coffin of a loved one since there is no longer any separation. Poverty, scarcity, and hunger are things of the past; all who dwell in God's house hold the key to His inexhaustible treasury. There, no icy winters and cold nights intrude; they are replaced by the eternal spring of heaven. What was low in the earthly world is now exalted to God's throne. In His heaven, all are priests, kings, and prophets. They are taught by God, clothed with priestly decoration, and crowned with the crown of the conqueror. All sighs and lamentations are silenced for the first things have passed away. Hallelujah!

Yes, there remaineth a still rest!
Arise, sad heart, that darkly pines,
By heavy care and pain opprest,
On whom no sun of gladness shines;
Look to the Lamb! In yon bright fields

Thou'lt know the joy His presence yields.
Cast off thy load and thither haste;
Soon shalt thou fight and bleed no more,
Soon, soon thy weary course be o'er,
And deep the rest thou then shalt taste.

(ELHB 566:1)

Come, O Christ, and loose the chains that bind us;
Lead us forth and cast this world behind us.
With Thee, th' Anointed,
Finds the soul its joy and rest appointed. Amen.

(TLH 589:6)

Sunday

Read John 8:47–59

"WHICH ONE OF YOU convicts Me of sin? If I tell the truth, why do you not believe Me?" (John 8:46). Here Jesus relates the reason why the Jews did not believe His Gospel. It was not because of a defect in that Gospel, since Jesus speaks the truth and no one could accuse Him of a sin. Jesus provides the true source of their unbelief: "Whoever is of God hears the words of God. The reason why you do not hear them is that you are not of God." He is saying that whoever has his mind on God accepts with joy the divine truth He preaches. Because the Jews did not have their minds on God, because they had an evil heart, and because they loved sin and darkness, they did not hear Christ's Word and therefore did not want to believe in Him.

If we want to identify the true source of unbelief, not only in the Jews but in all who reject the Bible and especially the Gospel of Christ, we need look no further than the corrupt heart of man. God has not given His Word so it can be understood and accepted only by those who are wise and highly educated. The key to receiving Christ's Gospel is a change in the corrupt heart. Whoever wants to accept that Gospel regards his own wisdom as foolishness and his own righteousness as a filthy garment. He gives God alone the glory in everything, and he becomes a fool before the world. Those who believe in the Gospel are poor in spirit and contrite of heart. They reject all their own light, all boasting of knowledge and culture, and all their own worthiness, glory, power, virtue, and good works. A thorough change is required not only in one's life and outward walk, but also in one's heart and mind with all their thoughts, desires, and powers. Above all, there must be humility, a virtue the world despises, which is of crucial importance in sanctification. The mind must be purified from everything earthly and vain, and the soul must be born again to a spiritual, divine, and heavenly inclination.

By nature, the heart of man dreads the kind of changes that the Gospel of Christ requires. The heart is disposed to love what it must hate when it accepts the Gospel, and that Gospel brings to shame those things in which the natural man takes pride. If unbelievers could conquer their pride, if they could rip the love of the worldly out of their hearts, and if they could depart from sin, all of their doubts regarding the divinity of the Bible and especially the Gospel would disappear.

Jesus says to the unbelieving Jews: "It is My Father who glorifies Me, of whom you say, 'He is our God.' But you have not known Him." He tells them they are completely blind.

They speak much of God as their Father, but they do not know Him, and that is why they do not want to believe in the Son of the Father. This, then, is the second reason for unbelief: the natural blindness of all people.

Christ's Gospel is such that it cannot be understood by the natural man; instead, it appears as foolishness to him. If he is to believe, God must enlighten him. He must expose to man the misery of his sin. He must make known to him that all human righteousness and respectability are worthless before God. God must, by this, show man how desperately he needs a Savior. His sins have offended and angered his heavenly Father, and on his own he cannot reconcile himself to God and so save himself.

If a person is to be cured of the blindness of his sinful heart, God's light must reveal to him that he is both erring and lost. When the light does this, the greatest hindrance to spiritual sight has fallen. Those in whom this light shines find the Gospel so full of wisdom, comfort, power, and salvation—so sublime and yet so perfectly suited to them—that all doubts vanish. Such people then fall as shamed sinners at Christ's feet, and like Thomas, they cry out with bitter tears of repentance, "My Lord and my God!" (John 20:28).

Wisdom's highest, noblest treasure,
Jesus, lies concealed in Thee;
Grant that this may still the measure
Of my will and actions be,
Humility there and simplicity reigning,
In paths of true wisdom my steps ever training,
Oh, if I of Christ have this knowledge divine,
The fulness of heavenly wisdom is mine. Amen.

(TLH 366:5)

Monday

Read Mark 3:28–29

THERE IS ONE SIN that cannot be forgiven, either in this world or in the next, either by God or by man. It is the sin against the Holy Spirit. Repentance and conversion are impossible for one who has committed this sin. Although this person still lives on earth, the time of grace has expired, and every door of grace is closed to him. God no longer calls him, enlightens him, chastises him, or has mercy on him. God has given him up to his wrong mind, and he is already cursed for eternity and irretrievably lost.

Those who commit this sin are seldom frightened about it. On the other hand, many who are far from sinning in this way torment themselves thinking that they have done so. It is therefore vital that every Christian know precisely what sin against the Holy Spirit is. Some suppose it is persistent impenitence until death. Others think it is each denial of the truth and each wanton sin committed after conversion. Still others believe it has to do with swearing an oath either falsely or to the devil. Christians who have fallen or who are repeatedly attacked by the devil sometimes experience all kinds of terrible thoughts. They cannot rid themselves of these thoughts despite their sighs, prayers, and battles against them. These thoughts accompany and persecute them everywhere, even to the altar of the Lord. Such Christians usually think they have committed the sin against the Holy Spirit. Indeed, many Christians who experienced the sweetest movements of the Holy Spirit immediately after their conversion later find that these impulses have ceased and then think they have fallen into that unforgivable sin.

But who, according to the Word of God, is guilty of that terrible sin against the Holy Spirit? It is not those who, out of ignorance and blindness, blaspheme the divine doctrine, like Saul. It is not those who, fearing death, deny the faith in the anguish of their soul, like Peter. It is not those who, after their conversion, are overcome by the desires of the flesh and fall into sin and disgrace, like David. It is not even those who, out of the blindness of their heart, commit all kinds of abominations, like Manasseh. All of these have come to the grace and forgiveness of their sins. Nor are the offenders those precious souls into whose heart Satan fires his blasphemies that sting like fiery darts, who still long from their heart to be rid of the spiritual misery in which they languish.

No, those who sin against the Holy Spirit are the ones whose hearts have been convinced by Him of the divine truth yet reject that truth out of their hatred of God. They are driven, by an impenitent, satanic evil, to blaspheme the truth as lies. God surrenders such people to the judgment of the obdurate. They no longer have another sacrifice for sin, but instead they await the fire that will consume God's opponents. Even Christ, the High Priest and Intercessor of all sinners, no longer prays for them. The Holy Spirit no longer works in them. Their names are removed from the list of those who can still find grace. Their sin cannot be forgiven in this world or in the world to come, and they will be condemned in the eternal judgment.

Then on Him I cast my burden,
Sink it in the depths below.
Let me know Thy gracious pardon,
Wash me, make me white as snow.
Let Thy Spirit leave me never;
Make me only Thine forever. Amen.

† *(TLH 326:4)*

Tuesday

Read John 6:67–68

PETER SAYS: "Our hearts long for truth and peace. We have found both with You. If we wanted to forsake You now, where should we go? We could go to the schools of the Pharisees, but they could not remove our present burden; indeed, they would only burden us with new laws. We could go to the sect of the Sadducees, but they have already given up trying to find the truth for which we long, and they are seeking in the pleasures of this world the rest that nothing temporal or earthly can grant us. Or we could go to the wisdom of the heathens, who in their search for truth may deride the many gods and superstitions of their people, but their altars are inscribed, 'To the unknown god.' Nowhere do we find what we need except with You. Therefore, we want to remain with You, for You have the words of eternal life."

On that day, so many wanted to desert Him who said, "I am the way, and the truth, and the life. No one comes to the Father except through Me" (John 14:6). The holy apostles, though, did not fall into this temptation nor were they led to doubt the divinity of Christ's Word. What about us, who live at a time when so many deny the divinity of the Holy Scriptures? If the Lord lays before us the question, "Do you want to go away as well?" we must answer with Peter, "Lord, to whom shall we go? You have the words of eternal life."

We, too, are in need of truth and peace. Without them, we would be the most miserable of creatures. Without truth and peace, no kingdom, no glory, no earthly desire can make us happy. God, who gave us a soul that cannot be happy and blessed without truth and peace, must also have provided us with the means of finding both. Where shall we now go to find them? Should we return to the heathen religions and philosophies? No! Even in the first century, they could not provide the apostles with what they were seeking. Should we turn to the Mohammedan religion, which arose later? No! What Muslims have of the truth they have taken from our Bible. Everything else is heathen and obvious delusion. Or should we consult the philosophers of our day? Woe to us, in that case! They know about God and know man must be just before Him, but they know nothing of reconciliation with God. Their philosophies are idle speculations that show man the goal and advise him, "Help yourself!" But they cannot provide the power to attain that goal. They are wells without water where the thirsty languish without comfort and help.

Away with all the deceptions of the wisdom of this world! The Bible alone has "words of eternal life," and this is what we are seeking. It shows us reconciliation with God through Christ. It shows us the way the sinner can be justified and saved. And by this, it gives us the power to walk here on earth, in a new, holy, and blessed life.

Thus my longings, heav'nward tending,
Jesus, rest alone on Thee.
Help me, thus on Thee depending;
Savior, come and dwell in me.
Although all the world should forsake and forget Thee,
In love I will follow Thee, ne'er will I quit Thee.
Lord Jesus, both spirit and life is Thy Word;
And is there a joy which Thou dost not afford?
Amen.

(*TLH 366:4*)

Wednesday

Read John 7:17

THERE ARE MANY STRONG, undeniable proofs from reason for the divinity of the Holy Scriptures. Nevertheless, although a person can know these proofs, he can still be easily thrown into grave doubt by subtle opposing arguments, and even by insolent mockeries and blasphemous talk. If there were no certain means of attaining a firm faith in the divinity of the Bible, we would be in a dismal state. But God Himself has provided that means, and Christ reveals it to us with the words of our text: "If anyone's will is to do God's will, he will know whether the teaching is from God or whether I am speaking on My own authority."

The certain means is by experience, learning in the heart that Christ's Word is not man's word but God's Word. If a person is only told that a certain food or drink is delicious, he can still be dissuaded from believing it. But if he partakes of that food or drink and experiences the pleasing taste himself, will he then let himself be talked out of sampling it again? Certainly not! No matter how many opinions are voiced against it, he will not listen. It is the same way with the Bible. As long as a person is convinced of its divinity solely by proofs of reason, other proofs of reason can cause him to waver in his conviction. But when he experiences the Bible in his heart, he learns its divine enlightening, divine comforting, and divine sanctifying power. No other book has these qualities, and once they are experienced, the believer can reply to all opposing arguments, "Say what you want. I have experienced—and still experience daily—the Bible as God's Word. As it is written with living letters in my heart, 'There is one

God,' so also the Holy Ghost has written in it, 'And the Bible is His holy Word.' You can rip the heart out of my body before you rip this faith out of my heart!"

How is it that a man such as David could so firmly adhere to God's Word until his death? It was because he could say: "If Your law had not been my delight, I would have perished in my affliction. . . . How sweet are Your words to my taste, sweeter than honey to my mouth!" (Psalm 119:92,103). The Word of God had been like a sweet, heavenly honey to him. How could the holy apostles have held so unshakably fast to Christ's doctrine before the whole world's wisdom and threatening power? It was because all of them could say with Peter, "Lord, to whom shall we go? You have the words of eternal life, and we have believed, and have come to know, that You are the Holy One of God" (John 6:68–69). They had experienced the power of Christ's doctrine in their very souls, rather than just understood it with their minds. Finally, how is it that all true Christians have not allowed their faith in the holy Bible to waver? It is because they "have tasted the goodness of the word of God" and the "powers of the age to come" (Hebrews 6:5) that lie in it. It is because the Holy Ghost testifies in them that the "Spirit is truth," that is, that the Word of the Bible, this Word of the Spirit, is the truth from God.

Give to Thy Word impressive pow'r
That in our hearts, from this good hour,
As fire it may be glowing;
That we confess the Father, Son,
And Thee, the Spirit, Three in One,
Thy glory ever showing.
Stay Thou, Guide now
Our souls ever That they never

May forsake Thee,
But by faith their Refuge make Thee. Amen.

(TLH 235:2)

Thursday

Read John 5:39

HOLY SCRIPTURE DECLARES often and clearly that God not only permits—He commands—that whoever can read must read the Bible. In our text, Christ instructs us to "search the Scriptures." The command is so clear that there is no possibility of misunderstanding. And to whom does He address this unambiguous command? Are they the so-called spiritual ones: the high priests, priests, and Levites? Or are they only the learned: the scribes, the elders of the people, the leaders of the Pharisees, and the like? No. In what precedes our text, we learn that Christ addressed the "Jews," that is, the entire people who surrounded Him. Christ demands not only that they read Scripture but also that they search it, that they closely investigate it and seek to learn it with diligence and zeal. According to Christ's command, all people, even the laity, are to read the Bible.

Do the prophets and the apostles declare something different? Not at all! Beginning with Moses, the prophets of every age allowed the whole of Scripture to be read to the whole people—men, women, and children. In their writings, they repeatedly and solemnly demanded that the whole world be hearers and readers of their Word. Isaiah writes: "Hear, O heavens, and give ear, O earth; for the LORD has spoken" (1:2). He thus insists that all people everywhere, Jews and Gentiles, hear what he has written. He continues: "Seek and read from the book of the LORD: Not one of these shall be missing; none shall be without her mate. For the mouth of the LORD has commanded, and His Spirit has gathered them" (34:16).

What do the apostles say? First, they directed almost all of their letters either to individual laymen or to congregations. But there can be no doubt that these writings were intended for all to read, as John confirms: "I am writing to you, fathers, because you know Him who is from the beginning. I am writing to you, young men, because you have overcome the evil one. I write to you, children, because you know the Father" (1 John 2:13). Paul concludes his First Letter to the Thessalonians with the earnest words, "I put you under oath before the Lord to have this letter read to all the brothers" (5:27), and at the end of his letter to the Colossians, he says, "And when this letter has been read among you, have it also read in the church of the Laodiceans; and see that you also read the letter from Laodicea" (4:16), that is, the Epistle to the Ephesians.

If there is any book that a person, following his natural understanding, would think should not be read by everyone because it is very hard to understand, it is certainly the Revelation of Saint John. But what does it say at the beginning of this book? Does it carry some sort of warning against many reading it? Not at all: "Blessed is the one who reads aloud the words of this prophecy, and blessed are those who hear, and who keep what is written in it, for the time is near" (1:3).

Whenever the apostles are commanded to preach the Gospel to all people, the people are commanded to receive and hear the apostles (that is, to read the Bible). They are thus instructed to base their faith, not on man's testimony, but on the Scriptures, and to fight with the sword of the Spirit. They are also commanded to examine and judge all teachers according to God's Word and not to let themselves be seduced by false prophets. Therefore, all who are enticed away are declared to be without excuse because they have the Scriptures. Indeed, whenever Scripture commands that all people read the Bible, they are then called upon to convert to the Lord and to care for the salvation of their soul. Scripture thus shows us the way to salvation.

A trusty weapon is Thy Word,
Thy Church's buckler, shield, and sword;
Lord, let us in this Word abide,
That we may seek no other guide. Amen.

(ELHB 110:8)

Friday

Read Hebrews 9:11–12

IN OUR TEXT, Christ is compared with the high priests of the Old Testament, and it shows that He is infinitely superior to them. It says, first, that "Christ appeared as High Priest." The high priests of the Old Testament were selected by men, consecrated to their office by men, and anointed with oil. But Christ is a different high priest. He did not attain this position on earth by the acclamation of men; instead, He came to earth to serve in this role. God Himself in eternity selected and anointed Christ as High Priest. He was born as our High Priest, in other words, as soon as He entered the world, He was already in that office.

The apostolic writer of the Book of Hebrews calls Christ "High Priest of the good things that have come." Here we are told a second way that Christ is superior to the high priests of the Old Testament. By their office, their sacrifices, and their sprinklings, they could declare that a person who had previously been regarded as impure should now be considered pure, and that one who had been excluded from the outward community of Israel should be reinstated. But Christ is an entirely different high priest. He has nothing to do with such temporal rights. By His office, He gains for us eternal, heavenly, and imperishable things. He is concerned with purity before God rather than men and with the inner rather than outward spiritual communion with the elect people of God. He bestows grace, forgiveness of sins, righteousness, the Holy Ghost, the peace of God, and, one day, eternal life.

The words "with the greater and more perfect tent not made with hands" points out another distinction between Christ and the high priests of the Old Testament. The latter carried out their office in the tabernacle and, later, in the temple in Jerusalem, both of which were built according to the plans God revealed to Moses on Sinai. But the setting in which Christ performs His office is much more glorious. Christ's tabernacle is His Church on earth, an invisible temple, a spiritual house, a kingdom of heaven and of God, and grace on earth. As High Priest, Christ directs a tabernacle that is "greater" than that of the Old Testament because it is spread all over the world and contains both Jews and believing Gentiles. The tabernacle of Christ is "more perfect" than that of the Old Testament because it is made up, not of gold, silk, wood, mortar, and stone, but of believers who, through faith, are holy people. Unlike the tabernacle of the Old Testament, Christ's tabernacle is "not made with hands"; it is raised up through the Holy Ghost by means of the Word and the Holy Sacraments.

The fourth way in which Christ's high priesthood is superior to that of the Old Testament is revealed with the words "[H]e entered once for all into the holy places, not by means of the blood of goats and calves but by means of His own blood, thus securing eternal redemption." When the high priests of the Old Testament entered the Most Holy Place, they carried with them the blood of mere animals, which in itself could not truly cleanse, reconcile with God, and redeem anyone. But Christ is a different high priest. With His own blood, He entered from the forecourt of His kingdom of grace in this world into the Most Holy Place of heaven and He appeared before God.

The high priests of the Old Testament were similar to Christ, but only as pictures and shadows. As the reality is incomparably more glorious than its pictures or shadows, so is Christ the High Priest incomparably more glorious than the Old Testament high priests.

Where should else my hopes be centered?
Grace o'erwhelms me with its flood;
Thou, my Savior, once hast entered
Holiest heaven through Thy blood.
Eternal redemption for sinners there finding,
From hell's dark dominion my spirit unbinding,
To me perfect freedom Thy entrance has brought,
And childlike to cry "Abba, Father," I'm taught.
Amen.

(ELHB 83:8)

Saturday

Read Hebrews 9:13–15

IS CHRIST THE TRUE High Priest for all sinners? The holy writer answers this question with a decisive "yes." He maintains that "He entered once for all into the holy places," that is, heaven, and, "by means of His own blood, thus secure[ed] an eternal redemption." The proof of this follows: "For if the blood of goats and bulls, and the ashes of a heifer sanctifies for the purification of the flesh, how much more will the blood of Christ, who through the eternal Spirit offered Himself without spot to God, purify our conscience from dead works to serve the living God?"

This argument is clearly directed toward believing Jews. The Jews readily admitted that a person who had outwardly defiled himself (by touching the dead or some other means) and was considered unclean according to the Mosaic Law was again made holy and clean through the blood of animals shed by the Old Testament high priests at sacrifices. But how should the blood of Christ not have much greater power? Wasn't Christ an innocent, pure, unblemished Lamb of God? Yes, but isn't it of infinitely greater worth that Christ is the Son of the eternal, almighty, most holy God Himself? What power must this have, that He sacrificed Himself for people, shedding His God-blood for their sins? Truly, whoever participates in this sacrifice will be purified, not only in the body, as in the Old Testament, but also in his soul from all his sins.

What about those who had already died in the time of the Old Testament, before Christ's sacrificial death occurred? Did they remain defiled by their sins? The apostle says, "Therefore He is the mediator of a new covenant, so that those who are called may receive the promised eternal inheritance, since a death has occured that redeems them from the transgressions under the first covenant." The old covenant of the Law afforded no forgiveness of sins, but even in the Old Testament a new covenant of grace was promised that the believers of that time waited and hoped for. So that this grace and forgiveness could be attained, Christ became both the true High Priest and, by His sacrificial death, also a Mediator of the promised new covenant of grace. Therefore, the Old Testament believers may not have found forgiveness, reconciliation, redemption, and peace of conscience in the Law or in the sacrifices of their high priests. But they did find all these in the New Testament that was promised them, that they faithfully hoped for, and that has finally been brought about by Christ. In their faith, they, too, attained all the fruits of His coming and His true sacrifice of atonement.

Whatever kind of sinner a person may be, he finds what he needs in Christ the true High Priest, who obtained an eternal redemption. Therefore, regardless of the time or place in which he lives, or the magnitude and duration of his sin, if Christ has become his High Priest, he has obtained an eternal redemption.

Not all the blood of beasts
On Jewish altars slain
Could give the guilty conscience peace
Or wash away the stain.

But Christ, the heav'nly Lamb,
Takes all our sins away;
A sacrifice of nobler name
And richer blood than they. Amen.

† *(TLH 156:1, 2)*

Sunday

Read 1 Peter 3:21

IF HOLY BAPTISM were something we do, then those who ask, "What use is a few handfuls of water to a person?" would have good reason to raise the question. Why is it a great help to someone to observe such a ritual? How can a person be allowed to place his trust in such a poor work that even the most godless can perform? However, Baptism is not a work a person does, but one God performs. It may always appear to be something very insignificant, but it is so great and full of grace that no human tongue can stop speaking about it. God gave up His only-begotten Son for the whole world and through Him reconciled all sinners to Himself, removed condemnation from them, gained for them eternal righteousness and salvation, and thus reopened heaven to them.

Holy Baptism is the means through which God offers, dedicates, and seals all that Christ acquired for people. It is the door through which a person enters the kingdom of grace. For this reason, Peter calls Baptism the covenant "of a good conscience." In this covenant of grace, God promises to give man the fruits of what Christ suffered for him: forgiving him his sins and receiving him as a child and heir of eternal life. Thus, in Baptism, a person receives a good conscience. He is then released from the servile fear of God and receives the Spirit of adoption so he can stand before God in childlike confidence and address Him as "Abba, dear Father!"

Peter expressly identifies in our text the blessed power that Holy Baptism really has: "Baptism . . . now saves you." But how are we supposed to believe that the grace offered, given, and sealed to us in Holy Baptism still applies to us poor, miserable sinners who have not kept what we promised God? Although we break the covenant we made with God in Baptism, God does not break His covenant with us. On His side, He stands firm. He will keep what He once promised. He is and remains faithful, even when we become unfaithful. May we not be sorry for God's gifts and calling. For this reason, the prophet Isaiah says, "'For the mountains may depart and the hills be removed, but My steadfast love shall not depart from you, and My covenant of peace shall not be removed,' says the LORD, who has compassion on you" (54:10).

Let us, then, confess with confident hearts, "The Lord has done great things for us, therefore we rejoice." We are baptized! Oh, inexpressible grace! God has thrown all our sins into the depths of the sea. Here God assures us that we should have a part in the redemption that was brought about by His Son. He assures us that He loved us from eternity and elected us to salvation before the foundation of the world was laid. He assures us that He is our Father and we are His children. In Baptism, God opened heaven to us and its door remains eternally open to us. Even if we are full of sins, our Baptism washes us clean. Even if the cloak of our own righteousness is a shredded, filthy garment, in our Baptism we are clothed with Christ in His holiness, righteousness, and innocence. Even if we easily stumble and fall, our Baptism stands firm for us. There, God began a good work in us, a work He promises to bring to completion. Oh, it is well with us! God Himself has made a covenant of grace with us. No world, no sin, no devil, no hell can annul our salvation. As soon as we, awakened by Him, come to Him in faith, He must accept us. When, in our hour of death, we remind God of His covenant, He cannot reject us. He will keep His covenant and take us up into His heavenly kingdom.

My faithful God, Thou failest never,
Thy cov'nant surely will abide;
Oh, cast me not away forever
Should I transgress it on my side!
Tho' I have oft my soul defiled,
Do Thou forgive, restore, Thy child. Amen.

† *(TLH 298:4)*

Monday

Read 1 Corinthians 11:23–25

WHEN CHRIST SAYS, "Do this in remembrance of Me," He demands that His guests use His Supper with holy devotion of the heart. This devotion is in His "remembrance." This does not mean they should vividly place before their soul the suffering of Christ in all its details that they might be moved to tears in sympathy. Instead, Christ's person is to be the focus of all their devotion, thoughts, and feelings at the use of His holy body and blood. Therefore, a right Communion guest is one who not only regards Christ's doctrine as true but also clings to Christ as the truth in person. He must be both a friend of Christ's doctrine and a personal friend of Christ Himself, one who stands with Him in a constant secret communication. While his body hurries to the Lord's table, his spirit is on Golgotha, kneeling there before Christ's cross, clasping His pale feet, and drinking there His blood streaming out of the five wounds.

Is it not strange that the humble Savior, who says of

Himself, "I do not seek My own glory" (John 8:50), nevertheless demands, at the institution of His holy Supper, "Do this in remembrance of Me"? Was this because Jesus would have to die a disgraceful death so His name would live on among people after His death? No, it is not for His sake but for that of His Supper guests that Christ places the demand "Do this in remembrance of Me." He says, "Take, eat; this is My body," and "Drink of it, all of you. For this is My blood of the covenant [testament], which is poured out for many for the forgiveness of sins" (Matthew 26:26–28). To these statements, He adds, "Do this in remembrance of Me."

Here Jesus says: "When you eat My body and drink My blood, you should not think about yourselves or your works, but you should concentrate on Me and My works—not on Me as I will come on the Last Day as a strict judge on the clouds of heaven, but as I hung on the cross as your Redeemer and Savior. Think of Me as I suffered there and shed My blood, not for Me or as a martyr for My doctrine, but for you, for the forgiveness of your sins."

A communicant honors Christ's demand, "Do this in remembrance of Me," when, at the reception of His body and blood, he not only recalls Christ's suffering but also thinks in his heart: "Oh, this is the body that was given into death for me! Oh, this is the blood that was shed for me! Oh, how blessed I am! Now I do not have to fear my sins, God's wrath, death, or hell. For now I have the precious, fully valid ransom by which Christ paid the debt of the whole world of sinners—even my debt. In that sacrificial act, He reconciled me to God and earned for me grace, forgiveness of sins, righteousness, life, and salvation. All doubts about my state of grace and my salvation are now removed!"

Receiving Christ's body and blood in remembrance of Him, then, means they are consumed both with the mouth and spiritually. In a word, they are eaten in faith.

For Thy consoling Supper, Lord,
Be praised throughout all ages!
Preserve it, for in every place
The world against it rages.
Grant that this Sacrament may be
A blessed comfort unto me
When living and when dying. Amen.

(TLH 306:8)

Tuesday

Read 1 Corinthians 11:26

THE APOSTLE PAUL demands that all communicants "proclaim" the Lord's death at their use of the Supper. Although they celebrate it, above all, for their own sake, they also celebrate it for the sake of their neighbor and the world, thereby preaching and extolling to them all the atoning death of the Lord. The altar on which the holy Supper is celebrated should also be the pulpit of the laity where they, as true spiritual priests, proclaim the virtues of Him who called them from the darkness into His wonderful light. The preacher proclaims the crucified Christ in his sermon from the pulpit, and when that sermon has ended, the believing congregation gathers at the altar to proclaim Him as well. By this, they demonstrate that they are part of the Church of Christ. If Christ had instituted only the office of preaching and not the holy Sacraments as well, no one would know where the Church or the congregation of believers is to be found. Many who do not want to be Christians, to whom the crucified Christ is foolishness, also hear the sermon. By their celebration of the Supper, those who have come to faith in Christ and have been baptized appear at the altar of the Lord to testify that they are still mindful of their covenant and that they remain His faithful disciples.

But our text also makes another demand. Saint Paul declares that our use of the holy Supper is a common confession of faith. Therefore, we should celebrate only with those who confess the same faith with us. If the Supper had been instituted for the sole purpose of eating the true body of Christ and drinking His true blood, we could then celebrate it wherever it is rightly carried out according to Christ's command. But Paul says that, by this act, we "proclaim the Lord's death," that is, we confess the faith. Thus it would be against Christ's will for us to celebrate the Supper where our confession of faith is contradicted.

Wherever it is celebrated, the holy Supper is the congregation's banner of faith. Just as a person enlists on the side of the army whose flag he supports, so also each Christian places himself on the side of the congregation in whose midst he eats the Supper. If that congregation confesses the true faith, the communicant, by his appearance at the altar, confesses the same faith with it. But if the congregation confesses a false faith, the communicant, by his participation in its celebration of the Lord's Supper, also confesses the false faith and thus denies the true faith. Therefore, whenever we approach the altar, let us appear before the world as confessors of the crucified Christ and as true spiritual priests of Him who called us from darkness to His wonderful light. Let us not gather around this banner of faith in the false church, but rather assemble where the true Christ and His whole, pure, and genuine Gospel is confessed and preached.

O Jesus, blessed Lord, to Thee
My heartfelt thanks forever be,
Who has so lovingly bestowed
On me Thy body and Thy blood.

Break forth, my soul, for joy and say:
What wealth is come to me this day!
My Savior dwells within my heart:
How blest am I! How good Thou art! Amen.

† *(TLH 309)*

Wednesday

Read Luke 22:19–20

THE MYSTERY OF THE LORD'S SUPPER does not consist in the body and blood of Christ working like a bodily medicine that makes a person healthy when taken. Many also imagine that Christ's body and blood mix with our body and blood, sanctifying us like a choice graft that ennobles a wild tree and planting in us the germ of the resurrection, so that, by itself, it makes us immortal and heavenly. No, the meaning of this mystery is something entirely different. When the Savior says, "Take and eat, this is My body which is given for you; this is My blood, which is shed for you," He shows that although we bodily eat the heavenly food and drink of His divine body and blood, we do this so our soul and our faith, not our body, may be fed and strengthened. Receiving the body and blood of Christ should thus make us participants in His Spirit, for as

Paul writes, in the holy Supper, we "all were made to drink of one Spirit" (1 Corinthians 12:13). When Christ says, "which is given for you" and "which is shed for you," He tells us that the most important thing about His Supper is not the presence of His body and blood, but the fact that it is the body that was given into death for us and the blood that was shed for us. The phrase "for you" is therefore the key to the mystery of grace embedded in the Lord's Supper.

Through the words "given for you" and "shed for you," Christ demonstrates that the use of this Sacrament depends not on eating and drinking with the mouth but on our recognizing and believing that the body and blood we have received were given and shed for us. The words "for you" call upon us to apply Christ's sacrificial death to ourselves in firm faith. Therefore, it says in our Small Catechism: "It is not the eating and drinking indeed that does them, but the words here written, 'Given and shed for you for the remission of sins.' For the words 'for you' require all hearts to believe." These words demand our faith and strengthen it as gloriously as anything contained in the Old and New Testaments. It is not difficult for the Christian to believe that the world has been reconciled with God, redeemed, and saved through Christ's sacrifice on the cross. This is clearly written in the Scriptures. But it is very difficult for the Christian to believe that this reconciliation, this redemption, and this salvation apply to him individually, for he does not find his own name in the Scriptures (and indeed, many people who are redeemed are not saved). If a Christian feels no working of the Holy Spirit's grace in him, but feels instead the movements of sin and the powerful threats of the Law in his heart, it is exceedingly difficult for him to believe he is reconciled, redeemed, and saved by Christ. In addition, he finds it almost impossible to comfort himself against sin, Law, death, judgment, God's wrath, Satan, and hell.

What more powerful, comforting, and glorious means can there be to make such a doubting Christian certain than when Christ's body and blood are given to him with the assurance that he should take, eat, and drink because they were given for him for the forgiveness of his sins, his atonement, his redemption, and his salvation! In his participation in the Lord's Supper, his doubts must be stilled. For there the redemption that our Lord has effected for all is given to him individually and sealed with the most glorious and certain pledge there is in heaven and on earth.

Thy body, given for me, O Savior,
Thy blood which Thou for me didst shed,
These are my life and strength forever,
By them my hungry soul is fed.
Lord, may Thy body and Thy blood
Be for my soul the highest good! Amen.

(TLH 315:11)

Maundy Thursday

Read 1 Corinthians 10:16–17

As the faith of the Christian is increased and strengthened by his participation in the Lord's Supper, so is his love. The fire of faith cannot exist without lighting and burning. These come from love, with its hidden glow on the inside and the shining of good works on the outside. As soon as a person becomes joyfully certain of his salvation, he cannot do otherwise. The ice of his heart melts away, removing anger and irreconcilability and replacing them with deeds that follow the example of Christ Himself, seeking to embrace all in love.

The Lord's Supper increases the Christian's love precisely because Christ's body and blood are present and received in it. As the apostle Paul explains in our text: "The cup of blessing that we bless, is it not a participation in the blood of Christ? The bread that we break, is it not a participation in the body of Christ? Because there is one bread, we who are many are one body, for we all partake of one bread." Paul is asking us, as we eat of the blessed bread and drink from the blessed cup, to remember that we are partaking of the body and blood of Christ. They are common to all of us, and by receiving them, we enter a body-and-blood fellowship. As bread comes from many pieces of grain, so in the holy Supper we become one body, one people, although we are many. Because we partake of the one bread, the same body and blood of Christ, the Supper is a meal of the most intimate communion, and thus it is a meal that demands and encourages an intimate love. We gather as equal children as at the family table of our common heavenly Father. We may be greatly different from other communicants in everyday life, but here, at the holy Supper, all of our differences disappear. We all share the same earthly and heavenly bread and drink—the subject and the king, the slave and the master, the beggar and the rich person, the young and the old, the woman and the man, the simplest and the most highly educated. Here, all communicants stand as sinners and beggars who are poor, hungry, and thirsty for grace. One of us may stand at the table in a coarse smock while another comes in velvet and silk adorned with gold and pearls, but when we depart, we are both clothed with Christ's blood and righteousness. All of us have received the same Jesus and the same righteousness from Him.

When we know, in departing from the table of the Lord, that our fellow communicants have the same Jesus in their hearts we do, this fosters the most intimate and fervent brotherly love. By eating the same body and drinking the same blood of Christ, we become one body and receive a common soul, Jesus. We must therefore love our fellow communicants as our second self.

May God bestow on us His grace and favor
To please Him with our behavior
And live as brethren here in love and union
Nor repent this blest Communion! O Lord, have mercy!
Let not Thy good Spirit forsake us;
Grant that heav'nly-minded He make us;
Give Thy Church, Lord, to see
Days of peace and unity: O Lord, have mercy!
Amen.

(TLH 313:3)

Good Friday

Read Luke 23:44–47

IF WE WANT TO KNOW the full magnitude of human sinfulness, we must go to Golgotha. For who is hanging there between heaven and earth, between two criminals, with outstretched arms, and with blood flowing over His whole body? Who is here mocked and given vinegar and gall to drink? Who is slowly being tortured to death? It is not a criminal suffering what his deeds earned, for He calls to His Father in heaven, "Father, into Your hands I commit My spirit." With a shaken heart, the centurion on duty called out after His death, "Certainly this man was innocent!" If the one who was crucified was only then first recognized as an innocent man, we must truly be alarmed at the wickedness of men, that they could bring Him to an agonizing death.

But this is more than an innocent man, more even than all the angels and archangels. He is the Son of the Most High God. He is the Lord of glory, the Creator of the world, and God of all men, who, out of eternal love took on human nature to redeem man. He traveled around, preached the Gospel, forgave sins, and healed all who were overpowered by the devil. And yet the people seized Him, hung Him on a wooden cross, and killed Him. This is the most shameful, vile, and cursed deed plotted in people's hearts and carried out by people's hands. Here we see human wickedness in the highest degree and most abominable form. We see that the heart of man is capable of the most horrible thing imaginable: killing his own Creator and the eternal Love. When the sun saw this, it ceased shining as if it could not bear to witness this agonizing scene. When the earth saw this, it quaked and tore its rocks as if in fury against this sacrilege toward its Creator.

On Golgotha, we see sin in the greatest magnitude and with the most horrifying result. For what Christ suffered here, He did not suffer for the sake of His own sin. Instead, He suffered voluntarily for the sake of our sin. "Surely," says the prophet Isaiah, "He has borne our griefs and carried our sorrows. . . . He was wounded for our transgressions; He was crushed for our iniquities" (53:4–5). What Christ suffered is what we should have eternally suffered for our sins. He endured the punishment, showing us that our sins merit eternal torment. He hung naked, disgraced, ridiculed, and shamed—the same condition our sins should have earned us. He thirsted and was not refreshed, demonstrating that our sins should have brought us eternal thirst and languishing. His cross was placed between the crosses of robbers and murderers, showing us that our sins should have excluded us from the communion of all holy creatures and consigned us instead to the company of the children of wickedness and condemnation. Christ was also forsaken by God, underscoring the fact that our sins merit eternal rejection by God. He hung there in awful darkness, telling us that our sins should have earned us no light of grace. Christ, the Life, died, and this is a stark reminder to us that our sins merit eternal death and damnation.

If we do not want to believe the terrible threats of the Law against sin, God has painted them on Golgotha for us in broad and bloody brushstrokes so all doubt and all excuses have been removed. On the cross of Christ, it is written before the eyes of all people: God does what He threatens. The sinner must die!

O Christ, Thou Lamb of God,
That takest away the sin of the world,
Have mercy upon us!
O Christ, Thou Lamb of God,
That takest away the sin of the world,
Have mercy upon us!
O Christ, Thou Lamb of God,
That takest away the sin of the world,
Grant us Thy peace! Amen.

(TLH 147)

Holy Saturday

Read 2 Corinthians 5:19–20

IN THE LIGHT OF THE CROSS, on which God permitted His only Son to bleed and die for our sins, no one can doubt that God will accept him when he returns to Him. What is left that can still fill a person with fear? His sins? They have been paid for by an immeasurable price: the blood of the Son of God. God's wrath? It has been appeased through the death of Christ. God's threats in the Law? They have been annulled through the cross on Golgotha and replaced with the clear promises of grace and salvation. As certain as it is that the earthly sun stopped shining at Christ's death, it is just as certain that the true Sun, the Sun of grace and righteousness, has risen. As certain as it is that the graves were opened and the dead went forth after Christ's death, it is just as certain that His death marked the end of our death and issued in a stream of eternal life flowing toward us. As certain as it is that the rocks split at Christ's death, it is just as certain that at that moment the ledger containing the debts of all people was torn by God's own hand. As certain as it is that the temple curtain was torn and revealed the Holy of Holies with the mercy seat, it is just as certain that the Holy of Holies in heaven was opened wide. God's messengers should now call to all people, "Come, come, be reconciled with God!" There is no need to ask, "How shall I be reconciled with Him, the Most Holy, whom I have offended?" It is already accomplished! God is gloriously, perfectly, and eternally reconciled to all. Let us also be reconciled with God!

Whoever does not want to come to God now, when will he want to do so? Whoever does not feel confident now, what would it take to change his mind? Whoever does not believe that the death of the Son of God Himself is enough, what would be required to satisfy him? Whoever does not want to accept this invitation from God to come to Him, what will attract him? If the love that inspired God's Son to die an atoning death on the cross cannot compel, with sweet omnipotence, a person to come to God, what can motivate him?

Some people allow the fear of their debt of sin to deter them from receiving reconciliation with God. Others hinder themselves by loving sin and the world. To all of these, God's Son urgently calls, "Oh, be reconciled to God!" You who want to remain God's enemies, what are you doing? How can you be unmoved by the greatness of the love God revealed for you through the death of His Son? Consider this: God did not need you, but even from eternity, He desired to draw you to Himself and to save you. He foresaw your fall, and He decided beforehand to redeem you and to reconcile you with Himself. You offended Him, but He did not wait for you to come to Him. He knew that if reconciliation depended upon you to make the first move, you would never seek Him. God the Most High, although He had been offended, took the initiative for your restoration by allowing His only Son to die for you. By this you are reconciled. Now His servants, with tears of love and sympathy, implore you to be reconciled with God. On the cross of the Reconciler is written in large, blood-red letters, "Be reconciled!" The blood that flowed from Christ's wounds on the cross calls, "Be reconciled!" The cherubim cry out from the uncovered mercy seat, "Be reconciled!" The dead who were resurrected from their graves cry, "Be reconciled!" The cracking rocks thunder, "Be reconciled!" This same invitation sounds from the mouths of all perfected spirits already taken up into heaven by the death of Christ.

Woe to him who remains deaf toward these thousands of voices! Woe to him who despises the Love that died for him!

Woe to him who will not let go of his enmity against God and who accounts the death of God's Son as futile to him!

O Jesus Christ, Thou only Son
Of God, Thy heav'nly Father,
Who didst for all our sins atone
And Thy lost sheep dost gather:
Thou Lamb of God, to Thee on high
From out our depths we sinners cry,
Have mercy on us, Jesus! Amen.

(TLH 237:3)

Sunday

Read Mark 16:1–8

EVERYONE KNOWS THAT EASTER is a true festival of joy. However, few know the real reason behind that joy. Does this ignorance apply only to those who do not seek that Easter joy in the houses of the Lord where the resurrected Christ is proclaimed, but look for it instead in the temples of worldly idols that know nothing about spiritual joy? No, this ignorance also applies to those who want to be Christians, who are acquainted with God's Word and derive joy from it. They know very well the source of the true joy of Christmas, but Easter is another matter altogether.

People usually think that on Easter Christendom rejoices that (1) the time of Christ's humiliation and great suffering has finally ended and His day of honor has arrived; (2) by His resurrection, His innocence was displayed before the whole world and both His divinity and the truth of His Word were undeniably confirmed; and (3) the resurrection of Christ establishes beyond doubt the immortality of the human soul and the future resurrection of human bodies. Holy Scripture certainly identifies all of these as fruits of the resurrection of Jesus. Regarding the first observation, it says: "He humbled Himself by becoming obedient to the point of death, even death on a cross" (Philippians 2:8). On the second observation, it notes, "Great indeed, we confess, is the mystery of godliness: He was manifested in the flesh, vindicated by the Spirit" (1 Timothy 3:16), and Christ "was declared to be the Son of God in power according to the Spirit of holiness by His resurrection from the dead" (Romans 1:4). Scripture says this about the third observation: "Now if Christ is proclaimed as raised from the dead, how can some of you say that there is no resurrection of the dead?" (1 Corinthians 15:12).

As important as all of this is, however, it does not encompass the full, true source of Easter comfort. For all three points—the glorification of Christ, the confirmation of His doctrine, and the assurance of the immortality of the human soul and the resurrection of the dead—Christ's resurrection was by no means absolutely necessary. God could have glorified Jesus in another way. Both His doctrine and His divinity had already been sufficiently confirmed by His glorious miracles. The immortality of man and the resurrection of the flesh were, without doubt, long established with the resurrection of Lazarus, the son of the widow of Nain, Jairus's daughter, and individuals whose stories are related in the Old Testament.

The true object of the Christian's Easter joy is something completely different. The points already noted are almost nothing more than the frame of the real picture. Holy Scripture presents the resurrection of Christ as absolutely necessary for the work of the redemption and salvation of man.

The apostle Paul clearly says: "And if Christ has not been raised, then our preaching is in vain and your faith is in vain. . . . Then those also who have fallen asleep in Christ have perished" (1 Corinthians 15:14,18). From this, we must conclude that Christ's resurrection is not only a stone in the building of our salvation, but the keystone of it. It is not a shining jewel in the crown of our redemption, but the crown itself. Without Christ's resurrection, the world would still not be redeemed.

With the resurrection of Christ, a person can rejoice in His birth, be comforted with His suffering and death, and boast in His cross. Therefore, the Christian church sings (and not only at Christmas), "Were this Child for us not born, We should all be lost, forlorn" (*TLH* 78:2). It also sings (and not only during the Passion season), "All sins Thou borest for us, Else had despair reigned o'er us" (*TLH* 146). At Easter, the church sings: "All our hopes were ended Had Jesus not ascended From the grave triumphantly. For this Lord Christ, we worship Thee. Lord, have mercy. Hallelujah! Hallelujah! Hallelujah! We now rejoice with gladness; Christ will end all sadness. Lord, have mercy" (*TLH* 187).

He is arisen! Glorious Word!
Now reconciled is God, my Lord;
The gates of heav'n are open.
My Jesus did triumphant die,
And Satan's arrows broken lie,
Destroyed hell's direst weapon.
Oh, hear What cheer!
Christ victorious Riseth glorious, Life He giveth—
He was dead, but see, He liveth! Amen.

† *(TLH 189)*

Monday

Read Romans 4:25

THE RESURRECTION OF JESUS CHRIST is the glorious end, not of Christ Himself, but of all people. He did not suffer, die, and rise for Himself, but for everyone. His suffering and dying were not for His own sins, but for those of the whole world. As the prophet Isaiah says, "But He was wounded for our transgressions; He was crushed for our iniquities" (53:5). When He rose from the dead, He no longer bore the form of a servant or of sinful flesh. He cast off the burden of sin and left it in His grave. This means that our sins have been removed from God's face; they are now eternally buried. Each Christian says, "What I have sinned, You have buried in the grave; there You have closed it; there is where it must also remain."

In suffering and dying, Christ wanted to pay the debt that we had accumulated, for He Himself says in Psalm 69, "What I did not steal must I now restore?" (v. 4). When He, as our pledge, then arose, He was released from the debtors' prison of death. Where is our ledger now? It is torn up. All of our debts have been paid. God the Father has now declared, by the resurrection of Christ, that He will no longer demand any payment from us.

When Christ suffered and died, He wanted to present Himself on the altar of the cross as the reconciliation of man to God. When God raised Him from the dead, God openly testified before heaven and earth that He had fully accepted the sacrifice of His Son.

In His suffering and dying, Christ began, as our army leader, as the Prince of our salvation, and as our David, the great struggle with our enemies: the Law, sin, death, and the devil. When He rose, He fulfilled the Law, conquered sin, stripped death of its power, and crushed the head of the devil as the old serpent, triumphing over the prince of darkness and all his servants. Since His battle was our battle, His victory is our victory and His conquest is our conquest. It is our enemies who lie under His feet. When Christ suffered and died, He was sentenced in our place and condemned to death. Who, then, was acquitted by God in the raising of Christ from the dead? Christ was in no need of acquittal, for no one could accuse Him of a single sin. Who was justified in Him? Who was declared in Him to be pure and innocent? We were; the whole world was. His life is our life and so are His absolution and justification.

Who can completely express what a great comfort lies in Christ's resurrection? It is the most glorious absolution, spoken by God Himself to all the world. Here, the eternal love of God is revealed in its complete abundance, its overflowing fullness, and its highest splendor. It was not enough for God to send His Son into the world to become man for us. It was not enough for Him to offer His Son into death for us. With burning love for us sinners, God did not wait for us to ask Him for His grace in Christ. Instead, He hurried to give us that grace through the resurrection of His Son, to absolve us of all our sins, and to declare publicly, before both heaven and earth, that we are redeemed, reconciled, pure, innocent, and just in Christ.

Oh, great comfort! It is eternally well with him who recognizes, has, and enjoys this comfort!

Thanks to Thee, O Christ victorious!
Thanks to Thee, O Lord of Life!
Death hath now no power o'er us,
Thou hast conquered in the strife.

Thanks because Thou didst arise
And hast opened Paradise!
None can fully sing the glory
Of the resurrection story. Amen.

† *(TLH 207:2)*

Tuesday

Read Romans 5:18

MANY SUPPOSE THAT IF GOD absolved the world by the resurrection of Jesus Christ from the dead, the entire world already has the forgiveness of its sins and, as a result, the entire world must be saved, for where there is forgiveness of sins, there is also life and salvation. While this doctrine is absolutely true, the conclusion is absolutely false. Whenever something is given, two people are involved: the one who gives the gift and the one who receives it. If a rich person gives something to a poor person, what is the benefit of that gift if the poor person refuses it out of either shame or false modesty? If an entire rebellious city is pardoned, what help is there for the individual rebel if he does not accept that pardon because of pride or defiance? If the release of an imprisoned criminal is announced to him, what good does it do him if he declines to leave his cell, perhaps out of the groundless fear of being bound in harder chains? If someone we have offended extends his hand to us in the hope of reconciliation, what help is that hand to us if we, holding fast to our hate and resentment, refuse to grasp it? If Christ is truly the Savior of the world, what help is He to a world that wants to know nothing about a Savior, that labors under the self-righteous delusion that it can redeem and reconcile itself?

Thus it is with the general absolution that God announced to the whole world by the resurrection of Christ. All of this is of no help to the poor world if it remains in unbelief. God has already given to each of us the forgiveness of sins, but He will not force any of us to accept it. We must accept it in order for it to be beneficial to us, and we can do that only through faith. The resurrected Christ did not offer a single word of condemnation against His disciples' sins—not against Peter's denial and not against the flight of all the others. The only thing He chastised in them was their unbelief: the women did not believe the angel, the apostles did not believe the women, Thomas did not believe the apostles, and the Emmaus disciples did not believe the prophets. And so it is with us as well.

God's absolution will remain valid and strong until the Last Day. However, that absolution is not given for eternity, but for this life on earth. As Christ expressly says, "Whatever you loose on earth shall be loosed in heaven" (Matthew 16:19). No one is allowed to think that God has already absolved him in Christ, together with the whole world, and so these places of refuge are always open. No one can suppose that there is thus no need to hurry to faith, that there is always time to believe and to be saved later on. For the sake of our salvation, none of us can think this way. Our death is certain, but the time and the manner of that death are unknown. And if we die without faith, we have eternally forfeited our absolution. The receipt God has held out to us in vain is torn to pieces, and our names, which God had blotted out of His book of debt, are again written in it because the time of grace has passed. Only those who accept the keys to the kingdom of heaven while they reside on this earth will find an open heaven and a merciful Judge in the life to come.

> *Oh, where is thy sting, Death? We fear thee no more;*
> *Christ rose, and now open is fair Eden's door.*
> *For all our transgressions His blood does atone;*
> *Redeemed and forgiven, we now are His own. Amen.*
>
> † *(TLH 198:4)*

Wednesday

Read Romans 1:4

JESUS' TESTIMONY about Himself was divinely and irrefutably attested to by the glorious miracles He performed. As great as those signs and wonders were, however, God provided a much more glorious and shining proof in the resurrection of His only-begotten Son, a proof that was not offered even to the greatest Old Testament ambassadors and prophets of God. Long before Easter, Jesus had proclaimed—both in private and in public and before both friends and enemies—His resurrection as a miraculous deed by which He would seal the truth of His testimony about Himself and the divinity of all of His other miracles. He had hardly begun His ministry to the Jews before He answered their question about the means He would employ to prove His divine power. "Destroy this temple," He said, referring to His body, "and in three days I will raise it up" (John 2:19). As the time of His crucifixion drew closer, He spoke often and clearly about the resurrection that would follow His death. Even in His last trial, Jesus showed His judges that His death and grave were the last steps of His humiliation, and that immediately thereafter His divine power and glory would be revealed.

Did Jesus keep this promise? He did indeed! With the first rays of morning on the third day after His shameful death on the cross, His glorified body penetrated the gravestone without breaking its seal as light penetrates glass without breaking it. An angel came down from heaven and, as the earth quaked, he rolled away the stone to demonstrate that the grave was empty. To those who sought Jesus' corpse to anoint it, he cried, "Why do you seek the living among the dead? He is not here, but has risen!" (Luke 24:5–6). And this word, "The Lord has risen!" went with lightning speed from mouth to mouth, sounding as a note from God's trumpet throughout all lands and all centuries until the present day. This word has proved itself true, by divine power, to million of hearts that have been awakened, enlivened, renewed, and given the peace of heaven.

Oh, what a good, firm, unshakable foundation to a joyful confession of our faith we Christians therefore have!

Jesus is God's Son. His resurrection shows, with invincible greatness, that His power did not end in death, which halts even the mightiest in the world. In death, all of our wisdom, projects, and designs come to an end, but not the decrees of Jesus. He decreed it, and His resurrection proved it. A man may rise to the highest positions of power on this earth, being worshiped either by others or by himself, and yet he remains a son of the dust who returns to dust. When death looms, he cannot help himself. Jesus, by contrast, although His human nature allowed Him to die, possessed another nature that could not be extinguished by death. This other nature was powerful enough to build up again, in three days, the destroyed temple of humanity—just as He promised. From the resurrection of Jesus Christ, we see that He is Lord over that king of terrors, death, and is the Prince of life. He is true God and eternal life itself.

But short was their triumph, the Savior arose,
And death, hell, and Satan He vanquished, His foes;
The conquering Lord lifts His banner on high.
He lives, yea, He lives, and will nevermore die. Amen.

† *(TLH 198:3)*

Thursday

Read 1 Corinthians 15:55–57

Because of the fall, we have come under the cruel tyranny of sin and we willingly obey it. Our desire, by nature, is to serve sin. Each of us serves certain sins that have full power over us. Like animals bound for sacrifice, we follow these sins wherever they lead us. We may be ruled by covetousness and avarice, drink or gluttony, lust and unchastity, vanity and the pursuit of pleasure, anger and vindictiveness, jealousy and envy, hypocrisy and falsehood, or the love of self and pride. Without reluctance, people by nature obey the commands of these vile tyrants. Often, both knowingly and deliberately, they sacrifice to them the peace of heart, body, mind, and soul that comes with God's grace and eternal salvation.

The most frightening thing about all of this is that when a person determines to free himself from this or that sin that is causing him such misery, he is utterly unable to do so. To be sure, he can occasionally ward off the outbreak of his sin, but he is not able to rid himself of the desire to sin. By nature, sin dwells in people's hearts like an invincible fortress. The garrison in this fortress, which defends it, is the indwelling evil inclinations, supported by worldly enticements and threats. That people by nature have a free will to choose good and to reject evil is an empty dream from which a person is awakened with every temptation.

Nevertheless, there is salvation for poor, imprisoned humanity. God created a means to free us from the power of sin. That means is the resurrection of Jesus Christ from the dead. As soon as a person believes in his heart that this resurrection absolves him from the debt of sin, sin is cast from its throne in his heart and its power is broken in his soul. The desire and joy of the heart were before directed toward sin and the world but are now focused on Christ and His glorious freedom and grace. Christ Himself enters into the heart of such a person, bringing with Him a new heavenly fire and life. From then on, He sits in the heart upon the throne that was vacated by sin, and He rules there by the prompting of His Holy Ghost. Such a person no longer needs to be told he must give up obedience to sin and serve Christ as his only legitimate Lord. He has already begun to do this, urged by a voluntary impulse now dwelling in him. The belief that he has been raised with Christ to His salvation moves him to walk with Christ in a new life.

Oh, precious, sweet freedom, which Christ has brought out of His grave to us poor people imprisoned and enslaved by sin! It makes us lords over sin, death, hell, and, more important, our own hearts. It makes us free citizens who, even if we submit to certain people, do so only for God's sake and are therefore really subject to no person but only to God Himself. Serving Him is no disgraceful servanthood, but true freedom, honor, and blessedness.

Then sing your hosannas and raise your glad voice;
Proclaim the blest tidings that all may rejoice.
Laud, honor, and praise to the Lamb that was slain,
Who sitteth in glory and ever shall reign. Amen.

† *(TLH 198:5)*

Friday

Read 1 Corinthians 5:7

IF WE WANT TO UNDERSTAND and apply these words correctly, we must first vividly imagine the situation in which the Israelites once found themselves when they received the command to slaughter their Passover lamb. At that time, they were in Egypt, where Pharaoh, a cruel tyrant, ruled the land. The children of Israel, who had been received so kindly in Egypt on account of Joseph, had been made slaves by unrighteousness. With strokes of a whip, they were forced by unfeeling taskmasters to intolerable services. They cried out to heaven, and through Moses God allowed the most horrible plagues to come upon the land of Egypt to persuade Pharaoh to allow the Israelites to emigrate. But Pharaoh's heart only became harder with each plague.

Yet the hour of redemption finally arrived for Israel. As the last of the ten plagues, God sent an angel of death through the land in a single night to slay every firstborn child in every house of the Egyptians. The Lord had commanded the Israelites to slaughter a lamb and to smear the lintel and doorposts of their houses with the blood, ensuring that the angel of death would pass over the houses marked with the blood and spare their inhabitants. In that terrible night, every house of the Egyptians, including that of Pharaoh himself, was full of wailing and lamentation. All of the Israelites' houses, on the contrary, resounded with exultation. The following morning, they marched off, driven in haste by Pharaoh himself, out of the land of their slavery to the Promised Land of freedom on the other side of the Red Sea.

All of these were but Old Testament foreshadowings, the fulfillment of which would take place in the New Testament. Egypt signified the whole world. The tyrant Pharaoh symbolized the prince of this world, the devil. The angel of death signified eternal death. The Passover lamb stood for Christ, sacrificed on the cross and resurrected. The blood of the lamb on the doorposts and lintel symbolized faith in Christ. Finally, the joyful exodus of Israel to the Promised Land signified the blessed death of the believing Christian, departing this world for an eternal heavenly homeland.

How blessed, therefore, are all those who in faith can call out triumphantly, "For indeed Christ, our Passover, was sacrificed for us." To be sure, believing Christians still find themselves in the Egypt of this world, where the hellish Pharaoh has erected his throne. But by the blood of their Easter Lamb, they are free, not from the devil's temptations, but from his tyranny. Believing Christians also retain their disposition to sin, but the Lamb's blood gives them the power to resist and overcome their sinful desires. The angel of eternal death appears before their hearts' doors, but because those doors are, through faith, sprinkled with the blood of the Easter Lamb, the angel of death must spare them. At last, believing Christians must depart from the Egypt of this world forever, walking through the Red Sea of their last trial to enter into the Promised Land of eternal life.

Thou our Paschal Lamb indeed,
Christ, today Thy people feed;
Take our sins and guilt away,
That we may all sing for aye: Hallelujah! Amen.

(ELHB 225:7)

Saturday

Read 1 Corinthians 5:6–8

OUR PROPER UNDERSTANDING and application of these words require us to go into the history of Israel. When God appointed the Passover lamb to protect the Israelites from the angel of death, he also decreed that they should sweep out all leaven from their homes and eat only unleavened, sweet bread. So strict was this obligation that God threatened to root out from Israel the soul of anyone who consumed leavened bread at the time of Passover.

This decree, like all other ceremonies pertaining to the institution of the Passover lamb, was a series of foreshadowings. The prescribed sweeping out of all leaven and the use of unleavened bread mean daily repentance and daily sanctification, respectively. For thus Paul writes, at the conclusion of our text: "Let us therefore celebrate the festival, not with old leaven, the leaven of malice and evil, but with the unleavened bread of sincerity and truth." Believing Christians are sacredly bound to daily repentance and daily sanctification in sweeping out the old leaven of malice and evil and in celebrating Easter with the unleavened bread of sincerity and truth!

Doesn't this demand for repentance and sanctification sound a sour note, a disturbing lament, in the midst of our Easter hymns of joy and exultation? Wouldn't this be contrary to the prohibition of the first church against fasting and praying on the knees at Easter? Not at all! Is it sad to be free of sins and to be clothed with everything that pleases God? Certainly not. If you would truly "cleanse out the old leaven," you must go into your heart, and even if you do not let sin rule in you anymore, you will still discover that there are many sins in you that have not been exterminated as they should be. The empty grave of Christ is the right time and the right place to search the most secret corner of your heart, and wherever you still find a sprouting weed of this or that sin, you will, as much as is possible by the power of faith, pull it out by the root. If we truly become more holy people, the more our hearts and lives will become a garden of God increasingly free of this poisonous weed!

But "let us keep the feast...with the unleavened bread of sincerity and truth." That is, let us examine our hearts and lives. There we will find—even if we have been purified by the blood of our Easter Lamb and given a new heart through faith—that there should be in us a much more fervent love and hope, a much deeper humility, a much greater patience, and a much more heavenly mind. In short, we need a much more glorious shining of all Christian virtues. Therefore, up, up! As our Lord waves His victory flag, let us begin to walk with Him more eagerly than before in a new, heavenly life.

May the Spirit of God Himself impress today's Easter word deeply in our hearts! Thus, as people doubly blessed, we will not conclude our dear Easter festival. Instead, we will, from now on, daily keep it, daily eat our Passover Lamb in faith, daily purge all leaven of sin from our hearts, daily eat the unleavened bread of sincerity and truth, and daily celebrate our resurrection with Christ and our new walk with Him. If, then, we were to die today or tomorrow, we would die in the

Lord and by this blessed death, we would enter with Him into a life of eternal glory.

May Jesus Christ, our precious Passover Lamb, help us all to this through the power of His bloody sacrifice and His victorious resurrection. To Him be thanks, praise, glory, and honor, both in time and in eternity.

The day of resurrection,
Earth, tell it out abroad,
The Passover of gladness,
The Passover of God.
From death to life eternal,
From this world to the sky,
Our Christ hath bro't us over
With hymns of victory. Amen.

† *(TLH 205:1)*

Sunday

Read John 20:19–23

THE POWER TO FORGIVE and to retain sins on earth is so clearly and uniquely attributed to the Church and its servants that it needs no other proof. Those who deny this power to the Church commit a great sacrilege. They oppose the Son of God to His face and declare His Word to be a lie. But, someone may ask, where have the apostles absolved like the preachers of the church? We respond that, although we do not find this ceremony of the Office of the Keys in the Apostolic Church, we do find something equivalent. Saint Paul writes to the Corinthians: "Do not be deceived: neither the sexually immoral, nor idolaters, nor adulterers, nor men who practice homosexuality, nor thieves, nor the greedy, nor drunkards, nor revilers, nor swindlers will inherit the kingdom of God. And such were some of you. But you were washed, you were sanctified, you were justified in the name of the Lord Jesus Christ and by the Spirit of our God" (1 Corinthians 6:9–11). Here Paul speaks of absolution for the fallen but repentant Corinthians. When the holy apostle affirms that "you are all sons of God, through faith [in Christ Jesus]" (Galatians 3:26), "by grace you have been saved through faith" (Ephesians 2:8), and the like, it is no different from what the Lord said to the paralytic: "Take heart, my son; your sins are forgiven" (Matthew 9:2). When Ananias baptized Saul, it is the same as if he had said, "Let me absolve you."

The apostles expressly attributed to themselves the power to forgive sins, and they employed this power with explicit words. We read about a man in the Corinthian congregation who had committed incest and was so severely punished by the entire congregation that he stood on the edge of despair. Paul writes to the congregation: "For such a one, this punishment by the majority is enough, so you should rather turn to forgive and comfort him, or he may be overwhelmed by excessive sorrow. So I beg you to reaffirm your love for him. . . . Anyone whom you forgive, I also forgive. What I have forgiven, if I have forgiven anything, has been for your sake in the presence of Christ" (2 Corinthians 2:6–8, 10). This testimony is so clear that even many enemies of absolution do not deny that at least the holy apostles had and used the power to forgive sins. But, they say, how can a person prove that present-day preachers of the Gospel also have this power?

Does not Saint Paul himself proclaim elsewhere, "Are all apostles?" (1 Corinthians 12:29). It is true that there is a great difference between an apostle and a present-day servant of the Church. The apostles were infallible, while today's servants of the Church are not. The apostles had the power to perform miracles and to prophesy, while present-day servants of the Church do not. The apostles were directly called by Christ, the Son of God, while the servants of the contemporary Church are called indirectly by Christ through the congregation. The apostles received the call to go into all the world, while the scope of the field addressed by today's servants of the Church is often limited to the congregation they serve. However, when it comes to the office of the preaching of the Gospel, there is no difference between them. The Word of the Lord instructs, "Preach the Gospel" (1 Corinthians 1:13). It also says, "Baptize them in the name of the Father and of the Son and of the Holy Spirit" (Matthew 28:19), and "Do this in remembrance of Me." Do these apply only to the apostles? No! Christ expressly tells the apostles, "Teaching them to observe all that I have commanded you" (Matthew 28:20). The commands to teach, baptize, and celebrate the holy Supper apply to the Church of all ages. All that was commended to the disciples should also be observed by the Church at all times. And this includes the Lord's instruction that "if you forgive the sins of anyone, they are forgiven; if you withhold forgiveness from anyone; it is withheld."

All praise, eternal Son, to Thee
For absolution full and free,
In which Thou showest forth Thy grace;
From false indulgence guard our race. Amen.

(TLH 331:7)

Monday

Read Matthew 16:13–19

TODAY'S READING COMES as a thunderbolt from heaven, exposing and condemning the lies on which the papacy has been built for more than 1,000 years. Christ asked His disciples, "Who do people say that the Son of Man is?" They responded by informing Him of the various opinions people held about Him. Jesus then asked them for their own opinion: "But who do you say that I am?" The fiery Peter, who was always ready to answer, replied in the name of all of the disciples who were asked, "You are Christ, the Son of the living God." In response, Jesus declared to Peter, "I will give you the keys of the kingdom of heaven." The sole reason for this, He quickly added, was the faith in Him that Peter had just expressed.

Let us consider Christ's words to Peter in their context. He begins His reply to Peter's confession with "Blessed are you, Simon Bar-Jonah!" We see here that the granting of the keys of the kingdom of heaven is a matter of being blessed and in no way a privilege of office. Jesus continues, "For flesh and blood has not revealed this to you, but My Father who is in heaven." He praises Simon, son of Jonah, because he recognized Christ in a faith worked by God Himself. Jesus then adds, "And I also tell you, you are Peter." The name refers to a rock or a rock-man, and Jesus selects it because, according to Simon's confession, he had built his faith, firm as a rock, upon Christ, the only and certain rock of salvation and blessedness.

Christ goes on to say, not "And upon you, Peter," as some would have it, but "And on this rock" (or, as it says in the original text, "And on this petra"), that is, on Christ Himself, "I will build My church, and the gates of hell shall not prevail against it." What Jesus indicates here is as clear as the midday sun. He is saying, in essence: "I rightly call you Peter for the sake of your firmly grounded faith upon Me, the Rock. But do not suppose that by this I have given you a special privilege belonging only to you, that you alone should be Peter, the rock or rock-man. No, just as you are built upon Me, the true Rock, and therefore stand firm, so I also want to build my whole church upon Me, that it may stand firm, defying all the gates of hell. As you, through the faith you have just confessed, are Peter, a rock-man, so also will my Church be an assembly of such clear believers, Peters, rock-men."

Here Jesus adds, "I will give you the keys of the kingdom of heaven." From the context, it undeniably follows that Jesus has not offered Peter these keys, any more than the blessedness He has already bestowed, as a reward, a privilege of office. Instead, both the blessedness and the keys of the kingdom of heaven were given to Peter as a right and property of his faith. Just as Christ first declared Peter, with all the members of the Church, blessed on account of faith, so He grants the keys of the kingdom of heaven to all who, like Peter, believe and confess Christ. Through faith, they are built upon the rock of Christ.

O faithful God, we worship Thee!
Thou pardon'st our iniquity,
Thou grantest help in sin's distress,
And soul and body Thou dost bless.

Thou, through Thy servant, say'st to me:
"Thy sins are all forgiven thee,
Depart in peace; but sin no more,
And e'er my pardoning grace adore." Amen.

(ELHB 425:1, 2)

Tuesday

Read Matthew 23:8

THE QUESTION CONCERNING the recipients of the keys of the kingdom of heaven is immensely important. If a person believes and teaches that Christ did not originally give the keys to the believers who constitute His Church but rather to those in office, then that person abolishes the equality of Christians in Christ, their brotherhood, and, consequently, their Christian freedom. For if preachers are the original, true holders of the keys of the kingdom of heaven, they would then be a self-transmitting spiritual peerage in the Church and greatly exalted over the common Christian. Thus, Christians in general would no longer have an open access to their Savior and His grace. Instead, the preachers would be their necessary mediators and lords rather than servants of the Church, while their congregations would be their subjects. In addition, preachers would then hold the authority to open heaven for the Christian or not to open it, for they alone would possess and preserve the blessed office that preaches the atonement. For if the preachers of the Church alone give or take, bind or loose, then Christians must beg for Christ's grace from them. They would also fear excommunication from them, whether it is just or unjust.

The Roman papacy demonstrates where this doctrine finally leads. This terrible empire, with its priestly rule and tyranny of consciences, is the consistent execution of the accursed doctrine that states that only preachers originally possessed all priestly glory, transmitted through ordination, and that they are therefore the priests of the New Testament. This belief, which invaded the Church even in its early years, is based on the anti-Christian claim that the pontiff and his so-called high clergy are the infallible lords and absolute rulers of the faith, installed by Christ Himself.

What we, with our dear Church, teach is completely different. According to God's Word, Christ did not originally give the keys of the kingdom of heaven to those holding public office, but to the Church of His believers. The Word of Christ stands firm with the doctrine in today's text. It tells us that Christ is the only King of Christians and that Christians are royal priests who are subject to no person, no angel, and no creature in heaven or on earth. With this doctrine, the glorious and blessed freedom of Christians is preserved. They remain the fellow dwellers of God, with the preachers serving as their stewards and the mere administrators of their goods. Therefore, with this doctrine, Christians have both the power and the right to install and depose preachers as their servants and the power and right to examine their doctrine and the management of their office and their life. No preacher has the authority to deny absolution to a repentant Christian; instead, it is his duty to speak it to the Christian as his appointed servant.

Therefore, it is essential that our Church does not fall back into the old papacy with its heathen clericalism, and so lose all fruits of the Reformation. In the Church, Christ must remain upon His throne, and preachers must remain servants rather than lords of Christians. Each congregation must be a flock of Christ, not a clerical empire. Faith has everything that Christ acquired for the sinner. All of this is summed up in the doctrine that Christ gave the keys of the kingdom of heaven to the Church of the believers, not to those who held public office.

Now, then, when the Antichrist roars like a lion, seeking to terrify Christ's sheep and to drag them into his cave, let us hold fast the high jewel of this doctrine against all attacks. Let us faithfully defend it and prefer to sacrifice everything rather than surrender even the smallest portion of it.

Lord, keep us in Thy Word and work,
Restrain the murd'rous Pope and Turk,
Who fain would tear from off Thy throne
Christ Jesus, Thy beloved Son.
Lord Jesus Christ, Thy power make known,
For Thou art Lord of lords alone;
Shield Thy poor Christendom, that we
May evermore sing praise to Thee. Amen.

(ELHB 274:12)

Wednesday

Read Revelation 1:18

SINCE CHRIST IS BOTH true man and the true, living God, He doubtless has held, from eternity, the keys of hell and death, having perfect power over them. It is evident that when He spoke the words of today's text, He wanted to announce that He had received the keys of hell and death as a fruit of His resurrection. Therefore, He now holds these keys in a different and very special sense.

What sort of key can unlock death and hell, restore a person to life, and remove him from hell to heaven? Since it is sin that brought us into the power of death and to the brink of hell, we cannot be rescued by anything other than the perfect righteousness that avails before God. This is the righteousness that Christ revealed when He returned to life and gloriously arose from His grave. God foresaw the fall of man, but He did not desire that even one being created in His image should perish and be lost. Out of His incomprehensible love, He made an agreement with His Son that the Son would assume the nature of fallen man, take upon Himself the sins of all people as if they were His own, and suffer and die in order to atone for them. In return, the Father would credit His Son's atonement to all people, declaring them just and receiving those who accept this through faith. And behold, the Son of God, with His unfathomable love, freely consented to this wonderful agreement, becoming man in the time that had been chosen for this from eternity. Whenever we consider the holy God-man from His conception in the womb of the blessed Virgin Mary to His rest in the bosom of the earth, we must regard Him as burdened with our sins and the need to atone for them.

Yet what happened? Awakened by God the Father Himself, Christ rose on the third day after His death on the cross. Formerly bowed down with the weight of our sins, He is now the comforted Head entirely free of those sins. At one time, He assumed, for the sake of our sins, the role of a servant, even walking humbly among His enemies, but today He is enthroned in kingly majesty, revealing Himself to His believers alone. Then, for the sake of our sins, He was condemned by the Father Himself as guilty and deserving of death, but now He is absolved of all debt and punishment before heaven and earth. For the sake of our sins, He was thrown into the debtor's prison of death and hell, but He was later released, having atoned for every debt. He who once was the object of God's wrath now shines like a thousand suns with His Father's complete favor and grace. For the sake of our sins, He once sighed, groaned, and struggled as One who had been conquered by the poisonous sting of the hellish snake in His heel. Today, however, we see Him triumphant while Satan writhes, powerless, his head crushed under the foot of the almighty Victor. For the sake of our sins, having once wrestled with death and having been swallowed up as death's prey with open vengeance, He is now clothed with a glorious body, and the sting of death has been broken. He who once cried, "I am a worm and not a man" (Psalm 22:6), now proclaims, in divine grandeur, "All authority in heaven and on earth has been given to Me" (Matthew 28:18).

It was a strange and dreadful strife
When Life and Death contended;
The victory remained with Life,
The reign of Death was ended;
Holy Scripture plainly saith
That Death is swallowed up by Death,
His sting is lost forever. Hallelujah! Amen.

† *(TLH 195:2)*

Thursday

Read 2 Corinthians 5:14

SOME PEOPLE THINK—and the rationalists truly teach—that Christ died for all only in the sense that He died for His doctrine for the good of all people. The reason for this, they maintain, is that Christ wanted to give all people an example of how they, too, should endure everything rather than forsake and deny virtue and truth. But, as Saint Paul says in today's text, the death of Christ is viewed by God as if all had died themselves. His death was substitutionary, a death in the place of, and instead of, all people. This death atones for and cancels their sins. It is like a payment of a debt, for when one person pays for all, no one remains a debtor.

This text contains a truth so pleasant and a joy so rich that we cannot stop talking about it. A person may say to himself that he is a sinner, and that punishment must follow sin, for God is just. Even before the first sin, He threatened that, on whichever day man would transgress His commandment, he must die. To this line of reasoning, Paul replies, "No! You shall not be punished because you have already suffered your punishment. You shall not die the death of the sinner because you have already died this death!" The person may then respond: "When was I already punished? And where did I die the death of the sinner?" The apostle supplies the answer in our text. After Christ died for all, all are considered to have died. What a substitute or guarantor does is accounted to those whom he represents as if they had done it themselves. After Christ died and bore the lawful punishment for the sins of all people, the Law, which threatened the sinner, was fulfilled in Him. Consequently, all have already paid the punishment that should have followed their sins. Before God, it is now as if all had already died the death to which they were sentenced. The judgment is already carried out in all and has been canceled, and every sinner is now free again. As Paul says elsewhere, "For he who has died has been set free from sin" (Romans 6:7). Whoever has suffered the punishment of death has also paid the price for his sins and is restored to the condition he enjoyed before he sinned.

If a person persists and asks what he should do to atone for his sins, the answer is: "Nothing more. You have already atoned for them. For it is written 'that if One died for all, then all died.'" What about reconciliation with God and salvation? Is there anything a person needs to do to attain those blessed goals? Again, the answer is: "Nothing more. You shall only believe that, as One died for all, thus you too have already died. You have paid your debt to God, and therefore you are justified. Your sins have been forgiven, and where there is forgiveness of sins, there is also life and salvation."

What an abundance of true joy resides in the words of today's reading!

He brings me to the portal
That leads to bliss untold,
Whereon this rime immortal
Is found in script of gold:
"Who there My cross hath shared
Finds here a crown prepared;
Who there with Me hath died
Shall here be glorified." Amen.

† *(TLH 192:8)*

Friday

Read 2 Corinthians 5:15

THE SIN OF LIVING for oneself is both the most common and the most hidden sin. By nature, all people live for themselves, but none recognizes that he is stuck in this sin and what a great abomination this is. This terrible, deep, inborn corruption of all people can be revealed only by God's Word through the illumination of the Holy Ghost.

What is it, then, to live for ourselves? It does not mean taking care of our own temporal and eternal welfare, for God Himself commanded man to have this care. Therefore, whoever cares for his own earthly and heavenly well-being, because it is God's will, does not live for himself, but rather, for God, His Lord. To live for ourselves is something completely different. It is doing some things and neglecting to do others precisely for our sake, not for God, so we gain some advantage: money, property, desire, pleasure, glory, or praise. Those who live by asking the question "What's in it for me?" live only for themselves. Whoever declines to do something sinful, either because it would bring him disgrace in this world or because he fears God would punish him for it in the next world, lives for himself. Whoever does something good, either because he expects much profit from it or because he anticipates a reward in the world to come, lives for himself. If a person's actions are not motivated by the pure love of God and his neighbor, he lives for himself.

What does Saint Paul have to say in today's text about all of this? He tells us that the Lord of glory emptied Himself, took the form of a servant, denied everything, and humbled Himself to death on the cross. He retained nothing, not even His life, shedding the last drop of His precious blood on the cross, all for us. He died to persuade us that we might become like Him, that we might again be glorified in His divine image, that we might no longer live for ourselves, and thus that we might participate in salvation and the eternal communion with God.

Oh, teach me, Lord, to love Thee truly
With soul and body, head and heart,
And grant me grace that I may duly
Practice fore'er love's sacred art.
Grant that my every thought may be
Directed e'er to Thee. Amen.

† *(TLH 399:5)*

Saturday

Read 2 Corinthians 5:15

THE HIGH DUTY OF CHRISTIANS is not only that they should no longer live for themselves, but also that they should live for Him who died and rose for them. How is it possible to live for Christ? How can a person serve Him? He is certainly in no need of our service. But this only demonstrates that we cannot serve Christ directly. We can, however, serve Him indirectly, and He has told us how we are to do this. On the Last Day, He will declare to those on His right, "Truly, I say to you, as you did it to one of the least of these My brothers, you did it to Me," but to those on His left, He will announce, "Truly, I say to you, as you did not do it to one of the least of these, you did not do it to Me" (Matthew 25:40, 45).

When our text tells us that Christ died for all and we should therefore live for Him, it says we should live for our brothers and sisters in this world, those who have been redeemed with us, our neighbors. For Christ will regard our actions as if we had directed them toward Him.

The Christian rejoices in the gifts God has given him, not because they can profit him, but because he can use them to serve others. Thus, if his actions can bring his neighbor greater advantage, he would rather be poor than rich, rather be humble than honored, rather have a low position than a high one, rather be unlearned than educated, rather be full of trials than temporally happy, rather be sick than healthy, rather even be dead than alive. He regards everything, then, in terms of serving his neighbor and bringing glory to God. He considers a day in which he has done everything for himself and nothing for his neighbor as lost. Far from being envious and taking joy in another's misfortune, he regards his neighbor's happiness or unhappiness as if it were his own. He rejoices with those who are joyful, and he weeps with those who mourn. He lives his life for the One who died and rose for him. He does not see himself as an owner, but rather merely as a steward, appointed by God to use everything he has been given for the benefit of the world. He neither seeks riches nor loves them, and if, by God's blessing, riches descend upon him, he employs them to care for the poor, widows, and orphans; to dry tears and to quiet sighing; to feed the hungry and give drink to the thirsty; and to clothe the naked. He admits the suffering and the forsaken into his home. He restores the sick and rescues those who are languishing in distress. And he does all of this good without tiring.

He sets his Christian walk, not in visible works of high spirituality, but in the faithful performance of his earthly calling. He does the work of his calling, not to gather temporal goods for himself, but in obedience to God, who tells us to eat our own bread, not someone else's. He chooses as his calling one that will allow him to offer the largest number of blessings to others. He does not seek a comfortable life, and if the necessity of a neighbor demands it, he sacrifices his comfort. He seeks no glory and no influence, but if both come to him without his assistance, he uses them to assist others. He forgets himself in his trade, in buying and selling, but looks out more for his neighbor than for his own advantage. He is more apprehensive about his neighbor's condition than about his own. Doing good, then, is his daily business and his life's joy. And thus he lives, both in his thoughts and in his deeds, for the One who died and rose for him.

Let me live to praise Thee ever,
Jesus, Thou my heart's Delight,
Thou who leadest me aright.

Let me cling to Thee forever,
All the fleshly lusts deny,
And the devil's hosts defy. Amen.

(TLH 408:2)

Sunday

Read John 10:12–16

"THERE WILL BE ONE FLOCK, one shepherd." For us to have a correct understanding of the words Christ speaks in our Gospel, we must go back to the time before Christ, in which what He predicts here had not yet occurred. In the time before Christ, all of humanity was divided into two flocks. One flock consisted of the great crowd of Gentiles, people without knowledge of salvation, without promise, and without hope. In short, they were without God. Making up the other flock were the families of the patriarchs and, eventually, the people of Israel. These are the people God chose, to whom He revealed Himself, with whom He made a covenant of grace, to whom He sent the prophets, and to whom He gave His Word and its promise of a Messiah—a Savior and Redeemer from sin, death, and hell.

Although the wall separating these two flocks was great and high, God revealed by the mouths of His holy prophets, long before the time of Christ, that this wall would not stand forever. In His time, the wall would fall and the Gentiles would have a share in the promised salvation. Then there would be one flock and one Shepherd. The words of the prophets were confirmed by these words of Christ: "And I have other sheep that are not of this fold; I must bring them also, and they will listen to My voice. So there will be one flock, one shepherd." With these words, Jesus announces that He is the Good Shepherd whom the prophets promised. He also says that the entire world of sinners constitutes the flock He wants to tend. Therefore, "I have other sheep that are not of this fold" are not of the people Israel, but rather poor, erring Gentiles. Until Jesus came, they stood outside the chosen community of Israel and the testaments of the promise were foreign to them. He intended to open the barriers that had separated them from the people of God. "And they will listen to My voice," He continues. The Word would be preached to these Gentiles, and they would receive it in faith. With this, the previous distinction between Jews and Gentiles, would cease, for Christ intended to build one Church that was no longer bound to any particular people, land, or law. The whole earth would be His Church, and the heavens would be its vault. The gates of this Church would be open everywhere, and through Baptism, all peoples would enter it as one people.

This promise of one flock and one Shepherd will not be fulfilled sometime in the future. The Holy Ghost revealed to the disciples that God does not regard the individual; instead, in every nation, whoever fears God and does right is acceptable to Him. A Gentile must not first become a Jew to belong to the people of God. Through faith in Christ, every person becomes a citizen with the saints and a member of God's household. From the moment all this was revealed to the apostles, they turned to the Gentiles and called to them, "Come, for everything is prepared!"

This call of God entered country after country. Everywhere, great multitudes of Gentiles became believers and were baptized. In all parts of the earth, Jews and Gentiles gathered in one Spirit and faith, glorified the God and Father of our Lord Jesus Christ. When this happened, the words that the Good Shepherd had proclaimed beforehand as the work He would bring to completion were fulfilled. He had called the sheep that were not from the fold of the Jewish Church, and they had heard His voice, becoming one flock with one Shepherd.

The Lord's my Shepherd, I'll not want;
He makes me down to lie
In pastures green; He leadeth me
The quiet waters by. Amen.

✝ *(TLH 436:1)*

Monday

Read John 10:16

IF, ACCORDING TO THESE WORDS, it is Christ's will that all people gather in one flock, it follows that there must be only one true Church of Christ on earth. We must therefore hold fast to the holy, apostolic faith, "I believe in one holy Christian Church." In our time, people frequently entertain the delusion that there are many true churches, each of which has a different form of the truth. Many maintain that the Christian religion is not the only saving faith. In fact, they claim that nothing depends on faith: if a person acts according to his conscience, if he loves his fellow man and treats everyone fairly, he may then believe whatever he wants, and he will be saved.

Many so-called Christian preachers misuse Bible verses to explain away such dreadful indifference to religion.

All of these pernicious thoughts undermine and overturn religion and godliness, and they are judged and rejected by the words of Christ: "There will be one flock, and one shepherd." Christ has one flock, and He is the only true Shepherd of peoples' souls. Therefore, if a person does not belong to this flock and this Shepherd, there is no second flock in which his soul can find pasture. Like a lost lamb, his soul restlessly wanders without water in the desert of this world, and it finally dies. A person who has not come to the communion of the Church is not on the path to heaven; instead, he is without God and without hope.

The true Church is bound to nothing except Christ and His holy Word, and since that Word has already sounded to the ends of the earth, His flock is to be found everywhere. While many falsely enlarge the Church of Christ, many others, on the contrary, falsely want to limit it. Roman Catholics bind the Church and salvation to Rome and the Roman pontiff, condemning all who do not want to subject themselves to his supreme power and the authority of the bishops appointed by him. The sectarians, on the other hand, bind the Church and salvation to their sect and its works and rituals, condemning all who do not want to subscribe precisely to what their sect believes. All of these limitations, which would separate people anew, cast to the ground these words of Christ: "And I have other sheep that are not of this fold; I must bring them also, and they will listen to My voice. So there will be one flock, one shepherd."

Only one thing is necessary to belong to the one flock that saves. A person must listen to the voice of Christ and recognize Him as the only Shepherd of his soul, accepting Him and remaining with Him. Whoever is with Christ is in the true

Church, and his salvation stands unshakably firm and certain.

The true application of these words of Christ, "so there will be one flock, one shepherd," consists, finally, in this: We must help to share the Gospel according to the call and relationship in which we stand and according to the gifts that have been given to us. For although Christ gloriously fulfilled His Word in the service of the holy apostles, He does not want it to cease being fulfilled as long as He preserves, by His intercession, the time of grace for the world. It is Christ's most gracious will that His call as Shepherd resound always more loudly in the wildernesses of this world, where unnumbered multitudes of miserable heathens continue to wander without God and without hope. By this sharing of the Gospel, more and more people are led to the green pastures of Christ's Church. And as His holy flock becomes more unified in Him, the fences Satan and his servants set up to separate believers will continue to be broken down.

O Christ, our true and only Light,
Enlighten those who sit in night;
Let those afar now hear Thy voice
And in Thy fold with us rejoice. Amen.

(*ELHB 475:1*)

Tuesday

Read John 17:20–21

"I BELIEVE IN THE HOLY catholic church, the communion of saints." So it says in the Apostles' Creed. This shows us that the Church of Jesus Christ, outside of which there is no life and salvation, is both invisible and extended over the entire world.

The Church is invisible because, according to the creed, it is an object of faith. God's Word defines faith as "the assurance of things hoped for, the conviction of things not seen" (Hebrews 11:1). The true Church is the communion of the hearts of all believers in Christ Jesus, their Lord. Now these believers, of course, are not invisible spirits, but visible people. However, who can see the faith worked in the soul by the Holy Spirit? We cannot tell merely by looking at a person whether he is a believer and a member of the Christian Church. But everyone can readily discern where the true Church is. It is wherever God's Word is purely and clearly preached, and wherever the holy Sacraments are administered according to Christ's institution.

However, true Christians, who alone belong to the true Church, are mixed with false Christians, like wheat with weeds. Who can now distinguish the true Christians from the false ones and thus recognize the Church? No one. The people among whom the Church is located can readily be seen, but those who alone make up the Church are seen and known only by Him of whom it is said, "But God's firm foundation stands, bearing this seal: 'The Lord knows those who are his'" (2 Timothy 2:19). Therefore, Christ calls His Church a kingdom of God on earth, which does not come with outward signs. The apostle Paul calls the Church the body of Jesus Christ, the bride of the Lord, a spiritual house, the Jerusalem from above, and the congregation of the firstborn who are written in heaven.

Despite its invisibility, the Church extends over the whole world. The apostles, following Christ's command, preached the Gospel among all peoples, and there are now, in all regions of the globe, souls that truly believe in Christ and therefore belong to His Church. That Church, therefore, is wherever the blessed sound of the Gospel has entered, according to that irrevocable and eternally certain promise: "So shall My word be that goes out from My mouth; it shall not return to Me empty, but it shall accomplish that which I purpose, and shall succeed in the thing for which I sent it" (Isaiah 55:11). Christ's Church does not belong to any particular people, city, or land. Thus, no single portion of the earth and no particular fellowship of churches can claim, "Here alone is the Church." One particular visible church may, above all others, preach God's Word purely, faithfully administer the holy Sacraments, and gloriously shine in good works. But it cannot say, "We alone are God's house," for God's Word tells us that Christ Himself rules in the midst of His enemies, that is, where unbelievers, mockers, tempters, heretics, and tyrants rage.

Wherever God's Word is still valued and reverenced, Christ has His believers, even if false teachers pervert and falsify it. Christ is not a poor king who reigns only in one city, province, or country. Wherever in all the world the Word of His grace sounds, there He makes subjects for Himself and establishes the holy kingdom of His Church in defiance of the gates of hell.

O Comforter of priceless worth,
Send peace and unity on earth.
Support us in our final strife
And lead us out of death to life. Amen.

(TLH 261:1)

Wednesday

Read Romans 16:17

It is a dangerous error when a person thinks that the visible Lutheran Church is the Church, outside of which there is no salvation, and therefore only those who call themselves Lutherans can be saved. Yet it is just as false to suppose that because many people who are not members of the visible Lutheran Church are saved, the visible church to which a person belongs is of no consequence. This erroneous notion also involves the belief that whoever finds himself in a heterodox Church can remain in it without danger to his soul, and whoever belongs to the right-believing Lutheran Church can, without danger to his soul, leave that church for another.

The true Church is both invisible and scattered over the entire world. However, this faith should in no way mislead us to leave the orthodox visible Church or to regard our fellowship with it lightly. Those who want to belong to the invisible Church have the holy duty to separate themselves from all who falsify God's Word and obstinately remain in their errors.

If we trace the entire history of the Church from Adam to the last apostle, John, we find that the orthodox always separated themselves from the heterodox when God commanded them to do so. When the orthodox let themselves be enticed into fellowship with the heretics, they were severely punished. After Cain performed false worship, the orthodox Church of Adam separated itself from Cain's church, and Cain had to depart. Later, at the time of Noah, the children of God united with the children of men, who had forsaken God's pure Word. As a result, the Church suffered such great distress that, in order to preserve it, God had to destroy the whole remaining world. When the orthodox Church of Shem had shrunk to the family of Abraham and false worship had arisen everywhere else, Abraham finally received the command to separate from the false church, to which even his father belonged.

God's leading of the people of Israel can be seen in His constant effort to keep the orthodox Israelite Church pure by causing it to separate from all of the world's false churches. The holy prophets of the old covenant constantly exhorted Israel to remove itself from the company of all who worship falsely. The New Testament, too, is full of divine commands concerning the separation of orthodox Christians from the heretics. Christ Himself says, "Beware of false prophets, who come to you in sheep's clothing but inwardly are ravenous wolves" (Matthew 7:15). Later, He cautions: "For false christs and false prophets will arise and perform great signs and wonders, so as to lead astray, if possible, even the elect. See, I have told you beforehand. So, if they say to you, 'Look, he is in the wilderness,' do not go out. If they say, 'Look, he is in the inner rooms,' do not believe it" (Matthew 24:24–26). The apostle Paul writes in today's text, "I appeal to you, brothers, to watch out for those who cause divisions and create obstacles contrary to the doctrine that you have been taught; avoid them."

Here we see that God clearly prohibits fellowship between orthodox Christians and the heretics. Whoever persists in that fellowship sins against the commandment of the Lord, and whoever does so knowingly and willingly sins grievously, even mortally.

The haughty spirits, Lord, restrain
Who o'er Thy Church with might would reign
And always set forth something new,
Devised to change Thy doctrine true. Amen.

(TLH 292:6)

Thursday

Read Galatians 5:9

EVERYONE WHO HAS MADE even the smallest start in Christian knowledge realizes that it is both dangerous and destructive to a Christian's soul to join a sect that publicly rejects God's Word and denies all the mysteries of the Christian faith. However, if the heretics of a particular sect are not so coarse and obvious, then many think there is no harm in joining it, since it still appears to subscribe to the principal Christian doctrines. Such heterodox fellowships often appear to be especially friendly, humble, and zealous, and many suppose that joining such a sect might result in even more blessing and edification than the orthodox Church could provide. To be sure, the truth as it is preached in the orthodox Church often seems to wear a rough garment.

But this temptation to associate with those outside the Church is only a delusion. In many places, God's Word earnestly warns against false doctrine because it is especially dangerous to the soul. Christ Himself says to His disciples, "Watch and beware of the leaven of the Pharisees and Sadducees" (Matthew 16:6). As Paul explains in today's text, even a little false doctrine permeates like leaven, ruining the unleavened bread of the clear, pure truth. Isn't it, then, a holy duty of those who want to belong to the invisible congregation of the elect, who should work out their own salvation with fear and trembling, to flee false doctrine and teachers like poison and plague?

Nevertheless, many continue to think it is contrary to love to reject all false doctrine and teachers so harshly, and to sever relationships with all heterodox. Love, they suggest, demands union. But this, too, is nothing but a miserable deception of the convoluted human heart. To be sure, even according to God's Word, love demands union. But which union?

Paul calls to all Christians, "[Endeavor] to maintain the unity of the Spirit in the bond of peace" (Ephesians 4:3), but he immediately adds, "One Lord, one faith, one baptism!" What kind of love acts against God's express prohibition? It is nothing but an appearance of love, an empty illusion of love, and a love that is sinful, godless, and idolatrous. Why?

Because it places the love of man over the love for God, the sinful creature above the Most High in heaven. O godless alliance! O damnable union! It is built upon a love that sacrifices the eternal truth of God and tramples upon God's eternal commandment. Union with the heterodox will only harm the Church. If the orthodox continue to separate themselves, the heterodox are continuously reminded that their teachings are not welcome and, in time, they may come to recognize and reject those teachings as utterly erroneous. In any event, separation denies them the opportunity to spread those false teachings further. Fellowship between orthodox and heterodox produces the following result: the orthodox become more indifferent to the errors of the heterodox, and the heterodox become more indifferent to the truth of the orthodox. Error triumphs, and the truth is lost. To the one who wanders along the path of error, love is not shown by accompanying him or even by only warning him, but by leaving him. This deed testifies to the seriousness of his error and the earnestness with which he should seek to rid himself of it.

O gracious Lord, direct us,
Thy doctrine pure defend,
From heresies protect us,
And for Thy Word contend,

That we may praise Thee ever,
O God, with one accord
And say: The Lord, our Savior,
Be evermore adored. Amen.

(TLH 544:3)

Friday

Read 1 Corinthians 1:10

WHOEVER WANTS TO BELONG to the one, invisible Church must be an upright Christian, striving with great earnestness to do what God has commanded and to leave undone what He has forbidden. Such a person also has the holy duty to belong, where he can, to an orthodox visible church because this, too, is a clear command of God. According to God's Word, a person should not only have the right faith in his heart, but he should also confess it with his mouth and his deeds. Therefore, whoever wants to belong to the true invisible Church also joins with those who confess the faith of this Church.

As soon as the family of Adam had divided, "Then people started to preach in the LORD's name" (Genesis 4:26 AAT). At that time, God instituted the public preaching of His Word and He has preserved this office ever since, announcing His anger to all who do not accept and listen to those who were called and sent by Him to preach His holy and pure Word. With the establishment and preservation of the preaching office, God clearly testified that, according to His holy will, there should be, in addition to an invisible kingdom of His children on earth, a visible Church of ordered congregations. In the midst of these congregations, God's Word is to be publicly, purely, and clearly proclaimed, and the holy Sacraments are to be faithfully administered. God's Word is thus to be preached both to those who have not yet heard it and in the assemblies of His children.

No one who wants to be saved is free to remain alone, to separate himself from the multitude of other confessors of the truth, and to keep the divine service only for himself. Instead, each person is bound to keep himself where the Word is preached in an open and orderly manner. As David testifies, "I hate the assembly of evildoers. . . . I wash my hands in innocence and go around Your altar, O LORD, proclaiming thanksgiving aloud, and telling all Your wondrous deeds" (Psalm 26:5–7). Christ says, "And if he refuses to listen even to the church, let him be to you as a Gentile and a tax collector" (Matthew 18:17). When the apostles converted 3,000 souls on the first Pentecost, the Book of Acts reports that "they devoted themselves to the apostles' teaching and fellowship, to the breaking of bread and the prayers" (2:42). Later, when those zealous for the faith wanted to go out, the apostles cautioned, "[Do] not [neglect] to meet together, as is the habit of some" (Hebrews 10:25). And as Paul exhorts in today's text, believers should tolerate "no divisions among you," but instead should be "united in the same mind and the same judgment."

Who, then, can deny God's express demand that those who want to belong to the true invisible Church must also belong to the orthodox visible Church?

Now we may gather with our King
E'en in the lowliest dwelling;
Praises to Him we there may bring,
His wondrous mercy forthtelling.

Jesus His grace to us accords;
Spirit and life are all His words;
His truth doth hallow the temple. Amen.

† *(TLH 467:4)*

Saturday

Read 1 Peter 2:25

WHEN GOD FIRST CREATED MAN, he was so good that all he required for blessedness was to remain as he was. However, after the first people allowed themselves to be tempted by Satan to fall from God into sin, all of their descendants are corrupt from birth. They can be saved only if they have converted to God from their heart. This conversion is required not just for coarse sinners who live in shame and vice, but also for subtle sinners who walk blamelessly before their fellow men. For this reason, Christ commanded His disciples to preach repentance as well as the forgiveness of sins. As Paul informed the Athenians, "The times of ignorance God overlooked, but now He commands all people everywhere to repent" (Acts 17:30). In our text today, Peter tells all true Christians that they "were straying like sheep" who "have now returned to the Shepherd and Overseer of your souls."

The blind, unbelieving world has a completely upside-down notion about conversion—and so do many who want to be good Christians. These people think that conversion occurs when a person begins to go to church faithfully, hears God's Word and reads it at home, and receives Holy

Communion. However, this is a great error. Going to church and hearing and reading God's Word are good and necessary things, but they do not constitute conversion. It is of no help to many thousands of so-called Christians that they have the Word of God if they do not use it rightly. Christ says, "Blessed rather are those who hear the Word of God and keep it!" (Luke 11:28). The Book of Hebrews reports, "For good news came to us just as to them, but the message they heard did not benefit them, because they were not united by faith with those who listened" (4:2).

The holy Sacraments are not conversion, but what follow from it. At the first Pentecost, Peter's hearers cried out, "Brothers, what shall we do?" Peter advised them repent and then to "be baptized every one of you in the name of Jesus Christ for the forgiveness of your sins" (Acts 2:38). The Ethiopian eunuch, talking with the evangelist Philip, said: "See, here is water. What prevents me from being baptized?" (Acts 8:36–37). Philip may have answered, "If you believe with your whole heart, you may." It is the same with Holy Communion. Eating and drinking, whether physically or spiritually, do not give a person life, but they do strengthen him. This Sacrament is instituted not for conversion but for those who have already converted as a means of strengthening them in their conversion, in faith, in love, and in patience. But if we ask how a person may recognize that he is a converted Christian, our text supplies the answer: "For you were like sheep straying, but have now returned to the Shepherd and Overseer of your souls."

Everything depends on the One to whom a person is converted. Converted Christians are not those who no longer sin. On the contrary, they are those who recognize themselves as sinners and who find God's grace and forgiveness through their Savior and Shepherd, Jesus Christ. They do not need to possess great knowledge or a strong, heroic faith. All they need to recognize is that Jesus is their Redeemer and that they must rely on Him alone. In heavenly things, they listen neither to the wisdom of this world nor to their own reason, but only to the voice of Jesus, their Good Shepherd. As our Lord says, "My sheep hear My voice" and "They do not know the voice of strangers" (John 10:27, 5). They are the ones who walk with Him on the road of suffering, but they enjoy, already here on earth, a blessed peace the world cannot give.

Who so happy as I am,
Even now the Shepherd's lamb?
And when my short life is ended,
By His angel host attended,
He shall fold me to His breast,
There within His arms to rest. Amen.

† *(TLH 648:3)*

Sunday

Read John 16:20–21

IN OUR GOSPEL, Jesus shows the disciples how their faith should be examined and exercised, and thus strengthened and preserved until they enter into eternal joy. The way this happens is the same way faith is first begotten and born. He tells them, "Truly, truly, I say to you, you will weep and lament, but the world will rejoice. You will be sorrowful, but your sorrow will turn into joy." Divine sorrow, not worldly sorrow, is the way to the joy of faith on earth. It cannot be otherwise.

way to the joy of faith on earth. It cannot be otherwise. True faith is not a passive adherence to the truth of everything in the Bible. Even a person who does not have a broken heart can do this much. True faith is a divine power worked by the Holy Spirit to comfort Christ's own in firm confidence against all uneasiness of conscience over sin, God's wrath, death, judgment, and hell. It is that power by which a person is born again, love of sin is rooted out of him, his heart is purified and renewed, and the love of God and neighbor is poured into his heart.

This wonderful change cannot take place in any person as long as he remains comfortable in his sins. Christ compares the birth of the joy of true faith in the heart of a person with the physical birth of a child, saying, "When a woman is giving birth, she has sorrow because her hour has come, but when she has delivered the baby, she no longer remembers the anguish, for joy that a human being has been born into the world." It is the same with the joy of faith. Without the birth pains of true repentance, faith does not come into the world. As God said, if true faith, with its heavenly joy, is to come into a human heart, the person must first "know and see that it is evil and bitter for you to forsake the LORD your God; the fear of Me is not in you" (Jeremiah 2:19). The individual who is contrite and sorrowful over his sins will not and cannot earn something from God because no person, as he is by nature, can truly believe. Only the one who is frightened by his sins can truly take hold of Christ in faith.

Unfortunately, there are many who want to be believing Christians but do not have an earnest grief over and an aversion to their sins. They do not conduct themselves conscientiously in their jobs but on occasion resort to dishonesty or, if they encounter a difficulty, lie. They are slanderers, gladly speaking evil of their neighbor behind his back or acting without love toward him. They align themselves with the vain world, secretly cling to the god of mammon, consider their own honor as their highest goal, make way for certain passions, nurse impure desires, engage in envy and hatred, and remain at enmity with those who offend them. Now and then, they experience a certain restlessness in their conscience over all this, but they easily convince themselves that this is just weakness and they can still stand with God in grace. They suppress their worry and try to get the matter out of their mind as rapidly as possible.

How can those who hobble between Christ and Belial think they still stand in faith? It comes from this: they have a faith that was not born of true sorrow over their sins. Instead, their miserable faith is one of delusion, which overcomes neither temptation nor death. Their faith is more dangerous than open unbelief.

From depths of woe I cry to Thee,
Lord, hear me, I implore Thee.
Bend down Thy gracious ear to me,
My prayer let come before Thee.
If Thou rememb'rest each misdeed,
If each should have its rightful meed,
Who may abide Thy presence?

Though great our sins and sore our woes,
His grace much more aboundeth;
His helping love no limit knows,
Our utmost need it soundeth.
Our Shepherd good and true is He,
Who will at last His Israel free
From all their sin and sorrow. Amen.

† *(TLH 329:1,5)*

Monday

Read John 16:22–23

WHEN THE LORD SAYS to His apostles, "A little while, and you will see Me no longer" (John 16:16), He gives a short biography of both the apostles and all Christians. Their life is not uninterrupted sorrow, but a constant changing from joy to sorrow. The reason for their joy is that they see Christ and in that they are certain of the nearness of His grace. The reason for their sorrow is that at times they do not see Christ; they become uncertain of the nearness of His grace.

Christians receive a portion of the trouble that comes to all people but also suffer disgrace, reproach, and persecution precisely because they are Christian. But this is not the object of the Christians' sorrow. If they sorrow over their cross, it is only a weakness of their flesh, a more worldly than godly sorrow. They should rejoice and boast in this instead of being sad. Their sorrow consists of something entirely different.

True Christians know no greater treasure in this world than that they have God's grace and live according to His will. It is this alone that makes life dear and valuable to them, and it converts a valley of misery into a place of joy. However, as long as they live on earth, they never manage to comfort themselves completely with God's grace and they cannot perfectly fulfill God's will. They long to be entirely spirit but they still have too much flesh. Today, they believe with full confidence but tomorrow their faith will seem to be in danger of being extinguished like a candle flame. Unbelief penetrates powerfully into the heart. And as soon as they become weak in faith, they lose their power to fight against their sins, to love God and neighbor, and to serve God and deny themselves. If this does not cause them to fall from faith quickly and completely, it nevertheless places them in a heavy battle so that, with Paul, they sigh, "Wretched man that I am! Who will deliver me from this body of death?" (Romans 7:24).

The Christian must spend many days of his life fighting this battle. Often, there are long periods when he feels almost nothing other than his unbelief and sinfulness; and this is so painful to him that his heart is almost always full of sighing. The remembrance of his past, the present condition of his heart and life, and his bleak thoughts of the future fill him with sorrow.

Whoever does not experience this on a daily basis can see evidence that his faith is only an empty, powerless delusion. As sad as this is for lukewarm Christians who do not engage in the battle, those who confess that they are almost never entirely free from the trial, care, and sorrow of the heart are in a happy condition. For if they squarely recognize their incurable corruption and regard any good they think, speak, or do as being entirely from God, it is well with them. Without misery about sin and sorrow of their heart, they would never remain in Christ. Instead, they would soon become secure, proud, and self-righteous. The sorrow with which they are continually visited is the means God employs to keep them with Christ.

Oh, blessed is he who is kept with Christ. By this he remains on the certain path to eternal joy. As Christ says: "So also you have sorrow now, but I will see you again and your hearts will rejoice, and no one will take your joy from you. In that day you will ask nothing of Me." Let us, then, gladly follow the way of godly sorrow on which the Lord leads us. His goal for us is peace in both time and eternity. While we reside on earth, our weak heart and the distress of our soul sometimes prompt us to ask, "O Lord, why?" But on that day when we behold God and the harvest of joy is gathered from our sowing of tears, we will ask nothing more. Then we will have nothing but praise for the One who has guided us through sorrow to eternal glory, through trouble and toil to eternal rest.

God knows full well when times of gladness
Shall be the needful thing for thee.
When He has tried thy soul with sadness
And from all guile has found thee free,
He comes to thee all unaware
And makes thee own His loving care. Amen.

† *(TLH 518:4)*

Tuesday

Read Philippians 3:1

THERE ARE PEOPLE who want to be Christians but they are almost always sad. Their faces almost never shine with peace and joy. They go around dark and sullen, a burden to themselves and others. And what is the reason? One is displeased because he sees others advance seemingly without difficulty, becoming rich and happy in the process, while he cannot prosper despite considerable effort. Another considers himself to be misjudged, denied the honor to which he thinks he is entitled. A third is disgruntled by enemies whose injustices are not suppressed by the authorities. These individuals are unhappy because things do not proceed according to their wishes.

Vain joy of the world is ungodly, but worldly sorrow is still more sinful and pernicious. Holy joy is the picture of God, while worldly sorrow is the picture of Satan and the exact opposite of faith. Although it often takes on the appearance of Christian earnestness, it is a secret murmuring against God, the Ruler of our life, and a fruit of pride and self-righteousness. For whoever has truly recognized that he has earned hell with his sins cannot possibly be dissatisfied with his lot, however unfavorable it may seem. He must remember that no matter his circumstances, they are better than he merits. As the Book of Lamentations expresses it, "Why should a living man complain, a man, about the punishment of his sins?" (3:39).

Worldly sorrow is also against the love of the neighbor. Whoever is almost always in a bad mood, dark and depressed, becomes a burden to those who deal with him. He should be a comfort and a help to his brothers on the difficult way to eternity. Instead, he serves only to make their pilgrimage through this world more difficult. Such a person eventually injures himself. When worldly sorrow dominates the heart, faith and love retreat and the Holy Ghost, the Spirit of joy and peace, no longer dwells there. Such sorrow, then, is a certain way to eternal sorrow in hell, for "worldly grief produces death" (2 Corinthians 7:10).

Therefore, Christ praises Christians as blessed when they are persecuted because of righteousness, hated on His account, slandered, and rejected as wicked. "Your reward is great in heaven" (Matthew 5:12). All of the apostles make the same demand on us. Peter writes, "Rejoice insofar as you share Christ's sufferings" (1 Peter 4:13). James says, "Count it all joy, my brothers, when you meet trials of various kinds" (1:2). These same apostles practiced what they preached. When the high council in Jerusalem flogged them because of they confessed Christ, they are not reported to have been sad and angry about it. Rather, "they left the presence of the council, rejoicing that they were counted worthy to suffer dishonor for the name" (Acts 5:41). Paul confesses, "In all our affliction, I am overflowing with joy" (2 Corinthians 7:4). This type of behavior was not reserved to the apostles, but was also followed by common Christians. The author of the Epistle to the Hebrews gives the converted Hebrews the glorious witness: "you joyfully accepted the plundering of your property, since you knew that you yourselves had a better possession [heaven] and an abiding one" (10:34).

If a Christian should be joyful and confident even amid the greatest afflictions and persecutions, is it not disgraceful when he indulges in sorrow and ill humor merely because things have not gone entirely according to his wishes? It is a truly terrible sign that he has lost the faith that overcomes the world.

O Friend of souls, how blest am I
Whene'er Thy love my spirit calms!
From sorrow's dungeon forth I fly
And hide me in Thy shelt'ring arms.
The night of weeping flies away
Before the heart-reviving ray
Of love that beams from out Thy breast;
Here is my heaven on earth begun.
Who is not joyful that has won
In Thee, O Lord, his joy and rest? Amen.

(ELHB 109:1)

Wednesday

Read Romans 13:1

ACCORDING TO GOD'S WORD, the governing authorities were appointed not because they acted piously, justly, fairly, and kindly, but because they were granted authority by God's governance and permission. Their authority is proof that God appointed them. At a time when the bloodthirsty Nero was emperor, Saint Paul did not advise Christians to be subject to the governing authority only if it was agreeable to them. Indeed, he says, "For there is no authority except from God, and those that exist," just or unjust, "have been instituted by God." As a good government is a blessing of God upon a people, a bad government is a divine punishment. Therefore God says to Israel, "I gave you a king in My anger" (Hosea 13:11). Furthermore, God says, "I will make boys their princes, and infants shall rule over them" (Isaiah 3:4). And, "a godless man should not reign, that he should not ensnare the people" (Job 34:30). As we now must suffer when God sends pestilence, flood, hail, crop failure, scarcity, and hunger upon a country, so too must we suffer when God lays the scourge of a tyrannical governing authority upon a land. In this, we must honor God's hand and holy order.

God is not the cause of sin. God can neither approve the unrighteousness of tyrants nor demand that people regard the unrighteousness as righteousness. However, while God rejects the person of unrighteous authority, He still confirms His order in His holy office. Thus, when the Israelites, tired of their republican state, deposed their judges and desired a king, God said to Samuel, "They have not rejected you, but they have rejected Me" (1 Samuel 8:7).

As a result of this revolution, Saul became king over the Jewish people and God Himself conferred on him all the rights of majesty belonging to a king. Later, when King Saul became a bloodthirsty tyrant, God rejected his person. But even David, who was persecuted by Saul, was not allowed to lay his avenging hand upon the king as one anointed of the Lord. Finally, when Jeroboam came to the throne as the result of a rebellion of the ten tribes following Solomon's death, God announced His judgment to him. However, when he had become king, God forbade the tribe of Judah to cast him from his throne. Christ Himself once said to His unrighteous judge, "You would have no authority over Me at all unless it had been given you from above" (John 19:11).

This shows that when God allows someone to come to power on earth, He wants those subject to him to subordinate themselves to this power. In time and in eternity, God punishes the sin of the tyrant. Nevertheless, He wants his power and his office to be honored. When the people rebel against an earthly ruler, they reject God and revolt against heaven. Yet when a revolution produces a new authority, God again seals it and demands obedience to it.

How could it be otherwise? Where would we be if God allowed those who deemed a government unjust to set themselves against it? Perpetual struggle, constant bloodletting, and continuous civil war would beset the people. No one could be certain of his life, his property, or his good name. Public rest and order, worship and instruction, trade and business, the cultivation of art and science—in short, everything that brings prosperity—would soon come to an end. To be sure, all this will be hindered by tyrannical government, but only occasionally since even the most unrighteous government must see to it that its citizens and subjects are cared for. Therefore, how could God better care for our well-being than by commanding that all be obedient to the government that has power over us?

Let our rulers ever be
Men that love and honor Thee;
Let the powers by Thee ordained
Be in righteousness maintained.
In the people's hearts increase
Love of piety and peace.
Thus united, we shall stand
One wide, free, and happy land. Amen.

† *(TLH 566:3)*

Thursday

Read 1 Peter 2:11

MUCH DEPENDS ON HOW a person sees his whole life on earth. The more an individual errs in how he judges his earthly existence, the more he misses the purpose God intends for him. The more vividly a person recognizes what his life in this world is, the sooner he attains the goal God sets for him.

How do most people view their lives in this world? They believe that God created them to enjoy, as much and as long as possible, the beauties, joys, and comforts of life and then pay the whole debt with death. Or they think they should remain here forever. The sad result of this is that these people totally forget about the salvation of their immortal soul and the eternity God plans for them. They never ask, "What must I do that I may be saved?" They conclude that they need no Bible, no divine revelation, no signpost to the heavenly fatherland, no Savior, and no Sanctifier. They seek only to become rich in earthly goods and attain high honor so they can live as happily as possible. Most do not care about God's holy will, do not heed their conscience, and are unafraid of sin and unrighteousness. They enjoy the earthly life and throw themselves into every fleshly amusement.

In our text, Saint Peter reminds Christians how they should correctly view their life on earth: "Beloved, I urge you as sojourners and exiles to abstain from the passions of the flesh, which wage war against your soul." The Christian should recognize that his entire life is a journey and he should abstain from every fleshly lust that fights against the salvation of his dearly paid for soul.

What traveler will reach his destination at the appointed time if he allows himself to dawdle along the way, if he is enticed by the amusements and attractions he encounters on his journey? It is important that he proceed directly, stopping nowhere, quieting only hunger and thirst, then, newly strengthened, set out again.

If a Christian recognizes that his life is nothing but a trip toward blessed eternity, this conviction will urgently compel him to refrain from the fleshly lusts that war against the soul. His flesh may tempt him to attach his heart to such earthly things as money and goods, house and property, glory and vain decoration, but if he recalls his journey, he will remember the words in the Epistle to the Hebrews: "For here we have no lasting city, but we seek the city that is to come" (13:14). Then the thoughts of fleshly delights and good days will cause him to become frightened and he will quickly tear the bands that ensnare his soul. Then he will set out again on his journey, saying, "It is not meant for me to sleep on soft pillows here. I have still not reached my destination. Perhaps the sun of my life will soon sink and the night will come, in which no one can work and no one can complete the way to the heavenly destination."

A pilgrim and a stranger,
I journey here below;
Far distant is my country,
The home to which I go.
Here I must toil and travail,
Oft weary and opprest;
But there my God shall lead me
To everlasting rest. Amen.

(TLH 586:1)

Friday

Read 1 Peter 2:12–17

TODAY'S READING INSTRUCTS the Christian to behave as a foreigner during his journey through this world. What is a foreigner's duty in a foreign land? Above all, he has to remember not to disgrace his homeland by his behavior. Others must see him as a praiseworthy representative of his country and his people. Saint Peter calls to us Christians, who confess that we are strangers on earth and children of God rather than the world, "keep your conduct among the Gentiles honorable," that is, among the people of the world. Whatever evil we may do is always an affront to our true King. Our smallest wrong dishonors both us and our brothers and sisters in Christ. The world will attribute our ungodly nature to the Bible because this is the book of the law in the holy city of God, whose citizens we confess to be. What kind of reception can we one day expect in our heavenly homeland if our behavior in this world caused God's kingdom to be slandered by its enemies? Therefore, wherever we Christians go and stay, we must prove ourselves to be subjects of a Lord in whose country justice and righteousness dwell and whose rule is grounded on love, truth, and holiness.

But there are many who are godly with the godly and godless with the godless. How much better it would be for such hypocrites if they did not pass themselves off as citizens of the heavenly kingdom, if they would completely renounce the Christian Church. Thus they would sin only for themselves and their behavior would not cause others to become vexed with God and His Word and so be lost. Therefore, let us never forget that we are here on a journey, and by our good behavior, we should also make a good name for our fatherland.

Christians everywhere should also conduct themselves as guests. A guest is unassuming. Wherever he is received, he does not behave as a lord of the house. Instead, he conforms himself to the regulations of the lord of the house so he does not become troublesome and risk being thrown out of the house that had welcomed him with hospitality. "Be subject for the Lord's sake to every human institution," Peter admonishes. "Honor everyone. Love the brotherhood. Fear God. Honor the emperor." On earth, we live in a foreign dwelling. Although we are free children of God, we submit ourselves to all human lords and laws as long as we do not infringe upon the obedience we have sworn to the eternal King in Holy Baptism. Let us show the world that, in our fatherland, the citizens have learned obedience and submission, that "they may see your good deeds and glorify God on the day of visitation."

But many make Christian freedom a cover for malice. When they hear that a person is righteous and saved through good works and not through faith in Christ, they believe they can live according to the free desire of their heart and God will overlook their deliberate sins. Oh, how they delude themselves! God wants to forgive them even for this sin so they can serve Him without fear throughout their life. They are created anew through faith to perform good works.

Lord Jesus Christ, my Life, my Light,
My Strength by day, my Trust by night,
On earth I'm but a passing guest
And sorely with my sins opprest.

Far off I see my fatherland,
Where thro' Thy blood I hope to stand.
But ere I reach that Paradise,
A weary way before me lies. Amen.

(TLH 148:1, 2)

Saturday

Read 1 Peter 2:18–20

WITH THE WORDS of our reading today, Saint Peter reminds Christians of the cross they must take up to follow their Savior. The conviction Christians have that they are only pilgrims in this world demands that they willingly bear the difficulties that arise during their pilgrimage.

There are many things to be endured on a journey. Sometimes there are unfriendly innkeepers, bad lodgings, dreary and rough regions, steep mountains, sudden slopes, marshes and bogs, burning heat of the sun, stiffening cold, and deluges without a protecting shelter. Sometimes forests must be traversed by night. Sometimes marauders attack in an attempt to take one's goods or life. Sometimes terrible storms arise on the sea under which the abyss opens like the vengeance of death.

It is both important and comforting for the Christian to remember that in the days of trial and tribulation, he is on a journey. For then he will understand that misfortunes are to be expected, and that the sad street on which he is traveling will finally lead to the heavenly homeland.

If the Christian has to deal with people who make life difficult for him, he comforts himself by recalling that he is on a journey. When he meets an unfriendly innkeeper, he knows that one day he will be welcomed with the hospitality of the heavenly Father. If his living conditions bring nothing but sorrow and trial, he can be comforted with the thought that he is merely staying overnight in a bad inn. It will last only until dawn, when he will find himself in heaven, to remain there eternally. If the Christian sees others living peacefully and moving upward while he himself cannot seem to get ahead, he views this as passing through a rough region. At such times, he must climb steep mountains and laboriously wend his way through marshes and bogs. But it is only a short stretch. The heavenly city already shines before him. There he will soon rest.

If the Christian here must earn his bread by the sweat of his brow, if he has the lowest wages for the hardest work, he asks, "How can it be otherwise for a traveler?" The warmth of the summer sun is soon followed by the icy cold of winter. If he cannot find suitable lodging, he can seek refuge under a foreign roof. He may be deprived of his own property and his body and life may even be in danger. But he remembers, "This is a discomfort of travel, yet no one can take my soul from me." Finally, if the Christian encounters the greatest temptation of his soul, even in the distress of death, he can say, "I am now on a ship surrounded by storms. But I can be comforted because God Himself is my Helmsman, and when the boat of my life is wrecked, He will carry me in His arms to the opposite shore of eternal life."

We must always remember to regard our life as nothing more than a journey to our true homeland. Then we would not so often stand still and engross our heart in the things of this world. Then we would not lose sight of heaven—we would consider the world to be as nothing. Then we would walk more carefully before the eyes of the enemies of God and His Word, as model citizens of a perfect kingdom so others might be awakened to walk the narrow path with us into the beautiful land we seek. Then we would conduct ourselves as guests who gladly accommodate ourselves everywhere and are happy even when we are merely tolerated. Then we would gladly surrender ourselves to God's will, even when He allows much trouble and suffering to be our portion.

There still my thoughts are dwelling,
'Tis there I long to be;
Come, Lord, and call Thy servant
To blessedness with Thee.
Come, bid my toils be ended,
Let all my wand'rings cease;
Call from the wayside lodging
To Thy sweet home of peace. Amen.

† *(TLH 586:6)*

Sunday

Read John 16:8–9

THE WORLD HOLDS various opinions on the subject of sin. Some think sin is nothing but a weakness and a sickness of human nature. They maintain that since a person cannot be punished when he suffers from a bodily sickness, he will not be punished for sins that result from sickness of the soul. Others attribute people's wicked and brutal lives to lack of education, bad upbringing, false principles, or temperament they inherited from their parents. God, they believe, will not hold such sins against them. Instead, when they die, He will make better people of them. Still others hold that sin is indeed something that damns people before God, but only coarse sins such as theft, public fraud, robbery, cruelty, murder, adultery, open fornication, false oaths, endless curses and slanders, daily drunkenness, gluttony, and the like. Such individuals contend that God does not impute to the weak person other, finer sins. Still others go somewhat further. They believe that even obvious sins against the love of God and neighbor do not damn; instead, if a person regrets his sins and seeks to better himself, his sins are forgiven.

What is the correct conviction of sin that the Holy Ghost alone provides? It is found in today's text. Does this mean the Holy Ghost will convince the world that, with the exception of unbelief, nothing is accounted as sin? Not at all! Rather, the Lord says, "When I have gone to the Father—that is, when I have completed My suffering and death, have been raised, and have ascended into heaven—then the Holy Ghost will preach through you, My dear apostles, in the whole world. He will say, 'You people, there are no differences among you. You are all sinners, and you lack the glory that you should have for God. But behold! God became a man, took all of man's sins upon Himself, and was punished for them. His bitter suffering and death blotted out all of those sins, so that all who believe in Him would not be lost, but would have eternal life. For whoever believes and is baptized will be saved, but whoever does not believe will be condemned'" (see Mark 16).

Jesus says that the Holy Ghost will first convict the world "concerning sin, because they do not believe in Me" (John 16:9). This means that the Holy Ghost will, by the preaching of the apostles, convict the people of the world who by nature lie in sin and condemnation. Precisely for this reason, the Son of God became a man, suffered, and died to blot out their sin and condemnation. Because He did, grace is offered to everyone. Now there is only one sin that has the power to condemn, and it, too, is a sin that rules in all people by nature: a failure to believe in Jesus Christ as our Savior from sin. As Saint Paul writes, "For God has consigned them all to disobedience [unbelief], that He may have mercy on all" (Romans 11:32).

Now to My Father I depart,
The Holy Spirit sending
And, heavenly wisdom to impart,
My help to thee extending.
He shall in trouble comfort thee,
Teach thee to know and follow Me,
And in all truth shall guide thee. Amen.

† *(TLH 387:9)*

Monday

Read John 16:10

MANY PEOPLE BELIEVE that no sin is damnable. Just as many hold that they do not need any righteousness to be able to stand before God and be saved. But most people will admit that for an individual not to be cast away by God, it is necessary that both his sins be forgiven and he be righteous before God.

Again, there is a great diversity of opinion about the righteousness that avails before God. One thinks he is righteous if he does what is demanded of a good citizen, a second believes he is righteous if he outwardly fulfills what his religion or his church prescribes, and a third maintains that a good heart is also required.

But what does the Holy Spirit say? The answer is supplied in today's reading. Christ's going to the Father—His life, suffering, death, resurrection, and ascension alone—is the source of our righteousness. It cannot be our works before we come to faith and are converted, for we are pure sinners by nature. It cannot be our faith, for faith is God's work alone. It cannot be our sanctification after we come to faith, for that is imperfect, stained with a thousand sins. There is only One out of all people who was perfectly righteous before God by His own work: the Man, Jesus Christ. He was not righteous for Himself, for He is God and does not require His own righteousness. He gives it away, gives it to all who desire it and will receive it. He gives it to all who believe in Him.

In order to convict us of this, the Holy Ghost calls to us, "For Christ is the end of the law for righteousness to everyone who believes" (Romans 10:4), and "For our sake He made Him to be sin who knew no sin, so that in Him we might become the righteousness of God" (2 Corinthians 5:21). This wonderful righteousness does not come from within a person, but from outside. He cannot gain or merit it; he must let it be given to him out of grace. Such righteousness cannot be found on earth, but only in heaven. No one who regards himself as godly can have it, but only the poor sinner who regards himself as lost and condemned.

Oh, poor person who does not want to be lost, do not laugh at this righteousness with which Christians comfort themselves. It may seem foolish to you, but it is the only righteousness with which you can stand before God. Do not attempt to plead your own righteousness before the holy God. You will only be shamed by it. Before God, even the heavens are not pure and all human righteousness is like a filthy garment. Even those of us who have become frustrated and who have called out, with David, "Enter not into judgment with your servant, for no one living is righteous before You" (Psalm 143:2), must not seek righteousness in anything other than Christ's going to the Father. Do not say, "How may I regard myself as righteous since I do not see in me any righteousness but only sin?" For this reason, Christ says that the Holy Ghost convicts the world of righteousness and that He goes to the Father and we see Him no more. This righteousness is not seen; it is grasped only through faith in the invisible Christ. Therefore, whatever your heart may say, Christ's suffering, death, and resurrection are your righteousness. This is the conviction the Holy Ghost holds out to you.

Naught have I, O Christ, to offer
Naught but Thee, my Highest Good.
Naught have I, O Lord, to proffer
But Thy crimson-colored blood.

Thy death on the cross hath Death wholly defeated
And thereby my righteousness fully completed;
Salvation's white raiments I there did obtain,
And in them in glory with Thee I shall reign. Amen.

(TLH 366:6)

Tuesday

Read John 16:11

AMONG THE UNBELIEVERS, the children of the world, there are those who are not afraid of God's judgment because they think either there will be no such judgment or God will not condemn them. There are only a few of these people, however, because the human conscience preaches too loudly that a day will come when God will make known the hidden things and reveal the counsel of hearts. Therefore, most people either try to avoid the vivid reminder of the judgment on the Last Day or regard it with fear and trembling. By his own natural understanding and power, no person is able to await the day of final judgment with joy.

About what does the Holy Ghost seek to convince the world regarding judgment? The words of today's text, as threatening as they sound, include an unspeakably great comfort. The Lord tells us here that through the Gospel the Holy Ghost will convince the redeemed world that Satan was overcome by Christ, rejected, and thrown into the abyss by God's judgment. Therefore, whoever is rid of sin through faith, thus sharing in Christ's righteousness, does not have to fear any judgment, any accusation of the devil, any hell, and any damnation. For him, the Last Day will be a day of complete redemption and victory. It will be the day when his freedom and glory in Christ, the conqueror of Satan, will be revealed.

It is well with him who has been brought to this belief by the Holy Ghost! He has thus come to the greatest height of faith. What the world must fear with trembling, he hopes for with joy. What embitters the mortal life of the world is a sweetening of the earthly life for him. What makes death hard and terrible for the world makes dying easy and precious for him. He can triumph in the face of death, saying, "For I am already being poured out as a drink offering, and the time of my departure has come. I have fought the good fight, I have finished the race, I have kept the faith. Henceforth there is laid up for me the crown of righteousness, which the Lord, the righteous judge, will award to me on that Day, and not only to me but also to all who have loved His appearing" (2 Timothy 4:6–8).

Now, then, let us rid ourselves of anxious thoughts on the subject of salvation. If we are here given the right conviction of the Holy Spirit by the Gospel, our path will go from sin to faith, from faith to righteousness, and from righteousness to glory. We will also discover that the golden chain wound by Paul has inseparable members: "And those whom He predestined He also called, and those whom He called He also justified, and those whom He justified He also glorified" (Romans 8:30).

To Him, the precious Holy Ghost, together with the Father and the Son, be praise, glory, and thanks in time and eternity. Amen.

O Jesus, who my debt didst pay
And for my sin wast smitten,
Within the Book of Life, oh, may

My name be also written!
I will not doubt; I trust in Thee,
From Satan Thou hast made me free
And from all condemnation.

O Jesus Christ, do not delay,
But hasten our salvation;
We often tremble on our way
In fear and tribulation.
Then hear us when we cry to Thee;
Come, mighty Judge, and make us free
From every evil! Amen.

† *(TLH 611:5, 7)*

Wednesday

Read Ephesians 2:3

IN OUR DAY, there is a frequently spoken principle that one person can demand nothing more of another than that he always acts according to his conviction. If it is asked whether someone has done right or wrong and whether that individual will be able to stand before God one day, the response is that it all depends on whether he followed his conviction. If a person does something believing it is good, this reasoning goes, then it is good.

The pursuit of this principle leads to great indifference toward religion. A person concludes that little or nothing depends on one's faith and religion. When a pagan worships the sun, moon and stars or people, animals and idols, it is thought to be just as pleasing to God as when a Christian worships the true God in true faith, as long as the pagan is of the opinion that those created things are his gods that he must serve. Actions based on convictions are also thought to justify a person before God and man. But if the believers of this principle read in God's Word that they, too, are great sinners and must repent, they often respond: "Why? What evil did I do? From my childhood on, I have behaved on the principle, Do right and offend no one. What more can God want from me?"

No matter how widespread it has become, the principle is still thoroughly false. It is true, of course, that when a person does something evil with the conviction that it is evil, it is a far greater sin than when he does evil in the erroneous belief that it is something good. Saint Paul says, for his own comfort, "formerly I was a blasphemer, persecutor, and insolent opponent. But I received mercy because I had acted ignorantly in unbelief" (1 Timothy 1:13). After Saint Peter tells the Jews in Jerusalem that they "killed the Author of life," he adds to excuse them and not to cast them down in doubt, "And now, brothers, I know that you acted in ignorance, as did also your rulers" (Acts 3:15,17).

There is no way, however, that we can conclude from this that what a person considers to be right is right or becomes right. Our Lord said, "And that servant who knew his master's will but did not get ready or act according to his will, will receive a severe beating" But he immediately added, "But the one who did not know, and did what deserved a beating, will receive a light beating" (Luke 12:47–48). God's Word goes still further. It shows us that godliness and the true fear of God are displayed when a person proceeds without following his thoughts, his discretion, his opinions, or his so-called conviction. The great corruption of people is that they act according to the desires of their heart and the judgment of their natural reason. In fact, God gives people up to the terrible punishment of doing exactly what they think is right. Isaiah therefore demands, "Let the wicked forsake his way, and the unrighteous man his thoughts" (55:7). Elsewhere, the Lord says, in wrath over His people, "So I gave them over to their stubborn hearts, to follow their own counsels" (Psalm 81:12).

Therefore, no person acting contrary to God's Word is justified because he acted according to his conviction. Instead of justifying him, this condemns him. The thoughts, opinions, and principles every person has by nature are precisely the things from which every person, if he wants to be saved, must turn away. It is not the conviction that natural reason provides about what is good and evil that will allow a person to stand before God, but the conviction that God Himself gives by His Holy Spirit.

From hearts depraved, to evil prone,
Flow tho'ts and deeds of sin alone;
God's image lost, the darkened soul
Nor seeks nor finds its heav'nly goal.

But Christ, the second Adam, came
To bear our sin and woes and shame,
To be our Life, our Light, our Way,
Our only Hope, our only Stay.

We thank Thee, Christ; new life is ours,
New light, new hope, new strength, new powers:
This grace our every way attend
Until we reach our journey's end! Amen.

† *(TLH 369:3, 4, 6)*

Thursday

Read Psalm 71:19

MAN FELL BECAUSE he wanted to be like God. Satan said to man: "You will not surely die. For God knows that when you eat of it your eyes will be opened, and you will be like God, knowing good and evil" (Genesis 3:4–5). At that point, the cunningly tempted people gave up all resistance. The thought that they could ascend as high as God, being completely free and no longer subject to God, was so enchanting they quickly forgot all of God's blessings and commands and eagerly seized the forbidden fruit. The thought of being their own rulers, and perhaps even of casting God down from His throne, penetrated their soul like a double-edged sword and severed the bond that had bound them to God.

The desire to be like God still lies hidden in each human heart. Every person by nature does not want to be subject to the divine law. He would like to be totally free to do or not do whatever he wants. Each person would like to be an absolute lord over everything. And when he hears the proclamation of God's wrath and punishment on transgressions of the divine law, he wishes he could cast God from His throne. The sin of man deifying himself is revealed in human arrogance and self-righteousness.

Unfortunately, we live at a time when people are not ashamed to exalt themselves. The sin of self-deification is clothed in the garment of science that man impudently wears for show and praises as the fruit of the most extensive research and highest wisdom. In the early eighteenth century, Christianity came under attack by so-called Christian preachers and the worldly-wise, who pretended to believe in

Scripture but explained away its truth and read into it all kinds of human errors. The distortions of these false interpreters disgraced them before the whole world. Now such people frankly and freely reject Scripture altogether, and teachers even in Christian higher education loudly proclaim that there is no God, that the whole world is God, and that this god reveals himself most gloriously in man and his reason.

With this reasoning, man has reached the lowest level in his fall from grace. Initially, he fell because he wanted to be like God. Now he maintains that the human spirit, especially human reason, is the true god. Man cannot distance himself further from his Creator. We can hardly expect a clearer sign that we live in the last days and that the Last Day is not far away. Therefore, if ever we had reason, we must use it now to pray earnestly:

Lord Jesus Christ, with us abide,
For round us falls eventide;
Nor let Thy Word, that heav'nly light,
For us be ever veiled in night.

Oh, keep us in Thy Word, we pray;
The guile and rage of Satan stay!
Oh, may Thy mercy never cease!
Give concord, patience, courage, peace. Amen.

(TLH 292:1, 4)

Friday

Read James 1:13–16

IN TODAY'S TEXT, Saint James warns us against the error that God tempts man to do evil and thus evil comes from God. This is confirmed by what follows where God says He is "the Father of lights with whom there is no variation or shadow due to change" (James 1:17). Scripture uses the images of light and darkness to describe good and evil. The apostle says God is a light that unlike the sun has no spots and unlike the moon is not subject to change. God is the "Father of lights;" He is the source of good and nothing evil can come from Him.

It seems unnecessary to impress this truth upon people since who would simultaneously believe in God yet be so deluded as to consider God the author of evil, the originator of sin? But many people often make this mistake, being tempted to this blasphemous thought. There is no one who is not tempted to think this. Christians must therefore arm themselves against it and always be firm in the truth: No evil comes from God.

Had God created people without the possibility of falling into sin, like the animals, neither sin nor trial would have entered the world. But then people would never have been able to come to eternal blessedness by beholding God. Wouldn't it be frightening to make God the originator of sin and trial in the world when He appointed us for blessedness, creating us so we could attain both life and death, both misery and blessedness?

Many may interject here, "Does it not say in the Scriptures, 'Does disaster come to a city, unless the Lord has done it?' [Amos 3:6], and 'I am the Lord, and there is no other; I form the light and create darkness, I make well-being and create calamity; I am the Lord, who does all these things' [Isaiah

45:6–7]?" To understand this correctly, we must know that at all times there have been people who believed there are two gods, one good and the other evil. These Scripture passages are directed against this false faith. They teach that without God's will, nothing happens; that God is and remains the Highest and He cannot be compelled against His will by any creature; and that while evil cannot happen without God's will, God allows it and permits good to come from it. God permits evil to punish the godless and to reveal His judgment on them, and to test believers and glorify His grace and love to them.

There is still more. God created everything, not only the good, but also the evil—but it is the fault of man that it is evil. God created the freedom, but it is the result of sin that it contaminates us. God created the body, but it is the result of sin that it is sick. God created the killing poison and everything that brings death, but it is the result of sin that it kills us. God created the fire that consumes our homes, the flood that devastates our fields, the murderer who thrusts his dagger into our heart, and even Satan, who seeks to destroy both our soul and our salvation. However, it is the result of our sin that all these bring death and destruction. The truth remains: Nothing evil comes from God.

O God, thou faithful God,
Thou fountain ever flowing,
Who good and perfect gifts
In mercy art bestowing,
Give me a healthy frame,
And may I have within
A conscience free from blame,
A soul unhurt by sin! Amen.

(*TLH* 395:1)

Saturday

Read James 1:17–18

AS LONG AS A PERSON believes in God, it is impossible for him not to recognize that all bodily and earthly goods come from Him. For it is God who made everything—the sky with its sun, moon, and stars, and the earth with everything that lives on it. God gave and continues to preserve body and soul, powers and gifts, and reason and all senses for each person. What good is the waking of the watchman, the work of the laborer, the plowing and sowing of the farmer, and the planting and watering of the gardener if God does not watch, protect, and prosper the work, commanding the sun to warm and the rain to give drink to our fields and gardens? Is it not God who has given sharpness to our understanding and skill to our hand? Does He not govern everything in that, without His blessing, all our thoughts, actions, and wisdom would be lost? He alone must give the growth, make us prosperous, and bring us honor.

But what do most people do when they have become rich and have been honored? Do they give God the glory? No! The more God gives a person, the more pride seizes him, and the more people honor him, the more honor he desires. For this reason, we must listen carefully to our text: "Every good gift . . . is from above." James also says "every perfect gift" (that is, every spiritual, heavenly gift) "is from above." While many people fail to recognize that all bodily and earthly goods come from God alone, they also do not want to regard Him as a source of spiritual and heavenly goods. Some may attribute earthly gifts to God but give themselves credit for heavenly gifts. Is not truth a spiritual, heavenly gift? But most people investigate the truth themselves instead of humbly receiving it from the revealed Word of God. Are not virtues and good works spiritual and heavenly gifts? But most people ascribe their alleged virtue and good works to themselves, hoping to earn something before God by them. Are not repentance and conversion spiritual, heavenly goods? But most people want to repent and convert by means of their own power. Are not the peace of God, the rest of the conscience, the grace of God, the forgiveness of sins, and righteousness before God all spiritual, heavenly gifts? But most people want to obtain them by themselves. Finally, are not heaven and salvation the greatest spiritual, heavenly gifts of all? But most people want to earn their own salvation by their virtue and godliness, their good works, their penitence, and their self-improvement. Oh, dreadful delusion!

James declares boldly, "Every good gift and every perfect gift is from above, coming down from the Father of lights." Therefore, whoever seeks the perfect, spiritual, and heavenly gifts in himself will never attain them. If he thinks he has attained them by his own merits, he is mistaken. James continues, "Of His own will He brought us forth by the word of truth, that we should be a kind of firstfruits of His creatures." The apostle says to the deluded ones that every spiritual and heavenly gift begins with the new birth. As little as a person can give bodily birth to himself, so little can he cause himself to be born again. The beginning of every spiritual good, as well as its continuation and completion, is utterly beyond our power. Everything good and perfect comes from God. And for this reason, we must give Him all glory!

Lord, 'tis not that I did choose Thee;
That, I know, could never be;
For this heart would still refuse Thee
Had Thy grace not chosen me.

Thou hast from the sin that stained me
Washed and cleansed and set me free
And unto this end ordained me,
That I ever live to Thee. Amen.

† *(TLH 37:1)*

Sunday

Read John 16:23–30

BELIEVING CHRISTIANS HAVE the comforting confidence that their prayers in the name of Jesus are always heard. Their faith has irrefutable grounds that make them absolutely certain they are not deceiving themselves.

The first reason on which the certainty their prayers are heard is based is God's clear command. Had God never commanded prayer, it would be a shocking audacity for a person to speak with God, the creature with the Creator, the clay with the Potter. To pray to Him involves wanting to prescribe something to Him. After all, a subject can confidently request something from even the strictest king and not offend him if the king himself has invited the subject to ask. Servants of God can confidently ask Him for everything they need because in numerous places in His Word He commands His servants to call upon Him. In today's reading, the Son of God says, "Ask, and you will receive." Elsewhere, we are invited to "call upon Me in the day of trouble; I will deliver you, and you shall glorify Me" (Psalm 50:15). David certainly recognized the immutability of this reason. He appealed to God's own command when he prayed, "You have said, 'Seek My face.' My heart says to You, 'Your face, LORD, do I seek'" (Psalm 27:8).

The second reason for the Christians' certainty that God hears their prayers is that He not only commanded us to pray, He also lovingly promised to hear. Christ asserted this with a double oath: "Truly, truly, I say to you, whatever you ask of the Father in My name, He will give it to you" (John 16:23). David goes further: "LORD, You hear the desire of the afflicted; You will strengthen their heart; You will incline Your ear" (Psalm 10:17). If a Christian considers God's promise that He hears his prayers, he cannot doubt. Even if his reason objects with "How can you force God to do what you desire?" he can respond confidently, "I do not need to compel God. From His ceaseless love, He has already voluntarily bound Himself by His own clear promises. He is faithful and true. What He promises, He must keep. The divine glory of His own name demands it. He cannot be unfaithful to the believer who prays."

As irrevocable as these reasons are for hearing the prayers of all believers, no one who prays would remain confident if there were not a third reason: Christ's merit and intercession. If a person wanted to rest upon God's command and promise, the knowledge of his unworthiness and sinfulness would continue to frighten him. But it is well for us! God's Word in no way bids us to look upon our own righteousness and worthiness in order to pray. In fact, it tells us just the opposite—that we should base the worthiness for our prayers entirely on Christ's merit and intercession. Therefore, Christ says in our text, "I do not say to you that I will ask the Father on your behalf; for the Father Himself loves you, because you have loved Me and have believed that I came from God" (John 16:26–27). Christ is not declaring here that He does not want to intercede for His dear apostles. Instead, He is pointing out that believing Christians should not think that only Christ can pray and be heard and they are not permitted to pray. Because they believe in Him, their prayer is pleasing to God on account of Christ, and what they pour out before God is certainly heard.

Oh, how blessed, then, is the believing Christian! There is no necessary bodily or spiritual good that he cannot attain through prayer, and there is no trial so great that he cannot overcome it for his prayer is always heard.

O bliss! in Jesus' name I've tendered
My prayer; He pleads at Thy right hand for me.
Yea and amen in Him is rendered
What I in faith and spirit ask of Thee.
O joy for me! and praise be ever Thine
Whose wondrous love has made such blessings mine!
Amen.

(ELHB 67:8)

Monday

Read 1 John 5:14–15

GOD'S FIRST MANNER of answering prayer consists in giving the praying believer what he asks when and how he desires it. If God sees, in His eternal wisdom, that what we ask from Him, the desired timing, and the manner of response is beneficial for us, He acts according to our will. He often helps our cause in ways no one can imagine. Circumstances and people that were opposed or seemed to be opposed to our will end up furthering it. When it is necessary, God spares no small miracle so our hope in Him is not brought to shame. How many examples of such remarkable answers to prayer do we find in Holy Scripture and in the history of the Christian Church! Through them, God irrefutably revealed His truthfulness and He continues to reveal it to those who notice.

Of course, God does not always answer prayers immediately. He sometimes lets the petitioner wait for a longer or shorter time. When Mary says to Jesus, "They have no wine," He replies, "My hour has not yet come" (John 2:3–4). But this is only another way of hearing, for "Though awhile it be delayed, / He denieth not His aid; / Though it come not oft with speed, / It will surely come at need" (*ELHB* 516:2). God often allows such delays for the wisest reasons. He alone knows the hour in which the requested help or the good will be salutary. He also uses the delay to awaken us, perhaps for the first time, to true earnestness in our asking.

God has still another wonderful way of hearing. He does not always give us what we ask for, but substitutes something else—and that something else is invariably better than what we requested. A person can often think God does not want to answer him at all. Job sighs: "I cry to You for help and You do not answer me; I stand, and You only look at me. You have turned cruel to me" (30:20–21). Jeremiah groans, "You have wrapped Yourself with a cloud so that no prayer can pass through" (Lamentations 3:44). We sometimes encounter times of profound testing when things do not seem to improve—indeed, they sometimes appear to be worse—after we pray. However, we must notice the hand of the Lord here. For God helps us continually but not always as we think He should. Isn't it still an answer when God gives us something better than what we desired? If He gives us a palace instead of the hut we prayed for, much instead of little, something great instead of something meager, something eternal instead of something temporal, isn't that an answer?

But many may object, "As good as this is, it still isn't a true answer if we do not receive what we prayed for." To this, Saint Paul replies: "For we do not know what to pray for as we ought, but the Spirit Himself intercedes for us with groanings too deep for words. And He who searches hearts knows what is the mind of the Spirit" (Romans 8:26–27). Here we see that we often do not understand our own prayers. With our words we ask for something that may be harmful to us, but the Holy Ghost, who dwells in us, groans without our knowing for something more beneficial. God, who understands this mind of our prayers, which is hidden even to us, gives us the better response. Isn't this a true answer? We certainly must guard ourselves against wanting to ask for some nonessential earthly good or to demand something from God when we have no idea whether it will be beneficial for us. Nevertheless, we should always ask God with certain faith. Faithful prayer is never offered in vain. Every such prayer is a sowing from which a precious fruit follows, an empty bucket let down into the fountain of divine goodness and filled to the top when it comes out again. Therefore, in all the cares and distress of this life, let us confidently take refuge in prayer for it is never for naught.

And what Thy Spirit thus hath taught me
To seek from Thee must needs be such a prayer
As Thou wilt grant, through Him who bought me
And raised me up to be Thy child and heir.
In Jesus' name I boldly seek Thy face
And take from Thee, my Father, grace for grace.
Amen.

(TLH 21:6)

Tuesday

Read James 1:22–25

JAMES SAYS IN OUR TEXT, "But be doers of the word, and not hearers only, deceiving yourselves." Whoever diligently hears, reads, and considers the Gospel but does not believe it with his heart only deceives himself with his hearing, reading, and considering. Is this admonition necessary? Will not those who fail to believe the Gospel also fail to hear it diligently? And shouldn't those who do diligently hear it also believe it? One would think so. But doesn't our daily experience teach just the opposite? Many are diligent hearers of God's Word but are not doers of it. They let themselves be preached to about Christ, but they still do not believe in Him. They hear about grace, but they do not take hold of it. They learn the way of salvation, but they do not walk in it. Although they may be moved by what they hear, they remain, as Saint James says in today's reading, "like a man who looks intently at his natural face in a mirror. For he looks at himself and goes away and at once forgets what he was like." The church service is hardly concluded when they may say, "That was a beautiful (or a provocative) sermon," but as they exit the church, they speak about something else and their hearts are engaged in earthly thoughts. So quickly forgotten are the instruction, comfort, and chastisement in that sermon!

What benefit do such people derive from the hearing, reading, and considering of God's Word? It is totally lost on them. It is not the hearing of the sermon that saves a person, but the doing of what was preached, the keeping of the Word. In short, the doing of the Word is faith. Christ tells us: "This is the work of God, that you believe in Him whom He has sent. . . . Truly, truly, I say to you, if anyone keeps My word, he shall never see death" (John 6:29, 8:51).

Therefore, James adds, "But the one who looks into the perfect law, the law of liberty, and perseveres, being no hearer who forgets but a doer who acts, he will be blessed in his doing." The one who hears the Gospel should not be like a man who, passing by a mirror, only glances into it. Instead, he should be like one who remains standing before the mirror and carefully considers the image shown in it. He will look at himself in the mirror of the Law as a sinner, a sinner for whom Christ obtained reconciliation with God, redemption from hell, grace, forgiveness of sins, righteousness, life, and salvation. This will kindle faith in him and he will grasp it and apply it to himself, taking comfort in it as it is given to him. He will "be blessed in his doing."

Let us not deceive ourselves by thinking it is enough when the Gospel is merely heard with the ears. We must hear it as the Word that opens heaven for us. If it now kindles only a spark of faith, may we persevere so our faith is not easily extinguished but rather grows strong until we have reached the goal of faith: the salvation of our soul.

How blest are they who hear God's Word
And keep and heed what they have heard!
They wisdom daily gather;
Their light shines brighter day by day,
And while they tread life's weary way,
They have the oil of gladness
To soothe their pain and sadness. Amen.

† *(TLH 48:1)*

Wednesday

Read James 1:26–27

ALTHOUGH GOD HARDLY needs our work, He nevertheless welcomes works that are done for Him. He has told us in His Word what these works are. God wants to be served by holy love for the neighbor, a love unstained by worldly love, and by the works that derive from that love. Because we cannot serve God by ourselves, He has arranged it so our neighbor's need is also our need. We consequently serve our neighbor and as we do, God regards it as a work done for Him. Christ tells us there will come a day when false Christians will say to Him, "'Lord, when did we see You hungry or thirsty or a stranger or naked or sick or in prison, and did not minister to You?' Then He will answer them, saying, 'Truly, I say to you, as you did not do it to one of the least of these, you did not do it to Me'" (Matthew 25:44–45). But to the true Christians, He will say, "Truly, I say to you, as you did it to one of the least of these My brothers, you did it to Me" (Matthew 25:40).

Those who think they serve God with the mere hearing of His Word are deceiving themselves. Now is the time for us to mark this truth and impress it upon the heart. In our country, most of the people are divided into two parties. One consists of those who no longer believe in God, who make their own understanding their god, who regard service to God as unimportant. The other party is made up of those who believe in God and in serving Him, but consider this service to be the mere hearing of the Word, prayer, singing, godly conversation, and other pious exercises. They regard lightly the works of love toward others according to the second table of the Ten

Commandments, suggesting these are common works that even the heathen could perform. The result is that nonbelievers often far surpass the apparently pious Christians in works of love for the neighbor. But what shame is there when a nonbeliever can say to a seemingly zealous Christian: "You have faith without works; I have the works without faith. You have what you call God's Word yet you do not do it. I do not hear your Word of God yet I do it. You go to church and want to serve God by that, but you do not serve your neighbor. I, on the other hand, do not go to church yet I serve my neighbor. Who, then, is better?"

Let us be properly alarmed by the words of the apostle: "If anyone thinks he is religious and does not bridle his tongue but deceives his heart, this person's religion is worthless." Arise! If we want to serve God, let us not only hear His Word but also act by the faith that is active in love. Let us not suppose we have already served God merely by going to church, partaking of Holy Communion, confessing our sins, and returning to our home where we speak pious words on our knees. Let us practice love for our neighbor. Let us visit the orphans and widows, armed with a mouth full of comfort and a hand full of works of love. Let us clothe the naked, feed the hungry, give drink to the thirsty, receive the needy into our home, visit the sick, and help those in distress, including the oppressed Church of Christ. Then one day we will all hear the joyful voice proclaiming, "Truly, I say to you, as you did it to one of the least of these My brothers, you did it to Me" (Matthew 25:40).

In sickness, sorrow, want, or care,
Whate'er it be, 'tis ours to share;
May we, where help is needed, there
Give help as unto Thee!

And may Thy Holy Spirit move
All those who live to live in love
Till Thou shalt greet in heaven above
All those who live to Thee. Amen.

† *(TLH 439:5, 6)*

The Ascension of Our Lord

Read Mark 16:14–20

CONSIDERING CHRIST'S ASCENSION is like staring at the sun: the more closely a person looks into it, the worse his eyes become and finally he cannot see anything at all. This work of Christ is for those who do not need to investigate but who simply want to believe with childlike faith what Scripture says about it. The more simply we regard the biblical description of this event, the more it strengthens our faith.

Scripture does not say the ascended Christ is confined like the saints. Instead, He fills everything. It does not tell us that He was received by the heavens but that He received heaven, even that He ascended far above the heavens where He sits "at the right hand of God."

The Bible conveys "the right hand of God" to refer to God's omnipotence, omnipresence, dominion, eternality, and divine majesty. Saint Paul declares: "He raised [Christ] from the dead and seated Him at His right hand in the heavenly places, far above all rule and authority and power and dominion, and above every name that is named, not only in this age but also in the one to come. And He put all things under His feet and gave Him as head over all things to the Church, which is His body, the fullness of Him who fills all in all" (Ephesians 1:20–23).

All of this is said not about Christ's divinity but about His human nature, assumed in the form of a servant. After all, the divine nature could be neither humbled nor exalted, nor could it experience a decline in or an increase of glory. As the psalmist reports in considering God's divinity, "But You are the same" (102:27).

Christ left the world. He would no longer walk among us as a mortal man, natural, visible, tangible, and spatial as He once did with His disciples. But let us not conclude that Christ is the King of a kingdom from which He is separated and which He can rule only at a distance. He spatially departed from the disciples. With His glorified body, He raised Himself higher and higher until the disciples could no longer see Him. But as soon as the gate of clouds closed behind Him, He entered into a state of divine majesty, appearing full of glory to all angels and saints who were welcoming Him with their hymns of triumph. Then, as Man, He commenced His almighty and omnipresent dominion over heaven and earth and all creatures.

When we consider Christ's ascension according to the clear witness of Holy Scripture, we find a certain foundation for a joyful faith. He has not removed Himself from His Church. Instead, He is now, as God and Man, extending His grace, help, and protection in all places. As Aaron wore on his breastplate the names of the tribes of Israel when he entered the Holy of Holies, so Christ, appearing as the true High Priest before God in heaven, wears the names of all believers on His heart. There, He prays without ceasing for His own, and He rules them, cares for them, and protects them so the gates of hell cannot overpower them.

We thank Thee, Jesus, dearest Friend,
That Thou didst into heaven ascend.
O blessed Savior, bid us live
And strength to soul and body give.
Hallelujah! Amen.

(TLH 223:1)

Friday

Read Acts 1:1–11

TO SOME EXTENT, Christ's ascension, as it took place before the eyes of the disciples, is only a representation of the actual event. He raised Himself like an eagle into the air, contrary to what one would expect of a human body. By this, He shows us how our bodies will be constituted after the resurrection. They will be proper bodies with flesh and bone but will no longer be as heavy and stiff as they are now. With our thoughts, we can now quickly imagine ourselves in distant places, but one day we will be permitted to do this with our bodies. After Christ's resurrection, the stone on His grave and the locked doors of the upper room did not prevent Him from passing through, although no one could tell how He had done this. Thereafter, He allowed Himself to be seen then made Himself invisible again, just as He wanted. At one moment, He was in one place and in another moment He was somewhere else. He could travel through air or on water as readily as upon earth. We will have to wait until after this life to experience this glory ourselves. For then our bodies will be like Christ's glorified body, according to the work by which He can make all things subject to Him.

But this is not the most important sign of the ascension. That Christ was received into heaven and separated from the earth on the clouds indicates that His spiritual kingdom is, as Paul indicates, above this one (Acts 1:9). It is a heavenly kingdom and it will remain invisible until it is revealed.

By His resurrection, Christ was made Lord over everything according to His human nature so He could say, "All authority in heaven and on earth has been given to Me" (Matthew 28:18). The attributes Christ possessed from eternity, according to His divine nature, were retained by His human nature but He used them only rarely during His humiliation. Even after the resurrection, Christ, according to His human nature, did not immediately assume dominion over all things. This took place after the ascension when, also according to His human nature, He entered into full use of the same majesty and power the Father exercises.

Our human understanding cannot grasp all of this, of course. The ascension of Christ remains an article of faith we do not comprehend with our intellect but believe in our hearts with humility. We should note both the greatness and the spiritual nature of the kingdom of Christ. Our King, as He entered into His governance, left the world, thereby clearly announcing that His kingdom is not of this world and has nothing to do with temporal and visible things. The ascension should dispel any thought that a person could seek worldly power, goods, and glory from Christ or that an outward, worldly works righteousness avails before God. In His kingdom, Christ distributes to us heavenly goods, grace, forgiveness, righteousness, redemption from sin and death, and eternal life.

The ascension demands of us that if we want to live under Christ in His kingdom, we must keep our minds focused on heaven and not seek salvation in the goods of this world. As Christ Himself says, "For where your treasure is, there your heart will be also" (Matthew 6:21). As Christ sits on His throne in heaven, so should our hearts be moved by a constant longing for heaven.

Grant that I only Thee may love
And seek those things which are above
Till I behold Thee face to face,
O Light eternal, through Thy grace. Amen.

† *(TLH 398:4)*

Saturday

Read Ephesians 4:8–10

IF WE WANT to correctly understand the fruit and power of Christ's ascension, we must consider it in its connection with His descent, that is, with the deepest humiliation in which Christ, true God and true man, placed Himself.

Since the fall of Adam, all people lie in the prison of sin, Law, death, and devil. Out of His eternal love and mercy, the Son of God freed us in this manner: He took human form and let Himself be placed in our prison for us. He remained in this prison during His entire earthly life, especially when He sweated blood on the Mount of Olives, hung on the cross, and finally gave up His innocent life. Death and the devil viewed these events with joy, for it appeared that they had triumphed over Christ.

Even when Christ came to the deepest places of the earth, He did not lose His divinity. Instead, He willingly gave up the use of His divine glory to offer Himself as an atoning sacrifice for our sins. When He did this, He experienced what a powerful master it was who made this prison for his prisoners. With that divine power, Christ broke all the bands of death, for, as Peter said in his Pentecost sermon, it was impossible for death to hold Him. Victorious, He arose from the grave and publicly defeated all enemies who wanted to hold Him prisoner. Only one thing remained for Him following His resurrection: His entrance to full dominion. This occurred with His glorious ascension and His sitting at the right hand of the Father.

What a glorious work, rich in comfort and joy, is Christ's ascension for all who believe in Him! It turned everything that had previously bound our soul into our prisoner. By our nature, we are all prisoners and servants of sin so we must do what sin wants. But by Christ's ascension, sin is now our prisoner and it must do what we want. It can still tempt us, but even this must turn out for the best for us. For if there were no longer any temptations to sin, our faith would soon grow cold, prayer would become lukewarm, and the Word would be considered and studied lazily. Sin must serve to double our zeal against it and to grasp Christ and His grace all the more firmly so it may be said even of sin, "For those who love God all things work together for good" (Romans 8:28).

So it is also with death, that frightful enemy of the human race, that vile poison, that most terrible punishment imposed by God for sin. But Christ's ascension makes death a prisoner to all believers as well. It can continue to terrify us, but it cannot defeat us. Its terrors prompt Christians to flee to their Savior all the more urgently to seek His help, protection, and rescue. It helps them prepare more earnestly for their departure from the temporal to enter the eternal. If there were no death, Christians would never seek comfort in God's Word.

This also applies to the Law. Its curse no longer harms the Christian; it only compels him to seek grace and blessing from Christ. The thunder of the Law has been transformed into a fruitful thunderstorm, after which the sowing of the Gospel sprouts and flourishes all the more gloriously.

Finally, it is also true that Satan himself is our prisoner. Our nature subjects us all to his tyranny. But now that our Savior, Christ, sits on His heavenly throne, Satan is our prisoner. Now, a little word—Jesus—can fell him. His cunning and power work nothing except to prevent believers from becoming secure so they entrust themselves all the more diligently to God's protection and walk all the more bravely (but carefully).

We thus consider Christ's ascension rightly when we regard it as the means by which all the enemies of our soul were taken prisoner by His victorious death and resurrection. Let us, then, give Christ thanks for the glorious completion of the work of our redemption. Let us, in faith, take hold of His mighty protection and thus remain safe from all our enemies. Let us open our hearts to Him and be filled with the richness of His gifts. To Him be praise and glory and adoration forever!

Since He returned to claim His throne,
Great gifts for men obtaining,
My heart shall rest in Him alone,
No other rest remaining;
For where my Treasure went before,
There all my tho'ts shall ever soar
To still their deepest yearning. Amen.

† *(TLH 216:2)*

Sunday

Read John 16:2

MOST PEOPLE HAVE good intentions in the sinful acts they commit. Good intentions are the fruitful mother of countless sins. They are the main comfort when people give in to sin and hold off true repentance. Therefore, good intentions are one of the mightiest snares with which Satan captures souls, keeps them in self-deception, and draws them always deeper into sin.

What Christ told the disciples in advance, as reported in today's reading, was fulfilled all too quickly. The Jews who laid hands on the apostles did not in any way intend to commit a sin. Rather, they had good intentions. They wanted to fight against the enemies of God, carry out their holy duties according to the Law, promote the right church, and offer true service to God.

Why did numerous believers throughout the world become martyrs in the famous persecution of Christians during the first centuries of the Church? Almost all of them fell as a sacrifice to good intentions. Even heathens believed they had to wipe out the Christians because they were enemies of the state, enemies of the human race, and enemies of the gods. They also believed the Christians were atheists since they had no temple, no altar, and no sacrifice. These deniers of the gods were considered to be the cause of all the plagues supposedly inflicted on the land by the angry gods.

And how was it possible that, in the history of Christian Church, a papacy with all of its anti-Christian superstitions was able to get a footing and both preserve and reproduce itself? This papacy promoted clerical dominion and tyranny of the soul. It rejected Christ and His merits, offering instead an idolatrous worship of the saints. It established monasteries and pilgrimages, banned the Bible, distorted the institution of the testament of the Lord, committed abominations of the mass, and presented a variety of other anti-God and anti-Christian actions. An obvious display of wickedness and cunning would not have suitably positioned the papacy to seize throughout the centuries so many millions of souls striving for salvation. The first root of the papacy was the good intentions that nevertheless opened the way to wicked abuse.

Even among Protestants, good intentions have brought about unspeakable harm. While promoting holiness in the world, fanatical sects fight against reliance upon the means of grace, that is, the Word of God and the holy Sacraments. The idea that all churches and sects should outwardly unite without oneness in the truth originated in the good intention of opposing, with combined strength, the obvious enemies of the Church and helping to prepare the way for the kingdom of God by removing those things that hinder it, thus expanding the borders of Christ's dominion.

No error is as evident and pernicious, no fanaticism is as insane, and no principle is as false and perverted as this: All of the horrors described in today's meditation grew out of the good intention of serving God and pleasing Him.

Therefore, Jesus, my salvation,
Thou my One, my All, shalt be.
Prove my fixed determination,
Root out all hypocrisy.
Look well if on sin's slipp'ry paths I am hasting,
And lead me, O Lord, in the way everlasting!
This one thing is needful, all others are vain;
I count all but loss that I Christ may obtain. Amen.

(ELHB 83:10)

Monday

Read John 16:3

WITH THESE WORDS, Christ testifies to the disciples for their comfort that their persecutors will not be regarded as God's friends because of their good intentions. Their intentions will reveal that they are still subject to their natural blindness, without knowledge of God and salvation, and thus are still God's enemies. By their continued resistance to the enlightening power of the Gospel, they have come into the judgment of a delusion and hardness that can no longer be overcome. Therefore, Christ would never pardon or justify sins committed with good intentions. Instead, He declares them to be revelations of a sinful condition, evil outlets from an evil source, and fruits of the most terrible slavery to sin.

There are, however, considerable differences among those who do evil with good intentions. The first category of such people is made up of those who have God's Word but wantonly resist the Holy Spirit. They remain in their blindness and finally are so deluded that they regard the greatest of crimes as a service to God. The Jews about whom Jesus speaks in today's reading were this way. In the preceding text, He said, "But when the Helper comes, whom I will send to you from the Father, the Spirit of truth, who proceeds from the Father, He will bear witness about Me" (John 15:26). He goes on to say, concerning the Jewish persecution of the apostles, "And they will do these things because they have not known the Father, nor Me." He thus declares that their good intentions are a fruit of their wanton opposition to the Holy Ghost. False churches also belong in this category. Therefore, woe to those who, like the fallen Jewish church, reject God's Word with good intentions, intending to replace it with the doctrine of man. They persecute the true Church, sometimes even with fire and sword! Their good intentions will not excuse them before God any more than did those of the Jews who rejected Christ. Indeed, they will damn them for wanton blindness and enmity against God and against Christ's Word and grace.

A second category consists of those who know nothing of God's Word and therefore regard the most terrible sins as if they were virtues. But even these people are not excused for this reason. We cannot forget that even the most ignorant heathen and all nonbelievers have God's Law and voice inside them via their conscience. Paul writes that they "are a law to themselves, even though they do not have the law. They show that the work of the law is written on their hearts, while their conscience also bears witness, and their conflicting thoughts accuse or even excuse them" (Romans 2:14–15). But the apostle adds that they "suppress the truth" that has been dwelling in them from their birth "by their unrighteousness" (Romans 1:18). They act so long against the better voice of their conscience that they finally become blind and dead, regarding even the greatest abomination as if it were meritorious service to God.

The third and final category comprises those Christians who have and accept God's Word, but who now and again act unrighteously with good intentions. They will not be excused either. They may indeed accept God's Word, but they do not conform to it in all things. God demands that everyone be guided by His Word, deviating neither to the right nor to the left. He expressly warns against following the heart and human opinions. When Christians fail to serve God according to His Word, even when their intentions are good, they fall short. They may demonstrate great zeal in their self-chosen service to God, but all such service is futile and rejected. The reason is that they are following a leader, a tempter, against whom God has repeatedly and earnestly warned them in His Word.

It is on God's Word alone that we will one day be judged, so it must now guide our faith and life. If we allow it to light our path continually, we will not go astray. And if we have strayed from the path out of weakness, this light will always bring us back. Therefore, we must let the humble prayer of the faithful Samuel be our prayer as well: "Speak, LORD, for Your servant hears" (1 Samuel 3:9).

Thou art the Truth, Thy Word alone
True wisdom can impart;
Thou only canst inform the mind
And purify the heart. Amen.

† *(TLH 355:2)*

Tuesday

Read 1 John 3:4–5

EACH SIN, a transgression of the divine Law, is an offense to the high majesty of the eternal, holy, and just God and thus merits eternal rejection by God. Nevertheless, there are degrees of offense. A person who is continually plagued by certain sins can still receive forgiveness and stand in God's grace, while other sins necessarily exclude a person from God's kingdom and His holy fellowship.

There are great distinctions among actual sins. These are not to be confused with original sin, with which all people are born. Original sin is an utterly sinful corruption of the entire human nature according to body, soul, reason, will, and impulse. Among the so-called actual sins are sins of weakness, malicious or wanton sins, sins of rashness, dominant sins, grievous and less grievous sins, and voluntary and involuntary sins.

Sins of weakness are those that arise out of the weakness of the human nature, even among those whose earnest desire is to serve God entirely without sin. Such people bear sorrow over the smallest error and seek forgiveness for it, and they always become more careful and watchful after they stumble. Malicious or wanton sins are deliberate sins in which a person takes pleasure. They may be such that a person would receive a worldly punishment except that he knows how to escape them, like the innocently shed blood of Abel. Or they may involve oppressing the poor and forsaken, the sweat of the poor extorted by the profiteer, and the tears of defrauded widows. Such sins, finding no judge on earth, cry to the omniscient and righteous Judge in heaven for vengeance. Sins of rashness are those by which a person is thrown down, either by his temper or by a sudden and unexpected heavy temptation, but from which he quickly rises with sincere repentance. Saint Peter offers us an example of this type of sin: fearing man and death, he was suddenly plunged into denial by the tempter.

Dominant sins are those a person willingly follows even without being strongly tempted. These are also called grievous sins because the person who is ruled by them cannot have faith and a place in God's communion of grace. He cannot be ruled by God's Spirit and he is therefore spiritually dead. Less grievous sins are those in which a person has not so hardened himself and made himself impenitent that he could not come to remorse and repentance. For him, there is hope of a longing for grace and faith. The grievous sin, on the contrary, is such a terrible hardening against all impulses of the Spirit of God that the individual despises, derides, and blasphemes all grace, comfort, and forgiveness throughout his life. Such an individual wants to know nothing about Christ, His blood, and His atonement. Scripture calls this the sin against the Holy Spirit and it is the sin that leads to eternal death.

Voluntary sins are those a person commits even against his better judgment and despite all warnings from the voice of his conscience. Involuntary sins, by contrast, are committed without one's thinking about them. A person who commits such sins may even think he is doing something good and pleasing to God.

Although the variety of sins is great and sad, from careless and vain thoughts to the obstinate hardness of Pharaoh and Judas, each demonstrates an uprising of our heart against God, the Father of light. Some may appear to be ever so small, but not one sin can be forgiven—except for the sake of Christ, the Son of God.

Thy love and grace alone avail
To blot out my transgression;
The best and holiest deeds must fail
To break sin's dread oppression.
Before Thee none can boasting stand,
But all must fear Thy strict demand
And live alone by mercy. Amen.

(TLH 329:2)

Wednesday

Read 1 Peter 4:7

After only a few years of public ministry, Jesus departed from the earth. Since then, about 2,000 years have passed and no sinner has been honored by seeing the Lord of glory. He now dwells in a light no one can share, but that will not always be so. The day will come when Christ will step out of His hidden light and appear once again in this world full of sin. As certainly as He once came in fulfillment of 4,000 years of Old Testament prophecy to redeem the world, He will come again to judge the living and the dead, according to the prophecies of the apostles and evangelists of the New Testament.

Following Christ's ascension to heaven, the first sermon God proclaimed to the world was "Christ will come again!" The apostles were still gazing in wonder toward the cloud that had just received Jesus and hidden Him from their eyes when, as Saint Luke relates, two angels in white garments said, "Men of Galilee, why do you stand looking into heaven? This Jesus, who was taken up from you into heaven, will come in the same way as you saw Him go into heaven" (Acts 1:11).

From that hour, the apostles themselves preached everywhere that Christ would return on the Last Day. They said, "But our citizenship is in heaven, and from it we await a Savior, the Lord Jesus Christ" (Philippians 3:20). With this blessed hope, the apostles consoled and comforted themselves and others in all their tribulations. This hope was sealed with their blood as they died a martyr's death, steadfast and with joy.

The apostles maintained that Christ's return at the end of the age was not only certain, but also near. Saint John wrote, "Children, it is the last hour" (1 John 2:18). Saint James preached, "Behold, the Judge is standing at the door" (5:9). In today's text, Saint Peter proclaimed, "The end of all things is at hand." Saint Jude testified, "Behold the Lord came with ten thousands of His holy ones" (14). We are not permitted to think that the apostles were in error in making this proclamation. Although they cried, "The Lord is at hand!" they well knew that millenniums could pass before Christ returned.

When, for example, Peter spoke about Christ's return being "at hand," he added, "But do not overlook this one fact, beloved, that with the Lord one day is as a thousand years, and a thousand years as one day" (2 Peter 3:8). And Saint Paul said, "Let no one deceive you in any way. For that Day will not come, unless the rebellion comes first, and the man of lawlessness is revealed, the son of destruction" (2 Thessalonians 2:3).

How, then, could the apostles speak so clearly about the end of the world being at hand? They did not speak the language of men, but of God. In God's reckoning of time, the end is always near, even if by our manner of telling time it is millenniums away. God desires that at all times His servants, the Christians, should cry out, "The Lord is near!" that each one might be ready to meet Him if He should come today. We should live each day as if it were the last day of the world. The coming of the Last Day may still be delayed for a long time, but we do not know this; and it could just as readily overtake us with all of its terrors before the next setting of the sun.

Therefore, all true prophets of the Lord have at all times proclaimed His nearness. Martin Luther, as a good watchman, continually announced this to sleeping Christians. All pure teachers have followed in this. As our whole Church has sung for centuries:

The world is very evil,
The times are waxing late;
Be sober and keep vigil,
The Judge is at the gate;
The Judge comes in mercy,
The Judge comes with might,
To terminate the evil,
To diadem the right. Amen.

† *(TLH 605:1)*

The Bridegroom will call us:
Come, all ye wedding guests!
May not His voice appall us
While slumber binds our breasts!
May all our lamps be burning
And oil be found in store
That we, with Him returning,
May open find the door! Amen.

(TLH 67:1)

Thursday

Read 1 Peter 4:7

ACCORDING TO THE TESTIMONY of the Word of God, the closer we come to the end of all things, the greater the world's security and lust will become. As the terrible hour nears, an hour in which all things visible and all the glory of the earth will suddenly be swallowed up, more and more people will, as the prophecies of Scripture inform us, immerse themselves in worldly goods. The more signs God sends to all His children, warning that the world will soon be destroyed and the Judge of the living and the dead will soon appear in the clouds of the heavens, the less people will believe them. Everything will continue secure and carefree, as if the world were to stand forever and the Last Day were nothing more than a fairy tale.

Our present age seems to fit perfectly the descriptions of the last days found in Scripture. All of the signs in nature, in the kingdoms of the world, and in the Church which, according to biblical prophecy, must precede the end of all things, have taken place during of the past centuries and especially in recent years. By the most terrible events, God has loudly proclaimed the imminent destruction of the world. But what has been the response? With each passing year, the world sinks deeper and deeper into false security. At no time has the notion of the Last Day appeared to be more laughable than it is now. Almost universally, people have denied the Christ who has already come, and they greet with even greater mockery the preaching that says He will return soon. Even those who believe God's Word consider those who preach the nearness of Christ's return to be fanatics. We have obviously entered that midnight hour when even the wise virgins sleep.

What does Peter say in cautioning Christians about such a time? He says, "The end of all things is at hand; therefore be self-controlled and sober-minded for the sake of your prayers." This does not mean that when the end of all things is near, Christians should no longer make use of the world, that they should deprive the body in self-chosen spirituality and humility and not provide for the necessities of the flesh. Nor does it mean they are not allowed to rejoice in the bodily refreshment God gives them in this last time. No, says the apostle, we should be serious and watchful only in our prayers. Even in the nearness of the Last Day, we can eat and drink, but we should not weigh down our hearts in these pursuits. We can like something in this world, but we must be prepared to sacrifice it readily to God. We can have and continue to accumulate gold and silver, but we should not attach our heart to them, not rely upon them, and not mourn when we lose them. We can build dwellings for ourselves, but they must be considered as lodgings for the night from which we will set out on the following morning (in other words, we must always prefer to go to the house of our heavenly Father than cling to our earthly abodes). We can continue to plant and sow in the face of the Last Day, but we must be prepared not to reap the harvest, if that is what the Lord desires. We can also care about the future, but only in such a way that our heart does not become burdened with worry. We are serious and watchful in prayer when our heart is not trapped by any earthly thing. It must always be free to be lifted up to God in prayer. In the midst of the things, business, cares, goods, and pleasures of this world, our deepest desire must be for salvation and for heaven. We must seek first the kingdom of God and His righteousness. And we must pass through this world like strangers and pilgrims, pausing here and there to rest and refresh ourselves, but soon thereafter hastening on toward our heavenly goal. Our entire life must be, as Luther expressed, an eternal Lord's Prayer in which our principal desire is for God to deliver us from evil. And may we add, "Come, Lord Jesus, take us out of this evil world, and take us to Yourself."

O Jesus Christ, do not delay,
But hasten our salvation;
We often tremble on our way
In fear and tribulation.
Then hear us when we cry to Thee;
Come, mighty Judge, and make us free
From every evil! Amen.

† *(TLH 611:7)*

Friday

Read 1 Peter 4:8

ACCORDING TO OUR LORD'S prophecies, the closer we draw to the end of all things, the greater will be the bodily and spiritual distress, especially among Christians. Increasingly, Christians will be hated, rejected, excluded, and forsaken by the world. They will be abandoned to misery and everywhere denied their right. One persecution and affliction after another will rise up against them. Satan will summon all his hellish powers to plague and torment Christians because he knows his time is short. More false christs will arise. Trials and temptations to error and sin will grow and become more dangerous, so that, if it were possible, even the elect would be led astray. The pure Word of God and the right worship will become rare.

In the last time, even Christians will be exceedingly weak. For this reason, Christ asks, "Nevertheless, when the Son of Man comes, will He find faith on earth?" (Luke 18:8). Therefore, precisely at that time, it will be urgently necessary for Christians to demonstrate a mutual brotherly love. As they are oppressed on all sides by the world, they cannot forsake one another. Instead, they must stand by one another in their trouble and be patient with one another in their mutual weakness.

Do we not see the signs of these prophecies in our own time? Do not Christians today lament over deep distresses, misery, and needs of all sorts? Does not the world live splendidly and in joy while poor Christians lie before its doors and live by its grace? Is not the flock of Christ both small and scattered in the face of poverty and want? And where can a person confess Christ in a setting in which hate and persecution do not arise? Do not Christians consider themselves fortunate in our day when they are not driven away, but instead are allowed to eat the crumbs that fall from the tables of the gluttons?

But isn't the spiritual distress of our day even more frightening? How scarce is God's Word now! How few are those who have good biblical knowledge and a firm grounding in the faith! Where are the fathers in Christ, the good spiritual leaders? So often they turn out to be only wolves in sheep's clothing. How strong are the errors that now prevail! How numerous are the false prophets who have gone out! How hard it is for those who do not wish to be led into error to remain firm in their faith! How many who read the Bible continue to struggle with fears, uncertainty, and doubt! How many continue to fall away after only a short distance in their Christian walk! Oh, great distress!

But God knew all of this beforehand. Therefore, the Holy Spirit moved the apostles to call to all Christians who would live in the end times, "Above all, keep loving one another earnestly." Let this also be said to us in these last, evil days. We Christians, who see and feel our common distress, who know we are increasingly forsaken by the world, must not forsake one another. We must extend helping hands, not shut our hearts before our poor brothers. Let us not become tired in giving and in comforting one another so no brothers or sisters sigh and lament to God that they have been abandoned even by other Christians. Let us also, in the midst of our joyful giving and helpful works, ask God to kindle in us an "earnest love" that would inspire us to persevere in the face of manifold difficulties.

Thou Fountain whence all wisdom flows
Which God on pious hearts bestows,

Grant us Thy consolation
That in our pure faith's unity
We faithful witnesses may be
Of grace that brings salvation.
Hear us, Cheer us
By Thy teaching; Let our preaching
And our labor
Praise Thee, Lord, and serve our neighbor. Amen.

† *(TLH 235:3)*

Saturday

Read 1 Peter 4:10–11

IN TODAY'S READING, Christians are admonished, in the last days, to be faithful in the use of their gifts and in the works of their office and calling. This warning is especially necessary now. As soon as a person understands that the end of all things is near, he is tempted to lose heart and believe it is too late to establish or to rescue anything.

Our text tells us how wrong these thoughts are. God has not revealed to us the misery of the last days so we would become despondent and idle. His threats will be fulfilled without our help. The horror and devastation of this age have been shown to us so that, in a time when everything appears lost, we might still more earnestly work to save that which can be saved and preserve that which can preserved, according to the gifts we have received. When God gives us the opportunity, we must help to build up the deteriorating walls of the

Church. As Saint Peter noted in his second letter, God has patience with people, not wanting anyone to be lost but everyone to repent. For this reason, He delays His frightening judgment until the last person who can be rescued is rescued. Therefore, Peter says in today's reading, "As each has received a gift, use it to serve one another, as good stewards of God's varied grace."

If God has given you the gift of knowledge, do not keep it to yourself in this dark time, but instead, use it for the common good of your poor fellow Christians. Wherever God offers you an opportunity in your station and calling, instruct the ignorant by virtue of your spiritual priesthood. If you have the gift of interpreting Scripture, unlock God's holy Word to your brothers. If you have the gift of comforting, seek out the sick, the sad, and the dying and console them. If you have the gift of silencing those who contradict the truth, allow yourself to be a good fighter for that truth, never forgetting the warning of the apostle, "whoever speaks, as one who speaks oracles of God." Woe to him who utters his own wisdom instead of God's Word. If you have the gift of ruling, do not deprive the Christian congregation of your counsel. If you have the gift of reconciling torn hearts, help to heal wherever the bond of peace has been severed.

If you think you have no gift, remember this: When you believe in Christ, you receive, as a member of the body of Christ, gifts for the common use. Even when you are unable to discover any gift in you, you are still able to pray effectively in Jesus' name. In the quiet of your room, pray for your brothers and for the preservation of the Word and the holy Sacraments. Place yourself, with only your sighs, in the breach and make yourself to be a wall opposing the spread of corruption. In the last times, when all corners of the earth are filled with cursing, you will become a great blessing.

As the Last Day draws ever closer, let us not forsake our

calling but firmly remain where God has placed us. Our text tells us that as miserable as the last times will seem, the office of the Church will not entirely cease since the admonition "whoever serves, as one who serves by the strength that God supplies" applies to these times.

Therefore, may we all remain in our callings and offer help wherever we can. We should do everything, not in our own power, but in the power the Lord alone supplies, "in order that in everything God may be glorified through Jesus Christ. To Him belong glory and dominion forever and ever. Amen."

Thou holy Fire, Comfort true,
Grant us the will Thy work to do
And in Thy service to abide;
Let trials turn us not aside.
Lord, by Thy pow'r prepare each heart
And to our weakness strength impart
That bravely here we may contend,
Thro' life and death to Thee, our Lord, ascend.
Hallelujah! Hallelujah! Amen.

† *(TLH 224:3)*

Sunday

Read Acts 2:1–13

PENTECOST IS A GLORIOUS EVENT for which Christians should be eternally thankful, an event that prompts them, as rejoicing multitudes, to enter their houses of God for a festive celebration. It marks the visible outpouring of the Holy Ghost upon the Lord's disciples. Christ had promised the disciples, "For John baptized with water, but you will be baptized with the Holy Spirit not many days from now" (Acts 1:5). Then, blessing them, He majestically ascended from the earth, higher and higher, until a cloud, like a victory carriage, received Him, and He withdrew from the longing gaze of His followers. Ten days after Christ's ascension, the Jewish festival of Pentecost arrived and the disciples gathered, with one accord, in prayers and supplications. And behold! There was a sound from heaven as of a mighty wind and it filled the whole house where they were sitting. Here, the Holy Ghost appeared visibly in the form of tongues of fire that burned over the heads of the disciples. The disciples were filled with the Holy Ghost and to the amazement of a great crowd of onlookers, festival guests from every nation under heaven, they suddenly proclaimed in fiery speech in all the languages of these foreigners the great deeds of God.

Through this act, the Holy Ghost revealed Himself, gloriously and majestically, before all the world as true God and the Third Person of the Holy Trinity. He now demands that the world recognize that He, with the Father and Son, is God, equally eternal and mighty, and that all should honor and worship Him on earth as in heaven.

By this miraculous public outpouring of the Holy Ghost upon the disciples, Christ also revealed before the whole world that He is truly risen, that He ascended into heaven, and that He now sits as God and Man at the right hand of the Majesty on high. He rules from His abundance, and according to His good pleasure He pours out the Holy Ghost over His elect children. For the disciples, this not only equipped them for their great office, but it also transformed their human weakness and despondency into divine strength and unconquerable courage. Their imperfect knowledge was changed into infallible, perfect enlightenment. Their simplicity and awkwardness were turned into heavenly wisdom. The descent of the Holy Ghost publicly and solemnly confirmed them in their heavenly calling before all the nations of the earth, attesting them as teachers of all people, God's messengers to the whole sinful world, and representatives of Christ.

We cannot think that the miracle of the outpouring of the Holy Ghost we celebrate today is something that happened to the apostles only. This is the especially glorious thing about the feast of Pentecost: the same thing that happened to the apostles, which we celebrate with a great festival, repeats itself each year. It is true that the apostles were endowed on that first Pentecost with certain extraordinary gifts of the Holy Ghost that were promised to them alone and were necessary for them alone. Nevertheless, we, along with all people at all times and in all places, can share in the main gift the apostles received: the gift of the Holy Ghost Himself.

O Holy Spirit, enter in
And in our hearts Thy work begin,
Thy temple deign to make us;
Sun of the soul, Thou Light Divine,
Around and in us brightly shine,
To joy and gladness wake us
That we In Thee
Truly living, To Thee giving
Prayer unceasing,
May in love be still increasing. Amen.

(TLH 235:1)

Monday

Read Acts 2:1–2

SAINT LUKE informs us here that the Jews in Jerusalem had hardly begun their celebration of the festival of Pentecost when they were reminded of the giving of the Law on Sinai amid lightning, thunder, and smoke. At 9 a.m., there was a loud sound coming down from heaven. The sound got louder until it could be heard throughout the entire city. It sounded like a whirlwind and it filled the house where the disciples had gathered. This was a bell God sounded to awaken the inhabitants of Jerusalem and summon them to the house where they could behold the great miracle of Pentecost and hear the first Christian Pentecost sermon. But it was also an announcement to the disciples of the coming of the Holy Ghost. What they experienced then is a picture of what every person who shares in the Holy Ghost must experience.

By nature, a person is incapable of being a dwelling place for the Holy Ghost. Each of us lies in a deep sleep of security from which we must be awakened. By nature, we are completely unconcerned about salvation. Even if we recognize that we are great, lost sinners (and this is the exception rather than the rule), we do not regard our sins as something frightening or we retain a greater concern for earthly comfort and bodily well being than heavenly comfort and spiritual joy for our soul. Whoever remains in this condition keeps his heart shut to the Holy Ghost and He is unable to enter it. Such a person cannot be saved.

If, then, a person is to be filled with the Holy Ghost so he can be saved, the Law of God must first sound through his heart like a rushing wind coming down from heaven, awakening him from his spiritual sleep. The words "You shall love the Lord your God with all your heart and with all your soul and with all your mind … [and] you shall love your neighbor as yourself" (Matthew 22:37–39) must strike his heart like a thunderbolt, causing him to lament, "Oh, what a great sinner I am! I have loved neither God nor my neighbor!" This must be followed by the recognition that "whoever keeps the whole law but fails in one point has become accountable for all of it" (James 2:10). This word, like a bolt of lightning from God's hand, strikes the person to the ground so he calls, in the fear of his soul: "I am lost! O God, what should I do that I might be saved?"

This rushing wind was unnecessary for the apostles for they had already recognized, with terror, that they were poor sinners, and they had already implored God for peace and comfort for their fearful hearts. But for the 3,000 who received the Holy Ghost on Pentecost, we read that they first had to experience the mighty, rushing wind of the Law in their hearts. In his Pentecost sermon, Peter held before the crowd their sin with great earnestness, declaring that they had murdered the Son of God. Scripture tells us they "were cut to the heart" by what they heard (Acts 2:37). Peter's words struck them like lightning. They suddenly recognized that they were lost sinners worthy of damnation and this caused them to call out, "Brothers, what shall we do?" (Acts 2:37).

Let us consider this well. If we want to be saved, we too must receive the Holy Ghost. And His entrance into us must be preceded by the mighty, rushing wind of the Law that leads us to recognize that we are poor sinners so we call out from the depths of our soul, "Lord, what shall we do that we might be saved?"

Oh, enter, let me know Thee
And feel Thy pow'r within,

The pow'r that breaks our fetters
And rescues us from sin!
Oh, wash and cleanse me
That I may serve Thee truly
And render honor duly
With perfect heart to Thee! Amen.

(TLH 228:2)

Tuesday

Read Acts 2:3–4

THE HOLY GHOST did not begin His work on the first Pentecost. Not only did He speak and write through the holy men of God in the Old Testament, the prophets, but also in everything truly good that was worked in the hearts of men after the fall. During that 4,000–year period, He did His work in secret. But on that first Christian Pentecost, He came out of concealment, audibly in the form of a mighty, rushing wind and visibly in the form of fiery tongues. He then revealed His divine power and glory by distributing His most glorious gifts to the people from all nations under heaven. If the Holy Ghost had previously trickled like a heavenly dew, He now poured Himself out in mighty streams. Until then, He had had His workshop almost exclusively among the chosen people of God, the people Israel; now He expanded that workshop to encompass all of humanity.

Why was the Holy Ghost publicly poured out at that time? It was to show that we owe the high, heavenly gift of the Holy Ghost alone to the redemption brought about by Christ. It was obtained by Christ's life, suffering, death, resurrection, and ascension. We had to be reconciled to God the Father, through the Son, before the Holy Ghost could do His work publicly. Thus, the true means by which the Holy Ghost enters the heart of man is not by the frightening preaching from the smoking and quaking Sinai but by the preaching of grace about Golgotha and the great deeds of God. It is not by the damning Law of our works, but by the sweet and comforting Gospel of free grace in Christ. The picture of the Baptism of Spirit and fire, which the dear apostles once experienced, demonstrates that God distributes the greatest of all His gifts, His Holy Ghost, not according to the measure of our merit, but according to the measure of His most generous and tender grace in Christ Jesus.

Which of us, having truly experienced the power of the Law like a mighty, rushing wind, would not like to experience the gentle, tender rustling of the Spirit of grace? Who, having felt his death, does not desire to receive the Spirit of life? Who, having felt his powerlessness, does not wish to obtain the Spirit of strength? Who, going about in restlessness and discord of conscience, does not long for the Spirit of comfort, rest, and peace? Who, tormented and harassed by doubts about God's grace and His blessedness, would not gladly welcome the Spirit of righteousness and confidence? Who, having become weary of the pursuit of the goods and joys of this world, would not wish for the Spirit of a true heavenly joy that is eternal?

The answer is: All of those who feel the misery in which they lie, all whom the Law has visited and thrown into despair, and all who hunger and thirst in spirit for the water of life would earnestly desire all of this. They should not lose heart or exert themselves to work on their own behalf. They should not think they are unworthy of the high grace of the Baptism of the Spirit, and they should not believe they must first prepare themselves to receive it. They should do nothing except have faith in the true and precious Word that teaches that Christ Jesus came into the world to save sinners, including them. They will then immediately experience the heart of God opening over them and the streams of the Spirit flowing down from it to fill their poor, aching hearts. To those who in their hearts are the most wretched of sinners, the promise of God applies: "I have blotted out your transgressions like a cloud and your sins like mist" (Isaiah 44:22), and "Come, everyone who thirsts, come to the waters; and he who has no money, come, buy and eat! Come, buy wine and milk without money and without price" (Isaiah 55:1).

Despite the trials of the world and Satan, whenever a poor sinner ventures by faith to receive Christ, the dove of the Holy Ghost comes at once to hover over him and to grant him the peace that God alone can give.

Thou holy Light, Guide Divine,
Oh, cause the Word of Life to shine!
Teach us to know our God aright
And call Him Father with delight.
From ev'ry error keep us free;
Let none but Christ our Master be
That we in living faith abide,
In Him, our Lord, with all our might confide.
Hallelujah! Hallelujah! Amen.

(TLH 224:2)

Wednesday

Read Acts 2:4, 6–7, 11, 13

From the moment the disciples were filled with the Holy Spirit, they recalled nothing about their own works, good or evil. Instead, only God's great deeds became important and comforting to them. And when they opened their mouths, the tongues of fire that had descended upon them spoke what was in their hearts.

We see here a picture of how the Holy Ghost works in every person in whose heart He abides. He does not awaken in a person great thoughts about himself, thoughts about his holiness, his worthiness, or the merits that make him better than others. Just the opposite! As soon as the Holy Ghost enters into the heart of an individual, he becomes smaller and more modest. He no longer knows anything about himself in which he can boast, and he no longer despairs on account of his sins. He is insignificant in his own eyes, but he recognizes how great is the love of God—the patience of the Father, the redemption of Christ, and the comfort of the Holy Ghost. He is unable to conceal from others the joy that now dwells in his heart. He says with David, "I believed, even when I spoke" (Psalm 116:10), and "Come and hear, all you who fear God, and I will tell what He has done for my soul" (Psalm 66:16). Those without the Spirit are at their most eloquent when they speak about their great deeds or about the things of this world. The person who has the Holy Ghost in his heart, by contrast, speaks only of what the eternal Love has done for the world of sinners, including that person himself.

The sermon of the apostles, which the Holy Ghost gave them to declare, produced two effects on its hearers. Some were full of astonishment, recognizing that the apostles were speaking in their own language. Others mocked them, saying, "They are filled with new wine." It is always the same with the testimony of those who are filled with the Holy Ghost. When the children of God hear about His great deeds, they immediately recognize this as being in their own language and they respond, "Truly, it is just as I have also experienced." Such Christians, even if they gather from the most remote regions, immediately become one heart and one soul as if they had drunk from the same mother's breasts. But when the children of the world hear a Christian speaking about the great deeds of God, they respond, "He is full of new wine, a fanatic, or mentally unwell."

Let us examine ourselves according to this. Have we already received the Holy Ghost? Had we earlier heard the rushing of that mighty wind that comes from Sinai? Had the Law thrown us to the ground and revealed our nakedness as sinners? Had we then heard the tender, enlivening, and restoring whisper of the Holy Ghost as He entered our hearts by the sweet Gospel? Finally, have we experienced the workings the Holy Ghost produces in a person when He takes up residence in that individual's heart? Have our hearts and tongues become inflamed to proclaim the great deeds of God in thoughts and words? Have we, then, experienced how true Christians react by saying "Yes and Amen" to our witness while the children of this world mock us as foolish fanatics?

Oh, may Pentecost not pass without allowing us to receive its blessing! In sermons at this glorious festival time, God opened all of heaven to let His grace stream down upon all people everywhere. Let us, then, open our hearts so this heavenly rain may penetrate. If we have already received this heavenly gift, let us go as true priests of God and preach to our unenlightened brothers, with burning hearts and fiery tongues so our fire may always produce a spark in others.

Come, Holy Ghost, God and Lord!
Be all Thy graces now outpoured
On each believer's mind and heart;
Thy fervent love to them impart.
Lord, by the brightness of Thy light
Thou in the faith dost men unite
Of ev'ry land and ev'ry tongue;
This to Thy praise, O Lord, our God, be sung.
Hallelujah! Hallelujah! Amen.

† *(TLH 224:1)*

Thursday

Read John 14:23–24

THIS IS A MOST remarkable statement. The Lord attributes everything else to faith, but here He does not say, "Whoever believes in Me," but rather, "If anyone *loves* Me." But even that is not enough! He adds, "He will keep My word, and My Father will love him, and We will come to him and make Our home with him." Christ means that the individual who loves Him will be made a member of the Church.

Jesus does not say here that true faith is not sufficient to make one a member of the Church, for elsewhere in Scripture the indwelling of God is directly attributed to faith and with it both membership in the Church and salvation. Here, however, He emphasizes that not every faith makes one a member of His Church. The powerless imaginings of the heart and the dead knowledge of the intellect will not suffice. Instead, the faith that avails is one in which a divine living power changes the heart of a person, softening it and filling it both with a holy aversion to every sin and with love for Christ. This love does not consist merely of words; instead, it is an inner, living impulse that also reveals itself in deeds. It is a love that makes a person both willing and able to keep Christ's Word, doing it and bringing it to completion. Therefore, the Lord adds, "Whoever does not love Me does not keep My words." Such a person cannot be a dwelling of God or a member of His Church.

It is not only the heathens, the Jews, and the Muslims who do not belong to the Church of Christ. Other nonmembers are all those who find themselves in the Church but do not abide in the love of Christ and do not keep His Word. Just as there is much in a stone church building that does not belong to it—a decoration, equipment, or a shameful stain—so the spiritual house of the Christian Church can contain people who do not belong to it. Such people may be in the Church because of their gifts or because they seek a respectable life, but if they do not love Christ and do not keep His Word, they are not a part of the Church. They are only an instrument, and if they conduct their life in a manner that is not Christian, they are only a shameful stain.

The Christian Church is like a field of grain. The weeds grow alongside the wheat. Like the wheat, the weeds often make a colorful display. Dew from heaven moistens them, the sun shines on them, and they are brought to maturity for the harvest. In the same way, many people are only weeds in the intangible wheat field of the Church. They do not belong to it, although they, like the true members, are moistened by the heavenly dew of the Gospel, shone upon by the rays of the sun of eternal truth, and brought to maturity for the eternal harvest. As weeds at the time of the harvest that are not brought into the barns but are instead bundled and thrown into the ovens, so will be those who did not love Christ and keep His Word. They may have been baptized, they may have known Christ, they may have developed a kind of faith in Him, and they may have even led an outwardly honorable Christian life. But they will one day find themselves thrown into the fiery oven of hell.

Let us not become secure about our membership in the Christian Church. Instead, let us examine ourselves regarding our love for Christ and our adherence to His Word so when we fall, we may awaken again in true repentance and return to earnest love. Then, when the cry "Here is the Bridegroom!" (Matthew 25:6) is heard, we may arise with rejoicing and follow Him into the wedding hall of the Church triumphant.

Pour down Thy grace in cheering streams
And warm my heart with mercy's beams
From heav'n, Thy throne of beauty;
Thy Spirit ever lead and guide
That in my calling I abide
And find my joy in duty.
Send light and might
That each measure,
Plan and pleasure,
Heav'nward tending,
E'er in Thee may find its ending. Amen.

† *(TLH 546:4)*

Friday

Read John 14:24–26

SINCE ONLY THOSE who love Christ and keep His Word belong to the Christian Church, that Church is made up of a host of people who are known only to God. For only the Lord, the

One who knows the heart, knows His own. No person can see into the heart of another or behold the living love of Christ in the soul of another. No person can discern the motives for the actions of another, which alone determine whether that individual truly or only apparently keeps the Word of Christ. Therefore, the Church, although it is made up of visible people, remains an invisible multitude because no person can distinguish those who love Christ from those who do not. It may seem to be impossible to tell where the Church can be found, although it extends over the entire face of the earth.

Nevertheless, there is one sign that makes the location of the Church unmistakable. The Lord Himself declares this sign in today's text. As His ascension neared, Christ comforted His own with this sign. Although He would no longer be a visible presence in their lives, He would send the Holy Spirit to teach them everything and remind them of all He had spoken to them. What He declared to be inseparable from His Church, something that would never be taken from it, was His Word, His Gospel. This is the certain sign by which the Church can be recognized.

The Church is the fellowship of all true believers and the body of Christ, and nothing except the Word makes a person a true believer and a member of that fellowship. Therefore, the Church of true believers can be found only where the Word is also found. As one may look for stalks of wheat to spring up only where wheat seeds have been sown, so also can one seek the sprouting of invisible true Christians only where the heavenly seeds of grain from the Word have been sown.

Because a crop can be suffocated, we cannot be sure good fruits will necessarily be found wherever good earthly seeds have been planted. But in this connection, the spiritual seed of the Word differs from earthly seed: "so shall My word be that goes out from My mouth; it shall not return to Me empty, but it shall accomplish that which I purpose, and shall succeed in the thing for which I sent it" (Isaiah 55:11). Therefore, God's Word is never preached in vain. Wherever He allows His Word to be preached, some will certainly be converted. Wherever He gives His means of grace, are those who will be pardoned. Wherever people are called by God's Word, we can be certain they include a number who are elected to eternal salvation. Wherever the candle of the Gospel burns, there the Lord has a number of His own. In short, wherever there is a visible congregation in which God's Word is taught purely and distinctly, there may be found the invisible Church of true believers who lie like the heavenly kernel lies hidden in the earthly shell. Everything else that is extolled as a mark of the Church—outward holiness, good works of its members, long duration of its existence, derivation of its origin from the holy apostles in unbroken succession—can deceive, but the mark of the preaching of the pure Word is infallible. Wherever it is found, we can be sure there is the workplace of the Holy Ghost. There we can hear the mighty, rushing wind in which the Spirit descends. Through the preaching of the Word of Christ, He continues to call, gather, enlighten, sanctify, and preserve the one holy Christian Church with Jesus Christ in the one true faith.

O mighty Rock, O Source of Life,
Let Thy dear Word, mid doubt and strife,
Be strong within us burning
That we be faithful unto death,
In Thy pure love and holy faith,
From Thee true wisdom learning.
Thy grace And peace
On us shower; By Thy power
Christ confessing,
Let us win our Savior's blessing. Amen.

(TLH 235:6)

Saturday

Read John 14:27–28

ACCORDING TO TODAY'S READING, what is the first good possessed by all those who love Christ and keep His Word, that is, the members of His Church? It is peace.

In this passage, Christ mentions none of the things man usually regards as great. He says nothing about high honor before men; nothing about earthly riches; nothing about a life rich in pleasure and enjoyment; nothing about being spared suffering, poverty, dishonor, and death. Instead, He expressly says, "Not as the world gives do I give to you. Let not your hearts be troubled, neither let them be afraid." Far be it that Christ should promise the glory of the world to those who belong to His Church. Rather, He assures them they will experience much because of the One in whom they believe; they must be troubled and afraid.

But is that which Christ offers to those who love Him and keep His Word, His Christians, something less than glorious, desirable, and enticing? To be sure, it is something inexpressibly great. When He says, "Peace I leave with you; My peace I give to you," He declares that God has concluded an eternal peace with the person who loves Him, keeps His Word, and belongs to His Church. God has eternally forgiven him all his sins and has become his covenant partner. God sees everything that is done to such a person, good or bad, as if it were done to God Himself. God considers such a person as His dear, elect child, and therefore as an object of His most hearty Fatherly love and care. From this outward peace with God arises the sweetest inner peace of the heart and conscience, the knowledge that there is nothing to fear, and the hope of everything good, now and through all eternity.

Yet this peace is not the only treasure the Church possesses. In our text, Christ continues: "You heard Me say to you, 'I am going away, and I will come to you.' If you loved Me, you would have rejoiced, because I am going to the Father, for the Father is greater than I." In this, Jesus says it is in no way a sad thing for the members of His Church that He does not visibly remain with them because He goes to the Father. In this, they are supremely fortunate for the "Father is greater than I." Christ does not mean that the Father is greater than Christ is Himself, for He clearly and precisely states elsewhere in John's Gospel, "I and the Father are one" (10:30), "Whoever has seen Me has seen the Father" (14:9), and "All may honor the Son, just as they honor the Father" (5:23). No, He is saying, in essence, it is more beautiful with the Father than below in His kingdom of peace because there with the Father is the kingdom of the destination: perfection and glory. Therefore, rejoice that Christ went there as He went ahead of us to prepare a place there for all us and to bring us along after Him.

This is the highest good and the most glorious treasure the Church has. It is a ship in which a person has peace and safety from the storms and waves of the world. In that ship, a person will certainly arrive in the harbor of a blessed world. The Church is also like a tree that stands as in a garden. One day, it will be taken out of this garden and transplanted in the ground of heaven. Finally, the Church is like the entrance hall of the eternal temple in which all of the saints will eventually gather to behold God face to face and to live a life in perfect peace for eternity. Outside the Church, there is no salvation, but in it, there is all salvation.

It is well, therefore, with all of those who find themselves in the ship of the Church as immigrants from the old world to the true new world. This ship will not be wrecked. Instead, in defiance of all the gates of hell, it will happily come to rest at the proper time on the shores of the land where only the saints may dwell. It is well with those who are living branches of the tree that is the Church. They will one day bloom and be displayed in the garden of eternal paradise. It is well with all who worship in the entrance hall of the Church of grace. Their praise on earth will one day become an eternal hallelujah in the most holy place of heaven.

Our place He is preparing;
To heav'n we, too, shall rise,
With Him His glory sharing,
Be where our Treasure lies.
Bestir thyself, my soul!
Where Jesus Christ has entered,
There let thy hope be centered;
Press onward toward the goal. Amen.

† *(TLH 214:4)*

Sunday

Read John 3:1–6

ACCORDING TO TODAY'S READING, the new birth is not something a Christian may or may not have. It is not a praiseworthy quality, the experience only of a strong Christian that a weak one would lack. It is not a high level of Christianity all do not have to attain. Our text does not say the new birth is good, desirable, salutary, and right. Instead, it says, "unless one is born again he cannot see the kingdom of God." Whoever is not born again does not belong in God's kingdom but in the kingdom of Satan. Indeed, he has not even seen God's kingdom and thus is still far from God's grace. His sins are not forgiven; he cannot come to God and be saved in this condition. He is lost.

It is striking that Jesus asserts this with a fourfold "truly," a fourfold oath. He takes before all the world God Himself as a witness, emphatically declaring this statement as irrevocably and eternally resolved: without the new birth, no one will come into God's kingdom or even see it.

Jesus continues, "That which is born of the flesh is flesh, and that which is born of the Spirit is Spirit." He reveals here for whom the new birth is necessary: all people. Through the natural birth of the flesh, by which all people come into the world, we are not spiritual and therefore not suited to the kingdom of God. We do not inherit divine life and Spirit from our parents, but only natural life, flesh, and sin. That is, we are conceived and born in sin, full of darkness, blindness, and enmity against God. Thus, every person is in need of a new birth. Whoever is not born again, in a completely different way by the power of the Holy Spirit from heaven, cannot attain eternal life.

The necessity of the new birth becomes even clearer to us when we consider Nicodemus, to whom Jesus spoke the words of today's text. Nicodemus was already outwardly a member of the true Church. God had already received him into the covenant of grace through the sacrament of circumcision. He was an old, experienced man. He was a ruler of the Jews, a strict Pharisee, but not as hypocritical and arrogant as most. Unlike them, he did not despise Christ much less persecute Him. Instead, he regarded Him as "a teacher come from God." He gladly listened to Christ's teaching and even went to Him at night to talk about the way of salvation. Moreover, as a learned man, Nicodemus was well versed in the Scriptures. In short, he was an excellent man about whom everyone likely thought, *If he does not go to heaven, who can?*

Yet what does Christ say when Nicodemus approaches Him? He shuts heaven to him before his eyes, declaring that if he will not be born again spiritually, he will be eternally condemned and lost despite all his knowledge, virtues, works, holiness, righteousness, worthiness, godliness, and experience.

It is clear from this that a person can outwardly be a member of the true Church. He can also have been born again by Holy Baptism. He can have had many experiences in the world and have achieved maturity. He can gladly and diligently hear God's Word and know the right, pure doctrine, holding it to be true and defending it. Indeed, he can be so godly that he is looked upon as a living saint. Yet such a person can still be a natural man, shut out of God's kingdom, unless he has a newborn heart from the Holy Ghost. Outwardly, a person can appear to be a thousand times better than a true born-again Christian. But this does not help him at all unless he is born again, for it is the heart that matters, and God alone sees what is in his heart.

Oh, enter, Lord, Thy temple,
Be Thou my spirit's Guest,
Who gavest me, the earthborn,
A second birth more blest!
Thou in the Godhead, Lord,
Tho' here to dwell Thou deignest,
Forever equal reignest,
Art equally adored. Amen.

(TLH 228:1)

Monday

Read John 3:14–15

CHRIST CALLS ATTENTION to the words "born again." These words refer to the new life of true faith in our hearts. This much is clear from today's text. But we must not think that because being "born again" is nothing else than faith there is no problem, for who would not believe? We must understand that true faith cannot be mere imagination and powerless conviction that can result from understanding the truth of the Gospel. Instead, it must be something living, powerful, always active and busy. It is something that changes and renews our hearts and minds, making us into totally new people.

Being born again is a complete renewal of the whole person. As our bodily birth gives us a bodily life and natural movements, desires, wills, understanding, and powers, so does the new birth give us these same qualities in a spiritual sense. By nature, we stand outside God's kingdom of grace; we are without a true knowledge of God and His will. We do not know the way of peace, and we do not and cannot trust, love, and fear God with all our heart as instructed by His holy Word. Rather, we are hostile to Him. However, if a person comes to true faith in Christ, he is the recipient of a new birth. He is transformed from a child of wrath into a child of grace, from a sinner into a person who is declared to be righteous, from a condemned person into a saint. Thus, from the kingdom of darkness he enters the kingdom of light. He awakens from his natural spiritual death and comes to spiritual life. In his mind, a new heavenly light shines and he vividly knows God and the right way to Him. The Gospel is no longer foolishness to him but a blessed revelation in which he finds pure truth, written clearly and enlightening him more and more. The innermost depths of his heart are stirred and he is filled with love, fear, and trust in God. Such a person, when he truly begins to believe, becomes a temple of the Holy Ghost who ceaselessly drives him to all good works. This individual no longer judges spiritual things according to his natural understanding but on the basis of God's Word, which totally occupies his soul. The Word is now his light, his wisdom, his counsel, his comfort, his hope, his shield, and his refuge. It becomes his second life, his second soul, and is indelibly written in his heart with the flames of the Holy Ghost. For these reasons, a born-again person is a totally new creature. He thinks, judges, speaks, and lives according to the Word. He is prepared to endure and suffer everything, even death, for the Word, which is spirit and life in him.

Outward changes do not help us at all. Together with our imagined good works, we remain lost. We must be born again, for as Christ says, "Truly, truly, I say to you, unless one is born of water and the Spirit, he cannot enter the kingdom of God" (John 3:5).

Hallelujah! Let praises ring!
Unto the Holy Ghost we sing
For our regeneration.
The saving faith in us He wrought
And us unto the Bridegroom bro't,
Made us His chosen nation.
Glory! Glory!
Joy eternal,
Bliss supernal;
There is manna
And an endless glad hosanna! Amen.

(TLH 23:3)

Tuesday

Read John 3:8

THE NEW BIRTH is a mysterious, incomprehensible work of the Holy Ghost. No person can do this work in himself. Just as we are unable to play even the most insignificant role in receiving natural life and bodily birth, we are unable to participate in being born anew spiritually. However, it is not necessary for us to put our hands in our lap and wait quietly until the Spirit of new birth comes upon us. The Holy Ghost works that change—but He does so through the means of the Word and the holy Sacraments. Christ says we must be born again of water and the Spirit. He names the Sacrament of Holy Baptism because it is the door through which we enter into the kingdom of grace. Why does the water of Baptism have the divine power to bear our souls to the entrance to God's kingdom? Because it is connected with the Word of God. Luther says: "It is not the water indeed that does them [works forgiveness of sins, delivers from death and the devil, and gives eternal salvation to all who believe], but the Word of God which is in and with the water, and faith, which trusts such work of God in the water. For without the Word of God the water is simple water and no baptism. But with the Word of God it is a Baptism, that is, a gracious water of life and a washing of regeneration in the Holy Ghost" (Luther's Small Catechism, 22).

Thus, the Word of God, the doctrine of the Gospel, is the true means by which a person is born again by God's Spirit. Saint James says, "Of His own will He brought us forth by the word of truth, that we might be a kind of firstfruits of His creatures" (1:18). Saint Peter says we have "been born again, not of perishable seed but of imperishable, through the living and abiding Word of God" (1 Peter 1:23).

How does the new birth take place? Only by God's Word. As the sinful person hears, reads, and learns God's Word, he becomes convinced that he is a sinner and God's enemy. He understands that a thousand times over he has offended the One who loved him from eternity and therefore has forever earned God's wrath in the form of both temporal and eternal punishment. Now he becomes terrified of his sins from his heart and, afraid for his soul, he groans, "Where shall I flee, since I am so weighed down with so many great sins? Where shall I find rescue? If all the world approaches, it would never take away my fear!" Those whom the apostles' preaching of repentance cut to the heart found themselves in this condition and it prompted their cry, "What shall we do?"

But it is well for the person who, with humbled spirit, full of fear and timidity from the feeling of his sins, asks this question. He then hears in the Gospel the comforting answer, "Believe in the Lord Jesus," the Savior of sinners, "and you will be saved" (Acts 16:31). If a sinner, in his fear, clings to this Word, even if only weakly at first, God's Spirit has overcome him. This holy wind arrived without the sinner's realizing it and gave him new birth. From this moment on, a new light shines in that individual and he has a new heart, a new life, and a new spirit.

Therefore, let us all see if we stand in the faith that cleanses the heart and if we bring forth the fruits of the Spirit that always follow faith. As Saint Peter says, "For whoever lacks these qualities is so nearsighted that he is blind, having forgotten that he was cleansed from his former sins. Therefore, brothers, be all the more diligent to make your calling and election sure" (2 Peter 1:9–10). Thus, the irrevocable judgment of Christ sounds, "Unless one is born again he cannot see the kingdom of God" (John 3:3).

Holy Ghost, with pow'r divine
Cleanse this guilty heart of mine;
In Thy mercy pity me,
From sin's bondage set me free. Amen.

† *(TLH 234:3)*

Wednesday

Read 1 Corinthians 1:27–28

Many believe that nothing should be preached to the common Christian about the mysterious election of grace because only the learned can comprehend this doctrine. But this is a great error. "All Scripture is breathed out by God and profitable for teaching, for reproof, for correction, and for training in righteousness" (2 Timothy 3:16). And so, when the doctrine of election of grace is rightly taught, it can never be harmful. Instead, it is thoroughly profitable. Holy Scripture mentions this doctrine often in words that are never hard to understand.

Christ Himself repeatedly pointed to the election of grace. He summarized the content of two of His parables (the workers in the vineyard and the royal wedding) with words of warning: "For many are called, but few are chosen" (Matthew 22:14). When He wanted to comfort the disciples against the hatred of the world, He said, "If you were of the world, the world would love you as its own; but because you are not of the world, but I chose you out of the world, therefore the world hates you" (John 15:19). When Christ wanted to humble His followers and suppress any presumption and boasting on their part, He said, "You did not choose Me, but I chose you" (John 15:16). When He wanted to strengthen them against the great danger of temptation in the last days, He said, "For false christs and false prophets will arise and perform great signs and wonders, so as to lead astray, if possible, even the elect" (Matthew 24:24), thus assuring them that this deception would be impossible. After prophesying the great miseries that would characterize that time, He added, "And if those days had not been cut short, no human being would be saved. But for the sake of the elect those days will be cut short" (Matthew 24:22). To imbue His disciples with certainty that their prayers would be heard, He said, "And will not God give justice to His elect, who cry to Him day and night?" (Luke 18:7). To prepare them for the falling away of Judas Iscariot, the betrayer, so they would not take offense and stumble over this terrible fall, Jesus declared: "I am not speaking of all of you; I know whom I have chosen" (John 13:18). Finally, to offer assurance that His followers would enter into eternal life on the Last Day, He said, "And He will send His angels . . . and they will gather His elect from the four winds, from one end of heaven to the other" (Matthew 24:31).

The apostles, by the enlightening and the impulse of the Holy Ghost, followed entirely in Christ's footsteps concerning the doctrine of the election of grace. In our text, for example, Saint Paul refers to God's election and warns the Corinthians, so rich in knowledge and other gifts, not to be presumptuous. In comforting the Thessalonians, he wrote, "we know, brothers loved by God, that He has chosen you" (1 Thessalonians 1:4), and "But we ought always to give thanks to God for you, brothers beloved by the Lord, because God chose you as the firstfruits to be saved" (2 Thessalonians 2:13). In the same way, to stir up the Colossians, he offered this advice: "Put on then, as God's chosen ones, holy and beloved, compassion, kindness . . ." (3:12). Saint Peter termed all believing Christians "a chosen race" (1 Peter 2:9), and he greeted the believers living here and there as "elect exiles" (1 Peter 1:1). Finally, to protect the wealthy from pride, Saint James wrote, "Has not God chosen those who are poor in the world to be rich in faith" (2:5)?

The doctrine of the election of grace is woven as a golden thread throughout Scripture. The holy apostles used this doctrine as Christ Himself did: sometimes for strengthening faith, sometimes for reviving hope, sometimes for humbling, sometimes as an incentive for prayer in firm faith, and sometimes as a warning against unbelief, sin, and apostasy. How profitable and salutary this doctrine is!

Hallelujah! Let praises ring!
Unto the Lamb of God we sing,
In whom we are elected.
He bo't His Church with His own blood,
He cleansed her in that blessed flood,
And as His Bride selected.
Holy, holy,
Is our union and communion.
His befriending
Gives us joy and peace unending. Amen.

(TLH 23:2)

Thursday

Read Ephesians 1:3–4

ACCORDING TO TODAY'S READING, who are the people God has chosen? The apostle Paul says, "even as He chose us." To whom does "us" refer? Paul includes himself, obviously, as well as those he addresses in his letter—the Ephesians who became believers. But how does Paul conclude that they are part of the chosen group? He bases his statement on what he had already written: "Blessed be the God and Father of our Lord Jesus Christ, who has blessed us in Christ with every spiritual blessing in the heavenly places," adding, "even as He chose us." Paul wonders how he or the Ephesians could doubt they are among the chosen ones since God had already blessed them "with every spiritual blessing in the heavenly places" in Christ. Indeed, Christ had already redeemed all people, but the Ephesians and others had also been called by the Word of the Gospel and enlightened with the gifts of the Holy Spirit. They had come to true faith in Christ, and through that faith they were made righteous and justified. In this way, he argues, it is certain that they may count themselves among the people God has chosen.

The doctrine of the election of grace is not a frightening doctrine that stirs up doubt in those who want to be saved. It is, on the contrary, full of comfort in that it should make believers absolutely certain of their salvation. The election of grace does not hang over believing Christians like a threatening thundercloud so they must always ask, "Am I also an elect one?" No, this doctrine is a bright, shining sun of grace and joy that rises over each person as soon as he is called by the Gospel and becomes a believer.

Who are the people God has chosen? They are the true believers. The Formula of Concord states, "The eternal election of God or God's predestination to salvation does not extend over both the godly and the ungodly, but only over the children of God, who have been elected and predestined to eternal life" (FC SD Article XI, paragraph 5).

In our reading, Paul says, "even as He chose us in Him *before the foundation of the world*." Holy Scripture tells us that

God did not wait until the first people were living in this world then choose them when He saw they would convert and keep the faith until their death. No, even before they were born and could have done something good—even before God laid the foundation of the world and created the sun, moon, and stars—the election of grace took place. The omniscient God, who rules everything, knew from eternity everything He would do in time, and it was then that He decided to do it.

On the Last Day, Christ will say to the elect, "Come, you blessed of My Father, inherit the kingdom prepared for you from the foundation of the world" (Matthew 25:34). For this reason, our Church confesses before all Christendom, "For not only before we had done any good, but even before we were born (in fact, 'before the foundation of the world was laid') God elected us in Christ" (FC SD XI 88).

Oh, what kind of hot and inexpressibly great fire must burn in God's heart toward us Christians that He resolved before we were born—even from eternity—to choose us. This is a love that is higher than the heavens, wider than the earth, deeper than the ocean, and as long as eternity.

Thou, mighty Father, in Thy Son
Didst love me ere Thou hadst begun
This ancient world's foundation.
Thy Son hath made a friend of me,
And when in spirit Him I see,
I joy in tribulation.
What bliss Is this!
He that liveth To me giveth
Life forever;
Nothing me from Him can sever. Amen.

(TLH 343:5)

Friday

Read Ephesians 1:4–6

WHEN OUR TEXT SAYS God chose us "that we should be holy and blameless before Him," it means God chose us to convert to Him from our heart. Only by a true conversion of the heart is a person "holy and blameless before Him." The text continues, "He predestined us for adoption." This means God chose us to become His dear children through faith in Christ. A person becomes a child of God only through faith.

It is a glorious fact that we were chosen by God from eternity for repentance, conversion, and holiness and were predestined for adoption and for faith. If we are chosen and predestined for this, then we are also chosen and predestined for salvation. Christ says, "Whoever believes and is baptized will be saved" (Mark 16:16). The apostle Paul also says we are chosen for salvation when he writes, "But we ought always to give thanks to God for you, brothers beloved by the Lord, because God chose you as the first fruits to be saved, through sanctification by the Spirit and belief in the truth" (2 Thessalonians 2:13). In the confession of our Church in the Formula of Concord, we read: "God's eternal election, however, not only foresees and foreknows the salvation of the elect, but by God's gracious will and pleasure in Christ Jesus it is also a cause which creates, effects, helps and furthers our salvation and whatever pertains to it. Our salvation is based on it in such a way that 'the gates of [hell]' are not able to do anything against it, as it is written, 'No one shall snatch my sheep out of my hand,' and again, 'As many as were ordained to eternal life believed" (FC SD XI 8).

The apostle writes, "He predestined us for adoption

through Jesus Christ, according to the purpose of His will, to the praise of His glorious grace, with which He has blessed us in the Beloved." This tells us that God had two reasons for choosing the elect for adoption and eternal salvation. The first was "the purpose of His will" or "His glorious grace," through which He made us His adopted children. The second reason was the holy merit acquired for all people through the life, suffering, and death of Jesus Christ.

God did not foresee something good in His elect that prompted Him to choose them. On the contrary, He saw them in the blood of their sins and yet declared, "You shall live!" God did not determine that they were already acceptable to Him but instead He "blessed us in the Beloved." God did not choose them because they had already forsaken the world by repentance and conversion. Rather, as Christ informs His disciples, He chose them "of the world." God did not even elect us for the sake of our faith. No person can give himself faith. So He decided from eternity to work faith in us by the Gospel and to keep us in that faith until the end of our days. Therefore, our Church confesses: "As it is written, 'He destined us in love to be His son through Jesus Christ, according to the purpose of His will, and to praise of His glorious grace which He freely bestowed on us in the Beloved.' It is therefore false and wrong when men teach that the cause of our election is not only the mercy of God and the most holy merit of Christ, but that there is also within us a cause of God's election on account of which God has elected us unto eternal life. For not only before we had done any good, but even before we were born (in fact, 'before the foundation of the world was laid'), God elected us in Christ" (FC SD XI 88).

From eternity, O God,
In Thy Son Thou didst elect me;
Therefore, Father, on life's road

Graciously to heav'n direct me;
Send to me Thy Holy Spirit
That His gifts I may inherit. Amen.

† *(TLH 411:1)*

Saturday

Read Ephesians 1:3–6

HOW SHOULD A CHRISTIAN correctly use the doctrine of the election to salvation? Our text does not give an explicit answer, but from the manner in which Saint Paul uses and applies this doctrine in the text, we clearly see how every believing Christian should use it.

When the apostle says to the Ephesians, "even as He chose us," he shows that the believers should comfort themselves with the election of grace and should certainly regard themselves as belonging to the elect. However, they should not seek to judge this plan according to their reason, the Law, or some other outward appearance. Nor should they attempt to plumb the hidden abyss of divine providence. Instead, Paul relates this doctrine to the "spiritual blessing in the heavenly places," a blessing with which God has already blessed them and through which He has already revealed His will toward them. All true Christians should use the doctrine of the election of grace this way. They should say to themselves, "God has already called me by the Gospel, enlightened me with His gifts, and sanctified and kept me in the true faith. I can conclude from this, then, that I, too, am an elect."

There is no other way by which God leads His elect to salvation. In Christ, the Book of Life, they are chosen. In Him alone can they find the cause of the eternal election of the Father. As God reveals this to them by the Gospel, they should recognize His hidden counsel and speak confidently: "Lord, in Thy nail-prints let me read / That Thou to save me hast decreed" (*TLH* 148:7). They should also exult with Paul: "Who shall bring any charge against God's elect? It is God who justifies. Who is to condemn? Christ Jesus is the one who died—more than that, who was raised—who is at the right hand of God, who indeed is interceding for us. . . . For I am sure that neither death nor life, nor angels nor rulers, nor things present nor things to come, nor powers, nor height nor depth, nor anything else in all creation, will be able to separate us from the love of God in Christ Jesus our Lord" (Romans 8:33–34, 38–39). Blessed are the Christians who use the doctrine of the election of grace this way and apply it to themselves! In it, they find comfort in every temptation of the flesh, the world, and the devil.

Paul also tells the Ephesians that they are chosen by God so they "should be holy and blameless before Him." The right use of the doctrine of the election of grace by believing Christians includes the admonition to pursue holiness with all earnestness, and so, by good works, "to make your calling and election sure" (2 Peter 1:10). This comforting doctrine cannot be used to further a sense of carnal security. If you regard yourself as one of the elect, do not forget that you have been chosen not only for adoption and salvation but also for holiness. Remember that you cannot do anything to be saved but there is much you can do to forfeit that salvation. God earnestly desires that all people be saved. He has not appointed a single individual for damnation. Calvinists deny the Word of God, which is as clear as the sun, when they teach this. No, all people are redeemed by Christ, and for this reason, the

Gospel should be preached to everyone. God wants to give faith to all through the Gospel and wants to preserve all who have come to faith through His grace. Therefore, whoever is lost has only himself to blame. He is not lost because God failed to grant him His grace but because of his stubborn unbelief and opposition. Therefore, God says, "He destroys you, O Israel, for you are against Me" (Hosea 13:9).

The Lord forsaketh not His flock,
His chosen generation;
He is their Refuge and their Rock,
Their Peace and their Salvation.
As with a mother's tender hand
He leads His own, His chosen band—
To God all praise and glory. Amen.

† *(TLH 19:4)*

Sunday

Read Luke 16:19–31

THE RICH MAN had lived his entire life gloriously confident and carefree. Because he was happy, he assumed God was his Friend. But when it was time for him to die and to leave all his earthly wealth behind, he discovered he had been terribly deceived. To his horror, he realized that God was his enemy, just as he was God's enemy. Instead of being received into heaven as he had hoped, he saw himself cast into hell. The man who had been so rich was now eternally poor. The man who had formerly dressed only in purple and fine linen was now naked and surrounded by the fires of hell. The man who had once indulged in all the pleasures of the earth now longed in vain for a drop of water to cool his parched tongue. When he was denied this relief, he thought about his five brothers, who also lived in the mistaken belief that they had nothing to worry about regarding the future of their soul. He feared that his distress would be magnified when they came to him in this place of torment. He therefore asked Abraham to send him from eternity so, as an eyewitness, he could describe to his brothers the pain of damnation he was suffering and move them to convert while they remained on earth.

But what did Abraham say? "They have Moses and the Prophets; let them hear them" (Luke 16:29). Then the suffering man remembered that he, too, had heard the Word of God but failed to convert. He responded, "No, father Abraham, but if someone goes to them from the dead, they will repent" (Luke 16:30). But Abraham remained unmoved. "If they do not hear Moses and the Prophets, neither will they be convinced if someone should rise from the dead" (Luke 16:31). Abraham thus declared that nothing in heaven and on earth could save a person who is not saved by God's Word.

Today, many people still believe as the rich man did. The Word of God, they are convinced, is not sufficient to convert and save. Many upright people, they say, find much in the Bible that is offensive to them, and knowing that their reason is a gift from God, they cannot believe that Scripture, which is incomprehensible and contradictory to them, has any value at all. Therefore, if God wanted all to believe in Christ, they conclude that the Word is not sufficient and some completely different means is necessary for conversion and salvation. Surely they would see the light if they witnessed an undeniably great miracle, if the dead rose to report on the fate of believers and nonbelievers on the other side of the grave, or if a multitude of angels clothed in heavenly glory came into the world to announce the eternal will of God regarding man. Of course, the best scenario, in their mind, would be for God to present Himself visibly to people and tell them what He expects in order for them to be saved. This, undoubtedly, would bring all doubters and unbelievers to faith instantly, as well as transform all enemies of Christianity into its best friends.

But all of this is the product of twisted thinking in the unrepentant human mind. When Israel was in doubt about its future, the prophet called: "And when they say to you, 'Inquire of the mediums and the necromancers who chirp and mutter,' should not a people inquire of their God? Should they inquire of the dead on behalf of the living? To the teaching and to the testimony! If they will not speak according to this word, it is because they have no dawn" (Isaiah 8:19–20).

Therefore, what Abraham replied to the rich man in our text remains true for all: "If they do not hear Moses and the Prophets, neither will they be convinced if someone should rise from the dead."

Help us that we Thy saving Word
In faithful hearts may treasure;
Let e'er that Bread of Life afford
New grace in richest measure.
Yea, let us die to ev'ry sin,
For heav'n create us new within
That fruits of faith may flourish. Amen.

† *(TLH 293:2)*

Monday

Read Numbers 23:19

WHAT MEANS WOULD God supply to bring to faith a person who could not be persuaded by His written revelation? Despite all the signs and wonders, the heavenly appearances, the risings from the dead, and the pronouncements of angels, it would be very easy for doubts to arise anew. A person might well wonder if he had been deluded by these things or if he had merely imagined them. God's Word, on the other hand, provides irrefutable certainty. It is our heavenly Father's letter and seal regarding what a person must believe. God can indeed be taken at His Word. Faith grounded on passing wonders or appearances can be easily lost, but not so the faith that comes from reading and understanding God's Word. Instead of merely passing by, it remains with us. It is a source from which we can daily draw truth and clarity. Scripture offers us a collection of counselors who can supply us with the very best advice on how we should conduct our lives. After witnessing the heavenly appearance on the Mount of the Transfiguration, Peter declared, "We have something more sure, the prophetic word" (2 Peter 1:19).

Aside from God's Word, there is nothing we can rely upon. We cannot trust our heart, for it always wants to follow the erring path. Scripture says that whoever relies upon his heart is a fool. Our own understanding is equally fallible. What one worldly wise man declares to be high wisdom, another dismisses as foolishness. We cannot depend on the testimony of people, for their judgments can be both errant and deceptive, sometimes by mistake and sometimes wantonly. All people are liars, the Bible teaches, and experience confirms this.

But God is wisdom itself, as Moses emphasizes in today's reading. Unlike men, God does not err, lie, or deceive. His Word is truth, and He Himself is reliable, making good on whatever He promises. The Word is an eternal rock upon which we can build with confidence and to which we can appeal on the Last Day. God cannot deny His Word. As surely as God is God, He must acknowledge it. We can look to Christ as our example here. When He battled the prince of lies and darkness, He repelled every attack with three simple words: "It is written" (Luke 4:4). He knew there is nothing more certain, nothing more firm, nothing more irrefutable than the Word of God.

We must remember that the closer we come to the Last Day, the more cunningly our evil enemy will attempt to deceive us into thinking that the treasure of the Word is uncertain and suspect. Let us, then, be on our guard! Our adherence to the Word is crucial for our salvation. If the Word were taken from us, the sun that lights our path to heaven would be extinguished and we would inevitably stumble in the darkness. If the Word were taken from us, the only staff on which we could lean while journeying to our heavenly Zion would be broken. It remains our only fortress, and that fortress is invincible. Let us not discard the only weapon that guarantees victory in our battle against Satan. Let us not be like ships without compass, rudder, or sail, tossed in every tempest and waiting to be dashed to pieces upon the rocks. God's Word is the lone certainty amid a sea of uncertainties.

How precious is the Book Divine,
By inspiration giv'n!
Bright as a lamp its doctrines shine
To guide our souls to heav'n. Amen.

† *(TLH 285:1)*

Tuesday

Read 1 Corinthians 1:18

GOD IS ABSOLUTELY holy and just. Therefore, He cannot pardon fallen people and make them holy in their present condition. However, it is His immutable will, purely from His grace, to admit into heaven those who humble themselves before Him, who seek His grace with contrite hearts, and who, with hearts of faith, avail themselves of the reconciliation brought about by Christ's sacrifice on the cross. A person who would be saved is not in need merely of instruction. Instead, he requires some means with the power to remove his natural blindness so he clearly recognizes his sin and his misery. He needs some way to awaken him from spiritual death to spiritual life. His heart of stone needs to be shattered and replaced by a heart of repentance. When he struggles with doubt, he needs to find heavenly comfort and cling with childlike confidence to the promise that his sins are forgiven him for Christ's sake. Finally, he needs a key to unlock the thousand chains by which every person, by nature, is bound to sin and the world so he can walk in the love of God and his neighbor.

Where, in heaven or on earth, is there a power that can regenerate and renew the human heart? As we discover with the rich man (Luke 16:19–31), the heart is not softened when a person is overwhelmed with earthly goods. How easy it is for such a person to deceive himself into thinking that such good fortune leaves him with no need to repent (for surely, by His abundant blessings, God has already declared Himself to be his Friend). Trouble and distress, on the other hand, have the power to make a person meek and embitter him toward the world and sin. But, as the way of the heathens demonstrates, without the Word there is nothing to drive a person to God. Instead, troubles cause an individual to bemoan his fate and eventually to despair.

The Word of God alone has the power to bring a person to true repentance and true faith. Because it proceeds from God's mouth, it is almighty. God is in heaven, where He reigns supreme. When He speaks, things happen. When God said, "Let there be light" (Genesis 1:3), there was light. When He said, "Let there be an expanse in the midst of the waters" (Genesis 1:6), an expanse resulted. When He said, "Let the waters under the heavens be gathered together into one place" (Genesis 1:9), they did so. When He said, "Let the earth sprout vegetation" (Genesis 1:11), it produced what it should. When He said, "Let there be lights in the expanse of the heavens to separate the day from the night" (Genesis 1:14), the land was illuminated. God's Son said to the storm, "Peace! Be still!" (Mark 4:39), and the waters were calmed. He told the lepers to be clean, the spirits of hell to depart, the blind eye to see, the deaf ear to hear, and even the dead to rise from the grave. And in each case, it happened just as our Lord commanded. This same Word of God is written in the Scriptures of the prophets and apostles, and it continues to be preached today by God's true servants. It has the power to make the dead soul alive, soften hearts that are as hard as stone, change unbelievers into joyful believers, and transform the children of sin and wrath into the holy children of God.

Let nothing make us doubt the Word of God so it is snatched away from us. If we surrender God's Word, we lose heaven, salvation, and our very soul. Rejection of the Word is also a rejection of God, for it is by the Word alone that He comes to us and we to Him.

Precious Jesus, I beseech Thee,
May Thy words take root in me;
May this gift from heav'n enrich me
So that I bear fruit for Thee!
Take them never from my heart
Till I see Thee as Thou art,
When in heav'nly bliss and glory
I shall greet Thee and adore Thee. Amen.

† *(TLH 296:4)*

Wednesday

Read 1 John 2:15

IF WE WERE TO ASK someone who believes in God whether he also loves God, surely he would not reply that he hates God. He would quickly answer, without thinking, "Indeed, who should not love God?" But how great is the deception that afflicts so many who think like this. For they fail to realize that the love of God is something much different, much higher, and much nobler than they think it is.

The manner of love is to love the beloved more than the self. If, then, we love God, we will hate, deny, and crucify ourselves. Love unites with the beloved. If we love God, we will also be one spirit and heart with Him, as Saint Paul declares, "But he who is joined to the Lord becomes one spirit with Him" (1 Corinthians 6:17). Love renounces all other friendships and clings alone to the beloved. If we love God, we will not have illicit relations with the world. Instead, like Paul, we will regard everything else as loss against the excellent knowledge of Jesus Christ. The love of the Father is not in him who loves the world. Love reveals one's heart to the beloved and expects every good from Him. If we love God, we will have a joyful confidence in Him. Praying to Him will be our heart's desire and in all trials we will call to Him in childlike faith, "Abba, dear Father!" Love devotes itself entirely to the beloved. If we love God, we will offer Him everything we have—our body and our soul. Love denies its own will and fulfills the will of the beloved in all things. If we love God, we rejoice only when His gracious will—be it sweet or bitter, easy or difficult—is completed in or through us. When the true love of God dwells in the human heart, that heart is cleansed from all wanton sins and all worldly lusts so it seeks only what is heavenly. True love draws the soul, with all its inclinations and thoughts, up to God so all its thoughts and desires are focused on Him. For what would a person who has everything in God need to seek outside of God?

Love even awakens in the soul a desire to suffer on account of God, extols itself as blessed when it has many burdens, rejoices with Christ's apostles when it is deemed worthy to suffer disgrace and blows, and boasts with Paul over affliction received because of adherence to Christ. This love was found in David, who called out: "I will love You, O LORD, my strength. The LORD is my rock and my fortress and my deliverer, my God, my rock, in whom I take refuge, my shield, and the horn of my salvation, my stronghold" (Psalm 18:1–2), and "As a deer pants for flowing streams, so pants my soul for You, O God. My soul thirsts for God, for the living God. When shall I come and appear before God?" (Psalm 42:1–2). Asaph, who also had this love, declared: "Whom have I in heaven but You? And there is nothing on earth that I desire besides You. My flesh and my heart may fail, but God is the strength of my heart and my portion forever" (Psalm

73:25–26). Saint Augustine, who wished to be a light that kindled God's love and consumed itself in this love, was also marked by true love.

Examined in this way, how many would come to recognize that their love for God is nothing but a dead thought? How many would hear from Jesus the words He once spoke to the Jews: "But I know that you do not have the love of God within you" (John 5:42). And how many of us who have made a beginning, by God's grace, to separate from sin and immerse ourselves only in the love of God, would nevertheless sigh, with Saint Augustine: "I have loved you too late, my Beauty, oh, too late have I loved You, my God! In Your creation I have too long sought my peace, until You, my Love, called me to You."

Lord, Thee I love with all my heart;
I pray Thee, ne'er from me depart,
With tender mercy cheer me.
Earth has no pleasure I would share,
Yea, heav'n itself were void and bare
If Thou, Lord, wert not near me.
And should my heart for sorrow break,
My trust in Thee no one could shake.
Thou art the Portion I have sought;
Thy precious blood my soul has bought.
Lord Jesus Christ,
My God and Lord, my God and Lord,
Forsake me not! I trust Thy Word. Amen.

(TLH 429:1)

Thursday

Read 1 John 4:16–18

WHAT MUST I DO to be saved? If we ask this, the Word of God gives only one answer: "Believe in the Lord Jesus, and you will be saved, you and your household" (Acts 16:31). No work can blot out our sin and no love can reconcile us with God. Only faith in Christ makes us just and holy before God. But what makes up the blessedness to which faith leads us? Above all else, it is blessed communion with the Triune God. If we do not love God, we can never be in communion with Him. As today's text teaches, "God is love, and whoever abides in love abides in God, and God abides in him" (1 John 4:16). Therefore, if the love of God does not reside in a person's heart, he boasts of faith and relies upon it in vain. Faith is not an intention to acquire all the comfort of the Gospel. It is a heavenly light, a divine power that God, with His grace, implants in the heart. Faith without love for God is an empty product of our imagining, a hull without fruit, a shell without a kernel, a painted picture without life. Wherever there is true faith, love comes forth like the shining of the sun. Wherever love is absent from the heart, God, the eternal love, cannot be found there. And where there is no God, there is also no faith. Darkness and light cannot coexist; it is the same with the loveless person and God.

Therefore, if you want to come to God and be saved, you must throw yourself down before Him with all your sins, lament your misery, and call upon Him for mercy. Then His Holy Spirit will comfort you and work true faith in your heart. Through the faith that dwells in you, He will pour out His love that you will taste and experience. But know this: If you do not remain in love, you also will not remain in faith.

You must allow the heavenly plant of love to take root in you so it can grow and produce its fruits. If love ceases in you, God will withdraw from you, for God is love. Forsaking love means forsaking God, for "God is love, and whoever abides in love abides in God, and God abides in him."

Saint John has more to say regarding the necessity of love. He says: "By this is love perfected with us, so that we may have confidence for the day of judgment. . . . There is no fear in love, but perfect love casts out fear. For fear has to do with punishment, and whoever fears has not been perfected in love" (1 John 4:17–18). How true this is! Nothing but the Word of forgiveness can heal our wounded conscience. Nothing but faith in the One who made the godless just can console us in the trials of sin and doubt. In the hour of our death, nothing will be able to give us peace except looking in faith to the crucified Christ, who bore our sins. No work and no love will stand on the Day of Judgment. But we must also know this: If our faith has not worked love in us, it has been nothing but a dream and a sham.

How many who continually live in sin against their conscience comfort themselves with their faith! But when death comes, their peace will depart, for those who were misused by that sin will come forward as witnesses to testify that there was no true faith in these hearts. Indeed, it is impossible now to have a joyful confidence in God by faith as long as a person realizes he is still not justified before Him. It is not possible to be calm while a person lives in sin against his conscience. A good conscience and faith are inseparable. Therefore, whoever pretends to believe in Christ but goes about dishonestly, gratifying the desires of the flesh in secret and being irreconcilable, arrogant, vain, unfaithful, miserly, slanderous, and insincere, is destroying the comfort of his faith and robbing himself of confidence in his heavenly Father. God will put him to the test in His time and he will see that his faith has no roots. In eternity, he will hear: "Not everyone who says to Me, 'Lord, Lord,' will enter the kingdom of heaven. . . . I never knew you; depart from Me, you workers of lawlessness!" (Matthew 7:21, 23).

Holy Ghost, with light divine
Shine upon this heart of mine;
Chase the shades of night away,
Turn the darkness into day.

See, to Thee I yield my heart,
Shed Thy life through every part;
A pure temple I would be,
Wholly dedicated to Thee. Amen.

† *(TLH 234:1, 6)*

Friday

Read 1 John 4:19

GOD DID NOT CREATE us for this transitory world as He did the animals. For this reason, He did not fill the earth with His goods in order to satisfy our immortal spirit. No, God had an inexpressibly higher, more glorious intention in creating us. He wanted to make us blessed, not by the enjoyment and love of the creature, but by the enjoyment and love of God Himself. Poor, humble man was born with the high destiny to embrace the greatest good with his love and to be eternally blessed in communion with God. But man fell into sin, and with that fall a terrible change occurred in his heart. Ever since that moment, no man is born with knowledge of his high destiny; and when that destiny is proclaimed to him, he has no urge to obtain it. All people retain the urge for rest, for peace, for blessedness. But after the fall, none of us, by nature, seeks blessedness in God but in the world. God's holy law stands like an enemy between God and the natural depravity of people. Therefore, a person sins boldly and wantonly against God or he merely submits himself outwardly to God's order, seeking to keep His commandments because he is afraid of wrath and punishment. Now, by nature, no person wants to enter heaven because he loves God and finds his blessedness in Him, but because he does not want to be condemned.

Oh, miserable people, how deeply have we fallen! God does not want to satisfy us with visible, temporal, perishable goods. He wants to give us Himself, the eternal, highest good. But we would rather satisfy ourselves with the fleeting things of this world! How can the love of God, for which we were created and in which we alone can be truly blessed, come into our hearts once again?

Saint John answers this question in today's reading. He shows us how God wants to come into our hearts when he says, "We love because He first loved us" (1 John 4:19). The Lord indeed loved us first, and we have not loved Him at all, but rather hated Him. By nature, we are enemies of God, worthy only of His vengeance and not His love. Yet God loved us from eternity, before we were born. He loved us so much that He gave His only begotten Son. Formerly, we were under the terror of our conscience, death, and hell, but now we are restored and consoled with the comfort that Jesus Christ, the Son of God, came into the world to save sinners. When, by the working of the Holy Ghost, we believe all of this from the heart, when we experience, by faith, the love of God in Christ amid the knowledge of our wickedness, then the love of God is again poured out into our heart.

It is impossible to draw near to the great fire of the love of God in Christ without becoming warmed by it in fervent mutual love. Why do so few people love God? It is because they have not tasted in their heart the love He has for them. Had they done so, they would truly burn with love for God. They would love Him more than the miser loves his earthly goods, than the mother loves her child, and than the bride loves her bridegroom. Whoever knows how great a sinner he is, and yet that he is received in Christ, will reject the whole world for Christ. Everything else is small, stale, and bitter to him. He recognizes that God alone is worthy of his love. In Him, he finds everything for which his heart wishes. As a result of his reconciliation to God, heaven with all its blessedness already stands open to him.

Oh, teach me, Lord, to love Thee truly
With soul and body, head and heart,
And grant me grace that I may duly
Practice fore'er love's sacred art.
Grant that my every thought may be
Directed e'er to Thee. Amen.

† *(TLH 399:5)*

Saturday

Read 1 John 4:20–21

ACCORDING TO TODAY'S TEXT, love for God must reveal itself in love for the brethren for two reasons. The first is that a person who does not love his neighbor certainly cannot love God.

Saint John writes: "If anyone says, 'I love God,' and hates his brother, he is a liar; for he who does not love his brother whom he has seen cannot love God whom he has not seen?" (1 John 4:20). It is easier to love what we can see than what we cannot see. A person can love something he has only heard about so long as he regards it as worthy of his love. Nevertheless, how much more will he be moved to love it when he can see it! Conversely, if a person does not love something that is worthy of love, although he has seen it, how much less will he love it if he has not seen it! We can see our brother or our neighbor, but we cannot see God. If, then, we love God, how much more should we love our brother or neighbor! If we do not love our neighbor, how much less will we love God!

John continues, "And this commandment we have from Him: whoever loves God must also love his brother" (1 John 4:21). Here is the second reason the love of God must reveal itself. It is because God has commanded us to love our brothers just as He commanded us to love Him. A person cannot possibly love someone and not want to do his will. Can we believe that one who continually does the opposite of what we want, and so vexes and offends us, loves us? Certainly not! Instead, we will conclude from such behavior that he hates us. God has written in every human heart the commandment to love the brother as well as God Himself. This same commandment is repeatedly emphasized in Scripture. God testifies that He does not need our service but He wants us to serve Him by serving our brothers. Christ tells us that, on the Last Day, He will say, "As you did it to one of the least of these My brothers, you did it to Me" (Matthew 25:40). James testifies, "Religion that is pure and undefiled before God and the Father is this: to visit orphans and widows in their affliction" (1:27).

There is more. God does not want to know of any worship as long as we do not perform the necessary service of love to our brothers. Christ says: "So if you are offering your gift at the altar and there remember that your brother has something against you, leave your gift there before the altar and go. First be reconciled to your brother, and then come and offer your gift" (Matthew 5:23–24). If love of the neighbor requires it, we should omit the outward service to God and serve the neighbor, knowing that, in this, we serve Him as well.

May God let His love be known to us all in Christ! Let the fire of our love for Him burn in our hearts and it will overflow toward our neighbor in our good words and works. May God also preserve us in this love through faith until the end of our days. Thus we will also enjoy God's love in eternity. For "God is love, and whoever abides in love abides in God, and God abides in him" (1 John 4:16).

Thou sacred Love, grace on us bestow,
Set our hearts with heav'nly fire aglow
That with hearts united we love each other,
Of one mind, in peace with ev'ry brother.
Lord, have mercy! Amen.

(TLH 231:3)

Sunday

Read Luke 14:16–20

THIS PASSAGE DESCRIBES how the Jews, who had already been invited to the Great Supper by the Old Testament prophets, received a new invitation via the Gospel when Christ appeared and the table was finally set. Yet one after another excused himself, hindered by the things of the world.

It has always been this way. Most people still refuse the invitation of the Gospel. Why do most so-called Christians want to know nothing about the preaching of Christ? Why does the call, "Repent, for the kingdom of heaven is at hand" (Matthew 4:17), repel many? Why do some gladly hear the invitation, "Come, for everything is now ready" (Luke 14:17), and faithfully come to church, but fail to really come to Christ? Why do so few truly convert? Why do so many take a certain pleasure in the comforting Gospel, but never let it become their daily bread, the life of their soul and the soul of their life?

As in the Gospel, many today ask to be excused and say, with their hearts if not with their mouths, that they have things to do, have taken a husband or a wife, have bought something that requires attention, or the like. Such people find they cannot separate themselves from the things of this world, whether they are earthly goods or earthly desires or earthly honors. They do not wish to turn away from the happiness they find in the world. They are so entangled in the cares of the world they find no time to go to Christ daily, fearing they might lose too much or gain too little in such an effort. They do not regard Christ and His kingdom as worthy of the sacrifice of their whole life. They even consider life in Christ's kingdom to be a difficulty bound to make them unhappy.

How foolish such thoughts are! How foolish are all those who allow the things of this world to prevent their entrance into Christ's kingdom. It is the world that is not worthy of a person's trust; the kingdom of Christ is worth the surrender of everything else so one can enter by its narrow gates. For what is life in this world? It is as Christ describes it in today's reading: the joy and care for field, cattle, wife, and child. As

Moses says, "The years of our life are seventy, or even by reason of strength eighty; yet their span is but toil and trouble; they are soon gone, and we fly away" (Psalm 90:10). Therefore, what can be more foolish than letting the miserable things of this world prevent us from entering into Christ's kingdom?

Whoever enters that kingdom hardly embitters his life. It is, as Christ describes it in our text, a supper. It is not difficult work or service, but, as it is called elsewhere, righteousness, peace, and joy in the Holy Ghost. Whoever leaves the world and clings to Christ with his whole heart finds a gracious and kind Father who does not remember His children's sin, who takes all worries from their hearts, and who lets them dwell in His house, eat at His table, and drink from His cup. He provides for them, daily and richly, restoring them in body and soul. Whoever leaves the world and clings to Christ truly begins to live, experiencing what it means to be happy. He discovers how wonderful it is to be free of the chains that bound him when he served sin. He now recognizes the darkness in which he once languished and how blessed he is now that the Sun of grace has risen.

The world with wanton pride
Exalts its sinful pleasures
And for them foolishly
Gives up the heavenly treasures.
Let others love the world
With all its vanity;
I love the Lord, my God—
What is the world to me! Amen.

† *(TLH 430:6)*

Monday

Read Luke 14:21–24

THE INVITATION TO ENTER Christ's kingdom was first extended to all Jews, but the rich despised it. Now, we learn in today's reading, the Gospel is to be preached mainly to the poor and wretched. The Jews had rejected the Gospel, and now Christ's servants would extend the invitation to the Gentiles. Here we also learn the true state of Christ's kingdom. Those who despise His grace cannot be saved even if they should love ever so uprightly, and those who long for His grace cannot be lost no matter how poor they are in spiritual things. Even if they are still great, miserable, and shameful sinners, who are rejected by all and comforted by none, the invitation to enter Christ's kingdom of grace remains open to them.

All who by God's grace recognize that they are completely unworthy sinners and who long to be received into Christ's kingdom should rejoice, for Christ calls, "Come, for everything is now ready" (Luke 14:17). He commands His servants to compel them to come in. They are not to listen to the voice of their heart that says grace is denied them. The heart is not the judge, but rather the Word of God, which extends the invitation. They are also not to be terrified by the Law, losing heart when they read in Scripture how much God demands from people and how severely He wants to punish all sins. The Law has no power over those who flee to Christ, for "Christ is the end of the law for righteousness to everyone who believes" (Romans 10:4). They are not to become discouraged when Satan raises doubts in their heart by suggesting they have sinned too much or too long to be worthy of consideration as a guest as Christ's table. The invitation, "Come, for everything is now ready," extends until the Last Day and even to the last hour of life. When we hear that call and recognize our sin, we can and should come that we might receive grace upon grace.

Many may say: "I wanted to come gladly, but I am afraid. I lack the necessary true knowledge of my sins." You who so lament consider: A person finds grace not by the knowledge of his sin but through belief in Christ. Therefore, grace does not depend upon the degree of your knowledge of your sin. If, without feigning, you can say you recognize yourself as an entirely unworthy sinner who can be saved only by grace, you should hurry to save your soul. "Come, for everything is now ready."

Another may say: "I fear deceiving myself. There have already been too many who intended to comfort themselves with the grace of Christ but in the end were lost." This is true. But all of these were lost because they only imagined the comfort of Christ and therefore did not turn their hearts to Him. Whoever from his heart turns to Christ truly attains grace from Him, the One who does not deceive.

Thy great love for this hath striven
That we may from sin be free
And forever live with Thee;
Yea, Thy Son Himself hath given
In His grace an earnest call
To His Supper unto all.

Lord, Thy mercy will not leave me—
Truth doth evermore abide—
Then in Thee I will confide.
Since Thy Word cannot deceive me,
My salvation is to me
Well assured eternally. Amen.

(TLH 384:2, 4)

Tuesday

Read 1 Corinthians 15:22–24, 28

God did not create everything because He was forced to or because He wanted to be useful. He was motivated solely by His eternal love. David says: "The heavens declare the glory of God, and the sky above proclaims His handiwork. Day to day pours out speech, and night to night reveals knowledge. There is no speech, nor are there words, whose voice is not heard. Their measuring line goes out through all the earth, and their words to the end of the world" (Psalm 19:1–4). All creatures have tongues with which they should praise their Creator day and night. God's glory is the purpose and goal of their existence. God was free either to create the world or to leave it in its nonexistence. In addition, His perfect glory is not enhanced by the praise of His creatures, so it was not necessary for Him to create the world for this. God did not need creatures. He is an ocean of eternal love that overflowed in the creation of countless beings to whom He revealed His love and with whom He shared His goodness.

From eternity, God decided to send down the full stream of His goodness especially on mankind. He decided to establish a kingdom of blessedness and glory and to gather all people into it. God created man in His image to make him capable of an eternal joy and blessedness in Him. But man fell into sin. This caused him to lose the image of God in which he had been created. Now he is, by nature, unfit for the holy kingdom of God. For this reason, God's Son came into the world: to establish a kingdom of grace for fallen people that they might one day enter into God's kingdom of perfect blessedness and glory.

To enter that perfect, holy kingdom, one must first become a subject in Christ's kingdom of grace. "I am the way, and the truth, and the life," Christ said. "No one comes to the Father except through Me" (John 14:6). He also said: "I am the door. If anyone enters by Me, he will be saved" (John 10:9). Saint Peter testifies, "And there is salvation in no one else, for there is no other name under heaven given among men by which we must be saved" (Acts 4:12). In today's text, Saint Paul teaches that the kingdom of Christ on earth will one day be absorbed into the kingdom of the triune God in heaven. We see here that there is only one city of God in heaven and on earth. Whoever wants to dwell in heaven must already inhabit its earthly suburb. There is only one temple of God on earth and in heaven. Whoever wants to enter into the holy of holies must already have entered the courts of grace on earth. And whoever wants to take part one day in the glorious entry into the heavenly Jerusalem must have become a citizen of Christ's kingdom on earth, in company with the saints and the household of God. For this reason, when Christ appeared among the Jews, His first statement to them was "The time is fulfilled, and the kingdom of God is at hand; repent and believe in the gospel!" (Mark 1:15).

This invitation into Christ's kingdom is extended to us, but have we accepted it? Is sin no longer our queen, having been replaced by Christ as our Lord of all? Have we embraced the Gospel's call of grace? Can we say with Paul and without contradicting our conscience, "But our citizenship is in heaven, and from it we await a Savior, the Lord Jesus Christ" (Philippians 3:20)? May God in grace grant that the call, "Come, for everything is now ready" (Luke 14:17), becomes so powerful in our hearts that we set out to walk the path to the heavenly Zion in faith.

Now keep us, holy Savior,
In Thy true love and fear
And grant us of Thy favor
The grace to persevere
Till, in Thy new creation,
Earth's time-long travail o'er,
We find our full salvation
And praise Thee evermore. Amen.

† *(TLH 32:4)*

Wednesday

Read Romans 10:17

IF A PERSON WANTS to be saved, he must first diligently hear, read, and examine God's Word. Whoever does not want to do this cannot be helped, despite his prayers and concerns, for he remains in his natural darkness, in sin, and under God's displeasure.

The Holy Spirit, who must work everything that is good in a person, does not work without means. God's Word is the only means of grace through which He works. Even Baptism and Holy Communion have power only because the earthly elements are connected with the heavenly Word. Without the Word, Baptism would be mere water and no Baptism, and Holy Communion would be nothing more than bread and wine rather than Christ's body and blood. The Word of God is the hand God extends to us from heaven to draw us to Him. Whoever does not hear His Word turns away from the divine hand and therefore cannot be saved.

The Word of God not only shows us the way to heaven, but it alone awakens people who by nature are spiritually dead. It enlightens them so they rightly learn to know themselves and Christ, and it works faith in Christ in them. Therefore, Saint Paul says, "So faith comes from hearing, and hearing through the word of Christ" (Romans 10:17). As long as a person continues to hear God's Word, he cannot give up hope that he can still be converted even when everything else appears utterly futile to him. But if an unconverted person flees every opportunity to hear God's Word, it is impossible for him to be saved unless the Word eventually awakens him in the distress of death.

The hearing, reading, and examination of the Word are also required for a converted Christian to remain in the faith. If someone has awakened from the sleep of his soul, he is in great danger of falling asleep again or sinking back into spiritual death. The Word of God must both awaken him and keep him awake. Even if someone has come to the knowledge of his sins and the danger they pose to his soul, he remains in great danger of relapsing into blindness. The Word of God must continually remind him of his sins and their danger. Someone who has experienced the comfort that comes from knowing his sins are forgiven is still in constant danger of losing this comfort. The Word must keep filling him with that divine comfort. The person who has started to walk the path of faith and evangelical sanctification can still easily lose his way and return to an errant path. For this reason, he must rely upon the Word as his road map to keep him on the correct path or to restore him to that path.

What earthly food and drink are to the body, the Word of God is to the soul. As the body loses its powers and finally dies when it is deprived of food and drink for only a short time, so also the soul of the Christian loses its spiritual powers and sinks back into spiritual death when he fails to study God's

Word zealously on a daily basis. What wood and coal are to the fire in the fireplace, the Word is to the fire of faith and love in the Christian's heart. As the fire in the fireplace immediately goes out when it is not carefully tended, so the fire of faith and love in the Christian's heart is extinguished when he ceases to study God's Word. A tree withers not just when it is cut down but also when it is no longer watered. Likewise, a Christian falls from grace not just when he returns to the world and falls into obvious sin, but also when he ceases to hear and examine Scripture diligently. When he makes the study of Scripture his constant concern, he is like a tree, planted by streams of water, that brings forth its fruit in its season, and its leaves do not wither.

Preserve, O Lord, Thy children,
Thine own blest heritage;
Resist, disperse, and scatter
Those who against Thee rage.
Let Thy commandments guide us,
Grant us Thy heav'nly food;
Clothe us in Thy rich garments,
Bought with Thy precious blood. Amen.

† *(TLH 264:4)*

Thursday

Read 1 John 4:7

BIBLICAL AND CHURCH history informs us that when things have gone well in the Christian Church or in individual congregations, this has been revealed through love. By God's grace, there have been great awakenings in the Church and in individual congregations as He gloriously built up His fallen Zion by gracious visitations. And as God's Word has been brought to light and been made powerful in many hearts, it has always resulted in the demonstration of an inner, heartfelt, mutual brotherly love. Whenever God has given entire congregations a better understanding of evangelical knowledge and their members have faithfully gone around in this light, they have invariably displayed a great, fervent love.

When, on the first Christian Pentecost, the Word of God achieved such a glorious victory that a Church of 3,000 souls was gathered, both the faith and the love of these individuals were noted. "Now the full number of those who believed were of one heart and soul, and no one said that any of the things that belonged to him was his own, but they had everything in common" (Acts 4:32).

As it was in the apostolic age, so it has been ever since. Whenever the tree of the Church has blossomed in faith, the fruits of brotherly love have appeared right away. During the first three centuries of the Christian era, when so many thousands of believers sealed their faith with their blood under the persecutions of heathen emperors, love was stronger than it has been at any time since. Although Christians were scattered in many countries, they were still bound by love as to a great family. They called themselves brothers and sisters whether they were of high or low estate. If one Christian was distressed, all felt that distress. They mourned together and they rejoiced together. No brother was ashamed of another. Sparing no danger, Christians visited those who were in prison on account of their confession. Often, an entire multitude of believers crowded into a prison to comfort and restore with their tears, words, and gifts of love.

This was also the experience of the Church centuries

later. When the pure doctrine and the right faith were lost, the first love was also lost in Christianity. But when, in the darkest times, by the reading of the Bible, true Christian congregations arose again, the confessors of the truth were recognized again by their love. Often, their persecutors in the Church put away their instruments of martyrdom, having been moved by the true love exemplified by these believers.

At the time of the Reformation, when the apostolic doctrine appeared again in its purity, love was awakened with faith. When Luther fearlessly went into the midst of his angriest enemies, placing himself in Worms before emperor and empire and expecting nothing but death, all the believers in Germany prayed to God for the safety of this man. Nine years later, when the Protestant estates in Augsburg laid down their undying confession, strong bonds of love showed themselves among those who were united by one faith. No one abandoned another in his distress. Instead, the greater the danger, the stronger the bond of love that was demonstrated. This was the time during which love founded most of the charitable establishments for churches, schools, the poor, widows, and orphans, whose blessings are still felt today in countries where the legacy of the Lutheran Reformation is felt.

As it is with the Church as a whole, so it is with the individual believer. As soon as he becomes a true Christian, he is filled with the true love. Therefore, whoever has love has the witness that he stands in the true faith and stands with God in grace.

Jesus, all Thy children cherish
And keep them that they never perish
Whom Thou hast purchased with Thy blood.
Let new life to us be given
That we may look to Thee in heaven

Whenever fearful is our mood.
Thy Spirit on us pour
That we may love Thee more—
Hearts o'erflowing;
And then will we
Be true to Thee
In death and life eternally. Amen.

(TLH 444:4)

Friday

Read 1 John 3:16

TRUE LOVE for our neighbor is not an inheritance from our parents. By nature, no one recognizes what true love really is or how high it ascends. "By this," John says, "we know love, that He laid down His life for us" (1 John 3:16). Only in Christ can we recognize the kind of love God requires of us.

Whoever has true love directs his love not only at those who love him and do good to him, but, like Christ, also at his enemies, the children of the world who carry hatred and resentment in their hearts. Whoever has true love makes no distinctions among people and considers love to be a debt he daily pays to all of his brothers according to the flesh. He regards everyone as a creature of God, who loved that person so much that He gave His Son to death on the cross. He regards that person as a possession of the Lord Jesus, bought with His own blood, and as a dwelling place of the Holy Spirit. Whoever has true love does not despise even the most wretched and godless; instead, he holds the souls of all people in high regard, for he knows how precious each individual is to God. Whoever has true love wishes evil for no one in the world. Rather he prays from his heart that all will go well, both temporally and eternally, for his brothers and does whatever he can to promote their well being. He rejoices even when things go well for his enemies, and their distress goes to his heart. He would rather suffer himself than see others suffer. When he has the goods of this world and sees his brother in want, he does not close his heart but extends an open, generous hand to assist. But he does not give to be seen or to receive something good in return. Indeed, he gladly gives even when he does not expect anything but ingratitude in return.

Whoever has true love does not consider himself to be a lord over his goods but a steward of them, and he wishes, according to God's Word, to distribute those goods to his brothers in need. If he is generous, he does not boast about it but continues to regard himself as an unworthy servant who is doing only what he is obligated to do. If someone treats him unjustly, he is not troubled that he was wronged but that his enemy sinned against God and thereby lost His grace. For this reason, he is always ready for reconciliation and he gladly lays aside his rights to bring about peace. Whoever has true love does not rejoice over his enemy's downfall. He does not gladly speak about the sins and failings of others, and he excuses them as much as he can in good conscience, seeking only the betterment and the conversion of the sinner. He also seeks to benefit his neighbor, even at the cost of his own life.

By nature, this love for the neighbor does not reside in any human heart. This love is a daughter of faith, a fruit of the Holy Ghost. Only one whose heart has been changed by God can love so universally, so sincerely, so heartily, so unselfishly, so self-sacrificially, so humbly, so purely, so untiringly, and so faithfully until death. No one can give himself this love. When he is awakened from his sins and comes to recognize his inexpressible misery without Christ, he seeks to find peace for his restless heart, grace for his debt, and forgiveness for his sin. Then, having found these in Christ, he discerns that God is no longer angry with him, that in Christ he is accepted as His child, and that despite his unworthiness life and salvation are given to him freely. This causes the heart of the sinner to be opened to love Him who loved him from eternity. Then the love of God is poured into that heart by the Holy Ghost and the individual is sweetly compelled to do good to his fellow men and to seek, with his whole heart and according to all his abilities, their temporal and eternal welfare.

All love is Thine, O Spirit;
Thou hatest enmity;
Thou lovest peace and friendship,
All strife wouldst have us flee.
Where wrath and discord reign,
Thy whisper kindly pleadeth
And to the heart that heedeth
Brings love and light again. Amen.

† *(TLH 228:6)*

Saturday

Read 1 John 3:14–15

LOVE IS NOT the feeling of a strong faith, a high and deep knowledge, a great and glittering work, and a great sanctification of life. Instead, it is the mark of our state of grace. For this reason, a Christian who is weak in the faith need not be intimidated when he hears about the strong faith of Abraham, David, Peter, and Paul. He need not fear when he cannot sing triumphantly with Job, "For I know that my Redeemer lives" (19:25); cry out with Paul, "I have fought the good fight, I have finished the race, I have kept the faith. Henceforth there is laid up for me the crown of righteousness, which the Lord, the righteous Judge, will award to me on that Day" (2 Timothy 4:7–8); and rejoice with Luther, "Tho' devils all the world should fill, / All eager to devour us, / We tremble not, we fear no ill, / They shall not overpow'r us" (*TLH* 262:3). Many Christians around him may cheerfully confess that they are godly minded, that they stand with God in grace, that they look forward to death and the Last Day, and that they are ready at any moment to appear before God's throne. He, by contrast, perhaps can only weakly grasp Christ and often cries out, "I believe, Lord, help my unbelief!" (Mark 9:24). However weak his faith may be, if it has worked love in him, he has a certain and comforting mark of his state of grace.

Perhaps he lacks a rich knowledge, understanding only a little of what he reads in God's Word. He sees that other Christians have a much greater knowledge of Scripture, while he himself is unable to answer important questions about spiritual and church-related subjects. But he cannot imagine that because of this his salvation is somehow compromised for it is his love that marks his state of grace.

He may be troubled that he cannot show great, shining works, being limited to the earthly vocation he pursues from morning to night. He cannot point to great deeds completed for the Savior or to great suffering endured for Christ's sake. Yet he can be comforted because God does not judge according to outward things. If he is faithful in his earthly calling, doing everything in the fear of God and in hearty love for his neighbor, then his seemingly humble works are great, holy, and pleasing to God. The most meager and despised works performed in love are as holy as the building of churches and the rescuing of souls by apostolic preaching.

The truth that brotherly love is a mark of our state of grace is also a warning to those who nurse hatred and enmity and who have no forgiveness in their hearts. Today's text tells us, "everyone who hates his brother is a murderer" (1 John 3:15). This judgment pertains to all the loveless. A person can speak beautifully about Christianity; he may have unmatched knowledge of the Word of God; he may think he is strong in faith; he may seemingly perform Christian works. He may appear to be friendly, humble, patient, generous, and zealous for pure doctrine. He may separate himself from the world and lead a chaste, moderate life of self-denial in the eyes of man. He may appear to take upon himself shame and suffering for Christ. But in all of this, if he is without love for others, he is no Christian, no child of God. He does not stand in grace but instead lies in spiritual death. One without love may seem to be holy but it is only appearance. Such a one remains a murderer before God, for our text adds, "Everyone who hates his brother is a murderer, and you know that no murderer has eternal life abiding in him" (1 John 3:15).

Thy light to every thought impart
And shed Thy love in every heart;
The weakness of our mortal state
With deathless might invigorate. Amen.

(TLH 233:4)

Sunday

Read Luke 15:1–10

CHRIST SEEKS ALL who have gone astray. Who are they? Some wander around in the deserts of the heathen without any knowledge of God and their Savior. Others are on the path of obvious unbelief, living in open vice. Still others, like the prodigal son, forsake the house of their pious parents and the fellowship of Christians, reject the Christian instruction they received, ignore the compelling admonitions given to them, and forget their confirmation vows. They go with the godless world on the path of all vanity, no longer caring at all about God's Word, the Church, Holy Communion, prayer, heaven, and hell. People who go astray can even include those who walk in the midst of Christians, enjoying a close fellowship with them, outwardly living and speaking as Christians, and being zealous for God's kingdom.

Those who go astray are all acting naturally for each of us arrives in the world without a true love of God, a true fear of God, and a true trust in God. Instead, we have a false love of ourselves, sin, the world, and vanity. No one, by nature, lives in fellowship with God. But people go astray in different ways. One gets tangled in the thorns of covetousness and the love of money. Another falls into the swamp of lust. A third tries to ascend the steep heights of pride, self-righteousness, and the like. They go equally far away from God. Yet Christ seeks all of them. He seeks the whole world.

For this reason, the only begotten Son of God decided from eternity to become a man and to lower Himself to share our misery. He carried out this eternal, blessed decree. By His blood and His death on the cross, He atoned for the sins of all people and redeemed them to bring them back into the arms of His heavenly Father. This is precisely Christ's office: to seek all who have gone astray. As the Old Testament high priest wore the names of all the tribes of Israel on his breastplate, so Christ wears the names of all lost people on His heart. They are written in the book of His omniscience and engraved in His pierced hands. He seeks all who stray, the rich and the poor, the lowly and despised as well as the high and respected, the simple and the learned, the children and the grownups. He searches ceaselessly until the end of days in every land and every nation.

No person is too insignificant to be included in this search and to be part of Christ's effort to rescue souls. No person has strayed so far he cannot be found and raised up. No one has caused so great an offense that the Father and the Savior no longer want to receive him. No person is such a great sinner that Christ would be ashamed of him. No, as Christ confesses before the haughty, hypocritical, and self-righteous Pharisees, He loves and is a Friend of all sinners and His heart breaks over the distress of each of them. He seeks them all. He does not cast away any who come to Him; instead, He accepts them all.

Oh, what a comfort this is! Each of us is under the watchful eye of the Good Shepherd. He and His mercy follow us from the first moment of our life. He wants to bring us back to His Father and finally to gather us in His heaven. He looks with tender love on those who have already recognized the error of their ways. He does not calculate the quantity, magnitude, and severity of our sins in order to weigh the grace He shows us. The fact that we are lost sinners is what moves Him to accept us.

Sheep that from the fold did stray
No true shepherd e'er forsaketh;

Weary souls that lost their way
Christ, the Shepherd, gently taketh
In His arms that they may live—
Jesus sinners doth receive. Amen.

† *(TLH 324:3)*

Monday

Read Ezekiel 34:11–12

CHRIST SEEKS THE LOST by means of His sweet Gospel. It is His voice, His shepherd's horn, His bait. We see this, not only from His own example, when He preached His Gospel of grace to poor sinners and tax collectors, but also when He compared Himself with a shepherd who pursues and calls to the lambs that have strayed in the wilderness. When the Gospel—the doctrine that Christ came into the world to save sinners—is preached, it is nothing else than the sound of Christ's own voice.

Jesus has the Law, the doctrine of sin, preached first to the people He is seeking. This is because most people do not recognize they are on the path of error; rather, they delude themselves into thinking they are on the right path. The Law must first reveal to people that they are poor, erring, and lost sinners. But the Law is not the true voice of Christ. It can reveal that a person has gone astray, but it offers nothing regarding a way out or a way back. It calls: "You have distanced yourself from God by your sin and have become His enemy. Do you not see that you are going astray? What will become of you? Do you not see the abyss you are hurrying toward? Woe to you! You are lost!"

To this, the Gospel responds: "Be comforted, you straying lamb. You are not yet lost. See, here is your Shepherd. You need only to run back to Him confidently and you will receive eternal help. Your Good Shepherd will bring you to His flock, lead you to the green pastures of His grace, protect you from all dangers, and finally take you through the gates of death into His heavenly fold."

So all who had gone astray might hear this blessed voice of the Gospel, Christ sent His apostles into the world to preach the good news. He also instituted the holy office of the ministry through which His voice would resound everywhere until the end of days. Christ often goes to people in exceedingly wonderful ways that they may hear the voice of their Good Shepherd in the desert of this world. Christ gives many people parents who lay them as infants in the Shepherd's arms through Holy Baptism and who give the sweet milk of the Gospel to their children to nourish them. Christ sends others into schools where, as young lambs, they are led to the pasture of the Gospel by Christian educators. In other cases, He may let people wander around in the world without knowledge of Him, perhaps even adopting a false religion until they encounter a good book, a Christian friend, or a spouse that points them to Christ. Sometimes, when the pure Gospel is not proclaimed in their native city, Jesus sends the erring into another place where they finally hear His voice and are found by Him.

Christ's act of seeking involves even more. Because most who hear His voice prefer to remain in their erring ways rather than forsake them, He sees to it that they not only hear His Gospel but also are awakened and moved to abandon those ways. Therefore, He takes their destinies in His hand and seeks them until He finds them. Many attach their heart to money and earthly goods. Christ may then allow such people to become or remain poor so they can receive the desire for heavenly riches. Others seek their heaven in good days and a comfortable life. Christ may send them all kinds of crosses—sickness, pain, and the like—so they turn to seek their true joy in Him. Those who attach their heart to honor before people may come into disgrace and contempt. Those who are overly bound to wife, children, and good friends may see them die and mourn their loss. In short, whatever a person pursues in this world that hinders him from the pursuit of Christ is eventually taken from him so he can become embittered toward the world and awakened to the love of Christ.

We see from this that Jesus has always sought all of us from our childhood on. He sought us when we were baptized. He sought us as His sweet Gospel was proclaimed to us. He sought us in our schools, at confirmation, and whenever we came to His table. He sought us at all times and in all the circumstances of our life. How wonderful it is, then, when He finds us!

I am Jesus' little lamb,
Ever glad at heart I am;
For my Shepherd gently guides me,
Knows my need, and well provides me,
Loves me ev'ry day the same,
Even calls me by my name. Amen.

† *(TLH 648:1)*

Tuesday

Read John 6:37

With an air of contempt, the Pharisees and scribes said Jesus receives sinners (see Matthew 9:11). Jesus not only confirmed their observation, but He also made no attempt to amend it. He testified that He receives without exception all sinners who come to Him in whatever condition they happen to be. These include young sinners and old sinners, coarse sinners and fine sinners, sinners not already converted and sinners who have converted but fell away, honorable sinners and infamous sinners, sinners He knows will remain with Him and sinners He knows will sooner or later fall away from Him. Jesus receives all sinners, wherever they may be and at whatever time they come to Him, whether it is in the blossom of their life or the hour of their death.

Christ says in our text, "All that the Father gives Me will come to Me, and whoever comes to Me I will never cast out." He refuses no one who comes to Him. Everyone is welcome. The Gospels are filled with examples. When mothers brought their little children to Jesus, He received them kindly. When a notoriously great sinner in the city approached Him, kissed His feet, moistened them with her tears, and dried them with her hair, He welcomed her graciously despite the Pharisees' comment that "if this man were a prophet, He would have known who and what sort of woman this is who is touching Him, for she is a sinner" (Luke 7:39). When the ten lepers came to Him, He accepted them all although He knew nine of them would fall away again. When the thief on the cross next to Him, a robber and murderer who was receiving the punishment his deeds warranted, turned to Jesus in the hour of his death, Jesus received him and opened the gates of paradise to him. When the fallen Peter returned to Christ, He welcomed him and reconfirmed him in his apostolic office.

There is not one person who comes to Jesus that He will not accept. If people have not yet turned to Him, being too timid or perhaps even afraid because of their many and great sins, He invites them with the words, "Come to Me, all who labor and are heavy laden, and I will give you rest. . . . And you will find rest for your souls" (Matthew 11:28–29). When sinners are scattered far from Him, He pursues them until He finds them. How does He do this? The parables of the lost sheep and the lost coin supply the answer. How does a shepherd receive a sheep that was lost but has been found? Exactly as he finds it. If it is sick, it does not first have to be restored to health. If it is wounded, it does not have to wait until its injuries heal. If it has broken limbs, it is not left to languish until those limbs mend. No, the shepherd receives the sick, wounded, or lame sheep just as it is, carrying it home on his shoulders to rejoin the flock in a secure pen. And how does the poor woman receive a coin that fell from her hand and was lost? Exactly as she finds it. If the coin is full of the dirt into which it fell, it does not need to be cleaned before she accepts it. If it is corroded, a good shining is not required. If the inscription has faded, it does not need to be restored. No, the poor woman takes the dirty, corroded coin just as it is, clutching it in her hand and joyfully placing it in her treasure chest.

We see from this that nothing is necessary for Jesus to receive us except that we approach Him as a sinner to the Savior, as a sick person to the doctor, as a lost sheep to the shepherd. That alone suffices. Jesus then receives us. The prodigal son did not buy himself a grand garment before returning home because he could not afford one. He came to his father just as he was, torn and tattered, and was embraced by him. So, too, must we approach Jesus in the filthy garments of our unrighteousness or even naked. He will embrace us in that very condition in His saving arms.

I, a sinner, come to Thee
With a penitent confession;
Savior, mercy show to me

Grant for all my sins remission.
Let these words my soul relieve:
Jesus sinners doth receive. Amen.

(*TLH* 324:5)

Wednesday

Read Matthew 9:12–13

THE FIRST AND MOST earnest truth in the words "Jesus receives sinners" is that Christ does not want to have anything to do with people who do not recognize themselves to be sinners. This does not mean, of course, that He takes no pleasure in the company of the truly pious and just and derives satisfaction from evil and godless people. As the psalmist says, "For You are not a God who delights in wickedness, evil may not dwell with You" (Psalm 5:4). If we were as pious and just as when God first created man, we would still be dear and pleasing to the Son of God. (But in that case, He would not have become man and entered the world since there would have been no need of a Savior and Redeemer.) Jesus came to earth because, as Saint Paul said, all men are sinners and fall short of the glory of God. We were sick in our souls, fatally and eternally sick; and Christ came as a physician to restore us to health.

By nature, we are great, lost, and condemned sinners, and neither we nor any other creature under heaven has the power to heal us. As long as we pretend to be self-righteous, Christ does not concern us. What does our going to church avail if we do not call out from the depth of our heart, "God, be merciful to me, a sinner" (Luke 18:13)? What good is Baptism or the Gospel or the Holy Meal if we do not embrace it as sinners? To those who continue to think they can cleanse themselves and do not need to be washed pure by Christ, the word He spoke to Peter applies: "If I do not wash you, you have no share with Me" (John 13:8). In short, if we are unwilling to acknowledge that we are poor, lost sinners, we renounce Christ. The truth that "Jesus receives sinners" remains for us, as it did for the Pharisees and scribes, a stumbling block and a hindrance to salvation. It remains a thunderbolt of the Law from Sinai underscoring our judgment to eternal damnation. How good it is, then, when we admit our sinful state and draw inexpressible comfort from the words "Jesus receives sinners."

When the Pharisees and scribes called those who approached Jesus "sinners," they were absolutely right. Some of them were great sinners. Tax collectors, for example, were manifest deceivers of the people. The woman who washed Jesus' feet with her tears and dried them with her hair was a notorious prostitute. The only thing that distinguished the sinners who drew near to Christ from those who did not was not that their sins were less significant than others, but that they vividly recognized themselves as sinners and sought forgiveness from Jesus.

What a great comfort, then, lies in the words "Jesus receives sinners"! No matter how great the sins you have committed, do not harden your heart but recognize your sins and go to Jesus. He will receive you. Do not hesitate because you have sinned for a long time or because you believe your sins are so great that you are beyond forgiveness. Remember Peter, who denied his Lord three times. Remember Saul, who persecuted the Church of God and ridiculed His Word. Remember the thief on the cross, who was a robber and a murderer. Jesus received each of them graciously and so will

He receive you. Even if your sins are as many as the hairs on your head and as numerous as the grains of sand on the beach, you can find forgiveness in Christ.

"Jesus receives sinners." May these words comfort us at all times, even until the hour of our death. He is always ready to receive us and to help us enter His heavenly kingdom.

Though great our sins and sore our woes,
His grace much more aboundeth;
His helping love no limit knows,
Our utmost need it soundeth.
Our Shepherd good and true is He,
Who will at last His Israel free
From all their sin and sorrow. Amen.

† *(TLH 329:5)*

Thursday

Read Luke 19:10

THESE WORDS ARE WORTHY of being written with golden letters on the walls of every house of God in which Christ and His Gospel are preached. They should be engraved by the Holy Ghost on the heart of every individual. They are a dynamic summary of the entire Christian religion, a little Bible every Christian should have in hand day and night. They are so rich in doctrine, comfort, and admonition that no preacher of the Gospel could ever exhaust them. Let us examine this clear and pure source of light and life.

The first thing Christ is saying here is that no one should marvel over His receiving of the lost Zacchaeus as if it were something strange. No one should grumble about it or look on with envy. The seeking and saving of lost souls is Christ's proper office. He is the promised Messiah, the Savior of sinners, and the Redeemer of the lost.

But this seeking and saving constitutes more than an office. It is also Christ's joy and desire. He is saying here, in essence: "Consider how much it has cost Me to be able to seek the lost and save them. On account of that, I left heaven and came to earth. On account of that, I emptied Myself of My divine glory, taking the form of a servant and becoming a man just like you. On account of that, I took upon Myself lowliness instead of grandeur, poverty instead of riches, suffering and persecution instead of joy. On account of that, I am going to Jerusalem to face the deepest shame, even death on the cross. Should I have suffered—and continue to suffer—for no reason? No. It all depends upon Me to seek the lost souls. It cannot be anything else but My joy and desire to save them, for the souls that were lost and found again are the only compensation of My difficult work. They are the only fruit of My tremendous suffering. They are the only reward of My fierce battle. They are the only pearls I have found since lowering Myself into the abyss of human misery."

Jesus also says here that if He had not wanted to seek Zacchaeus because he was lost, then He would not have been able to seek anyone—for all are lost. By nature, every person is like a little child who has become separated from his mother in the dark forest. Having strayed from the heavenly path, a person wanders in the desert of this world lost from his heavenly Father, without light and without hope. Like a lone sheep separated from the flock and in constant danger of being attacked, being torn apart by wolves, or falling into an abyss, a person without Christ is equally defenseless and utterly unable to rescue himself. There are really only two kinds of people: those who are lost and those who are found. A person who has not yet been found can appear to live respectably, while another who is lost is immersed in vice. The world can praise the former as virtuous, while the other is despised by as a great sinner. But before God, both the virtuous and the coarse sinner are still lost. This is as true of Saul, who according to the Law was blameless, as it is of Zacchaeus, who could hardly boast of keeping the Law. Christ came to seek and to save all of the lost, including Zacchaeus and Saul.

There is one more thing Christ tells us in these words. He most diligently seeks those who, because they have fallen deeply into sin, cannot attempt to justify themselves as the virtuous do. Feeling the weight of their sins, they humble themselves before God and desire nothing except His grace and mercy. Let us not think that Jesus prefers the virtuous to those who recognize how far they have fallen. He lets go the virtuous who do not desire to be with Him, and He seeks those who are overwhelmed by the guilt of their sins. He makes sinners of saints and saints of sinners. He lets the self-righteous perish and saves those who are honest enough to recognize that they are lost.

O Thou Physician blest,
Make clean my guilty soul
And me, by many a sin opprest,
Restore and keep me whole. Amen.

† *(TLH 322:3)*

Friday

Read Luke 18:24–27

If we compare the condition of the poor and the rich according to Holy Scripture, we find that the poor are preferred. As far as temporal things are concerned, God has already received the poor. In His Word, God calls Himself the Protector of the poor, the Father of orphans, and the Judge on behalf of widows. He says none of these things about the rich. God gives many laws intended to care for the poor. He declares severe threats against all who oppress the poor. And He says that what is given to them is deemed as given to Him and the one who does this will be richly rewarded. None of this applies to the rich. Even in spiritual things, the poor are blessed above the rich. Whenever God has done great things in His kingdom of grace, He has used the poor as His instruments. When He wanted to exalt His people in the Old Testament, He turned not to a king's son or offspring of a prominent family, but to David, a poor shepherd boy, and made him a mighty king over Israel. And when God's only begotten Son became man, God chose as our Lord's mother not the wife of a rich and powerful prince, but a poor maid, the betrothed of a humble woodworker, Joseph. Finally, when the heavenly hosts announced the most important of all events on earth, the birth of the Savior of the world, their audience was not the rich and famous of Jerusalem and Judea, but the poor, simple shepherds of Bethlehem.

When Scripture reveals to whom the Gospel should be brought, it declares, "The poor have good news preached to them" (Matthew 11:5). When the apostles speak about those God has chosen for salvation, they say, "Has God not chosen those who are poor in the world to be rich in faith?" (James 2:5).

But what is said in Scripture about the earthly rich? Even their goods have evil names. Sometimes they are referred to as the uncertainty and deceitfulness of wealth, sometimes they are called unrighteous mammon, and sometimes they are compared to thorns among which the good seed of the divine Word is choked. About those who want to become rich, Scripture says that they "fall into temptation, into a snare, into many senseless and harmful desires that plunge people into ruin and destruction" (1 Timothy 6:9). Wealth and wickedness are often equated in the Bible. Isaiah says about Christ, "And they made His grave with the wicked and with a rich man in His death" (53:9).

The salvation of the rich is spoken about very doubtfully in God's Word. Today's text underscores the difficulty the rich face in getting into heaven. These words should frighten every rich person to the heart. Can those who seek to become rich truly care for their soul at the same time? It is impossible. They may seem to be interested in their salvation, but their pursuit of wealth does nothing but impede their progress to heaven.

Is it impossible to be rich in an earthly and heavenly sense? Not at all! When the Lord told His disciples how hard it is for the rich to enter heaven, they were terrified and exclaimed, "Then who can be saved?" (Luke 18:26). How did Christ answer them? He said, "What is impossible with men is possible with God" (Luke 18:27). Here we see that, if a person, by God's blessing and without his own anxious seeking and striving, becomes wealthy, he can also, by God's grace, become rich in heavenly goods. Even the godless rich person is not excluded from God's grace on account of his wealth. If he, from the heart, converts to God, he can retain his earthly riches and still be saved.

What to me may seem a treasure
But displeasing is to Thee,
Oh, remove such harmful pleasure;
Give instead what profits me.
Let my heart by Thee be stilled;
Make me Thine, Lord, as Thou wilt. Amen.

(TLH 348:3)

Saturday

Read Luke 1:67–79

ZECHARIAH CALLS OUT, both to his neighbors and to us, "Blessed be the Lord God of Israel, for He has visited and redeemed His people" (Luke 1:68). The rich Lord of heaven and earth visited poor sinners just as a doctor visits the sick, and He continues to visit us today through His Word and Sacraments. Through the preaching of the Gospel, the Sacraments of Holy Baptism and the Lord's Supper, He announces, dedicates, and seals His grace to us.

Zechariah continues, "And has raised up a horn of salvation for us in the house of His servant David" (Luke 1:69). Christ is the horn of salvation. The horn means strength and power. Thus, if we are weak, Christ wants to be our Horn, our Strength. Zechariah adds, "That we should be saved from our enemies and from the hand of all who hate us" (Luke 1:71). Here he speaks not about our bodily enemies but about our spiritual foes—sin, death, Satan, and hell. All of us have these enemies and without Christ we have no strength to overcome them. Instead, sin rules in us, death terrifies us, Satan holds us in his kingdom, and hell finally devours us. But Christ has overcome all of these mighty enemies of our soul. Therefore, if, through faith in Christ, we enter His kingdom, sin cannot harm us, death cannot kill us, Satan does not hold us prisoner, and hell does not frighten us. Our faith is the victory that overcomes sin, death, hell, and all of our other enemies.

Zechariah says, "Blessed be the Lord . . . to show the mercy promised to our fathers and to remember His holy covenant, the oath that He swore to our father Abraham, to grant us" (Luke 1:68,72–73). With these words, he describes to us in greater detail the state of the kingdom, whose nearness his son John would proclaim. He says that mercy will bring it about and mercy will govern it. Therefore, the Christian, who is received by Baptism into Christ's kingdom, is blessed. If, through faith, he remains in that kingdom, grace and mercy will hold sway over all his sins, his works, and his words. In that case, he is not in the covenant of the Law but in the covenant of grace God made with our fathers. God also keeps the oath He swore to Abraham that in his descendant, Jesus Christ, he and all nations of the earth should be blessed.

Zechariah adds, "That we, being delivered from the hand of our enemies, might serve Him without fear, in holiness and righteousness before Him all our days" (Luke 1:74–75). Here he tells us that all who want to remain in Christ's kingdom of grace should serve Him in holiness, which is pleasing to Him. Thus a Christian should daily seek to purify himself from sin. He should walk before God by pursuing sanctification. But how weak we are! How easily flesh and blood lead us to sin!

What should we do when we fall? Is there no more help for us? Oh, yes, Zechariah says. He places the righteousness of Christ beside the holiness of our life. If we stumble and fall, we should immediately recognize our sin, repent of it, and seize the righteousness of Jesus. Then that righteousness will cover our unholiness, restoring us before God and giving us clear conscience.

After Zechariah emptied his heart in joy over Christ and His kingdom of grace, he turned to his newborn son and said, "And you, child, will be called the prophet of the Most High; for you will go before the Lord to prepare His ways, to give knowledge of salvation to His people in the forgiveness of their sins" (Luke 1:76–77). These words define for us the office of John the Baptizer. He is called a prophet of the Highest, but John was even more than all prophets. They showed Christ only from afar, but John was called to be the first servant in the kingdom of grace, to precede the entry of the King of heaven. As the close friend of the Bridegroom, he was to invite the guests to the heavenly wedding. He was also to point to the Christ, who was already among the people but unknown to them. John was chosen to give people knowledge of their salvation that lies in the forgiveness of sins by the mercy of God, in which the Dayspring from on high, the Son of righteousness, has visited us. He was chosen not to proclaim a new law but to convince all people that they cannot keep the Law, that they lie in sin and sit in darkness and the shadow of death—and that Christ alone is the way of peace.

O God, my sin indeed is great;
I groan beneath the dreadful weight.
Be merciful to me, I pray;
Take guilt and punishment away.

Saint John the Baptist points to Thee
And bids me cast my sin on Thee;
For Thou hast left Thy throne on high
To suffer for the world and die. Amen.

(TLH 328:2, 3)

Sunday

Read Luke 6:36

THE MERCY OF GOD the Christian enjoys is the first thing that must move him to be merciful to his erring, sinful, and thirsty neighbor. For that reason, in our text, Jesus bases His exhortation "be merciful" on the Father's mercy (Luke 6:36). Whoever is a true Christian, a blessed child of God, did not become one by his own merit but by God's incomprehensible compassion alone. For if God were only righteous and not merciful, no one could be saved. Because a Christian has God's grace, he cannot maintain that he is better than those without God's grace and still mired in their sins. Instead, he must confess that although he is the greatest of sinners, God accepted him and out of pure and free grace for Christ's sake made him His child. Whoever thinks he can become a Christian by some other means is not yet a Christian. Being a Christian can never be separated from being merciful. Whatever other characteristics are found in the Christian, they are invalid if he lacks mercy. He can be weak in knowledge, weak in overcoming the world, weak in restraining his behavior, and weak in confidence, yet he can stand in the faith. But it is impossible for God's grace to have dawned in a person who is unmerciful.

Whoever has experienced the bottomless love of God in Christ knows that his sins are forgiven and that, out of His free grace, God made him His blessed child. The heart of such a person has to be moved and softened by this knowledge. Experiencing the mercy of God makes the stony heart sensitive and the natural stubborn disposition easily pliable. Through grace, a person who is cruel by nature becomes compassionate, one who is very reserved becomes open for every trial, the hardened soul is transformed into wax-like softness, and the lion is turned into a lamb.

A Christian knows that, by God's mercy, he is free from judgment. Therefore, he cannot judge his fellow sinner lovelessly. A Christian also knows that, by God's mercy, he is free from damnation. Therefore, he cannot condemn his fellow sinner. A Christian realizes that, by God's mercy, all of his sins are forgiven. Therefore, he cannot remain unreconciled to those who have sinned against him. A Christian understands that, out of His unfathomable compassion, God gave him His dear Son, righteousness, heaven, and eternal life. Therefore, he cannot close his heart and hand to his thirsty neighbor. A Christian knows that not a moment goes by in which he does not offend God anew with his sins. He is therefore in need of God's mercy at every moment and he richly enjoys it. For this reason, his heart is always like a broken vessel and false courage is removed from him. He can no longer be obstinate toward his neighbor. Tenderness dwells in his soul and does not allow him to provoke or grieve another willfully. He would rather hurt himself than injure another. Even the world can readily see that Christians are not vindictive; instead, they have in their hearts good will toward everyone.

If a Christian lets himself be carried along to an unmerciful judgment, he very quickly feels inside how greatly he has sinned and is ashamed of himself. With contrition, he comes to God and laments how he has made himself so unworthy of God's mercy. He humbly asks for new grace, then watches more earnestly and carefully over his evil heart. Let us not deceive ourselves! If we are Christians, we are children of God and thus will direct our minds toward the heavenly Father and show mercy to our neighbor. If we do not do this, we are not yet Christians. As Christ says, he who has been forgiven much also loves much.

Forgive our sins, Lord, we implore,
Remove from us their burden sore,
As we their trespasses forgive
Who by offenses us do grieve.
Thus let us dwell in charity
And serve our brother willingly. Amen.

(*TLH* 458:6)

Monday

Read Luke 6:37–38

WE SHOULD IN NO WAY conclude from today's passage that we can earn God's mercy by showing mercy toward our neighbor. God had to send us His love before we could know what it is to love our neighbor. Thus, if we are still unmerciful, it is a sign that we do not stand in the faith, that our sins are not forgiven, and that if we ever had God's grace, we have lost it. For God is righteous, and He cannot absolve us from our sins while our neighbor groans against us and accuses us before Him. God must do to us as we do to our neighbor.

Some continue to judge their sinful neighbors in an equally sinful manner. As soon as they spot something unrighteous in them, even if it only looks suspicious, they pounce in accusatory tones instead of chastising in a loving manner. Such people judge their neighbors in their heart, looking down on them and regarding them as non-Christians. They may even defame their neighbors behind their back, making their sins greater than they are. These malicious souls need to know that God will measure to them according to the measure they employ with their neighbors. On the Last Day, those who magnified the sins of others while dismissing their own will find that God will restore the balance by putting the spotlight on their sins, even their most secret sins.

If someone condemns his neighbor lovelessly, failing to show mercy when he has deeply fallen, condemning him by insisting he is not worthy of any grace from God, and thinking himself worthy of salvation while denying it to his neighbor, God will judge him as he has judged. He who condemns others will be condemned by God. Therefore, condemn not, and you will not be condemned.

God will judge accordingly the person who does not want to forgive his neighbor, who refuses to be reconciled to him, who does not ask forgiveness from one he has offended. God will take notice of someone who has been sinned against by his neighbor but refuses to pursue reconciliation with him. God will not hear those who do not try to pursue peace with their neighbors when they pray for forgiveness. Moreover, God will one day call those neighbors as accusers and refuse to be reconciled forever to the ones who refused to reconcile with others. Therefore, forgive, and you will be forgiven.

Finally, those who remain hardened toward the bodily distress of their neighbors, lending them nothing, failing to help them in their trouble, refusing to be generous toward them in their want, declining to comfort them in their misfortune, and preferring to live well while those around them suffer, need to be aware that God will pour out the same measure to them. In eternity, they will be like the rich man who was unable to obtain even a droplet of water for his burning tongue. They could have used their temporal goods to dry tears, still sighs, ease suffering, and rescue the unfortunate. Instead, they chose to embrace their money and goods in a miserly way. Their earthly stinginess will become a crushing weight upon them in eternity. Therefore, give, and it will be given to you.

God is indeed just. To the merciful, He will be merciful. To the good, He will be good. To the reconcilers, He will be reconciled. To the generous, He will be generous. "For with the measure you use it will be measured back to you" (Luke 6:38). Both God and His Word are holy and true.

O grant that from my very heart
My foes be all forgiven;
Forgive my sins and heal their smart,
And grant new life from heaven.
Thy Word, that blessed food, bestow,
Which best the soul can nourish;
Make it flourish
Through all the storms of woe
That else my faith might overthrow. Amen.

(ELHB 365:3)

Tuesday

Read Luke 6:39–42

IT IS OFTEN THE CASE that those who are the harshest judges of others are themselves burdened with the greatest defects. The heterodox usually behave this way. If they discover only the smallest weakness in the doctrine or life of the faithful, they will make it out to be so terrible that every Christian heart is horrified by it. If the unbelieving, godless world sees only the smallest splinter in Christians, it accuses them of being the worst villains. These accusers, however, fail to discern the great planks in their own eyes. They wantonly falsify and twist God's Word, making God out to be a liar in His Word, and destroying the most holy Sacraments of Jesus Christ.

We should not be surprised that the children of the world and the heterodox are such proud hypocrites. If God passes judgment on them in Scripture, how much more will they dare to judge their neighbors!

Christians themselves are hardly free of such weaknesses. Their righteousness and holiness are not theirs, but Christ's. They, too, must cry, "If You, O Lord, should mark iniquities, O Lord, who could stand?" (Psalm 130:3), and "Enter not into judgment with Your servant, for no one living is righteous before You" (Psalm 143:2). They must daily pray, "Forgive us our trespasses, as we forgive those who trespass against us." They are righteous before God only because they believe in Christ. Without faith, their sins would damn them just as readily as the sins of others condemn them. A Christian may progress only so far in sanctification during his life; he must still appear daily as a poor sinner and beggar before God.

If a Christian does not do this, he begins to admire himself because of the improvement in his life and then loses the poverty of the spirit. He tends to judge others severely while saying in his heart, "God, I thank You that I am not like other men" (Luke 18:11). He ceases to be a Christian at all and instead becomes a hypocritical, proud Pharisee. This spiritual pride causes many so-called Christians to return outwardly to the world they once renounced.

Christians must continue to recognize that they are sinners and this must move them to be merciful toward their neighbors. If they see sins in others they do not have, they must remember that they may have sins that are just as reprehensible before God, sins that are perhaps even more punishable than those of their neighbors. Their neighbors may sin lightheartedly, but they themselves may sin by unfriendliness and a gloomy character. Their neighbors may not know how to keep their earthly goods, but they themselves may have too great an attachment to their possessions. Their neighbors may not seem to be sufficiently industrious, but they themselves may sin by overexertion in their temporal vocations. Their neighbors may seem too forward in professing the truth before their enemies, but they themselves may sin by timidity and subtle denial. Their neighbors may be too often openly angry, but they themselves may harbor secret resentment and envy. Their neighbors may pride themselves overmuch on fashionable clothes, money, or property, but they themselves may consider too highly their gifts of the Spirit, their understanding, and good works. In short, Christians may find things that are blameworthy in their neighbors but if they truly know themselves, they will find a thousand shortcomings in themselves that will make them feel ashamed.

Should not all of this move us to be merciful, lenient, and humble toward our erring, sinning, and thirsty neighbors? Certainly! Whoever judges a speck in another's eye develops before God a plank in his own. His sins that God would otherwise gladly forgive become magnified and more damnable by his behavior, and he forfeits God's grace and his soul's salvation.

Oh, let me never speak,
What bounds of truth exceedeth;
Grant that no idle word
From my mouth proceedeth;
And then, when in my place
I must and ought to speak,
My words grant pow'r and grace
Lest I offend the weak. Amen.

† *(TLH 395:3)*

Wednesday

Read 2 Timothy 2:25–26

AN ACCUSATION commonly made against preachers who strictly adhere to pure doctrine is that they are condemning, loveless men who ignore the Savior's command to not judge and condemn. This command of our Lord, their accusers say, will condemn them on the Last Day. Many allow themselves to be deceived by this reasoning, but the accusation rests upon a false interpretation of our Lord's command.

When Christ tells us not to judge and condemn, it does not mean no one is permitted to judge and condemn false doctrine or openly proclaim God's judgment of unbelieving and wicked people. To do this is Scripture's clearest command given to all of Christ's servants repeatedly in God's Word. Christ told His servants to "go into all the world and proclaim the gospel to the whole creation. Whoever believes and is baptized will be saved, but whoever does not believe will be condemned" (Mark 16:15–16). According to this, every preacher should preach salvation to believers but condemnation to unbelievers. In the Book of Isaiah, an affliction is pronounced over all those who do not want to condemn the ungodly: "Woe to those who call evil good, and good evil; who put darkness for light, and light for darkness, who put bitter for sweet, and sweet for bitter" (5:20). Another of God's prophets wrote: "Son of man, I have made you a watchman for the house of Israel. Whenever you hear a word from My mouth, you shall give them warning from Me. If I say to the wicked, 'You shall surely die,' and you give him no warning, nor speak to warn the wicked from his wicked way, in order to save his life, that wicked person shall die for his iniquity, but his blood

I will require at your hand" (Ezekiel 3:17–18). About preachers who do not proclaim the condemnation of the impenitent, but instead prefer to preach sweet things that are pleasing to men, Scripture says this: "They are all silent dogs; they cannot bark, dreaming, lying down, loving to slumber" (Isaiah 56:10).

This applies not only to preachers but also to the laity. They, too, should confidently reject and condemn false doctrine and a godless life. The Lord says to all Christians, "Beware of false prophets, who come to you in sheep's clothing but inwardly are ravenous wolves" (Matthew 7:15). How could the hearers beware of false prophets if they are not permitted to judge, reject, and condemn their false doctrine? Furthermore, Christ says that the members of the congregation should regard as heathens and tax collectors those who despise all their admonitions. Must they not pass the judgment of condemnation upon them? Saint Paul writes, "Take no part in the unfruitful works of darkness, but instead expose them" (Ephesians 5:11). How can the laity expose the godlessness in the world if they are not allowed to say it is leading its practitioners to condemnation?

Christ, the prophets and apostles, and the early Christians provide us with examples to imitate. Christ many times pronounced woes upon the Pharisees and scribes, those false teachers. Saint Paul wrote that "if anyone is preaching to you a gospel contrary to the one you received, let him be accursed" (Galatians 1:9). Paul also said that the end of the enemies of Christ's cross is destruction (Philippians 3:19), and he delivered Hymenaeus and Alexander to Satan so they might learn not to blaspheme (1 Timothy 1:20). Saint John wrote, "If anyone comes to you and does not bring this teaching, do not receive him into your house or give him any greeting" (2 John 1:10). John also praised the Ephesian congregation with these words: "But have tested those who call themselves apostles and are not, and found them to be false" (Revelation 2:2).

The rebuking, criticizing, judging, and condemning of false doctrine and an obviously godless life are not forbidden by Scripture. Indeed, whoever fails to do this acts most lovelessly. For the Christian who sees his neighbor sinning, heading for destruction, and does not warn him about the great danger in which his soul lies, is viewed no differently by God from the one who is lost in sin because he failed to receive a warning.

Would to God that I might even
As the martyred saints of old,
With the helping hand of Heaven,
Steadfast stand in battle bold!
O my God, I pray Thee,
In the combat stay me.
Grant that I may ever be
Loyal, staunch, and true to Thee. Amen.

† *(TLH 470:4)*

Thursday

Read Matthew 18:20

ACCORDING TO THE CONTEXT of today's reading, the first thing necessary for Christian fellowship is that those in fellowship are true Christians. They do not all have to be strong in the faith, advanced in love and holiness, or particularly rich in knowledge. If they have a living faith in their Lord Jesus Christ, that is enough.

Our text also indicates that Christian fellowship requires that all things be done in a Christian manner, that is, in Christ's name. But when are Christians gathered in Jesus' name? It is not only when they attend public or private worship services together, hear or read God's Word together, partake of the holy Sacraments together, pray and sing together, or consider the things of salvation together. It is also whenever a Christian seeks out another Christian because of his beliefs, because he shows him love as a brother, because he receives a blessing from him, or because he wants to rejoice or mourn with him. Christians who foster fellowship in the name of Jesus often take the opportunity to speak together about divine doctrines, experiences of the heart, signs of the times, and events in the kingdom of God, so as to instruct, admonish, chastise, and comfort one another. Christians also gather in Jesus' name when they speak of earthly things, eat and drink together or relax after the work of the day. Wherever Christians gather, even without spiritual reasons, their fellowship is still a true Christian fellowship if it results from God's Word and the fear of God. If love for Christ and for others rules their hearts and tongues and if their speech is lovely to hear, theirs is a Christian gathering.

In contrast, pious speech without a living and believing heart in one accord is nothing before God except a hypocritical abomination. Christian fellowship is founded on the promise from Christ Himself, as our text makes irrefutably certain. No Christian can say: "I prefer to remain alone. Why should I have fellowship? I derive no blessing from it." Whoever speaks like this contradicts Christ and questions His faithfulness.

What is the blessing Christ promises? "Jesus himself stood among them" (Luke 24:36). Can anyone think of a greater blessing than that Christ wants to be in the midst of His followers as often as they gather in His name, even if they are only two or three in number? Could Christ ever be present among His gathered followers with empty hands, without distributing gifts of His grace among them? Just as light cannot be present without illuminating its surroundings, just as fire cannot fail to provide warmth, and just as rain certainly moistens the dry land, so Christ cannot come among His own without blessing them.

Let us recognize, with hearty thanks, the blessing we receive in Christian fellowship. And let us diligently use this blessing. But above all, let us ask God to help us remember to assemble always in Jesus' name so we may not anger one another with our speech and behavior, but instead support and edify one another.

The whole wide world, O Spirit,
Upon Thy hands doth rest;
Our wayward hearts Thou turnest
As it may seem Thee best;
Once more Thy power make known,
As Thou has done so often,
Convert the wicked, soften
Thou all hearts of stone. Amen.

(ELHB 252:8)

Friday

Read Romans 14:14, 22–23

AT THE BEGINNING of today's text, Saint Paul writes, "I know and am persuaded in the Lord Jesus that nothing is unclean in itself, but it is unclean for anyone who thinks it unclean"

(Romans 14:14). The apostle testifies here that, in the New Testament, nothing is profane and unclean merely because it is declared to be so in the Law of Moses. However, if a person does not recognize this and still regards something as profane and unclean, then it is profane and unclean for him. Nevertheless, he sins if he permits such things. We see from this that in all our doings God does not consider the work we do as much as He regards the disposition with which we do it. If we deem something to be wrong and still do it, then it is sin for us even when God permits it.

It is extremely sad when someone wants to be a Christian but permits himself to engage in certain behaviors merely because he sees that most people do so. He may think, "Doing this or that is not something terribly wrong, since so many people—even smart and respected people—do it." What makes this sad is that a Christian should know that, according to God's Word, the entire world is immersed in evil and most people are on the wide path to destruction. Isn't it frightening when someone who wants to be a Christian judges himself according to popular behavior instead of letting God be his Judge?

It is equally wrong when a person judges himself according to what those who are considered Christians allow. Is not the reliance upon man in matters of conscience tantamount to idolatry? Cannot Christians also err and sin? Does not God's Word expressly say that Christians lack manifold things?

Proper caution in using Christian liberty amounts, above all, to refusing to consider anything right if one does not know it from God's Word, even if the rest of the world (including all Christians) is accustomed to doing it. Holy Scripture, not the world and not other Christians, is to govern us.

In our text, Paul says he is "persuaded in the Lord Jesus that nothing is unclean in itself" (Romans 14:14). If a person wants to allow something, he should not make his judgment on superficial knowledge or on the hearing that it is neither condemned nor commanded according to God's Word, but on the certainty of faith by the working of grace from the Lord Jesus. To make this absolutely clear, the apostle concludes: "Blessed is the one who has no reason to pass judgment on himself for what he approves. But whoever has doubts is condemned if he eats, because the eating is not from faith. For whatever does not proceed from faith is sin" (Romans 14:22–23). A person does not sin only when he does something he knows is sinful. He also sins when he does something about which he is doubtful. Whoever is unsure if something is right or wrong but does it anyway, shows he is unconcerned whether this behavior is contrary to God's desires. Is this not opposed to the fear of God that should dwell in the heart of every Christian?

Let us, then, be careful in the use of our Christian freedom! If there is even the smallest doubt in our heart and conscience about whether what we want to do is right according to God's Word, even if the whole world regards it as right, we should prefer to die rather than to do it. For, as Saint Paul says, "But whoever has doubts is condemned if he eats, because the eating is not from faith. For whatever does not proceed from faith is sin" (Romans 14:23).

Oh, that the Lord would guide my ways
To keep His statutes still!
Oh, that my God would grant me grace
To know and do His will. Amen.

† *(TLH 416:1)*

Saturday

Read Romans 14:15–22

MANY PEOPLE THINK that if something is neither commanded nor forbidden by God and is not a sin in and of itself, they can do it at any time and under any circumstances. If they are admonished by someone to stop, they reply, "Are you suggesting that what I am doing is sinful?" These activities include such things as playing cards and frequenting taverns. Since it has to be granted that such things themselves are not sin, they think they have won and respond, "Do you want to make a sin of something God has neither commanded nor forbidden?" How wrong they are! People who do these things and reason that they should be free to pursue them fail to make a necessary distinction between activities that are not in themselves sinful and the select use of Christian freedom.

This is the lesson Paul teaches in today's text: "For if your brother is grieved by what you eat, you are no longer walking in love" (Romans 14:15). Here, Paul reminds the Roman Christians that under the new covenant there are no longer prohibitions regarding food, but if, in their Christian liberty, they eat anything placed before them, even meat dedicated to idols, without considering that weaker Christians who are present might be offended, they have grieved and offended those who regard such things as sinful. Isn't this an act against love?

It is not enough for a Christian to know that such an act is not in itself sinful. He must also ask, *But do others, such as weaker Christians, regard this as sinful? Would they take offense and stumble in their faith if they were to see me doing this?* For this reason, no one may look to himself alone. He must also consider the feelings of the entire congregation. He should avoid everything offensive to any one of them. He must also remember Paul's words: "By what you eat," that is, on account of something that might be construed as offensive to others, "do not destroy the one for whom Christ died. . . . Do not, for the sake of food, destroy the work of God" (Romans 14:15, 20). By the inconsiderate use of Christian liberty, a Christian can be responsible for the eternal loss of a precious soul redeemed by Christ's blood and the destruction of a glorious work of God for the salvation of people.

Someone may ask if it is necessary for people to hold firmly to their precious liberty attained by Christ? This is certainly necessary to counteract, for example, the work of false teachers who try to make free things no longer free and so rob the Christian of the freedom of the Gospel. Paul did not give in to these erring spirits, "to them we did not yield in submission even for a moment, so that the truth of the gospel might be preserved for you" (Galatians 2:5). However, when the love of the weak neighbor was involved, Paul always surrendered his liberty, becoming all things to all men—to the Jews a Jew, to the Greeks a Greek, and to the weak a weak one—so he would offend no one. As he wrote, "Therefore, if food makes my brother stumble, I will never eat meat, lest I make my brother stumble" (1 Corinthians 8:13). The concern here is not his insistence upon his freedom but his self-restricted freedom on behalf of the weak, prompted by love. With such restriction, a Christian does not give up his freedom. Rather, he chooses to not use it outwardly even while holding it all the more firmly in his mind. Therefore, Paul writes, "It is good not to eat meat or drink wine or do anything that causes your brother to stumble" (Romans 14:21). But he immediately adds, "The faith that you have, keep between yourself and God" (Romans 14:22).

Here he means that when he requests that his dear Christians refrain from using their liberty before certain people, he is not asking them to give it up entirely. They should continue to hold that freedom in their hearts and minds before God, even at times when, out of love, they choose not to employ it.

May we Thy precepts, Lord, fulfill
And do on earth our Father's will
As angels do above;
Still walk in Christ, the living Way,
With all Thy children and obey
The law of Christian love. Amen.

† *(TLH 412:1)*

Sunday

Read Luke 5:1–11

IN TODAY'S READING, we encounter Saint Peter working diligently in his earthly calling. He explains to Christ that he has worked patiently through the entire night. Although he has caught nothing, he does not give up the difficult vocation of fishing to seek something more rewarding. Instead, we find him the next morning washing his nets with his partners and preparing to try again.

Every true Christian will work diligently and untiringly. He will not leave his chosen vocation without real cause, recalling the words of the apostle Paul: "So, brothers, in whatever condition each was called, there let him remain with God" (1 Corinthians 7:24). This is not, however, a distinguishing mark of the Christian since unbelievers can also pursue a vocation with dedication and endurance. In some cases, a non-Christian may even surpass a Christian in his devotion to his work.

How, then, does the true Christian show himself to be such by his earthly work? The first thing we notice from Peter's example is that, although he was very industrious, he laid his net aside and carefully listened to Jesus as soon as He began to preach. Moreover, he permitted Jesus to use his boat as a pulpit when the people on the shore crowded Him from all sides. Finally, when Jesus called him to be a fisher of men, Peter immediately "left everything and followed Him" (Luke 5:11).

In the midst of his earthly work, a true Christian shows that it is not the principal activity of his life. Indeed, he places his heavenly calling above his earthly one. He seeks first the kingdom of God and His righteousness. He does not let his bodily work be a hindrance in caring for his soul. He would rather interrupt his bodily support than be without nourishment for his soul from the precious Word of God.

Today's text tells us even more about Peter. When he let down his net and caught such a great number of fish that the net tore, he did not in any way attribute the success to himself, his diligence, his wisdom, or his worthiness. Instead, "he fell down at Jesus' knees, saying, 'Depart from me, for I am a sinful man, O Lord'" (Luke 5:8). He regarded his great success as a blessing of Christ alone that he did not earn. Here we see the second way a person reveals in his earthly work that he is a true Christian. He does not believe he can preserve himself by his work, his diligence, and his wisdom, but only by awaiting his daily bread from God's faithfulness. He does not lose heart if his work proves fruitless, but instead places his reliance upon God. If his work is crowned with success, he receives it as a gift of grace from His heavenly Father. He does not bind himself to earthly things, but separates himself from them that he might be drawn to Christ all the more.

There is one more way in which Peter demonstrated in his work that he was a true Christian. When Jesus had stopped speaking, "He said to Simon, 'Put out into the deep and let down your nets for a catch'" (Luke 5:4). His command was completely contrary to the rules of fishing and Peter's own experience. The best fishing is not in the depths of the open sea but close to the shore; it is also not during the day but at night. How does Peter respond? "And Simon answered, 'Master, we toiled all night and took nothing! But at Your word I will let down the nets'" (Luke 5:5). This is how all true Christians work. They are motivated by God's command because His Word says, "By the sweat of your face you shall eat bread" (Genesis 3:19). Christians therefore daily say, in the conviction of their heart, "But at Your word I will let down the nets."

And gently grant Thy blessing
That we may do Thy will,
No more Thy ways transgressing,
Our proper task fulfill,
With Peter's full assurance
Let down our nets again.
Success will crown endurance
If faithful we remain. Amen.

(TLH 544:5)

Monday

Read Proverbs 11:18

AN IDLE PERSON is certainly no true Christian. But diligence in work is no guarantee of true Christian faith either. A non-Christian can work very diligently, toiling his whole life, and yet, in the end, he receives eternal torment as his wage. It is not the work, but how and why one works that reveals who is a Christian and who is not.

Many work so zealously it appears as if they are on the earth merely for the sake of their vocation. They are so engrossed in their work they think little, if at all, about the salvation of their immortal soul. They forget God's Word, and they forget to pray. They work on the Lord's Day even when they are not in need as if they had no soul that needs to be fed and no God who wants to be worshiped. Even if such people take time to read the Bible, offer morning and evening prayers, and go to church, they do so only half-heartedly. In the midst of the worship service, their heart is still at their business. Their concern is directed more toward the temporal than the eternal, more toward the body than the spirit, and more toward the earthly than the heavenly. They think more about what they want in this life than about how they can enter into heaven. These are obviously non-Christians—fleshly, earthly minded people who bury themselves ever deeper in their trade and thus work themselves into damnation.

Since they are not motivated by the command of God and by love for their neighbor, there are four main reasons why non-Christians work. The first is need. Many people would work little or not at all if they did not know that without work there is no bread. They are thus compelled to work. The craftsman, merchant, and servant who work only for this reason receive their wage.

A second reason people work is avarice. They are zealous in their earthly vocation because they want to amass money and acquire possessions. If they could accomplish this by being idle, however, they would prefer idleness. Where there is little profit, there is little zeal in such people. They do not seek to serve their neighbor but themselves. God's Word says that the Christian should create something good with his hands so he has something to give to the thirsty, but thousands seek to enrich themselves at the expense of the thirsty. They, too, have their reward for their labor. As non-Christians, bound by temptation and other snares, they sink into destruction and damnation.

Ambition is the third basis for some people's work. Although this motivates workers in all trades, it is especially prevalent among artists and the learned. They want to make a name for themselves in the world. That others behold and praise their art and knowledge is their overriding goal. If their work is successful, they do not attribute it to God but to themselves. They are their own idols and their work is the sacrifice they offer themselves. Their wage is solely this. All their work is sin, and they gain only God's wrath by it. God resists the arrogant and gives grace to the humble.

Finally, some people work simply because of the pleasure it gives them. They have been used to working since childhood and are at a point where they cannot live without work. As laudable as it is to take pleasure in one's work, if it is not motivated by obedience to God and love of the neighbor, it remains a sinful pursuit before God.

But whoever, with Peter, forsakes everything and follows Christ will never regret it. Jesus gives His own everything they need and they do not have to worry. One day, He will give them the ultimate reward: eternal life. For, as Scripture says: "Write this: 'Blessed are the dead who die in the Lord from now on.' 'Blessed indeed,' says the Spirit, 'that they may rest from their labors, for their deeds follow them!'" (Revelation 14:13).

Crown all our labors with success,
Each one in his own calling bless.
May all we do or think or say
Exalt and praise Thee, Lord, this day! Amen.

(TLH 547:4)

Tuesday

Read Matthew 12:33

IF A PERSON BECOMES a true Christian, he does more than lay aside vices and take on virtues. He becomes a totally new person in his heart and in his mind. A true Christian is a child of God, born anew by the Holy Ghost. Just as a child, though small and weak, enters the world as a complete person, so the Christian, though weak at the beginning of his spiritual pilgrimage, is not half-Christian and half a child of the world. No, he is a Christian throughout. Being a Christian does not mean doing a certain number of so-called good works and walking honorably. Instead, it is a complete change in a person's thoughts, desires, words, and works.

While it is difficult to discern that a person is a true Christian, there are telltale signs that one is not. Certainly it is evident enough if the whole direction of a person's life is toward wickedness, but it can also be shown with a single deed and even a single word. It is true that no Christian becomes perfectly holy in this life and completely free from all sins of weakness. However, there are certain sins that drive away faith and define a person as something other than a true Christian. If he sins wantonly, if he does not want to be held responsible for a sin he has committed, if he stubbornly defends a sin of which he has been convicted, if he boldly speaks against God's Word, if he is not reconciled toward an offender, if he knowingly and willfully deceives someone, or if he seeks an unjust gain, he has shown that he is not a true Christian. Just as a fire must give off light rather than darkness, the true Christian cannot wantonly sin, persistently excuse and defend known sins, contradict God's clear Word, remain unreconciled to those who have injured him, and deceive others.

Christ shows us all of this with the words of today's reading. A thistle cannot be regarded as a fig tree, and a person who produces bad fruit can hardly be considered a Christian. Someone may argue, "Have I not shown myself a true Christian in every other way? Should I be condemned on account of only one sin? This is entirely too harsh." But it is not. One single wanton and malicious deed or one single godless word is a wolf's paw that suddenly appears out of the sheep's clothing of a holy and pure life. A non-Christian can behave like a true Christian in a hundred cases, but a true Christian cannot behave in even one case like a non-Christian. A bad tree cannot produce good fruits and a good tree cannot bring forth evil fruits. True Christianity is not a series of individual good fruits, but rather a new, divine seed in a person that produces an entirely new tree full of good fruits that signify a new life.

Thou art the Vine—O nourish
The branches graft in Thee
And let them grow and flourish,
A fair and fruitful tree.
Thy Spirit pour within us
And let His gifts of grace
To such good actions win us
As best may show Thy praise. Amen.

(ELHB 21:7)

Wednesday

Read Acts 4:32

WHEN GOD CREATED the world, all creatures stood in the most beautiful, purest harmony without the slightest discord. God was the universal sun around which all creatures revolved. His will was the motivating power that placed all spirits in harmony. His love was the sea in which angels and men lived and were united. Heaven and earth were like a temple in which everything that had breath praised the Creator. People were one holy, intimately bound family, fervently loving one another as children of one Father, and they were blessed in that love.

What upset this happy balance? People fell into sin and destroyed the harmony. Man was ripped away from God and from his fellow man. The children of Adam still understand that they are descendants of one set of parents and are all brothers and sisters, but their love for one another has vanished. When people fell away from God, the bond that joined them to their fellow man was also severed. Man now loves only himself, even if he deludes himself into thinking he cares for and looks after others. He coldly passes by his neighbor as if he were a foreigner. Instead of love, indifference and hate dwell in his heart. The unity of God has been transformed into endless discord. God's blessed peace has been changed into ceaseless fighting.

From eternity, God saw that His glorious work of creation would be corrupted by sin, and out of His bottomless love, He determined to renew that work, still the discord, and establish a new kingdom of grace and peace. He then carried out this plan to the eternal admiration of all reasonable creatures. Even when man did not desire to be connected with God, God bound Himself to man. By an act of divine mercy, God Himself became a man who was capable of suffering so He could atone for man's rebellion against Him. He redeemed all and united all who would be sought and found by Him, by the working of His grace, into His congregation of pardoned children bound together in holy love and unity.

Through Christ, the Son of God, a holy Church of the redeemed was established. Among the members of this Church, the pure harmony that existed before the Fall has been reestablished. God is again a sun around which all revolve, the sole power that moves all hearts, and a sea in which all live in blessed union. With His Church, God has again built Himself a temple in which all unanimously praise Him with one voice as the Father of their Lord Jesus Christ. The Church is a holy, intimately bound family whose members fervently love one another as children of one Father and they are blessed in this love. There is no envy, fighting, hatred, or indifference among the members of the Church. Instead, there is love, joy, peace, and harmony for all stand in one faith and in one hope. They are all dwellings of the same God, the same Savior, and the same Holy Ghost. It is as if they had one heart and one soul.

But it is true that as long as the members of the Church remain on the earth, they are not entirely spirit. Instead, they retain something of the old man and his corrupt nature. This makes it appear that true unity and true peace are still elusive. For this reason, members of the Church are continually exhorted in Scripture to pursue unity and peace.

Thou sacred Love, grace on us bestow,
Set our hearts with heav'nly fire aglow
That with hearts united we love each other,
Of one mind, in peace with ev'ry brother.
Lord, have mercy! Amen.

(TLH 231:3)

Thursday

Read 1 Peter 3:8

IT IS ABSOLUTELY NECESSARY to be informed about the true unity Scripture says should be pursued and cultivated in the Church. "Union," "unity," and "church peace" are buzzwords uttered by many thousands of people and are regular themes in religious media. But what is the nature of this unity so routinely spoken about and sought? It is this: People should stop fighting because of differences in faith; they should leave one another in peace; they should either remain silent about the errors of others or set themselves against only the greatest of deviations from God's Word; they should extend a brotherly hand to all others; and they should unite into one great Church where they worship together, celebrate together the supper of reconciliation at the Lord's Table, struggle together against coarse unbelief, and work together in building the kingdom of God. Love rules, so the thinking goes, and religion should give way to it if God is to work unity in faith and in doctrine.

This is the kind of unity that pleases the heart and mind of the natural man. This is a unity the world desires. But this is hardly the unity to which God's Word so often and so urgently exhorts the Church. Far from it! This is nothing but a semblance of unity. It marks a surrender to the notion that no true peace can be brought about here on earth. It is not a healing of the wounds of the Church, but only a bandage on the festering abscess so it is not seen although it penetrates the heart all the more deeply. It does not join the stones in the walls of a church to form a solid building, but it is instead the whitewashing of the schisms that have arisen so the building will fall all the harder.

The unity toward which the Church is to strive is completely different. "Finally, all of you, have unity of *mind*" (1 Peter 3:8), Peter admonishes. The first thing necessary if true Christians are to be united is to be of the same mind. All should have the same faith, principles, views, and hope. What one Christian recognizes as true in matters of faith should be the conviction of every other Christian. And all should judge and act accordingly.

The apostle adds, "Let him seek peace and pursue it" (1 Peter 3:11). From the root of the one faith, a tree filled with the fruit of a hearty, fervent brotherly love should blossom in the Christian. The one truth should motivate a common work that is built in peace. This is the unity the Church should cultivate. Unity in mind produces unity in works. The Church should be one in faith, and unity should follow in love. The Church should recognize, from the heart, the right doctrine, and from this unity in doctrine, confession with the mouth should result. The Church should be convicted of one truth, and unity in peace should come forth. The Church should be one in hope, and this should produce a unity in the brotherly walk toward the same goal. The Church should be one in heart and in soul, and it should, with one spirit and one mouth, praise God, the Father of our Lord Jesus Christ. All the members of this one body should help one another and join in battle against their common enemy.

Oh, keep us in Thy Word, we pray;
The guile and rage of Satan stay!
Oh, may Thy mercy never cease!
Give concord, patience, courage, peace. Amen.

(TLH 292:4)

Friday

Read 1 Corinthians 1:10

IF CHRISTIANS DO NOT cultivate unity in doctrine and in life among themselves, they are misled by their flesh and blood, standing by peacefully as divisions arise and discord grows day by day. God did not give His gifts to only one Christian or to one Christian congregation. Instead, He distributes them in such a way that all must work together to succeed. When divisions surface, success is hindered—errors increase, quarrels become more passionate, confusion grows, false judgments and a spirit of condemnation ensue, and sects become more numerous. When this happens, how many lose the foundation upon which their faith is built! When the poor world sees how disunited Christians are among themselves, it finds little reason to embrace the faith and is even comforted in rejecting it. Many are offended who might have been won to Christianity. Who can count the souls that perished in the battle Zwingli launched against the doctrine of the holy Sacraments that divided churches of whole nations? Who can count the souls that now stumble over the hundreds of sects within Christianity, hindered from seeking the truth and remaining in their unbelief, lost eternally? How can one hope to stand before God one day when he is guilty of discord and division within the Church? How necessary it is, then, that the Church cultivate with the greatest care and zeal unity and peace among its members.

Christian unity always produces a blessing. If the Church is one in doctrine and life, in faith and love, it shares its gifts and knowledge. It then grows in the wealth of knowledge, the power of faith, the fervor of love, the comfort of the Holy Ghost, and the liveliness of hope. It grounds itself ever more deeply and builds itself ever more gloriously, adorned with all sorts of gifts of the Spirit. It then extends its hands to raise up shepherds and soldiers who pursue the work of converting those who sit in darkness and in the shadow of death and who struggle against the enemies of the truth. How many who have been offended by such discord of Christians might have been drawn to the Church by its unity in truth and its fervor in brotherly love, and so won by the Word! When the first Christian Church stood in blessed unity, Scripture said of its members, "And walking in the fear of the Lord and in the comfort of the Holy Spirit, it multiplied" (Acts 9:31). The Church also had "favor with all the people. And the Lord added to their number day by day those who were being saved" (Acts 2:47).

Satan knows all too well what kind of power the Church exercises when it is united. It then not only greens and bears fruit, but it also stands invincible against all of its enemies, conquering them and extending its borders. Therefore, Satan's most important and dangerous strategy, which he employs to damage the Church, is destroying its unity and sowing discord among its members. And how easily he succeeds! How quickly is the holy bond that binds Christians together torn apart! How quickly an ember of discord among the ashes is fanned into a bright flame that seizes and lays waste entire congregations! How necessary it is, then, that the Church carefully cultivate unity, pursuing it as a precious jewel!

O Comforter of priceless worth,
Send peace and unity on earth.
Support us in our final strife
And lead us out of death to life. Amen.

(TLH 261:3)

Saturday

Read Philippians 2:1–2

THE BELIEVING CHRISTIAN recognizes that he has a duty to cooperate so the whole Church can be built in unity of faith and love. For this to take place, a Christian cannot be satisfied by knowing just enough of God's Word that is absolutely necessary for his salvation. God does not desire that His children remain children in knowledge, being tossed to and fro by every wind of doctrine. Instead, if the Church is to remain unified, each member must diligently and daily, with prayer and great earnestness, seek to grow in God's Word by studying the writings of enlightened teachers, listening attentively to public sermons, and using all means at their disposal to grow in the knowledge of salvation. They must train themselves to distinguish between good and evil and to judge between truth and error. The office of the pastor is, above all else, to investigate the Law of the Lord, judging doctrine and rejecting error. As the prophet Malachi says, "For the lips of a priest should guard knowledge, and people should seek instruction from his mouth, for he is the messenger of the LORD of hosts" (2:7).

If the Church is truly to grow in unity of faith and love, it is not enough that teachers alone should be grounded in God's Word. Instead, the entire congregation must stand as witnesses for the truth and as fighters against error. As soon as the laity begins to become lukewarm and lazy in their investigation of the truth, relinquishing the judgment of doctrine to their pastors, the unity of the Church is lost and God will soon open the floodgates through which false doctrine will come. What faithful teachers built over many years with great effort will then quickly be destroyed.

Our work toward unity is not finished when we strive after greater knowledge. It is equally necessary that each member of the Church guard his heart so he does not arrogantly extol himself. Rather, he must become more humble so he is always ready to recognize his error when he is convicted of it, confessing it, surrendering it, and giving honor to the truth. History teaches that most errors in the Church arose and spread not because people did not know better, but because they were too proud to admit their errors. Saint

Augustine said, "Pride is the mother of all heresies." A heart that is humble and open to the truth is thus the second prerequisite for cultivating and furthering of Church peace.

The third and final necessity is love that pursues the erring, leaving no stone unturned in the effort to turn him from the wrong path. Christians cannot be satisfied when they have recognized the truth and know how to protect themselves against prevailing errors. Their love for erring souls compels them to use every means to combat error wherever they find it and to let the truth shine unmistakably. What a glorious example we have in our forefathers! How they worked for the spread of the truth and fought to overcome error! How they sought, lovingly and earnestly, to preserve the unity of faith in their conversation and writing! Because of their faithful struggle, thousands slander them as miserable, quarrelsome people. But how inexpressibly God blessed their work and their struggle. Millions thank them for deliverance from pernicious error and for the treasure of the pure, clear truth. Who can calculate the blessing that has flowed out upon Christianity from their polemical writings, from their devotional books, and from the confessions of the Church? Indeed, the blessings of their work continue to flow until this very hour, long after they have rested from their work!

Therefore, let us follow them as faithful sons and daughters. God has also sent us the light of His pure Word. Let us spare no effort to share this light with others.

Preserve, O Lord, Thine honor,
The bold blasphemer smite;
Convince, convert, enlighten,
The souls in error's night.
Reveal Thy will, dear Savior,
To all who dwell below—

Thou Light of all the living—
That men Thy name may know. Amen.

(*TLH* 264:2)

Sunday

Read Matthew 5:20–22

EVERY PERSON who believes in God and eternal life after death will admit that a certain righteousness is required to enter the kingdom of heaven. A person's own conscience taunts him that because of his sins he cannot enter that kingdom. But what righteousness do most people hope to obtain that will one day allow them to stand before God and gain entrance into heaven? They think that if they can fulfill the Law of God to some extent, at least as much as is possible with the weak powers of man, they will satisfy the requirement of righteousness God imposes on those who want to be received by Him into heaven.

What does Christ say in response to this? In our Gospel reading, He says, "For I tell you, unless your righteousness exceeds that of the scribes and Pharisees, you will never enter the kingdom of heaven" (Matthew 5:20). Here Matthew strikes to the ground all the thoughts of those who believe they can somehow earn their way to heaven. For what did the scribes and Pharisees do that Christ here excludes from heaven? As much as it was in their power, they sought to fulfill the literal reading of the Law.

What could Christ have meant when He referred to another, better righteousness that without no one can enter heaven? He tells us in today's text: "You have heard that it was said to those of old, 'You shall not murder; and whoever murders will be liable to judgment.' But I say to you that everyone who is angry with his brother will be liable to judgment; whoever insults his brother will be liable to the council; and whoever says, 'You fool!' will be liable to the hell of fire" (Matthew 5:21–22). These verses tell us that those who want the righteousness that avails before God must not concentrate on attempting outward fulfillment of the Law. The Law is spiritual and, therefore, its fulfillment requires the whole person: thoughts, words, and deeds. According to the Law, only the person who has fulfilled it in its true spiritual sense, even its strictest demands, is righteous before God.

But the Law forbids all sins without exception: "For whoever keeps the whole law but fails in one point has become accountable for all of it" (James 2:10). Thus, anyone who can be accused of even a single sin is not righteous before God. The world maintains that a single word is not significant, but Christ replies, "I tell you, on the day of judgment people will give account for every careless word they speak" (Matthew 12:36). Thus, not just obvious sins but even an idle word renders one unrighteous before God. The world argues that thoughts are free, but the Law says, "The Lord . . . will bring to light the things now hidden in darkness and will disclose the purposes of the heart" (1 Corinthians 4:5), and "You shall not covet" (Exodus 20:17). Therefore, the one the Law can accuse of evil thoughts and sinful longings in his heart also is not righteous before God.

The Law also says, "For this is the message that you have heard from the beginning, that we should love one another. . . . Everyone who hates his brother is a murderer, and you know that no murderer has eternal life abiding in him" (1 John 3:11, 15). Thus, the one the Law accuses of loving something more than God and of loving himself more than his neighbor is not righteous before God. The Law adds, "So whoever knows the right thing to do and fails to do it, for him it is sin" (James 4:17). If the Law accuses someone of having left undone some good deed he might have done, then he is again lacking in righteousness. Finally, the Law demands, "You shall be holy, for I the LORD your God am holy" (Leviticus 19:2), and "you therefore must be perfect, as your heavenly Father is perfect" (Matthew 5:48). Those who are not perfect remain unrighteous before God.

The Law may threaten endless death
From awful Sinai's burning hill,
Straightway from its consuming breath
My soul through faith mounts higher still;
She throws herself at Jesus' feet
And finds with Him a safe retreat,
Where curse and death can never come.
Though all foes threaten condemnation,
Yet, Jesus, Thou art my Salvation,
For in Thy love I find my home. Amen.

(ELHB 109:3)

Monday

Read Romans 4:5

BY THE WORKS of the Law alone, no one can attain the righteousness that avails before God. The Law certainly reveals the righteousness God demands from us, but it gives us no power to produce it. It shows us our death, but it cannot make us alive. Therefore, Saint Paul says to the Galatians, "For if a law had been given that could give life, then righteousness would indeed be by the law" (3:21). Many have tried to make themselves righteous before God by diligent good works, being pious, turning their back to the world, praying, fasting, and all kinds of self-torment. But all of this work is futile.

No one can change his own heart. Our heart is corrupt by nature, inclined to sin, and full of sinful desires. Thus it is impossible for anyone to appear completely pure before God as He demands. Paul writes about the Jews: "but that Israel who pursued a law that would lead to righteousness did not succeed in reaching that law. . . . I bear them witness that they have a zeal for God, but not according to knowledge. For, being ignorant of the righteousness that comes from God, and seeking to establish their own, they did not submit to God's righteousness" (Romans 9:31; 10:2–3).

Just as the hypocritical Pharisees and scribes, together with the poor and ignorant souls around them, sought in vain to obtain righteousness by their works of the Law, so also did those who lacked true earnestness. David, who had deeply fallen, had to cry out, "Enter not into judgment with Your servant for no one living is righteous before You" (Psalm 143:2). Even Job, whom Scripture calls "a blameless and upright man, one who fears God and turns away from evil" (1:8), was forced to exclaim, "How then can man be in the right before God? How can he who is born of woman be pure?" (25:4), and "If I wash myself with snow and cleanse my hands with lye, yet you will plunge me into a pit, and my own clothes will abhor me" (9:30–31). Isaiah echoes: "We have all become like one who is unclean, and all our righteous deeds are like a polluted garment" (64:6). As the saints in Scripture speak, so too have all the saints at all times.

How, then, can a poor, weak, sinful person attain the righteousness that God accepts? The only path is the one the Gospel shows: the way of faith in Jesus Christ. Whoever despairs of his own righteousness—his works, wants, abilities, and deeds—and turns instead to Christ, who perfectly fulfilled the Law for all people, bearing and atoning for their sins by His innocent suffering and death, will be declared righteous by God in His grace and absolved from all his sins. It is as if he had perfectly fulfilled the Law as Christ did. Whoever stands in great guilt before God but believes in Christ receives a perfect acquittal from God Himself. Even the one who has nothing good within him can, through his faith in Christ, receive a fully valid merit so God cannot condemn him but must instead declare him to be fully righteous before all angels and creatures. In short, whoever believes in Christ has the righteousness without which no one can enter into the kingdom of heaven.

Oh, it is well with all poor sinners who, tired of vainly seeking rest and peace through their own methods, finally seize Christ by faith and say to Him: "Lord, I am a sinner, but You are holy for me. My life and suffering are pure unrighteousness, but Your life and suffering are my righteousness!" Then they can joyfully and confidently turn to all the world, and even to God's Law, and boldly say, with Paul, "Who shall bring any charge against God's elect? It is God who justifies. Who is to condemn? Christ Jesus is the one who died—more than that, who was raised—who is at the right hand of God, who indeed is interceding for us" (Romans 8:33–34). Hallelujah!

My faith looks up to Thee,
Thou Lamb of Calvary,
Savior divine.
Now hear me while I pray;
Take all my guilt away;
Oh, let me from this day
Be wholly Thine! Amen.

† *(TLH 394:1)*

Tuesday

Read Matthew 5:23–26

FEW WHO REGARD the Bible as true do not believe they have obtained righteousness before God through Christ. Whoever deceives himself in this is a thousand times more accursed than the obvious sinner who knows he has no part of Christ. There are certain marks, however, that make it obvious that someone already has the imputed righteousness of grace.

The person who has grasped Christ as his righteousness is no longer occupied, as Saint Paul says, with works. That is, he does not seek any merit, comfort, or righteousness before God by his own works. One who has the righteousness of faith is also zealous in regard to the righteousness of life, is no longer motivated by compulsion but rather by a free heart. He does not hope for a reward, but he demonstrates instead a hearty, thankful love toward God not for his own honor but to honor His God and Savior, who has forgiven him all his sins and clothed him in the cloak of His innocence.

As soon as a person believes this from his heart, his faith becomes the germ of a new, divine life within him. The Holy Spirit chastises him, fights against even the smallest movement of sin, and so propels his will to every good work. If God's severe Law is preached to such a person, he does not resist when sin is exposed to him. He does not deny it or attempt to excuse it, but humbly confesses it and asks for forgiveness. He does not seek to reject the severe demands of the Law; rather, he gives himself up. He is ready to die rather than to do something if he is uncertain whether it is a sin.

Luther describes the manner of this faith very beautifully: "Faith, however, is a divine work in us. It changes us and makes us to be born anew of God (John 1); it kills the old Adam and makes altogether different men, in heart and spirit and mind and powers, and it brings with it the Holy Ghost. Oh, it is a living, busy, active, mighty thing, this faith; and so it is impossible for it not to do good works incessantly. It does not ask whether there are good works to do, but before the question rises, it has already done them, and is always at the doing of them" (Preface to *Commentary on Romans*).

In this, it is evident if someone has the righteousness that avails before God. Whoever can speak beautifully about faith and justification and Christian liberty but fails to show these fruits only deceives himself in thinking that he will one day be able to stand before God.

In our text, Christ gives us an important example of this: "So if you are offering your gift at the altar and there remember that your brother has something against you, leave your gift there before the altar and go. First be reconciled to your brother, and then come and offer your gift. Come to terms quickly with your accuser while you are going with him to court, lest your accuser hand you over to the judge, and the judge to the guard, and you be put in prison" (Matthew 5:23–25). These words show us the disposition of those who are righteous in Christ. Such people not only are diligent in serving God, but also have tender love for the brethren. They want to be reconciled both with God and with their neighbor. They regard all their worship as futile if their neighbor should have something against them. They go to their neighbor and seek to be reconciled, even when they are the innocent victims of an offense.

Let us examine ourselves against today's reading. When we say that Christ is our righteousness, can we show that we are speaking the truth? Do we produce the fruits that are never absent whenever there is true faith? Or do we want to do only certain things but not bear a cross that seems too heavy? In this life, Christians have only the first fruits of the Spirit. They are still flesh and blood that fight against the Spirit. There is a struggle that goes on inside the Christian but the flesh does not get the upper hand.

Oh, may each of us truly receive Christ from the heart, for whoever appears before God in his own righteousness, without Christ, will not stand.

Faith clings to Jesus' cross alone
And rests in Him unceasing;
And by its fruits true faith is known,
With love and hope increasing.
Yet faith alone doth justify,
Works serve thy neighbor and supply
The proof that faith is living. Amen.

† *(TLH 377:9)*

Wednesday

Read Romans 4:16

MANY THINK THAT a person is righteous before God through faith and nothing else, since faith is a good work and a glorious virtue. They maintain that a person makes himself acceptable and pleasing to God by his faith, which cleanses his heart, unites him with Christ, and brings forth the fruit of good works.

It is true that faith has all of these glorious qualities, but it is false to say this makes a person righteous before God. Scripture never says a person is righteous before God *because of* or *on account of* his faith. Instead, he is righteous *through* faith. Faith, then, is not the cause of our justification but only its instrument. It is the means by which we receive righteousness from God.

Faith does not make us righteous before God because it is such a good work and such a beautiful virtue. Precisely the opposite is the case. As today's reading informs, faith makes a person righteous before God because righteousness can be obtained solely by grace.

God created man in His image, in perfect righteousness. But when the first people fell, they and all their descendants without exception lost that righteousness. All have become sinners who lack the glory they should have in God. But behold! When we had plunged ourselves into a destruction so complete that no person, angel, or other creature could rescue us, God had already decided from eternity to restore us to righteousness and save us by His grace. But because God could not simply revoke His Law; something had to happen so our just and holy God could declare us righteous without offending the Law. He did this by giving up His only begotten Son for all people to pay the price of our redemption and to lay upon Him the burden of our debt.

God's Son became a man, allowed all the sins of all the people to be attributed to Him, placed Himself under the Law, and by His suffering and death bore our punishment. He became obedient even unto death on the cross. When He cried out, "It is finished" (John 19:30), He referred to the completion of His great sacrifice for the atonement of all sin. And on the third day after His death, God the Father raised Him from the dead, thereby confirming the Redeemer's word of victory at Calvary. With this, He said, in essence: "Yes, it is finished! I am appeased! You are redeemed! Your debt is paid, and the righteousness that avails before Me has been acquired for you!"

What, then, is necessary for a person to be righteous before God? Since our debt is already paid, it is necessary for us only to believe and accept it happily. What does a prisoner need to become free when the doors of his cell are already open? He needs only to acknowledge this and exercise his freedom. What does one who has been reprieved from the sentence of death require to embrace his pardon? He must accept it and that is all. The sin debt of all people has been paid by the work of Christ, and if we believe this from our heart, all the benefits of His sacrifice will be ours.

Why does faith make one righteous before God? Is it, perhaps, because a person must still contribute something, even if it is just a little, toward his justification? Perish the thought! We can contribute absolutely nothing to our salvation for Christ has already done everything for us. He made the perfect atonement for our sins, redeemed us, and obtained a perfect righteousness for us before God. We are blessed solely by grace because God alone wants the glory that attends our justification and salvation. Therefore, let us accept what Christ acquired for us, dedicate ourselves to it, comfort and gladden ourselves in it, and believe in the One who worked all of this for us.

I fall asleep in Jesus' wounds
There pardon for my sins abounds;
Yea, Jesus' blood and righteousness
My jewels are, my glorious dress.
In these before my God I'll stand
When I shall reach the heav'nly land. Amen.

† *(TLH 585:1)*

Thursday

Read Romans 4:16

MANY PEOPLE BELIEVE the proclamation of the Gospel is nothing more than a report of what Christ has done and a lesson in what we must do to redeem ourselves, with Christ's help. They also think the holy Sacraments are merely empty signs of the grace a person has already obtained. But, God be praised, this is not so! Christ has indeed already perfectly reconciled the whole world with God, redeeming it and acquiring for it an eternal righteousness. The Gospel and the holy Sacraments are divine promises to all who hear the Gospel and use the Sacraments. The Father, the Son, and the Holy Ghost are the three divine witnesses in heaven who testify to the righteousness obtained for all sinners. And the Spirit, the water, and the blood—that is, the Gospel, Baptism, and Holy Communion—are three divine witnesses on earth (1 John 5:6–8).

Wherever the Gospel is preached, God absolves people and Christ's righteousness is offered and delivered to them. Whenever people are baptized, God declares Himself to be their Father, Christ to be their Savior, and the Holy Ghost to be their Comforter. Whenever people partake of Holy Communion, Christ gives them His redemption, forgives their sins, and offers them eternal righteousness, sealing this, His promise, with the presentation of His true body and blood. What God once promised Abraham with the words, "[In your Seed] all the families of the earth shall be blessed" (Genesis 12:3), He now promises to all people through the Word and the holy Sacraments.

No person can then say, "Oh, that God would come

from heaven and Himself speak with me and promise me righteousness and eternal life! Then I would believe and be joyful!" For God truly speaks with every person through the Gospel. In it, He promises righteousness and eternal life and seals this promise with the holy Sacraments. These three means of grace are the audible and visible representatives of the triune God on earth—God's mouth, voice, and hand—and they give Christ's righteousness. They are the receipt God makes out and delivers after Christ paid the debt of all people.

What else but faith is necessary for a person to be righteous before God? Where there is a free promise, faith alone is the means to rejoice in that promise. In the Word and in His holy Sacraments, God promises to grant righteousness freely to all who use it. Thus, love, hope, humility, patience, or any other virtue is not the means of attaining righteousness. It comes by faith alone. As soon as a person determines to attain righteousness by some other means, God's promise is no longer sure to him; he makes it a lie and he grounds his righteousness on the quicksand of his own works.

Let us never forget what the holy apostle writes in today's text: "In order that the promise may rest on grace and be guaranteed to all his offspring—" (Romans 4:16). This doctrine of justification through faith alone contains the only foundation of all hope and salvation. It is the crux of the entire Bible and the key to all other mysteries of faith that are revealed in Holy Scripture. It is the article on which the Church stands or falls. It is the sun that alone gives us light in the darkness of life and in the night of trial and death. Where this sun no longer shines, nothing but hellish darkness overtakes us. Whoever does not cling to this doctrine is not safe against error. But he who holds it firmly can certainly distinguish between true and false prophets, pure doctrine and erring spirits, and the true and false churches.

Oh, it is well with him who holds fast to this doctrine! He has a right indicator of the way against all temptation, a firm comfort against all anguish of sin, and an open door through death into eternal life.

And Thou, O Holy Spirit,
My Comforter and Guide
Grant that in Jesus' merit
I always may confide,
Him to the end confessing
Whom I have known by faith.
Give me Thy constant blessing
And grant a Christian death. Amen.

(TLH 334:3)

Friday

Read Ephesians 2:20

A CHURCH THAT WANTS to be a Christian church maintains that the faith it confesses is the true one. A church that lays no such claim renounces itself as a branch of the true Christian faith. Yet not every church that claims to have the true faith actually possesses it. Everything depends on the foundation on which its doctrine and faith are built. Truth is eternally unchanging, not wavering or flexible or yielding. Therefore, anything that has an uncertain foundation cannot be the eternal truth. What, then, is the foundation on which the Church confesses its faith?

It is, first of all, not its own reason or the reason of any person. To be sure, earnest Christians ask these questions: "From where does man come? Where is he going? What is his relationship to the Creator of the world? How does he find rest from the accusations of his conscience? What is his destiny after death?" These are the questions of religion that human reason cannot answer. Thus, reason cannot be the foundation of true faith. It cannot be the sun from which the light radiates, but only the eye that receives the light.

Second, the foundation of what the Church confesses as its faith is not the traditions of the Church, not the decisions of some member of the Church, not the decrees of faith from some church assembly. While some continue to maintain that the promise of infallibility is given to members of the clergy, the history of all ages has undeniably shown that this is empty pretense. Church traditions and decrees of faith have repeatedly contradicted one another. The indispensable mark of truth, on the other hand, is that it agrees with itself. Therefore, contradictory Church traditions, council decisions, and the like cannot possibly be the foundation of true doctrine and true faith.

Finally, new revelations are not the foundation on which the Church is established. The truth is always the same, as old as God Himself. Accordingly, a truly new divine revelation can be nothing but a confirmation of the old. All would-be new revelations want to be viewed as corrections of the old, and thus they already carry on their forehead the brand of lie or self-deception.

What, then, is the only foundation upon which the Church grounds its faith? It is, as Saint Paul tells us, the "foundation of the apostles and prophets" (Ephesians 2:20), that is, the apostolic and prophetic Scriptures of the Old and New Testaments. "The Bible, nothing but the Bible, and the entire Bible" is our most supreme principle. What the Bible declares to be the truth is accepted as such by our Church, and we firmly cling to it even if the rest of the world declares it to be false. In addition, whatever the Bible declares to be an error is rejected by our Church, even if the rest of the world or an angel from heaven would praise it as high wisdom. The Bible alone is our guide and judge in every dispute that arises.

The evangelical Church stands on a rock solid foundation. "Heaven and earth will pass away," Christ says, "but My words will not pass away" (Matthew 24:35). These words are as certain today as they were 2,000 years ago. In fact, this has been confirmed, over and over again throughout all these centuries. All of the systems of philosophy propounded during antiquity and once much admired have plummeted like falling stars. The Bible and its doctrines have remained. Likewise, new systems of human wisdom will not stand the test of time. Even the gates of hell will be unable to destroy the Church, which is built upon the eternal, unshakable ground of Holy Scripture.

Preserve Thy Word, O Savior,
To us this latter day
And let Thy kingdom flourish,
Enlarge Thy church, we pray.
Oh, keep our faith from failing,
Keep hope's bright star aglow.
Let naught from Thy Word turn us
While wand'ring here below. Amen.

(TLH 264:1)

Saturday

Read Ephesians 2:20

THE TASK OF EVERY Christian church that rightly bears this name is to provide eternal comfort. Every person has within himself an accusing conscience and longs in his heart to know his condition before the holy God. He wants to know if he, a sinner, can and will one day die a blessed death. To still this longing of man, God has established the holy Christian Church. It should be a garden of heaven on earth, full of living springs at which the tired earthly pilgrim can rest and out of which he can draw the comfort that heals his wounded conscience and fills him with the hope of eternal life. A church that does not provide this comfort, one that acts instead like a school of morals, preaching only one's duties, awakening a servile fear of God, and leaving doubt about eternal salvation, is a church in name only.

What value is this comfort if it is not grounded on a good foundation? What good is the comforting word that God is a person's friend and that he can expect a better life after this one, if that word is not based on an irrefutably solid foundation? What good does it do someone to hear that he will be saved if he keeps the commandments of God because who can keep them perfectly? What good is it for him to hear that he will be saved if he truly repents of his sins from his heart because who has perfect repentance? What comfort is it to be told that salvation can result from a life of good works because who can believe that the holy God will let His eternal heaven be purchased with our imperfect works? Oh, accursed are the people who have no other foundation for their comfort!

What is the foundation of the comfort to which the evangelical Church firmly holds? The apostle Paul answers this question in today's text. He tells the Christians at Ephesus that they are "built on the foundation of the apostles and prophets," adding, "Christ Jesus Himself being the cornerstone" (Ephesians 2:20). Christ alone is the foundation of the comfort of our Church.

All true Christians believe, teach, and confess that all people are lost sinners. God, who is the eternal love, does not want even one person to be lost, however. Therefore, according to an eternal decree, He sent His only begotten Son into the world for its deliverance. He became a man, and by His life, His suffering, and His death, acquired for mankind complete forgiveness of sins and eternal life. God the Father publicly confirmed the reconciliation that was brought about on the cross when He raised Christ from the dead. Then Christ has commanded His messengers to go into all the world and to preach the Gospel to every creature. The Gospel is the joyful message that God is already reconciled with all people and the blessed announcement that the gates of heaven are already opened to them. There are no conditions attendant on His proclamation of peace; otherwise, that proclamation would not be grace. A person need do nothing more than believe the message that God wants to be his Father, that all his sins are forgiven, and that he is an heir of heaven.

We confess, "And there is salvation in no one else, for there is no other name under heaven given among men by which we must be saved" (Acts 4:12), except the precious name of Jesus. We also confess that "[Christ is] the way, and the truth, and the life. No one comes to the Father except through [Him]" (John 14:6). Moreover, we believe that there are untold souls outside the visible church who ground their faith on God's Word alone and who, therefore, will be saved. The Church of the Bible according to its faith, also is the Church of grace according to its comfort.

In Thee alone, O Christ, my Lord
My hope on earth remaineth;
I know Thou wilt Thine aid afford,
Naught else my soul sustaineth.
No strength of man, no earthly stay,
Can help me in the evil day;
Thou, only Thou, canst aid supply.
To Thee I cry;
On Thee I bid my heart rely. Amen.

(TLH 319:1)

Sunday

Read Mark 8:1–4

IN TODAY'S READING, we see people filled with a zeal for God's Word that is unequaled anywhere else in the New Testament. Jesus had returned to Galilee after traveling in the region of the Gentile cities of Tyre and Sidon, and here He and His disciples climbed a mountain in a desert region that is not far from the Sea of Galilee. Although it was the hot time of year, the people still followed Jesus, coming from all sides in great numbers. Some came to have Him heal their sick while others came to hear His Word. A number of them traveled great distances to see Him. They set out on the long, difficult journey to Christ through the desert to a mountainous region in the hot glare of the sun. Some even carried their infant children with them. The audience swelled to 4,000 men; women and children were not counted.

The day passed quickly as the crowd heard Jesus speak the words of eternal life. Evening came, but no one made arrangements to return home. So they could hear Jesus preach again the next day, all gladly preferred to take a night's lodging on the hard ground under the open sky. Even on the second day, they could not separate themselves from Christ. They held out until the third day. At that point, a great need arose. The people, probably not anticipating that they would stay with Jesus so long in the wilderness, had taken along only a few provisions and these had been consumed during these three days.

If judged solely by human logic, it would seem the people had gone too far in their zeal for God's Word. Where would the many thousands obtain food in the wilderness? Were the men, women, and children able to make the long trek back to the cities without food? The danger was so great the Lord Himself said, "And if I send them away hungry to their homes, they will faint on the way. And some of them have come from far away" (Mark 8:3).

These people provide us with a marvelous example. True Christians would rather suffer earthly harm than lack something spiritual. False Christians also want to hold Christ and serve Him, but only as long as they can do so without sacrificing time, money, rest, honor, or any other favorite thing. The true Christian is completely different. He prefers in every case the spiritual to the bodily, the eternal to the temporal, and the heavenly to the earthly. He would gladly forsake something earthly to gain something spiritual. Like the people who, awakened by the Spirit of God, listened to Jesus that day, a true Christian gladly sacrifices time and earthly gain to hear and examine God's Word. For this purpose, he happily endures burdens and surrenders bodily peace. A true Christian would even give up a lucrative vocation, selecting a career that affords fewer earthly goods, if by doing so he could care for the nourishment of his soul. A lord would become a servant if that work would benefit him spiritually.

To the true Christian, faith is a serious matter. He would never abandon his country and move to another merely to become rich there. But he would easily leave a place where he had great prospects of wealth and move to a place where he did not have such prospects if there would be greater benefit to his soul and those of his children. Being heavenly minded, he is generous in his support of the poor and in helping to spread the good news of the kingdom of heaven. The richer he becomes, the greater the gifts he provides. Like the people in today's reading, he may sometimes even encounter discomfort as a result of his zeal for the spiritual. In short, he considers every earthly gain as loss when it takes away from spiritual pursuits, and he deems every earthly loss as gain when he grows spiritually as a result.

Christ Himself, my Shepherd, feeds me,
Peace and joy my spirit fill;
In a pasture green He leads me
Forth beside the waters still.
Oh, naught to my soul is so sweet and reviving,
As thus unto Jesus alone to be living;
True happiness this, and this only, supplies,
Through faith on my Savior to fasten mine eyes.
Amen.

(*ELHB* 83:9)

Monday

Read Mark 8:5–9

MANY WHO HEARD about the men, women, and children who braved the inhospitable terrain and the heat of the day and follow Christ into the wilderness to hear His Word must have considered them to be fools. False saints would surely have come to this conclusion, but not Christ. He was pleased with the people's zeal, which had been awakened by God Himself. Therefore, when their need arose, He said, "I have compassion on the crowd" (Mark 8:2), and He ordered the people to sit down. The people, whose faith had been strengthened by what they had heard, obeyed and sat at Christ's empty table. Christ then took the seven loaves of bread and a few fish the disciples had left over for themselves, and He blessed them, broke them into pieces, and gave them to the disciples to distribute. And behold! In Christ's hands, the food miraculously multiplied. The distribution continued until every last one of the thousands gathered there had been fed. In fact, after all had eaten, seven baskets full of fragments remained. All of the people departed, having been strengthened both in body and in spirit.

Like the people in today's reading, all true Christians gladly sacrifice the bodily for the spiritual. In this, the world may regard them as foolish, even hypocritical, since in order to pursue nourishment for their soul, they forget worldly cares. But their God and Savior regards them with pleasure. Who can be happier than the one who has God on his side, even if the whole world is against him? As Saint Paul says, "If God is for us, who can be against us?" (Romans 8:31). The world may look on in malicious delight when zealous Christians lag behind in earthly things. Indeed, they may even come into need because they will not use sinful means to enrich themselves and because they sometimes spend considerable time feeding their souls, sharing their wealth with poor brothers and sisters, and spreading the kingdom of God. Yet, despite such discomforts, they do it. In their poverty and temporary distress, Christ looks on them with great pity. He values every bodily deprivation they incur for the sake of the Gospel, and He gives them in heavenly comfort and refreshment a hundred times what they lose in bodily and temporal things. He leads them through all their distress so that, in the end, they always have whatever they need. When distress is at its greatest, so is the help He supplies. In them, the old proverb is confirmed: "Going to church does not delay; giving alms does not make one poor."

If we want to better understand why true Christians are so willing to sacrifice bodily things for spiritual things, we must look from the vantage point of eternity. Whoever would prefer to give up something spiritual for something bodily in this life will come to regret his decision when he sees how little he has harvested in the world to come. Conversely, whoever gladly sacrifices the bodily for the spiritual in this life will find that even the most meager self-denial is capital to which God adds and for which God eternally pays interest. The nature of this interest is yet unknown to us, but we can be sure it will far exceed whatever we have measured out in the way of earthly sacrifice.

What is the world to me
With all its vaunted pleasure
When Thou, and Thou alone,
Lord Jesus, art my Treasure!
Thou only, dearest Lord,

My soul's Delight shalt be;
Thou art my Peace, my Rest—
What is the world to me! Amen.

(*TLH* 430:1)

Tuesday

Read Matthew 16:26

A TRUE CHRISTIAN is not what most people think he is. Some suppose a Christian distinguishes himself from others merely by guarding himself against all coarse sins, declining to participate in the amusements of the world, hearing and reading God's Word more diligently than others, and, of course, patiently waiting for Christ's return. This notion, however, is completely false. A person can do all of these things and still not be a true Christian. As Saint Paul writes, in Christ Jesus "neither circumcision counts for anything, nor uncircumcision, but a new creation" (Galatians 6:15).

A true Christian is a new creation, a new person who has been inwardly changed, in both heart and mind, by the Holy Spirit. This change shows itself chiefly in his attitude toward sin. A true Christian wants to recognize ever more thoroughly and vividly everything that is sin according to God's Word, and he hates and fears even the seemingly smallest sins in word, in deed, and in desire. For this reason, his main concern upon awakening each morning is to keep himself that day from every sin, no matter how small it may seem. Whenever he is tempted to sin, he thinks, "How then can I do this great wickedness and sin against God?" (Genesis 39:9).

One mark of a true Christian, then, is not just that he does not wish to enrich himself through some sinful activity, but also that he would prefer to endure the greatest loss to keep the burden of something sinful from his conscience. If he is deceived with counterfeit money or buys something defective, for example, he does not try to make good on his loss by getting even. Instead he endures the loss so he will not risk committing a sin. If he is uncertain about whether he can make a gain in a certain situation without sinning, he is not content with the possibility that it might not be sinful. He forgoes the doubtful in order to do only that which he knows is proper. And he keeps company with those who think just as he does in this regard, lest he face another temptation in bad advice.

Regarding earthly goods, then, the true Christian is governed by today's text: "For what will it profit a man if he gains the whole world and forfeits his life? Or what shall a man give in return for his life?" (Matthew 16:26). Speculation that could reward him handsomely in earthly goods although it bothers his conscience, or contemplating a sin by which he could avoid a great loss and be easily excused by man is regarded by him as a trap laid by the world, flesh, and the devil. And he flees from this as from the jaws of hell opening before him.

The world, of course, will regard him as a fool. But what does that matter? In eternity, everyone will see who made the wiser choice. There, many false Christians will wish they could hide their gains from God's eyes, gains to which sin clings like an unwashable bloodstain. The sinful gain will then hang around their neck like a boulder, pulling them into the abyss of hell. This will be the portion for all hypocrites, while the one who, for God's sake, refused the risky gain and endured the loss for the sake of the joy of his conscience, will see that loss converted into imperishable riches that will last for all eternity.

Hence, all earthly treasure!
Jesus is my Pleasure,
Jesus is my Choice.
Hence, all empty glory!
Naught to me thy story
Told with tempting voice.
Pain or loss, Or shame or cross,
Shall not from my Savior move me
Since He deigns to love me. Amen.

(TLH 347:4)

Wednesday

Read Psalm 38:18

THE IMPENITENT PERSON who is not anxious about his sins is more than happy to join the chorus that proclaims, "We are all sinners; we are all poor, weak men; each one has his faults." When such a person joins in this song, he thinks he has enough knowledge of his sins. The anguish over sin that dwells in the heart of a penitent person shows itself differently. This individual is in no way satisfied with coldly joining in the confession of the whole world. He is anxious to recognize his sin rightly. To do this, he examines all the works of his daily life to see if he has done and is doing what God's Word commands in the vocation and position in which God has placed him. He examines himself to see if he has fulfilled all of his duties as a spouse, parent, employee, boss, citizen, member of his congregation, and the like. He examines even his seemingly good works to make sure they were not grounded in evil motive or impure purpose, such as self-advancement or self-praise. He asks himself if he has left undone some good he could have and should have done. And he does not stop with works. He also reviews his words, his thoughts, and his desires—everything, in fact, in his heart—to make sure nothing in his behavior contradicts the Word of God.

A penitent and godly person needs to conduct this self-examination with a hearty and sincere earnestness. He turns to God and implores Him for the enlightenment and desire of His Holy Spirit. Thus he will daily find a multitude of great and serious sins in himself.

His anguish over sins also consists in making certain he obtains forgiveness. When the impenitent person remembers his sins, he usually comforts himself by thinking God is kind and therefore He will not be so particular, or that he will improve, or even that the presence of Jesus in the world means an individual doesn't need to worry about sins.

The penitent person knows otherwise. He knows God is indeed particular. He knows his future improvement does not exonerate him from past sins. He knows that hasty thoughts about Jesus do not constitute faith. He refuses to build the forgiveness of sins upon such an uncertain and false foundation. To him, the forgiveness of his sins is the most necessary, important, and precious thing in this world. Therefore, he says, "I must become certain of my state of grace with God. It may cost me a great price, but what does it help me if I win the whole world yet lose my soul?" Therefore, he diligently reads God's Word, listens to evangelical preaching, and inquires of experienced pastors and other longtime Christians how he can be certain he has God's forgiveness. When he hears he must simply believe in the Word, which offers the forgiveness of sins to all people, he does not soothe himself with a fleeting devotion to Jesus. Instead, he turns to God in prayer and implores, "O God, give me the right faith in Your Word. Protect me from empty self-deception. Let Your Word of grace sink to the bottom of my heart so I may know You have also received me. Give me the testimony of Your Holy Ghost!" Such a penitent person does not rest until he knows for certain that his faith is no self-deception, that by it he has truly grasped Christ and His righteousness, that his sins have been forgiven by God's grace, and that he has been received as a child of God.

Whoever truly anguishes over his sins does not think he has reached his goal even if he already knows his sins are forgiven. His anguish displays itself, finally, in his seeing to it that he is completely cleansed and redeemed. When the impenitent person believes he has obtained forgiveness for his sins, he becomes secure. The penitent person, on the other hand, can finally cry, "I am under grace!" But he immediately adds, "What shall I render to the LORD for all His benefits to me?" (Psalm 116:12). He capitalizes on his holy intentions, praising God's eternal faithfulness. He then conspires with his heart and all his faculties against sin and the world. He relinquishes his sins and fights against them with all earnestness. He even asks other Christians to admonish him and chastise him in order to keep him on the proper path. He goes out of his way to avoid temptations, watching and praying that he does not succumb to those he cannot avoid. He also faithfully uses the means that keep him upright. He walks in hearty fear and sacrifices his whole life to his Savior and brethren. If he stumbles again, he is deeply grieved and quickly casts himself down before God and asks for grace.

Let us take to heart the words of David in today's reading!

Create my nature pure within
And form my soul averse to sin;
Let Thy good Spirit ne'er depart
Nor hide Thy presence from my heart.

I cannot live without Thy light,
Cast out and banished from Thy sight;
Thy holy joys, my God, restore
And guard me that I fall no more. Amen.

† *(TLH 325:2, 3)*

Thursday

Read Matthew 18:7

One of the greatest and strongest dangers and temptations for Christians to depart from the path of godliness is the evil example set by the children of this world. It is easy enough to see that, for the most part, it goes well for the children of the world in their sinful life. They hurry from desire to desire, and from pleasure to pleasure. Those who care nothing about God and His Word are among the most loved and honored people in the world. Even those who are not conscientious in their trade seem to profit thereby. By this enticing appearance of earthly happiness, which surrounds the children of the world, many a pious person is blinded, deceived, and tempted to fall into sin.

Many such believers were faithful for a time, looking to God and their Savior, but like Eve at the forbidden tree, they were overcome by their eyes of desire as they gazed upon the apparent happiness of the children of the world and said to themselves: "Why do I still plague myself with piety? Behold, all these, too, want to be saved and still enjoy the world, and God lets it go well with them. I don't want to be a fool any longer!" The glory of the world is a great attraction, especially to the young. Many of them were raised as Christians who carried the Lord Jesus in their hearts long before they learned to recognize the pleasures of the world. But once they tasted those pleasures, they readily fell away. Saint Paul writes about one young Christian whose godly walk and desire to become a preaching helper to the apostle went awry. His name was Demas, and Paul says of him, "For Demas, in love with this present world, has deserted me" (2 Timothy 4:10).

For this reason, Saint John admonishes his spiritual children: "Do not love the world or the things in the world. If anyone loves the world, the love of the Father is not in him. For all that is in the world—the desires of the flesh and the desires of the eyes and pride in possessions—is not from the Father but is from the world. And the world is passing away along with its desires, but whoever does the will of God abides forever" (1 John 2:15–17). Christ Himself warns, even more earnestly, of the tempting example of the world in the words of today's reading, which He prefaces with this caution: "but whoever causes one of these little ones who believe in Me to sin, it would be better for him to have a great millstone fastened around his neck and to be drowned in the depth of the sea" (Matthew 18:6).

We must not think that the evil example of the world is such a strong temptation that a Christian, by God's grace and power, cannot resist it. Oh, no! Countless people in the midst of the severest temptations of the world have remained faithful to their God. The Bible offers some examples. Lot and his family were in grave danger of falling away in the rich but godless city of Sodom, but he remained true to His God. So also was Joseph tempted from the path of godliness in the company of his brothers and in the plotting of Potiphar's lewd wife, but he stood firm, saying, "How then can I do this great wickedness and sin against God?" (Genesis 39:9). Moses, too, was surrounded by the idolatry and voluptuousness of the Egyptian court in which he was raised. He might well have fallen away from the religion of his fathers and become ashamed of his despised Israelite brethren according to the flesh. But it says of him in the Epistle to the Hebrews, "By faith Moses, when he was grown up, refused to be called the son of Pharaoh's daughter, choosing rather to be mistreated with the people of God than to enjoy the fleeting pleasures of sin. He considered the reproach of Christ greater wealth than the treasures of Egypt, for he was looking to the reward" (11:24–26).

Watch and pray, watch and pray!
Zion, ever watch and pray
Lest the wicked world misguide thee
From the narrow path to stray
And thy God reprove and chide thee.
Zion, work with zeal while it is day.
Watch and pray, watch and pray! Amen.

† *(TLH 479:3)*

Friday

Read Romans 6:19–21

THERE CANNOT BE a more faithful and vivid picture of the true condition of slavery to sin than that which Saint Paul, by the inspiration of the Holy Ghost, has sketched here.

As long as a person has not, from his heart, turned to God, he continues to serve sin, not by force, but freely. A servant of sin is a slave who does not hate sin, his master, but instead loves it with his whole heart. He is driven to the service of sin more by his heart and inner preference than by outward compulsion. The servants of sin do not serve sluggishly and carelessly, but are highly diligent and untiring in their service. Whoever is engaged in sin carries in his heart the desire to perform it day and night. Therefore, wherever the servant of sin finds an opportunity to engage in it, he seizes this chance without first considering it.

It is remarkable that despite the difficult and disgraceful situations in which the servants of sin find themselves, they continue to serve with joy and avoid no sacrifice they must endure on its behalf. This seems incomprehensible, yet it is so. Sin is the cruelest of tyrants, and it makes its servants the most accursed of slaves. Yet they serve it willingly! The sensual person sacrifices the health of his body as well as the peace of his soul to indulge in his sins, and for the purchase of a single hour of pleasure, he endures a life of misery. The drunkard also sacrifices his health in pursuing his pleasure, but that often comes at the expense of his family's happiness, the loss of his good name, and the incurring of the deepest shame and contempt. The covetous person, in order to serve sin, denies himself refreshment and exerts himself day and night, sometimes dying in the process and leaving to his heirs the fruits of his worries. As these examples demonstrate, no one serves a crueler master or lives in such miserable slavery as the servant of sin.

To what end does a person thus serve sin? Is the final reward so glorious it outweighs all the troubles of the service? Oh, no! The most terrible thing about serving sin is the meager payment one receives for his hard service. For what is the wages of sin? It is, as Saint Paul says in today's text, eternal death and damnation. O shameful payment! O bitter fruit! O horrible end! If, during his earthly life, the servant of sin has to sacrifice the health of his body, rest and refreshment, peace of conscience, good name—in short, everything that has value in this life—what lays in store for such an individual as the end of his life draws near? Will sin merely dismiss its servant without paying him? No; the wages are only more torment: on his deathbed, the sinner is taunted with a foretaste of hell. Sin then reminds the sinner how he has wantonly transgressed God's eternal Law, angered and offended Him, and taken upon himself God's wrath and curse. If at that time the sinner wants to turn to God, sin gleefully cries, "It is too late!" and the sinner, standing before the gates of eternity, is cast into a hell of doubt. Then, when that tormented person wrests himself free from the body covered with the cold sweat of death, sin accompanies him even to the throne of God, where it accuses him, recounting every evil thing the person did or even thought in life. At that time, of course, it is indeed too late. The time of grace, the time of repentance and conversion, has passed. All requests and sighs and tears of the servant of sin will prove futile. God, who is righteous, will pronounce the sentence of eternal death and damnation over him. Then sin will take its pale, trembling servant, carry him away from the presence of God, and cast him into the furthest darkness, where there will be weeping and gnashing of teeth. At last, he will be tossed into the fiery sea, where the smoke of his torment will ascend forever.

This is the horrifying but true picture the holy apostle draws to show how the service of those who traffic in sin will be rewarded.

Grant steadfastness and courage
That bravely we contend
Against the wiles of Satan;

O Lord, Thy flock defend!
Help us to battle well,
To triumph o'er the devil,
To overcome the evil
And all the powers of hell. Amen.

(ELHB 252: 12)

Saturday

Read Romans 6:22–23

IF A PERSON truly wants to be a Christian, he must always fight against sin, watch and pray, and strive after sanctification. At the same time he often has to endure ridicule and disgrace. Some Christians are troubled by this thought, especially when they see how well things appear to go for the children of the world. Asaph found himself in this position, and he noted: "But as for me, my feet had almost stumbled, my steps had nearly slipped. For I was envious of the arrogant when I saw the prosperity of the wicked. … All in vain have I kept my heart clean and washed my hands in innocence. For all the day long I have been stricken and rebuked every morning" (Psalm 73:2–3, 13–14).

Christians who struggle with this should look more closely at the children of the world and their service. If, in contemplating their own difficulties, they are tempted to conclude that the children of the world are more fortunate, they should consider this: Do not the children of the world have to serve, just as Christians do? And what lord do they serve? Sin, the most horrible and vile tyrant, the mother of all misery in the world. And what does the Christian do? He serves the Lord, who is most worthy of love. He is the highest good, the source of all holiness, and the fountain of all blessings. Now if the world serves its vile lord so zealously, shouldn't Christians serve their Lord even more zealously? If the servants of sin serve so eagerly, shouldn't Christians be much more diligent in their service to God? Moreover, what do the children of the world have for all their service? Aside from a few hours of sinful pleasures, the fruit of their service is the destruction of their soul and body, their goods and honor. These are replaced by anxiety, unrest of conscience, sickness, poverty, and shame.

And how is it with Christians, by contrast? Although their service to righteousness is not performed without some suffering and disgrace before man, the fruit they receive in return is peace and joy in their heart and conscience, the certainty of divine pleasure and protection, and honor with God and with all the children of God. Now if the world serves sin so faithfully despite the bitter fruit it harvests, shouldn't Christians serve righteousness with even greater faithfulness? Thus they will be happy even in the midst of outward misfortune, rich in soul even if they reside in bodily poverty, and divinely joyful even in the presence of earthly sadness.

The main thing is this: If the world serves sin without finding true joy and true peace, what does it find instead? It is death, rejection from heaven, and eternal agony in the flames of hell. The children of the world do not want to believe this, of course. Nevertheless, it is unceasingly preached to them, they read it in Holy Scripture, and even their conscience proclaims it, sometimes so loudly they fall into anxiety and sorrow over it.

And what is the end Christians can expect from their service to righteousness? They cannot earn eternal life, but God, in His kindness, gives it to His faithful servants as a gift of free grace for Christ's sake. O blessed, glorious end! You Christians who groan under your burden, consider: The children of the world earn eternal death and hell with a heavy and shameful service to sin. To you, by contrast, eternal life and heaven will be a free gift of grace after you complete your honorable service to righteousness. Therefore, do not let it be said that the world brings more sacrifices to its disgraceful lord, sin and death, than you do to your good Lord, your God and Savior, who saves you by His grace. Do not let the world work more untiringly, suffer more patiently, and struggle more earnestly, only to gain hell, than you do to enter heaven. The world devotes itself to sin with its whole heart. You, however, need to give your heart totally to God.

Faith and hope and charity
Graciously, O Father, give me;
Be my Guardian constantly
That the devil may not grieve me;
Grant me humbleness and gladness,
Peace and patience in my sadness. Amen.

† *(TLH 411:6)*

Sunday

Read Matthew 7:15

IN THESE LAST DAYS, there are people who, although they have been baptized in Christ, deny His divinity and atonement, slander the triune God, and declare the Bible to be a book of fables. These are wolves in wolves' clothing. If a person blasphemes the Most High, he must already have lost the true faith from his heart and wantonly turned away from God. A Christian can protect himself against such prophets of Satan.

These individuals are not the subject of today's reading. Jesus is talking about the most dangerous false prophets, those who have a good appearance. If Satan wants to lead the children of God astray, he disguises himself as an angel of light. If the wolf wants to go into the flock, it puts on sheep's clothing.

What Jesus is saying here is that true prophets appeal to God's Word in all their doctrines. But if a person appeals to God's Word, teaches the divine truth in many places, and pretends to announce nothing but the pure doctrine of the Bible, he should not immediately be embraced as a true prophet. Be wary, Jesus suggests; he may be a wolf in sheep's clothing. Heretics in the Church have always appealed to Scripture. Even the prince of darkness, when he wanted to tempt the Son of God, said, "For it is written," (Luke 4:10), but the Lord answered him, "It is said, 'You shall not put the Lord your God to the test.' " (Luke 4:12). Therefore, if the Scripture is held out to someone, he should be careful. By testing the offered doctrine against Scripture, he will soon discover whether an individual is to be believed.

True prophets do not appoint themselves. Instead, they are rightly called to their office by the Christian congregation. If a preacher appeals to the office to which God has assigned him, one should not reject that office since it remains mighty and valid even if a Pharisee or Sadducee holds it. But we must not be deceived here. Perhaps the preacher's office is only sheep's clothing. The call can be right but the doctrine can be false. If those who are rightly called turn out to be wolves, Christ orders us to flee from them.

True prophets should walk in a godly way. They should be

examples to the flock. If we see a preacher who walks around in outward piety and holiness, who is friendly toward everyone, gentle toward his offenders, charitable toward the poor, helpful to those who are mired in misery and misfortune, diligent in his office and calling, and unselfish in all of his activities, we should certainly not reject him. But we still must be wary because all of this may be sheep's clothing.

The life of a teacher can be blameless before men, but his teaching can still be objectionable. What help is his shining life if his preaching leads people away from simple faith in Jesus Christ? Countless inexperienced people have seen an appearance of holiness, zealousness, love, and humility and have been overcome by it. They think that, with all this evidence of goodness, true Christian doctrine must also be present. But it is not necessarily so. They see the sheep's clothing and are enticed by it, but when they give themselves up to it, they may discover a wolf hidden inside and thus their souls are torn and ruined.

God often endows true prophets with great gifts of the Spirit. We may hear a preacher with shining gifts, whose eloquence shakes the hardest of hearts, who knows how to move even the most sluggish individuals to great zeal in pious exercises, and who shows a deep knowledge of Christian doctrine. This preacher may console the despondent, comfort the distressed, and refute certain arguments conclusively. But we must not be deceived by this. False prophets can also have great natural gifts. These gifts are sheep's clothing and we must be cautious of them.

No matter how great an appearance is offered by a shepherd in terms of his knowledge of the Word of God, his office and call, the holiness of his life, and his gifts of the Spirit, Christians should not let themselves be deceived. Oh, let us remember the words of Christ in today's reading and be ever on our guard!

The haughty spirits, Lord, restrain
Who o'er Thy Church with might would reign
And always set forth something new,
Devised to change Thy doctrine true.

And since the cause and glory, Lord,
Are Thine, not ours, to us afford
Thy help and strength and constancy.
With all our heart we trust in Thee. Amen.

† *(TLH 292:6, 7)*

Monday

Read Matthew 7:16–23

WITH THE WORDS of today's reading, Christ appears to teach that true prophets are recognized by their good works. When He speaks about fruits a teacher should bring, the first fruits are not the fruits of life but the fruits of doctrine. If a teacher does not bring the fruit of pure doctrine, he is a false prophet. The teacher sent by God is the one who proclaims to poor sinners that His dear Son, Jesus Christ, is the only way to salvation. For this is the will of the heavenly Father, "that everyone who looks on the Son and believes in Him should have eternal life" (John 6:40). Saint John says, "By this you know the Spirit of God: every spirit that confesses that Jesus Christ has come in the flesh is from God, and every spirit that does not confess Jesus is not from God" (1 John 4:2–3). A called teacher who does the will of God, purely preaching His Son to the world, is a true prophet, for to Christ "all the prophets bear witness that everyone who believes in Him receives forgiveness of sins" (Acts 10:43). But where souls are not helped because the preaching about Christ has been impure, there are false prophets, no matter how wise, gifted, or holy they may seem. Christ says, "Many will say to Me, 'Lord, Lord, did we not prophesy in Your name, and cast out demons in Your name, and do many mighty works in Your name?' And then will I declare to them, 'I never knew you; depart from me, you workers of lawlessness'" (Matthew 7:22–23).

Wherever false teachers have arisen, they have always lacked one thing. They have not proclaimed Christ alone, how He was made by God to be our wisdom, our righteousness, our sanctification, and our redemption. But where this article of faith has been preached correctly, all soul-destroying errors have retreated like the fog before the sun. If an individual's preaching shows people how they can come to Christ, remain with Him, suffer with Him, and die blessed through Him, they are listening to a true prophet. For if they receive Christ, they have received enough. If they have Him, they have everything.

A pious life that is not accompanied by pure doctrine cannot make a true prophet. On the contrary, the godly life of the orthodox preacher is a glorious confirmation and ornament of pure doctrine. The good works of a false teacher are like the passing flower on thorn bushes, but the good works of a pure teacher are good fruits of a good tree. For "a healthy tree cannot bear bad fruit, nor can a diseased tree bear good fruit" (Matthew 7:18).

Wherever pure doctrine is preached, some listeners will not take it to heart, but at least a few of them will become fruitful trees of righteousness and produce the fruits of the Spirit, "love, joy, peace, patience, kindness, goodness, faithfulness, gentleness, self-control" (Galatians 5:22–23). Wherever false prophets prevail, a person may show much love but it will be limited, displaying a love only for those who belong to the party. But when the love of God, through the Gospel, is poured out into a person's heart, that person will love both those who follow Christ and the erring and fallen, his fellow-redeemed.

Grant honor, truth, and purity,
And love Thy Word to ponder;
From all false doctrine keep me free.
Bestow, both here and yonder,
What serves my everlasting bliss;
Preserve me from unrighteousness
Thro' out my earthly journey. Amen.

(TLH 406:2)

Tuesday

Read 1 Corinthians 11:19

THE CHURCH OF GOD on earth has always been a fighting one. It has always been oppressed and persecuted, both by those in the world and by those in the Church itself who spread false doctrine. These false prophets secure followers and then cause separations in the Church. In the Church of Adam, self-righteous Cain stirred up dissension; in the Church of Noah, it was Ham, who despised his father; in the Church of Abraham, it was Ishmael the mocker; in the Church of the prophets, there were many who falsely comforted the people and led them into idolatry. Even in the apostolic Church, in almost every place where the Gospel was preached, heretics arose to stir up schisms and even to destroy flourishing congregations. Saint Paul names among them Alexander the smith, Hymenaeus, and Philetus, and Saint John accuses the entire sect of the Nicolaitans. And so this tension continues to the present day. Satan has never been content to let the Church be in peaceful possession of its heavenly goods; wherever pure doctrine has been preached, opponents have arisen to challenge it. For this reason, the Church has always had to use the Word of God, not only as nourishment for the soul, but also as a weapon to combat the instruction of false teachers. If the Church ceases to fight, it will not survive for long. For just as the springtime sun coaxes both the plants and the vermin out of their wintry sleep, so too does Satan arise with the blessed preaching of God's Word in an attempt to sow his weeds amid the wheat and thereby suffocate it.

We may ask why God would allow His flock to be fed by true shepherds and, at the same time, attacked by wolves cunningly disguised as shepherds in order to seize the sheep and tear them to pieces. Since God can prevent this, why doesn't He? Scripture supplies two reasons. God allows this both to test His children and to punish unthankful hearers. Saint Paul tells the Corinthians, "For there must be factions among you in order that those who are genuine among you may be recognized" (1 Corinthians 11:19). If the jewel of pure doctrine were never disputed, those who firmly hold to it would never be recognized. However, if false teachers and enthusiasts appear in the Church, it becomes obvious who believes in the pure Word. In this confrontational atmosphere, the faith of the upright is tested and confirmed. If the pure doctrine were never attacked, Christians would soon become lazy, lax, and lukewarm. Whenever people deviate from God's Word, the faithful are driven to investigate it more diligently and carefully, paying attention to every word. When a pure teacher is challenged by those who promote other doctrines, he will search the Scriptures and thereby grow in divine knowledge and certainty. Therefore, heretics are nothing but the whetstone of the Church by which it learns to use the sword of the Spirit all the more sharply.

God knows how to lead the evil to good. However, He often carries out His severest judgment through false teachers. God often sends His faithful servants to another country or another church for a time. People there may have little regard for the pure preaching that results. They do not thank God for these ministers, they continue to regard earthly goods as of more value than the pure Word and Sacrament, they begin to be ashamed of the right doctrine before the world, and after hearing the Word with a sleepy heart, they finally come to despise it. Then God permits these unthankful souls to lose their heavenly treasure. Those who despise the bread of the precious divine Word must be fed with the stones of man's powerless doctrines. Thus Saint Paul speaks about Christians in the last times, "they refused to love the truth and so be saved. Therefore God sends them a strong delusion, so that they may believe what is false" (2 Thessalonians 2:10–11).

Preserve, O Lord, Thy children,
Thine own blest heritage;
Resist, disperse, and scatter
Those who against Thee rage.
Let Thy commandments guide us,
Grant us Thy heav'nly food;
Clothe us in Thy rich garments,
Bought with Thy precious blood. Amen.

(TLH 264:4)

Wednesday

Read 1 Peter 2:2

IT IS IMPOSSIBLE for a person to become a Christian without the Word of God, and it is just as impossible for him to remain in the faith without it. For this reason, Saint Peter calls Scripture the imperishable seed from which one is born again, and also the pure milk by which newborn children are enabled to grow to a saving knowledge and a true faith. If we want to retain this spiritual life, this right knowledge, and this true faith, it must happen by the precious Word of God. Our body requires daily nourishment, and so does our soul, lest it sink back into spiritual death. No earthly fire maintains itself, and in like manner, the heavenly fire of true faith is soon extinguished if it is not fed daily by Holy Scripture. A person may stand for a time in a great zeal for godliness, and the bright light of a saving knowledge may burn in him, but if he becomes lazy in using Scripture, neglecting to read it or hear it for weeks and even months, his zeal will grow cold and the old darkness will again cover his soul. If he then ceases to associate with the Bible, he is bound to experience a complete fall from divine grace.

A Christian who recognizes his own weakness and corruption knows how easily a person can become lukewarm and forget the danger of losing his soul. He will also know how necessary it is for him to contemplate Scripture daily so his heart is continually awakened to receive its instruction, exhortation, warning, and comfort. It is all too easy to be led away by the laziness of the flesh, but if the Christian will take care to consider, earnestly and attentively, something from God's Word on a daily basis, he will not easily lose his way from the path of truth and godliness.

Therefore, God said to Joshua, "This Book of the Law shall not depart from your mouth, but you shall meditate on it day and night, so that you may be careful to do according to all that is written in it. For then you will make your way prosperous, and then you will have good success" (1:8). David calls, "Blessed is the man who walks not in the counsel of the wicked, nor stands in the way of sinners, nor sits in the seat of scoffers; but his delight is in the law of the LORD, and on His law he meditates day and night. He is like a tree planted by streams of water that yields its fruit in its season, and its leaf does not wither. In all that he does, he prospers" (Psalm 1:1–3). And, "if Your law had not been my delight, I would have perished in my affliction. . . . Your word is a lamp to my feet and a light to my path" (Psalm 119:92,105).

The apostles call to converted Christians, "Let the word of Christ dwell in you richly, teaching and admonishing one another in all wisdom, singing psalms and hymns and spiritual songs, with thankfulness in your hearts to God" (Colossians 3:16). They also show, by their own example, how necessary it is for converted Christians to continue to receive admonition and encouragement from the Holy Scriptures. The Epistles are the clearest evidence of this.

O grant that from my very heart
My foes be all forgiven;
Forgive my sins and heal their smart,
And grant new life from heaven.
Thy Word, that blessed food, bestow,
Which best the soul can nourish;
Make it flourish
Through all the storms of woe
That else my faith might overthrow. Amen.

(ELHB 365:3)

Thursday

Read Romans 8:12

SAINT PAUL had the same sad experiences in preaching the Gospel that its proclaimers encounter today. He preached that a person is saved not by works but by grace alone through faith in Christ Jesus. Many who wanted to be Christians were pleased by that precious, comforting doctrine, but they then misused it in carnal security and regarded their sin lightly. "Now then," many of them said, "if we cannot earn heaven by any work, if everything is grace alone, then there is no danger in sin. It would indeed be foolish to battle with sin. If we wanted to call in our last hour, 'Lord Jesus, have mercy on me,' we would still have heaven."

In his Epistle to the Romans, Paul squarely confronts this horrible misuse of the doctrine of grace. He attempts to show, in various ways, that the grace of God offers us forgiveness of sin but in no way grants us permission to sin. In fact, the final goal of the grace that God established in Christ for our redemption, atonement, deliverance, and salvation is that we might be wholly cleansed from sin and perfectly hallowed by His Spirit. In that way, the divine image might be restored in us and our spirit might again become capable of eternal perfect union with the Holy Ghost.

Today's text marks Paul's effort to incite the Christians in Rome to a holy walk. It is a reminder to them that they are still truly obligated to God. Jesus came into the world to save sinners. They need not lose heart, even if their sins are especially great and terrible. With their works, they can earn nothing. Nothing except faith in Christ makes them blessed and righteous. God has freely offered grace and forgiveness for all their sins. Why, then, do they want to insist on abusing that precious gift to persevere in sin? Why would they want to anger God anew when He has expressed His desire to forgive and forget everything? Should a continued effort to serve fleshly desires and despise God be the thanks He receives?

If we can earn nothing by works, it is equally certain that we are in debt to God. After all, He created us. Everything we have—body, soul, and life—is His gift to us. Does not this alone make us His debtors and obligate us to serve Him with all our energies and faculties? But even this is not enough. God has made us His debtors in another sense as well. By sin, we fell away from Him and entered the kingdom of death and eternal damnation. But behold! God has graciously received us once again. He gave His Son for us that He might bring us back into His blessed kingdom and receive us into it. Thus we are doubly in debt to God. He has done great things for us, granting us life and rescuing us from eternal corruption by surrendering His Son into death. Is He worthy of no thanks for all of this? By what right are we entitled to reply, "since I cannot earn heaven with works, I won't do any"? No, no! We are truly bound to live according to God's Word and not according to our own flesh. Since everything is by grace alone, God must be our God and our souls must be His sacrifice and property.

Oh, grant that in Thy holy Word
We here may live and die, dear Lord;
And when our journey endeth here,
Receive us into glory there. Amen.

(*TLH* 292:9)

Friday

Read Romans 8:13–14

IN TODAY'S READING, Saint Paul reminds us that true Christians continue to be tempted by all kinds of evil thoughts and desires. However, they have within them a new spirit, a new divine power, a new holy impulse that sets itself unceasingly against the desire to sin. The heart of a true Christian is no longer dead. He no longer willingly obeys the promptings of his flesh and blood, but instead he constantly battles sinful lusts, suppressing and overcoming them. To be sure, sin does not give the true Christian an hour's rest, but as soon as it arises in the heart, the good spirit dwelling therein is active to meet the invading enemy.

Whoever does not stand in this constant battle of flesh and spirit, knowing grace in his mind but not in his heart, is devoid of all spiritual life. If he does not fight against sinful impulses, sin will continue to rule over him, rendering him spiritually dead and eventually wresting his hope of eternal life from him. To such a person, eternal death is already adjudged, and he can only abandon the sweet dream that he stands in God's grace. As Paul says, "For if you live according to the flesh you will die" (Romans 8:13).

Eternal judgment is irrevocably pronounced on all false Christians. If they still live according to the flesh, if sin remains so dear to them that they do not earnestly want to kill it, God declares that it is they who will die. With their love of sin and their false reliance on God's grace, they have rejected true grace, voluntarily renouncing the redemption of Jesus Christ, who came to free them from the prison of sin and to destroy the works of the devil. Oh, foolishness! They want to comfort themselves with the redemption of Christ while remaining a servant of sin. Oh, foolishness! They retain the hope of eternal life while they daily sink ever deeper into the death of sin. Oh, foolishness! They want to dream about grace while they daily provoke God's wrath against them by their sins. What good does cleansing by the blood of Jesus do them if they insist on daily polluting themselves again? Of what value is the cross of Christ when they do not desire to crucify their flesh, but instead continue to crucify Christ by their walk according to the flesh? If Christ were to die a thousand times more for the sin of the world, it would still be impossible for a person who continues in sin to attain heaven and salvation.

With the closing words of today's reading, Paul gives us a new touchstone of our Christianity. If we want to be Christians, we must declare ourselves to be children of God. But children of God are those who are led by the Spirit of God. Oh, how the reputation of many Christians defies these words! What kind of spirit leads us to works of the flesh? It is truly not the Spirit of God, but the evil spirit, the spirit of uncleanness, of darkness, of the world and sin. Wherever this spirit leads the heart, there is no grace and it is futile to boast that one is a Christian. As Paul emphasizes, only those who are led by the Spirit of God are sons of God. Therefore, let each of us ask this question: "Which spirit leads me?" Only one spirit can rule over us. It is either the spirit of sin or the Spirit of God. If the Spirit does not continually awaken us, chastise us, and guide us, He cannot be dwelling in our heart, and we must confess that we are being led by our own spirit—to our peril.

Create in me a new heart, Lord,
That gladly I obey Thy Word
And naught but what Thou wilt, desire;
With such new life my soul inspire. Amen.

(*TLH 398:3*)

Saturday

Read Romans 8:15–17

WHAT SAINT PAUL SAYS in today's text is this: If neither the obligation to serve God nor the certainty that he is going astray can move a person to give up the sinful life according to the flesh, then he should be motivated by the condition of those who walk according to the Spirit as children of God. Their condition is exceedingly blessed and glorious. Whoever sins against his conscience strives in vain to maintain a childlike confidence in God and to believe that God's threats against sin will not come upon him. For a time, he may enjoy a false comfort and a false peace, but they are only temporary. Soon the wounds of sin, inwardly festering, break forth with a pain that is greater than before. A single word can penetrate so deeply into the hypocrite's soul that all at once he sees the complete nothingness of his self-made faith, his imagined hope, and his false comfort. Out of habit, he may bend his knee for prayer or sigh to God in servile fear, but he is in no state to unburden his heart before God in childlike confidence. He pretends to love God, but his heart is full of servile fear before Him. The Law of God, with all its threats, still lies upon him, and if he does not change his ways, death will eventually lead him into an accursed eternity that is horrible above all imagining.

But whoever, in his alarm over sin, does not wait until the hour of his death, but instead recognizes the magnitude of his sin and his worthiness of condemnation, can be led by the Holy Ghost, through the Gospel, to Christ. Then, by the power of faith, he will be strengthened daily so as to kill sin in himself, crucifying his fleshly desires and walking in truth and righteousness. Such a person has protection against all accusations of his conscience, and peace and rest for his soul. He can daily approach God as his dear heavenly Father. If he is in trouble, God is his refuge and his help, and he knows God will never forsake him. If he falls again into sin because of his weakness, he quickly hurries to God and is reconciled to Him by Christ's blood. Then he can comfort himself with God's grace and forgiveness. Everything else may condemn and reject him, but he can remain joyful because the Spirit of God gives him an assurance that conquers everything else: He is God's child.

How blessed, therefore, are all who rightly bear the name "children of God" (Romans 8:16)! They do not need to envy the world and its glory, for their glory is greater. They can laugh at sin, Satan, and death because they have overcome them all. They need not fear the future, for if God is on their side, who can be against them?

Nevertheless, on earth, the life of the children of God is still hidden with Christ in God. The world has no idea of the Christian's glory and blessedness. But when Christ reveals that life, then everyone will know of it. This is why Saint Paul says at the close of today's reading, "And if children, then heirs—heirs of God and fellow heirs with Christ, provided we suffer with Him in order that we may also be glorified with Him" (Romans 8:17). Oh, let us long for that glorious day when God will break open the seal of His eternal testament and distribute the heavenly inheritance among His children! In the meantime, let us be faithful until death, that we, too, may obtain the crown of life. Let us cling to Christ, who grants us aid in life and in death.

For He can plead for me with sighings
That are unspeakable to lips like mine;
He bids me pray with earnest cryings,

Bears witness with my soul that I am Thine,
Joint heir with Christ, and thus may dare to say:
O heav'nly Father, hear me when I pray! Amen.

(*TLH* 21:4)

Sunday

Read Luke 16:1–2

FROM THE MOMENT mankind fell, the reason for man's destruction has been that he wants to be his own lord. Every person, by nature, thinks or lives as if he were convinced he is an absolute lord over everything that belongs to him. If someone has excellent gifts, a wonderful knowledge, and the like, he thinks these are his property and he can therefore appropriate them for his own use, his own glory, and his own desire. No one, he believes, is allowed to ask him, "What are you doing?"

This is especially true with a person's earthly goods. If he has gained something by the work of his hands, by exchange, by inheritance, or as a gift, he thinks he is free to act according to his pleasure and can say, like God, "Do I not have the power to do what I want with my own?" But what does the Lord say about this in our Gospel? He speaks a parable to the disciples, which He begins with the words, "There was a rich man who had a manager" (Luke 16:1). According to this, what is man in relation to his temporal goods? He is not a lord of everything he has, but merely a steward, a manager. The Lord of all things is God and man in himself is desperately poor. Before God, he can call nothing his own except his guilt of sin. His body and his soul are not his, but the Lord's alone. Indeed, a person has nothing from himself. Whatever he has, he has from God. It is God's gift, and God can take it back at any moment. God makes rich and makes poor. He raises and humbles. He gives and takes as it pleases Him. Therefore, everything a person has is only a good God has lent and entrusted to him for management. Although someone may have many thousands or even millions of dollars at his disposal, he is only God's treasurer with respect to that money. He may have a very profitable business and a great stock, but he is still only God's steward. Although he may live in many houses and palaces and show indisputable title to great stretches of land, he is nevertheless only God's tenant and leaseholder.

Why, then, does a person consider himself to be someone special merely because God has given him a good understanding or other gifts? Why does such an individual, so richly blessed by God, despise those who have not acquired similar skills and proudly look down on them? Why does he think he is worthy of special honor and able to rule over others because God has allowed him an abundance of earthly goods? A person who is proud in any of these divine gifts, instead of being humbled by them, and who despises others and exalts himself because of them, is like a treasurer who, having fallen deeply into debt, thinks he can simply take his lord's money and pay up. What could be more foolish and even more laughable than such pride?

Christ continues His parable in our text, saying, "There was a rich man who had a manager, and charges were brought to him [that is, the lord] that this man [that is, the steward] was wasting his possessions. And He called him and said to him, 'What is this that I hear about you? Turn in the account of your management, for you can no longer be manager'" (Luke 16:1–2). We see from this that because a person is only a steward of his goods, he cannot use them according to his pleasure or for his own honor. Instead, he must deal with them as with foreign goods. He must use them according to the instruction of the Lord his God, and this Lord will one day demand from him a strict accounting of the manner in which he has used His goods and gifts.

Yea, Lord, 'twas Thy rich bounty gave
My body, soul, and all I have
In this poor life of labor.
Lord, grant that I in ev'ry place
May glorify Thy lavish grace
And serve and help my neighbor.
Let no false doctrine me beguile,
Let Satan not my soul defile.
Give strength and patience unto me
To bear my cross and follow Thee.
Lord Jesus Christ,
My God and Lord, my God and Lord,
In death Thy comfort still afford. Amen.

(TLH 429:2)

Monday

Read Luke 16:3–9

WHY WOULD CHRIST praise a person who tries to help himself out of his dilemma by deception? Should He really have offered this parable as an example for His Christians to imitate?

Not at all! No, with this story, the Lord says that just as this godless man knew how to deal with the goods of his lord to guarantee his temporal future, so should a person use the goods of the Lord His God in such a way that he secures an eternal future. As godless prudence was praiseworthy before the world, so is true prudence praiseworthy before God.

If God has placed you as steward over temporal, earthly goods and gifts, the danger for you lies in that one day, having become unfaithful, you are called to give a strict account and are rejected. You have also received the only means with which you can and should acquire eternal and heavenly goods. Thus you can rejoice if God has given you a good understanding, but do not seek personal glory in this. Instead, you must be content on earth with your steward's wages, with nourishment and clothing. Turn your gift to God's glory and to the good of your neighbor, and in heaven you will find a rich eternal harvest from your brief sowing. If God has helped you to obtain a useful skill, be joyful but do not seek to use it for yourself. Rather, be content with your steward's wages of nourishment and clothing and seek to serve the world with your gift. In heaven, you will have an abundantly rich interest to enjoy from every dollar you have expended in another's service. If you hold an important office and are thereby given high honor and considerable influence, you have another cause to be joyful. But you must give back to God the glory people have given to you, being content with the nourishment and clothing that are your steward's wages. Administer your office faithfully and honestly for the well being of your brethren, and all of the difficult works you undertake for them will one day shine as pearls in your crown. Finally, if God has blessed you with all kinds of goods, rejoice. But you must protect yourself from avarice and extravagance, being content with your steward's wages of nourishment and clothing. Make use of the goods entrusted to you whenever you find opportunity to do so, and make for yourself friends in heaven with the unrighteous mammon. When you suffer want and when, one day, in death, you lose everything and leave the world as poor as you entered it, they will receive you into the eternal habitations. As you were rich in temporal goods on earth, you will be rich in the eternal treasures of heaven.

But how? Doesn't Scripture teach that a person does not gain entrance into the eternal habitations by any work, but alone by grace through faith in Christ? Isn't this parable a contradiction of the Gospel? Not at all! There can be two reasons why one day Christ will receive us into heaven: because, as the Lord of heaven, He has earned our entrance for us and, as the Servant, He will testify to our claim at the entrance. Christ alone has earned our entrance into heaven for us, but no person will be admitted unless he has witnesses that he really believed in Him. These witnesses are among our brethren whom we have served with our goods and gifts on earth.

Let us poor sinners, then, seize Christ in faith and demonstrate that faith by responsible stewardship over all the gifts and goods entrusted to us. Let us make friends for ourselves with our unrighteous mammon and with everything we have. Then, one day, we will not stand in shame before the gates of eternity. All those we have served here without selfishness will there come to us rejoicing before all the inhabitants of heaven in all the good things we have done for them. Then the Lord Himself will say to us, "Ah! You godly and faithful servant. You were faithful over little. I will set you over much. Go in to the joy of your Lord."

Salvation free By faith in Thee,
That is Thy Gospel's preaching,
The heart and core Of Bible lore

In all its sacred teaching.
In Christ we must Put all our trust,
Not in deeds or labor;
With conscience pure And heart secure
Love Thee, Lord, and our neighbor. Amen.

† *(TLH 266:2)*

Tuesday

Read Proverbs 22:2

MANY BELIEVE THAT complete equality, especially in temporal goods, is the only means by which all people will be equally happy. They think that if one person would no longer be rich and another no longer poor, then the golden age prophesied by the poets would come: the earth would be changed into a paradise, every groaning of the numerous people in distress would be stilled, every tear of earthly misfortune would be dried, and all humanity would be one big, happy family.

Others go even further. They point to the disparity between the world's rich and poor. They note that one person possesses a magnificent palace, while another can hardly find housing in a homeless shelter. One person owns great tracts of land, while another cannot call a square foot of ground his property. One person controls considerable amounts of the earth's production, while another cannot pick the fruit of even one of the world's trees. One person can revel in abundant pleasures, while another must starve. One person can be arrayed in costly attire, while another is hardly able to cover his nakedness with coarse garments. All of this, they say, is a state of universal injustice. They maintain that all people, as inhabitants of this earth, come into this world with absolutely equal rights and consequently have equal claim to its ground, its production, and its goods. They draw no distinction between the rich person and the thief and dismiss the worldly authority that protects the property of the rich against the destitute as the appointed public preserver of flagrant injustice.

It is certainly true that if the human race had remained in the state it enjoyed when God created it, had sin not come into the world, there would be no inequality among the people, no circumstance in which one lives every day gloriously and joyfully while another starves and utters cries for help that go unheard. Instead, the whole earth, with all it goods and pleasures, would be a great common fountain from which each one could draw according to his desire and need. Without asking "What's in it for me?" each one would use his gifts, strength, and means to serve the whole; all would contribute and receive equally.

However, we are fallen creatures. By nature, self-love and selfishness dwell in our hearts. If there were no "mine" and "yours" in the world, there would be no order to make a person's possessions sacred and inviolable to another. If all of us had the same claim to everything, all would surely want the benefit of it but only a few would work for the well being of all.

Therefore, complete equality would hardly change earth into heaven; rather, it would make the earth a hell. God thus wrote the commandment "You shall not steal" (Exodus 20:15) into the hearts of all people, publicly and solemnly calling it down from fiery Sinai through His elect servant and messenger, Moses. And with this commandment, He erected a fiery wall around the property each person has earned or received. As the angel stood before the entrance to Eden with the flaming sword, so the commandment "You shall not steal" stands as a threatening watchman appointed by God before the house, yard, garden, field, and goods of every person.

Originally, all people were equal. No person had privilege before God. However, after God distributed and enclosed the goods of the earth by His wonderful direction and by His holy commandment "You shall not steal," no person can appeal to the original equal right of all people to the stores of the treasury of the earth. Rather, Solomon rightly says, "The rich and the poor meet together; the LORD is the maker of them all" (Proverbs 22:2). Therefore, whoever declares the difference between rich and poor, high and low, and commanding and obedient as a state of injustice, sacrilegiously declares God Himself to be unjust. But He has might to do what He wants with His own, since He Himself established this difference among us fallen people.

Preserve, O Lord, Thine honor,
The bold blasphemer smite;
Convince, convert, enlighten,
The souls in error's night.
Reveal Thy will, dear Savior,
To all who dwell below—
Thou Light of all the living—
That men Thy name may know. Amen.

(TLH 264:2)

Wednesday

Read 2 Timothy 3:15

NO BOOK REPORTS more crimes and horrors of sin than the Bible. Holy Scripture, especially the Old Testament, contains almost nothing in its accounts of mankind's deeds except a great and terrible register of sins. The first report of man's activity in the Bible is of the Fall that had consequences of sin and corruption for the entire human race at all times. It goes on to relate that the first son of the first parents murdered his brother and that people's wickedness increased from generation to generation. It became so great, in fact, that finally, in the seventeenth century after the creation of the world, God had to wipe out all the millions of incorrigible people who then lived on the earth. Only eight souls were saved in the universal flood. Even after this terrible divine judgment, the Bible does not present an encouraging picture of the world. It describes the heathen Sodom and Gomorrah as cities whose sins and abominations cried so loudly to heaven for vengeance that God had to destroy them in a storm of fire and sulfur. Later, Scripture characterizes the family of the holy patriarchs and the entire chosen people of God as seats of idolatry and every other sin. Even among those who extolled the Scriptures as holy, there were almost none who are not reported to have fallen into one sin or another. The Bible often describes the greatest sins so fully and bluntly that one cannot read the accounts without shuddering.

Many intelligent people have taken offense at this. They think that any book that dwells so much on sins, describing them so graphically, cannot possibly be the holy Word, the revelation of God. Any book that has been given by God Himself for the betterment of mankind, they believe, must concentrate solely on the lives of godly and virtuous people whose behavior is worthy of imitation. Such thoughts are thoroughly absurd. In great wisdom God sketched a dark, awful picture of humanity in His Word. All of Holy Scripture was written to bring people to faith in Christ, the Savior of the world. He is the heart of the Old and New Testaments. He even says of the Old Testament, "You search the Scriptures because you think that in them you have eternal life; and it is they that bear witness about Me" (John 5:39). Paul wrote to Timothy in today's text, "From childhood you have been acquainted with the sacred writings, which are able to make you wise for salvation through faith in Christ Jesus" (2 Timothy 3:15). Peter preached, "To Him all the prophets bear witness that everyone who believes in Him receives forgiveness of sins through His name" (Acts 10:43).

No one needs a passage to prove that the New Testament has this same goal, but to give just one example, John reports, "These are written so that you may believe that Jesus is the Christ, the Son of God, and that by believing you may have life in His name" (20:31). If the Holy Scriptures preached only how godly people were, would we be led to faith in Christ? Wouldn't we conclude, instead, that people are good and they could surely be saved by their own works, without the help of a Savior? Without a doubt. That is why we should never be offended by the fact that the Bible presents even the holiest of people as sinners. We must recognize God's great wisdom in portraying them in this way. By revealing the sins that have flourished among the people from the beginning of the world, God shows us that human righteousness and worthiness are nothing but an empty dream, that every person is a sinner, that even the most godly cannot stand before the heavenly Father in their own righteousness, that free grace is man's only refuge, and that there is no salvation and no blessedness outside of Christ. The ones whose horrible sins are related in the Bible should be a mirror for us, a mirror in which we learn to examine our own life and our own heart so we humble ourselves before God and flee to the cross of the Lamb of God who bears the sins of the world.

Speak, O Lord, Thy servant heareth,
To Thy Word I now give heed;
Life and Spirit Thy Word beareth,
All Thy Word is true indeed.
Death's dread pow'r in me is rife;
Jesus, may Thy Word of Life
Fill my soul with love's strong fervor
That I cling to Thee forever. Amen.

† *(TLH 296:1)*

Thursday

Read 1 Corinthians 10:6–11

IN THE VERSE immediately preceding today's reading, Saint Paul says about the Israelites, "Nevertheless, with most of them God was not pleased, for they were overthrown in the wilderness" (1 Corinthians 10:5). Our text then begins with the words, "Now these things took place as examples for us, that we might not desire evil as they did" (1 Corinthians 10:6). After the Israelites had been satisfied by the manna (bread) that fell from heaven, most of them remembered the many sorts of food they had enjoyed in Egypt. Then the distress from which God had rescued them was quickly forgotten and they called out greedily: "Oh that we had meat to eat! We remember the fish we ate in Egypt that cost nothing, the cucumbers, the melons, the leeks, the onions, and the garlic. But now our strength is dried up, and there is nothing at all but this manna to look at" (Numbers 11:5–6).

"Do not be idolaters as some of them were," Paul continues. "As it is written, 'The people sat down to eat and drink and rose up to play'" (1 Corinthians 10:7). When Moses ascended Mount Sinai to receive the Law and was delayed a long time, Aaron, according to the wish of the people, used the occasion to cast a golden calf, sacrifice to it, and even worship it. The apostle adds, "We must not indulge in sexual immorality as some of them did, and twenty-three thousand fell in a single day" (1 Corinthians 10:8). When the Israelites came near, the Moabites tried to overcome them by inviting them, through their daughters, to the festival of their idol, Baal Peor. What did the Israelites do? Forgetting that they should be a holy people, they accepted this invitation and were led into shameful unchastity at this festival to the glory of the idol. So those unfaithful ones of Israel fell there in horrible sin and shame.

Paul also writes, "We must not put Christ to the test, as some of them did and were destroyed by serpents" (1 Corinthians 10:9). The Israelites had wandered almost forty years, being led everywhere by the Son of God, the true spiritual rock, and experiencing numerous proofs of God's power and help all along the way. Having reached the border of the promised land, where the Edomites refused them passage through their land, the people at once spoke against God and Moses, saying: "Why have you brought us up out of Egypt to die in the wilderness? For there is no food and no water, and we loathe this worthless food" (Numbers 21:5).

The apostle names yet another sin: "Nor grumble, as some of them did and were destroyed by the Destroyer"

(1 Corinthians 10:10). When the spies, sent to scout the promised land, brought news that it was inhabited by a mighty people who would be difficult to conquer, all of the Israelites, great and small, forgot God and cried out in unbelief, "Would that we had died in the land of Egypt! Or would that we had died in this wilderness! Why is the LORD bringing us into this land, to fall by the sword? Our wives and our little ones will become a prey. Would it not be better for us to go back to Egypt?" (Numbers 14:2–3).

We see here what horrible sins—greater than those of the heathen—had come even into the midst of a church in which God Himself preached with His own mouth. Why has God allowed this to be recorded in His Word for all ages? Saint Paul tells us in our text: "Now these things happened to them as an example, but they were written down for our instruction, on whom the end of the ages has come" (1 Corinthians 10:11). This should serve as a warning for us, lest we be offended by the falls into sin that still take place in the true Church, as if the Church would be false because of this. It remains the true Church when God's pure Word is preached there and the Sacraments are administered according to His institution.

Grant that our days, while life shall last,
In purest holiness be passed,
Be Thou our Strength and Tower,
From sinful lust and vanity
And from dead works set Thou us free
In every evil hour.
Keep Thou Pure now
From offenses Heart and senses.
Blessed Spirit,
Let us heavenly life inherit. Amen.

(TLH 235:8)

Friday

Read 1 Corinthians 10:12

WE MIGHT WELL IMAGINE that the Israelites in the desert should have been the last people to fall into sin and unbelief. After all, in Egypt, for their sake, God did astonishing and terrible signs and wonders to move Pharaoh to let them go. He divided the Red Sea so they could cross with dry feet and escape those who were in hot pursuit of them, then He destroyed their mighty enemies in the sea. As on eagles' wings, God bore them to the glorious land that had been promised to their fathers. God escorted them visibly in a pillar of cloud by day and in a pillar of fire at night. God rained manna and quail upon them for their food, and He quenched their thirst by miraculously allowing water to flow out of the dry rock and turning the bitter water into a sea of sweet water. God Himself descended onto Sinai in the fire, and with His own voice He called out, among earthquakes and the sound of the trumpet, His holy commandments into the ears of the entire people. God opened the earth, and Korah's group, that had raised up prophets against Moses, was swallowed alive by hell. In one night, God made Aaron's dry staff blossom and bear almonds as a testimony that Aaron was the high priest appointed by God Himself.

Doesn't it seem impossible, after all this, that such a highly favored people—surrounded by a thousand miracles of God, even wandering in the company of the visibly present God Himself, led by His hand as dear children—could fall into unbelief and sin? Nevertheless, most of them immediately embraced the most terrible sins: homesickness for heathen Egypt, idolatry, sexual immorality, tempting God, and murmuring against His holy and gracious leading. Aaron, to whom God had entrusted the highest spiritual office in His Church, fell into the horrible sin of idolatry, and even Moses declined into doubt and unbelief.

What an example to warn us! "Therefore," Saint Paul admonishes in our text, "let anyone who thinks that he stands take heed lest he fall" (1 Corinthians 10:12). If you have forsaken the Egypt of this world and now enjoy fellowship with true Christians, good for you. But do not become secure in this. Instead, let the example of the ancient Israelites serve to remind you just how easy it is to fall into sin. Hardly had they passed through the Red Sea and entered the wilderness when a small privation soon awakened in them a greedy longing for the fleshpots of Egypt. If you do not earnestly watch, pray, and contend against your flesh and blood, you too will soon fall victim to a reawakening of the vain lust for the comforts and goods of this world you have now forsaken. When that happens, you will be, at least inwardly, a child of the world. If you now stand in the right faith and confess the pure doctrine from a living conviction by the Holy Ghost, good for you. But do not become complacent. Instead, let Israel warn you. As soon as Moses was delayed on Mount Sinai, the people became irritated and called to Aaron, "Up, make us gods who shall go before us. As for this Moses, the man who brought us up out of the land of Egypt, we do not know what has become of him" (Exodus 32:1). If you who are now firm in the faith do not watch and daily seek to strengthen yourself in the way of righteousness, you can certainly become offended and fall away into the idolatry of false doctrine, enthusiasm, and unbelief. Remember Aaron, and apply his example to yourself. If even he could fall, how much less secure is your own footing, no matter how highly enlightened you think yourself to be.

If you now hate sin and earnestly pursue sanctification,

good for you. But beware of becoming secure in this. Instead, let the Israelites' example be a warning to you. When they were tempted by lewd prostitutes, they fell into whoremongering, adultery, and sexually transmitted disease. If you do not watch, pray, and earnestly seek to shun the way of temptation, you can lose, suddenly or slowly, your present aversion to sin and zeal for holiness. When that happens, you can quickly fall into sins and shame of all kinds. If you are now satisfied with God's leading, if you are ready to suffer everything for Christ's sake, even preferring death to denying God, good for you. But do not attempt to find security in this. Rather, let the example of the Israelites make you ever cautious. When the Lord let His people encounter just a little difficulty, they immediately fell into terrible sin, tempting God and murmuring against Him. If you do not diligently pray and watch over your heart, if you do not daily draw strength from God's Word, you too can easily despair, murmur against Him, and finally give Him notice. "Therefore," as the apostle says, "let him who thinks he stands take heed lest he fall."

O God, forsake me not!
Take not Thy Spirit from me
And suffer not the might
Of sin to overcome me.
Increase my feeble faith,
Which Thou Thyself hast wrought.
Be Thou my Strength and Pow'r—
O God, forsake me not! Amen.

(*TLH* 402:2)

Saturday

Read 1 Corinthians 10:13

THE MORE PURELY, clearly, and richly the Gospel of Christ and His grace is preached, the more secure, thoughtless, and audacious many become in their sins. They think they can stand in grace, despite their prevailing sins, as long as they still believe in Christ. Or they imagine that, when death one day comes knocking for them, they will then quickly plead for grace and God will certainly receive them, like the thief on the cross.

The Israelites surely had similar thoughts about their sins, for the more God demonstrated His extraordinary grace to them, the more faithless they became. But did their sweet hope for grace find fulfillment? No! Three times Paul mentions God's judgment, which then passed upon Israel. He says, "We must not indulge in sexual immorality as some of them did, and twenty-three thousand fell in a single day. We must not put Christ to the test, as some of them did and were destroyed by serpents, nor grumble, as some of them did and were destroyed by the Destroyer" (1 Corinthians 10:8–10). To this, Paul adds, "Now these things happened to them as an example, but they were written down for our instruction, on whom the end of the ages has come" (1 Corinthians 10:11). Thus the mirror of God's wrath, which has always eventually fallen upon wanton sinners, is held out before us Christians in these last evil days that are full of temptation and danger.

"Do not be deceived," Scripture says, "God is not mocked" (Galatians 6:7). God did not spare the Israelites, before whose eyes and for whose sake He had done countless wonders of grace, and whom He had elected from all the people of the earth to be His own people. In His judgment, only two of the 600,000 men who left Egypt entered Canaan, the Promised Land, while all the others perished miserably in the wilderness. How, then, can you think you will be able to face the righteous judgment of God? God remains as He is. As terrible as His wrath once was against Israel, which wantonly sinned in the face of all His grace, it burns just as brightly today. His long-suffering certainly allows a person to persist for a time in despising Him and serving sin, dishonoring His Word and His Church, blaspheming with the enemies of the Lord, vexing thousands upon thousands of innocent souls, and persecuting the children of God. But one day, the measure of that sinner will become full. One day, God will grow tired of having mercy on him. One day, He will tear the sinner out of his life of shame, place him before the judgment seat, and throw him into the deepest hell. The greater the grace the sinner enjoyed, the more terrible the wrath that awaits him. Whoever has ears to hear, let him hear!

God is faithful. Whoever clings to Him in faith can find comfort in the words of the apostle, who says He "will not let you be tempted beyond your ability, but with the temptation He will also provide the way of escape, that you may be able to endure it" (1 Corinthians 10:13). Thus, whoever retains faith in this faithful God, daily seeking His grace and completely despairing of himself, is not lost. It is impossible that a person who completely rejects his own righteousness and embraces the righteousness of Christ alone would be rejected by God. God is indeed faithful. It is just as impossible for a person who does not struggle against sin with his own power, but in Christ's grace, to be dominated and overcome by sin. God has mercy on us all, and especially on all those who still wantonly sin. May He give us all repentance and lead us through the desert of this world with His elect into the heavenly Canaan. May He do all this through Jesus Christ, our heavenly Joshua, for the sake of His boundless mercy.

O God, forsake me not!
Lord, hear my supplication!
In ev'ry evil hour
Help me o'ercome temptation;
And when the prince of hell
My conscience seeks to blot,
Be Thou not far from me—
O God, forsake me not! Amen.

(*TLH* 402:3)

Sunday

Read Luke 19:41–48

AS HE WEEPS OVER JERUSALEM, Jesus tells the city's inhabitants that what serves for their peace and their salvation is completely hidden from them. For years, He kindly and clearly showed them the way to salvation and confirmed His Word with the most glorious miracles. But not only did they not want to accept His Word, in the end, they came to believe Jesus was a tempter and His doctrine was false and dangerous. Completely hidden from them was the fact that Jesus Christ is the Son of God and that faith in Him saves. Instead, this notion was an offense they abhorred and a foolishness they derided.

But Jesus continued to reach out to them: "For the days will come upon you, when your enemies will set up a barricade around you and surround you and hem you in on every side and tear you down to the ground, you and your children within you. And they will not leave one stone upon another in you" (Luke 19:43–44). The citizens of Jerusalem had no idea they would meet God's judgment for their rejection of Jesus and His Gospel. Their consciences had been silenced. Although Jesus, warning them with tears, announced beforehand God's inevitable and just punishment, they still did not believe it.

But there is still more. The conclusion of our Gospel says, "And He [that is, Christ] was teaching daily in the temple. The chief priests and the scribes and the principal men of the people were seeking to destroy Him" (Luke 19:47). After they had been blinded to the things that made for their peace, and after they had lost all fear of God's judgment, they proceeded to fall from one sin into another without regarding them as sin. The most bitter enmity followed their contempt for Christ, until they finally made room in their hearts for thoughts of murdering the innocent One. Even then they did not rest until their thirst for blood was quenched by the sight of Christ on the cross.

We see here a vivid example of the condition of a person who is obdurate. Such a person has fallen so far that he no longer knows what makes for his peace. The Word of God is preached to him in vain. It no longer makes an impression on him. His heart is as indifferent as a stone. The Gospel, with all its grace and comfort, may be preached to the obdurate, and Christ and His love of sinners may be explained very movingly, but such a person does not budge. The Law, in all its sharpness and with all its threats, may be preached to the obdurate, the righteous and holy God may be characterized in a frightening way, and all of this may be accompanied by earnest admonishment, but still he does not respond. Grace and wrath, life and death, blessing and curse, heaven and hell, and salvation and damnation may be placed before the obdurate, but they are all alike to him. Although the way to salvation may be mapped ever so clearly for him, he is not convinced. Light no longer shines into his soul and he remains in his darkness. The more he reads and hears God's Word, the more foolish and offensive it becomes to him. Hatred and enmity firmly establish themselves in his heart, and the Word then serves only to harden his heart until it becomes an anvil for the hammer.

Just as the Word of God cannot enlighten, awaken, and move an obdurate person to repentance, so the experiences of life fail to make a salutary impression on him. If all goes well for him, he does not allow his heart to be softened and brought to repentance. The more love God shows him, the more secure, proud, and impudent he becomes. When trouble is absent, he believes things will never change and he will never perish. On the contrary, if things go badly for such a person, he still refuses to humble himself. Instead, he complains about his lot and blasphemes the Almighty in heaven. He no longer has any feeling for his sins. His conscience becomes scarred, no longer accuses him, and finally falls silent. Then, without any fear of punishment from God, he becomes a professed enemy and, ultimately, a persecutor of Christ, His Word, and His Christians. The tears of grieving parents, siblings, former companions in the faith, and friends are futile. The obdurate person laughs at the ones who pity him. Then, on the day when the righteous judgment of God is revealed, the obdurate will meet hell and damnation with hurried steps.

By the love Thy tears are telling,
O Thou Lamb for sinners slain,
Make my heart Thy temple dwelling,
Purged from ev'ry guilty stain.
Oh, forgive, forgive, my sin!
Cleanse me, cleanse me, Lord, within!
I am Thine since Thou hast sought me,
Since Thy precious blood hath bo't me. Amen.

† *(TLH 419:2)*

Monday

Read Exodus 10:20

THE LARGE CHURCH fellowship known as the Calvinist Reformed maintains that all who become hardened come into this condition according to an eternal, absolute decree of God. They base this view on Holy Scripture, which says, "So then He has mercy on whomever He wills, and He hardens whomever He wills" (Romans 9:18), and notes that the Lord hardened Pharaoh's heart so he would not let the Israelites go. But this is a blasphemous use of these biblical remarks. We cannot attempt to make God the author of a person's sin and damnation. Indeed, Scripture expressly testifies, "For You are not a God who delights in wickedness," (Psalm 5:4), and "Let no one say when he is tempted, 'I am being tempted by God,' for God cannot be tempted with evil, and He Himself tempts no one" (James 1:13). Moreover, the Bible testifies clearly that God neither wants nor has decreed the destruction of any person: "As I live, declares the Lord GOD, I have no pleasure in the death of the wicked, but that the wicked turn from his way and live; turn back, turn back from your evil ways, for why will you die, O house of Israel?" (Ezekiel 33:11), and "He destroys you, O Israel, for you are against Me, against your helper" (Hosea 13:9).

But doesn't the Bible also clearly say that God had really hardened many people? Yes, but it also emphasizes that God hardens only those who have already hardened themselves by despising grace. Christ says that the citizens of Jerusalem had finally fallen into the judgment of obduracy, not because God had decreed it from eternity, but "because you did not know the time of your visitation" (Luke 19:44). If God ever visited any people in great grace, it was the citizens of Jerusalem.

The Son of God Himself, together with His twelve apostles, preached the Gospel among them and invited them a thousand times into the kingdom of His grace. Faithfully, as a Good Shepherd, He followed them for three years with words, works, and tears, admonishing and imploring them to turn from their wicked ways. But when they all despised this grace, declined His kind invitation, and ultimately murdered Him, God finally withdrew His hand of grace and gave them up to the judgment of total hardness.

God always acts in this way. No one who becomes hardened did not first experience a time of gracious visitation. God's Word may be preached to him for a long time. He may be exhorted countless times by teachers, pastors, parents, and fellow believers. His own conscience and the Holy Ghost may often admonish and chastise him. But if he wantonly and stubbornly resists all of this and remains in his sin, his pride, and his love of the world, God finally tires of extending him mercy and says, "Why will you still be struck down? Why will you continue to rebel? The whole head is sick, and the whole heart faint" (Isaiah 1:5). At that point, He removes His hand of grace from such a person. Holy Scripture calls this a hardening. For when God no longer works in a person, he is left to his own devices, and as a result, his blindness increases and he becomes more and more firmly bound to his sin and malice. As water freezes when the sun's warmth is withdrawn, and as a field grows wild when it is no longer cultivated, so also a person's heart becomes hardened when God no longer shines with the sun of His grace and His Word can no longer penetrate.

Yea, as I live, Jehovah saith,
I would not have the sinner's death,
But that he turn from error's ways,
Repent, and live through endless days. Amen.

† *(TLH 331:1)*

Tuesday

Read Hebrews 6:4–6

HERE IS A TERRIBLE TRUTH that is clearly taught in God's Word: There is a hardening from which deliverance is no longer possible. God says: "Because I have called and you refused to listen, have stretched out My hand and no one has heeded, because you have ignored all My counsel and would have none of My reproof, I also will laugh at your calamity; I will mock when terror strikes you. . . . Then they will call upon Me, but I will not answer; they will seek Me diligently but will not find Me. Because they hated knowledge and did not choose the fear of the LORD, would have none of My counsel and despised all My reproof" (Proverbs 1:24–26, 28–30).

The writer of the Letter to the Hebrews teaches us the same thing in today's text. We see here that there are those, such as the heathen, who have become hardened to such an extent that the Lord has given them up to a false understanding that prompts them to do things that are of no use. These individuals have severed the last thread that joined them to God. They are like a tree whose roots have rotted away and would never blossom and bear fruit, even if it were placed in the most fertile land and watered ever so diligently. The judgment is already spoken here upon those who have locked the door against grace. There is no help for such people. Some of them already endure hell in their earthly life in the form of despair in their hearts and death in lamentation and woe, anticipating their certain damnation. Others, however, continue to laugh and pursue pleasure until they die and then awaken in a pool of eternal death.

We cannot think, however, that on account of this doctrine, even one sinner, no matter how great and hardened, must doubt his deliverance, for God does not desire the death of any sinner. He wants to save them all. Those who are lost are lost solely because they did not want to be rescued. Therefore, whoever knows he has an obstinate heart but still feels a secret longing for God's grace and deliverance from sins is certainly not yet irretrievably lost. Every good thing in us—even the sinner's longing for deliverance—is a work of God's grace.

People who lie under the judgment of hardness, from which there is no help, are often terrified by the misery into which they have fallen. They, too, long for help, but the help they seek is to be free from their trouble, not from their sin. They, too, believe in the wrath of God, but not in God's grace. This was the state in which Judas found himself.

In contrast, if you long for grace and for freedom from sin, there is still help for you! Do not despair if you feel that your heart is like a stone. God has already promised, through the words of the prophet Ezekiel, that He wants to remove our heart of stone and replace it with a heart of flesh. Do not lose hope when it seems as if your heart has become as hard as a diamond. You have only to listen to God's Word, which He Himself characterizes as a hammer that smashes rocks to pieces. Do not give up even if you must admit that you have become as hardened as the citizens of Jerusalem. Remember that, when they heard the sermon accusing them of having killed the Prince of life and the Lord of glory, they were finally terrified and called out, "What shall we do?" (Acts 2:37). They repented and were saved.

Whoever has often been awakened by God's Word but always resisted God Himself, may he not add to his account the greatest of sins: doubting God's grace. May he turn back, no longer despising the grace offered to him, and throw himself as a lost sinner at Jesus' feet. Thus He will receive and save him.

Create in me a clean heart, O God,
And renew a right spirit within me.
Cast me not away from Thy presence,
And take not Thy Holy Spirit from me.
Restore unto me the joy of Thy salvation;
And uphold me with Thy free spirit. Amen.

(TLH, P. 22)

Wednesday

Read Acts 17:30

WHEN PAUL PREACHED the sermon from which today's reading comes, he was in Athens, a famous and distinguished city. With the words of our text, the apostle demanded repentance, a change of heart and mind, from all people. Isn't that remarkable? Shouldn't there be people who already have the correct mind and therefore do not need repentance and conversion? Shouldn't there be people who, from childhood on, are good and live morally so they do not need to change their mind and can continue to live as before?

If people were still as they were when they came forth from the creating hand of God, then, of course, there would be people who would not need to repent. In that event, each person would only be exhorted to remain in his holy and blessed condition, to use the powers bestowed upon him for good, and to live according to the regulations of the divine Law. But this is not so. The entire human race is fallen. We find the story of the fall in the first chapters of Holy Scripture.

Since then, every person from birth on has a mind with which he cannot please God, and therefore he cannot come into fellowship with God and be saved. By nature, every person does not truly make God his God. He does not regard Him as his highest good, and he does not fear, love, and trust him above all things. Moreover, he does not avoid the sinful deed and do the good deed since he is not motivated by a pure fear and love of God. Instead, every person now lives for this world above all else, and he seeks his happiness in its pleasures, goods, honor, and wisdom. By nature, he is ruled by self-love and selfishness. He seeks his own advantage, rather than that of his neighbor, and in all his dealings, he follows the selfish principle, "Each person is his own neighbor." This mind-set is not found in only a few people, the godless and wicked ones, but in all people, without exception—even those who claim to live in the strictest morality, those who are regarded as the best and noblest people, and those whose works the world regards as above reproach.

Therefore, no person can be saved in his natural condition. Everyone must first experience a thorough change in his heart, receive a thoroughly different mind, and obtain a completely different direction for his spirit. God must become his highest good. He must cease to live for this world, focusing instead on the world to come, where he will seek his happiness and rest for his soul. Thus, he must no longer live for himself; instead he must present his entire life as an offering in love to his neighbor. For this reason, Paul once preached in Athens, "But now [God] commands all people everywhere to repent" (Acts 17:30). All who have not yet experienced this repentance, this change of mind, although they may appear to live as angels in this world, are not true Christians and do not stand before God in grace. Therefore, they are not on the path to blessedness and eternal life.

"That which is born of the flesh is flesh," Jesus says,

adding, "Truly, truly, I say to you, unless one is born again he cannot see the kingdom of God" (John 3:6, 3). According to this, then, the number of true Christians must be extremely small! Even among so-called Christians, there are many who have not yet experienced the necessary change of heart.

Therefore my hope is in the Lord
And not in mine own merit;
It rests upon His faithful Word
To them of contrite spirit
That He is merciful and just;
This is my comfort and my trust.
His help I wait with patience. Amen.

† *(TLH 329:3)*

Thursday

Read 1 Corinthians 12:4

THE APOSTOLIC CHURCH (that is, the Church as it existed during the lives of the holy apostles) enjoyed far greater privileges than the Church at any other time. Both the apostles themselves and most of the common Christians were empowered with extraordinary gifts by the Holy Ghost, as later Christians never were. That fire of the Holy Ghost and His miraculous gifts, with which the disciples were baptized on the first Christian Pentecost, soon afterward blazed in all of the congregations they established. Wherever the apostles proclaimed the Gospel and baptized or laid hands on those who were believers, they usually imparted to them at the same time the wonderful gifts of the Holy Ghost. At the festival of Pentecost, the apostle Peter called to all his listeners, "Repent and be baptized every one of you in the name of Jesus Christ for the forgiveness of your sins, and you will receive the gift of the Holy Spirit" (Acts 2:38).

Furthermore, when the apostles in Jerusalem heard that Samaria had received the Word of God, they sent Peter and John to them. There, they laid their hands upon those who had come to faith and were already baptized, and they received the extraordinary gifts of the Holy Ghost. And when Peter preached the Word of God and it was received in faith by the Gentile centurion Cornelius and his household, Scripture reports, "while Peter was still saying these things, the Holy Spirit fell on all who heard the word" (Acts 10:44). All of them suddenly began to prophesy, to speak in foreign languages, and to praise God.

In the apostolic age, almost every congregation had at least several members who possessed special gifts of the Holy Ghost. One could speak in languages he had never learned, while another was quickly able to translate what his brother was saying and explain it to their hearers. One was a prophet and spoke of future events, while another had the gift of interpreting the most difficult passages of Holy Scripture. Others were enabled to perform miracles, heal the sick with a word, cast out devils, and even awaken the dead. Therefore, at that time, whenever the congregation assembled, the most remarkable scenes occurred. A member might come forward to preach in a language no one understood, with another member quickly rising to provide a translation. One person might prophesy what would happen, while another might interpret dark passages from Scripture in light of events that had already taken place. A blind person might be made to see, and a mute person might be enabled to speak.

All of these miraculous gifts had a purpose: to confirm and seal the new revelation before the world in a divine way. With the coming of Christ, that revelation was announced to the world, and the Christian faith spread rapidly into all lands. These miraculous gifts were to be an outward testimony that the Gospel of Christ preached by the apostles really was a message from God and that the Christian Church founded by the apostles is really the Church of God, the elect, and the saved.

It is not surprising that such miraculous gifts are no longer found in the Church. The New Testament has been divinely sealed, and the Christian religion has been firmly established as a divine revelation to the world. For this reason, there is now no need for miracles. However, the fact that the Christian Church has endured despite repeated assaults through all the centuries that followed the apostolic age, and that it continues to grow, is a greater miracle than all of those performed in the earliest years of the Church. Whoever does not believe the Gospel that was sealed by the old miracles would hardly be convinced by new miracles. Indeed, had God continued to work these gifts and miracles in the Church they would have become contemptible, dismissed as something commonplace and considered to be no longer convincing to most people.

Thy kingdom come. Thine let it be
In time and in eternity.
Let Thy good Spirit e'er be nigh
Our hearts with graces to supply.
Break Satan's pow'r, defeat his rage;
Preserve Thy Church from age to age. Amen.

† *(TLH 458:3)*

Friday

Read 1 Corinthians 12:8–11

GOD'S WORD is always mighty. It brings people to the living faith, causing them to convert to God from the heart and to become new people by the changing of their heart, mind, and intellect. Moreover, when the Holy Ghost works true faith in the heart of a person, He simultaneously adorns him with the most glorious and extraordinary supernatural gifts.

There is, however, a twofold distinction to be made concerning the gifts of the apostolic age, to which Saint Paul refers in today's text. Paul names nine gifts. Four of them have completely disappeared from the Christian Church, while the other five are still found among believers, but to a lesser degree. The gifts that have disappeared are healing without the use of a doctor, performing miracles, speaking a foreign language without studying it, and interpreting languages one has never learned. The five spiritual gifts that remain are speaking of wisdom, being able to speak intelligently, prophesying (that is, interpreting Scripture), maintaining an especially strong and heroic faith, and discerning spirits. Although these remaining gifts are present in smaller measure than during the apostolic age, no one can deny that they are gifts of the Holy Ghost rather than natural endowments. There are, for example, believing Christians who, in their unconverted state, were hardly able to utter a coherent sentence. However, after they were truly converted, they received the extraordinary gift of speaking of divine things in such a way that they make a deep impression on their hearers. Before their conversion, some believing Christians had to remain silent in every dispute because even the weakest arguments of their opponents confounded them. As true believers, however, they have a presence of mind and a sharpness of discernment that cause them not to fear any opponent, even the shrewdest and most learned one. Although they themselves may be simple and unlearned, they know how to defend their faith in compelling fashion.

There are Christians who, when they once stood without a living faith, were always timid, uncertain, anxious, and full of fear. Since they came to know Christ, they remained timid and undecided in worldly things, but in matters of faith and of the kingdom of God, they show bravery, certainty, and heroic faith that are surprising. Before they came to Christ, some Christians were always helpless and easily changed their opinion. Since their conversion, however, they are decided, certain, and firm in their faith. No one can make them back down, and they are easily able to discern false spirits. When faith was absent from their heart, some Christians could hardly pray three words. But now that they have embraced Christ and His righteousness, they have received the gift of praying. Still other Christians have a special gift of understanding doctrine, interpreting difficult passages of Holy Scripture, shaking and softening the hardened sinner, comforting the afflicted, convincing the doubter, or reconciling those who are at odds with one another. Who can count all these dear and glorious gifts?

Not everyone, of course, has all of these gifts, but each one has some gift of the Holy Ghost. Some have their gifts in larger measure, while others have theirs in smaller measure. But as ungifted as a Christian may appear to be, he still has some beautiful gift, as Saint Paul reminds us at the end of today's text: "All these are empowered by one and the same Spirit, who apportions to each one as he wills" (1 Corinthians 12:11).

With Thy gifts my heart endowing,
Make it new and clean and fair;
Let it in true love be glowing,
Living in Thy grace fore'er;
Give me courage bold and good,
Sanctify my flesh and blood,
Let me, trusting in Christ's merit,
Worship God in truth and spirit. Amen.

(ELHB 248:5)

Saturday

Read 1 Corinthians 12:7

WHEN A CHRISTIAN, through faith, attains God's grace, the forgiveness of sins, righteousness before God, comfort, and the hope of eternal life, these are fruits for him alone. But when a Christian, through faith, receives all kinds of gifts, this is not for his sake but for the profit of all. With these gifts, he should serve both the Church and the world. The eye has the gift of sight, the ear has the gift of hearing, the foot has the gift of walking, and the hand has the gift of handling. In short, all the members of the body have various gifts, not for themselves, but for the whole body. So, too, does a believer have his gifts, not for his own benefit, but for that of everyone.

Therefore, the right use of all gifts a Christian possesses consists in using them for the profit of all. He should assist the congregation in its preservation, expansion, and edification in unity, faith, and love. In addition, as long as there are always some who remain outside the Church, he should do everything he can to bring them to the right faith. The entire Christian Church should be a military camp of the Prince of salvation, ceaselessly fighting that the kingdom of Satan might be destroyed and the kingdom of Christ might continue to increase. Each Christian is a soldier in this army of God.

Each congregation is also a missions family and each member of that congregation is a missionary. He should not be isolated from the whole and uncaring about other Christians. The Church is the body of Christ, the communion of saints, and each of its members has a certain duty to perform. A Christian should therefore not think that he has done everything he is obligated to do if he himself is on the right path to salvation and serves his God privately. Instead, he should remember that bringing others onto the path of salvation and service is a holy duty. Moreover, he should not think that converting souls and caring for them are matters only for the preacher and not for the laity. Rather, he should recognize that he himself is a spiritual priest who should proclaim the virtues of the One who has called him from the darkness into His marvelous light.

Oh, if we examine ourselves in light of this, mustn't we all be heartily ashamed? Do we really use all of our gifts for the profit of all? Does each one show himself to be a spiritual priest, proclaiming first to the members of his own family, then to his neighbors and to all whom God brings to him, the virtues of God, the Gospel, and the divine works of redemption? Can each one point to souls to whom he showed the right way or helped to keep them on it, warning them against error and sin, comforting them in bodily and spiritual distress, and chastising them for the sake of their eternal salvation?

No person can say he has no gifts with which he can serve the Church and the world in spiritual things. If anyone attempts to say this, he merely reveals how ungrateful he is toward God. The true, living Christian has at least one gift of the Holy Ghost. If he lacks his brother's gift, he has one that his brother lacks. Let us, then, use our gifts for the profit of all! The one to whom God has given the gift of wisdom and good counsel should advise. The one to whom God has given the gift of knowledge should instruct. The one who has received from God a strong, heroic faith should display it and seek to inspire others wherever strong faith is necessary. The one to whom God has given the gift of especially fervent and mighty prayer should pray. If one has received the gift of comfort, he should comfort. Those who have the gifts of admonishment and persuasion should exercise them regularly.

In short, let each one seek to recognize the gift he has been given, not boasting of it or letting it remain unused. Instead, let him employ it for the benefit of all.

Yea, Lord, 'twas Thy free bounty gave
My body, soul, and what I have
In this poor life of labor;
O grant that I may through Thy grace
Use all my powers to show Thy praise
And serve and help my neighbor.
From all false doctrine keep me, Lord,
From Satan's lies and malice ward,
In every cross uphold Thou me
That I may bear it patiently.
Lord Jesus Christ!
My God and Lord, my God and Lord!
In death Thy comfort still afford. Amen.

(ELHB 366:2)

Sunday

Read Luke 18:9–13

EVERY RELIGION wants to show people a way they can be righteous before God and be saved. But what way do they offer?

The heathen says, "If you want to be righteous, give each person what is due him. If, however, you have not always fulfilled this duty, sacrifice to the gods." The Jew says, "If you want to be righteous, be circumcised and keep the Law of Moses and the traditions of the elders." The Muhammadan says, "If you want to be righteous, confess that there is only one god and Muhammad is his prophet, and conform yourself to the regulations of our Koran." The Roman Catholic says, "If you want to be righteous, keep the commandments of God and the Church. If you want to be absolutely certain of your salvation, forsake the world, go into a monastery, and keep the threefold vows of poverty, chastity, and obedience." The enthusiast says, "If you want to be righteous, pray and struggle until you have received another heart, and if you want to be absolutely righteous, do not rest until you are perfect and no longer sin." Finally, the rationalist, the believer in reason, says, "If you want to be righteous, exercise yourself in virtue and do noble works. But if you fail, regret it and better yourself."

The answers are diverse, but they are based on the same premise: A person can be righteous before God and be saved, partly by outward good works and partly by inward moral improvement. What does today's reading say in response to this? Just the opposite. A Pharisee and a tax collector are placed before us. The Pharisee is described as a man full of so-called good works, whereas the tax collector is characterized as a poor sinner without any good works. Of the Pharisee, it is said that he went into the temple to pray and there he said to God in his heart: "God, I thank You that I am not like other men, extortioners, unjust, adulterers, or even like this tax collector. I fast twice a week; I give tithes of all that I get" (Luke 18:11–12). However, the tax collector could not in any way boast of these things. On the contrary, he was ashamed because of his unrighteousness up to that point. He did not even want to raise his eyes toward heaven, but instead beat on his breast and sighed, "God, be merciful to me, a sinner!" (Luke 18:13). And yet—how wonderful!—Christ says this tax collector returned to his house justified, while the Pharisee, with all his good works and righteousness before men, was not righteous before God.

The justification of a poor sinner before God obviously does not require good works and a display of inner holiness. Rather, it derives from God's grace. The sinner remains a sinner, but God declares him to be just despite his sins. According to our Gospel, justification is not an act a person performs himself, but something done in him by God. It does not begin in a person's heart, but in the heart of God. It is not to be compared with the action of a doctor who restores a sick person to health, but with the action of a judge who acquits the accused criminal, not only releasing him from all punishment but also, despite his crimes, awarding him all the rights of an innocent citizen. In short, justification is the forgiveness of sins. God sees a justified person as if he had never sinned, as if he had perfectly fulfilled the demands of God's Law.

David and all the rest of the Old Testament saints understood the mystery of this justification very well. The psalmist writes: "Blessed is the one whose transgression is forgiven, whose sin is covered. Blessed is the man against whom the LORD counts no iniquity, and in whose spirit there is no deceit" (Psalm 32:1–2).

From depths of woe I cry to Thee,
Lord, hear me, I implore Thee.
Bend down Thy gracious ear to me,
My prayer let come before Thee.
If Thou remembʼrest each misdeed,
If each should have its rightful meed,
Who may abide Thy presence?

Thy love and grace alone avail
To blot out my transgression;
The best and holiest deeds must fail
To break sin's dread oppression.
Before Thee none can boasting stand,
But all must fear Thy strict demand
And live alone by mercy. Amen.

(TLH 329:1, 2)

Monday

Read Luke 18:14

THE PHARISEE was not justified. Why not? Not because he was free from coarse sins and was an honorable man before the world, but because he was one of those "who trusted in themselves that they were righteous, and treated others with contempt" (Luke 18:9). He was self-righteous.

Why did the tax collector go to his house justified before God? How did he obtain this highest and most precious of all goods? He did not think about doing something he could present to God to obtain justification from Him. Rather, he went as he was—as a poor, lost, and condemned sinner, burdened with his great sin, completely despairing, and doubting his righteousness and godliness—into the temple, which contained the mercy seat that foreshadowed the atonement of the Messiah. Here he sought the help he did not find in himself, beat his breast, and sighed, "God, be merciful to me, a sinner!" (Luke 18:13). Casting away all other comfort, he made the atonement of the Savior his only comfort. He seized it in faith, and behold! He then went, as the Lord clearly says in our text, down to his house justified.

Thus, how is justification obtained, according to the Gospel? It is by faith alone. What does a debtor have to do to be free of the debt that another has paid for him? He must accept that the payment has been made for him. What action must be taken by an offender, with whom the one he offended has already reconciled himself, so he is also reconciled? He has only to accept the reconciliation. What must the prisoner, whose cell door has already been opened, do so he may enjoy his freedom? He must simply accept the freedom he has been given and leave the prison. What must the pardoned criminal do to enjoy his pardon? He must merely receive it.

The debt of all people's sin has already been paid by Christ, God has been reconciled to them, the prison of God's wrath and hell has been opened, the pardon of everyone has been accomplished, and through the Gospel it has been proclaimed and offered to all. What must a person do to receive all of this with joy? Nothing, absolutely nothing, but receive it gratefully. Even this is nothing but believing it. Believing, according to the Gospel, is the only way justification is obtained. It is not that faith is such a good work or such a splendid quality of the heart that, because of it, God will consider the person as righteous. It is also not because a person must do something, even a small thing, in addition to what has already been accomplished. No, a person has nothing at all to do with his justification. It has already been acquired by Christ, and it is offered, presented, and distributed in the Gospel to all who hear it. For this reason, Saint Paul writes, "For Christ is the end of the law for righteousness to everyone who believes" (Romans 10:4), "For we hold that one is justified by faith apart from works of the law" (Romans 3:28), and "to the one who does not work but trusts him who justifies the ungodly, his faith is counted as righteousness" (Romans 4:5).

Isn't this a heavenly, inexpressibly sweet doctrine for us poor sinners? Can hell be deep and agonizing enough for the enemies of God? That is the rightful dwelling place of the ones who, out of pride and self-righteousness, reject this doctrine and do not want to be justified before God and saved. Oh, that there would be none among us for whom this doctrine is foolishness and offensive! It is the heavenly sun of the Christian religion that distinguishes it from all other religions just as the light distinguishes itself from the darkness. May this doctrine be a treasure preserved in all its purity. Let us hold fast to it! Thus, we will always have on earth the true ladder to heaven. And when we die, God Himself will say about us, "This one went justified," not down to his own house, but up into the house of heaven.

Just as I am, Thou wilt receive,
Wilt welcome, pardon, cleanse, relieve;
Because Thy promise I believe,
O Lamb of God, I come, I come. Amen.

† *(TLH 388:5)*

Tuesday

Read 1 John 1:9

WHOEVER IS A SINNER and still hopes to be saved because he relies upon God's goodness does not have his hope on a firm foundation. God is not only love but also holiness. He is not only good, gracious, patient, and forbearing, but also unalterably just. What does it help a sinful person if he thinks God regards him as righteous, but God's holiness and justice must nevertheless judge and condemn him? Doesn't justification stand in opposition to God's being, qualities, will, and unchangeable Law? It does appear so, but—praise God—appearances can be deceiving.

Justification has a firm foundation that nothing can invalidate. This was clearly indicated in last Sunday's reading. There we read that the tax collector sighed, "God, be merciful to me, a sinner!" (Luke 18:13). What he was really saying was that he took refuge, not in God's goodness and grace, but in His grace of the atonement through the work of the Savior. That is the firm foundation upon which justification rests. When we fell into the debt of sin, there was no help for us. Indeed, it appeared that even God Himself could not rescue us. For if, in grace, God had wanted to forgive us sinners, His strict, inviolable righteousness would have raised an eternal protest against it. But God's eternal wisdom had the solution. Since we could not pay the immense debt of our sins ourselves, and since God's righteousness could not declare us just without its payment, God allowed His only begotten Son Himself to become a man, and He imputed to Him our debt of sin. Thus, His Son, Jesus Christ, paid our debt in our place by His holy life and bitter suffering and death. When He had paid our debt to the very last cent, God the Father raised Him from the dead and gave Him might to proclaim this to all people in the form of forgiveness, righteousness, life, and salvation. Here, again, is the foundation for the justification of a poor sinner before God, according to the Gospel!

Is this foundation firm enough? Can we be in any doubt that our debt has been paid in full? Can righteousness still hinder the grace that declares the debtor to be debt-free? Or mustn't righteousness give way instead to the judgment of grace? Let us look to today's text, which attributes our justification not to grace, but directly to the faithfulness and righteousness of God: "If we confess our sins, He is faithful and just to forgive us our sins and to cleanse us from all unrighteousness" (1 John 1:9). Thus, it is certain: the justification of a poor sinner before God stands rock-solid, for it rests as much on God's righteousness, holiness, and faithfulness as on His goodness and grace. Its foundation is that God's Son already reconciled all people, already paid their debt of sin, and already acquired and offered them forgiveness and righteousness.

My guilt, O Father, Thou hast laid
On Christ, Thy Son, my Savior.
Lord Jesus, Thou my debt hast paid
And gained for me God's favor.
O Holy Ghost, Thou Fount of grace,
The good in me to Thee I trace;
In faith do Thou preserve me. Amen.

(*TLH* 375:5)

Wednesday

Read 2 Timothy 1:12

A PERSON WHO does not know if he has the true faith and stands in grace with God is certainly in a miserable state. Countless people have this uncertainty, and many of them do not even desire to resolve it. Their hope is founded on the most tenuous of grounds, and they must be prepared to accept damnation. But it is frightening not to know our standing before God, who created us, redeemed us, preserves us, and will be our judge at death. How can a person who is unsure of divine grace lie at night in peace? Mustn't he think, "How shall I fare if I fall asleep into death this night?" How can such a person awaken in the morning with joy? Mustn't he fear that he faces another unblessed day? How can he go to work with anticipation? Mustn't he fear that a curse will rest upon his labors? How can he rejoice when it goes well for him? Mustn't he fear that, in His wrath, God is sending him earthly wealth? How can he comfort and console himself when trouble oppresses him? Mustn't he regard everything as a punishment? How can he not despair when so many enemies set themselves against him? Mustn't he believe that God will inflict a punishment upon him, that he will fall into the hands of his opponents and come to shame before them? How can he endure sicknesses that befall him? Mustn't he think that God will completely forsake him because he despised God's grace? How frightful must each harbinger of death be to such a person! Mustn't he expect that it is a sign of his eternal rejection and expulsion from God's presence?

Truly, we may wonder how a person who does not know if he stands before God in grace is not terrified by every leaf that rustles near him. We may wonder if he can still raise his face to heaven, read or hear God's Word, enter a church, receive the holy Sacraments, and open his mouth for prayer or song without being alarmed.

Conversely, there is no one more fortunate than the one who knows he stands in grace before God. With joy he can lie down at night, for he knows he is placing himself in the arms of his God, who appoints His angels to watch over him. With joy he can awaken in the morning, for he knows God has preserved him in order to give him a new day with new grace. With joy he goes to his calling, for he knows God is with him. With joy he sees himself blessed on earth, for he knows God wants to make him happy. With confidence and courage, he looks forward to trouble, for he knows God wants to lead him to heaven along this path. Without dread, he sees himself surrounded by secret and public enemies, for he knows he has nothing to fear from them; without God's will, they cannot bend one of his hairs, for God stands with him in covenant. He gladly climbs into the sickbed God has prepared for him because there he can think, speak, and do to the glory of God. The news of the nearness of his death is a happy message to him, for he knows that "I long to be in heaven / In that untroubled sphere / Where they will be rewarded / Who served their God while here" (*TLH* 407:1). With joy he opens his Bible, for in it he finds light, power, comfort, and peace. With joy he enters into the house of God, for there his soul delights in the glorious worship of the Lord. He joins in the congregational hymns and prayers, and the use of the Holy Supper gives him a festive day.

Oh, how blessed is the one who knows he stands in the true faith and, for this reason, he stands with God in grace! He already has heaven on earth, despite its thousandfold trouble.

Help me, for I am weak; I fight,
Yet scarce can battle longer;
I cling but to Thy grace and might,
'Tis Thou canst make me stronger;
When sore temptations are my lot,
And tempests round me lower,
Break the power:
So through deliverance wrought,
I know that Thou forsak'st me not. Amen.

✝ *(ELHB 365:5)*

Thursday

Read 1 Corinthians 15:1–2

THIS IS A GLORIOUS DESCRIPTION of Christians who truly believe. Saint Paul says they received the Gospel and stand in it. These are not the words of man, but the words of the Holy Ghost, who speaks through the apostle. God's words are deep, rich, and comprehensive. Many think that if they call "good" what the Word of God says, if they are pleased with the beautiful doctrine of the Gospel, if they gladly and diligently hear and read the Bible, then they also received it. However, a person can have a certain pleasure in the Word of God and nevertheless be full of enmity against it when it touches a sore spot in his heart. It is said of Herod, "for Herod feared John, knowing that he was a righteous and holy man, and he kept him safe. When he heard him, he was greatly perplexed, and yet he heard him gladly" (Mark 6:20). However, when John chastised Herod for the sin of having his brother's wife, he had to die under the executioner's ax. In like manner, almost all of Germany once praised Luther's comforting teaching, yet we hear this man complained about everywhere; people did not accept his word, but rejected it instead.

By nature, no person is capable of receiving the Word in his heart. He must be brought to it by the Holy Ghost. As often as an unconverted person hears, reads, or examines the Word of God, the Holy Ghost seeks to convince him that he is a great sinner, that he does not stand in grace with God, and that God's wrath rests upon him. If, through this divine working, the person does not resist the Holy Ghost, his heart is filled with a deep sadness and his awakened conscience provokes anxiety and even terror in him. Then, through the Gospel, a heartfelt longing for grace, help, and mercy arises in the person. Oh, blessed is he who experiences this, for this longing for grace is the beginning of the true, saving faith. It begins as soon as the sinner reaches out with longing to Christ, the propitiation of all sins. If such a person remains under the cultivation of the Holy Ghost through the Word of the Gospel, he finally, in faith and confidence, embraces Christ so he can cry out with divine certainty: "Praise the Lord, O my soul! For I, a sinner, have found grace. I, a miserable person, have found mercy." The person who has had such an experience has received the Gospel and come to true faith.

Whoever has not experienced any of the pains of true repentance, whoever has not yet felt the force of the Law and regarded himself as a sinner through the enlightenment of the Holy Ghost, whoever has never groaned from the depths of his distressed heart for Christ's grace, and whoever still fails to recognize that a person cannot believe in Christ by his own powers but alone by the working of the Holy Ghost is certainly still without faith. The birth of faith in the soul of a sinner cannot leave him unmoved. Indeed, it is a work that transforms the whole person—from darkness to light, from spiritual death to spiritual life—and brings him out of powerlessness into a divine strength. Luther gloriously speaks about this in the preface to his commentary on the Epistle to the Romans: "This is the reason that, when they hear the Gospel, they fall-to and make for themselves, by their own powers, an idea in their hearts, which says, 'I believe.' This they hold for true faith. But it is a human imagination and idea that never reaches the depths of the heart, and so nothing comes of it and no betterment follows it. Faith, however, is a divine work in us. It changes us and makes us to be born anew of God" (John 1); it kills the old Adam and makes altogether different men, in heart and spirit and mind and powers, and it brings with it the Holy Ghost. . . . Pray God to work faith in you; else you will remain forever without faith, whatever you think or do" (xvi, xvii).

Now keep us, holy Savior,
In Thy true love and fear
And grant us of Thy favor
The grace to persevere
Till, in Thy new creation,
Earth's timelong travail o'er,
We find our full salvation
And praise Thee evermore. Amen.

† *(TLH 32:4)*

Friday

Read 1 Corinthians 15:3–4

WHEN SAINT PAUL tries to convince the Corinthians that he had planted the true faith in them, he says he laid the foundation for all of them with Scripture. In this we see a sure mark of the person who has true faith: his faith is grounded in God's Word alone. This is very important. In the 1700s, there was such a great falling away in Christendom that for forty years almost nothing about faith was preached. Instead, a comfortless heathen ethic resounded from most pulpits, especially in Germany. Then, from 1817 on, many began again to preach something about faith. Indeed, the great majority of teachers and hearers confess that faith is necessary for salvation.

But let us not deceive ourselves. Not everything a person would like to include under this term is really faith. Even true believers can fall into error. For instance, there is no true faith where a person knowingly errs or lightly regards his errors as small and not dangerous. There is no true faith where a person is careless or indifferent about whether a doctrine is correct or incorrect. There is no true faith where a person knowingly departs from one single Word of God. God is not satisfied when we accept only some of His holy Word, no matter how acceptable it appears to our reason and our feelings. Whoever thinks he is unable to accept some small part of Holy Scripture rejects all of it. Whoever does not want to recognize the Old Testament as God's Word thereby rejects the New Testament, for the latter is grounded in the former.

True, saving faith can exist only where a person vividly recognizes, by the enlightenment of the Holy Ghost, that all of Scripture is the revealed Word of God, the Most High, who will one day judge the entire world. Where there is true faith, there one is filled with the deepest reverence toward Scripture. In Psalm 119:120, David says he is so fearful before God and His laws that his skin trembles. Isaiah 66:2 says God regards the suffering of those with a broken spirit and those who fear His Word. Wherever there is true faith, a person does not knowingly depart from one letter of Holy Scripture; indeed, he would rather forsake goods, glory, even life itself. One single word of Scripture has more value to a true believer than all the wisdom and utterances of all the world's wise men. A true believer never asks, "How is that possible?" With him, the all-important question is, "What is written? What do you read?" If he has the clear Word of God, he humbly accepts it, even when his reason, his heart, and his feelings still seem to want to contradict it. Whatever conflicts with the clear Word of God, he knows, must be rejected as delusion and falsehood no matter how reasonable it sounds. Anything that has only the appearance of God's Word is insufficient. The true believer is cautious in matters of faith and filled with an earnest worry that he does not deceive himself. He grounds everything on God's Word. If one Bible text is against him, he cannot rest easy, even if all the world calls him blessed. But if he has God's Word for himself, nothing can disturb him, even if the whole world—yes, even his own heart—condemns him.

Guard, O God, our faith forever;
Let not Satan, death, or shame
Ever part us from our Savior;
Lord our Refuge is Thy name.
Though our flesh cry ever: Nay!
Be Thy Word to us still Yea! Amen.

(TLH 226:8)

Saturday

Read 1 Corinthians 15:8–10

WITHOUT DOUBT, Saint Paul stood in the true faith in Jesus Christ. How did it show itself in him? Before his conversion, he was arrogant and self-righteous, but after he became a Christian, he was humble, calling himself "one untimely born" (1 Corinthians 15:8) and "the least of the apostles" (1 Corinthians 15:9). He even said he was "unworthy to be called an apostle" (1 Corinthians 15:9). He considered all his former righteousness according to the Law as rubbish, and his boasts now were confined to the grace of his God of mercy. Before, he was a persecutor of the Church of God; now he gathered a holy Church to Christ, to His praise and honor, by his tireless preaching of the Gospel in all lands. Before, he tempted many souls, now he sought to rescue souls and bring them to Christ, showing himself to be a faithful shepherd of Christ's sheep. Before, he dishonored Christ, now he sought to promote Christ's glory. Before, in religious fanaticism, he persecuted the "heterodox," now he wished to be banished from Christ if it meant he could rescue the souls of his deluded brothers.

We see here the picture of a Christian who not only accepts the Gospel but also stands in it. Let us, according to this, honestly and earnestly examine ourselves. Wherever there is true faith, there will also be the proof of a new life. If you were once arrogant, you will now be humble before God and man. If you were once money-loving and miserly, you will now be generous and heavenly-minded. If you were once vain and a lover of the world, you will now be self-denying and godly. If you were formerly unchaste and lustful, you will now be chaste and moderate. If you were formerly bad-tempered, you will now be meek and kind. If you were formerly unfaithful and dishonest, you will now be honest and conscientious. If you were formerly lukewarm and lazy, you will now be zealous and fervent. If you were formerly careless and apathetic in your earthly vocation, you will now be earnest and diligent. If you were formerly full of jesting and things of folly, your mouth will now be filled with God's praise and edifying speech. If you were formerly full of murmuring against God and consumed by earthly worries, you will now devote yourself to your heavenly Father and be full of confidence. If you previously served sin, the world, and Satan eagerly, you will now earnestly serve righteousness, God, and your Savior. For "if anyone is in Christ, he is a new creation. The old has passed away; behold, the new has come" (2 Corinthians 5:17).

Whoever can say, with Paul, "But by the grace of God I am what I am, and His grace toward me was not in vain" (1 Corinthians 15:10), does not despair at the great weakness of his flesh. If he also says, with Paul, "For I do not do the good I want, but the evil I do not want is what I keep on doing" (Romans 7:19), he fights on uprightly and does not let sin rule over him. If, in the fight against sin here, grace is not futile in us, it is thus a sign to us that it will also not be futile when we one day appear before God's throne. It will absolve us from all sin and open to us the entrance to eternal blessedness.

Destroy in me the lust of sin,
From all impureness make me clean.
Oh, grant me pow'r and strength, my God,
To strive against my flesh and blood! Amen.

† *(TLH 398:2)*

Sunday

Read Mark 7:31–35

THE DEAF-MUTE was a very miserable person. He is a picture of how every man is by nature according to his soul. However, he was brought to Christ so He might help him. Christ graciously and kindly received him. This is a picture of how a person becomes righteous before God: "He put His fingers into his ears, and after spitting touched his tongue. And looking up to heaven, He sighed and said to him, 'Ephphatha,' that is, 'Be opened.' And his ears were opened, his tongue was released, and he spoke plainly" (Mark 7:33–35). Here we have a picture of sanctification. As the Savior received the deaf-mute in grace and healed his infirmities, so too does the Savior heal the soul of every person who has found grace with Him.

Justification occurs in heaven. A poor person, mourning over his sins, often does not know he has already been justified. He may continue to cry tears of repentance on earth while in heaven all the angels are already rejoicing over him. However, justification does not remain without effect on a person. Its first fruit is that such an individual is born again. He receives a new heart and a new mind that no longer loves sin but instead loves God and His Word. He now wishes to live a godly life. In justification, as that person is declared by the heavenly Father to be His child for the sake of Christ's atonement, the Holy Ghost begins the work of sanctification in his heart. It may begin very slowly, but the transformation is real. The person who is justified becomes a completely different person. He begins to live for Jesus instead of for himself. Concern for the salvation of his soul busies his heart endlessly. He would rather speak about heavenly things than about anything else. Even when he performs his earthly business, he does so with a mind directed toward God. He begins to keep watch over his thoughts and desires. He can no longer be indifferent as evil thoughts go through his mind. If they arise, he sighs and prays against them. He is hostile toward every sin. If, out of rashness and weakness, he falls into sin, he does not persist in it. Instead, he is ashamed. He confesses his sin to God and prays for forgiveness. He lets his fall serve as a warning, and he becomes more humble and watchful over himself.

A person in whom the process of sanctification has begun regards the pleasures of the world as vanity. Therefore, he no longer conforms himself to the world. The pleasure he receives from God's Word and edifying fellowship with zealous Christians is more dear to him. If the Christian has a day of joy, it is joy in the Lord. If he possesses earthly goods, his heart does not cling to them but to God alone. If suffering befalls him, he prays to God for patience, guards himself from murmuring against God, and comforts himself with the glory that awaits him in heaven. He seeks to devote his entire life to his neighbor. He loves his neighbor from his heart. He gladly helps him when he is in need, he rejoices in his happiness, and he sympathizes when misfortune befalls him. He happily covers his neighbor's weaknesses. He gladly reconciles with the person who has offended him. He is concerned for the salvation of his neighbor's soul.

Finally, the most precious thing about true sanctification is that a person comes to realize that this is worked in him by God's grace alone. Therefore, he regards himself as nothing before God. Such is the new heart and the new life that the Holy Ghost works in those who are justified through faith in Jesus Christ.

Let my soul, in full exemption,
Wake up in Thy likeness now;
Thou art made to me redemption,
My sanctification Thou.
Whatever I need for my journey to heaven,
In Thee, O my Savior, is unto me given;
O let me all perishing pleasure forego,
And Thy life, O Jesus, alone let me know. Amen.

(ELHB 83:7)

Monday

Read Mark 7:36–37

THOSE WHO BROUGHT the deaf-mute to Christ were already justified; God had begun the work of sanctification by His Spirit in their hearts. Undoubtedly they intended good when they publicly boasted of Christ's glorious, miraculous work, but they nevertheless sinned by it. Their zeal was not entirely pure as they transgressed a command of Christ by it. Their otherwise good deed was stained with self-will and disobedience. They acted without a call. Yet they did all this not out of wickedness but out of weakness.

Justification happens in a blink of an eye. As soon as a sinner, in despair, recognizes his sin and desires grace and redemption, God speaks a word in heaven and justification takes place. Sanctification, on the contrary, does not happen suddenly. It occurs gradually, and it continues until the end of our life. Justification is immediately perfect. Each one who is justified instantly receives the full forgiveness of his sins, the complete righteousness of Christ, and a new status as a child of God. Sanctification, which follows justification, begins weakly and grows until death, but it never comes to perfection. Unfortunately, there are enthusiasts who pretend that a person can bring sanctification to perfection. But only a hypocrite or self-deceiver can be bold enough to raise himself above the apostles and prophets and claim that he is perfect in sanctification. Whoever thinks that he is perfect can no longer pray the fifth petition of the Lord's Prayer; he is no longer in need of a Savior and the Gospel.

Saint Paul says this about perfection: "Let those of us who are mature think this way, and if in anything you think otherwise" (Philippians 3:15). How can this be? Earlier, he had said, "Not that I have already obtained this or am already perfect" (Philippians 3:12). Perfection for the Christian is the clear recognition that he is imperfect in himself, but nevertheless perfect in Christ Jesus. There are many who doubt that they properly display their state of grace because they continue to feel the life of sin in their heart. They think, "If I stand in grace, I must also have such a mighty feeling of grace in my soul that I could always overcome sin, the flesh, the world, and the devil victoriously and with joy. Instead, I must daily fight with sin and thereby feel that my faith has no conquering power over the world and sin."

When a person is justified, God generally lets him taste the sweetness of His grace in order to draw the sinner from the world to Himself. At this point, many a beginner in Christ thinks he is rid of the world, sin, and Satan. But if that were truly the case, it would not be long before such a person became secure and proud. Therefore, our faithful God removes the sweet feelings of grace and power from most of His believers, and from that time on, He bestows such blessings meagerly and allows His Christians to grow in humility. When a person becomes truly poor, he must daily beg God for everything and adhere to Jesus' word of grace so he is not lost. He also comes to realize that God's work of grace in sanctification is revealed in the fact that his spirit continues to struggle against his flesh. If he feels that sin rages in him, but something else in him prevents sin from gaining dominion over him, this moves him to prayer and to the Word of God. If he succumbs to sinful temptations, he goes to Jesus and prays to Him for forgiveness. Such a person is not dead, for a dead heart no longer beats.

Let us who are already engaged in this battle fight on courageously. Let us, however, not fight in our own strength, but daily draw power from the fountain of divine grace in Christ Jesus. Then we can be sure we will hold the field and attain victory.

Grant steadfastness and courage
That bravely we contend
Against the wiles of Satan;
O Lord, Thy flock defend!
Help us to battle well,
To triumph o'er the devil,
To overcome the evil
And all the powers of hell. Amen.

(ELHB 252:12)

Tuesday

Read Acts 20:28

THE OFFICE OF PREACHING is not merely a beneficial human office. Unlike the role of the teacher in the schools and the manager in the workplace, the preaching office was not instituted because people understood how necessary and useful it is to provide religious instruction. No, the preaching office has a higher source. It is a holy, divine office. God, the Most High, established it to be the proper means through which His people could be led to blessedness. The Old Testament testifies to this with the words, "And I will give you shepherds after My own heart, who will feed you with [doctrine and wisdom]" (Jeremiah 3:15); "O God, you provided for the needy. The Lord gives the word; the women who announce the news are a great host [evangelists]" (Psalm 68:10–11); and "Be glad, O children of Zion, and rejoice in the LORD your God [who gives you teachers for righteousness]" (Joel 2:23). The New Testament reports the same thing. Saint Paul writes, "And God has appointed in the church first apostles, second prophets, third teachers" (1 Corinthians 12:28); and "All this is from God, who through Christ reconciled us to Himself and gave us the ministry of reconciliation; that is, in Christ God was reconciling the world to Himself, not counting their trespasses against them, and entrusting to us the message of reconciliation" (2 Corinthians 5:18–19). What is attributed here to God the Father is attributed elsewhere also to God the Son. It is said of Him: "He who descended is the one who also ascended far above all the heavens, that He might fill all things.) And He gave the apostles, the prophets, the evangelists, the pastors and teachers" (Ephesians 4:10–11).

We must not think that this concerns only those who were once called directly into the preaching office by God and Christ and that preachers today are called by the congregation into their office as a work of man, a human contract. No, for this reason, Christ left behind to His Church the keys of the kingdom of heaven so that, in His name, it might administer the goods entrusted to it. In His authority, the Church can fill its offices with qualified people. Christ also exhorts His Christians to pray to the Lord of the harvest for faithful workers in His harvest. The preachers, called by God through the Church, stand in a divine office, not as slaves of men, but as servants of Christ and as ones sent by God the Most High. Therefore, Paul says of the servants of the Church at Ephesus, who were also called, not directly by God and Christ, but indirectly through their congregations, that the Holy Ghost Himself set them to be bishops to shepherd the Church of God, which He purchased with His own blood.

God has also irrefutably testified with deeds that the preaching office is not a changeable human ordinance, but His own holy institution. Despite the ragings of Satan and the world against this office, God has preserved it from the beginning of the world until this hour. In early times, the first-born of all families were also their priests. Later, God chose the tribe of Levi from among the Israelite people (and especially the family of Aaron) to be the exclusive holders of all priestly offices and rights. In the time of the New Testament, that role was assigned to the twelve apostles and the seventy disciples Christ sent out into all the world as heralds of His Gospel. But they appointed other persons as bishops and elders in the congregations they established, and so this office has remained until the present day.

Although many institutions of more recent founding have fallen over the years, the holy preaching office has never ceased to exist. God has proved that the preaching office is His work, in that He has mightily protected it so it might never be lacking in His Church. For the works of God must remain, even when the works of man must perish.

Yea, bless Thy Word alway,
Our souls forever feeding;
And may we never lack
A faithful shepherd's leading!
Seek Thou the wandering sheep,

Bind up the sore opprest,
Lift up the fallen ones,
And grant the weary rest. Amen.

† *(TLH 485:6)*

Wednesday

Read Acts 26:17–18

ACCORDING TO TODAY'S READING, the preacher has the task of fighting against the devil and rescuing and converting from his power all who called him to his office, bringing each one to faith, and then watching over him so he does not fall away. He is to counsel, admonish, and comfort his parishioners in good days and evil days, and he is to lead them through the last battle into the heavenly kingdom.

He should awaken from their spiritual sleep those who walk along secure and careless, not worrying about heaven or hell, that they become anxious about the salvation of their soul and the possibility of being lost. He should free those who love sin and are bound by it so they abhor their favorite sin, come to repentance, and weep, saying: "What have I done? Father, I have sinned in heaven and before You and am no longer worthy to be called Your child." He should persuade those who seek their heaven on earth and place their happiness in the goods or joys or honors of this world, so they are disgusted with the world and say: "World, farewell! I am tired of you. I want to go to heaven. O glory of the earth, I do not want, I do not like you!"

The preacher should persuade those who are self-righteous, regarding themselves as worthy of eternal reward because they live blameless before the world, so they beat their breast and learn to say, with the tax collector, "God, be merciful to me, a sinner!" (Luke 18:13). He should convince those to whom the Gospel is foolishness, who build upon their understanding and want to belong to the wise of this world, so they cry out, with Paul, "Indeed, I count everything as loss because of the surpassing worth of knowing Christ Jesus my Lord" (Philippians 3:8); and "He is the source of your life in Christ Jesus, whom God made our wisdom and our righteousness and sanctification and redemption" (1 Corinthians 1:30).

If a preacher has so snatched the booty of hell, and if the souls of all who are entrusted to him have been brought to Christ, he has in no way finished the work that has been charged to him. He must continue to watch day and night to see if the rescued soul is in danger of temptation and falling back. Moreover, as a spiritual father, he must try to feed, strengthen, and bring up his spiritual children. If wolves in sheep's clothing (that is, false teachers with a good appearance) draw near, he must, without hesitation, warn the souls entrusted to him, uncover the false doctrine, and rebuke and fight against it, all the while defending the pure doctrine with earnestness and not deviating one iota from it. Peace or discord may arise from it; one may then praise or scold him on account of it. If sins, offenses, dangerous practices, indifference to the world, and the like arise within his congregation, he must quickly place himself against them, admonishing his parishioners and halting the offenses, regardless of the personal cost to him.

If he sees a weak lamb in his flock, he must strengthen it. If he sees a sick one, he must nurse it. If he sees a troubled and afflicted one, he must rescue it. If he sees one that has fallen, he must help it up. If he sees that one has been lost, he must pursue it and not rest until he has found it and carried it home again. He must place himself before the breach in the congregation and make himself a wall against the destruction and against the punishment that will result from the judgment of God. He must be the light that shines into all houses. He must be the salt of the earth that wards off the decay of error and sin. He must be the doctor who binds up all wounds and gives the right medicine to cure all sicknesses of the soul. He must be the intercessor who daily places himself before God for all. He must be the mother who carries all in her heart with maternal love.

In a word, the preacher must be the good shepherd, who rightly tends, fights, teaches, and defends, never fleeing from any danger but always ready to give his life for the sheep. Therefore, one day he should be able to say to God, "Here I am and all the children that You have given me. Count them, Lord. See, I have lost none of them."

The servants Thou hast called
And to Thy Church art giving
Preserve in doctrine pure
And holiness of living.
Thy Spirit fill their hearts,
Endue their tongues power;
What they should boldly speak,
Oh, give them in that hour! Amen.

† *(TLH 485:5)*

Thursday

Read 2 Corinthians 5:18

WOE TO CHRISTIAN PREACHERS if they have nothing to preach but the Law! Their hearers will become hungry by it, but not satisfied. They will be startled out of their security, but they will never come to peace. They will learn to know their distress, but they will remain without help and rescue. They will be led to ask anxiously, "What should we do so we will be saved?" but the preachers will have no answer for them. Even if they would earnestly proclaim God's Law until the last day, no person's heart would become alive and no one would be truly converted to God.

But—thank God!—there is a glorious, precious, powerful means that will miraculously help all those who have been beaten down and killed by the Law. The means is the Gospel, the Good News, and it is entrusted to the evangelical preacher. His message is summarized in the following words: "The saying is trustworthy and deserving of full acceptance, that Christ Jesus came into the world to save sinners" (1 Timothy 1:15); "For God so loved the world, that He gave His only Son, that whoever believes in Him should not perish but have eternal life" (John 3:16); "[Jesus] receives sinners" (Luke 15:2); and "Those who are well have no need of a physician, but those who are sick" (Matthew 9:12).

This preaching of righteousness by grace makes the evangelical preaching office one of the Spirit, who makes alive. This gives it an exuberant clearness that makes it far superior to the office of Moses, the office of the Law. O, glorious office! If it falls hard upon a person's heart that he must perfectly keep God's commandments, though he is unable and asks,

"What should I do to become righteous?" the preachers should answer: "Christ is the end of the law. Believe on Him and so you are just." O glorious office! If a person has come to a vivid knowledge of sin and then asks, "What should I do to blot out my immense sin and become pure?" the preachers should answer, "The blood of Jesus Christ, the Son of God, makes you clean from all your sin." O glorious office! If a person who knows he has been pardoned cannot see any sign of sanctification in his life so that he asks, "Where do I get power for a new life?" the preachers should answer him, "Enter then through faith in Jesus, for without Him you can do nothing; but through Him, who makes you strong, you are able." O glorious office! If a person says: "I was once a believing Christian and was so blessed. But sin enticed me. I have fallen very deeply. Is there still help for me?" the preachers should answer, "Yes, indeed. Do not try, then, to help yourself. Hand yourself over to Jesus, for He has ascended on high and has led captivity captive, and He has received gifts for people, even for the unfaithful!

O glorious office! No matter how sick a person may be in his soul, the Gospel can heal him. No matter how deeply a person has fallen into the corruption of sin, the Gospel can pull him out. No matter how troubled, frightened, and afflicted a person may be, the Gospel can comfort him. Whatever the condition in which a person finds himself, even if he is convinced that he must perish because of it, the preachers can confidently oppose him, saying: "No, as certainly as God lives, He does not want the death of any sinner. You shall not perish; instead, you shall be saved. Turn to Jesus, who can evermore save all who come to God through Him." And if one who lies near death calls out: "God, what have I done? Woe to me! Now it is too late! I am lost!" the preachers should call to him: "No, no, it is not too late! Commit your departing soul to Jesus. You too shall still be with Him in paradise today."

O, glorious, high office, too high for the angels! May we always hold it in high regard, not looking at the person who bears it and despising his weakness, but looking instead at the Institutor of this office and His exuberant goodness. Let us turn to Him in faith so we can experience the blessings of which the preachers have spoken and, through them, be gathered together one day into the barns of heaven as a completely ripe sheaf.

And for this our soul's salvation
Voucheth Thy good Spirit, Lord,
In Thy Sacraments and Word.
He imparteth consolation,
Granteth us the gift of faith
That we fear nor hell nor death. Amen.

† *(TLH 384:3)*

Friday

Read 2 Corinthians 3:4–6

IN TODAY'S TEXT, Saint Paul humbly confesses that he would not have known how to separate the Gospel from the Law and so conduct himself correctly in his preaching office if God had not made him qualified for it. Behold, dear Christian, if you want to know how to divide and use the Gospel and the Law in your heart for salvation, you must ask God for this blessed ability. The Holy Ghost is the only teacher who can teach you correctly. No effort of our reason will help. Without the Holy Ghost, the entire divine revelation, Law as well as Gospel, remains dark, unclear, contradictory, and even foolishness to us. Without the enlightenment of the Holy Ghost, we can never rightly understand why either the Law or the Gospel was given to us.

Let us especially note the following in our heartfelt supplications for the light of the Holy Ghost. Both the Law and the Gospel are doctrines that have their source in God, and both must be preached in the Church if the people are to hear the whole counsel of God for their salvation. We must not believe that the stern Law cannot be heard in an evangelical sermon. We cannot think that a person who keeps the Law at least outwardly will be righteous before God. Anyone who wants to be justified by the Law does not know how much the Law demands from us. He is like the Jews, who, failing to understand the Law, thought they kept it and, for this reason, rejected Christ. No one becomes a Christian by doing good works according to the Law. Instead, he becomes a Christian through faith, and then he is able to do works that please God. Whoever thinks that keeping God's commandments makes him a good Christian does not know what a Christian is. A person becomes a Christian, not by doing, but by believing. Whoever thinks he can be certain of being saved, and so wants to believe in Christ and do good works, confuses Law and Gospel and has no idea what faith is. No law, no work, and no merit will avail here. In the article on the justification of the sinner before God, we must separate the Law from the Gospel as far as heaven is from the earth. To the questions "How do I become righteous before God?" and "How do I become a Christian?" God's Word gives no other answer than "Believe in the Lord Jesus." If one has come to true faith, truly good works will follow. One who has become a good tree will bring forth good fruits. One who has become a good fountain will pour forth good thoughts and a hearty love of God and His Word.

But one may interject at this point: why then has God given us His holy Law? We would be miserable and eternally lost if God had given us His Law that we should be saved by keeping it. Then no person would be saved. God had already given His Law in Eden, but man fell. Now he is born as a poor sinner and has no hope of keeping the Law perfectly. The Law is preached to us so we can recognize our revolt against it, feel the death and divine wrath that sin brings, and seek to embrace the better righteousness of Jesus Christ. He alone can help us out of our sin into righteousness, out of death into life, and out of wrath into grace in heaven.

Help us, Lord Jesus Christ, for we
A Mediator have in Thee.
Our works cannot salvation gain;
They merit but endless pain.
Have mercy, Lord! Amen.

(TLH 287:12)

Saturday

Read 2 Corinthians 3:6–11

"FOR THE LETTER KILLS, but the Spirit gives life," Saint Paul writes (2 Corinthians 3:6). This means that the Law shows a person that he is dead in his sins. Because of his sins, he has earned temporal and eternal death. But the Law leaves him standing in sin. It does not show him any way to come out of death. Instead, the deeper the Law penetrates into his heart, the more the person must despair of ever being rescued out of his misery and being saved. The Gospel, however, is the comforting message from God's mouth directed to poor, sinful, lost man: "When I passed by you and saw you wallowing in your blood, I said to you in your blood, 'Live!' I said to you in your blood, 'Live!'" (Ezekiel 16:6).

The Law tells us what we should do, but it immediately shows us that we cannot do it. On the contrary, the Gospel tells us what God has done for us, that He has fulfilled in our place what we are unable to do for ourselves. The Law reveals to us our sickness and makes us feel sin's fatal wound to our soul. The Gospel introduces us to the heavenly Doctor; it is the balm that quiets the pains of the soul and brings eternal healing. The Law shows us our poverty and the shame of our nakedness before God, but the Gospel opens to us God's heavenly charity, whereby we receive all of the garments of salvation to cover our soul so we can confidently appear before God's judgment seat. The Law calls out, "You are lost, for you have not done what God commanded!" But the Gospel says: "Do not despair, sinner. There is Help, for here is Jesus Christ, a Savior for all sinners, for the great and the small, for the old and the young."

Through the Law comes knowledge of sin and divine wrath; through the Gospel comes the knowledge of the atonement for sins and grace in Christ. Saint Paul says it even more clearly in our text when he writes that the Law is the office that preaches condemnation, while the Gospel is the office that preaches righteousness. Thus the divine Law is not a moral code that tells us only that we should live modestly, honorably, and justly before men. No, where the Law is truly preached in its purity, it preaches nothing but eternal damnation for all people because the Law is spiritual and addresses itself to the heart of the sinner. It preaches that people should be completely holy and pure in their thoughts, words, and works—holy just like the holy God and Father in heaven. And then it adds the terrible threat, "Cursed be everyone who does not abide by all things written in the Book of the Law, and do them" (Galatians 3:10). Therefore the apostle says that the Law preaches condemnation to all people, without exception, for no one can keep it. Each of our transgressions awards us condemnation. The Gospel, however, preaches righteousness to us. This righteousness is not ours, for we cannot earn it. The righteousness of the Gospel is Christ's righteousness, which God wants to give us freely when we believe in Him—our Substitute, Savior, and Redeemer.

But the most glorious distinction Paul makes in our text between the Law and the Gospel is that the former ceases but the latter remains. He says that the Law must be preached to us sinners in all its severity; we must recognize our misery in it and, with terror, feel the threats of God in our heart. However, the Law should not hold our death before us forever. It must cease, striking us only until we hurry to Christ. Precisely when the Law appears to have conquered us, when we want to know no more of its threats, then it must cease. For then the Gospel opens to us a refuge in Christ, the Crucified, where Moses with his curse can no longer reach in.

The Law may threaten endless death
From awful Sinai's burning hill,
Straightway from its consuming breath
My soul through faith mounts higher still;
She throws herself at Jesus' feet
And finds with Him a safe retreat,
Where curse and death can never come.

Though all foes threaten condemnation,
Yet Jesus, Thou art my Salvation,
For in Thy love I find my home. Amen.

(ELHB 109:3)

Sunday

Read Luke 10:25–33

MOST PEOPLE BELIEVE they are saved by fulfilling what they think are their duties toward their neighbor. They completely forget about the necessity of fearing, loving, and trusting God above all things. Yet focusing on the neighbor while ignoring God is nothing but self-deception. No one can fulfill the requirements of the Law this way. Much, much more is involved.

The lawyer who, according to our text, tested Jesus thought he had fulfilled the commandment of love for his neighbor. But what did our Lord answer him? He responded with a parable, saying that a Jew who traveled from Jerusalem to Jericho fell among robbers that stripped him, beat him, and left him half-dead. A priest and a Levite passed by without showing mercy to the suffering man. However, one of the Samaritans, to whom the Jews were so hostile, came by and "had compassion" on him (Luke 10:33). Although he saw his enemy lying in his own blood, he did not rejoice over his misfortune, but heartily cared for him. Why did Christ relate this parable? He wanted to show the lawyer that a person must love both his friend and his enemy if he is to fulfill his duty toward his neighbor.

This story shows that no person can justify himself before God and make himself holy, for no one can perfectly fulfill the commandment to love his enemy as his friend. Many people, even heathens, have shamed their enemies by the kindnesses they extend to them, but where is the person who can say he loves his enemy like a friend? All Christians must conquer their anger against their enemies and finally embrace them with love, but where is the person who can say that he never carried anger against his enemy in his heart? If he became angry with his enemy even once, he did not fulfill the commandment of love for the neighbor and he condemns himself as a transgressor of the Law.

The law of love for the neighbor demands that we rejoice in the happiness of our enemy as if it were our own and grieve over his misfortune as if it had befallen us. It requires us to be just as concerned for his temporal and eternal welfare as we are for our own, and to pray just as heartily for him as for ourselves. We must be more interested in our offender's obtaining forgiveness from God for his sin against us than in receiving an apology from him ourselves. Therefore, Christ says elsewhere, "But I say to you, Love your enemies and pray for those who persecute you" (Matthew 5:44).

Only Jesus Christ, the Son of God, demonstrated such love on earth. Only He always returned evil with good, wickedness with kindness, curses with blessings, and hate with love. He lamented, with great tears, the misfortunes of His persecutors, prayed for His murderers, and gave up His life on the cross for the salvation of all his enemies. Who has perfectly imitated the Savior? No one. For this reason, the commandment to love the neighbor shows that no person can justify himself before God and thus save himself.

Oh, that the Lord would guide my ways
To keep His statutes still!
Oh, that my God would grant me grace
To know and do His will! Amen.

† *(TLH 416:1)*

Monday

Read Luke 10:34

ALL WHO THINK they are able to justify themselves by fulfilling the commandment to love their neighbor are deluded. They think they have acted justly toward everyone, that no one can call them to account, and that all the world must recognize their actions as just. Thus, they believe, they have done enough to satisfy the commandment of love. They think this love demands that they give to each person what is his, return what they have borrowed, repay kindness with kindness and love with love, help their neighbor (if it isn't too much trouble for them), avoid placing their neighbor in danger or bringing upon him any disgrace, giving to the poor from their excess, and the like.

But they deceive themselves mightily. This is not love, but justice. True love is incomparably more than justice. Christ demonstrates this in the example of the merciful Samaritan. He did not think, "If the priest and the Levite passed by this suffering man, who is their brother in the faith, it isn't necessary for me to exert myself." He did not think, "It is unsafe in this forest. I must think about saving my own life so I may safely come to the inn." He did not think, "I am tired and need my beast of burden for myself. I will go to the inn and there summon people to bring in the half-dead man." No. Instead, he thought, "If the priest and the Levite passed by their distressed brother in the faith, let them see how they will answer for it before God. I feel myself obligated to help." He thought, "I too may be in danger of falling into the hands of robbers, but I have a duty to practice love. If God will not protect me now, may His will then be done. Why shouldn't I give my life for my neighbor?" Finally, he thought, "If I first hurry to the inn and fetch help, this poor man could die in the meantime and I would become his murderer by my negligence and convenience." So he poured oil and wine into his wounds, bandaged them, placed him on his animal, and accompanied him to the inn.

We see here how the commandment of love is fulfilled. A person must be ready and willing, out of love for his neighbor, to offer the greatest sacrifice. True love does not ask what other people ought to do. It thinks, "Even if no one else acts, I am still obligated." True love does not ask what can be demanded. It is not satisfied when it has merely acted justly, but it always asks, "How would I want others to act toward me if I were in the same situation?" True love causes an individual to love the neighbor as himself. It does not stop to think whether someone else should be obligated to respond. It responds immediately, and it would rather suffer shame than let the neighbor bear that shame. It is ready to help even when the task is difficult, when it has no surplus, and when it must give to the needy what it needs itself. It is ready to place goods, health, honor, and even life at stake for the neighbor whenever it is necessary.

Moses wrote, "If you see the donkey of one who hates you lying down under its burden, you shall refrain from leaving him with it; you shall rescue it with him" (Exodus 23:5).

The New Testament adds, "Let no one seek his own good, but the good of his neighbor" (1 Corinthians 10:24); "Bear one another's burdens, and so fulfill the law of Christ" (Galatians 6:2); and "We ought to lay down our lives for the brothers" (1 John 3:16).

Where is the person who leads such a life in love? There is no one. Only Christ lived, suffered, and died in this manner, not for Himself, but because of His love for sinners. True Christians, in whom Jesus lives, make a beginning of such love, but they never bring it to perfection. It is, therefore, evil delusion when a person thinks he is able to justify himself before God and make himself holy by the fulfillment of the commandment to love the neighbor.

Thou sacred Love, grace on us bestow,
Set our hearts with heav'nly fire aglow
That with hearts united we love each other,
Of one mind, in peace with ev'ry brother.
Lord, have mercy! Amen.

† *(TLH 231:3)*

Tuesday

Read Luke 10:35–37

THE COMMANDMENT to love the neighbor demands that a person must love his enemies and be ready to make the greatest sacrifice on behalf of them. In addition, it insists that a person must never tire of loving his neighbor. We see this in our

Gospel's model of the merciful Samaritan. He arrived at the inn with the wounded Israelite. Then what did he do? Did he think he had done his part and the innkeeper would care further for the Israelite? No. Although he was likely exhausted from the journey, he cared for the suffering man himself that night; and the next morning, when he had to continue his journey, he paid the innkeeper for the nursing care he had committed to the injured man. But he did not stop even there. The Samaritan promised to return and to pay the innkeeper for any costs incurred in the care of the Israelite beyond those for which he had already been compensated.

What is Christ saying here, both to the lawyer in our text and to us today? He is saying that only the person who never grows tired of loving carries in his heart the perfect, true love for his neighbor, which avails before God. But where is such a person? Who is always fervent in his love for his neighbor? Who has never felt cold and sluggish in this regard? Who does not become weary of generosity when he is approached, almost every day, by poor individuals? Who does not grow tired of being charitable when he sees how often he has distributed his money completely in vain? Who does not contemplate halting his works of mercy when he finds that people repay his goodness with shameful ingratitude? Who does not occasionally wonder why he should continue to forgive and reconcile when a person always offends and provokes?

Only one was able—Jesus Christ. Scripture says of Him, "having loved His own who were in the world, He loved them to the end" (John 13:1). He was just as untiring in love toward His enemies. Even the vile traitor could not exhaust the love of Christ with his devilish hypocrisy and wickedness. Christ received Judas's kiss with a kind face and called the disgraceful one "friend." He came, full of love, into a world of sinners to seek and to save what was lost. Although the world, for which He did only good, did not rest until it had nailed Him to the cross, He continued to bless it even as He was dying under the curse and mockery of His enemies.

Oh, may no one hope to be able to justify himself before God and save himself by his love for his neighbor. May we instead recognize how much we are lacking in the love God demands from us. May we learn to vividly recognize our loveless and cold heart, beat our breast, and mourn over it. There is only one love that saves us and that is the love of God in Christ Jesus. Whoever despairs of his own love and comforts himself with this love, begins to love a little. But one day he will arrive in heaven, where all live in perfect, eternal love and are blessed. For this reason, let us say to God, with the poet:

O Love, who madest me to wear
The image of Thy Godhead here;
Who soughtest me with tender care
Thro' all my wand'rings wild and drear—
O Love, I give myself to Thee,
Thine ever, only Thine, to be. Amen.

(TLH 397:1)

Faith clings to Jesus' cross alone
And rests in Him unceasing;
And by its fruits true faith is known,
With love and hope increasing.
Yet faith alone doth justify,
Works serve thy neighbor and supply
The proof that faith is living. Amen.

† *(TLH 377:9)*

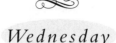

Wednesday

Read Psalm 111:10

"Act rightly, and avoid no one!" There are many who freely admit that their whole religion consists in these words. They say this especially when the doctrine of Holy Scripture—that a person shall be saved through faith—is held before them. This utterance shows how miserable is the religion of all who have made it their motto. Our forefathers said, "Fear God, act rightly, avoid no one!" But in our day, people leave off the "Fear God!" By this they show that they have a religion without God. But what is a religion without God but a house without a foundation, an ocean without water, and a person without a heart and soul? Isn't there a God whom we must fear, love, and trust above all else and whom we are obligated to honor, worship, and serve? Does a person have a duty only to people? Doesn't he have a duty toward God and is this not his foremost and most precious duty?

Truly, there can be no greater delusion for a person than wanting to be regarded as upright, as a good Christian, because he gives people what is due them while he lives as if there were no God, the Creator and Lord of all, to whom he is subject and whom he is obligated to serve. But those who preach virtue, reason, and nature think a person can be virtuous if he merely fulfills his duties to his neighbor, even if he does not trouble himself about God, does not want to hear God's Word, and completely neglects prayer.

The oddest thing about all this is that those who have chosen "Act rightly, and avoid no one!" as their motto think they can be blameless and exemplary in their relations with their fellow man. If you were to observe such people carefully, you would find that most of them *say* they do good works and love their neighbor, but the last thing they *think* about is doing good works and loving their neighbor. In the old days, the fear of God and faith stood first. Today, a person merely says, "Act rightly, and avoid no one!" At which time, do you suppose, love and good works were practiced more diligently?

It is true that people today build magnificent houses for the poor, the orphans, and the sick, but in many cases, these are but proud monuments that a boasting charity erects for its own glory. People are now so philanthropic that they would prefer to change prisons into comfortable houses and to stop punishing murderers with death. This seemingly greater humaneness fails to take sin and corruption seriously. There is today, finally, a great number of societies, both public and secret, that have mutual support as their main purpose. But they exist because no one wants to show love toward another unless he binds himself with an oath to him. Everything has now sunk so completely into selfishness, self-love, egotism, profiteering, and avarice that no one can hope for mercy from another in the time of need.

Those who know nothing about the fear of God will never be zealous in love for their neighbor. Indeed, those who incessantly talk about the love of man as the only mark of a good person and a true Christian are generally those who practice it the least. It cannot be otherwise. The flame of a pure, unselfish love of man can begin to burn only in a heart in which the fear and love of God already dwell, even if, in such a heart, this love remains imperfect until death.

O gentle Dew, from heaven now fall
With power upon the hearts of all,
Thy tender love instilling,
That heart to heart more closely bound,

In kindly deeds be fruitful found,
The law of love fulfilling.
Dwell thus In us;
Envy banish; Strife will vanish
Where Thou livest.
Peace and joy Thou givest. Amen.

(*TLH* 235:7)

Thursday

Read Romans 3:31

THE OLD AND NEW TESTAMENTS contain two doctrines that are completely different from each other: the doctrine of the Law and the doctrine of the Gospel. By the Law, God tells us we should perfectly do His holy will; by the Gospel, He says we should only believe and accept what He has done for us. By the Law, God promises us life and salvation under the condition of perfect obedience; by the Gospel, He offers life and blessedness without any condition, out of free grace and mercy for the sake of His dear Son, Jesus Christ. By the Law, God proclaims to all people that they are sinners, subject to temporal, spiritual, and eternal death; by the Gospel, He proclaims to all people grace and eternal life.

The Law and the Gospel are the chief components of the divine revelation, and they must always be well separated in doctrine and in practice by teachers and hearers. If they are mixed with each other, the entire divine order of salvation is perverted and all doctrines are falsified. On the contrary, the right distinction is a bright candle that casts light upon the entire way of salvation. When the Law and the Gospel are mixed, no one can be certain of his salvation. But when they are properly distinguished, we can readily see how even the greatest sinner can be just before God. Mixing produces confusion of conscience and anxiety, but the right distinction brings clarity and peace. If a person preaches the Law as if God were not strict about it, as if God could be satisfied with an outward fulfillment, and as if, as a good father, God demands nothing more than what we poor, weak people can do, he makes self-righteous hypocrites by mixing the grace of the Gospel with the thundering voice of the Law. If a person preaches that the Gospel requires good works, as if grace alone did not make us just and blessed, this throws the poor sinner into despair when he feels the great burden of his sin and senses that he is dead to all good.

No one can be helped when the Gospel is made into a new law or the Law is mixed with the preaching of the Gospel. Dr. Martin Luther rightly said: "This distinction between the Law and the Gospel is the highest art in Christendom, which each and all who pride themselves on or appropriate the name 'Christian' should know and be able to practice. For where there is a lack of this art, one cannot tell a Christian from a heathen or Jew; so absolutely everything depends on this discrimination" (quoted in Franz Pieper, *Christian Dogmatics*, v. 3, p. 244). He also said: "Now, him who is adept at this art of properly dividing Law and Gospel set at the head of the table and declare him a Doctor of the Holy Scriptures. Without the Holy Spirit it is impossible rightly to divide Law and Gospel" (*ibid.*, pp. 242–43). All teachers of our church praise God especially for the great blessing that, through the Lutheran Reformation, the great distinction between the Law and the Gospel was again brought to light. Since the age of the apostles, this distinction was never drawn more sharply than it was by Luther, that venerable reformer of the 16th century, by the enlightenment of the Holy Ghost. The confessional writings of our church gloriously spell out this distinction.

Therefore, no one should think that rightly dividing the Law and the Gospel is an easy task. A sermon can provide very little guidance on this subject. The main thing, however, remains this: each hearer must bow his heart before God and fervently implore Him that, by the Holy Ghost, He will teach him this distinction. It must be experienced in the daily struggle with the terrors of sin and conscience, and one who thinks he can grasp the distinction without experiencing it is blind. Luther, a highly enlightened man of God, called himself a pupil in the study of the Law and the Gospel. Where does that leave the rest of us?

The Law discovers guilt and sin
And shows how vile our hearts have been;
The Gospel only can express
Forgiving love and cleansing grace. Amen.

† *(TLH 289:2)*

Friday

Read Galatians 3:15–18

BY NATURE, people cannot know the Gospel, which God reveals only in His holy Word. There, we read that we have no other name by which we must be saved than that of Jesus. He, as God and man, reconciled fallen mankind with the angered God and redeemed them. Many take offense at this and think, "If there is no salvation outside of Christ, how could the fathers in the Old Testament, to whom the Law was proclaimed, be saved?"

This thinking rests upon a great error. Both in the Old and New Testaments, God showed that the only way to heaven was by faith in the Savior of the world, who is described as "the same yesterday and today and forever" (Hebrews 13:8). Although, in Eden, Christ had not yet died for our sins, the Gospel about Him was proclaimed there, and the first people were invited to believe in their future Messiah. God spoke to them in a comforting way: "He shall bruise your head, and you shall bruise His heel" (Genesis 3:15). This meant that, by a bloody sacrifice, the Son of a woman would one day blot out sin, together with all its misery. This precious promise was the Gospel of grace, upon which all godly people of the next age placed their trust. Abel, Seth, Noah, Shem, and Melchizedek held fast to this promise and died in this faith, confident and saved. Two thousand years later, God repeated this promise to Abraham, the father of all believers: "In your offspring [that is, by one Descendant from your family] shall all the nations of the earth be blessed" (Genesis 22:18).

This is the testament of which Saint Paul speaks in our text. He gives two reasons why the Law does not annul the Gospel: first, because God gave Abraham the Gospel as His testament, as His last, inviolable will, and second, because He first revealed the Law by Moses 430 years later. How can we believe that God, by His threatening Law, wants to annul His Gospel, which is rich in grace? Why, then, would He have first given the Law centuries after the Gospel? And hasn't God Himself declared that the promise of Christ is His testament, His last will, in which He has appointed all people of the earth to be heirs of His blessing? God may have given the Law on Sinai with great majesty, but it cannot overturn the testament of His Gospel for us. The Law came to us later than the Gospel, and it can thus be nothing more than a new seal for God's will that was finally broken in the apostolic age by the preaching, in all the world, of the holy absolution.

Oh, what a doctrine! It is rich in comfort for all who are terrified by the Law! Behold, dear Christian, if you have fallen, perhaps deeply, into sin, you may well fear drawing near the holy God because the Law says to you, "God is not a god whom the godless being pleases; whoever is evil, does not remain before Him." Know, then, that God's last will does not call for casting you away, as He threatens in His Law. Open the precious Gospel, read there the testament of your God, and you will find His final will, which shall not be changed: "Jesus sinners doth receive" (*TLH* 324:1), and "Believe in the Lord Jesus, and you will be saved" (Acts 16:31). In Him, all people are blessed. Believe the Gospel of your God, and behold with joy the seal of Holy Baptism and the Holy Supper, with which God has irrevocably ratified His precious testament to you.

My sins, O Lord, against me rise,
I mourn them with contrition;
Grant, thro' Thy death and sacrifice,
To me a full remission.
Lord, show before the Father's throne
That Thou didst for my sins atone;
So shall I from my load be freed.
Thy Word I plead;
Keep me, O Lord, each hour of need. Amen.

(*TLH* 319:2)

Saturday

Read Galatians 3:19–22

THROUGH THE LAW, no flesh is just. As Saint Paul says in today's text, the Law cannot make us alive. The Gospel, however, is a treasure chest full of divine grace for all people. No person, by nature, is capable of this grace. The natural man cannot recognize how greatly his sin has offended God, and that only through the blood of the Son of God can he again be reconciled with the Father.

The human heart, by nature, is surrounded by a diamond-hard wall of self-righteousness and security. There is no terror over sin and no hunger for grace. Instead, there is an arrogant mind in the midst of sin. As long as the heart and the mind of a person remain in this condition, the Gospel is preached to him in vain. The announcement of grace may sound in his ears, but his heart remains firmly shut against it. Therefore, the Law is the message that God must first send into the sinner's heart so it may prepare for the acceptance of the Gospel and open the entrance for Christ in that person's soul. If we ask, "What purpose, then, does the Law serve?" the apostle answers in our text, "It was added because of transgressions, until the offspring should come to whom the promise had been made" (Galatians 3:19). Thus, the Law shows the person the greatness of his sin, lets him feel God's displeasure, demands from him what he cannot keep, drives him into despair by its threats against all transgressors, compels him to accuse and reject himself, and lays him in the dust of death. Through the Law, then, the Holy Ghost makes the poor sinner feel himself to be lost.

But if the Law lets a person taste its terrible bitterness, it does so only to allow the Gospel to taste sweeter to him. The Law batters, wounds, and kills a person, but only so that when the merciful Samaritan, Jesus Christ, comes in the Gospel, the sinner gladly allows himself to be bandaged by Him and brought, out of grace and mercy, into the heavenly inn. The more unalterable and unrelenting the Law shows itself to the sinner in its demands, the more he is prepared to seek salvation, not in himself, but in his Savior and Substitute, Jesus Christ. For this reason, God revealed the Law with particular terror before Christ's entrance into the world. He had it preached in order to make His people long for their promised Redeemer. As the Israelites learned to pine for the Promised Land while they were under the tyranny of Egypt, God sought to bring them, by the unbearably heavy yoke of the Law, to a yearning for the promised Messiah.

The story of the people of God must repeat itself in each one who wants to experience the coming of Christ into his heart. It must be our life story if we want to be called "children of God" (1 John 5:2). We must first bow under the yoke of the Law until Christ enters our soul through faith. As our text says, "But the Scripture imprisoned everything under sin, so that the promise by faith in Jesus Christ might be given to those who believe" (Galatians 3:22). We must recognize that we lie in the bonds of sin that Christ alone can loosen; we must understand that we are imprisoned in a house of spiritual death that Christ alone can open. Therefore, Luther says, "It is not possible that the one who hears the Gospel and is made alive by the grace of the Spirit, did not first hear the Law and was not first killed by its letter: for grace is not given but to those who thirst after it. Life only helps the dead, grace only sinners, the Spirit only the letter, and no one may have one without the other."

Then on Him I cast my burden,
Sink it in the depths below.
Let me know Thy gracious pardon,
Wash me, make me white as snow.
Let Thy Spirit leave me never;
Make me only Thine forever. Amen.

† *(TLH 326:4)*

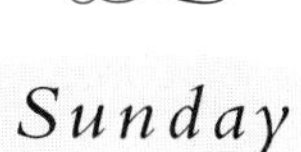

Sunday

Read Luke 17:11–19

EACH PERSON IS surrounded and covered by God's blessing even more than he is by the air. Body and soul are the basic blessings each individual has received from God. However, reason and every power of the soul, all understanding and every member of the body, every ray of light that falls into his eye, every sound that penetrates his ear, every breath of air that fills his lungs, every heartbeat, every bite of bread he eats, every drop of water he drinks, every slumber that comfortingly shuts his eye, every joy that refreshes his soul, every step he takes without misfortune, every moment he spends—in short, everything a person is and has—is a special blessing of God. In Him we live, move, and have our being. He has called us into existence, He preserves us and governs our life, and if He were to withdraw His hand from us, we would perish. It is, therefore, impossible for a person to count the blessings God shows him during even one hour!

Who vividly recognizes all these things as blessings from God? Most regard them as the inevitabilities of life. They do not regard them as things for which God is worthy of praise.

They enjoy all these blessings without thinking about the source of every good and perfect gift. If they meet with a little misfortune, their heart and mouth are filled with complaints, and when there is so much as one blessing they imagine they are lacking, they suddenly forget all the millions of other blessings they enjoy. Only when people lose a blessing do they come to realize how great it really was. They must lose their sight, hearing, or general health to learn what a blessing each of these is. Only when the heavens are shut do they remember the blessing of rain, and only when their crops fail do they recall how great is the gift of fruitful weather.

If, however, the bodily blessings of God are for the most part unrecognized by most people, the spiritual blessings are even more ignored. They almost never take time to consider how fortunate they are to have been redeemed, sanctified in Baptism, born into Christendom instead of among the heathen, called to the kingdom of heaven by the Holy Ghost, provided with a Bible, and given the holy Sacrament for their spiritual nourishment. No, most people take all of this with a hardened heart. They regard spiritual things as a yoke they must bear in this world and they would prefer it if there were no God they should serve, no Word of God they should hear and obey, and no eternity about which they should worry. They certainly do not want to thank God continually from the bottom of their heart.

Yet there are certainly blessings almost all of us recognize as worthy of great thanks: protection and deliverance from great bodily danger, the restoration of health after a long sickness, the revelation of innocence after a period of unearned shame and scorn, the receipt of temporal goods following a time of severe poverty, and the removal of strong pains and the fear of death. But while we may realize that these things merit loud and lifelong thanks, what do most of us do? We call upon God in a time of need and promise Him: "Lord, if You will help me this time, the thanks shall never cease in my heart. I will become a different person. I will totally convert to You and lead a holy life, forsaking the world and its vanity. I will serve You with body and soul, give You my heart, and become and remain Your servant now and forever." But what happens when God has heard our cry of distress and helped us? With most of us, it is the same as with the nine lepers in our Gospel. The heavenly Benefactor is quickly forgotten. We ascribe the help to chance and our recovery to the doctor, our good nature, or the right medicine. How many of us do not fall down before God in thanks, but persist in living our lives the way we did before? Oh, ingratitude of the human heart! How unbelievably great it is!

I praise and thank Thee, Lord, my God,
For Thine abundant blessing
Which heretofore Thou hast bestowed
And I am still possessing.
Inscribe this on my memory:
The Lord hath done great things for me
And graciously hath helped me. Amen.

(TLH 33:2)

Monday

Read Psalm 50:23

IT IS IMPOSSIBLE to be a Christian and not be thankful to God. Conversion involves beginning to recognize vividly God's blessings (especially His spiritual blessings), taking comfort in them, clinging to them with the whole heart, and no longer seeking hope and blessedness in the world's goods but in God's goodness in Christ Jesus. To become a Christian is to be thankful to God.

Psalm 50, which rejects all false worship by which people hope to be saved, concludes with the words of today's reading. It shows us that if a person has not yet converted to Christ and so has not received the greatest of blessings—the forgiveness of sins—he is incapable of thanking God from his heart. But as soon as he believes in Christ from his heart, his heart opens like a fountain and daily thanks rush forth like a stream. Then he says, with the psalmist: "Bless the LORD, O my soul, and all that is within me, bless His holy name! Bless the LORD, O my soul, and forget not all His benefits, who forgives all your iniquity, who heals all your diseases, who redeems your life from the pit, who crowns you with steadfast love and mercy, who satisfies you with good so that your youth is renewed like the eagle's" (Psalm 103:1–5).

A true Christian is one whose eyes have been opened so he vividly recognizes that he is a completely unworthy sinner and that everything temporal and eternal, in body and soul, and in earthly and heavenly goods is a pure blessing of grace that God gives him for Christ's sake. A true Christian does not merely grant this in humility. Instead, this knowledge illuminates his entire being like a new sun, and in this light he sees everything he is and has. Therefore, he lives in constant thanks and can say, with David, "when I remember You upon my bed, and meditate on You in the watches of the night" (Psalm 63:6). He does not need the sickbed to teach him that health is a great and unearned blessing of God, a roaring fire to remind him that it is the Lord alone who watches and protects his house, a devastating flood to convince him that the Lord protects the harvest for him, and the torch of war to enlighten him regarding the joys of peace and safety.

Even if each true Christian has begun to recognize God's blessings in his life and to praise Him on that account with words and deeds, he has only made a beginning. He must continue to lament his unthankful heart, for even the Christian is not perfectly enlightened. He still walks along among thousands upon thousands of unknown blessings from his God and Father. The Christian remains flesh and blood, and therefore he is often slow to offer praise and thanks. He may indeed have called upon God in a time of need, but when that time has passed, he has forgotten to keep his vow to the Most High and remained in debt. The Christian must especially regret that he has not thanked God often enough for his cross, need, sickness, poverty, ridicule, and disgrace, which are mostly a greater blessing of God than good days, health, wealth, and glory.

Although the true Christian still has much in common with a non-Christian, there is nevertheless a great difference between them. The ingratitude of the true Christian is one that he recognizes, laments, and daily wars against, and as he stands in faith, this is, in the end, not attributed to him, for Christ's sake. It is an ingratitude that is daily forgiven him. A Christian is an enemy to his unthankful heart. Therefore, he longingly looks toward heaven and says, with David, "My soul will be satisfied as with fat and rich food, and my mouth will praise You with joyful lips" (Psalm 63:5). The Christian says, "Here, the flesh still pulls me to the earth, but one day, when I will have escaped and risen into the temple of heaven, then I will perfectly praise and laud You from everlasting to everlasting with the whole choir of Your elect children."

O Father, deign Thou, I beseech Thee,
To listen to my earthly lays;
A nobler strain in heaven shall reach Thee,
When I with angels hymn Thy praise

And learn amid their choirs to sing
Loud hallelujahs to my King. Amen.

(TLH 30:6)

Tuesday

Read 1 Samuel 16:7

CHRISTIAN CHURCHES are the visible congregations in which the Word of God is preached and the holy Sacraments are administered. In these churches are found, not only true Christians, but also false Christians and hypocrites. Such congregations, made up of the godly and the ungodly, are called "churches" only in a figurative sense. The name applies only on account of the true and pious Christians, just as a field is called a "wheat field" because of the wheat in it, although wheat and weeds grow next to each other.

The Christian Church, which is the kingdom of Christ on earth, is essentially all the people who have received Christ as their King and are ruled by Him, who believe on Him from their heart, and who are thus true Christians. It is clear from this that the Church, in the proper sense of the word, cannot be seen. It is invisible. Therefore it says, in the Third Article of our Christian faith, "I believe in the Holy Ghost; one holy Christian Church, the communion of saints." What a person believes, he cannot see. A person can, of course, see the communion of people that is called the Christian Church, but the *proper* Church, which consists solely of true Christians, cannot be seen. The true Christians who make up the Church are not invisible spirits but visible people. No one can discern who in a congregation belongs to the true Church. There is nothing that visually distinguishes them from the false Christians.

According to love, whoever outwardly considers himself to be a Christian is regarded as a true Christian. However, a person cannot be certain that anyone is a true, born-again Christian. By nature, every person does not want to believe what is invisible; rather, he wants to be able to assure himself by means of sight. The Jews did not want to know anything about an invisible kingdom of the Messiah. Later, in Christian history, the desire to have a visible church led to the establishment of the papacy. In our day, the same desire can be found in the so-called Protestant church. The teaching that the Church of Christ is, in the proper sense, invisible is regarded as enthusiasm, and those who do not want to believe in it call to us: "Away with your invisible dream church! No, it is not invisible! Look! Here is Christ! There is Christ!'"

No matter how clever and sharp-sighted a person may be, he will never manage to make Christ's Church visible to the eye. It remains impossible to tell with complete certainty whether someone is a Christian. The privilege of knowing and seeing those who belong to the Lord is something the Lord has reserved for Himself alone. Holy Scripture tells us, "man looks on the outward appearance, but the LORD looks on the heart" (1 Samuel 16:7), "The Lord knows those who are His" (2 Timothy 2:19), and "I know whom I have chosen" (John 13:18). Neither man nor angel can determine who among the people are the elect ones. On the Last Day, Christ, as Lord of the Church, will reveal Himself to all people and angels, and at the same time He will present His Church visibly, prepared as a bride adorned for her husband.

We are God's house of living stones,
Builded for His habitation;

He through baptismal grace us owns
Heirs of His wondrous salvation.
Were we but two His name to tell,
Yet He would deign with us to dwell,
With all His grace and favor. Amen.

† *(TLH 467:3)*

Wednesday

Read 1 Corinthians 3:16

WHEN MAN WAS STILL in the state in which God had created him in Eden, his greatest blessedness consisted in God Himself dwelling in his soul. God was the light of his reason and the moving power of his will. Since all people fell into sin with the first father, Adam, man's greatest misery is that by nature he wanders around without God. What Isaiah once testified about the Israelites applies to all people in their natural condition: "but your iniquities have made a separation between you and your God, and your sins have hidden His face from you" (59:2). As long as a person belongs to the world, he is without God, for as Christ says, "The world cannot receive [the Holy Ghost]" (John 14:17).

Before they are converted to Christ, all people are separated from God by their unforgiven sins. But Christ came into the world to unite heaven and earth, to reconcile God and man, and to lead us sinners back into fellowship with God. Therefore, as soon as a person, in penitence, recognizes his fall from God and turns in faith to Jesus Christ, the Mediator of the New Testament, the wall of separation crumbles, his sins are forgiven him, and God unites Himself with him in grace. "He saved us," Paul wrote, "by the washing of regeneration and renewal of the Holy Spirit, whom He poured out on us richly" (Titus 3:5–6). He also said, "and [having] believed in Him, were sealed with the promised Holy Spirit, who is the guarantee of our inheritance until we acquire possession of it" (Ephesians 1:13–14). To these statements, the apostle added the words of today's reading.

We see from this how highly honored and blessed each true Christian is. Christians who see others around them who are honored while they sit in deep lowliness, should consider that the highest estate of the children of this world is as nothing compared with the honor in which all Christians share. The Most High God has, in grace, united Himself with poor sinners. The centurion from Capernaum did not consider himself worthy to have the Son of God come under his roof, but Christians have the inexpressible honor of providing a home for the Triune God in their poor hearts! True Christians will often hear the Holy Ghost sighing in them. He will continue to enlighten them by the Word of God, and He will move, comfort, admonish, and chastise their hearts. Why should any of them long for the honors of this world or worry because of the contempt they experience, when the great Lord, before whom everything in heaven and on earth must bow, dwells in their soul?

That Christians receive the Holy Ghost through faith is not only a great honor but also a wonderful comfort! For whoever is moved by the Holy Ghost also has an irrefutable divine testimony that he is a child of God and is with Him in grace. By this, Saint Paul says, he has a certain seal and guarantee of his eternal inheritance. But the apostle notes, "If the Spirit of Him who raised Jesus from the dead dwells in you, He who raised Christ Jesus from the dead will also give life to your mortal bodies through His Spirit who dwells in you" (Romans 8:11). A Christian cannot be sorrowful in affliction, grieved in contempt, and despondent in the trials of sin when he rightly considers how precious God must regard him. The heavenly Father not only looks down upon him from His throne, but He also makes His dwelling in the Christian's miserable heart.

Oh, enter, let me know Thee
And feel Thy pow'r within,
The pow'r that breaks our fetters
And rescues us from sin!
Oh, wash and cleanse Thou me,
That I may serve Thee truly
And render honor duly
With perfect heart to Thee! Amen.

† *(TLH 228:2)*

Thursday

Read Galatians 5:16

"WALK BY THE SPIRIT," Saint Paul instructs us (Galatians 5:16). Does this demand that whoever wants to call himself a Christian and be saved must be totally spiritual, pure, and holy, with no trace of sin? If so, one would search for a Christian in vain. Despite the work of the new birth, the abysmal corruption with which we entered this world is not completely removed. Grace may be strong within us, but it cannot wipe sin out of our heart. Even among the true children of God, evil thoughts still arise. Even the holiest people often feel the most shameful lusts in their soul. In fact, the holier one is, the more often he is visited with terrible trials and temptations to sin. Even the holy apostle Paul once had to confess, "For I know that nothing good dwells in me, that is, in my flesh" (Romans 7:18). David also sighed for justification: "Who can discern his errors? Declare me innocent from hidden faults" (Psalm 19:12).

Even the righteous, who walk in the Spirit, are tempted by the sin in them, and they also stumble and fall. True Christians are often so covered with weaknesses and defects that faultfinders deny that they can be in a state of grace. Although the true Christian who walks according to the Spirit continues to be a poor sinner, like the false Christian, and as much as the child of the world resembles the child of God in many respects, there is a difference between the two that is as stark as the distinction between life and death. Today's text spells it out for us. As long as a man lives in sin, having no power to hate it and to fight against it, the Spirit is not in him and he walks according to the flesh on the way to hell. Whoever walks in the Spirit still has fleshly desires within him, but he is also empowered to hate sin and fight against it so it does not gain dominion over him. If someone sins because he wants to, he walks according to the flesh. If someone walks in the Spirit, he, too, commits sin, but this is not what he wants to do and he abhors what he has done.

The one who can peacefully resolve to do something he knows is a sin thereby sins on purpose and walks on the path of the flesh, which leads to destruction. However, the one who walks in the Spirit, although he also sins, does so, not on purpose, but out of weakness and rashness. The one who takes pleasure in sin or is indifferent toward it thereby lives in the flesh. However, the one who walks in the Spirit daily bears sorrow over his sin, is filled with anguish and grief, and often laments his sins with a thousand bitter tears of repentance. Those sins are his greatest distress, his heaviest burden, and his greatest cross. The one who recognizes what he does as sin but regards it as of no importance is still living in the flesh. However, the one who walks in the Spirit considers even the smallest of sins as great and terrible. The one who seeks to excuse and defend his sins when they are held before him is still living in the flesh. However, the one who walks in the Spirit tries to recognize clearly the depth of his fall, and as soon as his conscience convicts him, he immediately declares his guilt before God and man, condemning himself before others can do so.

If someone has committed a serious sin and is at peace with it, if he has delayed repentance instead of earnestly seeking God's grace and forgiveness, he is still a child of sin and death and walking in the flesh. However, if someone is walking in the Spirit, he can, like Peter, quickly gather himself up after a fall, throwing himself before God with repentance and deep shame. He implores his heavenly Father for forgiveness and grace for Christ's sake, and he does not rest until his conscience has been cleansed and he is certain of reconciliation with his heavenly Father. If someone has sinned in such a way that the Spirit of God has retreated out of his heart, he still lives in the flesh. But if someone walks in the Spirit, he too can grieve the Holy Ghost at times, but he never expels Him from his heart by wanton sins. Sin can rise up in his heart against the Spirit, but it never usurps the Spirit's reign in the life of the true Christian.

But Thou hast raised me up
To joy and exultation
And clearly shown the way
That leads to salvation.

My sins are washed away,
For this I thank Thee, Lord;
And with my heart and soul
All dead works are abhorred. Amen.

(*TLH* 417:4)

Friday

Read Galatians 5:17

WHEN SAINT PAUL SAYS in our text that "the desires of the flesh are against the Spirit, and the desires of the Spirit are against the flesh" (Galatians 5:17), he is talking about Christians. We see here that, in a true Christian, there are two things, flesh and spirit. This means there is the old heart and a new heart, the old mind and a new mind, the old darkness and a new light, the old evil will and a new good will, the powerlessness of the old nature and the power of a new nature—in short, the old inborn sinful corruption and a new work that is being created by the Holy Ghost. The Bible speaks of all this as the old man and a new man.

Paul also points out that a struggle between the flesh and the spirit takes place in the Christian. We must understand, first of all, that not every battle against a person's flesh is a sign that he is a Christian, since even in non-Christians a certain struggle against the flesh often takes place. However, in the non-Christian, the combatants are either reason against flesh or flesh against flesh (that is, sin against sin). For example, there may be a battle between covetousness and wastefulness, pride and shameful vice, and laziness and avarice. If non-Christians are tempted to certain sins, they often say: "No, I cannot be induced to this sin, for what would the people say about it if it became known? I would put my good name, my honor, even my entire life's happiness at stake by it!" Or they might say, "I would destroy my health by this!" or "God would punish me temporally and eternally!" They do not struggle against any sin for God's sake alone.

A clear sign that such struggles are between reason and flesh, or even flesh (sin) and flesh (sin), is that the non-Christian does not struggle against all sins, especially his favorite sins. Moreover, these struggles are not continuous, but only occasional.

The struggle the apostle has in mind in our text is another matter entirely: "For the desires of the flesh are against the Spirit, and the desires of the Spirit are against the flesh, for these are opposed to each other, to keep you from doing the things you want to do" (Galatians 5:17). As soon as a person is converted to God from his heart and becomes a true, born-again Christian, he carries inside himself, next to the old flesh, the spirit, that is, a new divine light and power that are from the Holy Ghost. From the moment this spirit enters a person, it is continually active, proving itself to be an irreconcilable enemy of the flesh that remains in the Christian. Therefore, whenever a Christian is tempted to sin and whenever his flesh desires to succumb to this, the spirit immediately supplies the Christian with an impulse to resist. If the temptation arises, not from some external source, but from his own heart, which is evil by nature, the spirit dwelling within the Christian makes him restless and moves him to use every possible means to overcome the enticement to sin.

The spirit may often appear to have left a person or gone to sleep, but as soon as the Christian feels tempted to sin, it immediately springs to arms. The flesh, too, is never lazy. It never stops tempting the Christian. For this reason, the spirit is always active. It makes no distinction among sins. It chastises the Christian about his most secret sinful thoughts, and it fights ceaselessly, especially against favorite sins, since the more constant the temptation, the more dangerous it is.

Holy Spirit, strong and mighty,
Thou who makest all things new,
Make Thy work within us perfect
And the evil Foe subdue.
Grant us weapons for the strife
And with victory crown our life. Amen.

† *(TLH 226:7)*

Saturday

Read Galatians 5:18–24

WITH THESE WORDS, Saint Paul shows us the result of the battle between the flesh and the spirit within Christians. He begins with this: "But if you are led by the Spirit, you are not under the law. . . . And those who belong to Christ Jesus have crucified the flesh with its passions and desires" (Galatians 5:18, 24). In this battle, the spirit is the stronger and the flesh is the weaker of the combatants. Thus, the spirit, not the flesh, rules the man. The spirit wields the scepter and removes all desires of the flesh far away. Those desires may continually rebel against the government of the spirit but they are daily conquered by the spirit, taken captive, and nailed to the cross.

The believing Christian often receives many wounds in this battle. He may even lie bleeding on the ground, trampled by sin. However, the outcome of his battle is always victory over the flesh, the world, and the devil. Therefore, Paul continues in our text: "Now the works of the flesh are evident: sexual immorality, impurity, sensuality, idolatry, sorcery, enmity, strife, jealousy, fits of anger, rivalries, dissensions, divisions, envy, drunkenness, orgies, and things like these. I warn you, as I warned you before, that those who do such things will not inherit the kingdom of God" (Galatians 5:19–21). We see here that, although Christians are and remain sinners, there are certain obvious works of the flesh that lead toward death. One who commits such sins cannot be a Christian and stand in a state of grace. If someone peacefully allows himself to be ruled by any one of the sins named by the apostle, the battle of the flesh and spirit is not being waged within him and he is not a true Christian. He may believe that he is engaged in the battle, but the conflict is only a figment of his imagination or a battle of reason or flesh against flesh, and its outcome is certain defeat. As he falls into these sins, they rule over him, and he becomes their subject and their slave. The end of his battle is temporal captivity on earth and eternal captivity hereafter, for as Paul declares, "Those who do such things will not inherit the kingdom of God" (Galatians 5:21).

However, he hastens to add the following: "But the fruit of the Spirit is love, joy, peace, patience, kindness, goodness, faithfulness, gentleness, self-control. Against such things there is no law" (Galatians 5:22–23). Here we see that, in the battle of the flesh and spirit, in which true Christians stand, they not only overcome sins, they carry off all kinds of precious virtues as the booty of their combat. The longer they battle, the more universal, comforting, and untiring their love becomes. Their joy becomes purer, their peace becomes firmer, their patience becomes stronger, their kindness becomes more sincere, their goodness becomes richer, their faith and faithfulness become more constant, their gentleness becomes more unconquerable, and their self-control becomes more immaculate.

In short, the end of the true battle of the flesh and spirit is an advance in sanctification. This resulting sanctification is as far from perfect as the victory of the spirit over the flesh is complete. Instead, every Christian must confess, with Paul, "Not that I have already obtained this or am already perfect" (Philippians 3:12). Nevertheless, where that battle truly exists, a fighter must be able to add truthfully, as Paul does, "But I press on to make it my own, because Christ Jesus has made me His own" (Philippians 3:12). The apostle concludes our text with the words, "And those who are Christ's have crucified the flesh with its passions and desires" (Galatians 5:24).

Oh, may God grant that we all become and remain true fighters against the flesh and sin. May Jesus Christ, our eternal Prince of victory, help us all for the sake of His battle with death.

Let us also die with Jesus.
His death from the second death,
From our soul's destruction, frees us,
Quickens us with life's glad breath.
Let us mortify, while living,
Flesh and blood and die to sin;
And the grave that shuts us in
Shall but prove the gate to heaven.
Jesus, here I die to Thee
There to live eternally. Amen.

† *(TLH 409:3)*

Sunday

Read Matthew 6:24

A PERSON'S GOD is that to which he clings as the greatest and highest thing in heaven and on earth, that which he loves above everything else as the highest good, that which he fears losing more than anything else, that in which he trusts above everything else, and that in which he seeks his greatest joy. He expects this god to preserve his entire person, to be his protection in all danger, and to rescue him from all trouble. In short, he expects to receive from this god his true salvation. He believes in this god from his heart, and he serves it.

The real god of the world, in which it believes and which it serves, is not the true God, that invisible being who made heaven and earth. Instead, it is "mammon." In every land, mammon is the all-powerful god for which the hearts of the people beat and to which they pay the expected homage. It has its loyal slaves in every stratum of society. The richest people, who otherwise do not want to serve anyone, are the most zealous servants of mammon. Emperors, kings, and princes, who do not want to be subject to anyone else, remain the obedient subjects of this high monarch. Even most of those who are called as messengers of the heavenly King secretly stand in the service of mammon. Therefore, the world looks upon the poor, who are without mammon, as forsaken and rejected by God. Wealth grabs the attention of the world, and in its eyes the one who has mammon is worthy of honor. In every location, this god has its altars, as well as its priests who sacrifice to it.

What do most people seek and love above everything else? Isn't it mammon? Don't most human hearts rejoice more in a profit of temporal goods than in anything else? Don't most people find their greatest pleasure and comfort in gold and silver, in expanding and profitable businesses, and in beautiful houses and expansive tracts of land? Why do they rise so early in the morning and remain at their labors until nightfall? They eagerly and tirelessly pursue mammon. They sacrifice everything, even their other most loved things, in order to obtain it, worrying themselves sick in the process. They deny themselves a thousand joys, rest, and comfort. They sacrifice friendships, honor, a good conscience—even their very life. There is nothing people fear more than the loss of the favor of this god, this mammon. When they do lose it, they often fall into a fatal sadness. Countless people have committed suicide in their despair after they found themselves forsaken by the comfort and help of mammon.

In the end, what does the world trust? Does it not regard mammon as the key to true happiness? Does it not believe it can rest only when it possesses much mammon? Does it not therefore pursue it ever more avidly in the hope of avoiding worry about the future? Is it not the greatest wish of many people to obtain so much money that they could live entirely off the interest? How can we deny, then, that mammon is the god of this world, which it loves, fears, and trusts above all other things?

Hence, all earthly treasure!
Jesus is my Pleasure,
Jesus is my Choice.
Hence, all empty glory!
Naught to me thy story
Told with tempting voice.
Pain or loss, Or shame or cross,
Shall not from my Savior move me
Since He deigns to love me. Amen.

(*TLH* 347:4)

Monday

Read Matthew 6:25–34

CHRIST SAYS that whoever does not seek *first* the kingdom of God and His righteousness is no Christian. Such a person does not give himself up in true love and childlike faith to the governing and preservation of the heavenly Father, but worries about his body and his life for the next day. What he will eat, drink, and wear are his key concerns. This individual is still a heathen according to his faith and the condition of his heart. His god is still mammon. This is a hard and frightening judgment, but there are many miserly, avaricious, money-loving, earthly-minded servants of mammon who do not think so.

Only the one whose heart does not adhere to money and temporal goods is not a servant of mammon. When God blesses him with money, he sees it only as an opportunity to do good to others. He regards himself as an instrument of divine good, as God's almsgiver, and he finds his own happiness in making others happy. He works, not because he believes it is God's command, but because he recognizes that God wills it and it pleases Him. This individual does not worry about his sustenance and clothing, which are not the product of work and effort but a gracious gift of the heavenly Father. He considers temporal things to be meager matters that, although he must care for them, are entirely of secondary importance to seeking after God's grace and the salvation of his soul. He thus "seek[s] first the kingdom of God and His righteousness" (Matthew 6:33).

There are those who say they do not wish to become rich, but to have only as much as they need to ensure a worry-free livelihood. Such people do not think they are servants of mammon. But their goal is to have just enough so they no longer have to trust in God alone, like the birds in the branches that daily must wait to see where God has scattered food for them. That small sum they hope to get by on is more important to them than letting God provide for them. This little sum, then, is their god!

Others are content with what they have and so think they are not governed by avarice. But behold! Even the little they have is their comfort and thus their god!

Still others do indeed care about the kingdom of heaven. They pray, go to church, partake of the Holy Supper, associate with Christians, and separate themselves from the godless world. But their heart is still troubled by a greater concern about how they want to get by, how to improve their business, and how they can become richer. No matter how pious and Christian such people appear, their god is still mammon.

Many rejoice in God's Word and grace, and grieve at losing one or the other. But if they gain considerably in temporal goods, their joy is much greater, and if they lose their temporal goods, their grief is great and they do not let themselves be comforted. Such people are secret worshipers of the god of mammon, temporal goods, rather than the heavenly Father and His spiritual goods.

There are some who do not seek after wealth because they know their striving would be in vain. They are therefore very angry with those who want to become rich. They may not appear to be attached to earthly things but only because their heart still laughs at them when they think they, too, could obtain wealth. Mammon is still their god.

Some give, not much but only as little as they can give with honor. They can, out of love of money, let a person depart without having received the charity for which he asked. They can cruelly turn away from the needy individual who wants to borrow from them. They can gleefully pocket the fixed interest of the debtor who can present it to them only with groaning. They can conclude a hard bargain and even stop the wages of the poor.

Each person who fits this description is a servant of mammon. Money is his idol, to whom he has sworn his soul. The love of the true God may be on his tongue, but it does not dwell in his heart.

One thing's needful; Lord, this treasure
Teach me highly to regard;
All else, though it first give pleasure,
Is a yoke that presses hard.
Beneath it the heart is still fretting and striving,
No true, lasting happiness ever deriving.
The gain of this one thing all loss can requite
And teach me in all things to find true delight.
Amen.

(TLH 366:1)

Tuesday

Read 1 Timothy 6:10

WE SEE FROM THESE WORDS what a shameful thing the love of money or the service to mammon must be. What can be said about something that is more shameful than that it is a root of all evil? No evil is as great as that which service to mammon produces! From it grows love of self, lovelessness toward the neighbor, hatred, envy, and indifference toward Christ, His

Word, and His grace. It results in enmity against God, a despising of heavenly goods, deception, murder, and hardness against the impulse of the Holy Ghost.

Wherever the love of money and goods enters, the love of God departs. Wherever mammon builds itself an altar, the heart becomes the temple of an idol, from which the true God must retreat in a hurry. The servant of mammon may perform many outward works of service to God, but the heart does not participate. Instead, the heart that clings to mammon is turned away from God, and thus its worship is a miserable shadow that is an abomination before God. A servant of mammon may present himself as ever so godly, but he still hates God in the bottom of his heart. He hopes to be able to be saved without God's grace, and thus he does not at all concern himself about that grace. If he could eternally remain in the world in earthly joy, he would eternally remain far from God, gladly leaving Him heaven and satisfying himself with the world.

God's sharp Law or sweet Gospel is preached in vain to a servant of mammon. The care, the riches, and the lusts of this life choke the heavenly seed. The heart of a lover of temporal goods is occasionally moved, for he, too, would one day like to possess heavenly as well as earthly goods; but almost immediately his thoughts return to the temporal things that again engulf him like the waves of the ocean and extinguish the faintly burning spark. A servant of mammon may often come to an earnest resolution to become a true Christian and to follow Christ until death, but when he hears that he must "sell all that you have and give to the poor" (Mark 10:21), that is, that he must tear his heart away from all temporal things, that he must have money only to do good, he goes away grieved, like the young man in the Gospel. The gate is too narrow for him, the path too small, and the stipulation too difficult. But what is his destiny? Already, here on earth, it is sorrow, grief, worry, unrest, and discontent. He always says to himself, "If I only had this or that, then I would be content." But the more he has, the greater his wishes become.

Death is a terrible message to the servant of mammon. It is terrible to him because it means losing the world and its goods and because his condition before God is uncertain. He guesses that Christ will not acknowledge him as one of His own. He imagines that he has forgotten and forfeited the heavenly for the earthly. Many have already died in this state, without hope and comfort, and with lamentation and woe. But despair in the hour of death is only a foretaste of what awaits the servant of mammon in eternity. On earth, he did not seek his joy in God, but in shameful mammon. Thus, in heaven, God will say to him, "Depart! Now let yourself be saved by your dead idols!" God's wrath and damnation will be the eternal interest paid on the account of those who amassed temporal goods only for themselves, who feasted their eyes and did not make the most of their possessions for the sake of the poor and the spreading of the kingdom of God. Before God, the servants of mammon will attempt to excuse themselves and say, "What evil have we done that we should be damned?" God will answer them: "Indeed, you have done nothing evil, but where is the good you should have done? Not only the tree that brings forth bad fruit, but also the tree that does not bring forth any good fruit, shall be cut down and cast into the fire. I blessed you in temporal things, but where is the increase from the pound that I gave you? The undried tears of the poor accuse you before Me. The rust on the gold and silver in your chests, the groans of the oppressed and defrauded, and indeed, your entire life in pursuit of temporal goods testify against you that you gathered for yourself treasures, that you loved yourself, and that you did not serve Me but mammon. For this reason, depart from Me, you accursed, into the everlasting fire prepared for the devil and all his angels!"

Oh, may each of us be frightened of the shameful service to mammon! Sad is the time of service, and terrible is the wage. Here on earth, it deceives man out of rest and peace of heart, and there in heaven, he will lose God, his soul, and his salvation.

Give us this day our daily bread
And let us all be clothed and fed.
From war and strife be our Defense,
From famine and from pestilence,
That we may live in godly peace,
Free from all care and avarice. Amen.

(TLH 458:5)

Wednesday

Read Lamentations 3:40

UNFORTUNATELY, many people know less about themselves than they do about anything else. An individual may easily notice his neighbor's faults, readily discerning the smallest splinter in his brother's eye, but it is hopelessly difficult for him to sense the beam in his own eye. People think they should know themselves easily and so do not seek to penetrate the hidden depths of their soul. However, in today's text and in many other places in the Bible, we are urgently called upon to learn to know ourselves. That we are so often implored to do this suggests that it is not at all as easy to accomplish as we may think.

Indeed, Christ says: "Why do you see the speck that is in your brother's eye, but do not notice the log that is in your own eye? . . . You hypocrite, first take the log out of your own eye, and then you will see clearly to take the speck out of your brother's eye" (Matthew 7:3, 5). These words teach us that all other knowledge, intelligence, culture, and wisdom is of no help at all to us if we do not know ourselves. We may investigate the course of the stars or the inner parts of the earth, but what does it avail us if we remain ignorant of ourselves? Without self-knowledge, even the most precise literal knowledge of the truths of the revealed Word of God is like a tree whose fruits we cannot pick and enjoy. The person who has not examined his heart directs his eyes in vain toward God to recognize His glory. He hears the preacher say that Christ is his gracious Savior, but if he does not know himself, it makes no impression on him.

Self-knowledge is the first step that one who wants to reach the true light must climb. It is the door to true wisdom, a person's first and most necessary learning. As soon as an individual rightly knows himself, he becomes humble. He sees that he is nothing but dust and ash, a great sinner, a transgressor of all divine commandments, a rebel against God's kingdom, and an abomination before God. Oh, it is well for the person who recognizes this! When the Gospel of Christ is preached to him, he receives it with a thousand joys. He believes in the Savior of sinners, and he holds Him firmly. Daily growth in the knowledge of himself prompts him daily to humble himself anew and to seek the righteousness, power, strength, and blessedness of Christ.

But how does a person come to this self-knowledge, and how does he grow in it? When the prophet Jeremiah says, "Let us test and examine our ways" (Lamentations 3:40), he is not suggesting that we can attain it by our own powers. A person may be ever so discerning, intelligent, experienced, and learned in earthly knowledge, but this will not help him obtain true self-knowledge. No matter how high his education, he can remain completely blind about himself. By nature, we are so deluded by our love of self that we always regard ourselves as better than we are. God Himself must open our eyes in order for us to obtain a true knowledge of ourselves, and He wills to work this in us by His Holy Ghost whenever we read, hear, and examine His holy Word as we examine ourselves. No person can recognize himself outwardly without a mirror and this is also the case inwardly. The mirror for our soul is the Word of God. Most people look into the mirror of the world; that is, they judge themselves according to the thoughts and prejudices of thoughtless mankind. Whoever does this will never come to a right knowledge of himself. He will never understand the corruption of his heart. Therefore, he will reject the Gospel and its teaching that he is a poor, lost sinner.

We must not regard ourselves in the distorted mirror of the world, but peer into the mirror of the Word of God, especially the Ten Commandments. There we will see our true self. We must, however, examine ourselves in a right manner. When Scripture chastises us for our sins, we must heartily call to God. He wants to expose the wickedness of our heart rightly to us. He wants to enlighten us with His Holy Ghost. He wants to take from us all self-deception and place our sins before our soul.

Its light of holiness imparts
The knowledge of our sinful hearts
That we may see our lost estate
And seek deliv'rance ere too late. Amen.

† *(TLH 295:2)*

Thursday

Read Galatians 6:6

MOST PEOPLE BELIEVE they have fulfilled all of their duties when they cannot be charged before any human court on account of their actions. Since no one is compelled in our country by some sort of governmental law to contribute something toward the preservation and spreading of God's Word and public worship, they think they are free to contribute or not to contribute to this effort. They believe they can choose to attend and belong to a Christian church, but this is in no way required of them. Nevertheless for the Christian, there can be no doubt that he is obligated to sacrifice some of his earthly goods for the preservation and spreading of God's Word.

First, we have a clear commandment from God on this subject, such as is found in today's text. Elsewhere, Saint Paul writes, "The Lord commanded that those who proclaim the gospel should get their living by the gospel" (1 Corinthians 9:14). And when the Lord once sent His holy apostles to preach the Gospel, He said to them, "You received without paying; give without pay" (Matthew 10:8). Thus He forbade them to trade with the Gospel and spiritual goods, but He added: "Carry no moneybag, no knapsack, no sandals, and greet no one on the road. Whatever house you enter, first say, 'Peace be to this house!' And if a son of peace is there, your peace will rest upon him. But if not, it will return to you. And remain in the same house, eating and drinking what they provide, for the laborer deserves his wages" (Luke 10:4–7).

We see here that, in order for the preachers of the Gospel to rightly attend to their office, God has commanded that they are not to live off the work of their hands. Indeed, woe to them if they desire a quiet, comfortable life, even gold and silver for their enrichment! Such are not servants of Christ, but servants of the belly. Instead, they should receive their necessary sustenance and clothing from those to whom they preach.

Since this is the clear commandment of God, can a person be a Christian if he does not want to sacrifice any of his temporal goods so God's Word would be preached to him? Certainly not. But Scripture goes further. Christ says, "The harvest is plentiful, but the laborers are few; therefore pray earnestly to the Lord of the harvest to send out laborers into His harvest" (Matthew 9:37–38). He also teaches His Christians to pray daily, "Our Father, who art in heaven, hallowed be Thy name, Thy kingdom come." If, then, Christians diligently call to God for workers for the heavenly harvest and daily ask Him that His name be hallowed by all people and that His kingdom come everywhere, must they not also do everything they can so God may answer their prayer? Would it not be a hypocritical prayer if Christians asked God to send His holy, saving Word while they themselves failed to sacrifice anything on its behalf? Thus, isn't the commandment to pray for the salvation of all people also a commandment to do everything we can for it ourselves?

There is still more. Christ says that the commandment "You shall love your neighbor as yourself" (Leviticus 19:18) is like the main commandment, "You shall love God above all things," on which all the Law and the Prophets depend. But if we should love our neighbors as ourselves, don't we then have the precious duty to care that they, as well as we, have God's Word? There is no doubt. In addition to the clear commandment of God that we sacrifice some of our earthly goods for the preservation and spreading of His Word and that we pray for the advancement of His kingdom, we have the command to love our neighbors as ourselves. This is God's way of telling us that we must contribute from our own resources to the spreading of His Word and His kingdom until the end of the age.

Lord Jesus, help, Thy Church uphold,
For we are sluggish, thoughtless, cold.
Oh, prosper well Thy Word of grace
And spread its truth in ev'ry place! Amen.

(TLH 292:3)

Friday

Read Psalm 51:13

HOW MISERABLE are the people who have no Word of God! Wealth, honor, and earthly joys cannot make them really happy for they are lacking the best and most necessary thing: the peace of God, the rest of the heart and the conscience. Despite their riches, they remain full of gnawing worry, and for all their joys, they are often bitterly sad. And if these people come into distress, poverty, sickness, shame, or the death of loved ones, their misery is complete and inexpressible. They have no balm of comfort for the wounds of their grieved hearts, no hope for the dark future, no bright view over the valley of sorrows of this world into a blessed eternity.

Yet the most horrible distress of those who do not have God's Word is one they do not immediately recognize: the distress of their sins. They are under the wrath of God but they do not know it. Heaven and salvation are closed to them, and they cannot imagine the hell and damnation that await them. With their covered eyes, they die and fall into the abyss of eternal misery and corruption and are lost.

However, if such people hear the Word of God, a few will always receive it, for God has promised that His Word will never come back void but will accomplish the purpose for which He sent it. Those who receive the Word of God in faith certainly do not thereby receive earthly riches for their poverty, human honor for their shame, bodily health for their sickness, and temporal life for them and their loved ones. But through the Word, they receive, in their distresses, such sweet heavenly comfort that they, as the apostle Paul writes, "Rejoice in hope, be patient in tribulation" (Romans 12:12). They may even boast of their cross and their tribulation as their jewels. In the midst of misfortune, they are joyful, and in the midst of death, they are full of hope.

Yet the most glorious thing with those who receive God's Word and accept it is that it delivers them from sin and its bitter fruits. Their doubt and their unrest of conscience are removed from them, the wrath of God against them is extinguished, and hell and damnation are closed to them. Instead, they receive the grace and peace of God, the forgiveness of all their sins, the knowledge that they are children of God, and the hope of eternal life. Oh, it is a blessed change that takes place in the person who receives God's Word and accepts it. For him, this world loses its bitter woe and becomes a prelude of the blessed world that awaits him. He will be delivered from the greatest distress, the distress of sin, and the highest good, God Himself, will be given to him.

The faith-filled person who sacrifices some of his earthly goods for the preservation and spreading of God's Word also participates in all of the glorious things that the Word works. He has a share in bringing comfort to others in distress, in changing the vale of tears of this world into a temporal paradise of grace for them, in removing the burden of sin and God's wrath from them, in closing hell and opening heaven to them, and in successfully rescuing their lost souls. For the small earthly good we contribute to the preservation and spreading of the Word of God, we have a means of making a poor person's soul rich in imperishable treasure. With it we have a key to unlock eternal joy and a seed that will grow into a fruitful tree.

May our zeal to help the heathen
Be increased from day to day
As we plead in true compassion
And for their conversion pray.
For the many faithful heralds,
For the Gospel they proclaim,
Let us all be cheerful givers
To the glory of Thy name. Amen.

† *(TLH 498:5)*

Saturday

Read Galatians 6:7–10

THE PERSON WHO SACRIFICES something only because he expects to receive a reward for it one day will certainly lose his reward. God pays such servants of reward in this world, where they already have their reward. However, it is not wrong to incite people to do good by holding up the reward of grace before them. Even God Himself, in His Word, often holds before us the future reward of grace. It is written of Moses that he chose "rather to be mistreated with the people of God than to enjoy the fleeting pleasures of sin. He considered the reproach of Christ greater wealth than the treasures of Egypt, for he was looking to the reward" (Hebrews 11:25–26). This does not mean that the reason for his faithfulness was the anticipation of the reward of the life to come, but this view nevertheless strengthened him when the world wanted to entice him with its glory or frighten him with its wrath.

God has established a great reward when a person willingly sacrifices from his temporal things for the preservation and spreading of His holy Word. Saint Paul says this in our text: "Do not be deceived: God is not mocked, for whatever one sows, that will he also reap. For the one who sows to his own flesh will from the flesh reap corruption, but the one who sows to the Spirit will from the Spirit reap eternal life. And let us not grow weary of doing good, for in due season we will reap, if we do not give up" (Galatians 6:7–9). We see from this that everything a person does in this life is a sowing for eternity. Whoever uses his earthly goods only for himself—for his comfort, joy, and glory—sows to the flesh and shall harvest eternal corruption from it. But whoever uses his earthly goods to do good, to serve his brother and, above all, to further the kingdom of God, sows to the Spirit and shall harvest eternal life from the Spirit. The temporal gift shall bring him eternal fruit. For his small sowing, he will harvest without ceasing. All contributions for the preservation and spreading of the Word of God that are presented with believing, joyful hearts will, in the life to come, become trees of the heavenly paradise that will never wither, but will be eternally green, always bearing new blossoms and fruits.

It may often appear that our gifts are employed in vain when, despite our best contributions, we perceive no advance, and perhaps even a decline, of the kingdom of God. But in heaven, the fruit, the glorious reward of grace, is still certain. We may sometimes think our small gift falls as a drop into the large ocean and disappears into nothing. But in heaven, that small drop becomes a precious pearl in our crown. Like snowflakes that are gathered together then tumble down the mountain into the valley as a huge avalanche, so will even our smallest gifts, presented in love and faith, fall from the mountain of divine mercy into our lap as an immense treasure of heaven. Here on earth, no one may know what a great sacrifice our little gift was for us, and our kindness may soon be forgotten in the splendid works of the rich, as if it were nothing. But in heaven, we will discover that God has not forgotten what we sacrificed to Him. He does not weigh it on a human scale, but on the scale of His unending goodness, which sees the heart. In His Word, He says He wants to repay in heaven even the secret prayer that is offered in the small, hidden chamber.

When we consider all of this, and when we think that one day we will be unable to take any of our earthly goods with us into the grave, shouldn't we be filled with joy and an earnest desire to do good? Certainly! For this reason, arise! Let us listen to the voice of God in our text: "So then, as we have opportunity, let us do good to everyone, and especially to those who are of the household of faith" (Galatians 6:10). Let us not listen to the voice of our flesh that so gladly laments that there is no end to giving. Let us listen, rather, to the voice of the divine Rewarder that again calls to us today: "For in due season we shall reap if we do not lose heart."

Thou Fountain whence all wisdom flows
Which God on pious hearts bestows,
Grant us Thy consolation
That in our pure faith's unity
We faithful witnesses may be

Of grace that brings salvation.
Hear us, Cheer us
By Thy teaching; Let our preaching
And our labor
Praise Thee, Lord, and serve our neighbor. Amen.

(TLH 235:3)

Sunday

Read Luke 7:11–17

TODAY'S GOSPEL READING presents a terrible situation for all unbelievers because it eliminates all their excuses. When Christ raised this young man from the dead, He demonstrated that He is who He declared Himself to be, namely, the Son of the living God. When mere prophets performed a miracle, most of them did so after having called upon God and invoking the name of God or Christ, never their own. However, Christ said, "Young man, I say to you, arise" (Luke 7:14). Thus He performed this miracle in His own name and by it He sealed these words: "I and the Father are one" (John 10:30), and "Believe in God; believe also in Me" (John 14:1).

Whoever can raise the dead with His own strength must be the true God and Life itself. But the day will come when Christ's words will raise not only the young man from Nain for the second time but also all the dead who sleep in their graves. God's trumpet will sound and Christ will call out: "You dead! Arise! The time of judgment has come! Appear, appear to receive your eternal judgment." This word of Christ will permeate heaven and earth, move all lands and seas, shake all mountains and valleys, open all graves, and in one moment place all the dead before the fiery countenance of the Most High Son of God, the Lord over death, and judge of all the world. Then even the unbelievers will finally be frightened. Shrieking, they will attempt in vain to flee from the face of Him whom they blasphemed. They will seek death, but they will not find it for they will have fallen into the hand of the Almighty.

While Christ's resurrection of the young man from Nain is terrible to the unbeliever, it is highly comforting to all true Christians. Consider how great, how irresistible must be the power of Him before whom even the power of death is mere powerlessness. Do we, then, have cause to fear that Christ's many enemies in our day will finally destroy His Church? Not at all. Christ has protected His Church until now, and He will continue to do so. He will rescue His honor and bring to shame all the powerless ones who rebel against Him. If we become weak in our faith, we have only to go in spirit to Nain and behold how Christ there seized death and overcame it. We can then rejoice that we believe in a Savior who is so great that when He speaks, it is done and when He commands, the dead rise. When Christians are troubled by their sins, they can find comfort in the account of Nain. Whoever can overcome death must also be a Lord over sin. For death is the wages of sin, and sin is the sting of death. For this reason, we must cling to Jesus Christ in firm faith. With Him, we find the forgiveness of all our sins, victory over all the enemies of our soul, grace, life, and salvation.

If death seeks to terrify us, if we cry over the graves of our loved ones, we can again seek solace in the resurrection at Nain. Jesus Christ, who changed the widow's tears of sorrow into tears of joy, can also dry our tears. As certainly as the widow again embraced her beloved son, we will one day, by Christ's miraculous power, also joyfully embrace all our loved ones who have died in the faith. A blessed morning will come when Christ will say to all of His own, in a new earth and a new heaven: "Do not cry! All sorrow has come to an end. I have overcome for you! Now rejoice eternally with Me, for now there is no longer any separation, any parting."

Finally, if we are frightened by the thought of our own last hours, we must grasp in our heart the words of Christ: "I say to you, arise." At this word, death fled and life returned. In like manner, Christ has abolished our death and brought us life and immortality. We can sleep peacefully, for Jesus remains our ever-watchful Savior. One day, we will awaken, and then death will be no more, for the first things have passed away. Hallelujah!

My spirit I commend to Thee
And gladly hence betake me;
Peaceful and calm my sleep shall be,
No human voice can wake me.
But Christ is with me through the strife,
And He will bear me into life;
And open heaven before me. Amen.

† *(TLH 594:5)*

Monday

Read Psalm 23:4

BY NATURE, an individual's death is a terrible event. Natural man's highest good is his earthly life, with its goods and its joys. Departing from those joys is the saddest fate that can befall him. He vacates his house and moves into the small, dark chamber of the grave. It pains him to consider that, at his death, he will leave behind his money and his goods, which are the desire of his eyes. These will become the property of others and he himself will be completely impoverished. The thought that his body, which he now serves and adorns, will then lie as an ice-cold corpse on its final couch and finally rot in a moldy grave, decomposing and becoming the food of loathsome worms, shakes his entire soul and fills him with horror.

If the natural man now considers that death is not an annihilation but an earnest messenger of God calling him into the great judgment hall where he will receive what his deeds are worth, either an inexpressible blessedness and glory or eternal pain and punishment, then his false comfort disappears. He is now thrown into doubt and despair. With broken lips, he calls out, "Oh, may I live until tomorrow!" Even true Christians are frequently seized by fear when they approach the dark valley of death.

On account of this, no one can be secure. You may think you do not fear death, but have you ever looked directly into its smirking face, into its hollow, staring eyes? Truly, it is not the might of man, but God's grace alone, that can overcome this king of terror. We see this clearly in the words of today's reading. They show us that if a person wants to overcome the terror of death and even to climb down into the darkness of the grave with confidence, he must forsake the world from his heart and draw near to the Lord, choosing Him and His grace as his highest good and leaning on His Word as his staff. If an individual comes to the point where he can say, with David, "For You are with me" (Psalm 23:4), that is, I hold You to myself as my true treasure with the hand of my faith, and "Your rod and Your staff, they comfort me" (Psalm 23:4), that is, I build upon and hope in the promises of Your Gospel, then he can also add, with David, "Even though I walk through the valley of the shadow of death, I will fear no evil" (Psalm 23:4). These words signify that he does not fear any separation, any grave, any hell, or any damnation, for by God's grace, the grave is a cottage of peace and death is the portal of life, the departure out of this world, and the entrance into heaven.

The German proverb says it well: "A clear conscience is a soft pillow." But where is the person who has never stained his conscience? Who can be pure when no one is pure? Where is the one who is not a sinner? Oh, miserable is the one who relies upon his conscience, who hopes to slumber upon this pillow at his death. At the moment of death, the conscience, which had fallen asleep during life, will awaken in most people and change into a pillow thorns of doubt and terror.

There is only one way a person can die gently, confidently, and blessed. He must learn to go to God as a poor sinner and to call upon Him for grace for Christ's, His Savior's, sake. He must learn to seize Christ and His promises of grace in faith. He must taste and see how friendly, how good, how gracious, and how merciful the Lord is. If he does all of this, he will despise the world and learn to long for heaven. Saint Paul had recognized and experienced God's grace in Christ. He certainly knew that he had a gracious God and that he would be saved. For this reason, the thought of leaving this poor world did not cause him any grief. He was not afraid of death. Instead, he longed for it from his heart and said, "[I have a desire] to depart and be with Christ" (Philippians 1:23).

Since Thou the power of death didst rend,
In death Thou wilt not leave me;
Since Thou didst into heaven ascend,
No fear of death shall grieve me.

For where Thou art, there shall I be
That I may ever live with Thee;
That is my hope when dying. Amen.

(TLH 594:4)

Tuesday

Read 1 Corinthians 15:54–55, 57

DEATH IS THE LOUDEST and strongest preacher to the unbelieving world. That world may shun all churches and avoid all preachers of the Word of God, but there is one preacher it must hear. Death's church is the whole earth and the heavenly vaults above it; its pulpits are the deathbed, the coffin, the hearse, the grave, and the cemetery. With a piercing voice that penetrates marrow and bone, this preacher calls into the world's ear wherever it goes: "Man, you must die! There is no remaining abode here. The earth is not your homeland. This life is not the destiny given to you. You must finally go out of this world, with all its glory, at an hour unknown to you. Oh, repent! Repent!"

But in incomprehensible delusion, the world does not want to hear death's call to repentance. It must then experience the great might of the king of terrors. If its loved ones die, it cries tears of doubt, then looks on as the grave locks up the corpses forever and their souls flutter and disappear like fog in the air. It looks into eternity as into an unknown land, tormented by doubt.

How differently believers stand by the coffins and graves

of their loved ones who have fallen asleep in the faith! While their poor hearts bleed for them and their grieved eyes cry, their spirits exult with Paul in the words of today's text. Those words assure us that our lives only appear to be swallowed up by death. For Christ, in whom we have believed, has swallowed up death and removed its power, and He has brought life and immortality to light. Death has become a little bee that has lost its sting, and now it carries nothing but sweet honey in its mouth. The death day of our loved ones is actually their most blessed birthday, for their death marks their entrance into true life. Their corpses lie before us like those of all people—cold and stiff, forsaken by the soul. Nevertheless, they are precious seeds of grain planted in God's field. On the day of the heavenly harvest, these bodies will sprout again and their dear souls will return to their former dwellings that will then be gloriously transformed, shining as the sun.

There is certainly a hell, but not for our loved ones who have fallen asleep in the faith. Christ has risen from the dead, ascended into heaven, and taken captivity captive. The precious souls of our loved ones who have fallen asleep in the faith are no longer with us, but they have gone up to Christ and now dwell in the house of His Father. They have already arrived in their true homeland. They have now joined the heavenly Jerusalem, with all its blessed ones who have gone on before and with all holy angels, and there they all sing a new song at the throne of the Lamb. For this reason, believers can jeer at the coffins and graves of their loved ones who have fallen asleep in the faith and call out, with Paul, "O death, where is your sting?" (1 Corinthians 15:55). You have lost it! "O death, where is your victory?" (1 Corinthians 15:55). It is snatched away from you. You are now eternally conquered!

In his song of joy, Paul includes the words, "But thanks be

to God, who gives us the victory through our Lord Jesus Christ" (1 Corinthians 15:57). This hymn of joy is not only a hymn of victory, but also a hymn of thanksgiving. The unbelieving world thinks it is impossible to sing a hymn of thanksgiving at the coffins and graves of its loved ones. Rather, it wants to quarrel with its Creator and Ruler, cursing God as a cruel tyrant who has jealously taken from it its dearest on earth and, with a merciless hand, destroyed its life's happiness. But believers, standing at the coffins and graves of their loved ones who have fallen asleep in the faith, have a completely different outlook. They humbly submit themselves to the wondrous counsel of their God and Father. They sing, in firm faith, "What God ordains is always good." But they also thank Him that, out of His eternal goodness, He created them, preserved them, governed them, and redeemed them by His Son. By pure grace, He brought them to faith, sanctified them, and preserved them in the faith until the end. They know that their loved ones are among the elect from eternity for salvation. Therefore, even the gates of hell cannot rob them of their salvation.

It was a strange and dreadful strife
When Life and Death contended;
The victory remained with Life,
The reign of Death was ended;
Holy Scripture plainly saith
That Death is swallowed up by Death,
His sting is lost forever. Hallelujah! Amen.

† *(TLH 195:2)*

Wednesday

Read Song of Solomon 4:14

WHEN GOD TAKES adults out of this world quickly, when He pulls fathers or mothers from their family circles, when He suddenly extends the cold hand of death to a young man or woman, this is not always a sign of His grace. If these individuals sought only to gather for themselves treasures of this world, forgetting to seek the treasures that do not rust, are not consumed by moths, and are not dug up by thieves, their early death is then a work of divine wrath. God has said: "Fool! This night your soul is required of you, and the things you have prepared, whose will they be?" (Luke 12:20). If these people sought a comfortable life or honor before men while ignoring the matters of eternal life and honor with God in true repentance, then their early death is a sign of the end of divine long-suffering, the most terrible punishment of the holy God, who throws them into eternal misery and disgrace. If young men or young women thought only of enjoying their youth and rejoicing in life, if they sacrificed the fragrant blossom of their young life to the world and its vanity, and if they thought they could later give the withered leaves of their old age to their God and Savior, then their early death is a flash of lightning from the hand of the angry, eternal Judge, who casts them into the outermost darkness, where there is weeping and gnashing of teeth. For this reason, all true Christians daily pray: "Protect us, dear Lord God, from an evil, sudden death. My God, I pray, through Christ's blood, make my end a good one!"

However, this is not the case when God suddenly takes baptized children from this world. Here, He is not motivated by wrath. Although our children, having been born into sin, are not innocent beings, they have been washed clean from all their sins by Christ's death and their own Holy Baptism. Christ has made them children of His Father and heirs of eternal life. Therefore, their heavenly Father loves them infinitely more dearly than their earthly fathers and mothers are able to love them. He carries them in His heart as a mother does in her womb. He gives them to drink of His Spirit of grace, as a mother does with the milk of her breast. He gives them the holy angels to be their guardians and attendants, and He keeps His eye upon them day and night. He is angry with those who cause them even the smallest sorrow and prompt them to sin. It would be better for such people if a millstone were hung around their neck and they were drowned in the depth of the sea. For He says, "Whoever receives one such child in my name receives Me" (Matthew 18:5). How, then, could it be wrath if He quickly takes His dear one out of this world?

The Book of Wisdom speaks truly when it says about such children, "For his soul pleased the LORD: therefore hasted He to take him away from among the wicked" (Wisdom of Solomon 4:14 KJV). What could it be but love if someone were to free us from a solitary, dark underground prison and lead us into a hall of light where we would be united with our best friends? What else could it be but love if someone were to bring us from a place full of danger into a perfectly secure castle? What else could it be but love if someone moved us from bitter poverty to riches, from the deepest shame to the highest honor, from misery and distress to joy, from continual sickness into lasting health, from dying into never-ending life?

What is this evil life but a lonely, dark underground prison where our soul languishes and lies captive in the bonds of sin? And what is heaven but a hall of light into which all the elect are gathered? What is this evil life but a place full of the greatest dangers, in which even the just are hardly preserved, a great Sodom and Gomorrah? And what is heaven but a solid, perfectly secure castle into which no enemy of our soul, no danger, can come? What is this evil life but bitter poverty in which we must daily come before God as naked beggars? And what is heaven but immense riches? What is this evil life but misery, trouble, sickness, and death? And what is heaven but a constant joy, eternal health, and blessed life?

With peace and joy I now depart;
God's child I am with all my heart.
I thank thee, Death, thou leadest me
To that true life where I would be.
So cleansed by Christ, I fear not death.
Lord Jesus, strengthen Thou my faith. Amen.

(TLH 585:2)

Thursday

Read Ephesians 3:13–17

THERE IS A TIME when a person's body ceases to grow. This is not so in spiritual things. If a person has become a Christian, a new spiritual being (or, as our text says, a new "inner being") is created in him by God through faith and the growth of this being never ceases until death. In Christianity, there is no standing still. Whoever does not go forward, goes backward. The life of a Christian is not marked by being, but by growing. The goal toward which he strives is so high that he can never say he has reached it and can rest from his efforts. Even Saint Paul says, "Not that I have already obtained this or am already perfect, but I press on to make it my own, because Christ Jesus has made me His own" (Philippians 3:12).

Of what does the strengthening "in your inner being" (Ephesians 3:16), the spiritual growth of the Christian, consist? Paul shows us in today's text when he says, "That Christ may dwell in your hearts through faith" (Ephesians 3:17). An ever growing and stronger faith, through which Christ dwells in our hearts, is necessary, above all else, for the strengthening of the inner being. A person becomes a Christian through faith. Once he vividly recognizes that he is a sinner, it is obvious to him that he cannot stand before God with his own righteousness and cannot atone for his sins himself. Instead, he needs a Reconciler, a Redeemer, a Savior—One who brings salvation. The knowledge of this hopeless condition alarms him and in his fear, he turns in faith to Christ, who in the Gospel offers all sinners grace, forgiveness of sins, life, and salvation. Thus, he becomes a Christian.

The new Christian usually thinks he has a great, strong, and firm faith. He feels so blessed in his new experiences. His anxiety over his sins has disappeared, and his conscience, which previously accused him, has been silenced. But, despite appearances, the beginner in Christ is weak. His confidence in his faith is based upon the feeling of grace he has in his heart and the sense of joy he had never before experienced. However, if he loses these sweet feelings, his faith usually disappears with them. Then he may wonder: "How can Jesus dwell in me when I feel nothing but sin and sadness? How can God have become my Father and I His child when it goes so badly with me?"

If a person remains weak in the faith, his faith will finally be overcome and extinguished. Therefore, if he is to remain a Christian, his faith must grow and become firmer. His faith must be built on the Word alone so he can comfort himself with that mere written Word even when he feels no joy in his heart. Then he will believe in the forgiveness of his sins even when he senses the presence of sin still dwelling in him. He must also comfort himself with the grace of God that is preached to him, even when he experiences God's wrath. Then he can regard God as his gracious Father and himself as His child even when it appears God has forsaken him. Even in bitter want, he can rely upon God's supply. In the greatest danger and distress, he can be confident of God's help and rescue. And, in the midst of death, he can trust in his certain redemption by God. That is the essence of becoming firm in the faith.

Thou holy Fire, Comfort true,
Grant us the will Thy work to do
And in Thy service to abide;
Let trials turn us not aside.
Lord, by Thy pow'r prepare each heart
And to our weakness strength impart
That bravely here we may contend,
Thro' life and death to Thee, our Lord, ascend
Hallelujah! Hallelujah! Amen.

† *(TLH 224:3)*

Friday

Read Ephesians 3:17

PAUL SAID HE OFTEN PRAYED to God that He would make the Ephesians stronger. By this he meant that Christ might dwell in their hearts by faith and that they might be "rooted and grounded in love" (Ephesians 3:17). We see here that, through love, Christianity becomes akin to a firmly rooted tree and a house on a solid foundation. Should this really be attributed to love? According to Holy Scripture, isn't it faith alone that makes one just and blessed before God? Isn't it faith alone that gives life, light, comfort, and power? Isn't it, then, faith alone that rightly roots and grounds the Christian?

This is true, of course, but Scripture says that faith without works is dead, a mere empty picture of faith. True, living faith is active through love. Therefore, as there is warmth and light in the presence of fire, there are love and good works in the person whose heart has been warmed by the sun of faith. As the tree is recognized by its fruit, faith is recognized in love. The person who is weak or lacking in love cannot be a strong, firm Christian. He may call himself a Christian, but where is the proof that he stands in the faith? Therefore, in the hour of his death, woe to the Christian who boasted of faith but did not show any love. It will probably be difficult for him to show that he comforted himself with Christ and did not doubt because, although faith alone avails before God, we owe love to our neighbor and need love ourselves so we are strong.

The individual who wants to become inwardly strong must always become more zealous in love. He must also extend the scope of his love. He cannot say: "What does this one or that one concern me? This one is a stranger; he is not worthy of my love." With each person who is in need of his love, he must remember that this individual is also a possession of Christ, one for whom God's Son shed His blood, one who was created by God and called by Him to eternal life. Thus, even if this person is his enemy, he must love him for God's sake as his brother.

A Christian must also become purer and more unselfish in his love. He must not ask, "What's in it for me?" He must not do good for the sake of the thanks he hopes to receive, the reward he expects, or the praise that might result. His left hand must not know what his right hand is doing. He must learn to endure ingratitude and not allow his love to grow cold on account of it. He must keep a heart full of love toward those who offend and provoke him—even those who have done flagrant wrong to him, hated him, and persecuted him.

He must always become more tender, holy, and godly in his love. He must have patience with his neighbor's weaknesses, sins, and defects. He must also not be ashamed of the greatest sinner, but have mercy on him. He must, above all, see to the rescue of his soul. He must chastise him out of love, even if he would lose his favor by it, even when this love would be interpreted as hate and he would be despised and rejected as someone malicious.

The Christian must rejoice over his neighbor's happiness as over his own, and grieve over his neighbor's misfortune as over his own. To have a brother who is grieved or irritated must cut his heart. He must, finally, arrive at the point where he strives to let his entire life be a life of service to his neighbor, being ready to give up his possessions and even his life for his brothers. Oh, it is well for such Christians! They have become, "through faith," as it says in our text, rightly "rooted and grounded in love."

Faith clings to Jesus' cross alone
And rests in Him unceasing;
And by its fruits true faith is known,
With love and hope increasing.
Yet faith alone doth justify,
Works serve thy neighbor and supply
The proof that faith is living. Amen.

† *(TLH 377:9)*

Saturday

Read Ephesians 3:18–21

WITH THESE WORDS, Saint Paul identifies something that is a part of the necessary strengthening of a Christian in the inner man: always becoming richer in knowledge and experience. "[So that you] may have strength to comprehend with all the saints what is the breadth and length and height and depth, and to know the love of Christ that surpasses knowledge, that you may be filled with all the fullness of God" (Ephesians 3:18–19). Paul is not talking about an always greater knowledge of Christian doctrine and its truths, for knowledge often serves only to puff up. No, the apostle is speaking here about the knowledge and experience of the unsurpassable love of Christ.

Experiencing this love is a main part of the necessary strengthening of a Christian. He may know everything else, but it will not help if he does not know Christ's love. Whoever knows Christ's love, knows enough, even if he knows nothing else. Thus, if we want to become inwardly strong, we must learn more and more to recognize Christ's love. We must learn to recognize its "width" that it is wider than the whole world; it embraces all sinners and, indeed, everything that lives in heaven and on earth. We must learn to recognize its "length" that this love is longer than the duration of the world; it is from eternity and extends until eternity. We must learn to recognize its "height" for this love is higher than all the mountains of the world; it reaches even to heaven. We must learn to recognize its "depth" for this love is deeper than the foundation of the earth; it is a deep, inexhaustible, unfathomable spring that flows from the depth of God's own heart.

Paul goes even further. We must learn that Christ's love surpasses all knowledge, that it can never be completely learned, explored, or studied. It is as great, as glorious, and as immeasurable as God is Himself. May we, then, continually open the book of Christ's love and study it with prayer and meditation! What we will then experience! How often will we enjoy a foretaste of eternal life! How strong will we become in the inner man! By it, we will, as the apostle says, "be filled with all the fullness of God." O blessed Christians, who daily seek to become firmer in faith, more zealous in love, and richer in the knowledge and experience of Christ's love! Let us all strive to become such Christians. To that end, let us hear and read God's Word, as well as pray, watch, and fight. We will then one day behold what we believed and enjoy that for which we hoped.

"Now to Him who is able to do exceedingly abundantly above all that we ask or think, according to the power that works in us, to Him be glory in the Church by Christ Jesus throughout all ages, world without end. Amen."

Oh, grant that nothing in my soul
May dwell but Thy pure love alone!
Oh, may Thy love possess me whole,
My Joy, my Treasure, and my Crown!
All coldness from my heart remove;
My ev'ry act, word, thought, be love. Amen.

† *(TLH 349:2)*

Sunday

Read Luke 14:1–11

HOW DID THE PHARISEES observe the Sabbath? Not by hearing the Word of God from the mouth of Christ, with whom they assembled in the house of one of their rulers. Instead, our reading today says: "They watched Him closely." They waited for Him to do something that would allow them to expose Him to the people as a violator of the Sabbath. For this purpose, they apparently brought along a man who had dropsy in order to lead Jesus, who they knew had already healed on the Sabbath, into temptation so He would do so again on this occasion. Jesus revealed their hypocrisy. But they did not receive God's Word. Instead, they became silent and hardened themselves against the salutary chastisement. Moreover, they demonstrated a completely childish pride and ambition, for when they wanted to sit at the table, "they chose the best places."

According to the law of the Pharisees, the main thing in the observance of the Sabbath was not working. Sanctifying was a matter of such secondary importance that it could even be omitted entirely. The Pharisees regarded the doing of a necessary work of love on the Sabbath, such as the healing of a sick person, as a great violation of the Sabbath. But they did not regard as a violation of the Sabbath their refusal to hear the Word of God, their enmity toward Christ, and their hypocrisy, pretense, vanity, and pride. If they appeared in the synagogue with open ears but deaf hearts, heard readings from the Law and the Prophets, recited some prayers, and abstained from all daily work, they believed they kept, in the best way, the Third Commandment, "Remember the Sabbath day, to keep it holy" (Exodus 20:8).

Unfortunately, such people are still among us. Here in America, there are only too many such Sabbath observers. Many still regard it as a great sin to work on Sunday, observing a strictness exceeding even that of the Jews, for they would reject the doing even of works of necessity and love on that day. But some do not regard it as a sin that they often neglect to attend worship services and to hear the preaching of God's Word. This, then, is a pharisaic, legalistic, hypocritical observance of the Sabbath.

There are many others who regard not going to church as a great sin, but they do not attend services to hear God's Word for the salvation of their souls, but only to perform what they think is a work for God. They imagine that if they have merely gone to church, they have completely kept the Sabbath. It doesn't matter to them whether they hear the pure Word of God or a falsified version of it, and whether they listen to the revealed truth or the mere doctrines of man. They do not examine what they hear; indeed, they are unreceptive toward pure doctrine and prefer to hear an interpretation of God's Word that is aligned with their own twisted understanding and distorted inclinations. Again, this practice is nothing but a pharisaic, legalistic observance of the Sabbath.

Finally, there are some who attend churches in which God's Word is purely and clearly preached, or where they *suppose* that it is purely and clearly preached. They listen with a certain attentiveness, and they are moved and shaken by it, as the Pharisees once were by Christ's chastisement of them. But despite all this, they remain unchanged. These are the so-called Sunday Christians, who on Sunday pass themselves off as holy, devout, and zealous Christians but their unchristian life begins anew when they return to work on Monday. This, too, is a hypocritical, pharisaic, legalistic observance of the Sabbath, in which a person fulfills the outward letter of the Law but denies its inner, true sense. Such an individual certainly celebrates the Sabbath, but he does not sanctify it. Rather, he breaks and violates it.

Blessed Spirit, Comforter,
Sent this day from Christ on high,
Lord, on us Thy gifts confer,
Cleanse, illumine, sanctify.
All Thy fullness shed abroad;
Lead us to the truth of God. Amen.

† *(TLH 8:3)*

Monday

Read Exodus 20:8

THE TRUE GOSPEL-MINDED CHRISTIAN outwardly keeps the Sabbath after the model of Christ. In the New Testament, the commandment to rest from work on that day was abolished, for Paul expressly wrote "Therefore let no one pass judgment on you in questions of food and drink, or with regard to a festival or a new moon or a Sabbath. These are a shadow of the things to come, but the substance belongs to Christ" (Colossians 2:16–17). But because it is necessary to rest from all work once in the week and to occupy oneself with spiritual things above all else, and because the Christian Church chose Sunday as the day for this, the Christian joyfully observes this necessary and salutary ordinance for the sake of love and peace. He will never work on Sunday except in an emergency. He will never neglect a worship service on

Sunday except in an emergency. He regards this not as a difficult duty but as a precious privilege. Although he knows he is free of the Sabbath obligations of the Old Testament, he still observes Sunday as the New Testament Sabbath with great care. To him, this day is the most precious day of the entire week, when he can step back from the daily grind and rejoice. He would not give up his dear Sunday, when he is permitted rest, for all the world's goods and money.

On the Sabbath, the true Christian studies God's Word. He reads it, hears it, considers it, and speaks with others about it. To him, it is more a matter of sanctifying Sunday than observing it. A Sunday without God's Word and worship is not a Sunday for him. It is essential that God's Word is preached purely and clearly. He flees all false prophets and all false churches, seeking a place where the true bread of life is distributed. The true Christian not only hears God's Word with his ears, but he is also sanctified by it, increasing in knowledge, in faith, in love, in hope, in humility, in patience, and in all other Christian virtues. For this reason, he prays to God, going to and leaving from church that he might continue to grow in His Word. At the same time, he investigates the Scriptures to see if what was preached to him is consistent with what they contain, and he repeats at home what he heard. If he receives chastisement from God's Word, he is not angry with the preacher. On the contrary, this chastisement is as dear to him as thorough instruction and sweet comfort.

As careful as the Gospel-minded Christian is to observe the Sabbath by bodily rest and to sanctify it by God's Word, his thinking is not so narrow that he would regard works of necessity and love done on Sundays to be sinful. He knows that to care for children, to visit and attend to sick people, to help someone in an accident, and to provide the body with the necessities are not violations of the Sabbath but rather God-pleasing works. Nor is the true Christian judged when, even on

Sundays, he enjoys his God-created natural surroundings, the company of dear brothers and sisters, or even a moderate banquet, if only he seeks to do everything in the fear and glory of the Lord, seasoning his conversation with spiritual words. Following Christ's model, he does not decline the invitation of the children of the world and the enemies of the truth if he can be among them without having to share in their sins. He then uses the opportunity offered to him to confess his Savior and His truth before both friends and enemies and to chastise all ungodly beings, if not with words, then by his entire behavior.

Oh, when the observance of the Sabbath happens in a Christian manner, then each Sunday illumines all other days with its heavenly shine, the pearl and crown of all days, the right Sabbath eve on earth, after which will come the eternal Sabbath in heaven.

In every season, every place,
May we regard Thy Word of grace
Until, when life's brief day is past,
We reach eternal joy at last. Amen.

† *(TLH 7:3)*

Tuesday

Read Colossians 2:16–17

As holy and inviolable as the Sabbath day must have been to the people of God in the time of the Old Testament, it was not established by God for all ages. According to God's will, the entire Old Testament, with its church and civil laws and institutions, was not designed to remain forever, but was to serve only as a preparation and equipping for the coming of the Savior of the world. The Sabbath was a model of the rest of Christ in His grave at the end of His work of redemption, as well as a model of the perpetual Sabbath Christ wants to bring about in the hearts of His believers until He brings them to the eternal Sabbath in heaven.

Therefore, with the coming of Christ, the entire scaffolding of the Old Testament was dismantled. By His coming in the flesh, Christ took away from us the oppressive yoke of countless outward rules. The time of the preparation ended, and with Christ, freedom from all servile service was granted to us. No appointed place, house, ceremony, or time of the Old Testament binds us. All shadows of Christ are put away because Christ Himself has come. All models of Christ are abolished because Christ has appeared. The Old Testament itself revealed that all its shadow-work would not last forever. Moses announced that, after him, the Prophet of God would be raised up, whom Israel should obey. Jeremiah prophesied that when all Gentiles would gather in Jerusalem for the sake of the Name of the Lord, there would no longer be an Ark of the Covenant and sacrifice. Isaiah foretold that, in the New Testament, there would no longer be an appointed Sabbath, but "from Sabbath to Sabbath" (66:23). The children of the New Testament would thus keep Sabbaths every day.

We find this abundantly confirmed throughout the New Testament. As soon as Christ entered His teaching office, He began to alleviate the strictness of the Mosaic Law. He not only healed the sick on the Sabbath, He also allowed His disciples to pluck grain on the Sabbath, showing that the end of the Mosaic Sabbath had come. Following the death of Christ, the curtain in the temple before the Holy of Holies was torn in two as a sign of the complete abolition of the Levitical worship. The holy apostles clearly taught that no Christian is any longer bound to the Jewish Sabbath. As Saint Paul says in our text, "Therefore let no one pass judgment on you in questions of food and drink, or with regard to a festival or a new moon or a Sabbath. These are a shadow of the things to come, but the substance belongs to Christ" (Colossians 2:16–17). Thus, freedom from the Jewish Sabbath was clearly proclaimed to all Christians, and the observance of an appointed day for duty, as a command of God, was not laid on their conscience. When false apostles convinced the Galatians to keep appointed days because God had commanded it, Paul informed them that they "observe days and months and seasons and years! I am afraid I may have labored over you in vain" (Galatians 4:10–11).

We see here that Christianity does not provide new laws about appointed times, places, and other outwardly things. Rather, all Christians have achieved a perfect freedom through Christ, and their only commandment is to love. In the Epistle to the Romans, Paul says that a person should not offend or judge those who are weak in faith, but endure and bear. Thus they still observed days, but he also said, "the one who abstains, abstains in honor of the Lord and gives thanks to God" (Romans 14:6). Therefore, Sunday is not a commandment of God but a free arrangement of the Christian Church for the remembrance of the resurrection of Jesus Christ and the institution of the holy preaching office. It is appointed for the holy assembling of Christians. Indeed, while Sunday is mentioned in Holy Scripture, it is nowhere commanded. It is a part of Christian freedom.

O God, our Lord, Thy holy Word
Was long a hidden treasure,
Till to its place It was by grace

Restored in fullest measure.
For this today Our thanks we say
And gladly glorify Thee.
Thy mercy show And grace bestow
On all who still deny Thee. Amen.

† *(TLH 266:1)*

Wednesday

Read Galatians 5:13

ACCORDING TO its spiritual understanding, the Third Commandment was given not just to the Jews, but also to all people, and it remains in force until the Last Day. The appointed outward form as to how this commandment was to be fulfilled, the appointed day and ceremonies, was, of course, given only to the Jews, but the core of the commandment still applies also to Christians. Luther explained it entirely according to the Gospel: "We should fear and love God that we may not despise preaching and His Word, but hold it sacred and gladly hear and learn it" (Small Catechism, 10). No person who wants to be saved is released from it. The Christian Church has not been freed from the use of the divine Word. It must preach it, hold it sacred, gladly hear it, and learn from it. If the Church is to survive, Christians must come together to study God's Word, pray jointly, offer praise and thanks to God, and use the holy Sacraments in common. If Christians did not do this, they would despise the Word and the Sacraments, which alone sanctify them, and they could not obtain the promise of Christ: "For where two or three are gathered in My name, there am I among them" (Matthew 18:20).

"Yes, this is true," someone may say. "But didn't Paul himself say that a person should not be judged regarding appointed holy days?" Without doubt. No one should believe that God binds us by law and commandment to any certain day. However, God not only commands that Christians hear His holy Word, but He also calls to them through the apostle, "But all things should be done decently and in order" (1 Corinthians 14:40). But how is it possible for this to be done in a decent and orderly fashion in the Church of God if Christians do not pursue an appointed day or days in which they lay aside the work of their earthly vocations and come together to exercise in common God's Word and prayer? What would become of the Church if one person wanted the Christian assembly, Sacrament, and preaching to be offered today, but another preferred a different day? The Church would be devastated and thrown into confusion, and no day would become a Christian Sabbath. Therefore, the Church was not freed from an order for coming together.

Someone else may say: "By God's grace, I have so much knowledge, so much faith, and so much zeal that I do not need an appointed day. I keep every day a Sabbath. Why should I have the yoke of a special day laid upon me?" If a Christian is as strong as he thinks he is, he should thank God for His great grace! But he should consider that he is still flesh and blood. He still has something in him that must be awakened and aroused, and for this reason, he should not feel secure and despise the public Sunday observance. But even supposing that he himself does not really need this means, there are many others in the Christian communion who do. Is he then allowed to exclude himself? Might he not, by his example, lead others to despise that means of edification? Is he allowed to offend even the smallest of them who believe in Christ? Must he not do everything he can to ensure that all are brought to faith by public preaching and public confession every Sunday?

The Christian is not free from this service of love toward his neighbor. Christ indeed freed His Christians, by the Gospel, from the curse and compulsion of all laws, but not so a person can do whatever he wants. On the contrary, by the Gospel, Christ changes the hearts of people so that, without the compulsion of the Law, they do good things with a willing and joyful heart, motivated by their love of God and by thanks for His grace. True Christians are, through faith, different people. They are not compelled by the Law. No, from a spontaneous impulse of love poured into their hearts, they do all sorts of good wherever they can. It is the same way with the command of the Sunday observance. A Christian knows it is not commanded, but he keeps it all the more willingly and joyfully. No one compels and moves him to it. Instead, he keeps it out of love for God's Word, for order, and for his weak neighbors. In the grace of the New Testament, he naturally keeps Sunday as holy, just as any believer of the Old Testament kept his Sabbath.

Thy name be hallowed. Help us, Lord,
In purity to keep Thy Word,
That to the glory of Thy name
We walk before Thee free from blame.
Let no false doctrine us pervert;
All poor, deluded souls convert. Amen.

(*TLH* 458:2)

Thursday

Read John 18:36

ACCORDING TO CHRIST'S INTENTION, His kingdom, or the Church, should not be bound, mixed, or mingled with the kingdoms of this world. According to God's Word, Church and state are as far from each other as the sky is from the earth. The state is a kingdom of this world, an earthly kingdom; the Church is a heavenly kingdom. It is, as the Lord so often said, the kingdom of heaven on earth (John 18:36). The state is an outward, bodily, visible kingdom; the Church is an inner, spiritual, invisible kingdom. Christ said, "The kingdom of God is not coming with signs to be observed, nor will they say, 'Look, here it is!' or 'There!' for behold, the kingdom of God is in the midst of you" (Luke 17:20–21).

The citizens of the state are all who have been outwardly taken into it, the evil as well as the good, the godless as well as the pious, unbelievers as well as believers, non-Christians as well as Christians. The members of the Church, on the contrary, are those who are Christ's sheep, who listen to His voice, and who believe in Him from their hearts. The sole purpose of the state is to maintain the earthly welfare of man, to protect its citizens, and to preserve peace, discipline, and order. The purpose of the Church, however, is establishing peace between man and God, protecting man against sin and death and hell, and securing eternal righteousness, eternal life, and eternal blessedness. The state is guided by the light of nature or human understanding; the Church is illumined by the light of the direct, divine revelation contained in Holy Scripture. The state makes its own laws; the Church is governed by the eternal law of God. The state punishes only the outwardly evil deed, but the Church also focuses on the ungodly disposition of the heart. The state permits everything that furthers its earthly goals, but the Church permits only what God has declared as permissible in His Word.

The state commands by its own authority and demands obedience for the sake of its office; the Church commands nothing by its own authority and demands obedience only of the commands of Christ. The state enforces its authority with the sword and outward force, while the Church wields only the sword of the Spirit, that is, the Word of God and its power of conviction. The state has, as its essential components, authority and subjects, those who give orders and those who obey. In the Church, all are equal and subject to one another by love alone.

Thus we see that, according to God's Word, Church and state are indeed separated by a great distance. Therefore, no Bible believer can yield the point that, according to Christ's intent, Church and state should not be intermingled. The Church exists in the state, for it is still the kingdom of heaven on earth. But the state is not in the Church, for it is certainly on earth but not in the kingdom of heaven, which is the exclusive territory of the Church. The Church is not in the state as Church, but as a group of individuals who remain citizens of the state. Officials of the state can be in the Church, not as authorities with their laws and outward power, but as Christians and brothers, and therefore alike in power and right with all other Church members. World leaders rule over the members of the Church, not as Christians belonging to the Church, but only as subjects of the state. Therefore, the state does not rule over the Church itself or over the conscience, faith, and worship of the Christians, but only over their mortal body and their earthly goods. Christ said, "Therefore render to Caesar the things that are Caesar's, and to God the things that are God's" (Matthew 22:21), making a sharp distinction between God's kingdom and earthly kingdoms, and between Church and state.

O Jesus, King of Glory,
Both David's Lord and Son!
Thy realm endures forever,
In heav'n is fixed Thy throne.
Help that in earth's dominions,
Thro'out from pole to pole,
Thy reign may spread salvation
To each benighted soul. Amen.

(TLH 130:1)

Friday

Read John 18:37

CHRIST IS A KING of truth, and therefore only those who obediently follow His voice should be recognized as members of His Church. There are two ways in which we faithfully employ our precious religious freedom: first, by preserving the truth of Christ, and second, by presenting a life that conforms to this truth in obedience to Christ.

When the worldly regents of state churches are not sincerely devoted to the truth, when they are even enemies of that truth, purity and unity of doctrine are the first things to die. In these churches, neither faithful teachers nor faithful hearers can prevent false teachers and false doctrines from sneaking in. But how does a person in the free church excuse himself when the King of truth alone does not carry the scepter? This incomprehensible responsibility lies completely with Him. Every pulpit in the free church from which false doctrine sounds, every schoolhouse in the free church in which children are given the poison of vain teachings of man instead of the pure milk of the Gospel, every church book and newspaper that does not present the unmingled truth and earnestly fight against all errors—all are loud accusers of the free church as a whole as are each of its preachers, teachers, and members. Woe to the free church that does not want to risk everything so it remains a church that is pure in doctrine. The Lord's word of judgment to the free church at Laodicea applies: "Would that you were either cold or hot! So, because you are lukewarm, and neither hot nor cold, I will spit you out of my mouth" (Revelation 3:15–16).

The same thing applies to life. Corruption flows like an endless mountain river from the state church, in which all who belong to the state are also numbered among the members of the church, where they are held fast with force. But how can a free church excuse itself when the discipline of life degenerates in it? The Word of the Lord is clear: "If your brother sins against you, go and tell him his fault. . . . If he refuses to listen to them, tell it to the church. And if he refuses to listen even to the church, let him be to you as a Gentile and a tax collector. . . . Do not give dogs what is holy, and do not throw your pearls before pigs" (Matthew 18:15–17; 7:6). Furthermore, how will a free church excuse itself when it does not regard the words of Saint Paul: "Your boasting is not good. . . . Cleanse out the old leaven. . . . Purge the evil person from among you. . . . If anyone does not obey what we say in this letter, take note of that person, and have nothing to do with him, that he may be ashamed" (1 Corinthians 5:6–7, 13; 2 Thessalonians 3:14)?

Woe to the free church in which the unorderly, deceitful, and deceptive ways of the children of the world are unchastised and unhindered, perhaps only pointed out in a sermon with the enthusiasm of an Eli. Woe to the free church in which the allies and associates of the world, which has no conscience, are willingly received. Woe to the free church in which the manifest, wanton transgressors of the commandments of God, the servants of vice, and those who openly do not listen to the voice of Christ are tolerated without censure. There the blessing of church freedom becomes a church curse. Such a free church is not a holy city on a high mountain, which shines into the godless, dark world, but a high pillar of shame, for whose sake the name of Christ and His pure Gospel is blasphemed among the heathen. The terrible Word of the Lord applies to such a free church, "What right have you to recite My statutes or take My covenant on your lips? For you hate discipline, and you cast My words behind you?" (Psalm 50:16–17).

Now then, let us not look down, proudly and self-righteously, upon the corrupt state churches, making our free apostolic condition a pillow of security, idleness, and self-presumption. Rather, with a holy zeal of fire, let us strive that the more complete our freedom is, the more we will faithfully employ it for the preservation of pure doctrine and for its presentation in a true Christian life.

And bid Thy Word within me
Shine as the fairest star;
Keep sin and all false doctrine
Forever from me far.
Help me confess Thee truly
And with Thy Christendom
Here own Thee King and Savior
And in the world to come. Amen.

(TLH 130:6)

Saturday

Read Ephesians 4:1–6

WITH THESE WORDS, Saint Paul does not exhort us merely to an outward unity, but to "the unity of *the Spirit*" (Ephesians 4:3). The true unity of the Christian Church is internal and unseen, a unity of heart, mind, soul, and spirit. The apostle defines this as "*one* body and *one* Spirit—just as you were called to the one hope that belongs to your call" (Ephesians 4:4). True unity lies, not in being outwardly joined together like dead stones into a lifeless house, but in being living members of a living body through which the one Spirit, the Holy Spirit, flows. Although their earthly callings and conditions differ, Christians who live in unity stand in the same call concerning heaven, for which they all hope, because it belongs to them all without distinction.

Today, of course, the foundation upon which church unity is generally built calls for letting each member believe what he regards as right, tolerating people of various faiths in the church, and covering the differences with the robe of love. People do not fight against false doctrine, and they even remain silent to the manifest falsifications of the Word of God. Attempting to prove that their practice is correct, they cite the words of our text: "Eager to maintain the unity of the Spirit in *the bond of peace*" (Ephesians 4:3). The bond of peace, they say, is nothing other than love. True unity, they insist, rests upon love.

But this is a great error. The apostle urges us to endeavor, not to bring about or to create, but to keep, that is, to preserve and to protect "the unity in the Spirit." The bond of peace and love, then, is not the basis on which true unity resides, but its precondition. It must exist before unity can be achieved. When unity already exists, it is preserved and nourished by the bond of peace and love. Our text tells us that true unity really rests alone upon "*one* Lord, *one* faith, *one* baptism; *one* God and Father of all, who is over all and through all and in all" (Ephesians 4:5–6). Truly unified Christians confess one Lord, that is, Jesus Christ. They carry one faith in their hearts, they are baptized with one Baptism, and they are children of one God and Father. Where this foundation is laid, unity rests upon a true foundation. Where, on the contrary, this foundation is lacking—where one confesses this and another confesses that, where one believes this and another believes that, where one regards Baptism as an empty ceremony and another regards it as a means of grace, the washing of regeneration—all outward unity is false. Where one faith and one confession do not take place, outward unity is really a mere facade of unity, an empty comedy, nothing but lies and deception.

If we wish to preserve true unity, the right instrument for this is "the bond of peace" (Ephesians 4:3). What Paul means by this is revealed in the preceding text, where he exhorts humility, meekness, patience, and love. When God has given the unity of the Spirit on the foundation of a unity of faith and confession, one person cannot judge and exalt himself above another. Instead, he must be ready to overlook much, to allow for all kinds of weaknesses and defects in another, and to give ground to him. In this—and in no other way—will the precious jewel of true unity be preserved and protected.

O Comforter of priceless worth,
Send peace and unity on earth.
Support us in our final strife
And lead us out of death to life. Amen.

(*TLH* 261:3)

Sunday

Read Matthew 22:34–40

THE FIRST AND GREATEST commandment in the Law is "You shall love the Lord your God with all your heart and with all your soul and with all your mind" (Matthew 22:37). Where this love is lacking, a person transgresses all commandments, no matter what else he does or doesn't do. But of what person can it be said that he loves God with his whole heart, whole soul, and whole mind? Only the one who loves God with his whole heart, his whole soul, and his whole mind does everything that pleases God and is displeased by everything that displeases God. He loves everything good because God loves it, and he hates everything evil because God hates it. When he loves a gift or a creature, he loves it only for God's sake. He has his greatest joy in God, and he therefore always desires fellowship with God. He finds joy in nothing without God, and even in misfortune he is content and joyful with God. When, for God's sake or according to God's counsel, he loses or suffers something, he regards it, not as his loss but as profit, not as sorrow but as joy. Not only is his love for God all-encompassing, but it is also ceaseless. In everything he thinks, speaks, and does, he is filled and ruled by the love of God.

The Law also demands that we love our neighbor as ourselves. But of what person can this be said? Every person loves himself, not ostensibly but rightly, not coldly or lukewarmly but fervently, not only occasionally but constantly, not only when he is godly but also when he is godless. He never seeks his own loss but always his advantage, even in the greatest trouble and danger. Only the person who regards others in the same way he regards himself, loving them sincerely, fervently, and constantly, can be said to have fulfilled the Law. He does not seek his own good, but that of others. His entire life is devoted to serving his neighbor, and he is ready not only to suffer loss on his behalf, but even, if need be, to forfeit his own life for him.

But where are the people who love God and their neighbor in this manner? The flame of true love for God and neighbor, even for the enemy, has been lit in the hearts of all true Christians, and where this heavenly fire does not burn, a person's so-called Christianity is nothing but self-deception. Even the holiest of Christians, were they to examine themselves according to the law of love, would bend their knees, with David, throw themselves onto the ground, and sigh, "Enter not into judgment with Your servant, for no one living is righteous before You" (Psalm 143:2).

If God should judge a person according to the Law, He must judge him according to the love he possesses, for love alone fulfills the Law. Were there no other divine doctrine but that of the Law, all people since the Fall would have to be eternally condemned and lost. And for this reason, it is foolish, even insane, to seek salvation in the Law.

Before Thee, God, who knowest all,
With grief and shame I prostrate fall.
I see my sins against Thee, Lord,
The sins of thought, of deed, and word.
They press me sore; I cry to Thee:
O God, be merciful to me! Amen.

† *(TLH 318:1)*

Monday

Read Matthew 22:41–46

HAVING ANSWERED THE QUESTION the Pharisees put before Him, Christ asked them: "What do you think about the Christ? Whose Son is He?" (Matthew 22:42). He wanted to convince the blind Pharisees that salvation, which they vainly sought in the Law, is found only in the Gospel of Christ.

The Pharisees deceived themselves by an entirely false notion about the Christ who had been promised them by the prophets. They thought He would be a mere man, establish only a glorious earthly empire, and permit the Jewish people to rule over all nations. Christ showed the Pharisees, who believed the promised Messiah would be David's Son, that He could not be merely a man, but only God's eternal Son, for David had called Him "Lord" even before He was born. From this, the Pharisees should have concluded that Christ's kingdom couldn't be a human, earthly, and temporal one. Instead, it must be a divine, heavenly, and eternal kingdom in which salvation and blessedness are to be found.

And so they are. As our love for God and our neighbor is the summary of the Law, so is Christ's love for us the sum of the Gospel. Therefore, a person will have to cast his eyes downward in shame at the question "Have you kept the Law?" But he can, joyfully and with his whole heart, answer the questions "What do you think about the Christ? Whose Son is He?" He can reply: "He is the Lord and therefore also my Lord. He has redeemed me, a lost and condemned creature, purchased and won me from all sins, from death, and from the power of the devil. He did this, not with gold or silver, but with His holy, precious blood and with His innocent suffering and death, in order that I might be His own, live under Him in His kingdom, and serve Him in everlasting righteousness, innocence, and blessedness. Even as He rose from the dead, He lives and reigns for all eternity."

Nothing can tear salvation from the person who, from his heart, can call Christ his Lord, although he has not fulfilled—and cannot fulfill—the Law. Despite great debts and many enemies, a poor servant need not be afraid if he has a loving, good, and rich lord who will pay for him and protect him. In like manner, no person must be fearful on account of his sins when he has received Christ, in faith, as his Lord. For Christ already paid all his debts of sin, and overcame the enemies of his soul. Let us not, then, be so foolish as to seek our salvation in the Law. Instead, let us recognize that we are already condemned by the Law, for we have not loved God above all things and have not loved our neighbors as ourselves (and indeed, we are unable to do so). Therefore, let us flee from the Law as from blazing Sodom, and seek our refuge in the quiet Zoar of the Gospel of Christ. Christ Himself called the hardened Pharisees to His Gospel, and He continues to call us there today. There we find what our souls, heavily laden with sins, seek: forgiveness, righteousness, peace, and joy in the Holy Ghost. There we are given, out of grace, what the Law demands from us with threats.

The most glorious thing about all of this is that whoever seeks from his heart salvation in the Gospel receives another heart that begins to glow in the love of God and neighbor. The one who has been forgiven much also loves much, and by this, he receives the first fruits of the harvest of eternal life. And when he dies, all residuals of sin also die. He awakens in heaven, perfect according to God's image. Then he beholds God face-to-face, and the eternal, triune sun of God illuminates his whole being, making all darkness of sin eternally disappear.

May Jesus Christ, God's and David's Son, praised eternally, help us all.

Lord, Thee I seek.
I merit naught;
Yet pity and restore me.
Just God, be not
Thy wrath my lot;
Thy Son hath suffered for me. Amen.

(*TLH* 317:3)

Tuesday

Read Hebrews 13:9

ONLY A PERSON who has a believing heart can have a heart established in doctrine. But, as today's text informs us, it is possible for a person to have a believing heart and still lack a heart established in doctrine. Daily experience also teaches us this. Many Christians believe with their whole heart that the writings of the apostles and prophets are the Word of the living God and that Jesus Christ is their Redeemer and Savior; but they are nevertheless carried about "by diverse and strange teachings" like a weak ship in the raging wind of a storm (Hebrews 13:9). They have willingly received the truth that was preached to them, but they see only a few people who confess that truth or many who fall away or many highly regarded people who embrace error. They are thus tormented by worry that their doctrine may not be right and, perhaps, the strange doctrine is the truth after all.

Every sect that comes on the scene, especially one with the appearance of great holiness, immediately throws such Christians into uncertainty. Although they see that God's Word does not refute their doctrine and that God's Word cannot prove the strange new doctrine, the manifold contradictions they experience make such a strong impression that they float about insecurely on the clouds of constant doubt. Why? They are lacking that precious thing of which our text speaks: an established heart. And what is the result? Such dear Christians will never be truly happy in their faith. Eventually, after an extended period in that erroneous faith, they may flounder and be lost.

The Christian who has an established heart presents a completely different picture. He and few others may confess the truth they recognize from God's Word while many adhere to the strange doctrine, but this does not make him waver. He clings to the word of Christ, "Fear not, little flock, for it is your Father's good pleasure to give you the kingdom" (Luke 12:32). Those who are one faith with him may be only lowly, despised, simple people, whereas those who cling to the false doctrine may be the most highly regarded and learned people, but even this does not make him uncertain. He holds fast to the word of Christ, "I thank You, Father, Lord of heaven and earth, that You have hidden these things from the wise and understanding and revealed them to little children" (Matthew 11:25). Finally, the little flock that confesses the truth may lack the appearance of great holiness and demonstrate few great works. Indeed, it may even reveal a Judas and so cover the truth with disgrace and shame, whereas the great number of its opponents may be surrounded by the appearance of great holiness and shine by great deeds.

But even this does not confuse the one who has an established heart. He looks alone upon the certain, never-changing

Word. This is the precious thing of which our text speaks: an established heart that is not carried about by various and strange doctrines. Blessed, blessed is the person who has attained this treasure! His ship of faith safely, unwaveringly, steers into the harbor of eternal peace, even if the stormy winds of false doctrine rage violently against it and even if the waves of persecution rise ever so high.

Jesus, who for my salvation
To the Father didst ascend.
Hear my earnest supplication,
Unto me Thy Spirit send;
Let the Comforter for aye
Bide with me, my Strength and Stay,
That in faith I may not waver,
Steadfast in the truth forever. Amen.

(ELHB 248:3)

Wednesday

Read Hebrews 13:9

IF A PERSON is to receive a heart established against all the strange doctrines in the world, one might think that the ability to discern them from truth requires a high degree of education or Christian knowledge. Surely such a precious aptitude must cost a great deal in terms of searching and effort. But this is not what today's reading teaches us. It says, simply, "by grace" (Hebrews 13:9). No person can give himself an established heart. God alone can and will do this. And He does not give this treasure in such a manner that a person has to work for it, that he makes himself worthy of it by good works or perfect sanctification. Instead, the Lord God provides it out of His pure, free, divine grace.

Thus the free, certain way of attaining an established heart is this: An individual must first recognize that, by nature, he is a thoroughly depraved, lost, and condemned sinner for whom there is help only in free grace. Second, he must understand that this free grace is available to all people solely in Jesus Christ. By His death on the cross, He acquired grace, and God the Father publicly and decisively confirmed this by raising Christ from the dead. Finally, he must recognize that the Gospel is the proclamation of this grace obtained for all and offered by God, that Baptism is God's addition of the Christian's name to the list of the pardoned, that the body and blood of Christ's atonement in the Holy Supper are the divine seal and pledge of his pardon, that the absolution is its presentation to him again, and that the Bible is God's letter of pardon for all of redeemed mankind, written by His Spirit with His own blood.

This knowledge, this grace, supplies the precious established heart. No other knowledge, however great, can help. Many seek to become certain of their doctrine by pursuing learning along various avenues yet they never come to a knowledge of the truth, or, if they ever attain it, they easily fall away from it. As long as the Gospel's sun of grace does not shine in a person's heart, his doctrine cannot make him certain of his state of grace. Until he can triumphantly call out, "I have now found the ground which eternally holds my anchor," he can have only a timid and wavering heart in doctrine. But as soon as his doctrine has become for him a rock when he is terrified before God and hell, a rock to which he can cling and be rescued from the shipwreck of his sin, and a rock of righteousness upon which he can find security and peace for his soul, then his heart will be firm and certain.

Let us, then, faithfully preserve this crystal-clear, precious well in the desert sand of this world, and daily drink from it often, so that the thirst of our soul is quenched and our weak heart is refreshed and restored. Then we, too, will also experience what our text says: "For it is good for the heart to be strengthened by grace" (Hebrews 13:9).

I will praise Thy great compassion,
Faithful Father, God of grace,
That with all our fallen race
And in our deep degradation
Thou wast merciful that we
Might bring endless praise to Thee. Amen.

(*TLH* 384:5)

Thursday

Read Ephesians 4:14

EXTENSIVE KNOWLEDGE is not a prerequisite for salvation. Whoever knows that, as a sinner, he is in need of grace and believes in Christ as his Savior, has knowledge enough to be saved. The child who knows no more than that he is sinful and that "Jesus, Thy blood and righteousness / My beauty are, my glorious dress" (*TLH* 371:1), stands in a saving faith as great as that of any other Christian. One who comprehends only the basics of the divine Word can stand in a faith that conquers the world and be God's dearest child, while one who has a great knowledge remains without faith and a child of hell. Knowledge puffs up, but faith alone saves.

We would be greatly mistaken, however, if we concluded from this that a thorough knowledge of the truth is unnecessary. When a person comes to faith, there is always the danger that he could lose both soul and salvation. Next to God's preserving grace, a thorough knowledge of the truth is the only certain means of avoiding the danger of deception by false teachers. Woe to those whose Christianity consists in nothing more than habitually going to church and other religious exercises or in experiencing a sense of excitement and a lasting interest in religion, without securing a clear knowledge of the right doctrine. Our text tells us that these are children who are "tossed to and fro by the waves and carried about by every wind of doctrine, by human cunning, by craftiness in deceitful schemes" (Ephesians 4:14).

Every appearance of wisdom, holiness, love, and works that a sect may offer, combined with the splendor of its temple and the glamour and fervor of its worship, can make an almost irresistible impression upon souls that are lacking a thorough knowledge. When they are seized by a deceiver, they may think that the true light has risen in them when, in fact, the small light that had already been burning in them has now been extinguished. They think they have discovered the truth, but they have only lost what little knowledge of the truth they possessed. They think they have experienced the miracle of true regeneration, but the weak life of faith that was in them has, in an instant, been stolen from their heart. They think they now stand on the firm ground of salvation, while the deceiver has really placed them, unnoticed, on slippery ground. Their supposed new truths are only old errors and their supposed better faith is the empty imagination of their deceived hearts.

Here we see the frightening result of the lack of clear knowledge derived from a good foundation.

For this reason, because our salvation is so dear to us, let us earnestly guard ourselves against the fashionable Christianity of our time, which consists of nothing more than a person's going to church on Sunday and experiencing religious feelings without the underpinning of a clear knowledge of biblical truth and an intense desire to grow in it. When our Christianity is grounded on mere feelings, no error is so foolish and horrible that a cunning deceiver cannot persuade us to subscribe to it. Let us, therefore, strive to become ever more deeply rooted in the pure doctrine of the divine Word as, by God's grace, our church has it, and as it is laid down in our confessional writings and in the writings of Luther and other faithful, enlightened witnesses of the truth. In this way, we will not be "led away by diverse and strange teachings" (Hebrews 13:9), but will instead receive a firm heart and a mind that is skillful enough to distinguish between the good and the evil.

Let me be Thine forever,
Thou faithful God and Lord;
Let me forsake Thee never
Nor wander from Thy Word.
Lord, do not let me waver,
But give me steadfastness,
And for such grace forever
Thy holy name I'll bless. Amen.

(TLH 334:1)

Friday

Read 1 Corinthians 1:4–7

IN THIS PASSAGE, Saint Paul tells us why New Testament Christians have nothing else to wait for but the revelation of Jesus Christ on the Last Day. He says that these Christians "were enriched in Him in all speech and all knowledge" (1 Corinthians 1:5), and they therefore have everything they need for this life and the one to come. Indeed they are, the apostle says, rich "in all [doctrine] and all knowledge."

In the time before Christ, most truths were enveloped in dark foreshadows, but with the appearance of Christ, all these shadows disappeared and the substance of the prophesied things, the body itself, appeared. Now, as Paul remarks elsewhere, the clarity of the Lord is reflected with an uncovered face in all believers. Here is a clear answer for those who are looking for the right faith, for a God-pleasing life, for complete comfort in all trouble, and for a joyful, peaceful death, whereas, in previous times, such concerns were often addressed in figurative speech. New Testament Christians are rich in all doctrine and knowledge.

Paul goes further, saying that "even as the testimony about Christ was confirmed among you—so that you are not lacking in any spiritual *gift*" (1 Corinthians 1:6–7). They have the Gospel and, through faith in it, God's grace, the forgiveness of their sins, a righteousness that avails before God, divine sonship, the peace of God, strength for everything required for a godly life and walk, and the hope of a blessed resurrection and eternal life. God has given them all this in His Word. But even this was not enough for God. To strengthen them in their certainty and to seal all this divinely, He also gave them Baptism, that is, His covenant of grace, the keys of the kingdom of heaven on earth, the holy absolution, as well as the Holy Supper or the communion of the body and blood of Jesus Christ. These are pure, divine pledges of the spiritual, heavenly goods that have already been promised and given in the Word.

There is still more. God also established a holy office for the Christians, the office of reconciliation, and He earnestly commanded the bearers of that office to preach His grace to Christians day and night and to pour all His gifts of grace into their laps. In addition, God has given the Christians prayer, through which they can obtain anything they think is needful. God has also supplied them with the holy angels and all creatures as their servants, for He has ordered that everything—even the world with its temptations and troubles, even the devil with his trials and fiery darts, and even their own sins with their humiliations—must serve them for the best. Finally, God has given the Christians Himself, making them temples of the Holy Ghost and dwellings of His entire most Holy Trining.

Who, then, can declare the extent of the riches accorded New Testament Christians? They are so rich they are utterly unable to survey or to calculate their riches. Only one thing remains in this world for which they hope: to behold what they believe and to perfectly enjoy what they already have. Paul says they are "wait[ing] for the revealing of our Lord Jesus Christ" (1 Corinthians 1:7), that is, the Last Day. They do not seek glory in the world, but deliverance from this world. They do not await a thousand-year kingdom on this old earth, but an eternal kingdom in the new earth and the new heaven, where righteousness dwells.

I praise and thank Thee, Lord, my God,
For Thine abundant blessing
Which heretofore Thou hast bestowed
And I am still possessing.

Inscribe this on my memory:
The Lord hath done great things for me
And graciously hath helped me. Amen.

(TLH 33:2)

Saturday

Read 1 Corinthians 1:8–9

WHILE THE CHRISTIAN waits for the revelation of Jesus Christ, there is one thing that could give him pause and cause him to worry: his doubt about whether he will endure to the end. He sees how so many have started well and believed for a time, only to fall way in the time of trial. He himself has daily experienced how cunning Satan is, how alluring the world is, and how mighty his flesh remains. Therefore, Christians sometimes fear the Last Day instead of looking forward to it with joy.

God has not given any Christian an unconditional guarantee that He will preserve him until the end so he may do exactly as he pleases until then. The Gospel provides no freedom for security, but instead calls us to work out our own salvation with fear and trembling. God has not promised to force anyone to faith by an irresistible grace and to save him despite his own desire to indulge wantonly in sin and unbelief. Yet these warnings apply only to those who in wantonness desire to tempt God's grace and to sin against it. When the justified Christian who fears sin and unbelief is tempted to sin, he thinks, with Paul, "How can we who died to sin still live in it?" (Romans 6:2), and when he painfully feels his unbelief, he sighs, "I believe; help my unbelief!" (Mark 9:24). He can and should, without fear of falling, look forward with joy to the revelation of Jesus Christ on the Last Day. Why? Because the promise of our text applies also to him.

Indeed, this promise applies to every person who believes. The main thing is to seize this promise in faith. According to this precious promise, the salvation of a believing Christian does not depend upon his wavering faithfulness, but upon the unwavering faithfulness of his God. His salvation does not lie in his weak hands (for then it would soon be lost), but in the strong hands of his God. A believing Christian may be ever so weak, but God Himself will be his strength. If, out of weakness, he still stumbles and falls, God's faithfulness will always raise him up again. If, out of weakness, he still goes far astray, God's faithfulness will always fetch and bring him back aright, as He did the erring Thomas. The battle may still be hot, but God's faithfulness will strengthen him for it, just as He strengthened Jacob, and He will fight with him unto victory. The devil and the world may still cunningly seek after his soul, but God's faithfulness will not bring him into disgrace.

God will lead His Christian through the thick darkness to a wonderful path. He will be his light and his faithfulness, as He was with Job, and in the end He will work out everything gloriously. Whatever is necessary for a Christian—that he speak with wisdom before kings and princes, that he exercise a heroic faith, that he receive the gift of performing miracles—God's faithfulness will supply his need, even as He once provided for the holy martyrs. The Christian may often be soiled in the dust of the earth on his way, but God will bring to completion on the day of Jesus Christ the good work that He began in him.

Therefore, a Christian should believe that he is, from eternity, elect to salvation, and because of this, his salvation stands so firmly that the gates of hell will not be able to overpower it. His salvation clings to that golden chain, the members of which the holy apostle connected, and they cannot be broken: "And those whom He predestined He also called, and those whom He called He also justified, and those whom He justified He also glorified" (Romans 8:30).

And Thou, O Holy Spirit,
My Comforter and Guide,
Grant that in Jesus' merit
I always may confide,
Him to the end confessing
Whom I have known by faith.
Give me Thy constant blessing
And grant a Christian death. Amen.

(TLH 334:3)

Sunday

Read Matthew 9:1–8

CHRIST USUALLY PROCLAIMED His grace to sinners in general. For example, when He wanted to comfort the chief tax collector, Zacchaeus, He said only that "the Son of Man came to seek and to save the lost" (Luke 19:10). But on the occasion recounted in today's text, He spoke the forgiveness of sins directly to a highly troubled sinner. Why didn't He speak the general preaching that every penitent can obtain forgiveness?

The reason is not difficult to find. The paralytic was so frightened by his sins that they created more affliction for him than even his severe sickness, and he was thus in need of a special comfort. For another example of this, consider Christ's dealing with a very sinful woman. When, with a contrite heart, she drew near to Jesus, crying bitterly, wetting His feet with her hot tears, and drying them with the hair of her head, Christ did not tell her that grace is for all sinners. Instead, He turned to her and said, "Your sins are forgiven" (Luke 7:48).

Here we see the very special comfort that lies in private absolution. This is not, of course, the only means by which God speaks forgiveness to the sinner, for He also does this by the general preaching of the Gospel, by the giving of Holy Baptism, and by the eating and drinking of the body and blood of His Son in the Holy Supper. Whoever, in faith, holds firmly to these three testimonies of God's grace toward all penitent sinners has the forgiveness of sins and can be joyfully certain of it. But Christians know from experience that even among those who hold God's Word as true, those who do not doubt that God wants to be gracious to all sinners when they believe, there can be doubt in an individual's heart as to whether he, too, is in this happy state. When that happens, he may need to be comforted with more than general promises of grace.

When a true Christian reads that such great sinners as David, Manasseh, and Peter obtained forgiveness, he may say in his heart, "Yes, if I were a David or a Peter and my repentance were as thorough as theirs, then I might well believe that my sins, too, have been forgiven." The Christian may read that God does not desire the death of any sinner, that He wants to have mercy on all, and that He loved the whole world so much that He gave His Son for it, but he may then be inclined to think, "Yes, I know that God wants to save me, but have I not, by my sin, excluded myself from universal grace?" The Christian may hear preachers proclaim the wealth of divine mercy, the kindness of Christ, the faithfulness of the Shepherd toward His lost sheep, and His burning desire for the salvation of even the greatest sinners, but he remains assailed by many doubts and he sighs, "Oh, that I could believe that God has such a burning desire even for *my* salvation!" He may also say to himself, "Oh, that Christ Himself would come and say to me in particular, as He did to that paralytic, 'Be of good cheer; your sins are forgiven you'!"

Is it not, then, a great comfort that Christ said to the apostles, and consequently to His whole Church, "If you forgive the sins of anyone, they are forgiven" (John 20:23), and "Whatever you loose on earth shall be loosed in heaven" (Matthew 16:19)? When a Christian receives and rests upon private absolution, is he not raised above all doubt? Must he not say that when forgiveness is spoken to him in Christ's name, it is just as if Christ Himself had come down from heaven and spoken it to him with His own mouth? What more certain comfort can there be than when it says, "Your sins are forgiven" when Christ has declared that such an utterance shall also be valid in heaven (Matthew 9:2)?

Thou, through Thy servant, says't to me:
"Thy sins are all forgiven thee,
Depart in peace; but sin no more
And e'er my pardoning grace adore."
O Lord, we bless Thy gracious heart,
For Thou Thyself dost heal our smart,
Through Christ our Savior's precious blood,
Which for the sake of sinners flowed. Amen.

(ELHB 425:2,3)

Monday

Read 2 Corinthians 2:10

MANY UPRIGHT LUTHERANS have an aversion to private confession and absolution. This is because, first of all, they regard its institution partly as something new and partly as a return to papal institutions. But this is not true. Private confession was in use long before the rise of the papacy, and until the eighteenth century, it existed in all Lutheran congregations in all countries. Only a few enthusiasts openly rejected it, and only after the Rationalists (that is, the preachers of reason of the new age) had increased in the Lutheran churches was private confession abolished and the general confession introduced in its place.

A second reason why so many inveigh against private confession derives from their belief that the Christian Church does not have the power to forgive sins on earth. These individuals have become just like the Pharisees, who, after hearing of One who forgives sin, thought, "This Man is blaspheming!" (Matthew 9:3), for "Who can forgive sins but God alone?" (Mark 2:7). Either such people do not believe in God's Word or they do not consider that forgiving sins in their own name and in the name of God are two different things. In His own name, of course, only Christ could speak the absolution, for only to Him did God say, "Sit at My right hand" (Psalm 110:1), but in God's and Christ's name, the servants of the Church also loose and bind, for Christ Himself has commanded them to do so. Therefore, Saint Paul offers the words of today's text. What further proof does one need?

A third reason why so many fail to recognize the special comfort that lies in private absolution is that they do not vividly recognize their sins. They may say: "I have no need of this. I can sufficiently comfort myself with the general absolution." However, is it not possible that a true Christian would not at times be so weighed down by his sins that from his heart he would gladly hear the voice, "your sins are forgiven you"? Or are there today Christians with the kind of strong faith that people sought in vain at the time of the Reformation? Indeed, is there anything more lacking today than strong faith? Everyone who wants to be sufficiently comforted should examine himself closely to see if this contentment has arisen from the strength of his faith or if it has resulted from his own disregard for his sins. It is no wonder that thoughtless Christians do not desire private absolution. The wounds of their sins do not burn them, and thus they do not desire the soothing balm.

A fourth reason why so many do not want to use private confession is because it was not generally introduced into the contemporary Church. Instead, private absolution was granted mostly to gross sinners who returned penitent. "Therefore," one may say, "is not every Christian free to use or not to use the human institution of seeking private absolution before every use of the Holy Supper?" This is truly a part of Christian freedom. Therefore, no Christian should and can be compelled. But we might well ask ourselves if that which a person can do is also godly.

A fifth and final reason why so many oppose the use of private absolution is because they suppose that it must be preceded by a detailed confession of their sins. "How," they say, "should I uncover to a man the secrets of my heart, in whose experience or honesty I perhaps have no confidence at all? Must I not fear that a dishonest father confessor would misuse my confession?" There is no demand that the special absolution be preceded by a special confession of sin. Does not Christ absolve the paralytic without such a confession? Was it not enough for Him that the paralytic came to Him as a poor sinner with a believing heart? In the same way, an enumeration of sins is never demanded by a right-believing servant of Christ. Indeed, it is forbidden, as the words of the twenty-fifth article of the Augsburg Confession make clear: "And it is taught about confession, that one should not compel anyone to specify the sins."

All praise, eternal Son, to Thee
For absolution full and free,
In which Thou showest forth Thy grace;
From false indulgence guard our race. Amen.

(ELHB 426:11)

Tuesday

Read Acts 13:38

INSTRUCTION FOR A PIOUS and virtuous life is the central teaching of every religion except Christianity. But in the kingdom established by Christ, the main thing is the forgiveness of sins. In order for all people to obtain this forgiveness, the Son of God became a man and died on the cross. This was the real purpose of His entire great work on earth. After Christ's life, suffering, and death gained for all people the forgiveness of all their sins, all His additional works and institutions have no purpose other than to bring all people to believe in the forgiveness gained for them.

First, Christ had His Gospel written and He instituted the holy office of preaching so the forgiveness of sins could be preached in His name among all people in all ages until the end of time. The sins of anyone who believes this preaching, from his heart, are forgiven, as God's Word proclaims. According to His Gospel, God demands no work or suffering on our part by which we must blot out our own sins or earn remission from them ourselves. God alone wants the honor of our soul's rescue and salvation. Therefore, He wants to give us everything for nothing, without our merit and worthiness, out of pure grace and mercy alone.

But Christ knows how difficult it is for us, when we recognize how great our sins are, to believe firmly that despite our transgressions we are children of God and received into His kingdom of grace. For that reason, Christ added Holy Baptism to His Word, as a seal to a letter. He commanded, "Go therefore and make disciples of all nations, baptizing them in the name of the Father and of the Son and of the Holy Spirit" (Matthew 28:19), and He bound and adorned this command with the promise that "Whoever believes and is baptized will be saved" (Mark 16:16). Baptism is thus the visible pledge that Christ intends for all people to share in the forgiveness He acquired. When a baptized person believes, he can say: "If Christ, one day, wanted to condemn me, He cannot, for He has made a covenant of grace with me, and as its confirmation, He has given me the pledge of Holy Baptism. It is the first payment He has delivered for my salvation. I can already call upon it here, in all trial and doubt, and one day before His throne."

That our faith might always have a new pledge of the forgiveness of sins, Christ also instituted His Holy Supper. This Sacrament provides new support for our faith so it can remain firm against every wavering and weakening. Whoever has gone to Holy Communion can say, "How can I doubt, asking if I have a share in Christ's atonement for the world and if my sins are forgiven me? Christ has given me a share in His body, which He presented to God on the cross as a sacrifice for the sins of the world, and He has given me to drink of the blood that flowed on Golgotha for the universal forgiveness! What more could Christ do to convince me that I belong to those who have been pardoned by Him? Here all doubt must vanish."

Christ has provided for His redeemed, not only according to necessity, so they can believe the forgiveness of their sins. In addition, He has truly overwhelmed them with pledges of His grace. He has done exceedingly more than a human heart could ask for and understand. As Scripture says, He has proved that He is rich in mercy.

Finally, He has given His Church the power to say to every individual sinner in His name, "Take heart, my son; your sins are forgiven" (Matthew 9:2). Christ has promised that such an absolution, bestowed in His name on earth, should also be valid before Him in heaven, and He wants to confirm this on the Last Day.

I know not how to praise
Thy mercy and Thy love;
But deign my soul from earth to raise
And learn from Thee above. Amen.

† *(TLH 322:4)*

Wednesday

Read Matthew 9:8

THE MOST IMPORTANT THING every person needs is forgiveness of his sins. No matter how rich, healthy, and honored he may be, no matter how many goods he possesses, if he is without the forgiveness of his sins, he is like a person who sits at a well-set table while a deadly sword hangs by a hair above his head. He may have everything he desires, but without the forgiveness of his sins, he is like a criminal on the way to the gallows. Unless he knows his sins have been forgiven, he cannot have a certain, joyful conscience. He cannot know if God is his friend; instead, he must fear that God is his enemy. All the happiness the earth can offer is of no value, and all misfortune is without comfort and hope. Being without the forgiveness of sins and knowing he must soon die is the most terrible state in which a person can find himself.

Whoever does not try to conceal his true state must despair. The true God knows all of this only too well. And He responds by opening wide His fatherly heart and offering us forgiveness of sins in varied ways. Many heathens deny that God can and wants to forgive sins, but Scripture informs us otherwise and there can be no doubt. Today, many doubt that the forgiveness of sins is a power given to man, just as the scribes in Jesus' day denied this. When Christ forgave the sins of a paralytic, they said to themselves, "This Man is blaspheming!" (Matthew 9:3). But when Christ proved He could forgive sins by miraculously healing the paralytic with a word, the people were mightily convinced. Today's text says, "When the crowds saw it, they were afraid, and they glorified God, who had given such authority to men" (Matthew 9:8).

We must not think that these words were true only of Christ because He was both man and God. The people of that time, awakened by the Holy Ghost, praised God that such power is given to men. And so it is today. Christ, by His suffering and death, atoned for the sins of all the people, and by His holy life, He acquired for them a righteousness that avails before God. All people are thus perfectly reconciled with God and freed from their debt of sin. God the Father testified to this Himself when He raised Christ, our representative in His judgment, from the dead and set Him free as our guarantee.

If, today, an immensely rich man were to pay the debts of all the citizens of a city, and the creditor were to give all guarantees, wouldn't the proclamation of this forgiveness by those whose debts had been paid be just as valid as if the creditor himself had announced it? Certainly. So is it also with our sins. After Christ paid our debt and God the Father publicly announced this, all people were given the power to proclaim this forgiveness of sins.

Still, the question arises as to how we use this truth. It is not appropriate for a person to fold his hands in his lap and say, "Now then, if the absolution was so richly poured out for us, if the whole world is full of it, we have nothing else to do but to enjoy this and to hope for heaven." That is not so! What would it help a prisoner if he heard that he is pardoned but then refused to leave the prison and exercise his freedom? It would not help him at all. So it is with the forgiveness of sins, which can be spoken to us both by every preacher of the Gospel and by every Christian. If we want to use this forgiveness rightly, we must depart from the prison of our sins. We do this by heartily accepting our absolution, by comforting our self in it. In other words, it is by maintaining a firm and certain faith.

If we hear the preaching of the forgiveness of sins, let us believe that this preaching is God's forgiveness for us. If we hear a Christian comforting us with the forgiveness of sins, let us accept this as God's comfort. If a servant of the Gospel speaks forgiveness to us, let us receive this as a word from God Himself.

When ministers lay on their hands,
Absolved by Christ the sinner stands;
He who by grace the Word believes
The purchase of His blood receives. Amen.

† *(TLH 331:6)*

Thursday

Read Genesis 1:27

EVEN THE UNBELIEVERS of our day gladly accept the teaching that man is created in the image of God. They say this high nobility consists in the things by which man raises himself above the other visible creatures. God's image still shines in the spiritual being of our soul, in the light of our understanding, in the freedom of our will, and in the posture of our body directed toward heaven. However, all of these things are only shadows of our former glory, which had departed, like the footprints that remain in the sand after someone passes by.

According to God's Word, the image of God was a reflection of divine glory. The mind of man was filled with a pure light, in which man, without error, clearly recognized his Creator and His will. The boy Jesus could grow in wisdom without instruction, and that was the image of divine wisdom. God's holiness and righteousness were reflected in the will of man, God's goodness and patience were mirrored in his heart, God's love and mercy were revealed in his inclinations and desires, and God's truth and kindness were displayed in his words and deeds. There was nothing in man that would have struggled against the good; neither in his soul nor in his body was there an evil irritation or a sinful desire. That glorious knowledge in the mind and that pure righteousness in the will were the main parts of the divine image.

Many other glorious things were connected with it as well. God is almighty, one Lord of heaven and earth, and this He portrayed in man when he exercised a perfect dominion over all visible creatures. Then the lion followed his word and beckoning as willingly as the lamb. God is eternal, and this He portrayed in the immortality of man's body and soul. For as long as man carried in himself the image of God, death could not destroy his body, which was a pure temple of the Holy Ghost. God is blessed, with the fullness of joy and love eternally at His right hand. This was reflected in the blessedness of man. In his conscience were rest and peace. No fear and worry troubled the exuberant joy of his heart. Work was a desire, yet no weariness arose in his spirit and members. No pain and no sickness could touch him, and neither heat nor cold could injure him.

The earth, too, was full of the goodness of the Lord. Then it bore no thorns and thistles; instead, it offered only gifts of joy to man. The paradise in which man lived was the copy of God's heavenly dwellings, where He reveals His divine majesty. The world was a courtyard of heaven, in which man reigned as a visible regent of the invisible God, and man's soul was a quiet seat of the divine glory in which pure light, pure love, pure joy, and pure righteousness were found.

Where is this blessed state now? It has disappeared. Man, who at his creation bore the image of God in himself, now carries, from the moment he enters this world, the image of Satan: error, sin, misery, and death. By nature, our mind is darkened, our will is turned away from God, our heart is alienated from the life that is from God, our body is full of impure lusts, our conscience is full of unrest and mistrust of God, and our life is surrounded by distress and death. The proud man now boasts in vain of being created after the image of God, for this image has been lost. By the temptation of Satan, man fell into sin, and sin destroyed the glorious work of God. Oh, how deeply man has fallen! How much he has lost! How poor he is who once was so rich! How miserable is he who once was so glorious!

Yet it is well with us! God Himself took on the form of mortal flesh so we could be renewed to the lost image of God.

God has not changed His eternal will of love to let us have a share in His blessedness. He is ready, for the sake of Christ, His dear Son, to raise again in us, by His Holy Ghost, His destroyed work, beginning here and completing it in heaven.

Create in me a new heart, Lord,
That gladly I obey Thy Word
And naught but what Thou wilt desire;
With such new life my soul inspire. Amen.

(TLH 398:3)

Friday

Read Ephesians 4:22–24

When we are justified, Satan is cast down from the throne of our heart by faith, but this does not kill him. He continues to keep watch day and night, seeking, as Luther says, to gain a little room in which he can sink his claws, gradually penetrating us once again. And he does not cease until he has plunged us again into damnable unbelief, contempt for God, and disobedience. Because of this, our spirit is in need of daily renewal.

In justification, sin is forgiven, but it retains its roots in our heart. Therefore, if a Christian does not daily renew himself, his heart will again become wild, like a tree that is not pruned or a garden in which weeds are not removed. In justification and new birth, we are born as God's children, and so the beginning of the image of God is again restored in us. However, we are first weak children to whom daily nourishment and strengthening must be given so our faith does not dwindle and die. In justification, we are like the one who fell among the murderers: Christ had mercy upon us, and He bound our deep wounds of sin with the balm of His grace-rich Gospel. Now, in daily renewal, we must remain under the care of His Holy Ghost until we completely recover, when He comes again and calls us out of the hospital of this world to Himself by a blessed death.

Justification and new birth are spiritual creations, but the daily renewal of the Christian is the work of spiritual preservation. The created world would have perished long ago without God's preservation and government, and, in like manner, a Christian cannot remain born again without daily renewal. It is a good thing when faith is planted in the heart, but that faith must be watered if we are to finally obtain and enjoy eternal life.

What is daily renewal? It is the continuation of the work of grace that the Holy Ghost began in our soul by justification through faith. It is the hearty diligence that the believing Christian exercises daily in putting off, more and more, the old man, always striving to avoid error and suppressing sin in himself. It is the earnest daily effort to put on the new man, growing in doctrine and spiritual wisdom, so the Christian becomes conformed more and more to the image of Jesus Christ in thoughts, words, and deeds. In this daily renewal of the Christian, he must constantly war against his weakness and the great corruption in himself in order that they do not rule in him. Faithless people and those with hypocritical hearts may claim that they daily strive to become better and more godly, but they still let sin rule over them. When the true Christian awakens in the morning, his first care, which he takes to God in prayer, is, "Oh, may I be completely faithful today!" This care accompanies him in his work and, indeed, in all public and private settings. And finally, when evening comes, when he looks back over the day gone by, he confesses to God, with a broken heart, all his lapses. He sighs and prays for grace and forgiveness through Christ until, having been comforted, he can give himself up to rest.

Many hypocrites comfort themselves by recalling their former vivid experiences of divine grace, although they now practice godliness with a dead heart. With true Christians, Jesus Christ, the Sun of righteousness, who has risen in their heart, never completely sets again. Instead, He shines in their souls daily with His heavenly, illuminating, and warming rays. True Christians daily experience their own sin, God's kindness, and the power of His grace. Each day, they repent anew, believe anew, love anew, fight anew, and overcome anew. Whoever wants to be a Christian must be able to tell, not only of his former conversion, but also of how the work of God's grace continues daily in his heart.

Destroy in me the lust of sin,
From all impureness make me clean.
Oh, grant me pow'r and strength, my God,
To strive against my flesh and blood! Amen.

(TLH 398:2)

Saturday

Read Ephesians 4:25–28

SAINT PAUL BEGINS this passage by instructing us, "Therefore, having put away falsehood, let each one of you speak the truth with his neighbor, for we are members one of another"

(Ephesians 4:25). He places this first to show us that the first thing that must be seen in a renewed Christian is a love for truth and an aversion to everything false and hypocritical. Satan is the father of lies, and whoever takes refuge in lying continues to live under his dominion in the kingdom of darkness and divine displeasure. God is eternal truth and faithfulness. He destroys the liars and is outraged by the false ones. Therefore, whoever knowingly lies is no child of the faithful and true God. Jesus Christ testified before Pilate that He is the King of truth, and thus, anyone who does not love the truth above all else is no subject in His kingdom. The Holy Ghost leads into all truth, and whoever fails to walk by His guidance is motivated instead by the lies of his own heart.

Paul says we must speak the truth because "we are members one of another." Whoever wants to be a Christian must at all times speak as his heart and conscience give him witness. A person must be able to rely more surely upon the word of a Christian than upon a thousand oaths of one who does not fear God. His yes must mean yes; his no must mean no. A Christian must not be friendly and polite to a person to his face and hostile toward him behind his back. A Christian must not perform loving deeds with a heart full of bitterness and hate.

Paul continues in our text, "Be angry and do not sin; do not let the sun go down on your anger, and give no opportunity to the devil" (Ephesians 4:26–27). With these words, he reminds Christians that they will find enough cause and irritation for anger, hatred, and irreconcilability. He also indicates that even true Christians, on account of the weakness of the flesh, often feel the sinful movements of wrath. Thus, the one who wants to remain a Christian must retain God's forgiveness, and he does this, in part, by not holding wrath.

We must not deceive ourselves here. Many do not appear to be angry with their neighbors and their words and deeds directed toward them seem to be gracious, but they may retain anger in their heart. Therefore, if Christians are provoked to anger, they must pray to God that He would calm their heart so they would not repay evil with evil but bless those who curse them. However, if, by deception of their flesh, they have already been overcome by wrath, they must hurry to free themselves of it. If they intend to find rest, they must remember the words of the apostle: "Do not let the sun go down on your anger."

Finally, Paul tells us, "Let the thief no longer steal, but rather let him labor, doing honest work with his own hands, so that he may have something to share with anyone in need" (Ephesians 4:28). This verse tells us that anyone who pilfers another's property is obviously no Christian and has no share in the kingdom of God, that his theft continues as long as he keeps another's property as his own, that anyone who declines to work is not faithful in his earthly calling (and is a thief in God's sight, eating the bread of another), that those who do not acquire by the honest work of their hands (but instead by cunning and risky speculation) wantonly transgress the Seventh Commandment and are under God's curse, and that those who gather money for themselves while forgetting the needs of the poor have no inheritance in the kingdom of God.

On Christ, by faith, I fain would live,
From Him my life, my all, receive,
To Him devote my fleeting hours,
Serve Him alone with all my pow'rs. Amen.

† *(TLH 608:2)*

Sunday

Read Matthew 22:1–13

IN TODAY'S READING, Christ Himself gives us a brief but complete picture of a sham Christian. The sham Christian accepted the invitation to the heavenly wedding. He was a baptized Christian and boasted of his Baptism. He listened to the Word of God and confessed that he believed it and that he regarded Christ as the Son of God, who had come to establish a kingdom of heaven on earth. The sham Christian entered the wedding hall; that is, he adhered to the right church, confessed it, accepted its pure doctrine, and even defended it with great zeal. He mingled with the other festively adorned guests; that is, he no longer kept himself with the world, but had friendship and fellowship with true, believing Christians. He gladly spoke with them about spiritual subjects, visited them, and invited them to himself. He sat at the table with the other guests and ate and drank with them; that is, he used the means of grace like the true Christians. He ate the bread of life; that is, he diligently heard and studied God's Word, and he appeared at the table of the Lord. Finally, he acted like the other wedding guests; that is, he lived outwardly as pious Christians are accustomed to living. He could not be reproached for any obvious sins, he lived honorably, his speech was Christian and betrayed no haughtiness, his deeds were laudable and showed modesty, he spoke out against wrong, he was generous and accepted the common good, he gave each one his own and was no slack debtor, he was industrious in his work, he showed himself to be forgiving toward his offenders, and he allowed himself to be rebuked when he was in error.

What, then, is the outward form of a sham Christian? It is

the form of an upright, pious Christian. So what is it that all sham Christians lack? Despite their honorable life, their good works, their pious exercises, and their active zeal, why are they still not true Christians? Christ says they lack the "wedding garment" (Matthew 22:12). The sham Christian, despite his glorious outward appearance, does not wear the Christian faith in his heart. By this faith, true Christians put on Christ and His righteousness as a garment. The sham Christian appears to lead a Christian life, but before God's all-seeing eyes, his life has a form that cannot please Him, for Scripture says that "without faith it is impossible to please Him" (Hebrews 11:6). The sham Christian is rich in so-called good works, but because these works do not flow from the fountain of a heart purified through faith, they are, before God, nothing better than sins, for Scripture says that "whatever does not proceed from faith is sin" (Romans 14:23).

What will be the fate of the sham Christian in the world to come? There, his hands and feet will be bound. The time of grace will be cut off for him. He must go out from heaven, where God and the Lamb shine as the sun. He must be cast out into the eternal darkness, where no light of comfort rises upon him and where the praise of God will no longer be heard from his hypocritical lips; instead, the "weeping and gnashing of teeth" (Matthew 22:13), intolerable glowing heat and intolerable terrible cold will torment him. No true Christian, who here called him his brother, will then be around him; his fellowship will be with the damned and the spirits of hell. At that time, there will be no hope of a future redemption for the sham Christian; he will have to endure his torment for all eternity.

Oh, let us, then, examine ourselves before the Lord comes to inspect us. Let us not be content with the mere appearance of Christianity, but present ourselves to the Lord as we are. Let us, as poor sinners, daily fall at His feet, seek salvation with earnestness, follow Christ from our hearts, and serve Him. Thus He will one day also recognize us as His own.

Jesus, Thy blood and righteousness
My beauty are, my glorious dress;
Midst flaming worlds, in these arrayed,
With joy shall I lift up my head. Amen.

† *(TLH 371:1)*

Monday

Read Matthew 22:14

IT IS FRIGHTENING beyond all measure to hear that many—perhaps most—of those who called themselves Christians will be eternally lost. These people were once baptized, shared in the Christian fellowship, diligently heard and read God's Word, prayed and sang, were regarded by Christians as dear brethren, and partook of the Holy Supper. How, we may wonder, can this be? Isn't it enough that God eternally condemns all who obviously despise His Word and His grace? Must He also damn those who, at His invitation, appeared at the wedding of His Son?

Can we accuse God because He permits the loss of those who appeared at the wedding of His grace but who did not wear the wedding garment of true faith or sanctification? Instead, they appeared in the filthy garment of their own righteousness. Can we accuse God when He lets go those who confessed with their mouth that they were poor, lost sinners and that they believed in Christ as their Savior, but who in their heart did not regard themselves as so evil and therefore never earnestly believed in Christ as their Savior from sin? Instead, they relied upon this and that good work of theirs and thus did not give God the credit that He alone saves them. Can we accuse God when He allows to become lost those who outwardly presented themselves as Christians but in whose heart the old man remained?

These individuals really loved the world, let sin continually rule over them, and thus remained enemies of God. Whoever outwardly follows the Word of God but inwardly remains as he was is a much more disgraceful and godless person than the one who does not turn to God at all. Such a sham Christian not only commits the sin of obvious unbelief, but he also adds the sin of hypocrisy. He is no Christian, but he wants to appear as if he were. He is no believer, but he wants to be considered as one. With his mouth, he confesses God's Word as truth, but he still acts as if that Word were a lie. He calls himself an adherent of Jesus Christ, but he disgraces this name by a life dedicated to sin.

What should God do with such sham Christians? In the end, God must separate them from His Church so all the world may see that they, while professing to be Christians, were in fact Christ's most miserable enemies. They presented themselves as if they believed in the sacrifice of reconciliation offered for them, but in their hearts they despised it. Therefore, they appeared before the judgment throne without the Propitiator of eternal righteousness, and their judgment can only be damnation.

Thus we have heard why so many are called but few are chosen. We may have many more questions to ask on this subject, but as Scripture teaches us, it is perhaps better for us to remember what happened to the forward person who once asked the Lord Jesus, "Lord, will those who are saved be few?" (Luke 13:23). Did the Lord, on that occasion, answer all his questions and dispel all his doubts? Not at all! Rather, He said to him,

"Strive to enter through the narrow door. For many, I tell you, will seek to enter and will not be able" (Luke 13:24). Let that also be said to us. We know that many are called but few are chosen. Let us not muse over the how and why of this, but instead work out our salvation with fear and trembling so we may be found among those few who reach the heavenly goal.

God does not reject anyone who does not wantonly reject Him and His grace. Today, in this time of grace, God wants to have mercy even on the greatest of sinners. Therefore, as long as it is called today, let us seek the Lord while He is still to be found. Let us call upon Him because He is still near.

Finish, then, Thy new creation;
Pure and spotless let us be.
Let us see Thy great salvation
Perfectly restored in Thee,
Changed from glory into glory,
Till in heav'n we take our place,
Till we cast our crowns before Thee,
Lost in wonder, love, and praise. Amen.

† *(TLH 351:4)*

Tuesday

Read Psalm 18:36

TIMES OF SEVERE PERSECUTION for the Church (that is, for the communion of Christians) are always times of great blessing. They are like stormy days in which nature appears to be in an uproar and the heavens seem to want to pour death and destruction down upon the earth, but after the storm, the fields smile all the more cheerfully and the hardest rain leaves behind fruitfulness and life. In the same way, heavy persecution often seems to be the beginning of the destruction of the Church, but the Church is all the more firmly grounded and gloriously built by this transitory distress. As the early Church teacher Tertullian expressed it, "We Christians increase the more often people cut us down; the blood of Christians is a seed."

The faith grows in persecution more than at any other time. Faith perseveres in the most severe trials, and through exercise it becomes strong. Christians grow and become heroes in the faith. It is the same with love for the brethren. Like a herd that draws more closely together at the approach of a wolf, In the face of common persecution Christians unite as people who suffer alike. They become more aware of their holy fellowship in faith and hope. They feel more of their holy connection as servants of the one Lord, as wanderers toward one goal, and as fighters for one treasure, and this fans the fire of their brotherly love.

Times of persecution bless Christians by preserving them from security, from love of the world, and from a lust for its goods, joys, and glory. A desire to be out of the sinful world and in their true homeland with Christ is awakened in them. They experience the powerful, divine comfort of the Word of God, and a spirit of confession arises in them. Their prayers become fervent and, like incense thrown upon a fire, ascend as a pleasant odor to God. And we must not think that no one would want to become a Christian in times of great persecution, for it is precisely at such times that many are deeply convinced of the divine power of the Gospel through the examples of Christian courage and steadfastness, and they proceed to side with the Crucified.

The history of Christian persecution in all ages reflects this.

At no time has the Church groaned under a more difficult burden and a more gruesome persecution than during the first three centuries of the Christian era. But it was then that Christians displayed, as they have at no time since then, the strongest faith, the most burning love, the greatest freedom from affection with the world, the deepest hunger for the Word of God, and the highest fervency in prayer and confession. Never has the Christian Church shone more gloriously in its divine beauty than in the midst of that age of war and bloody persecution. The more people tried to exterminate the Church, the more wonderfully and quickly its members increased in number. On many occasions, those who were entrusted to carry out the death sentence on the Christians became sudden converts to the faith. When they saw how confidently the Christians looked death in the eye, how joyfully they scorned all torture, how unshakably they confessed their faith, how completely they displayed no malice toward their murderers (and even prayed for them while they themselves were dying), their executioners experienced a change of heart. Their courage sometimes failed them, and they declined to lay their hands on individuals who seemed to be from another world. Convinced of the heavenly power of Christianity, they asked the Christians to accept them and to teach them their wonderful mysteries of faith. And, having received that instruction, they pronounced themselves ready to live, suffer, and die as Christians.

Flung to the heedless winds
Or on the waters cast,
The martyrs' ashes, watched,
Shall gathered be at last.
And from that scattered dust,
Around us and abroad,
Shall spring a plenteous seed
Of witnesses for God.

The Father hath received
Their latest living breath,
And vain is Satan's boast
Of vict'ry in their death.
Still, still, tho' dead, they speak,
And, trumpet-tongued, proclaim
To many a wak'ning land
The one availing Name. Amen.

✝ *(TLH 259)*

Wednesday

Read Job 14:1–2

ACCORDING TO THE WORD OF GOD, our lifetime is both vain and important. It is vain because it is transitory and uncertain, and all of the goods and glories we have accumulated during our life will perish with us. As soon as we begin to live, we also begin to die. Whatever we do, with every passing moment, we are hastening toward our end.

Like Abraham, who had no heritage in the Promised Land except for a family grave, so man, even if he owns rich and expansive tracts of land, retains nothing in the end except a small plot for the burial of his decomposing body. So what does the person who seeks to become rich do? He exerts himself mightily to seize what is now a shadow and, at death, something that melts away into nothing. What, then, is all the glory in this world? How unstable it is!

Whoever is exalted by men today is often the object of

their deepest contempt tomorrow. Even if someone retains honor until he dies, what help is it to him if he must be ashamed of his own conscience? The person who seeks his own glory rather than God's may receive the esteem of others, but on the inside, he must be ashamed. This temporal glory is nothing but a dream.

In another respect, however, our earthly life is important. When God decided to create us, He also decided to save us eternally. By sin, we have lost all this blessedness and fallen under God's wrath. But God did not immediately award us the punishment our actions merit. In His unfathomable goodness and patience, He was pleased to establish a time of grace for us poor sinners in which we should return and find admission and salvation with Him. This time of grace is our lifetime in this world. God gave us His dear Son, Jesus Christ, to be Savior and Redeemer, and He now permits this to be proclaimed to us through His precious Gospel: *"O men, you have indeed fallen away from Me, and I could certainly have at once eternally rejected you. However, I do not want to do that. As long as I leave you here on this earth, the door of My grace still stands open to you. Whoever in his lifetime will still hear and accept My Gospel, turn to My dear Son, and persevere in faith shall again become My child, whose sins I will completely forgive, and he shall one day inherit the kingdom that was prepared for him from the beginning of the world."*

This is why our lifetime is both vain and important. With our every step, we draw closer to eternity, but our condition in the short term of our life determines our fate in the long term of the hereafter. Our life is the path by which Christ leads us into eternal life or the world and our own flesh and blood lead us into eternal death. How foolish, then, are those who waste their precious time on earth in the pursuit of vain things! Whoever has squandered his time of grace has no hope of buying it back in eternity. Gone is gone! If we have passed our time without Christ, we will have an eternity of sadness. Whoever still stands in this temporal life retains a precious, golden opportunity in which he can purchase eternal goods.

Direct our path in all things
According to Thy mind,
And when this life is over
And all must be resigned,
O grant us then to die
With calm and fearless spirit
And after death inherit
Eternal life on high. Amen.

(ELHB 252:13)

Thursday

Read Ephesians 5:16

IT IS PART of the natural corruption of all people that they do not consider the brevity and uncertainty of their time of grace and, therefore, always delay the concern for their salvation from one day to the next. There are few people who want never to convert, but most of them anticipate doing so tomorrow, or perhaps next year, or after this or that upcoming event in their life has passed.

Undoubtedly, the first reason for this procrastination is the delusion that now is not a good time; they must wait for an opportune moment. Those who are in their happy youth find it difficult to tear themselves away from the world. They think that an appropriate time to convert will arrive when they have attained full maturity. When they finally enter their years of adulthood, however, they discover that the obstacles to repentance have increased rather than diminished. Those who are enduring times of distress, poverty, and want think they do not now have time to seek heaven; they must first attempt to extricate themselves from their present predicament. Once they have attained peace, order, and the necessary means of this life, then they can begin to consider the salvation of their soul. But behold! Hardly has one episode of trouble passed when some new hindrance to their conversion arises. Days become months, and months become years, and still people wait for an opportune time to convert. Most people eventually decide to wait for their last sickness. At that moment, they imagine, their love of earthly and sinful things will magically disappear and nothing will hinder Christ from entering into their heart so He can bring them into His heavenly kingdom.

The operable word in all this delay is "later." The youth regards age as the right time to seek conversion, the poor person desires the time of prosperity, the miserable person awaits the time of joy, the healthy person anticipates a time of sickness, and the sick individual hopes for the time of recovery. Every time except the present seems to be the right time to become a disciple of Christ. But isn't all this a terrible deception of Satan and our own corrupt heart? Can there be a more inopportune time for conversion than old age and sickness? And yet most wait for it!

Whoever knows that, in his heart, he is still not right with God cannot afford to wait even a single day to address this matter. If he wants to wait for an opportune time, it will never arrive. May he recognize this evil deception of his heart. To our flesh and blood, there is no appropriate time for conversion. If it now appears difficult for a person to free himself from the fetters that preclude his conversion, he must not imagine that a better time will present itself. On the contrary, the longer he waits, the more deeply sin will take root in him, the more firmly the enticements of earthly goods will clasp him, and the more hardened his heart will become. Waiting for an opportune moment is a snare that has already dragged millions down into corruption.

For this reason, as dear as the salvation of our soul is to us, let us listen to the words of Saint Paul: "Making the best use of the time" (Ephesians 5:16). When we hear God's voice in our heart, when His Word proves its power in us, when we learn to recognize from that Word that all is not right with us, when it awakens our conscience so we feel our sins, and when, by the working of the Holy Spirit, we experience a longing for grace, redemption, and salvation, we must redeem the time. We must say to ourselves: "Today, today, when I hear God's voice, I must not harden my heart. I must not wait for an opportune time, for the opportune time has come! I must immediately seize it! I must cast myself down before God in my misery, confess my sins to Him, and grasp the grace Christ offers me in the Gospel." Once we have gone that far, with that spark of faith, we must remain faithful. As we continue to study and employ the Word and to seek God in prayer, we will see our weak faith becoming stronger, so nothing will be able to again tear us out of the hands of our God of mercy.

My end to ponder teach me ever
And, ere the hour of death appears,
To cast my soul on Christ, my Savior,
Nor spare repentant sighs and tears.
My God, for Jesus' sake I pray
Thy peace may bless my dying day. Amen.

† *(TLH 598:3)*

Friday

Read Ephesians 5:15–16

WITH THE WORDS in today's reading, Saint Paul warns all Christians that, in this life, they should never count on good, peaceful, and comfortable days, either for themselves or for their faith. Instead, they should expect to experience evil, dangerous, and woeful days. Where Christ is, there is also the cross. Therefore, as soon as a person has turned to Christ, he cannot think everything will go well with him as a child of God's grace. Rather, he must expect that the cross will now be his inseparable companion until his death.

As soon as a person sides with the Lord Jesus Christ, he breaks his peace with the world and Satan, and they arm themselves to conquer and reclaim the soul that has escaped from them. As soon as a person overcomes his evil heart through Christ's grace, he enters a battle with evil days. From God's perspective, time is a period of grace, but from mankind's point of view, it is evil. "The days are evil" (Ephesians 5:16), Paul tells the first-century Ephesians, and his words are applicable for all times.

Why is time so evil for Christians? Those who have found grace in time must battle, for the rest of their life, three mighty enemies that relentlessly seek to kill their treasure. They still have within themselves an evil heart that always wants to choose the wrong path. They continue to inhabit the world, which seeks to bring them to apostasy, either through the allurement of its goods and honors or through threats, ridicule, and persecution. Finally, they are still surrounded by Satan and his invisible helpers, who tempt them with evil thoughts, seek to make their soul weak by all kinds of misfortune, and confront them with false teachers and sects in order to wrest from them their soul and salvation. That is why Saint Paul says in our text, "Making the best use of time, because the days are evil" (Ephesians 5:16).

Above all, Christians should not be vexed in this evil time. They must not lose confidence in the truth of the divine Word when they encounter the travails of this world. They should not lose heart with all the hindrances to their faith. They must recognize that God, in His wisdom, does not immediately raise them to heaven. Instead, He wants to test their faith in the evil time, try their love for the truth and their steadfastness, strengthen their hope, and awaken their zeal. He desires to purify them, through their troubles, of all errors, wrong beliefs, and sin, just as impure gold is purified in the fire. The Christian redeems the time when he holds more firmly to the truth while others fall away from it, when he more joyfully confesses Christ as others deny Him, when his love grows warmer while that of others grows colder, when he denies the world and its vanity while others surrender to it, and when he becomes more zealous for God's honor and for the salvation of his neighbor while others become lukewarm.

Paul gives Christians an important rule that they should never forget, especially in evil times: "Look carefully then how you walk, not as unwise but as wise" (Ephesians 5:15). When they fight for the things of God, they should be led neither by the fear nor by the favor of men. Only those who are directed by Christian prudence and wisdom in everything can redeem the evil time. If they want to please God and bring about blessings, they must inveigh against every ungodly being, but they must do so with prudence and wisdom. In removing the weeds, they must be careful not to pull out the wheat and thereby destroy the work of God with that of man. They must confess the truth, but prudently, so the manner of their confession does not hinder others from accepting that truth. They must chastise their brothers as necessary, but with truth, so that, in attempting to rescue their souls, they do not destroy them. Good Christians must use every means to make improvements, but they must be careful not to become a stumbling block to the weak.

Help me speak what's right and good
And keep silence on occasion;
Help me pray, Lord, as I should,
Help me bear my tribulation;
Help me die and let my spirit
Everlasting life inherit. Amen.

† *(TLH 411:7)*

Saturday

Read Ephesians 5:18–21

WE SEE HERE how Christians should fill up the time they have been given by God: not with sinful and vain things, but with that which bring glory to their God. Christians should appreciate how valuable their lifetime is. They should not indulge in the time-killing amusements of this world; their time is too valuable for them to while it away with jesting and foolishness.

Christians should not sit where the mockers sit, where one slays his consciousness with drink and another removes from his tongue the bands of propriety and the fear of God. If Christians waste their time in places where people gather to present their idolatrous sacrifices to the flesh, how will they one day answer to God for it? When a certain heathen emperor could not recall in the evening having done a kindness during the day, he cried out, "Again I have lost a day!" How much more should Christians value their time as a pure and precious good, making the most of it, knowing that one day they will be asked to give account. Every hour is a time for sowing so they may find a rich harvest in eternity.

Oh, may our merciful God let this truth become alive in our hearts. For where are the Christians who redeem their precious time as they should, according to God's will? What kind of fruit can we expect to find in eternity, based on the way we spent so many hours of mortal life? When we assemble with others, do we speak about the one thing that is important or do we focus on the things of this world? Why are we silent about what the Lord has done for us? Why do we complain about how poorly we are doing or about how little money we make? Why do we not speak to one another, as it says in our text, "in psalms and hymns and spiritual songs" (Ephesians 5:19)?

Saint Paul gives us the antidote to all of this when he says, "Be filled with the Spirit" (Ephesians 5:18). The life of the Spirit has been extinguished in many of us, while in others it has at least been mightily suppressed. The mouth overflows with that which fills the heart. Since we have little time, we must not lose our focus on the salvation of our souls. We use so many hours for sleeping, for eating and drinking, and for friendly visits. Shouldn't we be able to find time for prayer, for praising God, and for examining His Word, which alone saves us? Consider the amount of time the children of the world expend in the service of their idols, the desires of their eyes, and the life of arrogance. Should the children of the Most High devote any less time to the service of their Father in heaven, who is rich in grace? The first Christians lived in a completely oppressive age, but we read of them that they were daily in one accord with prayers and petitions. For this reason, let us redeem the time! Let us do good and not become tired! Thus we, too, will one day harvest without ceasing.

May Jesus Christ help us all. May He give us the true faith and, through it, forgiveness of all of our sins. May He grant us His Holy Ghost and, through Him, work a new life in us. Finally, may He give us a blessed death and receive us into the kingdom of His glory.

O Father, draw me to my Savior
That Thy dear Son may draw me unto Thee;
Thy Spirit guide my whole behavior
And rule both sense and reason thus in me
That, Lord, Thy peace from me may ne'er depart,
But wake sweet melodies within my heart. Amen.

(TLH 21:2)

Sunday

Read John 4:47–49

THE FAITH OF THE NOBLEMAN was incomplete and burdened with want and infirmity. He did not simply want to comply with the Word of Christ. He wanted to experience Christ's help, to have something visible for his faith.

Such wants are still found among many Christians. As the nobleman desired Christ to come into his house, so many modern-day Christians believe God is gracious to them only if He immediately answers their prayers—if He blesses them with good health, earthly happiness, a successful business, and the like. If God deals differently with them, however, if He hides Himself from them and appears to fight against them, if many of their prayers do not seem to be answered, if He visits all their undertakings with sickness, poverty, and failure, and lets all kinds of misfortune overtake them, then they do not stand firm. Instead, they lose all confidence in their state of grace. They suppose that God is angry with them and their hope is lost.

As the nobleman did not want to believe firmly without witnessing signs and wonders, so today many Christians want to see first and then believe. They base the certainty of their state of grace on the joyful feeling and sweet sensation they have in their heart from God's kindness. On the other hand, if they no longer taste God's goodness, the staff upon which they lean is shattered and they think they have lost the Savior from their hearts. If God does not perform visible and tangible signs and wonders of grace in their heart so they can clearly see how much God's Word does in them, they do not want to believe.

The nobleman wanted to believe that Jesus could heal his deathly ill son, but not that He could raise him from the dead. In like manner, many Christians have confidence in God's grace and assistance when they can see that things are not going badly, when ways out of difficulties and remedies for distress are readily available. If they have good, dependable friends and financial resources of their own, they are joyfully confident that God will neither leave nor neglect them. But if all prospects vanish, that great confidence is suddenly lost. If they can feel the effects of the new heart God has given them, they can believe their sins have been forgiven. But if they sense the power of sin in themselves, if they see that they are still poor, vile sinners, then they believe their sins have not been forgiven and lie exposed before God's eyes. While they are still healthy, they can say they would gladly leave this world and look forward to the Last Day, but when death comes knocking for them, they surrender their faith before its terrors.

These are the great wants and infirmities from which the faith of even true believers often suffers. This is especially true with beginners in faith. Faith has to do with invisible and future things. It should not demand to see, feel, and experience. It is, as the Epistle to the Hebrews informs us, a certainty that the things hoped for will be realized and an absence of doubt about that which cannot be seen. True faith is a living confidence in God's Word and promise. Faith must rely on that Word even when everything else seen, felt, and experienced appears to contradict it. When a person is feeling lonely, true faith allows him to persist in the belief that God's grace is near. When he is feeling the effects of his sins, he must continue to believe in justification. When he senses God's wrath, he must recall that he is in a state of grace. When he thinks he is in the jaws of death, he must remember eternal life. May God give us grace to develop an ever firmer faith, whatever may befall us in this life.

In suffering be Thy love my peace,
In weakness be Thy love my power;
And when the storms of life shall cease,
O Jesus, in that final hour,
Be Thou my Rod and Staff and Guide
And draw me safely to Thy side! Amen.

† *(TLH 349:7)*

Monday

Read John 4:50–54

THE CONTINUING ACCOUNT of the nobleman shows us the love Christ sought to bring him. Jesus did not condone the infirmities of his faith; rather, He chastised them. But He also did not reject the man's imperfect faith; instead, He sought to purify it. As soon as the man had fallen into a great fear at the Lord's delay, Christ told him, "Go; your son will live" (John 4:50). This word penetrated the nobleman's heart and there it proved its glorious, divine power. For hardly had Jesus spoken it when, as our text says, "The man believed the word that Jesus spoke to him and went on his way" (John 4:50). All of his doubts quickly disappeared.

As firm as the man's faith then was, it awaited an even greater strengthening. At the seventh hour (that is, at one o'clock, according to our division of the hours of the day), the Lord told him his son was alive. When, on the next day, he completed his journey and drew near to Capernaum, his servants met him with the happy news, "Your son lives!" When he inquired at what hour his son had improved, they answered, "Yesterday at the seventh hour the fever left him" (John 4:52). With joy, he recognized that the miracle of the sudden recovery of his son at Capernaum had happened at the moment that Christ, at a great distance, had said to him, "Your son will live." Our text then says, "And he himself believed, and all his household" (John 4:53).

The spark of his faith had become a great fire on his journey. And upon his return, when his faith was confirmed in the most glorious way, that faith was even further intensified, so that he preached to his own and did not cease until he had led all to

Christ. Here we see the way every beginner in Christianity can be freed more and more from the wants and infirmities of his faith. The first and most important thing is that a Christian diligently hear and consider God's Word, especially the Gospel with its glorious promises. He must use it and let it penetrate his heart. Whoever wants to become stronger in faith must boldly grasp the promises God gives to all penitent sinners, comfort himself with them, build upon them, and ground himself upon them as upon an unshakable rock. Furthermore, as the nobleman did not wait until he could see the fulfillment of the Word of Christ, but began to believe as soon as he received Jesus' firm assurance that His word would be fulfilled, so now, when a Christian hears the Gospel, he must not wait even one moment to comply with it, but instead he must give God the glory. He must say: "Indeed, I, a poor sinner, have not earned grace and salvation, but only wrath and punishment. But because the Gospel is the Word of God and Christ, which cannot lie, I do not want my unworthiness to move me to make it a lie. I want to believe it until the hour comes when I will behold what I believed and enjoy that for which I hoped."

The nobleman not only believed the word of Christ, but he also considered how Christ confirmed and fulfilled His word. In like manner, beginners in Christianity and all who are weak in faith must firmly hold to the Word of the Gospel and notice every way Christ confirms His word to them. When a poor sinner begins to cling to the word of Christ, he often feels no change at all for a long time. At first, he has the word of Christ without comfort and without power. But if, in spite of this, he faithfully clings to the Word, he will eventually discover that all light, life, power, and comfort truly lies in Christ's word. He will find that everything the Word promises does indeed happen—that it gives rest to the soul, peace to the conscience, comfort in distress and death, and strength for a victorious battle against the world, sin, and Satan.

The Christian must note these experiences, and in this way, his faith will grow stronger and more confident. Then, like the nobleman, he will be able to tell others what great things the Lord has done in his soul. He will seek to bring others to Christ. And he will continue to grow and persevere in the faith until he reaches the end of his life and the goal of his faith—the salvation of his soul.

Visit, then, this soul of mine,
Pierce the gloom of sin and grief;
Fill me, Radiancy Divine,
Scatter all my unbelief.
More and more Thyself display,
Shining to the perfect day. Amen.

† *(TLH 359:3)*

Tuesday

Read Acts 15:11

THE DOCTRINE that a person is justified and saved alone through faith before God is very offensive to many people. This is because those people create for themselves a false notion of faith and its working. They think an individual should be saved *on account of* his faith. They say: "On account of faith, shouldn't a person be better before God because he believes exactly what is in the Bible? Shouldn't faith be a meritorious work before God, like love, meekness, humility, chastity, truthfulness, and other Christian virtues?" They want to make faith the *cause* of their salvation. But we know from Scripture that no virtue—not even that of faith—can earn heaven.

This belief rests upon an obvious misunderstanding. Nowhere in Holy Scripture is it taught that a person is saved on account of his faith or that faith is a meritorious cause of salvation. Instead, it says that he is saved *through* faith. Salvation is the *end* of faith. No one can earn his way into heaven by any work, virtue, or merit. Christ alone has done the work, He alone merited everything, and He alone prepared the wedding of the eternal blessed life. Therefore, a person can be justified and saved before God by grace alone. If he wants to enjoy this unfathomable benefit, he must seize it and believe it. Faith, then, is nothing but the hand with which a person grasps the salvation acquired by Christ, the vessel in which he gathers up the goods of grace, the key with which he opens the heavenly treasures. Faith can earn salvation for the believer as little as a beggar can earn a gift merely by stretching out his hand.

The Christian doctrine that faith justifies and saves is offensive only to those who are already offended that a person can obtain everything from God without any personal merit, but only by His grace and mercy. Those who perish, then, do so only because they refuse to receive the free gift of salvation. An important proof of the fact that faith does not save as a good and God-pleasing work is that, according to Holy Scripture, the faith of even true believers is never perfect, but always has certain wants and weaknesses. The Christian must not build his salvation upon his faith, but rather upon Christ, who is the reason for his salvation. Whoever thinks he can rely on his faith and earn something with it has not yet come to the true faith. Rather, he remains as self-righteous before God as the manifest unbeliever who wants to be saved through his virtues and good works.

Nay, too closely am I bound
Unto Him by hope forever;
Faith's strong hand the Rock hath found,
Grasped it, and will leave it never;
Even death now cannot part
From its Lord the trusting. Amen.

✝ *(TLH 206:3)*

Wednesday

Read 1 Timothy 6:12

TO EXPECT that a time will come before the Last Day when the Church will have peace and rest from all its enemies is a vain, groundless, and foolish hope. It is true that the holy prophets foretold a time when swords would be made into plowshares and spears into sickles. However, that time arrived long ago. It came when the angels sang, "Glory to God in the highest, and on earth peace" (Luke 2:14), ushering in the time of the New Testament, the Gospel that preaches and brings peace. This is not an earthly peace, but rather a peace that exceeds all human understanding, a spiritual and heavenly peace that stands firm even in the midst of war. It is peace of the heart and conscience with God despite sin, law, death, judgment, and hell.

Nevertheless, the Church of Christ on earth will remain a fighting Church until the end of days. It is God's army waging His war on earth. Christ, its Lord and head, is its commander in chief. To become a member of this army, a Christian must swear the oath of loyalty to the triune God, volunteer to serve among God's warriors, and place himself under the blood-red banner of Jesus Christ, the crucified Lord of glory and the Prince of life. Wherever a Christian finds himself, the entire world is his battlefield, and the entire Church, with all its spiritual and heavenly treasures, is the holy land whose borders he must defend. Each Christian family and congregation is a fortification and every revealed truth, every Bible verse, is an entrenchment he must guarantee with his blood.

In this battle, no one is neutral because this battle is for God's glory, for a person's own salvation, and for the salvation of the whole world. Here, neutrality is treason. Whoever does not join God's army and prepare to fight belongs to the enemy. Everyone, regardless of age, means, and social status, must bear arms. In this spiritual war, there is no peace treaty with the enemy. The Bible says "the one who endures to the end will be saved" (Matthew 10:22), and "Be faithful unto death, and I will give you the crown of life" (Revelation 2:10). On his deathbed, the Christian must be able to say, "I have fought the good fight, I have finished the race, I have kept the faith" (2 Timothy 4:7), that is, he never broke his baptismal oath.

Saint Paul wrote further, "An athlete is not crowned unless he competes according to the rules" (2 Timothy 2:5). Whoever fights but does not fight rightly, that is, whoever lets himself be overcome in the battle, whoever does not win a victory, will one day fail to go from the Church militant to the Church triumphant. He will not take part in the eternal peace and victory festival in the high vault of heaven. He will get nothing when the booty is distributed, and his brow will not be decorated with the imperishable wreath of glory of the conqueror.

Cast afar this world's vain pleasures,
Aye, boldly fight for heav'nly treasures,
And steadfast be in Jesus' might.

He will help, whate'er betide you,
And naught will harm with Christ beside you;
By faith you'll conquer in the fight.
Then shame, thou weary soul!
Look forward to the goal:
There joy waits thee.
The race, then, run;
The combat done,
Thy crown of glory will be won. Amen.

† *(TLH 444:2)*

Thursday

Read Ephesians 6:10

AN ARMY that lacks courage will not be victorious against the enemy, no matter how large its forces, how well armed it is, and how expertly it is directed by its field marshals. This is a truth confirmed by experience throughout the ages. The Lord says through Moses that warriors without courage, who may have a bad conscience that produces a cowardly heart, flee at the sound of a rustling leaf (Leviticus 26:36). Thus 135,000 cowardly Midianites once fled before Gideon's 300 brave warriors, whose battle cry was "For the LORD and for Gideon" (Judges 7:18).

Courage is the first and most important virtue of true people of war. This also applies to Christians in their spiritual battle. In his "army sermon," Saint Paul tells Christians to "be strong in the Lord and in the strength of His might" (Ephesians 6:10). If they want to reach the goal of their faith, that is, the salvation of their soul, then they must struggle. They cannot become cowardly, despondent, or timid. Instead, they must have a strong spirit and be brave. The true Christian will not allow himself to be frightened of anything, to flee as a coward before the enemies of his soul, to forsake faithlessly the army of the Church and the flag of its confession, to surrender to the enemy the fortress of the Word of God that has been entrusted to him, and to become a deserter to the enemy. The Christian wants to follow Christ, the Prince of his salvation and his heavenly Commander in chief, wherever He calls him. He wants to remain with His army, the Church, and with the flag of its confession. He wants to face the determined enemy, to fight bravely, and to defend the fortress of God's Word. He would prefer to die rather than surrender and reject even one little doctrinal concept or one short Bible verse. He must say to himself, "I will fight until I win, even if I must pay for my victory with my blood and life."

"But who can be so strong?" someone may say. "Aren't we all poor, weak creatures? Aren't we all powerless dust?" Yes, and precisely because of this, Paul says our strength resides "in the Lord and in the strength of His might." Paul is saying here that Christians, by nature, have no power to go confidently and joyfully with Christ into battle. But he is not asking them to be strong in themselves; rather, he desires that they completely despair of their own power and bravery and seek their strength in Christ alone. They must rely upon Him completely as their leader. They must have faith that, when they follow Christ, victory is certain. For He is the eternal Wisdom whom nothing outwits and the eternal Might whom nothing can overwhelm. Christians need to believe only that Jesus, their Savior, has wiped away all their sins, and so they can have a joyful conscience. In addition, it is He alone who really fights, and his forces stand secure under His shield. If they remember this, they will never lack for courage and strength.

Millions of Christians have fallen and deserted in the battle because they relied on their own strength. However, all who have become strong in the Lord, building upon Him alone, will hold the field, die blessed as victors, and attain everything for which they had hoped by faith. As the hymn says:

With might of ours can naught be done,
Soon were our loss effected;
But for us fights the Valiant One,
Whom God Himself elected.
Ask ye, Who is this?
Jesus Christ it is,
Of Sabaoth Lord,
And there's none other God;
He holds the field forever. Amen.

(*TLH* 262:2)

Therefore, the Christian can pursue the battle unafraid. Even in the face of death itself, he can retain a quiet courage for he knows his salvation is certain.

Grant steadfastness and courage
That bravely we contend
Against the wiles of Satan;
O Lord, Thy flock defend!
Help us to battle well,
To triumph o'er the devil,
To overcome the evil
And all the powers of hell. Amen.

(*ELHB* 252:12)

Friday

Read Ephesians 6:11–12

THIS PASSAGE TEACHES US, first of all, that it is not "flesh and blood"—men—against whom we as Christians have to fight. God's Word places us against completely different enemies: the "devil" and his angels, the "spiritual forces of evil in the heavenly places." These are God's sworn enemies forever. Cast out of heaven, they are, therefore, also the irreconcilable enemies of all of the children of God. In Eden, they tempted man, who had been created in the image of God, and led him to fall away from God. And ever since God reconciled Himself to fallen mankind and redeemed it, the devil and his angels have been striving, day and night, to deceive men and to drive them away from that reconciliation and redemption.

Since these enemies are invisible, we must always be armed and vigilant. If they were creatures with flesh and blood, we could defend ourselves against them by fleeing into a high fortress. But where can we flee to prevent evil spirits from entering? We know from other passages in the Word of God that these spiritual enemies are numberless. Thousands of them may lie in wait for a single person's soul to destroy it. Our text advises us to "put on the whole armor of God, that you may be able to stand against the schemes of the devil" (Ephesians 6:11). The evil spirits employ exceedingly cunning attacks against us. Satan disguises himself as an angel of light. If he wants to cast us down into error, he presents this error as truth and distorts God's Word in an effort to support his claim. If he wants to cast us down into sin, he presents the sin as a virtue or as something permissible, innocent, and unimportant. If he wants to persuade us to fall away from God, he tries to convince us, as he did Adam, that this is a way for us to draw closer to God and to become more like God.

When we think we are furthest from Satan—for example, when we are praying, reading or hearing God's Word, or when we are in the midst of upright Christians—there Satan is next to us, seeking to remove the seed of the Word from our heart and to annihilate the blessing of the communion. He does not attack us where we are strong, but where we are weak. Wherever he finds an opening in the wall of our heart, there he comes in.

Saint Paul calls the Christian's enemies "principalities" and "powers." Their cunning is thus united with great power. And there is an entire army of these hellish giants. Against them, we humans are powerless dust. If we wanted to fight them under our own power, it would be as if an unarmed child went to war against an entire well-armed army, as if a withered leaf desired to stand against the windstorm, and as if a straw wanted to fight against a fire. Paul also calls our enemies "the cosmic powers over this present darkness" (Ephesians 6:12). The entire world is the ally of Satan, for he governs it and leads it according to his will. All of the unbelievers, the unconverted, and the godless, who still belong to the world, are instruments our invisible enemies use to rob us of our faith, our love, and our hope, intending to lead us into unbelief, false faith, sin, and shame. Their ultimate goal is to cast us down into eternal damnation. Christians still carry something of the old Adam, of flesh and blood and the world, in their heart, and it is there in the midst of the fortress of our heart that our evil enemy has the most dangerous ally of all, which operates just like a secret traitor.

These, then, are the enemies against which Christians have to fight: evil spirits above and below them, the world next to them, and flesh and blood in them. Oh, it is well for the Christian who is strong in the Lord! Otherwise, he is certainly lost.

Friday

Read Ephesians 6:11–12

THIS PASSAGE TEACHES US, first of all, that it is not "flesh and blood"—men—against whom we as Christians have to fight. God's Word places us against completely different enemies: the "devil" and his angels, the "spiritual forces of evil in the heavenly places." These are God's sworn enemies forever. Cast out of heaven, they are, therefore, also the irreconcilable enemies of all of the children of God. In Eden, they tempted man, who had been created in the image of God, and led him to fall away from God. And ever since God reconciled Himself to fallen mankind and redeemed it, the devil and his angels have been striving, day and night, to deceive men and to drive them away from that reconciliation and redemption.

Since these enemies are invisible, we must always be armed and vigilant. If they were creatures with flesh and blood, we could defend ourselves against them by fleeing into a high fortress. But where can we flee to prevent evil spirits from entering? We know from other passages in the Word of God that these spiritual enemies are numberless. Thousands of them may lie in wait for a single person's soul to destroy it. Our text advises us to "put on the whole armor of God, that you may be able to stand against the schemes of the devil" (Ephesians 6:11). The evil spirits employ exceedingly cunning attacks against us. Satan disguises himself as an angel of light. If he wants to cast us down into error, he presents this error as truth and distorts God's Word in an effort to support his claim. If he wants to cast us down into sin, he presents the sin as a virtue or as something permissible, innocent, and unimportant. If he wants to persuade us to fall away from God, he tries to convince us, as he did Adam, that this is a way for us to draw closer to God and to become more like God.

When we think we are furthest from Satan—for example, when we are praying, reading or hearing God's Word, or when we are in the midst of upright Christians—there Satan is next to us, seeking to remove the seed of the Word from our heart and to annihilate the blessing of the communion. He does not attack us where we are strong, but where we are weak. Wherever he finds an opening in the wall of our heart, there he comes in.

Saint Paul calls the Christian's enemies "principalities" and "powers." Their cunning is thus united with great power. And there is an entire army of these hellish giants. Against them, we humans are powerless dust. If we wanted to fight them under our own power, it would be as if an unarmed child went to war against an entire well-armed army, as if a withered leaf desired to stand against the windstorm, and as if a straw wanted to fight against a fire. Paul also calls our enemies "the cosmic powers over this present darkness" (Ephesians 6:12). The entire world is the ally of Satan, for he governs it and leads it according to his will. All of the unbelievers, the unconverted, and the godless, who still belong to the world, are instruments our invisible enemies use to rob us of our faith, our love, and our hope, intending to lead us into unbelief, false faith, sin, and shame. Their ultimate goal is to cast us down into eternal damnation. Christians still carry something of the old Adam, of flesh and blood and the world, in their heart, and it is there in the midst of the fortress of our heart that our evil enemy has the most dangerous ally of all, which operates just like a secret traitor.

These, then, are the enemies against which Christians have to fight: evil spirits above and below them, the world next to them, and flesh and blood in them. Oh, it is well for the Christian who is strong in the Lord! Otherwise, he is certainly lost.

Abide with Thy protection
Among us, Lord, our Strength,
Lest world and Satan fell us
And overcome at length. Amen.

(*TLH* 53:5)

Saturday

Read Ephesians 6:13–17

THE HOLY GHOST, who spoke and wrote through the apostle Paul, knows better than we the great danger our souls are in. Therefore, He identifies the armor we must put on and use to hold the field against our spiritual enemies.

There are six things that constitute the armor of a well-equipped warrior. He has to gird himself with a belt so his long garments do not hinder his movement. He has to guard his chest with a breastplate. He has to put on iron-clasped boots as to cover his feet. He has to protect his body with a shield and his head with a helmet. Finally, he must be provided with a sword, his main weapon of attack. Paul then goes on to explain each of these means of protection.

First, he says, "Stand therefore, having fastened on the belt of truth" (Ephesians 6:14). "Truth" is to be understood here as conducting our lives in uprightness and sincerity. Hypocrites are incapable of fighting the holy battle of Christians because that battle can be waged only by those who have a spirit in which there is no deceit (Psalm 32:2). Our next means of protection, Paul tells us, is "the breastplate of righteousness" (Ephesians 6:14). This "righteousness" is in living a life that is just and inoffensive toward people. Whoever serves unrighteousness cannot fight against the unjust world. Paul identifies the third element in our arsenal as covering our feet "the readiness given by the gospel of peace" (Ephesians 6:15). The Christian walks in peace with everyone as a true confessor of the Gospel of peace. Oh, it is well for the Christian who is triple armed with truth, righteousness, and peace!

Yet each Christian wears these three means of protection only in great weakness. Therefore, the apostle continues: "In all circumstances take up the shield of faith, with which you can extinguish all the flaming darts of the evil one; and take the helmet of salvation, and the sword of the Spirit, which is the Word of God" (Ephesians 6:16–17). We should take great pains to maintain a sincere godliness and piety toward God and man, but this isn't so much a part of our weaponry as it is part of our comfortable dress in battle. Our true weapon of defense against all of the cunning attacks of the wicked one remains faith and salvation by grace in Christ Jesus, which is grasped in faith. Our only offensive weapon is the Word of God, the written word of the holy prophets and apostles. Whoever retains this faith and firmly holds to this Word will fight rightly and stand firm, even if all devils, the entire world, and his own flesh rage against him.

It is well for us that the Holy Ghost gives us such a short, blessed, and certain list of provisions for the battle. If we do not give up the faith in our salvation in Christ and throw away the weapon of the Word, then we will always hold the field.

Arm these Thy soldiers, mighty Lord,
With shield of faith and Spirit's sword.
Forth to the battle may they go
And boldly fight against the Foe. Amen.

† *(TLH 332:1)*

Sunday

Read Matthew 18:23–35

THE MOST WELCOME TEACHING the natural man could hear would be that he can do something for his salvation even after his death. As gladly and as customarily as he flatters himself with the hope that God will one day receive him in grace, no one who has not been born again by the Holy Ghost has the courage to believe this from his heart. But this hope of natural man—that after death there is still time to make up for whatever is missing for salvation—remains so dear to so many people that they comfort themselves with it even when they are also taught that they must atone for their sins, perhaps for centuries, in the terrible pain of a so-called purgatory. They can endure it only if they are assured they will finally be taken up into the place of eternal joy.

Although such people seek to soothe their conscience in this hope, it is nevertheless completely groundless. What reasons do they have for it? Some point to today's text, in which Christ says that the master delivered his servant to the torturers "until he should pay all his debt" (Matthew 18:34). They say, "Don't the words '*until* he should pay' clearly show that he should then be delivered after the time has passed in which he would have paid his debt?" But in Holy Scripture, the word *until* is often used in relation to things that not only last until a determined time but that never cease. For example, God the Father says to His eternal Son, "Sit at my right hand, until I make Your enemies Your footstool" (Psalm 110:1). Who will maintain that, according to this, Christ will no longer sit at the right hand of God when all His enemies have been conquered?

Although our text says that the unfaithful servant should be tortured "until he should pay," it does not say the time will ever come when he can pay his debt in full and therefore be released. To suggest otherwise is to suggest that God's Word contradicts itself. Doesn't the Bible clearly state that Christ alone bore and atoned for the sins of all people? Doesn't it say that man cannot be saved by his works, but alone by grace through faith in Christ?

There are others who, while recognizing that a person cannot atone for his sins following his death, cherish the delusion that, after this life, a person can still come to faith. Thus, even if an individual has died in unbelief, he can still finally be saved by Christ. But today's Gospel most definitely contradicts this notion. When Christ says that after the first grace was scorned and the unfaithful servant was required to pay, He shows us that, in eternity, grace has ended.

This is the teaching, not only in today's reading, but in many places throughout Scripture. The entire Bible is grounded on the teaching that now is the time of grace and that after this life the recompense, either eternal death or eternal life, is man's share.

Today Thy mercy calls us
To wash away our sin.
However great our trespass,
Whatever we have been,
However long from mercy
Our hearts have turned away,
Thy precious blood can cleanse us
And make us white today. Amen.

† *(TLH 279:1)*

Monday

Read Isaiah 55:6

IF THE HOPE OF ONE DAY being able to obtain God's grace truly had a basis, to wait one moment before seeking and accepting this highest of all goods would be the most foolish and godless thing imaginable. Would any person who wanted to be happy in earthly things prefer to remain in his present earthly unhappiness and postpone receiving happiness until tomorrow, or for several years, or until the last possible moment? Certainly no one would.

When it comes to earthly things, anyone who wants to obtain goods follows the principle "The earlier, the better." If he failed to follow this rule, the world would regard him as a fool. How foolish people are in spiritual things, then, when they want to wait until the last possible moment to obtain heavenly goods. They are content to remain under God's wrath while hoping someday to ask for His grace, to remain burdened with sin and a bad conscience while hoping someday to be delivered from them, and to remain on earth as a child of hell while hoping someday to become a child of heaven. Oh, the foolishness! Oh, the blindness! But the poor person is already so used to the misery of sin that he no longer considers it. Sin has become a darling he nurses and cultivates, and he can separate himself from it only with the greatest reluctance. He has become such an awful enemy of God that he wants to wait as long as possible to seek His grace.

But since the time of grace ends forever with a person's death, it is the height of insanity for him to postpone his concern about the salvation of his soul and seeking God's grace. Each person who does not stand with God in grace must hurriedly set out to seek His grace in eternity. We must remember that the unfaithful servant, whom Christ said owed his master the immense sum of ten thousand talents, is man. All of us are guilty before God of countless sins we have committed in thought, word, and deed against each of the holy Ten Commandments. God has reminded us of this every time His Word is preached to us and every time our conscience pricks us with the thought that we are indeed sinners. The verdict was pronounced over us long ago, as it was over the unfaithful servant.

Have you already fallen before your God and King and called upon Him for patience and grace? Have you already honestly confessed to Him your entire debt of sin? Have you already admitted to Him that your entire heart is corrupt and that your whole life is lost? Have you finally accepted, by faith, that God has taken pity on you and, for Christ's sake, He has forgiven you all of your great debt? And do you still fall before God daily, confessing your debt to Him with a broken heart and begging of Him His grace? Or have you imagined that you have had no time to do this before now? Have you, perhaps, regarded other things as more important? Have you first sought to put your temporal accounts in order, to enjoy the world, to earn your fortune, or to serve a certain pet sin awhile longer? Have you, therefore, put off from day to day the earnest seeking of God's grace, remaining uncertain of the status of your heavenly account?

What are you waiting for? Do you not consider the terrible danger your soul is in? Cannot death suddenly and unexpectedly claim you, as it has so many others, while you are yet unrepentant? What would then become of your soul? With your death, your time of grace quickly expires forever. If you were bound by sin on earth, you will be bound by sin in heaven. Your repentance and your hot tears will not move God's heart, for in heaven the day of recompense and righteousness will dawn. Oh, how you will then cry out the woe upon you! Here you could have found grace so easily; you needed only to sigh for it. However, in heaven, you can eternally cry out for grace and still hear the terrible voice, "Pay Me what you owe!"

If nothing else can move you to regard earthly things as of secondary importance and to make God's grace and the salvation of your soul your top priority, consider that only a short time has been allotted to you to settle your heavenly account. If you do not seek and find God's grace during that time, you will remain without it forever.

There still is time! The Master's voice still rings,
And all His heralds plead:
"Oh, hide beneath The covert of His wings
Against the time of need!"
The gracious call is still extended;
The day of grace is not yet ended.
There still is time! There still is time! Amen.

† *(TLH 509:2)*

Tuesday

Read 1 Corinthians 1:18

ISN'T THE CROSS A SYMBOL from which every eye turns away? Isn't the cross that terrible instrument of torture on which only the most vile criminals once suffered the most disgraceful death as the deserved payment for their crimes? Isn't the cross, then, an awful monument that man is a sinner, that there are people who, as a curse to the world, must be separated from the society of man, and who, by their torment, shame, and disgrace, serve as a lesson to others?

Indeed, the cross once had this frightening meaning. But we have only to look at Golgotha to recall that the only begotten Son of God, the Prince of life, and the Lord of glory Himself died upon a cross. Why did He once hang there, between heaven and earth, full of disgrace and pain, shedding His precious, divine blood and loudly crying out to heaven, "My God, My God, why have You forsaken Me?" (Matthew 27:46). The crucifixion, which ended with the triumphant cry, "It is finished" (John 19:30), was the offering of the all-sufficient sacrifice for the atonement of all sinners. The Man on the cross was the Lamb of God, who bears the sins of the world to carry them away from the face of God. The salvation of the whole world once hung by those three nails of the cross on Golgotha. As the fruit from the wood of the forbidden tree from which the first man once ate brought sin, death, and damnation upon the entire human race, so the fruits of the wood of the cross restored righteousness, life, and blessedness to all people.

On account of this, the cross is both holy and blessed! Once nothing but a dry piece of wood, it was changed, like Aaron's staff, into a green branch full of heavenly blossoms and fruit. Once an instrument of torment for the punishment of sinners, it now shines in heavenly splendor for all sinners as a sign of grace. Once the wood of the curse, it has now become, after the Promised Blessing for all people offered Himself up on it, a tree of blessing, an altar of sacrifice for the atonement, and a sweet-smelling aroma to God. Today, the cross is still a terror—but only to hell. It shines upon its ruins as a sign of the victory over sin, death, and Satan. With a crushed head, the serpent of temptation lies at the foot of the cross. It is a picture of eternal comfort upon which the dimming eye of the dying longingly looks, the last anchor of his hope and the only light that shines in the darkness of death.

Following Christ's death, the cross is now the only boat upon which even the greatest sinner can escape from the raging floods of his sins into the harbor of eternal salvation. It is a ladder ascending to heaven, upon which faith climbs confidently, as well as the key of heaven, with which the gates of paradise are opened. Once a sign of shame, the cross is now a sign of eternal honor and glory.

Therefore, Christians should never be ashamed of the cross. Instead, they should carry it secretly in their heart as their most precious treasure and they should carry it on their banner triumphantly throughout the world as a wonderful sign of the redemption of the world and as the dearest symbol of their holy religion, their faith, and their hope. Oh, holy, blessed cross! It is well with all who, in the distress of their sin-laden heart, chose the cross as their place of refuge, laid their load of sin at its feet, and embraced it with the arms of faith, saying: "My Love hangs on the cross. O Love, O eternal Love! Until my heart breaks me, I will never leave You!"

In our text, Saint Paul tells us that there are people to whom the Word of the cross is "foolishness." But who are these people? They are, as the apostle says, "those who are perishing" (1 Corinthians 1:18). They suffer from the incomprehensible delusion that they are not sinners, and so they do not want to be lifted up from their fall by grace. Paul adds, "But to us who are being saved it is the power of God" (1 Corinthians 1:18). To those of us who look to the cross in faith, daily experiencing it, the apostle says, "For I am not ashamed of the gospel, for it is the power of God for salvation to everyone who believes" (Romans 1:16).

When darkness round me gathers,
Thy name and cross, still bright,
Deep in my heart are sparkling
Like stars in blackest night.
O heart, this image cherish:
The Christ on Calvary,
How patiently He suffered
And shed His blood for me! Amen.

(TLH 407:3)

Wednesday

Read Galatians 6:14

TRUE GOOD WORKS and true virtue are not achieved by omitting this or that sin and doing this or that laudable work out of fear of punishment and the hope of reward. Instead, a person should omit sin and do good works because he hates all sin and loves every good. And in all of this, he should be motivated, not by concern about punishment or reward, but by the free, pure love of God.

What good is accomplished merely by continually preaching to someone, "You must put away your sin and walk on the path of virtue"? The resulting temporal and eternal death for sin may be described ever so vividly, and the resulting temporal and eternal reward for virtue and good works may be presented ever so enticingly. But the listener may remain as he was, saying to himself, "Who can be as godly as he should?" Or, in the best case, he may become a hypocrite who, fearing punishment for sin, protects himself by doing his "good works" in the hope of a reward, saying to himself, "Oh, that I could live as I want to!" With only the preaching of virtue, the person remains an enemy of the holiness of God and all of his works flow from the gloomy spring of a sin-loving heart. Who strove to live blamelessly according to the Law? The Pharisees! And, for the most part, they were hypocrites, who did not rest until they had brought Christ, the troublesome preacher of the truth, to the cross.

And how is it with those today to whom virtue and good works are continually preached and who still believe that "not creeds but deeds save"? Instead of loving God above everything else and their neighbors as themselves, they love all the world and themselves alone. There are some who really want to better themselves by their own power, who even mortify the most secret sinful desires in themselves in order to offer God a pure heart. But has any person ever achieved this goal by his own power? How earnestly Paul, when he was still Saul, exerted himself to walk blamelessly according to the Law. But when he thought he had attained the highest righteousness and holiness, he had become an enemy and a persecutor of Christians. While he was still a monk, Luther struggled and even wounded himself in his cloister cell in order to become holy by his own power. But all he achieved by this was doubt. All who have tried to become holy by their own power have experienced this.

Therefore, if a person is really to become holy, he is in need of a power other than his own. What he needs is a helping hand from heaven, the power of God. This sanctifying power is the Word of the cross. Certainly each person must pursue holiness, without which, Scripture says, no one will see the Lord. He begins by despairing of all his will and ability and by believing in the crucified One. The order of salvation is not that a person is first holy and then saved; rather, he is first saved and then made holy. "We love because He first loved us," John tells us (1 John 4:19), testifying that the love for God first comes into a person's heart when he recognizes and believes in the love God has for him in His heart. He learns to believe in the miracle of God's love: that God so loved him and the whole world that He gave up His Son to death on the cross for him and for the whole world.

Let my soul, in full exemption,
Wake up in Thy likeness now;
Thou art made to me redemption,
My sanctification Thou.
Whatever I need for my journey to heaven,
In Thee, O my Savior, is unto me given;
O let me all perishing pleasure forego,
And Thy life, O Jesus, alone let me know. Amen.

(ELHB 83:7)

Thursday

Read Acts 20:24

THE SALUTARY EFFECTS of the Reformation were so far-reaching that there is hardly a nation that was not affected by its mighty influence. It gave the entire Christian world a new form, and it ushered in a new age in the history of the world. Many respected members of the Roman Catholic Church acknowledge their church's debt to the Reformation, but it was the Protestants, above all others, who harvested and enjoyed the precious fruits of that movement. Even Protestants who possess only a little knowledge of history agree that the blessings of the Reformation are incalculable and that they are surrounded by them, as by the air.

The glorious fruit of the Reformation is considered to be the removal of the night of superstition that lasted for more than a thousand years. Mere outward ceremonies and worship services conducted in a foreign language were abolished. The Reformation put an end to the disgraceful dominion of the pope and priests, who lorded it over the laity. It banished the intolerable compulsion in the things of faith and the bloody horrors of the secret heresy courts of the Inquisition. The Reformation generally limited zealous religious persecution. It furthered enlightenment, championing the right to personal inquiry for knowledge and helping art and science to flourish. Religious freedom and tolerance for other beliefs became prevalent. For these glorious fruits, we cannot thank God enough.

But all of this does not include the most precious fruit of the Reformation. It would be a great error to maintain that Luther was pulled into this work because he yearned for freedom from the oppressive yoke of papal dominion and all that was directly connected with it. No, the true motive was this: Luther wanted to be certain of the grace of God and salvation but he did not know how to obtain them. After he had tormented himself for a long time by his own works, a strict monastic life, and constant prayer, fasting, vigils, and other mortifications, he found that he still had no peace. Indeed, he was led to the brink of despair by his failure. Then, by the reading of the Bible, which had come into his hands by God's miraculous providence, it gradually became clear to him that a person, according to the Gospel, should be righteous before God and saved, not by his own works, but by the faith given him by God. His righteousness and salvation depended, not on his worthiness, but only on grace; not on his own righteousness, but on an alien righteousness; not by his work and suffering, but by the work and suffering of Jesus Christ, the Son of God and the Savior of sinners. This discovery not only brightened Luther's outlook toward God (he wrote that he was like a hopeless person for whom the gates of paradise were suddenly opened), but it also made him happier and bolder toward all people, so that he felt a compelling need to proclaim the saving Gospel to the whole world. After all, it had given him such great comfort, heavenly refreshment, living hope, and rock-solid certainty that he simply had to share this good news. He would not be deterred, even if, as a defenseless monk, he was opposed by pope and emperor and threatened with excommunication, fire, and sword. The right understanding of the Gospel of the grace of God in Christ was the true treasure that the Reformation brought to Christendom.

When Rome had shrouded earth in night,
God said again, Let there be light!
And Luther with the Gospel came
To spread the truth in Jesus' name.

When Rome the saints of God oppressed,
And burdened souls could find no rest,
Through Luther God deliv'rance sent
By His pure Word and Sacrament. Amen.

† *(ELHB 283:1, 2)*

Friday

Read Philippians 1:3–6

THE APOSTOLIC PRAYER of thanksgiving in today's text should awaken us to say fervent thanks to God for fellowship in the Gospel. This doctrine is the certain, true, and precious teaching that Jesus Christ, the Son of God, came into the world to make sinners righteous and to save them. Every sinner who, from his heart, believes in this Son and Savior is declared righteous and saved. This doctrine distinguishes Christianity from every other religion. It alone makes a person a Christian. No other revealed doctrine offers us more help than this one, and all other doctrines perish when the pure doctrine proclaiming the justification of sinners through faith perishes.

If the Reformation had brought us nothing but freedom of religion and conscience, if it had given birth (as many now maintain) to the Enlightenment, it would not have rescued us from the pirate ship of the papacy and brought us safely to shore, but it would instead have thrown us into the sea. For the Enlightenment was nothing more than unbelief, rejection of the Gospel, renunciation of all bonds of the Word and the commandments of God, and the deification of man. But it is well with us! The Reformation brought us fellowship in the Gospel as the Philippians once enjoyed it. We cannot thank God enough for this.

Whoever possesses and rightly understands the Gospel has the highest treasure anyone can have in this world. He cannot despair of his sins, for the pure doctrine of the Gospel tells him that, when he believes it, those sins shall be and remain forgiven. He cannot be frightened by the demands and threats of the Law, for the pure doctrine of the Gospel tells him that, when he believes it, God regards him as if he had never transgressed the Law but had instead kept it perfectly. He cannot despair when his own heart and conscience accuse and condemn him and when he sees and feels nothing in himself except sin and unrighteousness, for the pure doctrine of the Gospel tells him that when he believes it, he obtains the righteousness of Christ, which alone avails before God. He cannot be afraid of death, for the pure doctrine of the Gospel tells him that when he believes it and clings to Christ's Word, he shall not see death eternally because Christ tasted death for him and brought life and immortality to light. Finally, he cannot fear judgment, hell, and damnation on the Last Day, for the pure doctrine of the Gospel tells him that when he believes it, he will not perish but have eternal life.

Whoever has the Gospel and the right knowledge of it dwells under an open heaven into which he can come at every moment. He also has the key to every grace of God, to every comfort, and to all of the goods of salvation, and he can use that key to unlock these gifts as often as he needs them. The most glorious thing is that whoever has the comfort of the Gospel does not worry himself with doubt about whether he will remain in that blessed state and reach the goal, for the Gospel gives him the gracious assurance that Paul gave the Philippians and gives us: "And I am sure of this, that he who began a good work in you will bring it to completion at the day of Jesus Christ" (Philippians 1:6).

Who can describe the great blessing enjoyed by those who possess the pure doctrine of the Gospel and the right knowledge of it! They know the way to heaven, and no false doctrine can lead them astray. They cannot despair in any trouble, and they cannot be overcome by any trial. Therefore, Luther writes, "If we understand this article correctly and purely, we have the right heavenly sun; if we lose it, however, we then have nothing else but hellish darkness."

But Thou hast raised me up
To joy and exultation
And clearly shown the way
That leads me to salvation.
My sins are washed away,
For this I thank Thee, Lord;
And with my heart and soul
All dead works are abhorred. Amen.

† *(TLH 417:4)*

Saturday

Read Philippians 1:9–11

SAINT PAUL lets the petition follow the thanksgiving. By his thanksgiving, he encourages the Philippians to thank God. By the content of his prayer, he tells them how they should show God their thanks for their fellowship in the Gospel. The first thing they should do is seek to grow in the knowledge and experience of the blessed Gospel. Far from becoming tired of it, they should become ever more zealous for it, delving into it and seeking to experience its divine power.

With such thanks, the Gospel was once received by thousands in Germany and other lands. In 1539, shortly after Easter, one of the greatest enemies of the Reformation, Duke Georg of Saxony, died and the Lutheran Duke Heinrich came to rule. Immediately the work of the Reformation began in the entire duchy. A few weeks later, on Pentecost Monday, Luther preached in Leipzig, where Georg had sorely oppressed

Lutherans. (Some had been executed; others had gone into exile.) By now, there was a great desire among the people to hear the blessed Gospel, and Luther's sermon made such a deep impression on them that, after he finished speaking, they publicly sank to their knees in the church and, with raised hands and streams of tears, they loudly thanked God that He valued them enough to make them aware of this blessed doctrine.

Luther himself was one who thanked God with a tireless zeal in contemplation of the Gospel. In the introduction to his exposition of the Epistle to the Galatians, he wrote, "In my heart alone rules and should also rule this one article, that is, faith in my dear Lord Christ, Who is the only beginning, middle, and end of all my spiritual and divine thoughts, which I may evermore have day and night." We see here how we, too, should demonstrate our thanks for the Gospel that has been given to us: it must always become more beloved, valuable, and precious to us. We must eagerly read, hear, and examine it so it fills and moves our whole heart and soul more and more, enlightens our understanding more and more, and changes our will more and more. In short, we must walk in the light of the Gospel, as the moon moves in the light of the sun.

Paul adds, "So that you may approve what is excellent, and so be pure and blameless for the day of Christ, filled with the fruit of righteousness that comes through Jesus Christ, to the glory and praise of God" (Philippians 1:10–11). We see here that our love for the Gospel and our zeal in learning it, experiencing it, and meditating on it should also be revealed in a sincere, honest, and holy walk before the world, and by all kinds of good works, such as being faithful in our vocation, patient in our trials, full of works of love toward our afflicted and needy neighbors, and eager to spread the blessed Gospel among those who still do not enjoy it.

If we examine ourselves as to how we have thanked God

for His precious Gospel, what must we say? Must we not lament all our idleness? And how about the sincerity and uprightness of our entire walk and our fruitfulness in all good works? Must not all of us, without exception, beat our breasts and cry out, "Lord, do not enter into judgment with Your servants"? Rise! Let us awaken from the sleep of idleness, into which the evil enemy would gladly lull us that we sleep through the salvation on the bright day of grace and lose, both for us and for our children, the treasure that has been given to us! For there is no greater sin than being ungrateful for the blessing of the Gospel, and for that the punishment will certainly not fail to come.

Thanks we give and adoration
For Thy Gospel's joyful sound.
May the fruits of Thy salvation
In our hearts and lives abound;
Ever faithful, Ever faithful
To the Truth may we be found! Amen.

† *(TLH 50:2)*

Sunday

Read Matthew 22:15–22

THE DELUDED JEWS believed that when the Messiah arrived, He would deliver them from the yoke of the Roman emperor and make them worldly lords to whom all other nations would be subject. Therefore, when Jesus came to Judea, declared Himself to be the Messiah, and then went about in a poor, lowly, and powerless manner, offering no provisions to rescue the Jews from the political oppression of Rome, many were offended and refused to recognize Him as the true Messiah. Foremost among these were the Pharisees. In order to trick Jesus, they once asked Him, "Is it lawful to pay taxes to Caesar, or not?" (Matthew 22:17). They said to themselves, "If Jesus says no, then we can accuse Him of revolt before the Roman authorities; if He says yes, we can then prove to our people that He cannot possibly be the true, promised Messiah." But our text says that Jesus "aware of their malice, said, 'Why put Me to the test, you hypocrites? Show Me the coin for the tax.' And they brought Him a denarius. And Jesus said to them, 'Whose likeness and inscription is this?' They said, 'Caesar's.' Then He said to them, 'Therefore render to Caesar the things that are Caesar's, and to God the things that are God's'" (Matthew 22:18–21).

By this, Jesus taught that if people live in a country in which the emperor has imposed a tax, they must prove they are his subjects and he has authority over them. For this reason, they should give the emperor what is his. If he is the ruler of the country, he should receive the tax, obedience, and honor due him. If we consider the motive behind Christ's saying, "Therefore render to Caesar the things that are Caesar's," and the context in which these words stand, we see quite clearly that Christ does not impress upon us mere obedience toward a sovereign prince. Instead, He declares that He did not come as the Messiah to abolish the orders of God among people. Therefore, the person who believes in Him is in no way freed from obeying those who have the right to command him according to God's order in His kingdom of power.

This command of Christ is applicable even today. We have both national and state authorities to whom we must be obedient. Without them, our nation could not exist, our property would be unprotected, we could not sleep peacefully at night, and our freedoms would be severely jeopardized or become a dangerous evil. Although our government is installed by the majority of the people and is accountable to them, it is still God's order and God's servant, into whose hands He Himself has given the sword of protection and the scales of justice. Its laws, then, should be holy and inviolable to us, and we should consider its decrees to be God's decrees. We should joyfully pay the taxes our government imposes upon us so its beneficial establishment is preserved and God's holy will is fulfilled. We should even be ready to sacrifice our life if, for the protection of the common welfare, our government calls upon us to march into the field against an enemy of our country. It is no small sin to transgress wantonly a command of the lawful government we have placed over ourselves and to defraud it of its taxes and duties. To be Christians, therefore, we must act conscientiously according to the word of Christ, "Therefore render to Caesar the things that are Caesar's." We must give the government whatever is due it.

The powers ordained by Thee
With heavenly wisdom bless;
May they Thy servants be
And rule in righteousness!
O Lord, stretch forth Thy mighty hand
And guard and bless our Fatherland. Amen.

† *(TLH 580:4)*

Monday

Read Matthew 22:21

JESUS HAD IMPORTANT REASONS for adding the words "and to God the things that are God's" to His command that we must "render to Caesar the things that are Caesar's" (Matthew 22:21). Many people want to give each person what is due him, but they do not think about the obligation they have toward the Most High God. They maintain that if they are honorable citizens, obedient children, and good workers, they are fulfilling everything expected of them, they are good Christians, and salvation is assured them. Some are hindered from service to God by their relationships with people, and they pay homage to the principle that "service to the lord comes before service to God." Christ's words in today's lesson contradict this as He reminds us that we must give "to God the things that are God's."

There is more to being a Christian than walking honorably before the world and being blameless before others. Today's text teaches that if we want to come to God, we must give Him everything that belongs to Him. But what belongs to God? He is due everything that we are and have: our body and soul, our heart, our life, our powers, our joys, and our honor. He is the Creator of all things, the Lord over all things, and the Fountain from which all things flow and to which they will return. By nature, however, every person lives for himself. By nature, he carries a certain enmity toward God in his heart. By nature, he seeks his rest and his heart's satisfaction in the goods and glories of the world. But when a person truly learns, by God's Word and the enlightenment of the Holy Ghost, to recognize Christ and His grace and His salvation, a great change occurs in him. He sees God as his highest good, and he seeks to become completely united with God and a sacrifice for Him.

Who among us has already experienced this change in his heart? Who among us no longer attaches his heart to the joys and goods of this world so he can say, "Whom have I in heaven but You? And there is nothing on earth that I desire besides You" (Psalm 73:25)? Who among us says in his heart, when he is praised and honored, "Not to us, Lord, but to Your name may glory be given"? May no one trust that he is giving each person what is due him if he fails to give God his whole heart and everything with it, for Christ has commanded that we do both.

Perhaps someone will respond, "I want to serve God with my whole heart, but I am surrounded by godless ones and must work the entire day, so I can think little about God and salvation." Another may add, "I desire to be a zealous Christian, but I have family members who love the world and whom I must live to please." Whoever excuses himself in this way must hear what Christ says elsewhere as a commentary on our text: "Leave the dead to bury their own dead" (Luke 9:60); "If anyone comes to Me and does not hate his own father and mother and wife and children and brothers and sisters, yes, and even his own life, he cannot be My disciple" (Luke 14:26); and "Whoever loves father or mother more than Me is not worthy of Me, and whoever loves son or daughter more than Me is not worthy of Me" (Matthew 10:37). Therefore, whoever has either not desired God at all or divided his heart between Him and some creature must tear himself away from his present entanglements and divided loyalties. If he does not do this, he will be deceived by his sham Christianity and, in the end, he will not come to God's heavenly rest.

But whoever is at peace with God through faith is already now blessed in God and already enjoying the peace that surpasses all understanding, a peace this world cannot give to anyone. His heart is full of comfort and hope. And when he dies, God will open to him the mansions of eternal peace and let him enter to perfect glory and blessedness forever.

Give unto God thy heart's affection,
Who else can claim thee as His own?
Should Satan hold thee in subjection?
With him but pangs of hell are known.
To Thee alone, O Lord divine,
My heart and all I now resign. Amen.

(TLH 404:2)

Tuesday

Read Psalm 87:1–2

IS THE CHURCH of believers really such a firmly established building? Doesn't it today more closely resemble a rotten mud-hut without a solid foundation that collapses with every gust of wind and every heavy downpour? Even if the Church has miraculously preserved itself until the present time, do we not retain only fragments and ruins that remind us of its former existence, as thousands upon thousands of worshipers leave it as a crumbling building? Isn't it foolish, then, to speak today of a glorious, miraculous building of the Church of God on earth?

No, because the Church is such a building. It appears to be weak, but as our text says, it stands unshakably firm upon the holy mountains. What are these holy mountains? The text tells us: "the LORD loves the gates of Zion more than all the dwelling places of Jacob" (Psalm 87:2). The high mountain upon which the Church stands is the love of God. Out of His unfathomable love, God gathered one Church of believers from the fallen and lost human race to preserve it and finally to lead it into a kingdom of eternal glory. This love is the diamond-like bedrock upon which the Church is established. What power of the world, of hell, and even of heaven can overturn this foundation? Everything else may, in time, sink to the ground, but time cannot crumble the foundation upon which the Church stands, for it was established even before the foundation of the world was laid. It was created, not in time, but before time as the world knows it, by the decree of eternal love. Upon every stone of this invisible building is written, "Everything lasts for its time, but God's love lasts forever."

What man has built can be broken down by man. But no person can demolish the foundation of the Church, for its Master Builder is the eternal God Himself. God permits the hellish powers of this age to destroy even the best works of people until the Last Day. However, they cannot destroy the work of the Church, for high above the seat of the powerless spirits of darkness reigns an almighty and true Love who has decreed that even the gates of hell will not overcome God's Church on earth. "Behold," He says, "I am with you always, to the end of the age" (Matthew 28:20).

Death removes all of those who established great empires, ruled them with might, and fortified them extensively. With their death, the proud work of their hands tumbles to the ground. But no death can bring down the Church, for the God who established and rules it is immortal. Death may devour everything that lives, and even heaven and earth will pass away. Yet God's love, which does not die (indeed, it is life itself), will lead the Church into the kingdom of heavenly glory, and there it will celebrate the feast of peace and the victory of eternal life.

But how can this be? Aren't all members of the Church still sinners? And isn't God holy and just? Wouldn't God's righteousness and holiness move Him, in His wrath, to smash the Church, which His love had built? No, for the love of God rests upon reconciliation. The watchword of the Church is "God is love!" (1 John 4:8). Upon its blood-stained banner is written, "Christ God was reconciling the world to Himself" (2 Corinthians 5:19). The holiness of God has been eternally satisfied, and His righteousness is thereby perfectly satisfied. He now extends hands of reconciliation to cover people's guilt. The sins of the believing Church, and even God's holiness and righteousness, cannot extinguish the fire of love, which has established the Church and wants to preserve it eternally.

What a glorious, miraculous building is the Church of God! As the earth is suspended freely in the air without a visible foundation yet does not sink into the bottomless pit because God's power is its invisible foundation, and as the starry sky arches over us without visible pillars yet stands firm because God's power invisibly supports the heavens, so also does the Church stand in this world. It has no visible foundation or pillars to support it, yet it does not sink because its invisible foundation is God's eternal love, revealed in the death and resurrection of Jesus Christ.

Glorious things of thee are spoken,
Zion, city of our God;
He whose word cannot be broken
Formed thee for His own abode.
On the Rock of Ages founded,
What can shake thy sure repose?
With salvation's walls surrounded,
Thou may'st smile at all thy foes. Amen.

† *(TLH 469:1)*

Wednesday

Read Psalm 87:3

THE PSALMIST KNOWS of no glorious thing the Church has to boast about other than the things preached in it, things it possesses only in faith. But we cannot conclude from this that the Church is not really rich. Its wealth is so great the human heart cannot comprehend it all!

What are the glorious things preached in the Church? They are the great and wonderful messages that God Himself came down from heaven, became a man, lived a holy life, died an innocent death, rose victorious, and ascended into heaven to redeem mankind from its sin. By that death and resurrection, Jesus Christ reconciled all people with God, blotted out their sins, overcame their death and hell, earned eternal salvation for them by grace, and opened to them the heaven of glory. These great deeds of God are what our text means when it says, "Glorious things of You are spoken, O city of God" (Psalm 87:3).

Who can measure the treasures the Church, through God, possesses? Who can calculate the value of its wealth? To the world, the Church appears as a beggar because the goods the earth presents to man are mostly in the hands of the world. They are the lords upon earth, and only here and there does a small crumb fall from their table to the Church! The wealth of the Church, then, is nothing but disguised poverty.

Why does the world, for all its riches, honor, and might, still restlessly strive after more? It is because the world has not found what the Church already has: God, happiness, and a peace that surpasses all human understanding. When, from time to time, the world momentarily thinks it has reached its goal, the thought of death always shakes it out of this dreamy state, for it knows that the end of its life is also the end of its phantom happiness. Poor and naked, it must finally go out into the dark eternity with nothing it can call its own. It will meet a God whose message of grace it despised on earth and who will cast it away from Himself forever.

What, then, is the wealth of the world? It is the wealth of a sailor who steers his ship, laden with great treasures, not into a safe harbor but into a bottomless whirlpool that destroys everything. How completely different is the wealth of the Church, which possesses glorious things that are preached in it and believed by it. It has a gracious God and Savior, forgiveness of all its sins, a peaceful conscience, the hope of eternal life, heavenly comfort in all its earthly distress, and true joy of the heart. The Church does not seek happiness, like the world, for it already has it. Even the poorest member of the Church knows he is richer than all the kings of the earth, and therefore he does not exchange his earthly want for all of the world's wealth, his lowliness for all of the world's grandeur, and his suffering for all of the world's joys.

The Church's goods are more valuable to it than its own life. While the world sacrifices all its goods in order to save its life, the Church readily sacrifices its life in order to save its goods. Unlike the world, the Church is not troubled by the thought of death. The certainty of death makes the Church certain of its happiness. For not only does the Church lose none of its goods in death, but the good works of the Church also follow it. And in the world to come, those goods will be gloriously transformed. The Church's beliefs will be changed into beholding what was believed, its hope will be changed into the enjoyment of what was hoped for, and its comfort in distress will be changed into a perfect, eternal joy and blessedness.

Oh, what a glorious, miraculous building is the Church!

Its temporal earthly poverty is only the coarse shell of the precious pearl of its eternal heavenly riches. Here, its life is still hidden with Christ in God. On earth, only the person who possesses wealth recognizes it. The worldly-minded heart that regards only temporal and visible goods as riches cannot understand the glory of the Church. However, the day is coming when the invisible Church will become visible, and then the world will be astonished to see how rich the apparently poor Church was. For the earthly beggar was really a disguised heavenly queen, receiving the kingdom that was prepared for it from the beginning of the world. Then the world will also learn that it did not subjugate the Church, but that it was subjugated by the Church; that the world did not tolerate and preserve the Church, but that the Church tolerated and preserved the world; that the Church was not the servant of the world, but that the world was the servant of the Church; that everything in the world, the great as well as the small, must stand in service to the Church. In short, the world will understand that Saint Paul spoke truly when he called the Church the poor one that yet makes many rich, saying of it, "For all things are yours, whether Paul or Apollos or Cephas or the world or life or death or the present or the future—all are yours!" (1 Corinthians 3:21–22).

Savior, since of Zion's city
I thro' grace a member am,
Let the world deride or pity,
I will glory in Thy name.
Fading is the worldling's pleasure,
All his boasted pomp and show;
Solid joys and lasting treasure
None but Zion's children know. Amen.

† *(TLH 469:4)*

Thursday

Read Psalm 87:4–7

ACCORDING TO its outward appearance, the Church has always been only a small flock. In the days of the Flood, it was made up of only eight souls. At the time of Elijah the prophet, it became so imperceptible that Elijah thought he was the only one remaining. When Christ the Lord walked upon the earth and gathered His Church, He called it a "little flock." On other occasions, He said: "For the gate is wide and the way is easy that leads to destruction, and those who enter by it are many. For the gate is narrow and the way is hard that leads to life, and those who find it are few" (Matthew 7:13–14).

The world has always taken offense at the small size of the Church. It says: "How should these few alone have the truth, go on the right path, and be saved? How can the world have been created for these few alone, that they alone should be the elect?" Many were vexed at this even at the time when today's psalm was written.

Our text addresses this stumbling block. The psalmist is saying, in essence: "The city of God, the glory of which I praise, may always appear to be small. But the eye of the spirit is opened in me, and looking into the future, I see an immense host. All the lands that have now shut their gates to the Word of Jehovah—wisdom-seeking Egypt, mighty Babylon, embittered Philistia, rich Tyre, far-off Africa—I see them all, their gates opening to the Lord, becoming citizens of Zion, and the Church of God flowing like a flood unto the ends of the earth" (see Psalm 87:4–7).

And behold! What our text once prophesied at a time

when no human spirit could have guessed it has today been perfectly and gloriously fulfilled. At Christ's command, the twelve apostles and their successors went out into all the world and preached the Gospel to millions upon millions of people who have become members of the Church.

Someone will ask: "Will this growth spurt end? Won't the Church become smaller?" It may appear, in these last, troubled days of the world, that the Church has dried up like a river in the desert. But if we consider it rightly, we must confess that the Church, even today, becomes larger with each passing day. For the Church is not an earthly kingdom, but a heavenly one; no time and no place limit it. The Church, which still fights on earth and is already triumphant in heaven, consists of the innumerable number of all believers. Its first members were Adam and Eve and its last member will be the last person who becomes a believer on the Last Day. It is a pilgrim throng, part of which still wanders abroad in this world and part of which has already arrived at its goal, the heavenly homeland. Even in death, the Church does not lose its members. Instead, in death, each of its members is recognized as one who cannot be lost eternally.

In vain, then, do the enemies of the Church rejoice at its seeming decline; in vain are its friends fearful because the number of its members appears to be dwindling. At no time has the Church included such a great host as it does today. Who can count the stars of heaven? So is the number of members of the Church today. All of the patriarchs of the first world, all of the prophets before Christ, all of the apostles and martyrs—in short, all who lived and died in the faith in the time of the Old and New Testaments—still belong to the Church, as do we. The building of the Church has not ended. Each day, more souls are brought into the Church by preaching and Baptism. And this will continue until the Last Day, when the last of the elect will be born. As the Lord says, many will come from the east and from the west and will sit with Abraham, Isaac, and Jacob in the kingdom of heaven.

What a glorious, miraculous building the Church is! It appears to be very small, but it comprises an innumerable multitude.

Draw us to Thee
Unceasingly,
Into Thy Kingdom take us;
Let us fore'er
Thy glory share,
Thy saints and joint heirs make us. Amen.

(TLH 215:5)

Friday

Read Philippians 3:17–18

SAINT PAUL considers the enemies of the cross of Christ to be those who are opposed to the doctrine that a person becomes just before God and is saved, not by the Law and his works, but through faith in the crucified Christ.

These enemies of the cross have not in any way died out in our day. Indeed, they do not merely creep around here and there, seeking to lead believing congregations astray. No, they have even come to power in the very midst of Christendom. What is the doctrine that now resounds from most so-called Protestant pulpits? Without shame, most preachers now teach, and their hearers gladly hear, that Christ is not the true God, eternally equal with the Father and almighty, but rather a son of God like all good people, only more enlightened, wiser, and godlier. Christ's death, they say, was only a martyr's death, a death for the sealing of the truth of His doctrine. Therefore, these preachers maintain, a person does not become clean by the blood of Christ, he is not reconciled by Christ's death, and Christ has not atoned for his sins by His suffering and death. Salvation, they say, does not depend on the faith of a person, but on his virtue, his upright mind, his good works, and his blameless life. By this alone, they claim, a person can make himself pleasing to God and just before Him; he thus makes himself worthy of salvation and gains a claim on heaven.

Thousands of preachers who call themselves Christian—Protestant, evangelical—teach this. Such preachers may hypocritically praise Christ and demand that people imitate His glorious example. However, they are nothing but enemies of the cross of Christ.

Those who all too clearly preserve and support the godless world by their unbelief, by their contempt of God and His Word, and by their earthly mind are manifest enemies of the cross of Christ, but their animosity is so overt that no believing Christian is led astray. There are, however, more subtle enemies of the cross who present a better appearance. They teach that Christ is God's only begotten Son, that He died a substitutionary death of atonement, and that a person becomes just before God through faith and not by works. But they proceed to deny grace and salvation to all who receive this doctrine at face value, without any personal claim of worthiness, in exclusive reliance upon the Word of the Gospel that is sealed to them by Baptism and Holy Communion. They do this by continually preaching about repentance, conversion, being born again, and sanctification, but they do not have mercy on the poor sinner and they do not want to give any comfort to those who can say nothing of themselves but that they are poor, lost sinners. They do this by describing the faith and justification and pardon of a person in such a way that the Gospel appears to show a person how he himself must earn grace and climb to heaven under an unbearable yoke. They do this by calling the Savior a hard Man and a Moses with thunder and lightning; they portray Him as ruling over His own with an iron scepter.

The preachers of these severe doctrines are the most dangerous enemies of Christ and His holy cross. They terrify sinners and keep them from Christ. Without saying it, they teach that Christians must build their state of grace and their salvation upon their own works. They drive the sheep of the Good Shepherd away from the sweet pasture of the life-giving Gospel and into the desert sand of the Law. They are thus guilty of causing thousands to go astray and to seek grace without ever finding it.

Preserve, O Lord, Thine honor,
The bold blasphemer smite;
Convince, convert, enlighten,
The souls in error's night.
Reveal Thy will, dear Savior,
To all who dwell below—
Thou Light of all the living—
That men Thy name may know. Amen.

† *(TLH 264:2)*

Saturday

Read Philippians 3:19–21

"Their end is destruction" (Philippians 3:19). Thus sounds Saint Paul's terrible judgment upon the enemies of Christ's cross. Should we be surprised by this judgment?

Surely not! Because of sin, each person is, by nature, an enemy of God. But what has God done? Despite our enmity toward Him, He has not put away His love for us. Instead, He used our enmity against Him to reveal, all the more gloriously, the greatness of His love to us. He became a man who, by dying in shame on the cross, atoned for our sins and reconciled us with God. As Paul says: "Christ God was reconciling the world to Himself, not counting their trespasses against them, and entrusting to us the message of reconciliation. Therefore, we are ambassadors for Christ, God making His appeal through us. We implore you on behalf of Christ, be reconciled to God" (2 Corinthians 5:19–20).

What should God do with a person who is hostile to Him because of the demands of His holy Law, and who is also now an enemy of His reconciliation, His redeeming love, His saving grace, and His merciful compassion? What should God do with a person who tramples the blood of reconciliation with his own feet, who wants no Savior and no Intercessor? What should God do with a person who, in order to fill his own belly or to appear holy, denies his enmity against the doctrine of the cross and of grace in Christ, and tears other souls from Christ? Who can measure the mountains of sin that such a despiser of grace loads upon his conscience?

The end of such an enemy of God can be nothing else but eternal damnation. The enemies of the cross of Christ may be highly regarded in the world and celebrated as men of peace, enlightenment, and progress. They may enrich themselves by the gifts of their poor, seduced hearers. They may live their life in splendor and in peace. But because of this, they are to be neither envied nor dismissed. Rather, they are to be pitied with hot tears. When the short time in which they stand under divine patience elapses, they will appear as enemies of the cross of Christ before the judgment throne of Him whose divinity they denied, whose majesty they blasphemed, whose grace they abused, whose divine blood they trampled, whose Gospel they falsified, and whose precious redeemed they tore from His arms and dropped into the pool of unbelievers and blasphemers. Then Christ will say to them: "Where are the souls that you should have led to Me? What have I done to you, you wretched one, that you have persecuted Me?" And behold! Hell will suddenly open up beneath them and devour them. They will suffer agony, and the smoke of their torment will ascend forever and ever.

Let us, then, in faith embrace the cross of our Savior, and let nothing tear us away from it. Although death may come and the world may perish, the anchor of the cross will not break. We will be drawn up on it, above the poor earth with its misery, into heaven, where the crucified One sits upon His throne, which beams with His eternal glory and is surrounded by all of the faithful. All of these should therefore say, "Our citizenship is in heaven, and from it we await a Savior, the Lord Jesus Christ, who will transform our lowly body to be like His glorious body, by the power that enables Him even to subject all things to Himself" (Philippians 3:20–21).

My Savior, wash me clean
With Thy most precious blood,
That takes away all sin
And seals my peace with God.
My soul in peace abideth
When in Thy wounds it hideth.
There I find full salvation
And freedom from damnation.
Without Thee lost, defiled by sin,
My Savior, wash me clean. Amen.

† *(TLH 335:2)*

Sunday

Read Matthew 9:18–26

FROM TODAY'S GOSPEL READING, we see what faith can do, what wonderful workings it produces, and what incomparable power it demonstrates. According to the detailed reports of the evangelists Mark and Luke, Christ expressly attributes both miracles—the healing of the woman and the raising of the ruler's daughter—to faith. However, it does not follow that because faith no longer demonstrates this power to heal and raise from the dead, it no longer has this power.

What separates faith from superstition is the certain divine promise to which the former can cling. Since believers no longer have the promise that God wants to heal them from every sickness and to raise all of the dead before the Last Day, faith cannot demonstrate its power in this way. But we cannot think that for this reason faith has less power than it did in the first century. No, it still has the same power. And the miracles true faith now performs are inexpressibly greater than all the healings of sickness and raisings from the dead about which the Gospel history speaks. Who can completely comprehend the glorious workings true faith produces when it begins to take root in a person's heart? As soon as he begins to believe, God's wrath, which had been directed toward him until that moment, is changed into grace and pleasure. God forgives him all his sins and declares him to be righteous, His child, and an heir of eternal life. Through faith, a person becomes so strong that, like Jacob, he can battle with God and overcome Him. Faith has the power to unlock God's heart, to shut the portals of hell and damnation, to open the gates of heaven and salvation, to give the heavenly hosts safe conduct through the world, and one day to gather them in the heavenly city.

Faith does not display this glorious power without allowing the believer to take some notice of it. It shows itself as "the assurance of things hoped for, the conviction of things not seen" (Hebrews 11:1). Faith makes a person divinely certain that he stands with God in grace. It fills him with the peace of God and gives him the Holy Ghost in his heart as a pledge and seal of his justification and salvation. Faith also creates a new heart in a person. It cleanses the heart from its natural love of sin, implants in it a sincere hatred of everything that displeases God and is forbidden in His Word, and gives the person power to fight earnestly against all sins and to love God as the highest good. Whoever stands in true faith can overcome all hatred toward his most bitter enemies so he loves them from his heart, forgetting their insults and supplying them with every good. He can lack all of the earthly things in which the natural man seeks his happiness, yet he can be joyful because he knows he stands with God in grace. He does not strive to become rich, but if riches nevertheless come to him by God's blessing, he does not attach his heart to them, but instead seeks to do good with them, drying the tears of the poor and helping to advance the kingdom of God. Faith makes a person so certain of his right standing with God that he cannot be shaken even if he were denounced by all of the world's wise and holy men as foolish and deceived. His faith makes him so courageous that he fears nothing from the world, even if it heaps scorn, threats, and persecution upon him. He is even ready, if necessary, to die for his faith to the glory of God. Oh, how great is the heavenly power of faith!

Increase my faith, dear Savior,
For Satan seeks by night and day
To rob me of this treasure
And take my hope of bliss away.

But, Lord, with Thee beside me,
I shall be undismayed;
And led by Thy good Spirit,
I shall be unafraid.
Abide with me, O Savior,
A firmer faith bestow;
Then I shall bid defiance
To ev'ry evil foe. Amen.

(*TLH* 381:2)

Monday

Read Luke 8:50

WHY DID THE FAITH of Jairus have the great power to obtain life again for his little daughter? Without doubt, its power lay in his seizing the word of Christ, "Do not fear; only believe, and she will be well" (Luke 8:50). Jairus complied, and thus it was impossible that what he believed should not have happened, for Christ cannot break His word.

Here we have the reason why there is such great power in believing in Christ. It is not that faith is a good work God must gloriously reward, that it earns something with God, and that it makes a person better and more worthy. Whoever believes in Christ is just as unworthy a sinner as the world's most godless person and most unbelieving mocker. Why, then, does faith in Christ produce great changes in heaven and on earth, turn God's wrath into grace, rescue the sinner from hell and open heaven to him, make him righteous and holy before God, create a new heart in him, and fill him with the Holy Ghost, comfort, joy, peace, power, and certainty? It is because faith grasps and dedicates itself to the Word of Christ and, with it, Christ Himself. The light and power of faith belong, not to faith, but to Christ. A lamp does not illuminate unless it is turned on, and faith shines only when it clings to Christ, the Light of the world. The earth becomes warm and fruitful only when it turns to the sun, and a believer becomes warm in love and fruitful in every good work only when he turns to Christ, the Sun of grace, who shines on him. For this reason, the natural man is presented in Scripture as a wild field that bears only weeds, and the Word of God is called the seed from which the fruitful plant of a new life grows. Faith receives the seed of the Word. Thus Christ also calls Himself the vine, and His believers the branches. Faith unites a person with Christ, binding them together as a branch to the vine. So it is not faith that does great things, but Christ, who is grasped through faith.

Those who pretend to have faith but who can overcome neither their indwelling sin nor the world and its enticements experience no such change. They remain the same as before, slaves of their passion and worshipers of the world's deceiving riches. They think they have sufficient faith and are lacking merely in sanctification. However, it is the other way around. What they lack, above all, is true faith. Their faith is a figment of their imagination. May they no longer shut their eyes to their lack of true faith. May they go to Christ as poor, empty, faithless sinners and implore Him to work the true faith in them. In this way, they, too, will experience His wonderful power with joy. And may those of us who grasp Christ daily in His Word, but only with a weak and trembling hand of faith, desire to stand firmly in faith! Let us write, deeply into our heart, the word Christ spoke to Jairus: "Do not fear; only believe." May this be our morning star in each of life's trials and our evening star in the hour of death, when the terrors of hell might otherwise overwhelm us. Let the world laugh at us because of our faith. Christ will keep His Word to us, rescuing us from the jaws of death and letting us behold in heaven, with eternal joy, what we here believed.

Just as I am, Thou wilt receive,
Wilt welcome, pardon, cleanse, relieve;
Because Thy promise I believe,
O Lamb of God, I come, I come. Amen.

† *(TLH 388:5)*

Tuesday

Read Jeremiah 5:3

THERE IS NO DOCTRINE of Holy Scripture more offensive to the world than the one that proclaims that a person becomes just and blessed before God merely through faith, and that, on the contrary, everyone who does not believe will be condemned. People cannot see that there should be any value attached to believing or disbelieving certain mysterious doctrines that are repugnant to our reason. "What will God one day care what a person has believed?" they say to themselves. "Rather, the question with God should be, 'How have you loved?' "

God is both just and impartial. It is therefore unthinkable to most people that He would receive a wicked person into heaven just because he believed everything in the Bible and that He would eternally cast away a virtuous, noble person because he was unable to believe everything. They remark that "every religion says to a person, 'Believe, and so you will be saved!' The Jewish rabbi demands faith in his Talmud, the Brahman in his Veda, the Muslim in his Koran, the heathen idol priest in his holy documents, and the Christian in his Bible. Among the Christians, there are numerous parties, each of which says, 'Believe what we believe, and so you will be saved.' Who would want to decide which faith is the right one?"

The best way out of this quandary, most people think, is that each one may believe what he wants, but everything depends on whether a person loves. If he leads a good life, then he may believe whatever he wants. He may be a Jew or a Muslim, a heathen or a Christian, a Bible believer or a believer of reason, a worshiper of God or an atheist, but he will still be saved. There is a widespread belief that the various religions are only different forms of the one true service to God, different paths that all lead to heaven. People reason that, one day, we will come to realize how foolish it was to worry about which faith is the right one, despising and rejecting all other faiths. In heaven, they maintain, God will say to the heathen, Jew, Muslim, and Christian alike: "You are all My children. You have given Me different names. The Christian calls Me Christ, the Jew calls Me Jehovah, the Hindu calls Me Brahma, the Muslim calls Me Allah, the Native Americans call Me the Great Spirit, and others call Me reason, nature, sun, moon, and stars. But you have all worshiped Me. For this reason, be reconciled and extend the hand of brotherhood to one another. Here there is no more strife!" Then, they imagine, all will sing, "We all believe in one God."

This is the faith that now fills so many hearts. In reality, it is naked unbelief. Whoever believes that all faiths are the same and have an equal claim on the truth basically believes nothing at all. Who would have thought that this type of reasoning would be found in Christendom? Yet according to the prophecies of Scripture itself, this must be the case. For it is said of the last time, "because they refused to love the truth and so be saved. Therefore God sends them a strong delusion, so that they may believe what is false, in order that all may be condemned who did not believe the truth but had pleasure in unrighteousness" (2 Thessalonians 2:10–12), and "In their case the god of this world has blinded the minds of the unbelievers, to keep them from seeing the light of the gospel of the glory of Christ, who is the image of God" (2 Corinthians 4:4).

The main reason why the doctrine that faith in Christ saves is now so offensive to so many is that these people are deluded and have never come to know the real quality of Christian faith. If the Christian faith were nothing but a dead adherence to certain mysterious doctrines as true, if a person could have the Christian faith and remain in his sins, then we could understand why many people think it makes no difference whether one's faith is Christian or Jewish or heathen or Turkish. But the true faith, to which Holy Scripture attributes salvation, is something completely different. This faith has such great power that the person who carries it in his heart is completely changed by it. He becomes a new person, who leads a truly pious life. True faith works what nothing else in the world can work in a person.

O Lord, in mercy stay my heart
On faith's most sure foundation
And to my inmost soul impart
Thy perfect consolation.
Fill all my life with love to Thee,
Toward all men grant me charity;
And at the last, when comes my end,
Thy succor send.
From Satan's wiles my soul defend. Amen.

(*TLH* 319:3)

Wednesday

Read Acts 17:26–27

PAUL ONCE PREACHED these great truths in the public market of the world-famous city of Athens, Greece. He taught that after God created the world, He did not depart, like a human builder. Instead, He continues to preserve and govern His work. If we consider the world only with the eyes of our understanding, it appears as if people determine for themselves and God is just an idle spectator. However, if we look at people's actions with the eye of faith, in the light of God's Word, we see something completely different. Paul says that everything that happens was appointed by God beforehand, even from eternity. God has set an end for everything and determined how long a person should live. While people seem to behave according to their own free will, God secretly has them in His hand and directs them so they do not carry out anything except His eternal decrees.

God has both the good and the evil in His all-directing hand. Either He places limits on them or He lets them happen and accomplishes His judgments of grace and wrath with them. We have a glorious example of this in the selling of Joseph by his brothers into slavery in Egypt. With this, they intended to do evil to Joseph, but God instead did good with it, and He carried out His eternal intentions of peace on Joseph and on His entire chosen people of Israel. While the world and hell raged against God, trying to take His glory from Him, to cast Him down from His throne, and to destroy His kingdom, these hostile powers unknowingly fought for God to promote His glory and to strengthen and increase His kingdom. We also see this in the bloody persecution of the first three centuries of the Christian era. This should have been enough to exterminate the Church, but like a tree moved by storms, it sent its roots deeper into the earth.

On the Last Day, when the play of the earthly life of humanity will have concluded, the enemies of God will clearly recognize with terror (but the elect with rejoicing) that nothing happened outside of God's will, that everything good and evil had to serve Him, and that He has led everything to a glorious and blessed end. How confident, then, a believing Christian can be! If something happens according to or against his will, he knows that it happened according to God's good and gracious will. Whether fortune or misfortune befalls him, he knows it is in accord with God's counsel. If he has many cunning and mighty enemies, he knows they cannot so much as bend a single hair on his head without being allowed by God to do so. If a person is robbed of everything—goods, honor, and joy—he knows all of it was taken from him by His God, through other people, but that God cannot have intended it as evil. If the future appears to be full of danger, he knows nothing will come upon him that God has not intended for him in grace.

Lord, as Thou wilt, deal Thou with me;
No other wish I cherish.
In life and death I cling to Thee;
Oh, do not let me perish!
Let not Thy grace from me depart
And grant an ever patient heart
To bear what Thou dost send me. Amen.

(*TLH* 406:1)

Thursday

Read Romans 1:19–20

THERE IS A NATURAL RELIGION or knowledge of God that a person can arrive at by himself, without the Bible. We know that there is but one God, that He is good and just, and that man is bound to serve and worship Him. We know these things because, when God created man, He gave him a soul and a heart on which His image was deeply impressed. Although man lost this divine image by his defilement with sin, he retains a spark of knowledge that tells him there is a God. This knowledge of God continues to be implanted in the soul and heart of every person. Thus, all people on earth, however cruel and undeveloped they may be, have some form of religion and worship. Even the mightiest of tyrants, who deny God with their mouth and have no fear of any person, are tortured after a life of shameful deeds by the most terrible torment of conscience and a fear of an unknown higher Judge. Where would this secret, gnawing fear have originated if not from the indelible writing in the heart of man that there is a God?

A second way that a person, even without Holy Scripture, can be convinced that there is a God is by contemplating the world. If he considers the great house of this world, his reason tells him that it could not possibly have arisen by itself; rather, there must be a great Builder who was there before it was established, an eternal, almighty God who built it and created everything. If the person then considers the wonderful order that exists among the millions of various beings—from the marvelous human body to the smallest insect—and the way they are harmoniously united into one great whole, he finds so many miracles of creation that they cannot have been conceived and constructed by any human mind. His reason tells him there must be an all-wise Being who called everything into existence with His wonderful wisdom. If the person then considers how every one of the earth's creatures is provided for—with nourishment, clothing, joy, and protection—his reason prompts him again to regard all of this as ordered by a divine Creator. Finally, if the person observes how his conscience accuses and chastises him as soon as he wants to transgress the law of righteousness, he reasons, "There must be a God who is holy and just, and who demands righteousness from me as well."

Paul writes, "For when Gentiles, who do not have the law," that is, the law given by special divine revelation, "by nature do what the law requires, they are a law to themselves, even though they do not have the law. They show that the work of the law is written on their hearts, while their conscience also bears witness, and their conflicting thoughts accuse or even excuse them" (Romans 2:14–15).

Praise to the Lord, the Almighty, the King of creation!
O my soul, praise Him, for He is thy Health and Salvation!
Join the full throng;
Wake, harp and Psalter and song;
Sound forth in glad adoration! Amen.

† *(TLH 39:1)*

Friday

Read Colossians 1:9

SAINT PAUL ADDRESSES the Colossians as if their knowledge of God had just dawned on them and only now could they grow in it. Man's natural knowledge of God has been so dimmed by sin, doubt, uncertainty, and false notions that it cannot give him peace or lead him to salvation. In his original state, man beheld God as in a picture, but now sin has blurred that image to the point that all he can see is God's footprints. The heathens, who had no immediate revelation of God, were able, by their natural knowledge, to come only to the point that they recognized that there must be an all-wise, good, and just Higher Being who is the originator and ruler of the universe, whom they are bound to worship in perfect righteousness. They did not, however, know precisely who God is and how He is disposed toward mankind. They knew they were obliged to serve Him and to live justly, but their conscience told them they did not, in fact, serve God and were not righteous as they should be. They knew God was good, but they continued to carry the knowledge of their own guilt and had no idea how they could be reconciled with Him. What good did this knowledge do them?

The natural knowledge of God is thus a limited knowledge, and His true being and will could not have been known had He not stepped out from His unapproachable light and revealed Himself to man. He would otherwise have remained an unknown God to all people, and all of the world's philosophers would have struggled in vain to investigate who He is. But behold! God has not left us orphans. He has indeed revealed Himself to us, and not just by raising up prophets, enlightening them with His Holy Ghost, and sending them out to preach His Word and the secrets of His essence and will. Above all, He Himself became a man, appeared on earth, and died for all people. In Christ, the secrets of all eternity and the will of God's own heart have been revealed to men. For in Christ we see what God has decreed from eternity for the salvation of humanity. Now no one can hopelessly cry out: "Oh, that I knew how God was disposed toward me! Oh, that I knew what God has decided about me!" Now each person can be answered: "If you want to learn to know God's heart and will toward you, look at Christ in the manger, in the circle of sinners that surrounded Him, in Gethsemane, and on the cross. There you can read God's heart as in an open book. For whoever sees Christ also sees God the Father. As you find nothing with Christ but kindness, love, and grace, so you can be certain that you will find all of this with the Father. Christ calls sinners to Himself, and He does not condemn them; instead, He forgives them their sins. And this is also what God does. He, too, wants to have mercy on you. Christ desires to take you up into His heavenly kingdom and so does the Father. To know the disposition of God's heart, you need only to look at how Christ is disposed toward you. His mercy is the reflection of the mercy of God. The sympathy of the Father is reflected in Christ's tears over the misfortune of the sinner. Christ's blood, which flowed for the atonement of the world, washed away the wrath of God, so He could proclaim, 'I am reconciled with men!' "

It is this knowledge of God and His will that Saint Paul is referring to when he declares in our text that he does not cease to pray that the Colossians may be filled with all kinds of spiritual wisdom and understanding. This is the knowledge of God in Christ.

Grant our hearts in fullest measure
Wisdom, counsel, purity,
That they ever may be seeking
Only that which pleaseth Thee.
Let Thy knowledge spread and grow,
Working error's overthrow. Amen.

(*TLH* 226:2)

Saturday

Read Colossians 1:10–14

TODAY'S TEXT DEMONSTRATES that the living knowledge of God in Christ produces glorious effects in each person in whose heart it has found room. Saint Paul says he prays that the Colossians will grow in the knowledge of God so they "walk in a manner worthy of the Lord, fully pleasing to Him, bearing fruit in every good work" (Colossians 1:10). This is the first result of the knowledge of God in Christ. As soon as it is revealed to a person that God has loved him from eternity—that He so fervently loved him He became a man and died on the cross for him—that person must love this good God in return. He then has a holy fear of offending his gracious God and Father in heaven by any sin. He also has a holy impulse to live to please Him in everything and to love his neighbor and to do good to him, as God loved and did good to him.

Paul continues, "[And that you be] be strengthened with all power, according to His glorious might, for all endurance and patience with joy" (Colossians 1:11). Here the apostle gives us the second result of a living knowledge of God in Christ: the might and patience for the glorious perseverance in the cross. The person who has not yet learned to know God as his Father in Christ will find it impossible to joyfully endure many, great, and lengthy sufferings and afflictions. But how completely different it is with those who vividly recognize that God is their dear Father and they are His dear children! People with this knowledge have a firm staff that will not let them fall. They have an unconquerable faith that God intends good for them and that their afflictions are fatherly disciplines rather than punishments, disciplines that lead to salvation, heaven, blessedness, and glory. For this reason, Paul says, in affliction and joyful in hope.

Our text concludes: "[And that you give] thanks to the Father, who has qualified you to share in the inheritance of the saints in light. He has delivered us from the domain of darkness and transferred us to the kingdom of His beloved Son, in whom we have redemption, the forgiveness of sins" (Colossians 1:12–14). Here we find the third and final effect of a living knowledge of God in Christ: a constant, fervent thanks. Praising and thanking God, which will be the main business of all saints in heaven, should also be the most precious occupation of all people here on earth. This is what distinguishes people from animals: people demonstrate their enjoyment of the gifts of God by thanking the Giver, whereas animals know nothing about the Giver. However, as long as a person does not vividly know God as his Father, his heart is cold in praise and thanks, for no matter how much he already has, he remains without happiness and thinks there is much more he needs to acquire to attain that happiness. However, as soon as he discovers the source of true happiness—the living knowledge of God in Christ—he finds himself so overwhelmed with inexpressible blessings that he must praise God even in the midst of poverty, shame, pain, sickness, and death. His heart cannot help but thank God for his wonderful deliverance from the power of darkness, for his translation into Christ's kingdom of grace, for his redemption by Christ's precious blood, and for Christ's gracious forgiveness of his sins.

My heart's Delight, My Crown most bright,
Thou, Jesus, art forever.
Nor wealth nor pride Nor aught beside
Our bond of love shall sever.
Thou art my Lord; Thy precious Word
Shall be my guide, Whate'er betide.
Oh, teach me, Lord, to trust Thee! Amen.

† *(TLH 383:4)*

Sunday

Read Matthew 24:15–28

THERE ONCE WAS A TIME when Christ was almost completely silenced in Christendom. This was the time before the Reformation. Mary and the so-called saints had almost entirely displaced Christ from Christianity and occupied His place. There is no longer such a silence about Christ. Indeed, He is preached everywhere. "Here is Christ! There is Christ!" many thousands of preachers exclaim.

Although the factions in Christendom have different beliefs, there is none that does not accord Christ His rightful place as the author and authority of its doctrines. Excluding the few in Christianity who speak disgracefully about Christ and are regarded by all civilized people everywhere as immoral and filthy deniers of God, almost all who praise something as moral, higher wisdom declare that the germ of it is hidden in the doctrine of Christ.

It would thus seem that the status of the Christian Church is now considerably better than it was before the Reformation. It even appears to be flourishing. Thus the person who regards the present as the horrible end times is thought to be greatly mistaken. But appearances can be deceiving. The cry of "Here is Christ! There is Christ!" that resounds from so many pulpits is precisely what makes our age so dangerous and abominable, and it demonstrates that the final, evil days of the world are approaching. For it is mostly a false Christ who is now being preached and praised in order to deceive even the elect. There are now many preachers and laity, both learned and unlearned individuals, who no longer believe the Bible is God's Word and faith in Christ is the only way to salvation. With their own imagined virtue and good works, they believe that they have made God their debtor, that He must rightfully receive them into heaven after their death, and that He must eternally reward them. They do not want to think of themselves as sinners who are in need of a Savior. The Word of the cross is foolishness and a stumbling block to them.

Nevertheless, despite their obvious rejection of Christ and His Gospel, they highly praise Him. They call Him the Wisest One, the Most Godly, and the Only Master, who stands far above all of the human teachers who ever lived. They present Him as the highest example of a truly virtuous person whom one must follow. They even grant that Christ can be called the Son of God in a special sense, for He must have stood in an especially close connection with the Divine. Thousands of those who hear Christ preached in this manner allow themselves to be tricked out of the salvation of their souls, God, heaven, and blessedness. For wherever one preaches Christ as a mere man and not as the true God, fully of the same substance, power, and glory as the heavenly Father, one preaches a false Christ. Wherever one presents Christ only as an example and as a teacher of wisdom and virtue, and not as the Lamb of God who died on the cross for the sins of the world and thereby reconciled mankind with the heavenly Father, one preaches a false Christ. And whoever accepts this Christ of the unbelievers has forsaken the true Christ and placed His confidence in a dream being, one who never existed except in the imagination of unbelieving fools. Christ Himself says, "I and the Father are one" (John 10:30), "Whoever has seen Me has seen the Father" (John 14:9), and "all may honor the Son, just as they honor the Father" (John 5:23).

The haughty spirits, Lord, restrain
Who o'er Thy Church with might would reign
And always set forth something new,
Devised to change Thy doctrine true. Amen.

(TLH 292:6)

Monday

Read 2 Corinthians 11:13–14

THERE ARE FACTIONS in Christendom that clearly and distinctly teach that Christ is the true Son of God, the Savior, and the Reconciler of sinners—but they still lead countless souls away from the only foundation of salvation. They confess with great zeal that Christ is the true God and eternal life who sacrificed Himself on the cross for the debt of the whole world's sins. If inexperienced believers hear such things, they are absolutely confident that these preachers are proclaiming the true Christ.

However, their Christ is a false one for two reasons. First, the true Christ imparts Himself alone through the Word and the holy Sacraments. He says, "You search the Scriptures because you think that in them you have eternal life; and it is they that bear witness about Me" (John 5:39). Saint Paul declares, "So faith comes from hearing, and hearing through the word of Christ" (Romans 10:17), and Saint Peter adds, "we have something more sure, the prophetic word, to which you will do well to pay attention as to a lamp shining in a dark place, until the day dawns and the morning star [that is, Christ] rises in your hearts" (2 Peter 1:19).

But what do the false believers do? They have little regard for the Word. They call it a dead letter, oppose it with the spirit, and say that not the Word, not the letter, but the spirit must do it! What kind of Christ can they have received without the Word? A false Christ. Scripture says further, "This is He who came by water and blood—Jesus Christ; not by the water only, but by the water and the blood. ... For there are three that testify: the Spirit and the water and the blood; and these three agree" (1 John 5:6–8). Saint Paul writes, "For as many of you as were baptized into Christ have put on Christ" (Galatians 3:27), and "The cup of blessing that we bless, is it not a participation in the blood of Christ? The bread that we break, is it not a participation in the body of Christ?" (1 Corinthians 10:16).

But what do the false believers do? They think little of Baptism and Holy Communion. They declare reliance upon them to be the deception of a fleshly heart. What kind of

Christ can they preach without the Sacraments instituted by Christ? A false Christ.

The second reason why the Christ of such sects is a false one is this: a person can acquire the true Christ only through faith. Christ says, "Blessed are those who have not seen and yet have believed" (John 20:29). Furthermore, Paul writes, "For by grace you have been saved through faith. And this is not your own doing; it is the gift of God, not a result of works, so that no one may boast" (Ephesians 2:8–9); "It is no longer I who live, but Christ who lives in me. And the life I now live in the flesh I live by faith in the Son of God" (Galatians 2:20); "And to the one who does not work but trusts Him who justifies the ungodly, his faith is counted as righteousness" (Romans 4:5); and "So then it depends not on human will or exertion, but on God, who has mercy" (Romans 9:16).

But what do false believers do? They teach that a person must earn grace. They prescribe a special degree of repentance that one must first experience. They maintain that only when a person has a special feeling of Christ's grace in his heart is he able to comfort himself with Christ. In short, they do not teach that a person acquires Christ through simple faith in His Word and His grace alone. They build upon what they do, what they experience, what they feel, and what they perceive, and they then call this "having Christ." What kind of Christ can this be? A false Christ.

As today's reading points out, such sham christs were already preached here and there in the apostles' own time. May the one who wants to be warned in this last, evil time be warned!

Thou holy Light, Guide Divine,
Oh, cause the Word of Life to shine!
Teach us to know God aright
And call him Father with delight.

From ev'ry error keep us free;
Let none but Christ our Master be
That we in living faith abide,
In Him, our Lord, with all our might confide.
Hallelujah! Hallelujah! Amen.

(*TLH* 224:2)

Tuesday

Read Galatians 2:16–17

A PERSON who outwardly adheres to the orthodox Church, who is convinced of the correctness of pure doctrine and confesses it with his mouth, is called an orthodox Christian. He thus also supports the doctrine that Christ is the Son of God and the Savior of sinners, that the Word of God and the holy Sacraments are the only means of grace, and that a person will be saved by grace through faith alone. Such an individual is generally regarded to be an orthodox Christian if he leads an outwardly decent life, and the last thing one would expect of him is that he secretly carries a false Christ in his heart.

But with so many so-called believers, this is entirely the case! There is a great difference between being convinced of something and carrying it in the heart, and regarding something as true and practicing it in life. A person may consider a certain way to be correct, and he may even show it to others, while he himself does not choose to pursue it. There are two classes of orthodox believers who still carry a false Christ in their heart. First, there are many who know that Christ receives all sinners if only they come to Him longing for His grace. These believers confess this grace and extol it to others who are anxious about their salvation. But if they are plagued by their sins and by a bad conscience, if they clearly see how corrupt their heart is and how reprehensible their entire life is, they say to themselves: "I cannot go to Christ. He will not receive me. Instead, He will be angry with me. He will send me away." Such Christians imagine Christ only as an angry Judge who does not want to have mercy on sinners, but only on the godly and worthy.

Isn't this an obviously false Christ? Doesn't Holy Scripture sketch a completely different picture of Him? Yes, indeed. It says He came into the world not to judge the world, but that the world might be saved through Him. It declares Him to be the most gracious Friend of sinners, noting, "The saying is trustworthy and deserving of full acceptance, that Christ Jesus came into the world to save sinners" (1 Timothy 1:15). Christ Himself says: "For the Son of Man came to seek and to save the lost" (Luke 19:10).

The second type of so-called orthodox Christians, on the contrary, maintains that with Christ, a person can continue to sin safely. These individuals portray Christ as a servant of sin. They, too, have a false Christ in their heart. Christ wants to cover our sins, but He also wants to take them away. He wants to clothe us with His righteousness, but He also wants to take shape in us, to be the High Priest who reconciles us with God, and to be the King who rules over and in us. He suffered and died to atone for our sins, but He also rose and ascended into heaven that He might live in us and we in Him and so we might walk in a new life. For this reason, "No one who abides in Him keeps on sinning; no one who keeps on sinning has either seen Him or known Him. . . . The reason the Son of God appeared was to destroy the works of the devil" (1 John 3:6,8).

Therefore, whoever has trusted in a Christ who would allow him to remain in his sins yet to come into heaven without repentance, without conversion, without sanctification, and without self-denial needs to know that there is no such Christ. His Christ is a false Christ, who will not rescue Him from death, damnation, and judgment, but will forsake him in the greatest distress. Whoever wants the right Christ must turn to Him whom God made our wisdom, righteousness, sanctification, and redemption. With Him there is salvation. He helps against sin, trouble, and death. To Him be praise and glory in eternity.

Lord, let Thy woes, Thy patience,
My heart with strength inspire
To vanquish all temptations
And spurn all base desire.
This thought I fain would cherish most—
What pain my soul's redemption
Hath Thee, O Savior, cost! Amen.

(ELHB 197:5)

Wednesday

Read Philippians 1:18

"ONLY THAT . . . Christ is proclaimed" (Philippians 1:18). These words are often heard, but how do people understand them? They think that as long as a preacher confesses in his sermons that Christ is God's Son and that He died for people, then this is enough. It does not matter how many errors he may have in regard to other points of Christian doctrine. Today, when a Christian insists upon pure doctrine and declines to have fellowship with false teachers and heterodox churches, people respond: "Have you not read what Saint Paul writes to the Philippians? Doesn't he say, 'Only that . . . Christ is proclaimed'? Paul was no narrow-minded man like you. He was satisfied if a preacher only proclaimed Christ. He declared this to be the main thing. Every other doctrine was of only secondary importance for him, and differences could be expected among Christians where they were concerned. Paul maintained fellowship with those who merely proclaimed Christ, and he declared them to be his brothers even if they deviated from him in other articles of faith."

Many well-intentioned people allow themselves to be deceived by this exposition of Paul's words. They believe they stand upon the foundation of the Word of God even when they do not hold fast to pure doctrine, choosing instead to participate in the outward union now established among various churches that are not unified in all articles of faith. Consider what Paul writes in the verses that precede today's reading: "Some indeed preach Christ from envy and rivalry, but others from good will. The latter do it out of love. . . . The former proclaim Christ out of rivalry, not sincerely but thinking to afflict me in my imprisonment" (Philippians 1:15–17). To this, he adds: "What then? Only that in every way . . . Christ is proclaimed, and in that I rejoice" (Philippians 1:18). Is Paul really saying here that it does not matter if a person preaches Christ purely or if he preaches Him with false doctrine? Of course not! Instead, as the context reveals, Paul is stressing that Christ is preached with a variety of intentions. Some preach Him rightly and purely, out of love, while others preach Him rightly and purely while they are motivated by insincerity, envy, and strife. The evil intention of some preachers does not make their good preaching of Christ evil or powerless. The preacher himself is certainly reprehensible, but his confession of Christ is not. It remains the power of God to save all who believe in it. For this reason, "Only that . . . Christ is proclaimed."

As sad as it is for the one who preaches Christ insincerely, we can still rejoice over the souls who are led to salvation by it. Paul confirms our interpretation with what he says elsewhere. To the Galatians, who were hearing about Christ with false doctrines mixed in, he writes: "A little leaven leavens the whole lump" (5:9), and "You are severed from Christ, you who would be justified by the law; you have fallen away from grace" (5:4). We can clearly see from this that it is not enough that Christ is preached. He must also be preached rightly and purely, for there is also a false Christ.

O mighty Rock, O Source of Life,
Let Thy dear Word, mid doubt and strife,
Be strong within us burning
That we be faithful unto death,
In Thy pure love and holy faith,
From Thee true wisdom learning.
Thy grace And peace
On us shower; By Thy power
Christ confessing,
Let us win our Savior's blessing. Amen.

(TLH 235:6)

Thursday

Read Psalm 11:3

AFTER A TIME of domination by rationalism, the Church has entered a period of more certain faith. From universities and pulpits and in religious newspapers, Christianity is once again frequently praised as a religion of supernatural, divine revelation and truth, whereas insolent unbelief repeatedly opposes all mysteries and miracles of Christianity. Unfortunately, representatives of the present so-called faith have not returned to the doctrines of the early Church, declaring instead that the "old system" can no longer be maintained in light of new research or science. Some say the old articles of faith must be abandoned, while others maintain that the old foundation must be built upon if the Church is to make progress. (Both views amount to the same thing, of course.) They claim that the time in which the emphasis was placed on preserving familiar doctrine was a time of strife and is now thankfully past, and they lament that others want to return to that "sad" age.

Under the name of Christianity, then, a new religion has appeared. It retains the title of the old articles of faith but attaches a completely different sense to them, thus deceiving countless inexperienced believers. Like the earlier paganism, it changes the truth into a lie. By the divinity of Christ, a certain godliness is understood. By the Church of the Third Article, which we believe, a visible institution is understood; that is, among the communion of saints and believers, there is a kingdom of rulers and subjects. By the office of ministry of servants of the Church, a special, privileged condition is understood. By the royal priesthood of Christians, the freedom in pious exercises is understood. By the hopes of the

Church, a future thousand-year visible glory on earth is understood. By the gracious, free gift of faith, the free decision of a person is understood. By death, departure to a middle kingdom is understood. The doctrine of justification alone by grace through faith is no longer considered the heart and soul of all doctrine; instead, it is now regarded in terms of holiness and good works as evidence of a Christianity that is more lively than in the so-called good old days.

The most frightening thing about this complete transformation of the Christian faith in our day concerns the role of the teacher. It is the total defection from the most supreme principle in all of Christianity: that Holy Scripture is the Word of the great God. Theologians declare that the idea that every word of Scripture is given by the Holy Ghost is no longer tenable. God's Word can indeed be found in the Scriptures, but these are two entirely different things. Therefore, the right doctrine of Christ cannot be established from individual verses of Scripture, but only from the whole of Scripture. Uncovering this right doctrine is therefore a matter for the learned ones of the Church. Thus, what David writes of the manifest enemies of the faith now applies to the so-called faithful: "The foundations are destroyed" (Psalm 11:3).

God's Word is our great heritage
And shall be ours forever;
To spread its light from age to age
Shall be our chief endeavor.
Through life it guides our way,
In death it is our stay.
Lord, grant, while worlds endure,
We keep its teachings pure
Throughout all generations. Amen.

† *(TLH 283)*

Friday

Read John 17:17

PEOPLE WILL READILY AGREE that God's Word is the truth, but they find much of it difficult to understand. Even heretics, they say, appeal to Scripture, but many thousands who have believed in the Word have been in error. It is true that a person who believes in the Word can be in error, but not in the basic doctrines of the faith if he firmly clings to them. God's Word is not dark and misleading; instead, it is clear and certain in all articles of faith. "We also have," Peter writes, "the prophetic word, to which you will do well to pay attention as to a lamp shining in a dark place" (2 Peter 1:19).

The fact that even those who believe in Holy Scripture err in articles of faith is not because God's Word is unclear and misleading, but simply because those believers too often follow their reason, their conceit, their heart, their prejudices, or the authority of man instead of the clear Word of God. Why, for example, do the Reformed churches not believe in the bodily presence of the body and blood of Christ in Holy Communion? Are Christ's words, "This is My body . . . this is My blood" (Matthew 26:26, 28), not distinct and clear? Why is there such uncertainty about the regenerating and saving power of Baptism? Aren't Christ's words, "unless one is born of water and the Spirit, he cannot enter the kingdom of God" (John 3:5) and "Whoever believes and is baptized will be saved" (Mark 16:16), distinct and clear? Why do so many fail to believe in the gracious, divine will and in the universal redemption of Christ? Aren't the words of God, "[God is] not wishing that any should perish" (2 Peter 3:9) and "[Christ Jesus] gave Himself as a ransom for all" (1 Timothy 2:6), distinct and clear? Why do so many fail to accept Christ's omnipresence according to His humanity? Aren't His words, which He spoke while in His state of humiliation, "No one has ascended into heaven except him who descended from heaven, the Son of Man" (John 3:13), distinct and clear?

Why do some believers continue to insist that the Christian is not free from the law of a special Sabbath day? Isn't the Word of God, "Therefore let no one pass judgment on you in questions of food and drink, or with regard to a festival or a new moon or a Sabbath. These are a shadow of the things to come, but the substance belongs to Christ" (Colossians 2:16–17), distinct and clear? Why is it that many deny that all faithful Christians of the New Testament possess the priestly office and, with it, all priestly rights, charges, and powers? Isn't the Word of God, "But you are a chosen race, a royal priesthood, a holy nation, a people for his own possession, that you may proclaim the excellencies of Him who called you out of darkness into His marvelous light" (1 Peter 2:9), distinct and clear? Why are so many reluctant to believe that the congregation has the final judgment in the Church? Isn't the word of Christ, "If he refuses to listen to them, tell it to the church. And if he refuses to listen even to the church, let him be to you as a Gentile and a tax collector" (Matthew 18:17), distinct and clear?

Why do so many deny the doctrine that the Church of Christ, in the proper sense, is not a visible institution but an invisible kingdom? Isn't Christ's word, "The kingdom of God is not coming with signs to be observed, nor will they say, 'Look, here it is!' or 'There!' for behold, the kingdom of God is in the midst of you" (Luke 17:20–21), distinct and clear? Why do so many dream of a special thousand-year glory of the Church at the end of days? Isn't Christ's word, "when the Son of Man comes, will He find faith on earth?" (Luke 18:8), distinct and clear? Finally, why do so many consider the doctrine of the divinity of the Word to be an open question, and why must this be endured in the Church? Isn't God's word, "Do you not know that a little leaven leavens the whole lump?" (1 Corinthians 5:6), and "but let him who has My word speak My word faithfully. What has straw in common with wheat?" (Jeremiah 23:28), distinct and clear?

As long as we stand upon God's Word without wavering, we can be confident, for in the clear Scriptures, we have the infallible truth.

How firm a foundation, ye saints of the Lord,
Is laid for your faith in His excellent Word!
What more can He say than to you He hath said
Who unto the Savior for refuge have fled?

† *(TLH 427:1)*

Saturday

Read 2 Peter 3:3–4

IN HOLY SCRIPTURE, the Christian Church is likened to a field in which weeds grew among the wheat until the end of days, to a wedding hall in which not all of those present wore a wedding garment, and to a net in which both good and rotten fish were caught. Therefore, it should not be difficult to understand that there never was a completely pure Church and that many in the Church who were baptized in the Church and bore the name Christian denied this name and their Baptism with their works. This corruption, which has always existed in the midst of the Christian Church, was never as great as it is today.

True, it was particularly frightening in Luther's time. The Abomination of Desolation, prophesied by Daniel and Christ, then stood in the holy place; the great falling away, which Paul had announced beforehand, took place; the man of sin and the son of perdition, the Antichrist, sat in the temple of God, was worshiped instead of Christ Himself, and introduced his human commandments in place of the Gospel. Although he had forbidden Christians to read the Bible, he still did not dare to annul Scripture itself, declaring it to be the word of man and a book of fables. Therefore, because God's Word was still valued in all of troubled Christendom, a reformation of the Church was still possible at that time. The foundation of the Church had not yet been pulled down, and thus, with God's help, it could again be built upon and the temple of God could be gloriously raised.

But what is the situation today? The prophecy of Saint Peter has been fulfilled: "scoffers will come in the last days with scoffing, following their own sinful desires. They will say, 'Where is the promise of His coming? For ever since the fathers fell asleep, all things are continuing as they were from the beginning of creation' " (2 Peter 3:3–4). Isn't Christendom full of scoffers who no longer believe in the promise and threat of God and to whom the thought of a Last Day is as ridiculous as the destruction of Sodom by fire and sulfur once seemed to the people of that city? Hasn't the foundation of the Christian Church now been pulled down? Are there not millions of people who were once baptized in the name of the triune God who no longer regard and declare God's Word to be God's Word but rather a miserable book of fairy tales and myths? Yes! In addition, are there not many who want to be faithful Christians, but who are so poisoned by unbelief and by the false explanations of our age that they can no longer believe much of what is written in the Bible, rejecting this or that portion, or preferring instead to follow their own reason, their own heart, or the principles of the world? Are there not many Christians who are ashamed to confess the sayings of the Old and New Testaments, which are troubling and offensive to arrogant and freedom-loving individuals?

Oh, that God in heaven would have mercy on us! Today, even the faithful have become unbelievers. A reformation, therefore, appears to be impossible. It is clear that the world is declining. The examples of the Flood, Sodom and Gomorrah, and the destruction of Jerusalem are being fulfilled before our eyes. The darkness of the midnight hour of the world has come upon us. The Judge already stands at the door. The hammer of the world's clock has been raised in order to announce the expiration of the last hour. God's army, the angels of the Lord of the heavenly hosts, stand in battle formation to fight the great battle of the Last Day. In but a few minutes of the world's time, God's trumpet will sound.

Though with a scornful wonder
Men see her sore oppressed,
By schisms rent asunder,
By heresies distressed,
Yet saints their watch are keeping;
Their cry goes up, "How long?"
And soon the night of weeping
Shall be the morn of song. Amen.

† *(TLH 473:4)*

The Purification of Mary February 2

Read Luke 2:22–32

On his deathbed, the person who has not thought about his death and his soul's salvation during his life, and who has served himself and the world instead of the Lord, is horrified to learn he has no hope of recovery and he must die. Compare this to the deathbed of one who has faithfully served the Lord during his life. Take old, pious Simeon, for example. Does he turn pale and appear frightened at the news that he will soon die? No! His weak eyes light up with joy at this announcement. Taking the Savior in his arms, he begins to praise God with an eloquent voice, saying, "Lord, now You are letting Your servant depart in peace, according to Your word; for my eyes have seen Your salvation that You have prepared in the presence of all peoples, a light for revelation to the Gentiles, and for glory to Your people Israel" (Luke 2:29–32).

This is the way in which a person who has served the Lord while he was healthy, perhaps even from his youth, dies. He has already experienced the horrors of death in his repentance, and he has overcome them by Christ's blood. Now death, disarmed of its horrors, comes to him as a messenger of peace. Old servants of the Lord, such as Simeon, are not distressed because they must be removed from the world by death. They have already forsaken this evil world and longed to be at home with the Lord. They do not grieve because they must leave their loved ones behind. They have loved them faithfully and heartily, but they have always loved their Savior more. If they leave behind sorrowing widows and crying children, they are still comforted. They have often experienced in this life how the

Lord never forsakes His own. They say to them, with Jacob: "Behold, I am about to die, but God will be with you" (Genesis 48:21); and they encourage them by saying, "remain faithful in love, suffering, and hope, and there we will see each other again and eternally rejoice with inexpressible joy."

The faithful servant of the Lord also does not sorrow because he must surrender the shell of his body to the dust and to worms for food. He has already often longed for peace in the grave. With his body, he lays aside a burden that often pressed hard upon him, and he says, with Job, "For I know that my Redeemer lives, and at the last He will stand upon the earth" (19:25). He is not frightened as he looks back on his life and looks ahead toward judgment and eternity. He remembers many sins of the past, yet he can say: "Who shall bring any charge against God's elect? It is God who justifies. Who is to condemn? Christ Jesus is the one who died—more than that, who was raised—who is at the right hand of God, who indeed is interceding for us" (Romans 8:33–34); and "There is therefore now no condemnation for those who are in Christ Jesus" (Romans 8:1).

When such a servant of the Lord looks ahead to eternity, he does not see anything dreadful. During his lifetime, he has made his calling and election sure. Thus he now stands before the gates of death without frightful expectation. He knows he will not come into judgment. He was not ashamed of Jesus here, but confessed Him before the world as his Savior. Thus he knows his Savior will not be ashamed of him in heaven, but will there confess him as one of His own before God and all of His angels. Therefore, his death is no death. It is a blessed journey into the mansions of eternal peace. Full of longing, he looks forward to his last breath. He stretches forth his arms of faith and sighs: "Come soon. Amen! Yes, come, Lord Jesus!" And so he slumbers gently and silently, and he goes over into the land of perfect joy.

There still my thoughts are dwelling,
'Tis there I long to be;
Come, Lord, and call Thy servant
To blessedness with Thee.
Come, bid my toils be ended,
Let all my wand'rings cease;
Call from the wayside lodging
To Thy sweet home of peace. Amen.

† *(TLH 586:6)*

The Annunciation to Mary March 25

Read Luke 1:26–38

THE EVENT REPORTED in today's reading is the greatest, most wonderful, and most incomprehensible of all the mysteries of the Christian religion. The Gospel says that an angel from heaven tells a virgin, named Mary, that by the power of the Most High and by the overshadowing of the Holy Ghost, she will become the mother of God's Son.

This is, indeed, a truly remarkable mystery. To consider it carefully is like looking into the flaming midday sun with the naked eye. The longer one looks at it, the darker it appears. But it retains all the marks of a great mystery worthy of God. It is, first of all, worthy of the divine wisdom, which does nothing idly or unnecessarily, but has a great and important goal for everything it undertakes. Everyone must admit that all people are sinful creatures, and no one can prove from his own understanding the manner in which a sinful person can become pleasing, just, and holy before God. Thus there is nothing more important for us than for God Himself to reveal how mankind could be reconciled with Him. This way of reconciliation was revealed in the incarnation. Scripture says that God became man in order to save fallen mankind and to make it pleasing to Him. Was this means unworthy of God? Certainly not! God Himself became a man in order to be able, by His suffering and death, to blot out the sins of all people and redeem them so all who believe can be saved. In the redemption of man, God revealed His holiness and His love, the magnitude of which is incalculable. How inviolable must be the holiness and justice of God if He could first forgive man only after the endurance of all the punishment their sins merited. And how unthinkably great must be His love, which caused Him to lay upon His only-begotten Son all of mankind's sins and to give Him up in disgrace, suffering, and death upon the cross to pay the penalty no creature was able to bear.

God had already revealed His holiness and righteousness when He gave the Law, with its strict demands and dire threats, and when He threw fallen man into distress and death by permitting terrible judgments to come. But what is this in comparison to God being unable to save any sinner unless His dear Son Himself had endured the punishments of their sin? And He had already revealed His love when He created man, gave him the whole earth with the fullness of its goods and pleasures, and preserved and provided for the human race after it fell away from Him. But what is this in comparison to God's becoming a man in order to reconcile all people with Himself by surrendering His own life?

In the mystery of the incarnation, God appears as a being of incomprehensible wisdom, of the highest holiness, and of eternal and all-encompassing love. What mystery could therefore be more worthy of God?

The Son obeyed His Father's will,
Was born of virgin mother,
And God's good pleasure to fulfill,
He came to be my Brother.
No garb or pomp or power He wore;
A servant's form, like mine, He bore,
To lead the devil captive. Amen.

† *(TLH 387:6)*

Saint John the Baptizer
June 24

Read Luke 1:57–66

THE CIRCUMSTANCES SURROUNDING the birth of John are extraordinary. First, his birth had been proclaimed 800 years before the fact. The prophets had said of him, "A voice cries: 'In the wilderness prepare the way of the LORD; make straight in the desert a highway for our God'" (Isaiah 40:3), and "Behold, I send My messenger and he will prepare the way before Me. And the Lord whom you seek will suddenly come to His temple; and the messenger of the covenant in whom you delight" (Malachi 3:1).

When the time drew near in which John, the forerunner of Christ, was to be born, the angel Gabriel proclaimed it to his father, Zechariah. Here, God revealed a wonder of wonders. Elizabeth, an old woman, was to become John's mother. When Zechariah, a priest, went to burn incense, as was his duty, Gabriel appeared to him and announced that he would have a son in his old age. The disbelieving Zechariah replied: "How shall I know this? For I am an old man, and my wife is advanced in years" (Luke 1:18). The angel answered him, "I am Gabriel, who stands in the presence of God, and I was sent to speak to you and to bring you this good news. And behold, you will be silent and unable to speak until the day that these things take place, because you did not believe my words" (Luke 1:19–20).

And it happened just as the angel had foretold. Zechariah came out of the temple, before which a crowd of people had gathered, but he could not address them because God had bound his tongue. When, finally, John was born, neighbors and friends rejoiced with the happy mother. On the day of his circumcision, ignorant of God's command, the people wanted to name the child after his father, but Elizabeth, to whom the decree of God had been revealed, said, "No; he shall be called John" (Luke 1:60). The guests were surprised and said, "None of your relatives is called by this name" (Luke 1:61). They then turned to the father and asked him what he wanted to name his son. Unable to speak, Zechariah took a tablet and wrote, "His name is John" (Luke 1:63). And at that very moment, his tongue was loosed, and he began to praise God. Astonished, the neighbors added their own chorus of praise to the One whose invisible hand they could not fail to recognize here.

Soon the wonderful story of the birth of John resounded throughout the Jewish community. But this did not happen for the glorification of John, but for the glorification of Christ, whom John would proclaim and reveal. Honor was accorded the servant only so we could recognize the infinitely greater glory of the Lord. Attention was paid to the forerunner only so we would be that much more attentive to the inexpressibly greater grandeur of the Coming One. Because Isaiah had already preached about John's coming, we can be sure that the sending of Jesus Christ had been decided from eternity. Gabriel had to announce John's birth, and from this we should recognize that all of the heavenly hosts must serve Christ. John was filled with the Holy Ghost and His joy even while he was still in his mother's womb. This is a reflection of the infinitely greater measure with which Christ was anointed with the Spirit at His conception.

An old woman was miraculously enabled to be John's mother, and Christ was born of the Virgin by the overshadowing of the Holy Ghost. According to God's command, the forerunner of Christ was named John, that is, "a pardoned one," and Jesus is the Savior, the Bringer of grace, as His name indicates. As soon as he returned to faith in God's promises, Zechariah was freed from his sins and filled with the Holy Ghost. This tells us that faith in Christ blots out all guilt and punishment, and adorns our hearts with the gifts of the Spirit. At the birth of John, the whole region was rocked with joy, and at the birth of Christ, the whole world should be filled with joy, wonder, and praise of God.

Oh, what an extraordinary preparation God thus made for us to extol His dear Son even before He was born!

Oh, grant, Thou Lord of Love,
That we receive, rejoicing,
The word proclaimed by John,
Our true repentance voicing;
That gladly we may walk
Upon our Savior's way
Until we live with Him
In His eternal day. Amen.

(TLH 272:5)

The Visitation
July 2

Read Luke 1:39–56

IF WE EXAMINE, in only a little detail, the picture that today's reading sketches of the three-month visit Mary paid to Elizabeth, we must wonder at the blessed time they spent together. They approached each other with the greatest of respect. As the mother of the Lord, Mary was more highly favored than Elizabeth, who was to become the mother of Christ's servant and forerunner, but she still greeted Elizabeth respectfully at the entrance to her house. And as soon as Elizabeth caught sight of Mary, she broke forth with the words: "Blessed are you among women, and blessed is the fruit of your womb! And why is this granted to me that the mother of my Lord should come to me?" (Luke 1:42–43).

Elizabeth, who could easily have claimed to be above the young girl, instead humbled herself most deeply and declared herself to be completely unworthy of a visit from the woman who carried the Lord in her womb. Each of them explained the great thing the Lord had done for them, and they took turns in praising and glorifying God. They did not speak a single idle word. Mary's entire hymn of praise was composed of passages from the prophets. God's Word, and above all the promise of the Messiah and the fulfillment of this prophecy, was the subject of all their conversation. How quickly the three months must have elapsed, and how sweet a time it must have been!

The relationships believing Christians cultivate among one another are always precious, and this is so for the same reason that made the relationship between Mary and Elizabeth so dear. First, they trusted each other and were confident that neither would be deceived by the other. A true Christian means what he says. If one is friendly, the other knows this friendliness comes from the heart. If one chastises the other, they both recognize that this is motivated by love and a concern for the soul. If one sins against the other, the one sinned against knows this was not done out of malice but as a result of weakness. The sinner is forgiven as soon as he recognizes his sin, and any possible brief disunity that can occur, even among Christians, results here in greater unity and love. True Christians, moreover, always approach one another with respect. None wants to offend another; rather, each is anxious to avoid any word or deed that could cause pain or grief for another. Each rejoices when another rejoices, and each regards himself as a greater sinner than another. He is therefore honored to receive a visit from even the humblest Christian, for he knows this individual carries within himself the Spirit of the Lord Jesus Christ, just as Mary carried Jesus bodily in her womb. He also knows that, in his fellow Christian, Christ is making a visit.

However, the one thing that, above all else, marks relationships among Christians is that they tell one another what has happened in their heart by God's grace and what the Lord has done for their soul. In general, they do not dwell on earthly things, but instead they focus on God's Word, spiritual matters, God's Church and kingdom—in short, on things that concern the salvation of the soul. Together, they praise and glorify God for every good thing He has shown to them and to others.

My soul doth magnify the Lord,
My spirit shall in God rejoice:
My low estate He did regard,
Exalting me by gracious choice. Amen.

† *(TLH 275:1)*

St. Michael and all Angels
September 29

Read Matthew 18:1–11

SCRIPTURE TEACHES US that there is another world, and just as the visible heaven surrounds the earth and gives it light and warmth, so the invisible heavenly world stands in closest connection with the earthly world. Scripture says that the angels are destined by God to be His instruments in the work of governing the world: "The angel of the LORD encamps around those who fear Him, and delivers them" (Psalm 34:7); "For He will command His angels concerning you to guard you in all your ways. On their hands they will bear you up, lest you strike your foot against a stone" (Psalm 91:11–12); and "Are they not all ministering spirits sent out to serve for the sake of those who are to inherit salvation?" (Hebrews 1:14).

In particular, today's text teaches us that God has commended to the angels the guardianship of our dear, weak, and often needy children. Nowhere in Scripture do we find a clear declaration that each person has a special guardian angel assigned to accompany him through life, but we do read that the godly are surrounded by a multitude of angels, that many angels protect each of the earth's cities and countries, and that, in war, the angels take the side that, according to God's will, should win.

Scripture gives us some glorious examples of the angels' activities. Angels led Lot out of Sodom to Zoar. Angels accompanied Eliezar and Jacob on their journey. Angels were appointed to protect the camp of the Israelite people. Angels guarded Job's house. Angels held the lions' mouths so they shut so would not devour Daniel. Angels protected the three faithful witnesses in the fiery oven. An angel opened the prison door for Peter and John. An angel struck down Herod, the enemy of Christ. The story of the prophet Elisha is especially lovely. The king of Syria had sent a great army, complete with horses and chariots, to surround the city of Dothan, in order to take Elisha prisoner. Trusting in the protection of the angels, Elisha took his servant and confidently went out into the city. The horrified servant saw the enemy warriors and didn't want to go on. But Elisha prayed to God that He would open the eyes of his servant's soul. And behold! He noticed that the mountain was covered with angels, horses, and chariots to protect Elisha.

The service angels perform continues without ceasing until the end of the world. If we believe this from the heart, mustn't this faith strengthen our trust in God's help in all situations? How alarmed do we become when we think of the constant dangers to which our helpless children are exposed? Who can watch over these inexperienced, inquisitive, and weak souls? How relieved we can feel if only we believe that the holy angels surround them, defend them, and rescue them! They are able to accomplish things that we, in our own weakness, cannot. How many dangers we have avoided in our vocation, thanks to their guardianship. With confidence and courage, we can pursue our calling, believing what Scripture teaches about the holy angels. They are God's hands by which we are continuously led. They are our invisible companions, receiving us upon our arrival in this world and continuing to accompany us throughout our life. They never leave us alone. They are with us each night so we can sleep peacefully. They encamp around our home like an army, ready to defend us against all evil. They are with us when our path leads us over mountains, through dark forests, and over rushing ocean waves. They protect us from precipices and false ways, and they prevent the bottomless depths from devouring our little ship. Even in the hour of our death, the presence and service of the angels continue, giving us ample reason for comfort and reassurance. As the angels refreshed the Savior when He struggled with death in the Garden of Gethsemane, so Christians, according to Scripture, can expect to receive the aid of the angels in their final battle. They gather around the deathbed, and when the soul leaves its mortal body, they bear it up into the blessed dwellings of the heavenly Father. Oh, what love of God we thus see revealed in the doctrine of the angels!

Lord God, we all to Thee give praise,
Thank-offerings meet to Thee we raise,
That Thou didst angel hosts create
Around Thy glorious throne to wait.

We also pray Thee to defend
By them unto the latter end
Thy fold, that little flock, O Lord,
That holds in honor Thy blest Word. Amen.

(ELHB 286:1, 12)

Reformation Day
October 31

Read Revelation 3:7–13

In today's reading, Christ clearly tells us how the true Church can be recognized: "I know that you have but little power, and yet you have kept My word and have not denied My name" (Revelation 3:8). Here we see that, outwardly, the

Christian Church has "a little power." It is powerless and insignificant before the world, but it keeps Christ's Word and confesses His name.

If we examine our Lutheran Church in light of this, we must say that it brightly bears these marks, as the sun does the light. If we consider the outward form of our Church, we must exclaim, with the prophet, "O afflicted one, storm-tossed and not comforted" (Isaiah 54:11). Nevertheless, Christ can say to us, as He did to the congregation at Philadelphia, "I know that you have but little power, and yet you have kept My word and have not denied My name." Why, then, did Luther separate himself from the church leaders in Rome? Was it because of misgivings of his reason? No. He was drawn into the great battle because he could not retreat from Holy Scripture. To cite only one example, what did he say when he stood before the emperor in Worms and was ordered to recant? He said: "Unless I am convinced by the testimony of the Holy Scriptures, or by patent, clear, and cogent reasons and arguments, and because the passages cited and quoted by me have convinced and grounded my conscience in God's Word, therefore I cannot and will not recant. Here I stand. I cannot do otherwise. God help me! Amen."

Luther was so minded, and this is also the mind of the Church that bears his name. This is not because Luther was the Church's leader, whom it unconditionally followed. It is not because it believed in Luther, but because it believes, as Luther did, in Christ's Word. The Lutheran Church was established upon the principle that the words of Scripture cannot be added to or taken away, and it still relies on that principle, which stands at the very top of its confession as its heart and life. If we are asked what a Lutheran is, we can offer no better answer than this: A Lutheran is a Christian who strictly keeps to the letter of the Scripture. This is the mark by which he is distinguished from all other Christians.

Just as our Church has kept Christ's Word, so it has also not denied Christ's name. Everyone who has read only a few pages of Luther's writings knows he faithfully confessed Christ's name. No other teacher since the time of the apostles has so clearly, comfortingly, and powerfully explained the doctrine of justification through faith in Christ. Luther wrote, "In my heart alone rules and should also rule this one article, that is, faith in my dear Lord Christ, who is the only beginning, middle, and end of all my spiritual and divine thoughts, which I may evermore have day and night." Our Lutheran Church has followed Luther's lead. Unlike any other church, it has, from its beginning, preached that a person becomes righteous only through faith in Christ, without the work of the Law. The eternal, golden foundation of faith and hope is not the work, repentance, contrition, betterment, sanctification, or suffering of man, but solely Christ's grace, merit, innocence, righteousness, active and passive obedience, suffering, and death. Our Church teaches all sinners to build upon this foundation.

Thus the Lutheran Church is the true Church of Christ on earth, for it has verified the praise that Christ, in our text, gave to His faithful church at Philadelphia: "You . . . have kept My word, and have not denied My name."

Lord Jesus Christ, with us abide,
For round us falls the eventide;
Nor let Thy Word, that heav'nly light,
For us be ever veiled in night.

Oh, keep us in Thy Word, we pray;
The guile and rage of Satan stay!
Oh, may Thy mercy never cease!
Give concord, patience, courage, peace. Amen.

(TLH 292:1, 4)

The Anniversary of a Church

Read Luke 19:1–10

IF IT WERE IMPOSSIBLE for a person to remain rich in earthly things and also obtain heavenly riches and salvation, a prime example of this would have been Zacchaeus. He resided in Jericho, a city cursed by God. Moreover, he was less likely than any other inhabitant of Judea to obtain eternal divine blessing because he was also a tax collector. Tax collectors were notorious in the ancient world. They took the tax the Romans levied upon the Jews, and they then used their office to enrich themselves at the expense of their own brothers in the faith. Not only did they mercilessly and forcibly collect high taxes from the poor as well as the rich, but they were accustomed to taking even more than what was demanded by the Romans in order to increase their own income. They were hard-hearted profiteers, liars, and frauds who had no mercy, even on widows, orphans, and the poor.

Zacchaeus was such a person. Indeed, our text reports that he was "a chief tax collector" (Luke 19:2), who had enriched himself not only by deceiving the citizenry himself, but also by the deceptions of the tax collectors who reported to him. Who would have thought that such a horrible sinner could come to faith and salvation? But he did so. Our text says Zacchaeus: "was seeking to see who Jesus was, but on account of the crowd he could not, because he was small of stature. So he ran on ahead and climbed up into a sycamore tree to see Him, for He was about to pass that way" (Luke 19:3–4). He may have said to himself: "Oh, if only I could see this Jesus just once and convince myself with my own eyes that He is really so kind and good, even toward great sinners! Perhaps this

Man could even help me out of my sins! If so, I would gladly give up my profession of sin!"

When Christ arrived in the city, Zacchaeus was waiting for Him. Christ called to him, "hurry and come down, for I must stay at your house today" (Luke 19:5). Zacchaeus quickly descended and "received Him joyfully" (Luke 19:6). The story of Zacchaeus ends with Christ's pronouncement, "Today salvation has come to this house, since he also is a son of Abraham. For the Son of Man came to seek and to save the lost" (Luke 19:9–10). Zacchaeus's desire to see Jesus was, at the same time, a desire to be delivered by Him from his sins and his misery. It was, in short, a desire of true faith. In this way, even a person who was godless and rich in earthly things was able to obtain heavenly riches and salvation. Zacchaeus heard of Christ's grace toward sinners, and this news so deeply seized his heart that he had an ardent longing to see this Jesus and to be rescued by Him. But Jesus did even more than Zacchaeus desired. He not only allowed Zacchaeus to see Him, but also invited Himself to be his guest. He entered the tax collector's home and assured him of salvation and blessedness despite the people's murmuring.

We see here how great is Christ's love for sinners and how great is the grace He acquires for His people. As soon as a person learns to recognize his misery and longs for Christ and His grace, he receives help, even if he is the greatest and most detestable of sinners. On the day when such a sinner gives up everything else and desires only to see Jesus in faith, then "salvation has come to [his] house . . . for the Son of Man came to seek and to save the lost."

Oh, draw us ever unto Thee,
Thou Friend of sinners, gracious Savior;
Help us that we may fervently
Desire Thy pardon, peace, and favor.

When guilty conscience doth reprove,
Reveal to us Thy heart of love.
May we, our wretchedness beholding,
See then Thy pardoning grace unfolding
And say: "To God all glory be:
My Savior, Christ, receiveth me." Amen.

(TLH 386:5)

The Day of General Confession

Read 1 Peter 4:4

THE FIRST CHRISTIANS seemed strange to the world because they did not participate in its works of vanity and its fleshly lusts. They were not indifferent to these things, but they separated themselves from them. Can we also say this about our Church? Unfortunately, no! There was a time when it seemed strange to the world that the members of our Church withdrew entirely, except in the civil realm, declining to cultivate any worldly fellowship. But now, it seems strange to the world that it meets members of our Church in its theaters, pleasure gardens, bars, and dance halls.

The first Christians also seemed strange to the world because they did not live in lovelessness and enmity, as the world does, but instead they were bound by heartfelt love for their brothers and sisters. Can we still say this about our Church? Unfortunately, no! Our old brotherly love has almost disappeared. What do we find in our congregations? Instead of covering our brother's sins, we uncover them and make them public. Instead of admonishing him to his face, like a brother, we slander him behind his back. Instead of seeking to save his good name, we ruin his reputation. Instead of excusing him, we take pains to make his guilt even greater. Instead of speaking good of him, we take pleasure in speaking evil of him. Instead of turning everything for the best, we interpret everything in the most evil way. Instead of grieving over the fall of our brother, we rejoice in having evidence to support our suspicions. Instead of chastising him out of love for his soul to improve, heal, and rescue him, we chastise him to take revenge on him. Brotherly love has so completely ceased to exist among many of us that some go before worldly authorities to make them arbitrators between brothers. The world is astonished to see that Christians are conducting themselves just like unbelievers—with slander, quarreling, hatred, and cruelty.

There was one more thing about the first Christians that appeared strange to the world. They were zealous for God and His Word. Can we say this about our Church today? Unfortunately, no! How many members of our congregations would be ready, like the first Christians, to gather daily, desiring not to neglect any instruction from God's Word? We hear complaints about too many gatherings, and people even stay away from worship services, especially when they are scheduled in the evening and on weekdays. It is getting to the point that we are beginning to fear that the more richly the Gospel is preached to us, the more many will say, as the Israelites once did, "we loathe this worthless food" (Numbers 21:5). The early Christians were ready to sacrifice their life to preserve even one of God's words in the Bible, but that can hardly be said about Christians today. Indeed, many find the old Lutheran strictness in doctrine and church discipline repugnant. Therefore, we have become ever more lax in raising our children. The terrible fruit of this is that our youth, having grown up without strict discipline, are inclined to say, "Let us burst their bonds apart and cast away their cords from us" (Psalm 2:3).

But it is still the day of salvation; it is still the acceptable time. Today, when we hear God's voice, let us not harden our hearts. If we have fallen, God wants to pick us up again. If we have strayed toward the path of error, God wants to lead us back to the path of righteousness. If we have sinned, God wants to forgive us. A day of repentance is a day of grace. God alone can help us. So let us, from the depths of our soul, call to Him for His mercy as we pray: *Kyrie eleison! Christe eleison! Kyrie eleison!* (Lord, have mercy! Christ have mercy! Lord, have mercy!).

Though alive, I'm dead in sin,
Lost to all good things by nature.
Holy Ghost, change me within,
Make of me a newborn creature;
For the flesh works ruination
And can never gain salvation.

Oh, create a heart in me
That in Thee, my God, believeth
And o'er the iniquity
Of my sins most truly grieveth.
When dark hours of woe betide me,
In the wounds of Jesus hide me. Amen.

† *(TLH 411:2, 4)*

Thanksgiving Day

Read Jeremiah 18:6

AMERICA IS ONE of the youngest nations on earth. It began toward the end of human history. This land was discovered only a little more than 500 years ago, and it was not even half a century ago that the last of our 50 states joined the union. However, as young as our country is, it has already surpassed most other nations, leaving them far behind in most important respects. It is certainly one of the world's most fortunate nations.

But what is the reason for this happy condition? When God wanted to show the prophet Jeremiah the ultimate reason for the destiny of His people, He led him into a pottery, where the potter, working at the wheel, threw away a marred vessel and made another, as it pleased him. The Lord said, "Behold, like the clay in the potter's hand, so are you in My hand, O house of Israel" (Jeremiah 18:6). The Lord said this, not only of Israel, but of all peoples and kingdoms. Thus, according to God's Word, our country, like all the others, is in God's hand; it, too, is like clay in the potter's hand. Who once put the idea in Columbus's heart that a land lay far to the west, on the other side of the Atlantic? Who safely carried his ships across that ocean, imbued him with courage to face the unknown, and gave him the resolve to continue his quest until the cry of "Land! Land!" sounded from the mast? Was it not God?

Who gave the authors of our Constitution the wisdom to draft that document? Was it not the Lord, from whom all wisdom comes? Who gave our land victory in the Revolutionary War? Was it not the Lord of Sabaoth, the Lord of hosts, who is the true Man of war, guiding the hearts of men, making one bold and another despondent? Have not many other countries that wanted to free themselves from tyrannical dominion, countries that had similar wise military leaders and that showed similar determination, strength, and willingness to sacrifice, been unable to accomplish this? Who has preserved America's freedom and blessed this nation so it has become a dwelling of earthly prosperity? Is it not the Lord, who nourished our love of freedom? Didn't the greatest and most glorious republics, like those of the Greeks and Romans, lose their freedom and decline? Didn't they willingly give up their freedom to one great leader for his strong government? And aren't there other republics that enjoy the same freedom as America, but harvest only the bitter fruit of intense party divisions? Who allowed the industry of America's citizens to triumph over all obstacles? Was it not the Lord, of whom it is written: "Unless the LORD builds the house, those who build it labor in vain. Unless the LORD watches over the city, the watchman stays awake in vain. It is in vain that you rise up early and go late to rest, eating the bread of anxious toil; for He gives to His beloved sleep" (Psalm 127:1–2).

Finally, who has given our country its geography, with its magnificent rivers, its fertile ground and manifold produce, and its seemingly inexhaustible sources of earthly wealth? Is it not the Lord, the Creator and Preserver of all things, who established this beautiful garden and kept it until this moment? Couldn't God have continued to keep the door of this western land shut, as He did for thousands of years? Couldn't He have let the Revolutionary War turn out miserably or, later, restored the land to European rule or surrendered it to a rebel conqueror? Couldn't He have depopulated the land and destroyed its wealth by a general crop failure or any number of other plagues on the land? Neither the wit nor the strength of man called our country into existence, but the

Lord. Neither the will nor the wisdom of man brought together people representing so many lands, ethnic groups, and languages, and united them into one great, free, and mighty nation, but the Lord. Neither reason nor the power of man preserved our country, bound its people together, and created its fortune, but the Lord. Our country was—and is—in His hand, as the vessel is in the potter's hand.

For this reason, away with all idolizing of man! Away with the thought that human wisdom, human courage, human power, and human righteousness produced the many blessings this land enjoys! Let us praise the Lord, who says, "My glory I give to no other, nor My praise to carved idols" (Isaiah 42:8). Let us also exclaim, "Oh give thanks to the LORD, for He is good; for His steadfast love endures forever!" (Psalm 118:1). He has done great things for us, and for that, we are grateful.

The nation Thou hast blest
May well Thy love declare,
From foes and fears at rest,
Protected by Thy care.
For this fair land,
For this bright day,
Our thanks we pay—
Gifts of Thy hand. Amen.

† *(TLH 575:2)*

Old Testament

New Testament

Hymns marked TLH are from *The Lutheran Hymnal.* Copyright © 1941 by Concordia Publishing House.

Hymns marked ELHB are from the *Evangelical Lutheran Hymn Book.* Copyright © 1931 by Concordia Publishing House.

Augustine. *Confessions.* R.S. Pine-Coffin, trans. NY: Dorset Press: 1986.

Luther, Martin. *Commentary on Romans.* J. Theodore Mueller, trans. Grand Rapids: Kregel Publications: 1976.

Luther, Martin. *Small Catechism.* St. Louis: Concordia Publishing House: 1943.

Pieper, Francis. *Christian Dogmatics.* Vol. 3. St. Louis: Concordia Publishing House: 1953.

Tappert, Theodore, Ed. *The Book of Concord: The Confessions of the Evangelical Lutheran Church.* Philadelphia: Fortress Press: 1959.

2nd week after Trinity
Wed. - Studying God's Word

p544 Christian fellowship
554 work
625 so much crime & sin in the Bible